Haynes

THE BOOK ®

Peugeot 206
Service and Repair Manual

Mark Coombs

Models covered

Peugeot 206 Hatchback models, including special/limited editions

(3757 - 8AF1 - 368)

Petrol engines: 1.1 litre (1124cc), 1.4 litre (1360cc) & 1.6 litre (1587cc) 8-valve engines
Diesel engines: 1.9 litre (1868cc) & 2.0 litre (1997cc), inc. turbo

Covers major mechanical features of Van
Does NOT cover models with 16-valve petrol engines (XSi, GTi, Grand Tourisme etc), or Cabriolet

© Haynes Publishing 2002

A book in the **Haynes Service and Repair Manual Series**

ISBN **1 85960 757 8**

British Library Cataloguing in Publication Data
A catalogue record for this book is available from the British Library.

ABCDE
FGHIJ
KLMNO
PQR

Printed in the USA

Haynes Publishing
Sparkford, Yeovil, Somerset BA22 7JJ, England

Haynes North America, Inc
861 Lawrence Drive, Newbury Park, California 91320, USA

Editions Haynes
4, Rue de l'Abreuvoir,
92415 COURBEVOIE CEDEX, France

Haynes Publishing Nordiska AB
Box 1504, 751 45 UPPSALA, Sverige

Contents

LIVING WITH YOUR PEUGEOT 206

MAINTENANCE

Routine Maintenance and Servicing

Contents

Advanced driving

Many people see the words 'advanced driving' and believe that it won't interest them or that it is a style of driving beyond their own abilities. Nothing could be further from the truth. Advanced driving is straightforward safe, sensible driving - the sort of driving we should all do every time we get behind the wheel.

An average of 10 people are killed every day on UK roads and 870 more are injured, some seriously. Lives are ruined daily, usually because somebody did something stupid. Something like 95% of all accidents are due to human error, mostly driver failure. Sometimes we make genuine mistakes - everyone does. Sometimes we have lapses of concentration. Sometimes we deliberately take risks.

For many people, the process of 'learning to drive' doesn't go much further than learning how to pass the driving test because of a common belief that good drivers are made by 'experience'.

Learning to drive by 'experience' teaches three driving skills:

☐ Quick reactions. (Whoops, that was close!)
☐ Good handling skills. (Horn, swerve, brake, horn).
☐ Reliance on vehicle technology. (Great stuff this ABS, stop in no distance even in the wet...)

Drivers whose skills are 'experience based' generally have a lot of near misses and the odd accident. The results can be seen every day in our courts and our hospital casualty departments.

Advanced drivers have learnt to control the risks by controlling the position and speed of their vehicle. They avoid accidents and near misses, even if the drivers around them make mistakes.

The key skills of advanced driving are **concentration,** effective all-round **observation, anticipation** and **planning.** When **good vehicle handling** is added to

these skills, all driving situations can be approached and negotiated in a safe, methodical way, leaving nothing to chance.

Concentration means applying your mind to safe driving, completely excluding anything that's not relevant. Driving is usually the most dangerous activity that most of us undertake in our daily routines. It deserves our full attention.

Observation means not just looking, but seeing and seeking out the information found in the driving environment.

Anticipation means asking yourself what is happening, what you can reasonably expect to happen and what could happen unexpectedly. (One of the commonest words used in compiling accident reports is 'suddenly'.)

Planning is the link between seeing something and taking the appropriate action. For many drivers, planning is the missing link.

If you want to become a safer and more skilful driver and you want to enjoy your driving more, contact the Institute of Advanced Motorists on 0208 994 4403 or write to IAM House, Chiswick High Road, London W4 4HS for an information pack.

Working on your car can be dangerous. This page shows just some of the potential risks and hazards, with the aim of creating a safety-conscious attitude.

General hazards

Scalding

• Don't remove the radiator or expansion tank cap while the engine is hot.
• Engine oil, automatic transmission fluid or power steering fluid may also be dangerously hot if the engine has recently been running.

Burning

• Beware of burns from the exhaust system and from any part of the engine. Brake discs and drums can also be extremely hot immediately after use.

Crushing

• When working under or near a raised vehicle, always supplement the jack with axle stands, or use drive-on ramps. *Never venture under a car which is only supported by a jack.*
• Take care if loosening or tightening high-torque nuts when the vehicle is on stands. Initial loosening and final tightening should be done with the wheels on the ground.

Fire

• Fuel is highly flammable; fuel vapour is explosive.
• Don't let fuel spill onto a hot engine.
• Do not smoke or allow naked lights (including pilot lights) anywhere near a vehicle being worked on. Also beware of creating sparks (electrically or by use of tools).
• Fuel vapour is heavier than air, so don't work on the fuel system with the vehicle over an inspection pit.
• Another cause of fire is an electrical overload or short-circuit. Take care when repairing or modifying the vehicle wiring.
• Keep a fire extinguisher handy, of a type suitable for use on fuel and electrical fires.

Electric shock

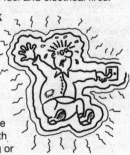

• Ignition HT voltage can be dangerous, especially to people with heart problems or a pacemaker. Don't work on or near the ignition system with the engine running or the ignition switched on.

• Mains voltage is also dangerous. Make sure that any mains-operated equipment is correctly earthed. Mains power points should be protected by a residual current device (RCD) circuit breaker.

Fume or gas intoxication

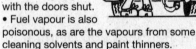

• Exhaust fumes are poisonous; they often contain carbon monoxide, which is rapidly fatal if inhaled. Never run the engine in a confined space such as a garage with the doors shut.
• Fuel vapour is also poisonous, as are the vapours from some cleaning solvents and paint thinners.

Poisonous or irritant substances

• Avoid skin contact with battery acid and with any fuel, fluid or lubricant, especially antifreeze, brake hydraulic fluid and Diesel fuel. Don't syphon them by mouth. If such a substance is swallowed or gets into the eyes, seek medical advice.
• Prolonged contact with used engine oil can cause skin cancer. Wear gloves or use a barrier cream if necessary. Change out of oil-soaked clothes and do not keep oily rags in your pocket.
• Air conditioning refrigerant forms a poisonous gas if exposed to a naked flame (including a cigarette). It can also cause skin burns on contact.

Asbestos

• Asbestos dust can cause cancer if inhaled or swallowed. Asbestos may be found in gaskets and in brake and clutch linings. When dealing with such components it is safest to assume that they contain asbestos.

Special hazards

Hydrofluoric acid

• This extremely corrosive acid is formed when certain types of synthetic rubber, found in some O-rings, oil seals, fuel hoses etc, are exposed to temperatures above 400°C. The rubber changes into a charred or sticky substance containing the acid. *Once formed, the acid remains dangerous for years. If it gets onto the skin, it may be necessary to amputate the limb concerned.*
• When dealing with a vehicle which has suffered a fire, or with components salvaged from such a vehicle, wear protective gloves and discard them after use.

The battery

• Batteries contain sulphuric acid, which attacks clothing, eyes and skin. Take care when topping-up or carrying the battery.
• The hydrogen gas given off by the battery is highly explosive. Never cause a spark or allow a naked light nearby. Be careful when connecting and disconnecting battery chargers or jump leads.

Air bags

• Air bags can cause injury if they go off accidentally. Take care when removing the steering wheel and/or facia. Special storage instructions may apply.

Diesel injection equipment

• Diesel injection pumps supply fuel at very high pressure. Take care when working on the fuel injectors and fuel pipes.

⚠️ *Warning: Never expose the hands, face or any other part of the body to injector spray; the fuel can penetrate the skin with potentially fatal results.*

Remember...

DO

• Do use eye protection when using power tools, and when working under the vehicle.

• Do wear gloves or use barrier cream to protect your hands when necessary.

• Do get someone to check periodically that all is well when working alone on the vehicle.

• Do keep loose clothing and long hair well out of the way of moving mechanical parts.

• Do remove rings, wristwatch etc, before working on the vehicle – especially the electrical system.

• Do ensure that any lifting or jacking equipment has a safe working load rating adequate for the job.

DON'T

• Don't attempt to lift a heavy component which may be beyond your capability – get assistance.

• Don't rush to finish a job, or take unverified short cuts.

• Don't use ill-fitting tools which may slip and cause injury.

• Don't leave tools or parts lying around where someone can trip over them. Mop up oil and fuel spills at once.

• Don't allow children or pets to play in or near a vehicle being worked on.

The Peugeot 206 range was introduced in the UK in the Autumn of 1998. Originally, the 206 was available with a choice of 1.1 litre (1124 cc), 1.4 litre (1360 cc), and 1.6 litre (1587 cc) petrol engines and a 1.9 litre (1868 cc) diesel engine. All models were available in both three- and five-door Hatchback form.

All petrol engines are derived from the well-proven TU series engines, which have appeared in many Peugeot and Citroën vehicles. The engine is of four-cylinder overhead camshaft design, mounted transversely, with the transmission mounted on the left-hand side. All models have a five-speed manual transmission; the 1.4 and 1.6 litre models also being offered with the option of a four-speed automatic transmission.

The diesel engine is from the new DW series of diesel engines. The engine has been derived from the original XUD diesel engines which were also well-proven units, having been fitted to many Peugeot and Citroën vehicles. The engine is of four-cylinder overhead camshaft design, mounted transversely, with the five-speed manual transmission mounted on the left-hand side.

In the Autumn of 1999, Peugeot introduced the 2.0 litre (1997 cc) turbocharged diesel engine into the 206 range. This engine is also from the new DW series of diesel engines and is fitted with a high-pressure direct injection (HDI) system which represents the latest in diesel technology. Other additions to the 206

range included the 2.0 litre (1997 cc) petrol engine GTi model and the Cabriolet model which are not covered in this manual.

All models have fully-independent front suspension. The rear suspension is semi-independent, with torsion bars and trailing arms.

A wide range of standard and optional equipment is available within the 206 range to suit most tastes.

Provided that regular servicing is carried out in accordance with the manufacturer's recommendations, the Peugeot 206 should prove reliable and very economical. The engine compartment is well-designed, and most of the items requiring frequent attention are easily accessible.

Your Peugeot 206 Manual

The aim of this manual is to help you get the best value from your vehicle. It can do so in several ways. It can help you decide what work must be done (even should you choose to get it done by a garage), provide information on routine maintenance and servicing, and give a logical course of action and diagnosis when random faults occur. However, it is hoped that you will use the manual by tackling the work yourself. On simpler jobs it may even be quicker than booking the car into a garage and going there twice, to leave and collect it. Perhaps most

important, a lot of money can be saved by avoiding the costs a garage must charge to cover its labour and overheads.

The manual has drawings and descriptions to show the function of the various components so that their layout can be understood. Tasks are described and photographed in a clear step-by-step sequence.

References to the left-hand and right-hand sides of the vehicle are always in the sense of when viewed by a person sat in the driver's seat, facing forwards.

Acknowledgements

Thanks are due to Champion Spark Plug, who supplied spark plug information. Special thanks to Bakers of Gillingham who provided several of the project vehicles used in the origination of this manual. Thanks are also due to Draper Tools Limited, who provided some of the workshop tools, and to all those people a Sparkford who helped in the production of this manual.

We take great pride in the accuracy of information given in this manual, but vehicle manufacturers make alterations and design changes during the production run of a particular vehicle of which they do not inform us. No liability can be accepted by the authors or publishers for loss, damage or injury caused by errors in, or omissions from, the information given.

Peugeot 206

The following pages are intended to help in dealing with common roadside emergencies and breakdowns. You will find more detailed fault finding information at the back of the manual, and repair information in the main chapters.

If your car won't start and the starter motor doesn't turn

☐ If it's a model with automatic transmission, make sure the selector is in P or N.
☐ Open the bonnet and make sure that the battery terminals are clean and tight.
☐ Switch on the headlights and try to start the engine. If the headlights go very dim when you're trying to start, the battery is probably flat. Get out of trouble by jump starting (see next page) using a friend's car.

If your car won't start even though the starter motor turns as normal

☐ Is there fuel in the tank?
☐ Is there moisture on electrical components under the bonnet? Switch off the ignition, then wipe off any obvious dampness with a dry cloth. Spray a water-repellent aerosol product (WD-40 or equivalent) on ignition and fuel system electrical connectors like those shown in the photos. Pay special attention to the ignition coil wiring connector and HT leads. (Note that Diesel engines don't normally suffer from damp.)

A Check the security and condition of the battery connections.

B Check the fuel cut-off inertia switch (where fitted) has not tripped. Reset the switch by depressing its button.

C Check that the ignition HT coil (where applicable) is securely connected by pushing it home.

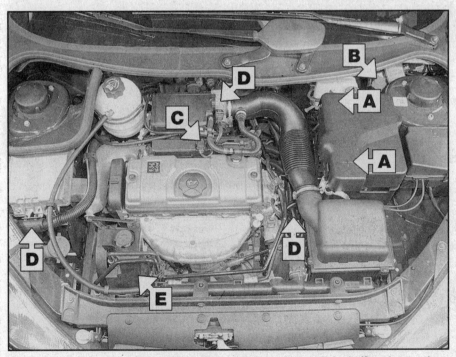

Check that electrical connections are secure (with the ignition switched off) and spray them with a water dispersant spray like WD40 if you suspect a problem due to damp

D On petrol engines, with the ignition switched off, check the various engine management sensor wiring connectors are all securely connected (crankshaft sensor shown).

E On diesel engines, check the injection pump wiring connectors are securely connected (remove the engine cover for access).

Jump starting

When jump-starting a car using a booster battery, observe the following precautions:

✔ Before connecting the booster battery, make sure that the ignition is switched off.

✔ Ensure that all electrical equipment (lights, heater, wipers, etc) is switched off.

✔ Take note of any special precautions printed on the battery case.

✔ Make sure that the booster battery is the same voltage as the discharged one in the vehicle.

✔ If the battery is being jump-started from the battery in another vehicle, the two vehicles MUST NOT TOUCH each other.

✔ Make sure that the transmission is in neutral (or PARK, in the case of automatic transmission).

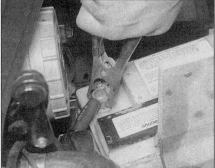

HAYNES HiNT *Jump starting will get you out of trouble, but you must correct whatever made the battery go flat in the first place. There are three possibilities:*

1 *The battery has been drained by repeated attempts to start, or by leaving the lights on.*

2 *The charging system is not working properly (alternator drivebelt slack or broken, alternator wiring fault or alternator itself faulty).*

3 *The battery itself is at fault (electrolyte low, or battery worn out).*

1 Connect one end of the red jump lead to the positive (+) terminal of the flat battery

2 Connect the other end of the red lead to the positive (+) terminal of the booster battery.

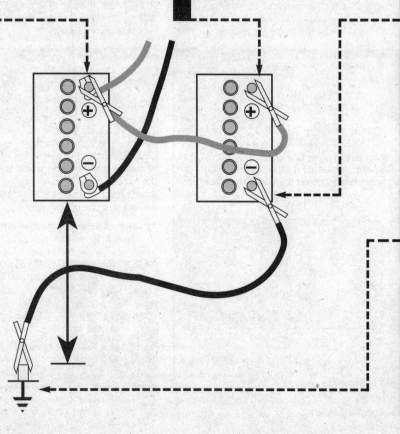

3 Connect one end of the black jump lead to the negative (-) terminal of the booster battery

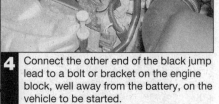

4 Connect the other end of the black jump lead to a bolt or bracket on the engine block, well away from the battery, on the vehicle to be started.

5 Make sure that the jump leads will not come into contact with the fan, drive-belts or other moving parts of the engine.

6 Start the engine using the booster battery and run it at idle speed. Switch on the lights, rear window demister and heater blower motor, then disconnect the jump leads in the reverse order of connection. Turn off the lights etc.

Wheel changing

Some of the details shown here will vary according to model. However, the basic principles apply to all vehicles.

Preparation

- ☐ When a puncture occurs, stop as soon as it is safe to do so.
- ☐ Park on firm level ground, if possible, and well out of the way of other traffic.
- ☐ Use hazard warning lights if necessary.

⚠ Warning: Do not change a wheel in a situation where you risk being hit by other traffic. On busy roads, try to stop in a lay-by or a gateway. Be wary of passing traffic while changing the wheel – it is easy to become distracted by the job in hand

- ☐ If you have one, use a warning triangle to alert other drivers of your presence.
- ☐ Apply the handbrake and engage first or reverse gear.
- ☐ Chock the wheel diagonally opposite the

one being removed – use the jack holder (as described below) or couple of large stones will do for this.
- ☐ If the ground is soft, use a flat piece of wood to spread the load under the jack.

Changing the wheel

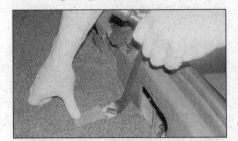

1 Unclip the wheelbrace from its holder at the rear of the luggage compartment. Lift the luggage compartment carpet to gain access to the spare wheel cradle bolt. Use the end of the wheelbrace to slacken the bolt sufficiently to be able to unhook the cradle from its retainer on the bolt.

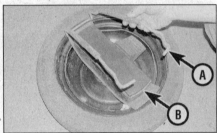

2 Unhook and lower the cradle then remove the spare wheel from underneath the vehicle. Where a space-saver spare wheel is fitted, unclip the spacer (A) from the top of the wheel. Remove the jack holder (B) then place the wheel under the sill as a precaution against the jack failing.

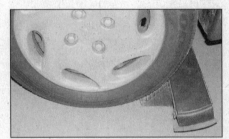

3 Use the jack holder to chock the wheel diagonally opposite the one being removed. Remove the wheel trim on the wheel to be replaced and loosen each wheel bolt by half-a-turn.

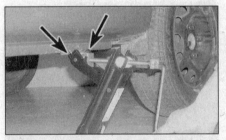

4 Engage the jack head with the reinforced jacking point nearest the wheel to be changed; the jacking point is the area in between the cutouts (arrowed) on the sill. Ensure the head of the jack is positioned centrally between the cutouts then raise the jack until its base is in contact with the ground. Ensure the jack base is located directly below the sill then raise the vehicle until the wheel is clear of the ground. If the tyre is flat, remember to raise the vehicle sufficiently to allow the spare wheel to be fitted.

5 Remove the bolts and lift off the wheel. Place the wheel beneath the sill as a precaution against the jack failing then fit the spare wheel. Fit the wheel bolts and moderately tighten them with the wheelbrace.

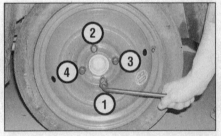

6 Remove the punctured wheel from under the sill then lower the vehicle to the ground. Tighten the wheel bolts in a diagonal sequence then refit the wheel trim. Note that the wheel bolts should be slackened and retightened to the specified torque at the earliest possible opportunity.

7 Remove the jack holder from under the wheel. Store the jack and space-saver wheel spacer (where fitted – it is not needed when a normal wheel is fitted to the cradle) in the boot then fit the punctured wheel to the cradle. Hook the cradle onto its retainer then raise the cradle fully and secure it in position by securely tightening the wheel cradle bolt.

Finally...

- ☐ Remove any remaining wheel chocks.
- ☐ Don't leave the spare wheel cradle empty and unsecured – it could drop onto the ground while the car is moving.
- ☐ Have the damaged tyre or wheel repaired as soon as possible.
- ☐ Check the tyre pressure on the wheel just fitted. If it is low, or if

you don't have a pressure gauge with you, drive slowly to the nearest garage and inflate the tyre to the right pressure.

- ☐ The space-saver wheel is only designed for emergency use; never exceed 50 mph (80 kph) whilst the wheel is fitted to the vehicle. Never carry the space-saver wheel in the cradle without the spacer being fitted.

Identifying leaks

Puddles on the garage floor or drive, or obvious wetness under the bonnet or underneath the car, suggest a leak that needs investigating. It can sometimes be difficult to decide where the leak is coming from, especially if the engine bay is very dirty already. Leaking oil or fluid can also be blown rearwards by the passage of air under the car, giving a false impression of where the problem lies.

 Warning: Most automotive oils and fluids are poisonous. Wash them off skin, and change out of contaminated clothing, without delay.

 The smell of a fluid leaking from the car may provide a clue to what's leaking. Some fluids are distinctively coloured. It may help to clean the car carefully and to park it over some clean paper overnight as an aid to locating the source of the leak.
Remember that some leaks may only occur while the engine is running.

Sump oil

Engine oil may leak from the drain plug...

Oil from filter

...or from the base of the oil filter.

Gearbox oil

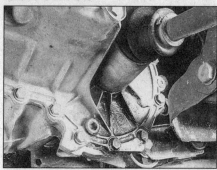

Gearbox oil can leak from the seals at the inboard ends of the driveshafts.

Antifreeze

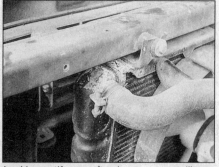

Leaking antifreeze often leaves a crystalline deposit like this.

Brake fluid

A leak occurring at a wheel is almost certainly brake fluid.

Power steering fluid

Power steering fluid may leak from the pipe connectors on the steering rack.

Towing

When all else fails, you may find yourself having to get a tow home – or of course you may be helping somebody else. Long-distance recovery should only be done by a garage or breakdown service. For shorter distances, DIY towing using another car is easy enough, but observe the following points:

☐ Use a proper tow-rope – they are not expensive. The vehicle being towed must display an ON TOW sign in its rear window.

☐ Always turn the ignition key to the 'on' position when the vehicle is being towed, so that the steering lock is released, and that the direction indicator and brake lights will work.

☐ Only attach the tow-rope to the towing eyes provided.

☐ Before being towed, release the handbrake and select neutral on the transmission.

☐ On models with an automatic transmission unit, the vehicle must only be towed forwards with the selector lever in the N position. Never tow the vehicle at speeds in excess of 30 mph (50 kmh) or over a distance in excess of 30 miles (50 km). Failure to observe these warning will lead to serious transmission damage.

☐ Note that greater-than-usual pedal pressure will be required to operate the brakes, since the vacuum servo unit is only operational with the engine running.

☐ On models with power steering, greater-than-usual steering effort will also be required.

☐ The driver of the car being towed must keep the tow-rope taut at all times to avoid snatching.

☐ Make sure that both drivers know the route before setting off.

☐ Only drive at moderate speeds and keep the distance towed to a minimum. Drive smoothly and allow plenty of time for slowing down at junctions.

Introduction

There are some very simple checks which need only take a few minutes to carry out, but which could save you a lot of inconvenience and expense.

These Weekly checks require no great skill or special tools, and the small amount of time they take to perform could prove to be very well spent, for example;

☐ Keeping an eye on tyre condition and pressures, will not only help to stop them wearing out prematurely, but could also save your life.

☐ Many breakdowns are caused by electrical problems. Battery-related faults are particularly common, and a quick check on a regular basis will often prevent the majority of these.

☐ If your car develops a brake fluid leak, the first time you might know about it is when your brakes don't work properly. Checking the level regularly will give advance warning of this kind of problem.

☐ If the oil or coolant levels run low, the cost of repairing any engine damage will be far greater than fixing the leak, for example.

Underbonnet check points

◀ Petrol engine

A *Engine oil level dipstick*

B *Engine oil filler cap*

C *Coolant expansion tank*

D *Brake fluid reservoir*

E *Screen washer fluid reservoir*

F *Battery*

G *Power steering fluid reservoir*

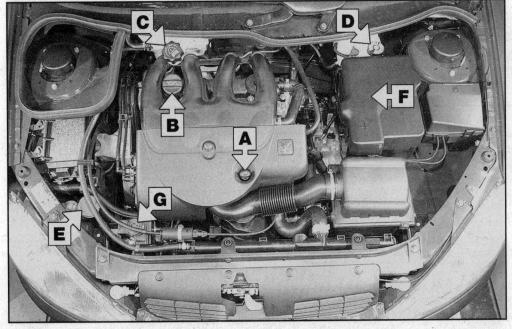

◀ 1.9 litre diesel engine

A *Engine oil level dipstick*

B *Engine oil filler cap*

C *Coolant expansion tank*

D *Brake (and clutch) fluid reservoir*

E *Screen washer fluid reservoir*

F *Battery*

G *Power steering fluid reservoir*

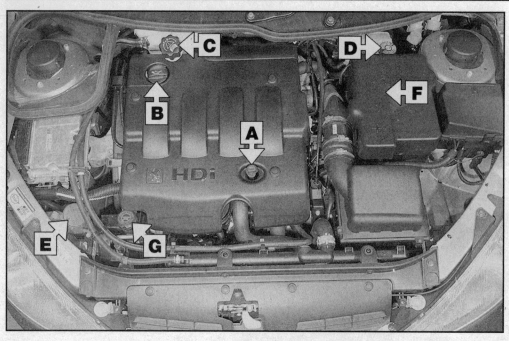

◀ **2.0 litre diesel engine**

A *Engine oil level dipstick*

B *Engine oil filler cap*

C *Coolant expansion tank*

D *Brake (and clutch) fluid reservoir*

E *Screen washer fluid reservoir*

F *Battery*

G *Power steering fluid reservoir*

Engine oil level

Before you start

✔ Make sure that your car is on level ground.
✔ Check the oil level before the car is driven, or at least 5 minutes after the engine has been switched off.

HAYNES HiNT *If the oil is checked immediately after driving the vehicle, some of the oil will remain in the upper engine components, resulting in an inaccurate reading on the dipstick!*

The correct oil

Modern engines place great demands on their oil. It is very important that the correct oil for your car is used (See 'Lubricants and fluids').

Car Care

● If you have to add oil frequently, you should check whether you have any oil leaks. Place some clean paper under the car overnight, and check for stains in the morning. If there are no leaks, the engine may be burning oil.
● Always maintain the level between the upper and lower dipstick marks (see photo 3).
● If the level is too low severe engine damage may occur. Oil seal failure may result if the engine is overfilled by adding too much oil.
On models equipped with an oil level gauge, don't be tempted to rely on the gauge alone – verify the level using the dipstick on a regular basis. Equally, don't ignore the gauge if it warns of low oil level.

1 The engine oil level is checked with a dipstick that extends through the dipstick tube and into the sump at the bottom of the engine. The dipstick is located at the front of the engine (see *Underbonnet check points* for exact location). Withdraw the dipstick.

2 Wipe all the oil from the end with a clean rag or paper towel. Insert the clean dipstick back into the tube as far as it will go, then withdraw it once more.

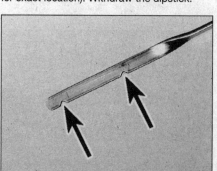

3 Note the oil level on the end of the dipstick. Add oil as necessary until the level is between the upper (MAX) mark and lower (MIN) mark on the dipstick. Note that approximately 1.0 litre of oil will be required to raise the level from the lower mark to the upper mark.

4 Oil is added to the engine via the filler cap on the cylinder head cover. Unscrew the cap and top-up the level. A funnel may help to reduce spillage. Add the oil slowly, checking the level on the dipstick frequently. Do not overfill.

Coolant level

 Warning: DO NOT attempt to remove the expansion tank pressure cap when the engine is hot, as there is a very great risk of scalding. Do not leave open containers of coolant about, as it is poisonous.

Car Care

● With a sealed-type cooling system, adding coolant should not be necessary on a regular basis. If frequent topping-up is required, it is likely there is a leak. Check the radiator, all hoses and joint faces for signs of staining or wetness, and rectify as necessary.

● It is important that antifreeze is used in the cooling system all year round, not just during the winter months. Don't top-up with water alone, as the antifreeze will become too diluted.

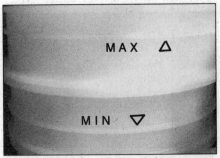

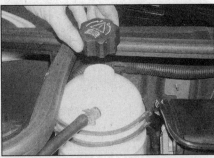

1 The coolant level varies with the temperature of the engine. The level is checked in the expansion tank located in the right-hand, rear corner of the engine compartment. When the engine is cold, the coolant level should be between the MAX and MIN level marks on the tank.

2 If topping up is necessary, **wait until the engine is cold**. Slowly unscrew the expansion tank cap, to release any pressure present in the cooling system, and remove it.

3 Add the specified coolant to the expansion tank until the coolant level is correct. Refit the cap and tighten it securely.

Brake (and clutch*) fluid level

On diesel engine models, the fluid reservoir also supplies the clutch master cylinder with fluid

 Warning:
● **Brake fluid can harm your eyes and damage painted surfaces, so use extreme caution when handling and pouring it.**

● **Do not use fluid that has been standing open for some time, as it absorbs moisture from the air, which can cause a dangerous loss of braking effectiveness.**

 HAYNES HiNT • **Make sure that your car is on level ground.**
• **The fluid level in the reservoir will drop slightly as the brake pads wear down, but the fluid level must never be allowed to drop below the DANGER mark.**

Safety First!

● If the reservoir requires repeated topping-up this is an indication of a fluid leak somewhere in the system, which should be investigated immediately.

● If a leak is suspected, the car should not be driven until the braking system has been checked. Never take any risks where brakes are concerned.

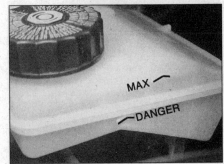

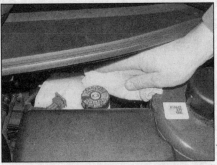

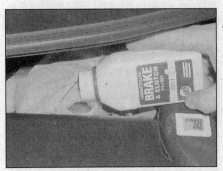

1 The brake fluid reservoir is located on the left-hand side of the engine compartment. The MAX and DANGER marks are indicated on the side of the reservoir. The fluid level must be kept between the marks at all times.

2 If topping-up is necessary, first wipe clean the area around the filler cap to prevent dirt entering the hydraulic system.

3 Carefully add fluid, taking care not to spill it onto the surrounding components. Use only the specified fluid; mixing different types can cause damage to the system. After topping-up to the correct level, securely refit the cap and wipe off any spilt fluid.

Tyre condition and pressure

It is very important that tyres are in good condition, and at the correct pressure - having a tyre failure at any speed is highly dangerous. Tyre wear is influenced by driving style - harsh braking and acceleration, or fast cornering, will all produce more rapid tyre wear. As a general rule, the front tyres wear out faster than the rears. Interchanging the tyres from front to rear ("rotating" the tyres) may result in more even wear. However, if this is completely effective, you may have the expense of replacing all four tyres at once! Remove any nails or stones embedded in the tread before they penetrate the tyre to cause deflation. If removal of a nail does reveal that

the tyre has been punctured, refit the nail so that its point of penetration is marked. Then immediately change the wheel, and have the tyre repaired by a tyre dealer.

Regularly check the tyres for damage in the form of cuts or bulges, especially in the sidewalls. Periodically remove the wheels, and clean any dirt or mud from the inside and outside surfaces. Examine the wheel rims for signs of rusting, corrosion or other damage. Light alloy wheels are easily damaged by "kerbing" whilst parking; steel wheels may also become dented or buckled. A new wheel is very often the only way to overcome severe damage.

New tyres should be balanced when they are fitted, but it may become necessary to re-balance them as they wear, or if the balance weights fitted to the wheel rim should fall off. Unbalanced tyres will wear more quickly, as will the steering and suspension components. Wheel imbalance is normally signified by vibration, particularly at a certain speed (typically around 50 mph). If this vibration is felt only through the steering, then it is likely that just the front wheels need balancing. If, however, the vibration is felt through the whole car, the rear wheels could be out of balance. Wheel balancing should be carried out by a tyre dealer or garage.

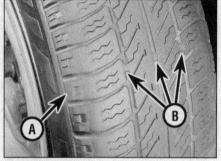

1 *Tread Depth - visual check*
The original tyres have tread wear safety bands (B), which will appear when the tread depth reaches approximately 1.6 mm. The band positions are indicated by a triangular mark on the tyre sidewall (A).

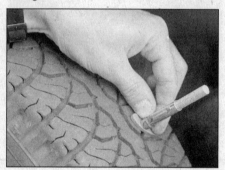

2 *Tread Depth - manual check*
Alternatively, tread wear can be monitored with a simple, inexpensive device known as a tread depth indicator gauge.

3 *Tyre Pressure Check*
Check the tyre pressures regularly with the tyres cold. Do not adjust the tyre pressures immediately after the vehicle has been used, or an inaccurate setting will result.

Tyre tread wear patterns

Shoulder Wear

Underinflation (wear on both sides)
Under-inflation will cause overheating of the tyre, because the tyre will flex too much, and the tread will not sit correctly on the road surface. This will cause a loss of grip and excessive wear, not to mention the danger of sudden tyre failure due to heat build-up.
Check and adjust pressures
Incorrect wheel camber (wear on one side)
Repair or renew suspension parts
Hard cornering
Reduce speed!

Centre Wear

Overinflation
Over-inflation will cause rapid wear of the centre part of the tyre tread, coupled with reduced grip, harsher ride, and the danger of shock damage occurring in the tyre casing.
Check and adjust pressures

If you sometimes have to inflate your car's tyres to the higher pressures specified for maximum load or sustained high speed, don't forget to reduce the pressures to normal afterwards.

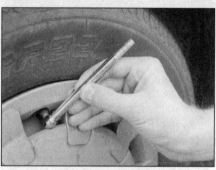

Uneven Wear

Front tyres may wear unevenly as a result of wheel misalignment. Most tyre dealers and garages can check and adjust the wheel alignment (or "tracking") for a modest charge.
Incorrect camber or castor
Repair or renew suspension parts
Malfunctioning suspension
Repair or renew suspension parts
Unbalanced wheel
Balance tyres
Incorrect toe setting
Adjust front wheel alignment
Note: *The feathered edge of the tread which typifies toe wear is best checked by feel.*

Power steering fluid level

Before you start:
✔ Park the vehicle on level ground.
✔ With the engine idling, turn the steering wheel slowly from lock-to-lock 2 or 3 times. Set the steering wheel straight-ahead position then switch off the engine.

HAYNES HiNT *For the check to be accurate, the steering must not be turned once the engine has been stopped.*

Safety First!
● The need for frequent topping-up indicates a leak, which should be investigated immediately.

1 The reservoir is located at the front of the engine on the right-hand side. Wipe clean the area around the reservoir cap, to prevent dirt entering the hydraulic system, then remove the cap from the reservoir.

2 Wipe all fluid from the cap dipstick with a clean rag. Refit the filler cap, then remove it again and note the fluid level on the dipstick. When the engine is cold, the level should be between the lower (ADD) mark and the middle (C) mark on the dipstick. If the engine is warm, the fluid level maybe up to the upper (H) mark.

3 If the fluid level is on or below the lower (ADD) mark, top up the fluid level to the middle (C) mark using the specified type of fluid (do not overfill). Once the level is correct, securely refit the filler cap to the reservoir.

Washer fluid level

Screenwash additives not only keep the windscreen clean during foul weather, they also prevent the washer system freezing in cold weather - which is when you are likely to need it most. Don't top up using plain water as the screenwash will become too diluted, and will freeze during cold weather. *On no account use coolant antifreeze in the washer system - this could discolour or damage paintwork.*

1 The screen washer fluid reservoir filler neck is located in the right-hand side of the engine compartment, behind the headlight. The screen washer level cannot easily be seen. Remove the filler cap, and look down the filler neck - if fluid is not visible, topping-up may be required.

2 When topping-up the reservoir, add a screenwash additive in the quantities recommended on the additive bottle. The exact level is not critical – add fluid slowly until the level reaches the base of the filler neck

Wiper blades

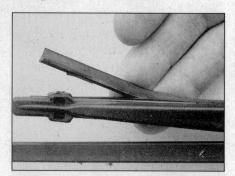

1 Check the condition of the wiper blades; if they are cracked or show any signs of deterioration, or if the glass swept area is smeared, renew them. For maximum clarity of vision, wiper blades should be renewed annually, as a matter of course.

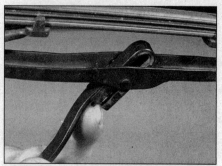

2 To remove a windscreen wiper blade, pull the arm fully away from the glass until it locks. Swivel the blade through 90°, then squeeze the locking clip and slide the blade out of the arm's hooked end. On refitting, ensure that the blade locks securely into the arm.

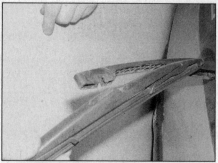

3 Don't forget to check the tailgate wiper blade as well. To remove the blade, pull the arm away from the glass then unclip the blade.

Battery

Caution: Before carrying out any work on the vehicle battery, read the precautions given in 'Safety first!' at the start of this manual.

✔ Make sure that the battery tray is in good condition, and that the clamp is tight. Corrosion on the tray, retaining clamp and the battery itself can be removed with a solution of water and baking soda. Thoroughly rinse all cleaned areas with water. Any metal parts damaged by corrosion should be covered with a zinc-based primer, then painted.

✔ Periodically (approximately every three months), check the charge condition of the battery as described in Chapter 5A.

✔ If the battery is flat, and you need to jump start your vehicle, see *Roadside Repairs*.

1 The battery is located on the left-hand side of the engine compartment. Unclip the cover from the battery tray to gain access. The exterior of the battery should be inspected periodically for damage such as a cracked case or cover.

2 Check the tightness of the battery cable clamps to ensure good electrical connections, and check the entire length of each cable for cracks and frayed conductors.

HAYNES
HiNT

Battery corrosion can be kept to a minimum by applying a layer of petroleum jelly to the clamps and terminals after they are reconnected.

3 If corrosion (visible as white, fluffy deposits) is evident, remove the cables from the battery terminals, clean them with a small wire brush, then refit them. Automotive stores sell tools for cleaning the battery terminals . . .

4 . . . and the battery lead clamps

Electrical systems

✔ Check the operation of all the electrical equipment, ie. lights, direction indicators, horn, etc. Refer to the appropriate Sections of Chapter 12 for details if any of the circuits are found to be inoperative.

✔ Visually check all accessible wiring connectors, harnesses and retaining clips for security, and for signs of chafing or damage

 HAYNES HINT *If you need to check your brake lights and indicators unaided, back up to a wall or garage door and operate the lights. The reflected light should show if they are working properly.*

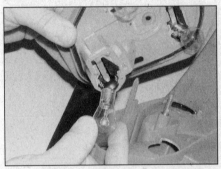

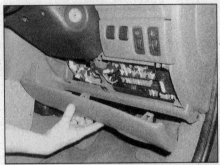

1 If a single indicator light, stop-light or headlight bulb has failed, it is likely that a bulb has blown and will need replacing. Refer to Chapter 12 for details. If both stop-lights have failed, it is possible that the stop-light switch has failed (see Chapter 9).

2 If more than one indicator light or headlight has failed, it is likely that either a fuse has blown or there is a fault in the circuit (see Chapter 12). The main fuses are located beneath the lower cover on the driver's side of the facia. Rotate the cover fastener 90° and remove the cover to gain access. Additional fuses and relays are located in the fuse/relay box located on the left-hand side of the engine compartment.

3 To replace a blown fuse, remove it using the plastic tool supplied (where applicable). Fit a new fuse of the correct rating, available from car accessory shops. If the new fuse blows immediately, there is a fault which must be traced and rectified (see *Electrical fault finding* in Chapter 12)

Lubricants and fluids

Engine

Petrol . . . . SAE 10W40, 5W40 or 0W40 Multigrade engine oil to ACEA A3 and API SH/SJ specification*
(Duckhams Fully Synthetic Engine Oil, or Duckhams QXR Premium Petrol Engine Oil)

Diesel . . . . SAE 10W40, 5W40 or 0W40 Multigrade engine oil to ACEA B3 and API CF/CD specification*
(Duckhams Fully Synthetic Engine Oil, or Duckhams QXR Premium Diesel Engine Oil)

Cooling system . . . . PROCOR 3000 or REVKOGEL 107 **only**

Manual transmission . . . . Esso Gear Oil BV 75W80 or Total Transmission BV 75W80 **only**

Automatic transmission . . . . Esso LT 71141 fluid **only**

Brake (and clutch) hydraulic system . . . . Hydraulic fluid to FMVSS 116 DOT 4
(Duckhams Universal Brake & Clutch Fluid)

Power steering . . . . Dexron type ATF to API GL5 specification
(Duckhams ATF Autotrans III)

*Due to the extended service intervals Peugeot specify, it is essential that semi-synthetic or fully synthetic engine oil is used.

Choosing your engine oil

Engines need oil, not only to lubricate moving parts and minimise wear, but also to maximise power output and to improve fuel economy. By introducing a simplified and improved range of engine oils, Duckhams has taken away the confusion and made it easier for you to choose the right oil for your engine.

HOW ENGINE OIL WORKS

• Beating friction

Without oil, the moving surfaces inside your engine will rub together, heat up and melt, quickly causing the engine to seize. Engine oil creates a film which separates these moving parts, preventing wear and heat build-up.

• Cooling hot-spots

Temperatures inside the engine can exceed 1000° C. The engine oil circulates and acts as a coolant, transferring heat from the hot-spots to the sump.

• Cleaning the engine internally

Good quality engine oils clean the inside of your engine, collecting and dispersing combustion deposits and controlling them until they are trapped by the oil filter or flushed out at oil change.

OIL CARE - FOLLOW THE CODE

To handle and dispose of used engine oil safely, always:

OIL BANK LINE
0800 66 33 66
www.oilbankline.org.uk

• **Avoid skin contact with used engine oil.** Repeated or prolonged contact can be harmful.
• **Dispose of used oil and empty packs in a responsible manner in an authorised disposal site.** Call 0800 663366 to find the one nearest to you. **Never tip oil down drains or onto the ground.**

Tyre pressures

Note: *Always refer to the tyre pressure data sticker on the rear edge of the driver's door (visible when the door is open) for the correct tyre pressures for your particular vehicle (**see illustration**). Pressures apply only to original-equipment tyres, and may vary if any other make or type is fitted; check with the tyre manufacturer or supplier for correct pressures if necessary.*

Chapter 1 Part A:
Routine maintenance and servicing – petrol models

Contents

Degrees of difficulty

Easy, suitable for novice with little experience	**Fairly easy,** suitable for beginner with some experience	**Fairly difficult,** suitable for competent DIY mechanic	**Difficult,** suitable for experienced DIY mechanic	**Very difficult,** suitable for expert DIY or professional 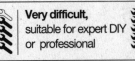

Lubricants and fluids

Refer to *Weekly checks*

Capacities

Engine oil

Including filter	3.2 litres
Difference between MAX and MIN dipstick marks	1.5 litres

Cooling system (approximate)	7.0 litres

Transmission

Manual	2.0 litres
Automatic:	
Refilling after draining	3.0 litres*
From dry	6.0 litres

If the torque converter is also removed and drained, add a further 2 litres

Power-assisted steering (approximate)	1.0 litre
Fuel tank	50 litres

Engine

Auxiliary drivebelt tensions (for use with special Peugeot tool – see text):

Models without power steering or air conditioning:	
Ribbed belt:	
New belt	120 SEEM units
Used belt	90 SEEM units
Vee belt:	
New belt	81 SEEM units
Used belt	67 SEEM units
Models with power steering or air conditioning:	
New belt	138 SEEM units
Used belt	103 SEEM units
Models with power steering and air conditioning	N/A – automatic tensioner fitted

Cooling system

Frost and corrosion protection	Refer to antifreeze manufacturer's concentration recommendations

Ignition system

Spark plugs:

1.1 litre engine	Eyquem RFC52LSP or Bosch FR7LDC
1.4 litre engine	Eyquem RFC52LSP or Bosch FR7LDC
1.6 litre engine	Eyquem RFC58LS or Bosch FR7KDC
Electrode gap	0.9 mm

Brakes

Brake pad friction material minimum thickness	2.0 mm
Brake shoe friction material minimum thickness	1.5 mm

Torque wrench settings

	Nm	lbf ft
Alternator mounting bolts	37	27
Automatic transmission:		
Filler plug	24	18
Level plug	24	18
Auxiliary drivebelt tensioner pulley nut	45	33
Manual transmission filler/level plug	25	18
Roadwheel bolts	85	63
Spark plugs	25	18
Sump drain plug	30	22

Note: *This maintenance schedule is a guide recommended by Haynes, for servicing your own vehicle. For the manufacturer's maintenance schedule, check with your local dealer.*
1 The maintenance intervals in this manual are provided with the assumption that you, not the dealer, will be carrying out the work. These are the minimum maintenance intervals recommended by us for vehicles driven daily. If you wish to keep your vehicle in peak condition at all times, you may wish to perform some of these procedures more often. We encourage frequent maintenance, because it enhances the efficiency, performance and resale value of your vehicle.
2 If the vehicle is driven in dusty areas, used to tow a trailer, or driven frequently at slow speeds (idling in traffic) or on short journeys, more frequent maintenance intervals are recommended.
3 When the vehicle is new, it should be serviced by a factory-authorised dealer service department, in order to preserve the factory warranty.
4 Valve clearance checking (Chapter 2A, Section 9) is no longer specified as part of the routine maintenance schedule. Check the valve clearances if there is any tapping or rattling from the top of the engine, or in the event of an unexplained lack of performance. The prudent owner may wish to check the clearances more often, perhaps at 40 000 mile (60 000 km) or four-yearly intervals.

Every 250 miles (400 km) or weekly
☐ Refer to *Weekly checks*

Every 10 000 miles (15 000 km) or 12 months – whichever comes sooner
☐ Renew the engine oil and filter (Section 3 – see Note below).
☐ Check all underbonnet components or fluid leaks (Section 4).
☐ Check the condition of the driveshaft rubber gaiters and CV joints (Section 5).
☐ Lubricate all hinges and locks (Section 6).
☐ Carry out a road test (Section 7).
☐ Reset the service interval indicator (Section 8).

Note: *Peugeot recommend the engine oil and filter are changed every 20 000 miles or two years. However, oil and filter changes are good for the engine and we recommend changing the oil more frequently, especially if the vehicle is used on a lot of short journeys.*

Every 20 000 miles (30 000 km) or two years – whichever comes sooner
☐ Renew the pollen filter (Section 9).
☐ Check the condition of the auxiliary drivebelt (Section 10).
☐ Check the condition of the front brake pads (Section 11).
☐ Check the operation of the handbrake (Section 12).
☐ Check the steering and suspension components (Section 13).

Every 40 000 miles (60 000 km)
☐ Renew the timing belt (Section 22).

Note: *Although the normal interval for timing belt renewal is 80 000 miles (120 000 km), it is strongly recommended that the interval is halved to 40 000 miles (60 000 km), especially on vehicles which are subjected to intensive use, ie. mainly short journeys or a lot of stop-start driving. The actual belt renewal interval is therefore very much up to the individual owner, but bear in mind that severe engine damage will result if the belt breaks.*

Every 40 000 miles (60 000 km) or two years – whichever comes sooner
☐ Renew the brake fluid (Section 14).

Every 40 000 miles (60 000 km) or four years – whichever comes sooner
☐ Renew the spark plugs (Section 15).
☐ Renew the fuel filter (Section 16).
☐ Renew the air cleaner filter element (Section 17).
☐ Check the manual transmission oil level (Section 18).
☐ Check the automatic transmission fluid level (Section 19).
☐ Check the condition of the rear brake shoes (Section 20).
☐ Check the exhaust emissions (Section 21).

Every 80 000 miles (120 000 km)
☐ Renew the timing belt (Section 22).

Note: *Although the normal interval for timing belt renewal is 80 000 miles (120 000 km), it is strongly recommended that the interval is halved to 40 000 miles (60 000 km), especially on vehicles which are subjected to intensive use, ie. mainly short journeys or a lot of stop-start driving. The actual belt renewal interval is therefore very much up to the individual owner, but bear in mind that severe engine damage will result if the belt breaks.*

Every 80 000 miles (120 000 km) or five years – whichever comes sooner
☐ Renew the coolant (Section 23).

1A

Underbonnet view of a petrol engine model (1.4 litre shown other models similar)

1 Engine oil filler cap
2 Engine oil dipstick
3 Battery
4 Brake fluid reservoir
5 Fuse/relay box
6 Air cleaner housing
7 Radiator
8 Power steering pump/fluid reservoir
9 Washer reservoir filler neck
10 Engine management ECU
11 Coolant expansion tank
12 Pollen filter
13 Ignition HT coil
14 Throttle housing
15 Cooling system bleed screws
16 Fuel cut-off inertia switch

Front underbody view (manual transmission model shown)

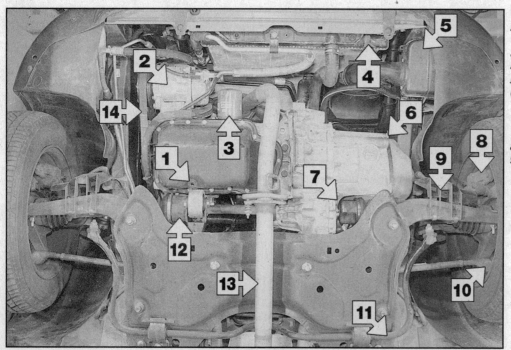

1 Engine oil drain plug
2 Air conditioning compressor (where fitted)
3 Oil filter
4 Coolant drain plug
5 Air cleaner intake duct
6 Manual transmission filler/level plug
7 Manual transmission drain plug
8 Brake caliper
9 Lower arm
10 Track rod balljoint
11 Anti-roll bar
12 Driveshaft inner CV joint
13 Exhaust system
14 Auxiliary drivebelt

Rear underbody view

1 Spare wheel
2 Exhaust system tailpipe
3 Fuel tank
4 Fuel filter
5 Handbrake cables
6 Rear axle front mounting
7 Rear axle rear mounting
8 Brake pipes
9 Rear shock absorber
10 Rear brake pressure
   regulating valve

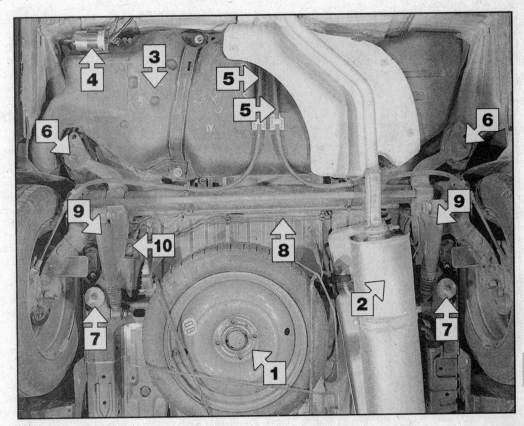

Maintenance procedures

1 General information

1 This Chapter is designed to help the home mechanic maintain his/her vehicle for safety, economy, long life and peak performance.
2 The Chapter contains a master maintenance schedule, followed by Sections dealing specifically with each task in the schedule. Visual checks, adjustments, component renewal and other helpful items are included. Refer to the accompanying illustrations of the engine compartment and the underside of the vehicle for the locations of the various components.
3 Servicing your vehicle in accordance with the mileage/time maintenance schedule and the following Sections will provide a planned maintenance programme, which should result in a long and reliable service life. This is a comprehensive plan, so maintaining some items but not others at the specified service intervals will not produce the same results.
4 As you service your vehicle, you will discover that many of the procedures can –

and should – be grouped together, because of the particular procedure being performed, or because of the close proximity of two otherwise-unrelated components to one another. For example, if the vehicle is raised for any reason, the exhaust can be inspected at the same time as the suspension and steering components.
5 The first step in this maintenance programme is to prepare yourself before the actual work begins. Read through all the Sections relevant to the work to be carried out, then make a list and gather together all the parts and tools required. If a problem is encountered, seek advice from a parts specialist, or a dealer service department.

2 Routine maintenance

1 If, from the time the vehicle is new, the routine maintenance schedule is followed closely, and frequent checks are made of fluid levels and high-wear items, as suggested

throughout this manual, the engine will be kept in relatively good running condition, and the need for additional work will be minimised.
2 It is possible that there will be times when the engine is running poorly due to the lack of regular maintenance. This is even more likely if a used vehicle, which has not received regular and frequent maintenance checks, is purchased. In such cases, additional work may need to be carried out, outside of the regular maintenance intervals.
3 If engine wear is suspected, a compression test (refer to Chapter 2A) will provide valuable information regarding the overall performance of the main internal components. Such a test can be used as a basis to decide on the extent of the work to be carried out. If, for example, a compression test indicates serious internal engine wear, conventional maintenance as described in this Chapter will not greatly improve the performance of the engine, and may prove a waste of time and money, unless extensive overhaul work (Chapter 2C) is carried out first.
4 The following series of operations are those often required to improve the performance of a generally poor-running engine:

Primary operations

a) Clean, inspect and test the battery (See 'Weekly checks').
b) Check all the engine-related fluids (See 'Weekly checks').
c) Check the condition and tension of the auxiliary drivebelt (Section 10).
d) Renew the spark plugs (Section 15).

e) Check the condition of the air cleaner filter element, and renew if necessary (Section 17).
f) Renew the fuel filter (Section 16).
g) Check the condition of all hoses, and check for fluid leaks (Section 4).

5 If the above operations do not prove fully effective, carry out the following operations:

Secondary operations

All items listed under *Primary operations*, plus the following:
a) Check the charging system (Chapter 5A).
b) Check the ignition system (Chapter 5B).
c) Check the fuel system (Chapter 4A).

Every 10 000 miles (15 000 km) or 12 months

3.3 Slacken the engine oil drain plug which is fitted to the rear of the sump

As the drain plug releases from the sump threads, move it away sharply, so the stream of oil issuing from the sump runs into the container, not up your sleeve.

3 Engine oil and filter renewal

Note: *A suitable square-section wrench may be required to undo the sump drain plug. These wrenches can be obtained from most motor factors or your Peugeot dealer.*

1 Frequent oil and filter changes are the most important preventative maintenance procedures which can be undertaken by the DIY owner. As engine oil ages, it becomes diluted and contaminated, which leads to premature engine wear.
2 Before starting this procedure, gather together all the necessary tools and materials. Also make sure that you have plenty of clean rags and newspapers handy, to mop up any spills. Ideally, the engine oil should be warm, as it will drain better, and more built-up sludge will be removed with it. Take care, however, not to touch the exhaust or any other hot parts of the engine when working under the vehicle. To avoid any possibility of scalding, and to protect yourself from possible skin irritants and other harmful contaminants in used engine oils, it is advisable to wear gloves when carrying out this work. Access to the underside of the vehicle will be greatly improved if it can be raised on a lift, driven onto ramps, or jacked up and supported on axle stands (see *Jacking and vehicle support*). Whichever method is chosen, make sure that the vehicle remains

level, or if it is at an angle, that the drain plug is at the lowest point.
3 Slacken the drain plug about half a turn **(see illustration)**. Position the draining container under the drain plug, then remove the plug completely. If possible, try to keep the plug pressed into the sump while unscrewing it by hand the last couple of turns **(see Haynes Hint)**. Recover the sealing ring from the drain plug.
4 Allow some time for the old oil to drain, noting that it may be necessary to reposition the container as the oil flow slows to a trickle.
5 After all the oil has drained, wipe off the drain plug with a clean rag, and fit a new sealing washer. Clean the area around the drain plug opening, and refit the plug, tightening it to the specified torque.
6 Move the container into position under the oil filter, which is located on the front of the cylinder block.
7 Using an oil filter removal tool if necessary, slacken the filter initially, then unscrew it by hand the rest of the way **(see illustration)**. Empty the oil in the old filter into the container.
8 Use a clean rag to remove all oil, dirt and sludge from the filter sealing area on the engine. Check the old filter to make sure that the rubber sealing ring hasn't stuck to the engine. If it has, carefully remove it.
9 Apply a light coating of clean engine oil to the sealing ring on the new filter, then screw it into position on the engine **(see illustrations)**. Tighten the filter firmly by hand only – **do not use any tools**.

3.7 Using an oil filter removal tool to slacken the oil filter

3.9a Lubricate the sealing ring of the new filter with clean engine oil . . .

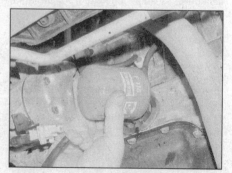

3.9b . . . then screw the filter onto the engine and tighten firmly by hand

10 Remove the old oil and all tools from under the car, then lower the car to the ground (if applicable).

11 Remove the dipstick, then unscrew the oil filler cap from the cylinder head cover. Fill the engine, using the correct grade and type of oil (see *Weekly checks*). An oil can spout or funnel may help to reduce spillage. Pour in half the specified quantity of oil first, then wait a few minutes for the oil to fall to the sump. Continue adding oil a small quantity at a time until the level is up to the lower mark on the dipstick. Adding approximately 1 litre will bring the level up to the upper mark on the dipstick. Refit the filler cap.

12 Start the engine and run it for a few minutes; check for leaks around the oil filter seal and the sump drain plug. Note that there may be a delay of a few seconds before the oil pressure warning light goes out when the engine is first started, as the oil circulates through the engine oil galleries and the new oil filter before the pressure builds up.

13 Switch off the engine, and wait a few minutes for the oil to settle in the sump once more. With the new oil circulated and the filter completely full, recheck the level on the dipstick, and add more oil as necessary.

14 Dispose of the used engine oil safely, with reference to *General repair procedures*.

4 Hose and fluid leak check

1 Visually inspect the engine joint faces, gaskets and seals for any signs of water or oil leaks. Pay particular attention to the areas around the cylinder head cover, cylinder head, oil filter and sump joint faces. Bear in mind that, over a period of time, some very slight seepage from these areas is to be expected – what you are really looking for is any indication of a serious leak. Should a leak be found, renew the offending gasket or oil seal by referring to the appropriate Chapters in this manual.

2 Also check the security and condition of all the engine-related pipes and hoses. Ensure that all cable ties or securing clips are in place, and in good condition. Clips which are broken or missing can lead to chafing of the hoses, pipes or wiring, which could cause more serious problems in the future.

3 Carefully check the radiator hoses and heater hoses along their entire length. Renew any hose which is cracked, swollen or deteriorated. Cracks will show up better if the hose is squeezed. Pay close attention to the hose clips that secure the hoses to the cooling system components. Hose clips can pinch and puncture hoses, resulting in cooling system leaks. If crimped-type hose clips are used, it may be a good idea to replace them with standard worm-drive clips.

4 Inspect all the cooling system components (hoses, joint faces, etc) for leaks (see Haynes Hint).

5 Where any problems are found on system components, renew the component or gasket with reference to Chapter 3.

6 Where applicable, inspect the automatic transmission fluid cooler hoses for leaks or deterioration.

7 With the vehicle raised, inspect the petrol tank and filler neck for punctures, cracks and other damage. The connection between the filler neck and tank is especially critical. Sometimes a rubber filler neck or connecting hose will leak due to loose retaining clamps or deteriorated rubber.

8 Carefully check all rubber hoses and fuel pipes leading away from the petrol tank. Check for loose connections, deteriorated hoses, crimped lines, and other damage. Pay particular attention to the vent pipes and hoses, which often loop up around the filler neck and can become blocked or crimped. Follow the pipes to the front of the vehicle, carefully inspecting them all the way. Renew damaged sections as necessary.

9 From within the engine compartment, check the security of all fuel pipe attachments and unions, and inspect the fuel pipes and vacuum hoses for kinks, chafing and deterioration.

10 Where applicable, check the condition of the power steering fluid hoses and pipes.

5 Driveshaft gaiter and CV joints check

1 With the vehicle raised and securely supported on stands (see *Jacking and vehicle support*), turn the steering onto full lock, then slowly rotate the roadwheel. Inspect the condition of the outer constant velocity (CV) joint gaiters, squeezing the gaiters to open out the folds **(see illustration)**. Check for signs of cracking, splits or deterioration of the gaiter, which may allow the grease to escape, and lead to water and grit entry into the joint. Also check the security and condition of the retaining clips. Repeat these checks on the inner CV joints. If any damage or deterioration is found, the gaiters should be renewed (see Chapter 8).

5.1 Check the driveshaft gaiters for signs of damage or deterioration

A leak in the cooling system will usually show up as white- or rust-coloured deposits on the area adjoining the leak.

2 At the same time, check the general condition of the CV joints themselves by first holding the driveshaft and attempting to rotate the wheel. Repeat this check by holding the inner joint and attempting to rotate the driveshaft. Any appreciable movement indicates wear in the joints, wear in the driveshaft splines, or a loose driveshaft retaining nut.

6 Hinge and lock lubrication

1 Work around the vehicle, and lubricate the hinges of the bonnet, doors and tailgate with a small amount of general-purpose oil.

2 Lightly lubricate the bonnet release mechanism and exposed section of inner cable with a smear of grease.

3 Check carefully the security and operation of all hinges, latches and locks, adjusting them where required. Check the operation of the central locking system (if fitted).

4 Check the condition and operation of the tailgate struts, renewing them if either is leaking or no longer able to support the tailgate securely when raised.

7 Road test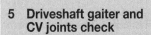

Instruments and electrical equipment

1 Check the operation of all instruments and electrical equipment.

2 Make sure that all instruments read correctly, and switch on all electrical equipment in turn to check it functions properly.

Steering and suspension

3 Check for any abnormalities in the steering, suspension, handling or road 'feel'.

4 Drive the vehicle, and check that there are no unusual vibrations or noises.

1A

8.2 Reset the service indicator as described in text

5 Check that the steering feels positive, with no excessive 'sloppiness', or roughness, and check for any suspension noises when cornering, or when driving over bumps.

Drivetrain

6 Check the performance of the engine, clutch, transmission and driveshafts.
7 Listen for any unusual noises from the engine, clutch and transmission.
8 Make sure the engine idles smoothly, and that there is no hesitation when accelerating.
9 Check that the clutch action is smooth and progressive, that the drive is taken up smoothly, and that the pedal travel is not excessive. Also listen for any noises when the clutch pedal is depressed.
10 Check that all gears can be engaged smoothly, without noise, and that the gear lever action is smooth and not vague or 'notchy'.
11 On automatic transmission models, make sure that all gearchanges occur smoothly,

without snatching, and without an increase in engine speed between changes. Check that all the gear positions can be selected with the vehicle at rest. If any problems are found, they should be referred to a Peugeot dealer.
12 Listen for a metallic clicking sound from the front of the vehicle, as the vehicle is driven slowly in a circle with the steering on full lock. Carry out this check in both directions. If a clicking noise is heard, this indicates wear in a driveshaft joint, in which case, the complete driveshaft must be renewed (see Chapter 8).

Check the operation and performance of the braking system

13 Make sure that the vehicle does not pull to one side when braking, and that the wheels do not lock prematurely when braking hard.
14 Check that there is no vibration through the steering when braking.
15 Check that the handbrake operates correctly, without excessive movement of the lever, and that it holds the vehicle on a slope.
16 Test the operation of the brake servo unit as follows. With the engine off, depress the footbrake four or five times to exhaust the vacuum. Start the engine, holding the brake pedal depressed. As the engine starts, there should be a noticeable 'give' in the brake pedal as vacuum builds up. Allow the engine to run for at least two minutes, and then switch it off. If the brake pedal is depressed now, it should be possible to detect a hiss from the servo as the pedal is depressed. After about four or five applications, no further hissing should be heard, and the pedal should feel considerably firmer.

8 Resetting the service indicator

1 On completion of the service, select the correct interval to the next service then rest the service interval indicator as follows.

Selecting the correct interval for the service indicator

2 With the ignition switched off, press and hold the trip meter button **(see illustration)**.
3 Turn on the ignition switch and release the trip meter button straight away. The indicator will now display the mileage interval to the next service, eg. 20 000. Scroll through the various mileage intervals by depressing the trip meter button. Once the correct interval is displayed, press and hold the trip meter button (the display will flash during this period). Once the display stops flashing, release the button and turn off the ignition switch.

Resetting the indicator

4 With the ignition switched off, press and hold trip meter button.
5 Turn on the ignition switch (the interval to the next service will flash on the display) and keep the trip meter button depressed for 10 seconds. After this period the display will indicate 0 and the service spanner symbol will disappear.
6 Turn off the ignition switch.
7 Turn on the ignition switch and check the correct mileage to the next service interval is displayed on the indicator.

Every 20 000 miles (30 000 km) or two years

9 Pollen filter renewal

1 Open the bonnet.
2 Reach in behind the right-hand suspension strut upper mounting and remove the pollen filter element from the heating/ventilation housing intake, noting which way around the filter is fitted **(see illustration)**.

9.2 Removing the pollen filter element

3 Wipe clean the inside of the housing and fit the new pollen filter element, making sure that it is correctly seated.
4 Close the bonnet.

10 Auxiliary drivebelt check and renewal

Note: *On models without power steering and air conditioning, Peugeot specify the use of a special electronic tool (SEEM C.TRONIC type 105.5 belt tension measuring tool) to correctly set the auxiliary drivebelt tension. If access to this equipment cannot be obtained, an approximate setting can be achieved using the method described below. If this method is used, the tension should be checked using the special electronic tool at the earliest opportunity.*

Check

1 Apply the handbrake, then jack up the front of the car and support it on axle stands (see *Jacking and vehicle support*). Remove the right-hand front roadwheel.
2 Undo the screws securing the front section

of the right-hand wheelarch liner to the base of the bumper. Remove the fasteners (pull out the centre pin then remove the complete fastener) securing the liner section to the body then manoeuvre the front section of the liner out from underneath the wing.
3 Using a suitable socket and extension bar fitted to the crankshaft sprocket bolt, rotate the crankshaft so that the entire length of the drivebelt can be examined. Examine the drivebelt for cracks, splitting, fraying or damage. Check also for signs of glazing (shiny patches) and for separation of the belt plies. Renew the belt if worn or damaged.
4 If the condition of the belt is satisfactory, on models without power steering and air conditioning, check the drivebelt tension as described below. **Note:** *On models with air conditioning and power steering, there is no need to check the drivebelt tension (an automatic tensioner is fitted).*
5 Refit the wheelarch liner, securing it in position with the retaining screws and fasteners.
6 Refit the roadwheel then lower the vehicle to the ground and tighten the wheel bolts to the specified torque.

Renewal – models without power steering or air conditioning

Removal

7 If not already done, proceed as described in paragraphs 1 and 2.

8 Disconnect the battery negative lead.

9 Slacken both the alternator upper and lower mounting bolts and the bolt securing the adjuster strap to the block **(see illustrations)**.

10 Back off the adjuster bolt to relieve the tension in the drivebelt, then slip the drivebelt from the pulleys **(see illustrations)**. Note: *If the belt is going to be re-used, mark the direction of rotation on the belt prior to removal. This will ensure it is refitted the correct way around.*

Refitting

11 If the belt is being renewed, ensure that the correct type is used and if the original belt is being refitted, use the mark made on removal to ensure it is fitted the correct way around.

12 Fit the belt around the pulleys, and take up the slack in the belt by tightening the adjuster bolt. Tension the drivebelt as described in the following paragraphs.

Tensioning

13 If not already done, proceed as described in paragraphs 1 and 2.

14 If the special measuring tool is available, fit the measuring equipment to the 'lower run' of the belt, approximately midway between the crankshaft and alternator pulleys. The belt tension should be set to the figure given in the Specifications at the start of this Chapter.

15 If the measuring tool is not available, the belt should be tensioned so that, under firm thumb pressure, there is about 5.0 mm of free movement at the mid-point between the pulleys on the lower belt run.

 HAYNES HiNT *Correct tensioning of the drivebelt will ensure it has a long life. A belt which is too slack will slip and squeal. Beware of overtightening, as this can cause wear in the alternator bearings.*

16 To adjust the belt tension, with the upper mounting bolt just holding the alternator firm, and the lower mounting bolt and adjuster strap bolts loosened, turn the adjuster bolt until the correct tension is achieved.

17 Rotate the crankshaft a couple of times, recheck the tension, then tighten both the alternator mounting bolts to the specified torque. Where applicable, also tighten the bolt securing the adjuster strap to its mounting bracket.

18 Refit the wheelarch liner, securing it in position with the retaining screws and fasteners.

19 Refit the roadwheel then lower the vehicle to the ground and tighten the wheel bolts to the specified torque. Reconnect the battery.

10.9a On models without power steering or air conditioning, slacken the alternator upper mounting bolt . . .

Renewal – models with power steering or air conditioning

Removal

20 If not already done, proceed as described in paragraphs 1 and 2.

21 Disconnect the battery negative lead.

10.10a Back off the adjuster bolt . . .

10.9b . . . the lower mounting bolt and adjuster strap bolt (arrowed)

22 Slacken the tensioner pulley nut and rotate the centre bolt to move the pulley away from the drivebelt until there is sufficient slack for the drivebelt to be removed from the pulleys **(see illustration)**. Note: *If the belt is going to be re-used, mark the direction of rotation on the belt prior to removal. This will ensure it is refitted the correct way around.*

10.10b . . . then remove the drivebelt from the engine

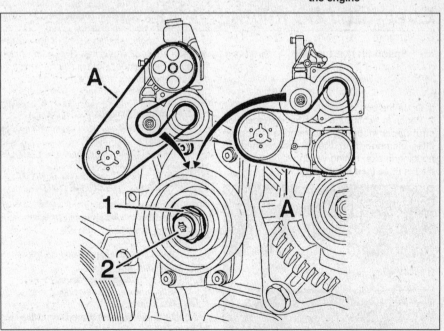

10.22 On models with power steering or air conditioning, slacken the pulley nut (1) and rotate the centre bolt (2) to adjust the drivebelt tension. Inset show belt tension checking point (A)

1A

10.34a Fit a 3/8 inch drive ratchet/bar (1) to the square-section backplate hole then pivot the tensioner away from the belt . . .

10.34b . . . and secure it in position by inserting a 6 mm diameter bolt/pin (2) in through the backplate hole (shown with the drivebelt removed for clarity)

Refitting

23 If the belt is being renewed, ensure that the correct type is used and if the original belt is being refitted, use the mark made on removal to ensure it is fitted the correct way around. Fit the drivebelt around the pulleys in the following order:
   a) Power steering pump and/or air conditioning compressor.
   b) Crankshaft.
   c) Alternator.
   d) Tensioner roller.

24 Ensure that the ribs on the belt are correctly engaged with the grooves in the pulleys, and that the drivebelt is correctly routed. Take all the slack out of the belt by turning the tensioner pulley centre bolt. Tension the belt as follows.

Tensioning

25 If not already done, proceed as described in paragraphs 1 and 2.

26 If the special measuring tool is available, fit the measuring equipment to the belt, approximately midway between the crankshaft and power steering pump/air conditioning compressor pulleys (as applicable). Check the belt tension is as given in the Specifications at the start of this Chapter.

10.35 With the tensioner pulley locked in position, the drivebelt can be slipped off the pulleys

27 If the measuring tool is not available, the belt should be tensioned so that, under firm thumb pressure, there is about 5.0 mm of free movement at the mid-point between the crankshaft and power steering pump/air conditioning compressor pulleys (as applicable).

> **HAYNES HiNT**
> *Correct tensioning of the drivebelt will ensure it has a long life. A belt which is too slack will slip and squeal. Beware of overtightening, as this can cause wear in the alternator bearings.*

28 To adjust the tension, slacken the tensioner pulley nut then rotate the centre bolt until the correct tension is achieved. Once the belt is correctly tensioned, hold the centre bolt stationary then tighten the pulley nut to the specified torque. Rotate the crankshaft a couple of times and recheck the tension.

29 When the belt is correctly tensioned, refit the wheelarch liner, securing it in position with the retaining screws and fasteners.

30 Refit the roadwheel then lower the vehicle to the ground and tighten the wheel bolts to the specified torque. Reconnect the battery.

Renewal – models with power steering and air conditioning

Note: *A 6 mm diameter bolt or pin will be required to lock the tensioner in position.*

Removal

31 If not already done, proceed as described in paragraphs 1 and 2.

32 Disconnect the battery negative lead.

33 Fit a 3/8 inch drive ratchet or bar to the square-section hole in the tensioner pulley backplate and have ready the 6 mm diameter bolt/pin.

34 Use the ratchet/bar to move the tensioner pulley away from the drivebelt and insert the bolt/pin through the backplate hole. Position the backplate so its hole aligns with the corresponding hole in the bracket then lock the tensioner in position by fully inserting the bolt. Ensure the bolt/pin is correctly located in the bracket then slowly release the tensioner backplate **(see illustrations)**. With the tensioner securely locked clear of the belt, remove the ratchet/bar from the backplate.

35 Disengage the drivebelt from all the pulleys, noting its correct routing, and remove it from the engine **(see illustration)**. Note: *If the belt is going to be re-used, mark the direction of rotation on the belt prior to removal. This will ensure it is refitted the correct way around.*

Refitting and tensioning

36 If the belt is being renewed, ensure that the correct type is used and if the original belt is being refitted, use the mark made on removal to ensure it is fitted the correct way around. Fit the drivebelt around the pulleys in the following order:
   a) Power steering pump.
   b) Alternator.
   c) Idler pulley
   d) Air conditioning compressor.
   e) Crankshaft.
   f) Automatic tensioner pulley.

37 Ensure that the ribs on the belt are correctly engaged with the grooves in the pulleys then refit the 3/8 inch drive ratchet/bar to the backplate. Move the tensioner away from the belt until it is possible to withdraw the locking bolt/pin then slowly release tensioner to tension the drivebelt.

Caution: Do not allow the tensioner pulley to spring forcefully onto the belt as this could result in damage.

38 Remove the ratchet/bar from backplate and refit the wheelarch liner, securing it in position with the retaining screws and fasteners.

39 Refit the roadwheel then lower the vehicle to the ground and tighten the wheel bolts to the specified torque. Reconnect the battery.

11 Front brake pad check

1 Firmly apply the handbrake, then jack up the front of the car and support it securely on axle stands (see *Jacking and vehicle support*). Remove the front roadwheels.

2 For a quick check, the pad thickness can be carried out via the inspection hole on the front caliper **(see Haynes Hint)**. Using a steel rule, measure the thickness of the pad friction material. This must not be less than the specified minimum given in the Specifications.

3 For a comprehensive check, the brake pads should be removed and cleaned. The operation of the caliper can then be checked, and the brake disc itself can be fully examined on both sides. Refer to Chapter 9 for details.

4 If any pad's friction material is worn to the specified minimum thickness or less, all four pads must be renewed as a set. Refer to Chapter 9 for details.

5 On completion, refit the roadwheels then lower the vehicle to the ground and tighten the wheel bolts to the specified torque.

12 Handbrake check and adjustment

1 Check and, if necessary, adjust the handbrake as described in Chapter 9.

13 Steering and suspension check

Front suspension and steering check

1 Raise the front of the vehicle, and securely support it on axle stands (see *Jacking and vehicle support*).

2 Visually inspect the balljoint dust covers and the steering gear gaiters for splits, chafing or deterioration. Any wear of these components will cause loss of lubricant, together with dirt

For a quick check, the thickness of the brake pad friction material can be checked through the aperture on the caliper body.

and water entry, resulting in rapid deterioration of the balljoints or steering gear.

3 On vehicles with power steering, check the fluid pipes/hoses for chafing or deterioration, and the pipe and hose unions for fluid leaks. Also check for signs of fluid leakage under pressure from the steering gear rubber gaiters, which would indicate failed fluid seals within the steering gear.

4 Grasp the roadwheel at the 12 o'clock and 6 o'clock positions, and try to rock it **(see illustration)**. Very slight free play may be felt, but if the movement is appreciable, further investigation is necessary to determine the source. Continue rocking the wheel while an assistant depresses the footbrake. If the movement is now eliminated or significantly reduced, it is likely that the hub bearings are at fault. If the free play is still evident with the footbrake depressed, then there is wear in the suspension joints or mountings.

5 Now grasp the wheel at the 9 o'clock and 3 o'clock positions, and try to rock it as before. Any movement felt now may again be caused by wear in the hub bearings or the steering track-rod balljoints. If the inner or outer balljoint is worn, the visual movement will be obvious.

6 Using a large screwdriver or flat bar, check for wear in the suspension mounting bushes by levering between the relevant suspension component and its attachment point. Some movement is to be expected as the mountings

13.4 Check for wear in the hub bearings by grasping the wheel and trying to rock it

are made of rubber, but excessive wear should be obvious. Also check the condition of any visible rubber bushes, looking for splits, cracks or contamination of the rubber.

7 With the car standing on its wheels, have an assistant turn the steering wheel back and forth about an eighth of a turn each way. There should be very little, if any, lost movement between the steering wheel and roadwheels. If this is not the case, closely observe the joints and mountings previously described, but in addition, check the steering column universal joints for wear, and the steering gear itself.

Suspension strut/ shock absorber check

8 Check for any signs of fluid leakage around the suspension strut/shock absorber body, or from the rubber gaiter around the piston rod. Should any fluid be noticed, the suspension strut/shock absorber is defective internally, and should be renewed. **Note:** *Suspension struts/shock absorbers should always be renewed in pairs on the same axle, or the handling of the vehicle will be adversely affected.*

9 The efficiency of the suspension strut/shock absorber may be checked by bouncing the vehicle at each corner. Generally speaking, the body will return to its normal position and stop after being depressed. If it rises and returns on a rebound, the suspension strut/shock absorber is probably suspect. Examine also the suspension strut/shock absorber upper and lower mountings for any signs of wear.

1A

Every 40 000 miles (60 000 km) or two years

14 Brake fluid renewal

⚠ *Warning: Brake hydraulic fluid can harm your eyes and damage painted surfaces, so use extreme caution when handling and pouring it. Do not use fluid that has been standing open for some time, as it absorbs moisture from the air. Excess moisture can cause a dangerous loss of braking effectiveness.*

1 The procedure is similar to that for the bleeding of the hydraulic system as described in Chapter 9, except that the brake fluid reservoir should be emptied by siphoning, using a clean poultry baster or similar before starting, and allowance should be made for the old fluid to be expelled when bleeding a section of the circuit.

2 Working as described in Chapter 9, open the first bleed screw in the sequence, and pump the brake pedal gently until nearly all the old fluid has been emptied from the master cylinder reservoir.

 Old hydraulic fluid is invariably much darker in colour than the new, making it easy to distinguish the two.

3 Top-up to the MAX level with new fluid, and continue pumping until only the new fluid remains in the reservoir, and new fluid can be seen emerging from the bleed screw. Tighten the screw, and top the reservoir level up to the MAX level line.

4 Work through all the remaining bleed screws in the sequence until new fluid can be seen at all of them. Be careful to keep the master cylinder reservoir topped-up to above the DANGER level at all times, or air may enter the system and increase the length of the task.
5 When the operation is complete, check that all bleed screws are securely tightened, and that their dust caps are refitted. Wash off all traces of spilt fluid, and recheck the master cylinder reservoir fluid level.
6 Check the operation of the brakes before taking the car on the road.

Every 40 000 miles (60 000 km) or four years

15 Spark plug renewal

1 The correct functioning of the spark plugs is vital for the correct running and efficiency of the engine. It is essential that the plugs fitted are appropriate for the engine (see Specifications). If this type is used and the engine is in good condition, the spark plugs should not need attention between scheduled replacement intervals. Spark plug cleaning is rarely necessary, and should not be attempted unless specialised equipment is available, as damage can easily be caused to the firing ends.
2 To gain access to the spark plugs, remove the ignition HT coil as described in Chapter 5B.
3 Unscrew the plugs using a spark plug spanner, suitable box spanner or a deep socket and extension bar **(see illustration)**. Keep the socket aligned with the spark plug – if it is forcibly moved to one side, the ceramic insulator may be broken off. As each plug is removed, examine it as follows.
4 Examination of the spark plugs will give a good indication of the condition of the engine **(see illustration)**. If the insulator nose of the spark plug is clean and white, with no deposits, this is indicative of a weak mixture or too hot a plug (a hot plug transfers heat away from the electrode slowly, a cold plug transfers heat away quickly).
5 If the tip and insulator nose are covered with hard black-looking deposits, then this is indicative that the mixture is too rich. Should the plug be black and oily, then it is likely that the engine is fairly worn, as well as the mixture being too rich.
6 If the insulator nose is covered with light tan to greyish-brown deposits, then the mixture is correct and it is likely that the engine is in good condition.
7 The spark plug electrode gap is of considerable importance as, if it is too large or too small, the size of the spark and its efficiency will be seriously impaired. The gap should be set to the value given in the Specifications at the beginning of this Chapter. **Note:** *The electrode gap on multi-electrode spark plugs cannot be adjusted.*
8 To set the gap on single-electrode plugs, measure the gap with a feeler blade, and then bend open, or closed, the outer plug electrode until the correct gap is achieved **(see illustration)**. The centre electrode should never be bent, as this may crack the insulator and cause plug failure, if nothing worse. If using feeler blades, the gap is correct when the appropriate-size blade is a firm sliding fit.
9 Special spark plug electrode gap adjusting tools are available from most motor accessory shops, or from spark plug manufacturers **(see illustration)**.
10 Before fitting the spark plugs, check that the threaded connector sleeves are tight, and that the plug exterior and threads are clean (see **Haynes Hint**).
11 Remove the rubber hose (if used), and tighten the plug to the specified torque using the spark plug socket and a torque wrench. Refit the remaining spark plugs in the same manner.
12 Refit the ignition HT coil as described in Chapter 5B.

16 Fuel filter renewal

⚠️ *Warning: Before carrying out the following operation, refer to the precautions given in 'Safety first!' at the beginning of this manual, and follow them implicitly. Petrol is a highly-dangerous and volatile liquid, and the precautions necessary when handling it cannot be overstressed.*

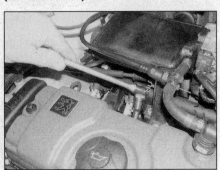

15.3 Unscrew the spark plugs using a deep socket and extension bar

15.4 Examine the spark plugs to check the condition of the engine – see text

15.8 Measuring the spark plug electrode gap with a feeler blade

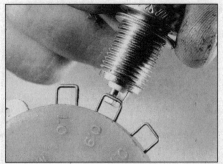

15.9 Measuring the spark plug electrode gap with a wire gauge

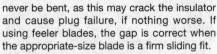
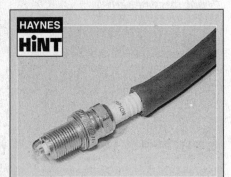

HAYNES HINT

It is very often difficult to insert spark plugs into their holes without cross-threading them. To avoid this possibility, fit a short length of rubber hose over the end of the spark plug. The flexible hose acts as a universal joint to help align the plug with the plug hole. Should the plug begin to cross-thread, the hose will slip on the spark plug, preventing thread damage to the cylinder head.

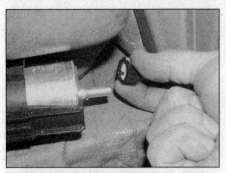

16.3 Depress the retaining clips and detach the fuel pipes from the fuel filter

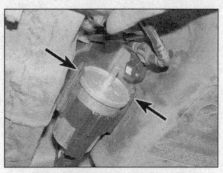

16.4a Release the retaining clips (arrowed) . . .

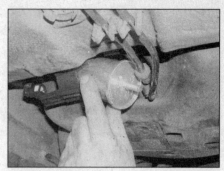

16.4b . . . then slide the filter out from its holder

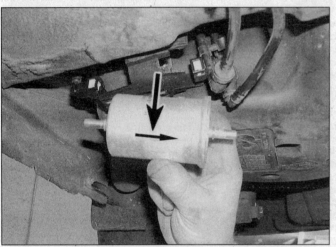

16.5 Ensure the new filter is installed with its arrow (shown) or OUT marking facing the right direction

17.1 Undo the retaining screws (arrowed) . . .

1A

1 The fuel filter is situated underneath the rear of the vehicle, on the right-hand side of the front of the fuel tank. To improve access to the filter, chock the front wheels, then jack up the rear of the vehicle and support it on axle stands (see *Jacking and vehicle support*).
2 Place a container beneath the fuel filter to catch all spilt fuel.
3 Position a large rag around the fuel pipe union, to catch any fuel spray which may be expelled as the fuel pressure is released, then depress the retaining clips and slowly disconnect the fuel pipe. Disconnect the other pipe from the opposite end of the filter and allow the filter contents to drain into the container **(see illustration)**.
4 Release the retaining clips and slide the fuel filter out of its holder, noting which way around it is fitted **(see illustrations)**. Dispose safely of the old filter; it will be highly inflammable, and may explode if thrown on a fire.
5 Slide the new filter into position, ensuring it is fitted the correct way around; the filter will either have an arrow on its body (indicating the correct direction of fuel flow) or be stamped OUT on one end (indicating the fuel outlet end of the filter) **(see illustration)**.
6 Ensure the filter is clipped securely in its holder then reconnect both fuel pipes. Ensure

the pipes 'click' into position on the filter and are securely retained by their quick-release fittings.
7 Start the engine and check the fuel filter for signs leaks.

17 Air cleaner filter element renewal

1 Undo the retaining screws securing the lid to the air cleaner housing **(see illustration)**.
2 Lift the lid and remove the air filter element

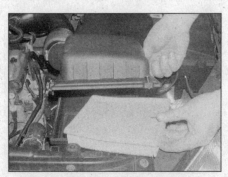

17.2 . . . then lift the lid and remove the filter element from the housing

from the housing, noting which way up it is fitted **(see illustration)**. If necessary, slacken the retaining clip securing the intake duct to the air cleaner housing lid then remove the lid to improve access.
3 Wipe clean the inside of the housing then fit the new element, ensuring it is correctly located.
4 Locate the lid correctly on the housing and securely tighten the retaining screws. Where necessary, reconnect the intake duct and securely tighten the retaining clip.

18 Manual transmission oil level check

Note: *A suitable square-section wrench may be required to undo the transmission filler/level plug on some models. These wrenches can be obtained from most motor factors or your Peugeot dealer.*
1 Park the car on a level surface. The oil level must be checked before the car is driven, or at least 5 minutes after the engine has been switched off. If the oil is checked immediately after driving the car, some of the oil will remain distributed around the transmission, resulting in an inaccurate level reading.

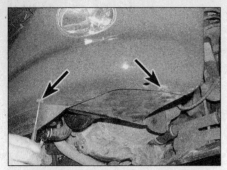

18.2a Remove the retaining screws (arrowed) . . .

18.2b . . . and fasteners . . .

18.2c . . . and remove the front section of the left-hand wheelarch liner

2 To improve access, undo the screws securing the front section of the left-hand wheelarch liner to the base of the bumper. Remove the fasteners (pull out the centre pin then remove the complete fastener) securing the liner section to the body then manoeuvre the front section of the liner out from underneath the wing **(see illustrations)**.

3 Wipe clean the area around the filler/level plug, which is on the left-hand end of the transmission. Unscrew the plug and clean it; discard the sealing washer **(see illustration)**.

4 The oil level should reach the lower edge of the filler/level hole. A certain amount of oil will have gathered behind the filler/level plug, and

will trickle out when it is removed; this does **not** necessarily indicate that the level is correct. To ensure that a true level is established, wait until the initial trickle has stopped, then add oil as necessary until a trickle of new oil can be seen emerging. The level will be correct when the flow ceases; use only good-quality oil of the specified type.

5 Filling the transmission with oil is an extremely awkward operation; above all, allow plenty of time for the oil level to settle properly before checking it. If a large amount is added to the transmission, and a large amount flows out on checking the level, refit the filler/level plug and take the vehicle on a short journey so that the new oil is distributed fully around the transmission components, then recheck the level when it has settled again.

6 If the transmission has been overfilled so that oil flows out as soon as the filler/level plug is removed, check that the car is completely level (front-to-rear and side-to-side), and allow the surplus to drain off into a container.

7 When the level is correct, fit a new sealing washer to the filler/level plug **(see illustration)**. Refit the plug, tightening it to the specified torque setting. Wash off any spilt oil then refit the wheelarch liner, securing it in position with the screws and fasteners.

19 Automatic transmission fluid level check

Note: *The transmission unit is equipped with a fluid wear sensor to inform the driver when the fluid needs replacing (the ECU flashes the Sport and Snow mode indicator lights when fluid replacement is necessary). Every time the transmission unit is topped-up, this sensor should be adjusted to compensate for the new fluid being added, however this can only be done using the Peugeot diagnostic test box. Adding fluid without adjusting the sensor will not cause any problems but will mean the sensor is giving an inaccurate reading, resulting in fluid renewal being recommended earlier than is actually necessary.*

1 Take the vehicle on a short journey, to warm the transmission up to normal operating temperature, then park the vehicle on level ground. Firmly apply the handbrake and place the selector lever in the P position.

2 Wipe clean the area around the filler plug, which is situated on the top of the transmission, directly beneath the battery. Unscrew the filler plug from the transmission and recover the sealing washer **(see illustration)**.

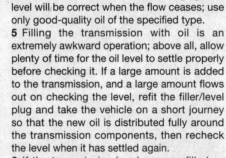
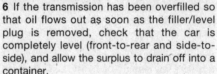

18.3 Unscrew the filler/level plug from the end of the manual transmission unit

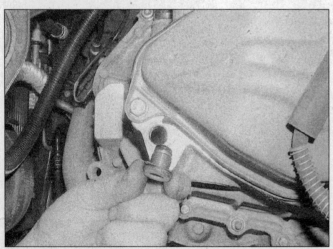

18.7 Once the level is correct, fit a new sealing washer then refit the filler/level plug to the transmission unit

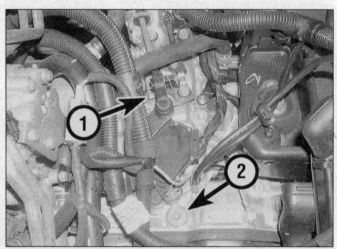

19.2 Automatic transmission unit filler plug (1). DO NOT remove the selector shaft bolt (2)

3 Carefully add 0.5 litre of the specified type of fluid to the transmission via the filler plug aperture. Fit a new sealing washer to the filler plug then refit the plug, tightening it to the specified torque.

4 Position a suitable container under the drain/filler plug arrangement, situated on the base of the transmission. The level plug is the smaller plug fitted to the centre of the larger drain plug **(see illustration)**.
Caution: Do not remove the drain plug by mistake.

5 Start the engine and allow it to idle. With the engine running, retain the drain plug then slacken and remove the level plug and sealing washer.

 Warning: The fluid will be hot, take precautions against scalding.

6 If there is sufficient fluid in the transmission unit, fluid should trickle out the centre of the drain plug before slowing to a drip. **Note:** *If no fluid trickles out, or just a few drips appear when the plug is removed, the fluid level is too low. Refit the level plug then switch off the engine. Add a further 0.5 litre of fluid to the transmission then refit the filler plug and*

repeat the check (see paragraphs 3 to 5).
7 Once the flow of fluid stops, the level is correct. Fit a new sealing washer to the level plug then refit the plug and tighten it to the specified torque. Switch off the engine.

20 Rear brake shoe check

1 Remove the rear brake drums, and check the brake shoes for signs of wear or contamination. At the same time, also inspect the wheel cylinders for signs of leakage, and the brake drum for signs of wear. Refer to the relevant Sections of Chapter 9 for further information.

21 Emissions control systems check

1 This check specified by Peugeot involves checking the engine management system by plugging an electronic tester into the system

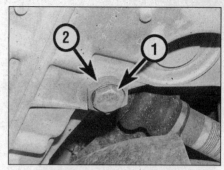

19.4 Unscrew the automatic transmission level plug (1) from the centre of the larger drain plug (2)

diagnostic socket to check the electronic control unit (ECU) memory for faults (see Chapter 4A).
2 In reality, if the vehicle is running correctly and the engine management warning light on the instrument panel is functioning normally, then this check need not be carried out.

Every 80 000 miles (120 000 km)

22 Timing belt renewal

Note: *Although the normal interval for timing belt renewal is 80 000 miles (120 000 km), it is strongly recommended that the interval is halved to 40 000 miles (60 000 km), especially on vehicles which are subjected to intensive use, ie. mainly short journeys or a lot of stop-*

start driving. The actual belt renewal interval is therefore very much up to the individual owner, but bear in mind that severe engine damage will result if the belt breaks.
1 Refer to Chapter 2A.

1A

Every 80 000 miles (120 000 km) or five years

23 Coolant renewal

 Warning: Wait until the engine is cold before starting this procedure. Do not allow antifreeze to come in contact with your skin, or with the painted surfaces of the vehicle. Rinse off spills immediately with plenty of water. Never leave antifreeze lying around in an open container, or in a

puddle in the driveway or on the garage floor. Children and pets are attracted by its sweet smell, but antifreeze can be fatal if ingested.

Cooling system draining

1 With the engine completely cold, unscrew the expansion tank filler cap.
2 Position a suitable container beneath the coolant drain outlet at the lower left-hand side of the radiator.
3 Loosen the drain plug (there is no need to remove it completely) and allow the coolant to

drain into the container **(see illustration)**. If desired, a length of tubing can be fitted to the drain outlet to direct the flow of coolant during draining.
4 To assist draining, remove the cooling system bleed cap/screw (as applicable) from the heater matrix outlet hose union on the engine compartment bulkhead, and the bleed screw and sealing washer from the top of the coolant housing on the left-hand end of the cylinder head **(see illustrations)**.
5 If the coolant has been drained for a reason other than renewal, then provided it is clean

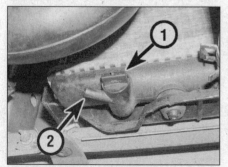

23.3 Loosen the drain plug (1) and drain the coolant via the drain outlet (2)

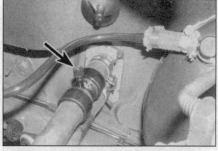

23.4a A bleed cap/screw (arrowed) is fitted to the heater matrix hose near the engine compartment bulkhead

23.4b Coolant outlet housing bleed screw (arrowed) – viewed from above

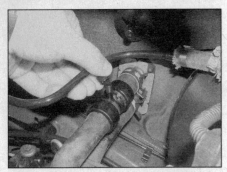

23.18 Remove the bleed cap/screw from the heater matrix hose

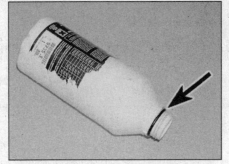

23.19 A plastic bottle and sealing ring (arrowed) can be used as a substitute header tank

23.20 Fit the header tank securely to the expansion tank and slowly fill the cooling system

and less than five years old, it can be re-used, though this is not recommended.

6 Securely tighten the radiator drain plug on completion of draining.

Cooling system flushing

7 If coolant renewal has been neglected, or if the antifreeze mixture has become diluted, then in time, the cooling system may gradually lose efficiency, as the coolant passages become restricted due to rust, scale deposits, and other sediment. The cooling system efficiency can be restored by flushing the system clean.

8 The radiator should be flushed separately from the engine, to avoid excess contamination.

Radiator flushing

9 To flush the radiator, first tighten the radiator drain plug.

10 Disconnect the top and bottom hoses and any other relevant hoses from the radiator (see Chapter 3).

11 Insert a garden hose into the radiator top inlet. Direct a flow of clean water through the radiator, and continue flushing until clean water emerges from the radiator bottom outlet.

12 If after a reasonable period, the water still does not run clear, the radiator can be flushed with a good proprietary cleaning agent. It is important that their manufacturer's instructions are followed carefully. If the contamination is particularly bad, insert the hose in the radiator bottom outlet, and reverse-flush the radiator.

Engine flushing

13 To flush the engine, remove the thermostat (see Chapter 3).

14 With the bottom hose disconnected from the radiator, insert a garden hose into the coolant housing. Direct a clean flow of water

through the engine, and continue flushing until clean water emerges from the radiator bottom hose.

15 When flushing is complete, refit the thermostat and reconnect the hoses (see Chapter 3).

Cooling system filling

16 Before attempting to fill the cooling system, make sure that all hoses and clips are in good condition, and that the clips are tight. Note that an antifreeze mixture must be used all year round, to prevent corrosion of the engine components (see following sub-Section). Also check that the radiator drain plug is in place and tight.

17 Remove the expansion tank filler cap.

18 Remove the cooling system bleed cap and screw(s) (see paragraph 4) **(see illustration)**.

19 Peugeot recommend the use of a 'header tank' when refilling the cooling system, to reduce the possibility of air being trapped in the system. Although Peugeot dealers use a special header tank which screws onto the expansion tank, the same effect can be achieved by using a suitable bottle, with a seal between the bottle and the expansion tank **(see illustration)**.

20 Fit the 'header tank' to the expansion tank and slowly fill the system whilst observing the bleed holes **(see illustration)**. Coolant will emerge from each of the bleed holes in turn, starting with the heater matrix hose. As soon as coolant free from air bubbles emerges from the heater matrix hose outlet, securely refit the cap/screw (as applicable) then watch the bleed hole on the coolant housing. Once coolant free from air bubbles emerges from the housing hole, refit the bleed screw and sealing washer and tighten securely.

21 Continue to fill the cooling system until bubbles stop appearing in the expansion tank. Help to bleed the air from the system by repeatedly squeezing the radiator bottom hose.

22 When no more bubbles appear, ensure the 'header tank' is full (at least 1.0 litre of coolant) then start the engine. Run the engine at a fast idle speed (do not exceed 2000 rpm) until the cooling fan cuts in and out TWICE, then when the fan has stopped for the second time, switch the engine off.

Caution: The coolant will be hot. Take great care not to scald yourself.

23 Allow the engine to cool, then remove the 'header tank'. Wash off any spilt coolant with cold water.

24 When the engine has cooled, check the coolant level with reference to *Weekly checks*. Top-up the level if necessary, and refit the expansion tank cap.

Antifreeze mixture

25 The antifreeze should always be renewed at the specified intervals. This is necessary not only to maintain the antifreeze properties, but also to prevent corrosion which would otherwise occur as the corrosion inhibitors become progressively less effective.

26 Always use an ethylene-glycol based antifreeze which is suitable for use in mixed-metal cooling systems.

27 Before adding antifreeze, the cooling system should be completely drained, preferably flushed, and all hoses checked for condition and security.

28 After filling with antifreeze, a label should be attached to the expansion tank, stating the type and concentration of antifreeze used, and the date installed. Any subsequent topping-up should be made with the same type and concentration of antifreeze.

29 Do not use engine antifreeze in the windscreen/tailgate washer system, as it will damage the vehicle paintwork. A screenwash additive should be added to the washer system in the quantities stated on the bottle.

Chapter 1 Part B:
Routine maintenance and servicing – diesel models

Contents

Degrees of difficulty

| Easy, suitable for novice with little experience | | Fairly easy, suitable for beginner with some experience | | Fairly difficult, suitable for competent DIY mechanic | | Difficult, suitable for experienced DIY mechanic | | Very difficult, suitable for expert DIY or professional | |

Lubricants and fluids

Refer to *Weekly checks*

Capacities

Engine oil

Including filter:
1.9 litre engine	4.75 litres
2.0 litre engine	4.50 litre

Difference between MAX and MIN dipstick marks:
1.9 litre engines	1.6 litres
2.0 litre engines	1.4 litres

Cooling system (approximate)
1.9 litre engine	8.20 litres
2.0 litre engine	6.25 litres
Transmission	1.9 litres
Power-assisted steering (approximate)	1.0 litre
Fuel tank	50 litres

Engine

Auxiliary drivebelt tensions (for use with special Peugeot tool – see text):

1.9 litre engine:
Models without power steering (with or without or air conditioning)	114 SEEM units*

Models with power steering (without air conditioning):
Models with a manual tensioner	114 SEEM units*
Models with an automatic tensioner	N/A – automatic tensioner fitted
Models with power steering and air conditioning	N/A – automatic tensioner fitted
2.0 litre engine	N/A – automatic tensioner fitted

This figure is only applicable when fitting a new auxiliary drivebelt – see text

Cooling system

Frost and corrosion protection	Refer to antifreeze manufacturer's concentration recommendations

Fuel system

Injection pump adjustment details – 1.9 litre engine:

Idle speed:
Models with air conditioning	875 ± 25 rpm
Models without air conditioning	800 ± 25 rpm
Anti-stall speed (3 mm shim in position – see text)	1700 ± 100 rpm

Brakes

Brake pad friction material minimum thickness	2.0 mm
Brake shoe friction material minimum thickness	1.5 mm

Torque wrench settings

	Nm	lbf ft
Auxiliary drivebelt tensioner:		
1.9 litre engine:		
Retaining bolts – models without power steering	25	18
Backplate bolt – models with power steering	95	70
Pulley bolt – models with power steering and air conditioning	50	37
2.0 litre engine (pulley bolt)	50	37
Roadwheel bolts	85	63
Sump drain plug	34	25
Transmission filler/level plug	22	16

1.9 litre engine maintenance schedule

Note: *This maintenance schedule is a guide recommended by Haynes, for servicing your own vehicle. For the manufacturer's maintenance schedule, check with your local dealer.*
1 The maintenance intervals in this manual are provided with the assumption that you, not the dealer, will be carrying out the work. These are the minimum maintenance intervals recommended by us for vehicles driven daily. If you wish to keep your vehicle in peak condition at all times, you may wish to perform some of these procedures more often. We encourage frequent maintenance, because it enhances the efficiency, performance and resale value of your vehicle.
2 If the vehicle is driven in dusty areas, used to tow a trailer, or driven frequently at slow speeds (idling in traffic) or on short journeys, more frequent maintenance intervals are recommended.
3 When the vehicle is new, it should be serviced by a factory-authorised dealer service department, in order to preserve the factory warranty.
4 Valve clearance checking (Chapter 2B, Section 11) is no longer specified as part of the routine maintenance schedule. Check the valve clearances if there is any tapping or rattling from the top of the engine, or in the event of an unexplained lack of performance. The prudent owner may wish to check the clearances more often, perhaps at 20 000 mile (30 000 km) or four-yearly intervals.

Every 250 miles (400 km) or weekly
☐ Refer to Weekly checks

Every 5000 miles (7500 km) or 12 months – whichever comes sooner
☐ Renew the engine oil and filter (Section 3 – see Note below).
☐ Drain the fuel filter (Section 4).
☐ Check all underbonnet components or fluid leaks (Section 5).
☐ Check the condition of the driveshaft rubber gaiters and CV joints (Section 6).
☐ Lubricate all hinges and locks (Section 7).
☐ Carry out a road test (Section 8).
☐ Reset the service interval indicator (Section 9).

Note: *Peugeot recommend the engine oil and filter are changed every 10 000 miles or two years. However, oil and filter changes are good for the engine and we recommend changing the oil more frequently, especially if the vehicle is used on a lot of short journeys.*

Every 10 000 miles (15 000 km) or 2 years – whichever comes sooner
☐ Renew the pollen filter (Section 10).
☐ Check the idle speed and anti-stall speed (Section 11).
☐ Check the condition of the auxiliary drivebelt (Section 12).
☐ Check the condition of the front brake pads (Section 14).
☐ Check the operation of the handbrake (Section 15).
☐ Check the steering and suspension components (Section 16).

Every 30 000 miles (45 000 km) or 4 years – whichever comes sooner
☐ Renew the fuel filter (Section 18).
☐ Renew the air cleaner filter element (Section 19).
☐ Check the manual transmission oil level (Section 20).
☐ Check the condition of the rear brake shoes (Section 21).
☐ Check the exhaust emissions (Section 22).

Every 40 000 miles (60 000 km)
☐ Renew the timing belt (Section 23).

Note: *Although the normal interval for timing belt renewal is 80 000 miles (120 000 km), it is strongly recommended that the interval is halved to 40 000 miles (60 000 km), especially on vehicles which are subjected to intensive use, ie. mainly short journeys or a lot of stop-start driving. The actual belt renewal interval is therefore very much up to the individual owner, but bear in mind that severe engine damage will result if the belt breaks.*

Every 40 000 miles (60 000 km) or two years – whichever comes sooner
☐ Renew the brake fluid (Section 17).

Every 80 000 miles (120 000 km)
☐ Renew the timing belt (Section 23).

Note: *Although the normal interval for timing belt renewal is 80 000 miles (120 000 km), it is strongly recommended that the interval is halved to 40 000 miles (60 000 km), especially on vehicles which are subjected to intensive use, ie. mainly short journeys or a lot of stop-start driving. The actual belt renewal interval is therefore very much up to the individual owner, but bear in mind that severe engine damage will result if the belt breaks.*

Every 80 000 miles (120 000 km) or five years – whichever comes sooner
☐ Renew the coolant (Section 24).

1B

2.0 litre engine maintenance schedule

Note: *This maintenance schedule is a guide recommended by Haynes, for servicing your own vehicle. For the manufacturer's maintenance schedule, check with your local dealer.*
1 The maintenance intervals in this manual are provided with the assumption that you, not the dealer, will be carrying out the work. These are the minimum maintenance intervals recommended by us for vehicles driven daily. If you wish to keep your vehicle in peak condition at all times, you may wish to perform some of these procedures more often. We encourage frequent maintenance, because it enhances the efficiency, performance and resale value of your vehicle.
2 If the vehicle is driven in dusty areas, used to tow a trailer, or driven frequently at slow speeds (idling in traffic) or on short journeys, more frequent maintenance intervals are recommended.
3 When the vehicle is new, it should be serviced by a factory-authorised dealer service department, in order to preserve the factory warranty.

Every 250 miles (400 km) or weekly
☐ Refer to *Weekly checks*

Every 6000 miles (10 000 km) or 12 months – whichever comes sooner
☐ Renew the engine oil and filter (Section 3 – see Note below).
☐ Drain the fuel filter (Section 4).
☐ Check all underbonnet components or fluid leaks (Section 5).
☐ Check the condition of the driveshaft rubber gaiters and CV joints (Section 6).
☐ Lubricate all hinges and locks (Section 7).
☐ Carry out a road test (Section 8).
☐ Reset the service interval indicator (Section 9).

Note: *Peugeot recommend the engine oil and filter are changed every 12 000 miles or two years. However, oil and filter changes are good for the engine and we recommend changing the oil more frequently, especially if the vehicle is used on a lot of short journeys.*

Every 12 000 miles (20 000 km) or 2 years – whichever comes sooner
☐ Renew the pollen filter (Section 10).
☐ Check the condition of the auxiliary drivebelt (Section 13).
☐ Check the condition of the front brake pads (Section 14).
☐ Check the operation of the handbrake (Section 15).
☐ Check the steering and suspension components (Section 16).

Every 36 000 miles (60 000 km) or two years – whichever comes sooner
☐ Renew the brake fluid (Section 17).

Every 36 000 miles (60 000 km) or 4 years – whichever comes sooner
☐ Renew the fuel filter (Section 18).
☐ Renew the air cleaner filter element (Section 19).
☐ Check the manual transmission oil level (Section 20).
☐ Check the condition of the rear brake shoes (Section 21).
☐ Check the exhaust emissions (Section 22).

Every 48 000 miles (80 000 km)
☐ Renew the timing belt (Section 25).

Note: *Although the normal interval for timing belt renewal is 96 000 miles (160 000 km), it is strongly recommended that the interval is halved to 48 000 miles (80 000 km), especially on vehicles which are subjected to intensive use, ie. mainly short journeys or a lot of stop-start driving. The actual belt renewal interval is therefore very much up to the individual owner, but bear in mind that severe engine damage will result if the belt breaks.*

Every 72 000 miles (120 000 km) or five years – whichever comes sooner
☐ Renew the coolant (Section 24).

Every 96 000 miles (160 000 km)
☐ Renew the timing belt (Section 25).

Note: *Although the normal interval for timing belt renewal is 96 000 miles (160 000 km), it is strongly recommended that the interval is halved to 48 000 miles (80 000 km), especially on vehicles which are subjected to intensive use, ie. mainly short journeys or a lot of stop-start driving. The actual belt renewal interval is therefore very much up to the individual owner, but bear in mind that severe engine damage will result if the belt breaks.*

Underbonnet view of a 1.9 litre diesel engine model (WJY engine shown)

1 Engine oil filler cap
2 Engine oil dipstick
3 Battery
4 Brake (and clutch) fluid reservoir
5 Fuse/relay box
6 Air cleaner housing
7 Radiator
8 Power steering pump/fluid reservoir
9 Washer reservoir filler neck
10 Injection system ECU
11 Coolant expansion tank
12 Pollen filter
13 Preheating control unit
14 Cooling system bleed screw

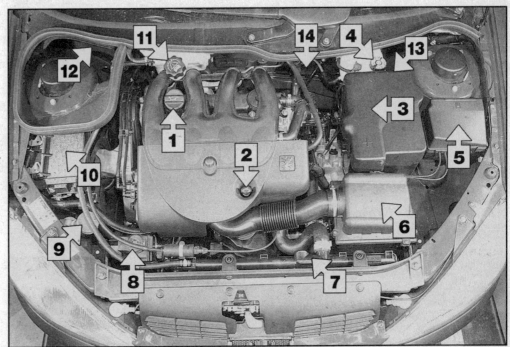

1B

Underbonnet view of a 2.0 litre diesel engine model

1 Engine oil filler cap
2 Engine oil dipstick
3 Battery
4 Brake (and clutch) fluid reservoir
5 Fuse/relay box
6 Air cleaner housing
7 Radiator
8 Power steering pump/fluid reservoir
9 Washer reservoir filler neck
10 Injection system ECU
11 Coolant expansion tank
12 Pollen filter
13 Preheating control unit
14 Cooling system bleed screws
15 Fuel cut-off inertia switch

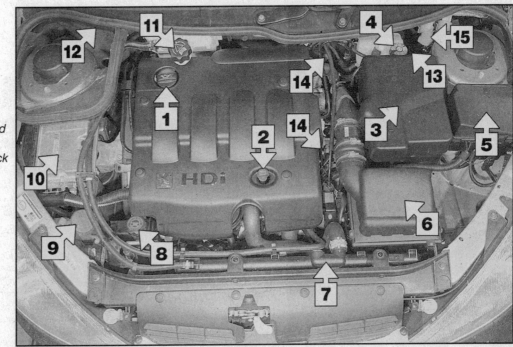

Front underbody view

1 Engine oil drain plug
2 Alternator
3 Oil filter
4 Coolant drain plug
5 Air cleaner intake duct
6 Transmission filler/level plug
7 Transmission drain plug
8 Brake caliper
9 Lower arm
10 Track rod balljoint
11 Anti-roll bar
12 Driveshaft inner CV joint
13 Exhaust system
14 Auxiliary drivebelt
15 Power steering pipes

Rear underbody view

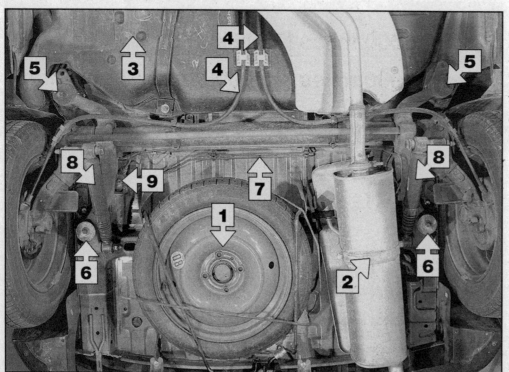

1 Spare wheel
2 Exhaust system tailpipe
3 Fuel tank
4 Handbrake cables
5 Rear axle front mounting
6 Rear axle rear mounting
7 Brake pipes
8 Rear shock absorber
9 Rear brake pressure regulating valve

Maintenance procedures

1 General information

1 This Chapter is designed to help the home mechanic maintain his/her vehicle for safety, economy, long life and peak performance.

2 The Chapter contains a master maintenance schedule, followed by Sections dealing specifically with each task in the schedule. Visual checks, adjustments, component renewal and other helpful items are included. Refer to the accompanying illustrations of the engine compartment and the underside of the vehicle for the locations of the various components.

3 Servicing your vehicle in accordance with the mileage/time maintenance schedule and the following Sections will provide a planned maintenance programme, which should result in a long and reliable service life. This is a comprehensive plan, so maintaining some items but not others at the specified service intervals will not produce the same results.

4 As you service your vehicle, you will discover that many of the procedures can – and should – be grouped together, because of the particular procedure being performed, or because of the close proximity of two otherwise-unrelated components to one another. For example, if the vehicle is raised for any reason, the exhaust can be inspected at the same time as the suspension and steering components.

5 The first step in this maintenance programme is to prepare yourself before the actual work begins. Read through all the Sections relevant to the work to be carried out, then make a list and gather together all the parts and tools required. If a problem is encountered, seek advice from a parts specialist, or a dealer service department.

2 Routine maintenance

1 If, from the time the vehicle is new, the routine maintenance schedule is followed closely, and frequent checks are made of fluid levels and high-wear items, as suggested throughout this manual, the engine will be kept in relatively good running condition, and the need for additional work will be minimised.

2 It is possible that there will be times when the engine is running poorly due to the lack of regular maintenance. This is even more likely if a used vehicle, which has not received regular and frequent maintenance checks, is purchased. In such cases, additional work may need to be carried out, outside of the regular maintenance intervals.

3 If engine wear is suspected, a compression test (refer to Chapter 2B) will provide valuable information regarding the overall performance of the main internal components. Such a test can be used as a basis to decide on the extent of the work to be carried out. If, for example, a compression test indicates serious internal engine wear, conventional maintenance as described in this Chapter will not greatly improve the performance of the engine, and may prove a waste of time and money, unless extensive overhaul work (Chapter 2C) is carried out first.

4 The following series of operations are those often required to improve the performance of a generally poor-running engine:

Primary operations

a) Clean, inspect and test the battery (See 'Weekly checks').
b) Check all the engine-related fluids (See 'Weekly checks').
c) Check the condition and tension of the auxiliary drivebelt (Section 12).
d) Check the condition of the air cleaner filter element, and renew if necessary (Section 19).
e) Check the idle speed and anti-stall speed – 1.9 litre engine (Section 11).
f) Renew the fuel filter (Section 18).
g) Check the condition of all hoses, and check for fluid leaks (Section 5).

5 If the above operations do not prove fully effective, carry out the following operations:

Secondary operations

All items listed under *Primary operations*, plus the following:
a) Check the charging system (Chapter 5A).
b) Check the preheating system (Chapter 5C).
c) Check the fuel system (Chapter 4B).

1.9 litre engine – every 5000 miles (7500 km) or 12 months

2.0 litre engine – every 6000 miles (10 000 km) or 12 months

3 Engine oil and filter renewal

Note: *A suitable square-section wrench may be required to undo the sump drain plug. These wrenches can be obtained from most motor factors or your Peugeot dealer.*

1 Frequent oil and filter changes are the most important preventative maintenance procedures which can be undertaken by the DIY owner. As engine oil ages, it becomes diluted and contaminated, which leads to premature engine wear.

2 Before starting this procedure, gather together all the necessary tools and materials. Also make sure that you have plenty of clean rags and newspapers handy, to mop up any spills. Ideally, the engine oil should be warm, as it will drain better, and more built-up sludge will be removed with it. Take care, however, not to touch the exhaust or any other hot parts of the engine when working under the vehicle. To avoid any possibility of

3.4 Slacken the engine oil drain plug which is fitted to the base of the sump

scalding, and to protect yourself from possible skin irritants and other harmful contaminants in used engine oils, it is advisable to wear gloves when carrying out this work. Access to the underside of the vehicle will be greatly improved if it can be raised on a lift, driven onto ramps, or jacked up and supported on axle stands (see *Jacking and vehicle support*). Whichever method is chosen, make sure that the vehicle remains level, or if it is at an angle, that the drain plug is at the lowest point.

3 Where necessary, slacken and remove the retaining screws, bolts and clips and remove the undercover from beneath the engine/transmission unit.

4 Slacken the drain plug about half a turn **(see illustration)**. Position the draining container under the drain plug, then remove the plug completely. If possible, try to keep the plug

HAYNES HINT

As the drain plug releases from the sump threads, move it away sharply, so the stream of oil issuing from the sump runs into the container, not up your sleeve.

pressed into the sump while unscrewing it by hand the last couple of turns **(See Haynes Hint)**. Recover the sealing ring from the drain plug.

5 Allow some time for the old oil to drain, noting that it may be necessary to reposition the container as the oil flow slows to a trickle.

6 After all the oil has drained, wipe off the drain plug with a clean rag, and fit a new sealing washer. Clean the area around the drain plug opening, and refit the plug, tightening it to the specified torque.

7 Move the container into position under the oil filter, which is located on the front of the cylinder block.

8 Using an oil filter removal tool if necessary, slacken the filter initially, then unscrew it by hand the rest of the way **(see illustration)**. Empty the oil in the old filter into the container.

9 Use a clean rag to remove all oil, dirt and sludge from the filter sealing area on the engine. Check the old filter to make sure that the rubber sealing ring hasn't stuck to the engine. If it has, carefully remove it.

10 Apply a light coating of clean engine oil to the sealing ring on the new filter, then screw it into position on the engine **(see illustrations)**. Tighten the filter firmly by hand only – **do not use any tools**.

11 Remove the old oil and all tools from under the car. Securely refit the undercover (where fitted) then lower the car to the ground (if applicable).

3.8 Using an oil filter removal tool to slacken the oil filter

12 Remove the dipstick, then unscrew the oil filler cap from the cylinder head cover. Fill the engine, using the correct grade and type of oil (see *Weekly checks*). An oil can spout or funnel may help to reduce spillage. Pour in half the specified quantity of oil first, then wait a few minutes for the oil to fall to the sump. Continue adding oil a small quantity at a time until the level is up to the lower mark on the dipstick. Adding approximately 1 litre will bring the level up to the upper mark on the dipstick. Refit the filler cap.

13 Start the engine and run it for a few minutes; check for leaks around the oil filter seal and the sump drain plug. Note that there may be a delay of a few seconds before the oil pressure warning light goes out when the engine is first started, as the oil circulates through the engine oil galleries and the new oil filter before the pressure builds up.

14 Switch off the engine, and wait a few minutes for the oil to settle in the sump once more. With the new oil circulated and the filter completely full, recheck the level on the dipstick, and add more oil as necessary.

15 Dispose of the used engine oil safely, with reference to *General repair procedures*.

4   Fuel filter draining

Caution: Be careful not to allow dirt into the fuel filter housing during this procedure or to spill fuel onto the clutch assembly.

3.10a Lubricate the sealing ring of the new filter with clean engine oil . . .

3.10b . . . then screw the filter onto the engine and tighten firmly by hand

Note: *On 2.0 litre models, fit a new drain screw and O-ring seal on reassembly. On completion, bleed the system of air (see Chapter 4B, Section 5) and check that there is no sign of fuel seepage from the filter drain screw once the engine is restarted.*

1 On 1.9 litre engines, release the fasteners from the right-hand side and top of the engine cover then lift off the cover, taking care not to lose its mounting rubbers **(see illustrations)**.

2 On 2.0 litre engines, remove the fasteners (twist the fasteners 90° to release them) and lift off the engine cover **(see illustrations)**.

3 On all engines, as a precaution, cover the transmission unit bellhousing with absorbent rags to catch any spilt fuel.

4 Wipe clean the exterior of the fuel filter housing then position a container beneath the drain screw on the base of the filter housing **(see illustrations)**. If necessary, attach a

4.1a On 1.9 litre engines remove the fasteners from the right-hand side . . .

4.1b . . . and top of the engine cover . . .

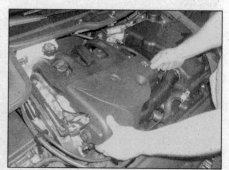

4.1c . . . then remove the cover from the engine

4.2a On 2.0 litre engines, remove each fastener by rotating it 90° . . .

4.2b . . . then lift off the engine cover

A leak in the cooling system will usually show up as white- or rust-coloured deposits on the area adjoining the leak.

short length of hose to the housing drain outlet to allow the flow of fuel to be directed into the container (on some models a hose may be fitted in production).

5 Unscrew the bleed screw and allow the contents of the filter housing to drain into the container. Note that it may be necessary to disconnect a fuel pipe from the filter housing cover to allow the contents of the housing to drain.

6 Once the housing is empty, securely close the bleed screw and securely reconnect the fuel pipe (where necessary) to the cover.

7 Remove the container and (where fitted) hose from the engine compartment. Mop up any spilt fuel then remove the rags from the transmission unit. Dispose of the drained fuel safely.

8 Prime the fuel system as described in Chapter 4B then securely refit the engine cover.

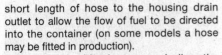

5 Hose and fluid leak check

1 On 1.9 litre engines, release the fasteners from the right-hand side and top of the engine cover then lift off the cover, taking care not to lose its mounting rubbers ills **(see illustrations 4.1a to 4.1c)**.

2 On 2.0 litre engines, remove the fasteners (twist the fasteners 90° to release them) and lift off the engine cover **(see illustrations 4.2a and 4.2b)**.

3 Visually inspect the engine joint faces, gaskets and seals for any signs of water or oil leaks. Pay particular attention to the areas around the cylinder head cover, cylinder head, oil filter and sump joint faces. Bear in mind that, over a period of time, some very slight seepage from these areas is to be expected – what you are really looking for is any indication of a serious leak. Should a leak be found, renew the offending gasket or oil seal by referring to the appropriate Chapters in this manual.

4 Also check the security and condition of all the engine-related pipes and hoses. Ensure that all cable ties or securing clips are in place, and in good condition. Clips which are broken or missing can lead to chafing of the hoses, pipes or wiring, which could cause more serious problems in the future.

5 Carefully check the radiator hoses and heater hoses along their entire length. Renew any hose which is cracked, swollen or deteriorated. Cracks will show up better if the hose is squeezed. Pay close attention to the hose clips that secure the hoses to the cooling system components. Hose clips can pinch and puncture hoses, resulting in cooling system leaks. If crimped-type hose clips are used, it

may be a good idea to replace them with standard worm-drive clips.

6 Inspect all the cooling system components (hoses, joint faces, etc) for leaks **(see Haynes Hint)**.

7 Where any problems are found on system components, renew the component or gasket with reference to Chapter 3.

8 With the vehicle raised, inspect the petrol tank and filler neck for punctures, cracks and other damage. The connection between the filler neck and tank is especially critical. Sometimes a rubber filler neck or connecting hose will leak due to loose retaining clamps or deteriorated rubber.

9 Carefully check all rubber hoses and fuel pipes leading away from the petrol tank. Check for loose connections, deteriorated hoses, crimped lines, and other damage. Pay particular attention to the vent pipes and hoses, which often loop up around the filler neck and can become blocked or crimped. Follow the pipes to the front of the vehicle, carefully inspecting them all the way. Renew damaged sections as necessary.

10 From within the engine compartment, check the security of all fuel pipe attachments and unions, and inspect the fuel pipes and vacuum hoses for kinks, chafing and deterioration.

1B

4.4a Fuel filter housing drain screw location – 1.9 litre engine

4.4b Fuel filter housing drain screw – 2.0 litre engine

6.2 Check the driveshaft gaiters for signs of damage or deterioration

11 Where applicable, check the condition of the power steering fluid hoses and pipes.
12 Once the check is complete, securely refit the engine cover.

6 Driveshaft gaiter and CV joints check

1 With the vehicle raised and securely supported on stands (see *Jacking and vehicle support*). Where necessary, remove the retaining bolts, screws and clips and remove the undercover (where fitted) from beneath the engine/transmission unit.
2 Turn the steering onto full lock, then slowly rotate the roadwheel. Inspect the condition of the outer constant velocity (CV) joint gaiters, squeezing the gaiters to open out the folds **(see illustration)**. Check for signs of cracking, splits or deterioration of the gaiter, which may allow the grease to escape, and lead to water and grit entry into the joint. Also check the security and condition of the retaining clips. Repeat these checks on the inner CV joints. If any damage or deterioration is found, the gaiters should be renewed (see Chapter 8).
3 At the same time, check the general condition of the CV joints themselves by first holding the driveshaft and attempting to rotate the wheel. Repeat this check by holding the inner joint and attempting to rotate the driveshaft. Any appreciable movement indicates wear in the joints, wear in the driveshaft splines, or a loose driveshaft retaining nut.

9.2 Reset the service indicator as described in the text

4 On completion of the check, securely refit the undercover (where fitted) then lower the vehicle to the ground.

7 Hinge and lock lubrication

1 Work around the vehicle, and lubricate the hinges of the bonnet, doors and tailgate with a small amount of general-purpose oil.
2 Lightly lubricate the bonnet release mechanism and exposed section of inner cable with a smear of grease.
3 Check carefully the security and operation of all hinges, latches and locks, adjusting them where required. Check the operation of the central locking system (if fitted).
4 Check the condition and operation of the tailgate struts, renewing them if either is leaking or no longer able to support the tailgate securely when raised.

8 Road test

Instruments and electrical equipment

1 Check the operation of all instruments and electrical equipment.
2 Make sure that all instruments read correctly, and switch on all electrical equipment in turn to check it functions properly.

Steering and suspension

3 Check for any abnormalities in the steering, suspension, handling or road 'feel'.
4 Drive the vehicle, and check that there are no unusual vibrations or noises.
5 Check that the steering feels positive, with no excessive 'sloppiness', or roughness, and check for any suspension noises when cornering, or when driving over bumps.

Drivetrain

6 Check the performance of the engine, clutch, transmission and driveshafts.
7 Listen for any unusual noises from the engine, clutch and transmission.
8 Make sure the engine idles smoothly, and that there is no hesitation when accelerating.
9 Check that the clutch action is smooth and progressive, that the drive is taken up smoothly, and that the pedal travel is not excessive. Also listen for any noises when the clutch pedal is depressed.
10 Check that all gears can be engaged smoothly, without noise, and that the gear lever action is smooth and not vague or 'notchy'.
11 Listen for a metallic clicking sound from the front of the vehicle, as the vehicle is driven slowly in a circle with the steering on full lock. Carry out this check in both directions. If a

clicking noise is heard, this indicates wear in a driveshaft joint, in which case, the complete driveshaft must be renewed (see Chapter 8).

Check the operation and performance of the braking system

12 Make sure that the vehicle does not pull to one side when braking, and that the wheels do not lock prematurely when braking hard.
13 Check that there is no vibration through the steering when braking.
14 Check that the handbrake operates correctly, without excessive movement of the lever, and that it holds the vehicle on a slope.
15 Test the operation of the brake servo unit as follows. With the engine off, depress the footbrake four or five times to exhaust the vacuum. Start the engine, holding the brake pedal depressed. As the engine starts, there should be a noticeable 'give' in the brake pedal as vacuum builds up. Allow the engine to run for at least two minutes, and then switch it off. If the brake pedal is depressed now, it should be possible to detect a hiss from the servo as the pedal is depressed. After about four or five applications, no further hissing should be heard, and the pedal should feel considerably firmer.

9 Resetting the service indicator

1 On completion of the service, select the correct interval to the next service and rest the service interval indicator as follows.

Selecting the correct interval for the service indicator

2 With the ignition switched off, press and hold the trip meter button **(see illustration)**.
3 Turn on the ignition switch and release the trip meter button straight away. The indicator will now display the mileage interval to the next service, eg. 20 000. Scroll through the various mileage intervals by depressing the trip meter button. Once the correct interval is displayed, press and hold the trip meter button (the display will flash during this period). Once the display stops flashing, release the button and turn off the ignition switch.

Resetting the indicator

4 With the ignition switched off, press and hold trip meter button.
5 Turn on the ignition switch (the interval to the next service will flash on the display) and keep the trip meter button depressed for 10 seconds. After this period the display will indicate 0 and the service spanner symbol will disappear.
6 Turn off the ignition switch.
7 Turn on the ignition switch and check the correct mileage to the next service interval is displayed on the indicator.

1.9 litre engine – every 10 000 miles (15 000 km) or 2 years

2.0 litre engine – every 12 000 miles (20 000 km) or 2 years

10 Pollen filter renewal

1 Open up the bonnet.
2 Reach in behind the right-hand suspension strut upper mounting and remove the pollen filter element from the heating/ventilation housing intake, noting which way around it is fitted **(see illustration)**.
3 Wipe clean the inside of the housing and fit

10.2 Removing the pollen filter element

the new pollen filter element, making sure that it is correctly seated.
4 Close the bonnet.

11 Idle speed and anti-stall speed check and adjustment – 1.9 litre engine

1 Release the fasteners from the right-hand side and top of the engine cover then lift off the cover, taking care not to lose its mounting rubbers **(see illustrations 4.1a to 4.1c)**.
2 With the engine cold, make sure that the accelerator cable and fast idle cables are correctly adjusted (Chapter 4B, Sections 3 and 10). Warm the engine up to normal operating temperature and check that the fast idle thermostatic sensor is functioning correctly. Rectify any problems before continuing **(see illustration)**.
3 Start the engine and warm it up to its normal operating temperature.
4 Insert a 3 mm shim in between the accelerator lever and the anti-stall adjustment screw (located on the back on the pump) **(see illustration)**.
5 Push the manual stop lever back against its stop, and hold it in position by inserting a 9 mm

diameter rod/drill through the hole in the fast idle lever.
6 The engine speed should be as specified for the anti-stall speed (see *Specifications*).
7 If adjustment is necessary, loosen the locknut, turn the anti-stall adjustment screw as required, then tighten the locknut.
8 Remove the rod/drill and the shim, and check that the engine is idling at the specified speed (see *Specifications*).
9 If adjustment is necessary, loosen the locknut on the idle speed adjustment screw (fitted to the fast idle lever). Turn the screw as required, and retighten the locknut **(see illustration)**.
10 Move the pump accelerator lever to increase the engine speed to approximately 3500 rpm, then quickly release the lever noting the time it takes for the engine to return to idle. This period should be between 2.5 and 3.5 seconds, and the engine speed should drop to approximately 50 rpm below idle.
11 If the deceleration is too fast and the engine stalls, unscrew the anti-stall adjustment screw a quarter-turn towards the control lever. If the deceleration is too slow, resulting in poor engine braking, turn the screw a quarter-turn away from the lever.

1B

11.4 Anti-stall speed adjustment screw (arrowed) is located on the rear of the injection pump – 1.9 litre engine

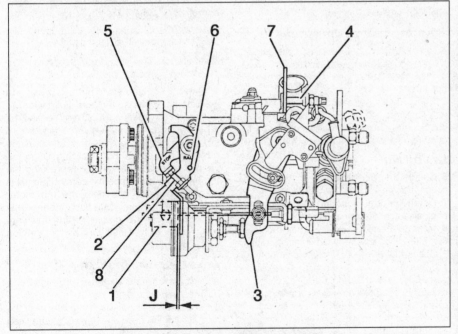

11.2 Injection pump adjustment details – 1.9 litre engine

1 *Fast idle cable end fitting*	5 *Manual stop lever*	8 *Idle speed adjustment screw*
2 *Fast idle lever*	6 *Fast idle lever hole*	
3 *Accelerator lever*	7 *Shim for anti-stall speed adjustment*	J *Fast idle cable end fitting clearance*
4 *Anti-stall adjustment screw*		

11.9 Idle speed adjustment screw and locknut (1) and manual stop lever (2) – 1.9 litre engine

12 Retighten the locknut after making an adjustment. Recheck the idle speed, and adjust if necessary as described previously.

13 With the engine idling, check the operation of the manual stop control by turning the stop lever clockwise. The engine must stop instantly.

14 On completion, ensure the mounting rubbers are all correctly fitted then install the engine cover, securing it in position with the fasteners.

12 Auxiliary drivebelt check and renewal – 1.9 litre engine

Note: *On models without power steering and air conditioning, Peugeot specify the use of a special electronic tool (SEEM C.TRONIC type 105.5 belt tensioning measuring tool) to correctly set the auxiliary drivebelt tension. If access to this equipment cannot be obtained, an approximate setting can be achieved using the method described below. If this method is used, the tension should be checked using the special electronic tool at the earliest opportunity.*

Check

1 Apply the handbrake, then jack up the front of the car and support it on axle stands (see *Jacking and vehicle support*). Remove the right-hand front roadwheel.

2 Undo the screws securing the front section of the right-hand wheelarch liner to the base of the bumper. Remove the fasteners (pull out the centre pin then remove the complete fastener) securing the liner section to the body then manoeuvre the front section of the liner out from underneath the wing.

3 Using a suitable socket and extension bar fitted to the crankshaft sprocket bolt, rotate the crankshaft so that the entire length of the drivebelt can be examined. Examine the drivebelt for cracks, splitting, fraying or damage. Check also for signs of glazing (shiny patches) and for separation of the belt plies. Renew the belt if worn or damaged.

4 On models with power steering (without air conditioning) which are equipped with an automatic belt tensioner, check the position of the wear indicators on the tensioner pulley arm and backplate (**see illustration**). The indicator mark on the backplate must be positioned between the two marks on the tensioner arm. If not the belt is stretched and should be renewed.

5 Refit the wheelarch liner, securing it in position with the retaining screws and fasteners.

6 Refit the roadwheel then lower the vehicle to the ground and tighten the wheel bolts to the specified torque.

Models without power steering

Removal

Note: *If the original belt is going to be re-used and the measuring tool is available, measure the belt tension prior to removal (see paragraph 13). On refitting, reset the tension to this same figure to ensure the belt is correctly tensioned.*

7 If not already done, proceed as described in paragraphs 1 and 2. Disconnect the battery negative lead.

8 Slacken the two bolts securing the tensioner pulley assembly to the engine (**see illustration**).

9 Back off the adjuster bolt on the base of the tensioner pulley bracket to move the pulley away from the drivebelt. Once there is sufficient slack in the drivebelt, slip the drivebelt off from the pulleys and remove it from the engine. **Note:** *If the belt is going to be re-used, mark the direction of rotation on the belt prior to removal. This will ensure it is refitted the correct way around.*

Refitting

10 If the belt is being renewed, ensure that the correct type is used and if the original belt is being refitted, use the mark made on removal to ensure it is fitted the correct way around.

11 Fit the belt around the pulleys. Ensure that the ribs on the belt are correctly engaged with the grooves in the pulleys then take up the slack in the belt by tightening the adjuster bolt. Tension the drivebelt as described in the following paragraphs.

Tensioning

12 If not already done, proceed as described in paragraphs 1 and 2.

13 If the special measuring tool is available, fit the measuring equipment to the 'lower run' of the belt, approximately midway between the crankshaft and alternator/air conditioning compressor pulleys (as applicable). If a new

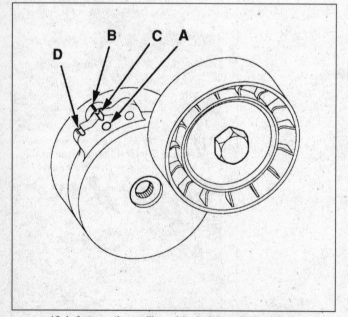

12.4 Automatic auxiliary drivebelt tensioner details

A *Tensioner arm locking pin hole*
B *Backplate indicator mark and locking pin locating hole*
C *Tensioner arm right-hand (zero) wear mark*
D *Tensioner arm left-hand (maximum) wear mark*

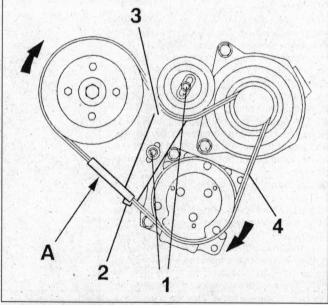

12.8 Auxiliary drivebelt and tensioner details – 1.9 litre engine with air conditioning

1 *Retaining bolts*
2 *Adjuster bolt*
3 *Tensioner pulley assembly*
4 *Drivebelt*
A *Tension checking point*

belt is being fitted, the belt tension should be as given in the Specifications at the start of this Chapter. If the original belt is being re-used, set the tension to the same figure as that noted prior to removal.

14 If the measuring tool is not available, the belt should be tensioned so that, under firm thumb pressure, there is about 5.0 mm of free movement at the mid-point between the pulleys on the lower belt run.

 Correct tensioning of the drivebelt will ensure it has a long life. A belt which is too slack will slip and squeal. Beware of overtightening, as this can cause wear in the alternator bearings.

15 To adjust the belt tension, with the tensioner pulley mounting bolts finger-tight only, rotate the adjuster bolt until the correct tension is achieved.

16 Rotate the crankshaft a couple of times then recheck the belt tension. Once the tension is correctly set, tighten both the tensioner pulley mounting bolts to the specified torque then lightly tighten the adjuster bolt.

17 Refit the wheelarch liner, securing it in position with the retaining screws and fasteners.

18 Refit the roadwheel then lower the vehicle to the ground and tighten the wheel bolts to the specified torque. Reconnect the battery.

Models with power steering (without air conditioning) with a manual tensioner

Removal

Note: *If the original belt is going to be re-used and the measuring tool is available, measure the belt tension prior to removal (see paragraph 24). On refitting, reset the tension to the same figure to ensure the belt is correctly tensioned.*

19 If not already done, proceed as described in paragraphs 1 and 2.

20 Disconnect the battery negative lead. Release the fasteners from the right-hand side and top of the engine cover then lift off the cover, taking care not to lose its mounting rubbers.

21 Slacken the tensioner pulley backplate bolt and back off the pulley adjuster nut, located behind the power steering pump, to move the pulley away from the drivebelt **(see illustration)**. Once there is sufficient slack in the drivebelt, slip the drivebelt off from the pulleys and remove it from the engine, noting its correct routing. **Note:** *If the belt is going to be re-used, mark the direction of rotation on the belt prior to removal. This will ensure it is refitted the correct way around.*

Refitting

22 If the belt is being renewed, ensure that the correct type is used and if the original belt is being refitted, use the mark made on

removal to ensure it is fitted the correct way around. Fit the belt around the pulleys in the following order.

  a) *Power steering pump.*
  b) *Tensioner pulley.*
  c) *Alternator.*
  d) *Lower idler pulley.*
  e) *Crankshaft.*
  f) *Upper idler pulley.*

23 Ensure that the ribs on the belt are correctly engaged with the grooves in all pulleys then take up the slack in the belt by tightening the adjuster nut. Tension the drivebelt as described in the following paragraphs.

Tensioning

24 If not already done, proceed as described in paragraphs 1 and 2. If the special measuring tool is available, fit the measuring equipment to the 'lower run' of the belt, midway between the alternator and lower idler pulley. If a new belt is being fitted, the belt tension should be as given in the Specifications at the start of this Chapter. If the original belt is being re-used, set the tension to the same figure as that noted prior to removal.

25 If the measuring tool is not available, belt should be tensioned so that, under firm thumb pressure, there is about 5.0 mm of free movement at the mid-point between the alternator and idler pulleys on the lower belt run.

 Correct tensioning of the drivebelt will ensure it has a long life. A belt which is too slack will slip and squeal. Beware of overtightening, as this can cause wear in the alternator bearings.

26 To adjust the belt tension, with the tensioner pulley backplate bolt finger-tight only, rotate the adjuster nut until the correct tension is achieved.

27 Rotate the crankshaft a couple of times then recheck the belt tension. Once the tension is correctly set, tighten the tensioner pulley backplate bolt to the specified torque then lightly tighten the adjuster nut.

28 Refit the wheelarch liner, securing it in position with the retaining screws and fasteners.

29 Refit the roadwheel then lower the vehicle to the ground and tighten the wheel bolts to the specified torque.

30 Ensure the mounting rubbers are all correctly fitted then install the engine cover, securing it in position with the fasteners. Reconnect the battery.

1B

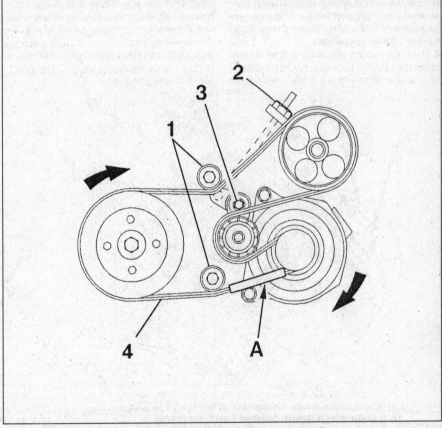

12.21 Auxiliary drivebelt and tensioner details –
1.9 litre engine with power steering fitted with manual tensioner assembly

1 Idler pulleys	*3 Tensioner pulley*	*4 Drivebelt*
2 Adjuster nut	*backplate bolt*	*A Tension checking point*

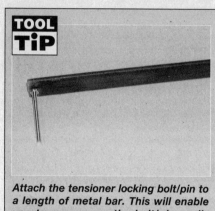

TOOL TiP

Attach the tensioner locking bolt/pin to a length of metal bar. This will enable you to manoeuvre the bolt/pin easily down between the engine and body and into position.

Models with power steering (without air conditioning) with an automatic tensioner

Note: A 4 mm diameter bolt or pin will be required to lock the automatic tensioner pulley in position (see Tool Tip).

Removal

31 If not already done, proceed as described in paragraphs 1 and 2.

32 Disconnect the battery negative lead.

33 Using a spanner/socket fitted to the spring-loaded tensioner pulley centre bolt, move the tensioner pulley away from the belt until it is possible to slip the drivebelt off one

of its pulleys. Once the drivebelt has been displaced, align the tensioner arm right-hand (zero) wear mark **(see illustration 12.4)** with the backplate indicator mark and lock the tensioner in position by inserting the 4 mm diameter bolt/pin **(see illustrations 13.11a and 13.11b)**. Ensure the bolt/pin is correctly located in the backplate then release the tensioner.

34 Disengage the drivebelt from all the pulleys, noting its correct routing, and remove it from the engine. **Note:** *If the belt is going to be re-used, mark the direction of rotation on the belt prior to removal. This will ensure it is refitted the correct way around.*

Refitting and tensioning

35 Manoeuvre the belt into position, using the mark made on removal to ensure it is fitted the correct way around.

36 Fit the drivebelt around the pulleys in the following order:
  a) Power steering pump.
  b) Upper idler pulley.
  c) Alternator.
  d) Lower idler pulley
  e) Crankshaft.

37 Fit the spanner/socket to the spring-loaded tensioner pulley belt. Move the tensioner pulley away from the belt until it is possible to withdraw the locking bolt/pin then slip the belt over the pulley. Ensure the belt ribs are correctly seated in all the pulley grooves then slowly release spring-loaded tensioner to tension the drivebelt.

Caution: Do not allow the tensioner pulley to spring forcefully onto the belt as this could result in damage.

38 Remove the spanner/socket and refit the wheelarch liner, securing it in position with the retaining screws and fasteners.

39 Refit the roadwheel then lower the vehicle to the ground and tighten the wheel bolts to the specified torque. Reconnect the battery.

Models with air conditioning

Note: A 6 mm diameter bolt or pin will be required to lock the spring-loaded tensioner pulley in position.

Removal

40 If not already done, proceed as described in paragraphs 1 and 2.

41 Disconnect the battery negative lead.

42 Slacken the manual tensioner pulley bolt.

43 Have ready the 6 mm diameter bolt/pin. Pivot the manual tensioner pulley in a clockwise direction, using a square-section key fitted to the hole in the pulley hub, to move the spring-loaded tensioner pulley. Position the tensioner pulley so the hole in its arm aligns with the corresponding hole in the bracket then lock the pulley in position by inserting the bolt/pin **(see illustration)**. Ensure the spring-loaded pulley is locked securely in position then release the manual tensioner pulley

44 Disengage the drivebelt from all the pulleys, noting its correct routing, and remove it from the engine. **Note:** *If the belt is going to be re-used, mark the direction of rotation on the belt prior to removal. This will ensure it is refitted the correct way around.*

Refitting and tensioning

45 Ensure the spring-loaded tensioner pulley is locked in position (see paragraph 43). **Note:** *The pulley arm has a square-section cut-out to allow the pulley to be moved using a ratchet/bar but this hole is only accessible with the belt removed.*

46 If the belt is being renewed, ensure that the correct type is used and if the original belt is being refitted, use the mark made on removal to ensure it is fitted the correct way around. Fit the drivebelt around the pulleys in the following order:
  a) Power steering pump.
  b) Manual tensioner pulley.
  b) Alternator.
  d) Air conditioning compressor.
  e) Crankshaft.
  f) Spring-loaded tensioner pulley.

47 Ensure that the ribs on the belt are correctly engaged with the grooves in the pulleys then rotate the manual tensioner pulley in a clockwise direction to remove all slack from the belt.

48 To correctly set the belt tension, position the manual tensioner pulley so that all spring pressure is removed from the locking bolt/pin fitted to the spring-loaded tensioner arm. Once the manual tensioner pulley is correctly positioned, tighten its retaining bolt to the specified torque.

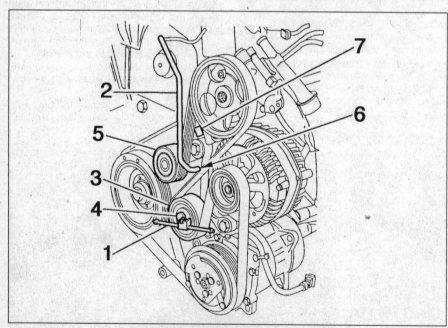

12.43 Auxiliary drivebelt and tensioner details – 1.9 litre engine with power steering and air conditioning

1 Peugeot tool for moving the manual tensioner pulley
2 Peugeot locking pin for spring-loaded tensioner
3 Drivebelt
4 Manual tensioner pulley
5 Spring-loaded tensioner pulley
6 Spring-loaded tensioner pulley arm locking hole
7 Spring loaded tensioner pulley arm square-section hole (only accessible with the belt removed)

49 Remove the locking bolt/pin then rotate the crankshaft through at four complete rotations. Check that the locking bolt/pin can still be easily inserted. If not, slacken the manual tensioner pulley bolt and repeat the adjustment procedure.

50 Once the belt is correctly tensioned, remove the locking bolt/pin and refit the wheelarch liner, securing it in position with the retaining screws and fasteners.

51 Refit the roadwheel then lower the vehicle to the ground and tighten the wheel bolts to the specified torque. Reconnect the battery.

13 Auxiliary drivebelt check and renewal – 2.0 litre engine

Check

1 Apply the handbrake, then jack up the front of the car and support it on axle stands (see *Jacking and vehicle support*). Remove the right-hand front roadwheel.

2 Unscrew the bolts securing the plastic inner cover to the wing valance and undercover and remove the cover to gain access to the crankshaft pulley.

3 To further improve access, undo the screws securing the front section of the right-hand wheelarch liner to the base of the bumper. Remove the fasteners (pull out the centre pin then remove the complete fastener) securing the liner section to the body then manoeuvre the front section of the liner out from underneath the wing.

4 Using a suitable socket and extension bar fitted to the crankshaft sprocket bolt, rotate the crankshaft so that the entire length of the drivebelt can be examined. Examine the drivebelt for cracks, splitting, fraying or damage. Check also for signs of glazing (shiny patches) and for separation of the belt plies.

5 Check the position of the wear indicators on the tensioner pulley arm and backplate.

The indicator mark on the backplate must be positioned between the two marks on the tensioner arm **(see illustration 12.4)**.

6 If the drivebelt shows signs of wear or damage or the backplate mark is aligned with, or beyond, the left-hand mark on the tensioner, the auxiliary drivebelt must be renewed.

7 On completion of the check, refit the wheelarch liner (where removed) and inner cover, securing them in position with the retaining screws and fasteners.

8 Refit the roadwheel then lower the vehicle to the ground and tighten the wheel bolts to the specified torque.

Renewal

Note: *A 4 mm diameter bolt or pin will be required to lock the spring-loaded tensioner pulley in position (see Tool Tip).*

Removal

9 If not already done, proceed as described in paragraphs 1 and 2.

10 Disconnect the battery negative lead.

11 Using a spanner/socket fitted to the spring-loaded tensioner pulley centre bolt, move the tensioner pulley away from the belt until it is possible to slip the drivebelt off one of its pulleys. Once the drivebelt has been displaced, align the tensioner arm right-hand (zero) wear mark **(see illustration 12.4)** with the backplate indicator mark and lock the tensioner in position by inserting the 4 mm diameter bolt/pin **(see illustrations)**. Ensure the bolt/pin is correctly located in the backplate then release the tensioner.

12 Disengage the drivebelt from all the pulleys, noting its correct routing, and remove it from the engine. **Note:** *If the belt is going to be re-used, mark the direction of rotation on the belt prior to removal. This will ensure it is refitted the correct way around.*

Refitting – used belt

13 Manoeuvre the belt into position, using the

TOOL TiP

Attach the tensioner locking bolt/pin to a length of metal bar. This will enable you to manoeuvre the bolt/pin easily down between the engine and body and into position.

mark made on removal to ensure it is fitted the correct way around.

14 Fit the drivebelt around the pulleys in the following order:
a) *Power steering pump.*
b) *Manual tensioner pulley.*
b) *Alternator.*
d) *Air conditioning compressor/lower idler pulley (as applicable).*
e) *Crankshaft.*

15 Fit the spanner/socket to the spring-loaded tensioner pulley belt. Move the tensioner pulley away from the belt until it is possible to withdraw the locking bolt/pin then slip the belt over the pulley. Ensure the belt ribs are correctly seated in all the pulley grooves then slowly release spring-loaded tensioner to tension the drivebelt.

Caution: Do not allow the tensioner pulley to spring forcefully onto the belt as this could result in damage.

16 Remove the spanner/socket then securely refit the wheelarch liner (where removed) and inner cover.

13.11a Using a spanner/socket on the tensioner pulley bolt, align the arm zero wear mark with the backplate indicator . . .

13.11b . . . and lock it in position by inserting the pin/bolt through the arm and backplate holes

1B

17 Refit the roadwheel then lower the vehicle to the ground and tighten the wheel bolts to the specified torque. Reconnect the battery and refit the engine cover.

Refitting – new belt

18 Ensure the spring-loaded tensioner pulley is locked in position with its right-hand (zero) wear marking correctly aligned with the backplate indicator (see paragraph 11).

19 Slacken the manual tensioner pulley bolt then fit the new drivebelt around the pulleys in the following order:

a) Power steering pump.
b) Manual tensioner pulley.
b) Alternator.
d) Air conditioning compressor/lower idler pulley (as applicable).
e) Crankshaft.
f) Spring loaded tensioner pulley.

20 Ensure that the ribs on the belt are correctly engaged with the grooves in the pulleys then rotate the manual tensioner pulley in a clockwise direction to remove all slack from the belt. Rotate the pulley using a square-section key fitted to the hole in the pulley hub.

21 To correctly set the belt tension, position the manual tensioner pulley so that all spring pressure is removed from the locking bolt/pin fitted to the spring-loaded tensioner pulley backplate **(see illustration)**. Once the manual tensioner pulley is correctly positioned, tighten its retaining bolt to the specified torque.

22 Remove the locking bolt/pin then rotate the crankshaft through at four complete rotations. Check that the locking bolt/pin can still be easily inserted. If not, slacken the manual tensioner pulley bolt and repeat the adjustment procedure.

23 Once the belt is correctly tensioned, remove the locking bolt/pin then securely refit the wheelarch liner (where removed) and inner cover.

24 Refit the roadwheel then lower the vehicle to the ground and tighten the wheel bolts to the specified torque. Reconnect the battery.

14 Front brake pad check

1 Firmly apply the handbrake, then jack up the front of the car and support it securely on axle stands (see *Jacking and vehicle support*). Remove the front roadwheels.

2 For a quick check, the pad thickness can be carried out via the inspection hole on the front caliper **(see Haynes Hint)**. Using a steel rule, measure the thickness of the pad friction material. This must not be less than the specified minimum given in the Specifications.

3 For a comprehensive check, the brake pads should be removed and cleaned. The operation of the caliper can then be checked, and the brake disc itself can be fully examined on both sides. Refer to Chapter 9 for details.

4 If any pad's friction material is worn to the specified minimum thickness or less, all four pads must be renewed as a set. Refer to Chapter 9 for details.

5 On completion, refit the roadwheels then lower the vehicle to the ground and tighten the wheel bolts to the specified torque.

15 Handbrake check and adjustment

1 Check and, if necessary, adjust the handbrake as described in Chapter 9.

16 Steering and suspension check

Front suspension and steering check

1 Raise the front of the vehicle, and securely support it on axle stands (see *Jacking and vehicle support*).

2 Visually inspect the balljoint dust covers and the steering gear gaiters for splits, chafing or deterioration. Any wear of these components will cause loss of lubricant, together with dirt and water entry, resulting in rapid deterioration of the balljoints or steering gear.

3 On vehicles with power steering, check the fluid pipes/hoses for chafing or deterioration, and the pipe and hose unions for fluid leaks. Also check for signs of fluid leakage under pressure .from the steering gear rubber gaiters, which would indicate failed fluid seals within the steering gear.

4 Grasp the roadwheel at the 12 o'clock and 6 o'clock positions, and try to rock it **(see illustration)**. Very slight free play may be felt, but if the movement is appreciable, further investigation is necessary to determine the source. Continue rocking the wheel while an assistant depresses the footbrake. If the

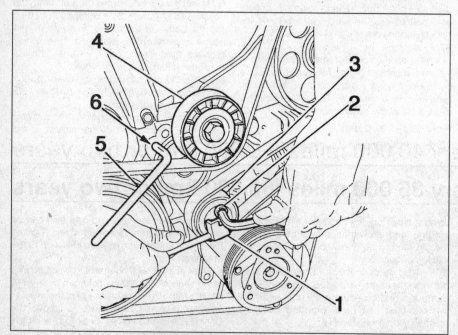

13.21 Auxiliary drivebelt adjustment details – 2.0 litre engine

1 Peugeot tool for moving the manual tensioner pulley
2 Manual tensioner pulley retaining bolt
3 Manual tensioner pulley
4 Spring-loaded tensioner pulley
5 Peugeot locking pin for spring-loaded tensioner
6 Spring-loaded tensioner pulley arm locking hole

For a quick check, the thickness of the brake pad friction material can be checked through the aperture on the caliper body.

16.4 Check for wear in the hub bearings by grasping the wheel and trying to rock it

movement is now eliminated or significantly reduced, it is likely that the hub bearings are at fault. If the free play is still evident with the footbrake depressed, then there is wear in the suspension joints or mountings.

5 Now grasp the wheel at the 9 o'clock and 3 o'clock positions, and try to rock it as before. Any movement felt now may again be caused by wear in the hub bearings or the steering track-rod balljoints. If the inner or outer balljoint is worn, the visual movement will be obvious.

6 Using a large screwdriver or flat bar, check for wear in the suspension mounting bushes by levering between the relevant suspension component and its attachment point. Some movement is to be expected as the mountings are made of rubber, but excessive wear should be obvious. Also check the condition of any visible rubber bushes, looking for splits, cracks or contamination of the rubber.

7 With the car standing on its wheels, have an assistant turn the steering wheel back and forth about an eighth of a turn each way. There should be very little, if any, lost movement between the steering wheel and roadwheels. If this is not the case, closely observe the joints and mountings previously described, but in addition, check the steering column universal joints for wear, and the steering gear itself.

Suspension strut/shock absorber check

8 Check for any signs of fluid leakage around the suspension strut/shock absorber body, or from the rubber gaiter around the piston rod. Should any fluid be noticed, the suspension strut/shock absorber is defective internally, and should be renewed. **Note:** *Suspension struts/shock absorbers should always be renewed in pairs on the same axle, or the handling of the vehicle will be adversely affected.*

9 The efficiency of the suspension strut/shock absorber may be checked by bouncing the vehicle at each corner. Generally speaking, the body will return to its normal position and stop after being depressed. If it rises and returns on a rebound, the suspension strut/shock absorber is probably suspect. Examine also the suspension strut/shock absorber upper and lower mountings for any signs of wear.

1B

1.9 litre engine – every 40 000 miles (60 000 km) or two years

2.0 litre engine – every 36 000 miles (60 000 km) or two years

17 Brake fluid renewal

 Warning: Brake hydraulic fluid can harm your eyes and damage painted surfaces, so use extreme caution when handling and pouring it. Do not use fluid that has been standing open for some time, as it absorbs moisture from the air. Excess moisture can cause a dangerous loss of braking effectiveness.

1 The procedure is similar to that for the bleeding of the hydraulic system as described in Chapter 9, except that the brake fluid reservoir should be emptied by siphoning, using a clean poultry baster or similar before starting, and allowance should be made for the old fluid to be expelled when bleeding a section of the circuit.

2 Working as described in Chapter 9, open the first bleed screw in the sequence, and pump the brake pedal gently until nearly all the old fluid has been emptied from the master cylinder reservoir.

> **HAYNES HiNT**
> *Old hydraulic fluid is invariably much darker in colour than the new, making it easy to distinguish the two.*

3 Top-up to the MAX level with new fluid, and continue pumping until only the new fluid remains in the reservoir, and new fluid can be seen emerging from the bleed screw. Tighten the screw, and top the reservoir level up to the MAX level line.

4 Work through all the remaining bleed screws in the sequence until new fluid can be seen at all of them. Be careful to keep the master cylinder reservoir topped-up to above the DANGER level at all times, or air may enter the system and increase the length of the task.

5 When the operation is complete, check that all bleed screws are securely tightened, and that their dust caps are refitted. Wash off all traces of spilt fluid, and recheck the master cylinder reservoir fluid level.

6 Check the operation of the brakes before taking the car on the road.

18.3 On 1.9 litre engines, release the retaining clip and disconnect the fuel outlet pipe from the filter housing cover

18.4 Release the retaining clip then lift off the cover . . .

18.5 . . . and remove the fuel filter from its housing

1.9 litre engine – every 30 000 miles (45 000 km) or 4 years

2.0 litre engine – every 36 000 miles (60 000 km) or 4 years

18 Fuel filter renewal

Caution: Be careful not to allow dirt into the fuel filter housing during this procedure or to spill fuel onto the clutch assembly.

1.9 litre engine

1 Release the fasteners from the right-hand side and top of the engine cover then lift off the cover, taking care not to lose its mounting rubbers (see illustrations 4.1a to 4.1c).
2 Remove all traces of dirt from the exterior of the filter housing then drain the fuel filter as described in Section 4.
3 Release the retaining clip and detach the fuel outlet pipe from the filter housing cover (see illustration).
4 Unclip the filter housing cover retaining clip then position the cover clear of the housing (see illustration). Discard the cover sealing ring; a new one must be used on refitting.
5 Lift the fuel filter and sealing ring out of the housing, taking care not to spill fuel everywhere (see illustration).
6 Remove all traces of dirt or debris from inside the filter housing.
7 Ensure the housing and cover are spotlessly clean then fit the new fuel filter.

8 Ensure the new small sealing ring is correctly fitted to the top of the filter then fit the new large sealing ring to the cover (see illustrations).
9 Locate the cover correctly on the filter housing and refit the retaining clip. Ensure the clip is correctly engaged with the housing and cover and secure it in firmly in position.
10 Securely reconnect the fuel outlet pipe to the cover.
11 Ensure the housing bleed screw is securely closed then prime the fuel system as described in Chapter 4B.
12 Once the engine is idling smoothly, ensure the mounting rubbers are all correctly fitted then install the engine cover, securing it in position with the fasteners.

2.0 litre engine

Note: Fit a new drain screw and O-ring seal on reassembly. On completion, bleed the system of air (see Chapter 4B, Section 5) and check that there is no sign of fuel seepage from the filter drain screw once the engine is restarted.

13 Remove the fasteners (twist the fasteners 90° to release them) and lift off the engine cover (see illustrations 4.2a and 4.2b).
14 Remove all traces of dirt from the exterior of the filter housing then drain the fuel filter as described in Section 4.
15 Release the retaining clips and detach the fuel outlet and return pipes from the filter housing cover (see illustration). Plug the pipe ends to minimise fuel loss and prevent the entry of dirt into the system.
16 Rotate the filter housing cover a quarter-of-a turn (90°) anti-clockwise to release it. To do this, simultaneously rotate the cover with one hand whilst apply the necessary extra force using a 22 mm socket/spanner fitted to the centre of the cover. Lift off the filter cover and remove the spring washer from the top of the filter (see illustrations).
17 Lift the fuel filter out of the housing, taking care not to spill fuel everywhere. Remove the cover sealing ring from the housing and discard it; a new one must be used on refitting.

18.8a Ensure the new small sealing ring (arrowed) is correctly fitted to the fuel filter . . .

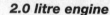

18.8b . . . and the larger sealing ring (arrowed) is correctly fitted to the housing cover

18.15 On 2.0 litre engines, disconnect the fuel outlet and return pipes (arrowed) from the filter housing cover

18.16a Remove the cover from the filter housing . . .

18.16b . . . and lift out the spring washer

18.19a Fit the new fuel filter . . .

18.19b . . . then fit the new sealing ring to the filter housing

18 Remove all traces of dirt or debris from inside the filter housing.

19 Ensure the housing and cover are spotlessly clean then fit the new fuel filter and new sealing ring to the housing (see illustrations).

20 Fit the spring washer to the top of the filter then refit the cover to the housing. Position the cover so the arrow on the cover is pointing towards the left-hand side of the engine compartment and the cover fuel unions are at a right-angle (90°) to the engine axis

21 Secure the cover in position by rotating it a quarter-of-a-turn (90°) clockwise; the arrow will now be facing forwards. Rotate the cover by hand, applying the necessary extra force using the 22 mm spanner/socket.

22 Securely reconnect the fuel pipes to the filter cover.

23 Ensure the housing bleed screw is securely closed then prime the fuel system as

described in Chapter 4B. On completion, securely refit the engine cover.

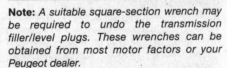

19 Air cleaner filter element renewal

1 On all engines, undo the retaining screws securing the lid to the air cleaner housing (see illustration).

2 Lift the lid and remove the air filter element from the housing, noting which way up it is fitted (see illustration).

3 Wipe clean the inside of the housing then fit the new element, ensuring it is correctly located.

4 Locate the lid on the housing and securely tighten its retaining screws.

20 Manual transmission oil level check

Note: *A suitable square-section wrench may be required to undo the transmission filler/level plugs. These wrenches can be obtained from most motor factors or your Peugeot dealer.*

1 Park the car on a level surface. The oil level must be checked before the car is driven, or at least 5 minutes after the engine has been switched off. If the oil is checked immediately after driving the car, some of the oil will remain distributed around the transmission, resulting in an inaccurate level reading.

2 On 2.0 litre engines, unscrew the bolts securing the plastic inner cover to the wing valance and undercover and remove the cover to gain access to the transmission filler/level plug.

3 On all engines, wipe clean the area around the filler/level plug, which is on the left-hand end of the transmission. Unscrew the plug and clean it; discard the sealing washer (see illustration).

4 The oil level should reach the lower edge of the filler/level hole. A certain amount of oil will have gathered behind the filler/level plug, and will trickle out when it is removed; this does **not** necessarily indicate that the level is correct. To ensure that a true level is established, wait until the initial trickle has stopped, then add oil as necessary until a trickle of new oil can be seen emerging (see illustration). The level will be correct when the flow ceases; use only good-quality oil of the specified type.

5 Filling the transmission with oil is an extremely awkward operation; above all, allow plenty of time for the oil level to settle properly before checking it. If a large amount is added to the transmission, and a large amount flows out on checking the level, refit the filler/level plug and take the vehicle on a short journey so that the new oil is distributed fully around the transmission components, then recheck the level when it has settled again.

6 If the transmission has been overfilled so that oil flows out as soon as the filler/level plug is removed, check that the car is completely level (front-to-rear and side-to-side), and allow the surplus to drain off into a container.

1B

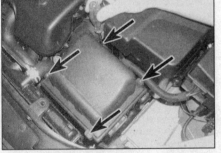

19.1 Undo the retaining screws (arrowed) . . .

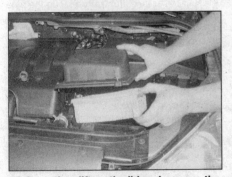

19.2 . . . then lift up the lid and remove the air cleaner filter element

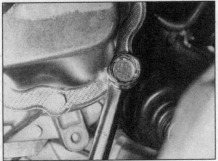

20.3 Removing the transmission filler/level plug

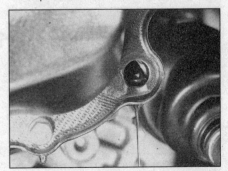

20.4 Oil level is correct when the oil stops flowing out of the filler/level plug hole

7 When the level is correct, fit a new sealing washer to the filler/level plug. Refit the plug, tightening it to the specified torque setting. Wash off any spilt oil. On 2.0 litre engines refit the inner cover.

21 Rear brake shoe check

1 Remove the rear brake drums, and check the brake shoes for signs of wear or contamination. At the same time, also inspect the wheel cylinders for signs of leakage, and the brake drum for signs of wear. Refer to the relevant Sections of Chapter 9 for further information.

22 Emissions control systems check

1 This check specified by Peugeot involves checking the engine management system by plugging an electronic tester into the system diagnostic socket to check the electronic control unit (ECU) memory for faults.

2 In reality, if the vehicle is running correctly and the injection system warning light on the instrument panel is functioning normally, then this check need not be carried out.

1.9 litre engine – every 80 000 miles (120 000 km)

23 Timing belt renewal

Note: *Although the normal interval for timing belt renewal is 80 000 miles (120 000 km), it is strongly recommended that the interval is halved to 40 000 miles (60 000 km), especially on vehicles which are subjected to intensive use, ie. mainly short journeys or a lot of stop-start driving. The actual belt renewal interval is therefore very much up to the individual owner, but bear in mind that severe engine damage will result if the belt breaks.*

1 Refer to Chapter 2B.

1.9 litre engine – every 80 000 miles (120 000 km) or five years

2.0 litre engine – every 72 000 miles (120 000 km) or five years

24 Coolant renewal

⚠ *Warning: Wait until the engine is cold before starting this procedure. Do not allow antifreeze to come in contact with your skin, or with the painted surfaces of the vehicle. Rinse off spills immediately with plenty of water. Never leave antifreeze lying around in an open container, or in a puddle in the driveway or on the garage floor. Children and pets are attracted by its sweet smell, but antifreeze can be fatal if ingested.*

Cooling system draining

1 With the engine completely cold, unscrew the expansion tank filler cap.

2 Position a suitable container beneath the coolant drain outlet at the lower left-hand side of the radiator.

3 Loosen the drain plug (there is no need to remove it completely) and allow the coolant to drain into the container **(see illustration)**. If desired, a length of tubing can be fitted to the drain outlet to direct the flow of coolant during draining.

4 To assist draining, remove the cooling system bleed cap/screw from the heater matrix outlet hose union on the engine compartment bulkhead. On 2.0 litre engines a bleed cap/screw is also fitted to the thermostat cover which is fitted to the top of the coolant housing on the left-hand end of the cylinder head **(see illustrations)**. Remove the fasteners (rotate the fasteners 90° to release them) and lift off the engine cover then remove the cap/screw and sealing washer (as applicable) from the cover.

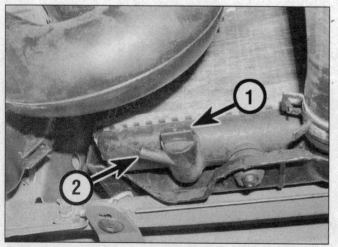

24.3 Loosen the drain plug (1) and drain the coolant via the drain outlet (2)

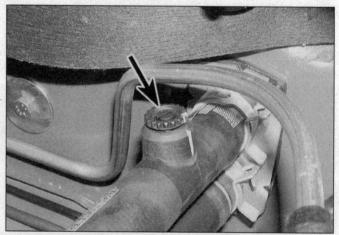

24.4a A bleed cap/screw (arrowed) is fitted to the heater matrix hose near the engine compartment bulkhead (1.9 litre engine shown)

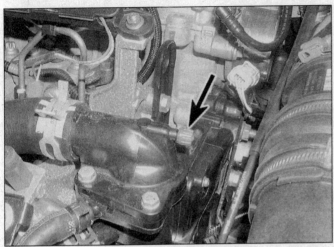

24.4b On 2.0 litre engines a bleed cap/screw (arrowed) is also fitted to the thermostat cover

24.5 Unscrew the coolant drain plug (arrowed) from the rear of the cylinder block

5 When the flow of coolant stops, reposition the container below the cylinder block drain plug. The drain plug is located at the rear of the cylinder block, on its left-hand end **(see illustration)**.

6 Remove the drain plug and sealing washer from the block and allow the coolant to drain into the container.

7 If the coolant has been drained for a reason other than renewal, then provided it is clean and less than five years old, it can be re-used, though this is not recommended.

8 Securely tighten the radiator drain plug on completion of draining. Fit a new sealing washer to the cylinder block drain then refit the plug, tightening it securely.

Cooling system flushing

9 If coolant renewal has been neglected, or if the antifreeze mixture has become diluted, then in time, the cooling system may gradually lose efficiency, as the coolant passages become restricted due to rust, scale deposits, and other sediment. The cooling system efficiency can be restored by flushing the system clean.

10 The radiator should be flushed separately from the engine, to avoid excess contamination.

Radiator flushing

11 To flush the radiator, first tighten the radiator drain plug.

12 Disconnect the top and bottom hoses and any other relevant hoses from the radiator (see Chapter 3).

13 Insert a garden hose into the radiator top inlet. Direct a flow of clean water through the radiator, and continue flushing until clean water emerges from the radiator bottom outlet.

14 If after a reasonable period, the water still does not run clear, the radiator can be flushed with a good proprietary cleaning agent. It is important that their manufacturer's instructions are followed carefully. If the contamination is particularly bad, insert the hose in the radiator bottom outlet, and reverse-flush the radiator.

Engine flushing

15 To flush the engine, remove the thermostat (see Chapter 3).

16 With the bottom hose disconnected from the radiator, insert a garden hose into the coolant housing. Direct a clean flow of water through the engine, and continue flushing until clean water emerges from the radiator bottom hose.

17 When flushing is complete, refit the thermostat and reconnect the hoses (see Chapter 3).

Cooling system filling

18 Before attempting to fill the cooling system, make sure that all hoses and clips are in good condition, and that the clips are tight. Note that an antifreeze mixture must be used all year round, to prevent corrosion of the engine components (see following sub-Section). Also check that the radiator and cylinder block drain plugs are in place and tight.

19 Remove the expansion tank filler cap.

20 Remove the cooling system bleed cap/screw from the heater matrix hose (see paragraph 4). On 2.0 litre engines also remove the cap/screw and sealing washer (as applicable) from the thermostat cover (remove the engine cover to improve access).

21 Peugeot recommend the use of a 'header tank' when refilling the cooling system, to reduce the possibility of air being trapped in the system. Although Peugeot dealers use a special header tank which screws onto the expansion tank, the same effect can be achieved by using a suitable bottle, with a rubber seal between the bottle and the expansion tank **(see illustration)**.

22 Fit the 'header tank' to the expansion tank and slowly fill the system whilst observing the heater matrix hose bleed hole **(see illustration)**. As soon as coolant free from air bubbles emerges from the heater matrix hose outlet, securely refit the cap/screw (as applicable).

23 On 2.0 litre engines then watch the bleed hole on the thermostat cover. Once coolant free from air bubbles emerges from the housing hole, refit the cap/screw and sealing washer (as applicable) and tighten securely.

24 On all engines, continue to fill the cooling system until bubbles stop appearing in the expansion tank. Help to bleed the air from the system by repeatedly squeezing the radiator bottom hose.

25 When no more bubbles appear, ensure the 'header tank' is full (at least 1.0 litre of

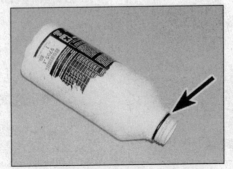

24.21 A plastic bottle and sealing ring (arrowed) can be used as a substitute header tank

24.22 Fit the header tank to the expansion tank and slowly fill the cooling system

1B

coolant) then start the engine. Run the engine at a fast idle speed (do not exceed 2000 rpm) until the cooling fan cuts in and out TWICE, then when the fan has stopped for the second time, switch the engine off..

Caution: The coolant will be hot. Take great care not to scald yourself.

26 Allow the engine to cool, then drain the contents of the 'header tank' and remove it from the expansion tank. Wash off any spilt coolant with cold water.

27 When the engine has cooled, check the coolant level with reference to *Weekly checks*. Top-up the level if necessary, and refit the expansion tank cap.

Antifreeze mixture

28 The antifreeze should always be renewed at the specified intervals. This is necessary not only to maintain the antifreeze properties, but also to prevent corrosion which would otherwise occur as the corrosion inhibitors become progressively less effective.

29 Always use an ethylene-glycol based antifreeze which is suitable for use in mixed-metal cooling systems.

30 Before adding antifreeze, the cooling system should be completely drained, preferably flushed, and all hoses checked for condition and security.

31 After filling with antifreeze, a label should be attached to the expansion tank, stating the type and concentration of antifreeze used, and the date installed. Any subsequent topping-up should be made with the same type and concentration of antifreeze.

32 Do not use engine antifreeze in the windscreen/tailgate washer system, as it will damage the vehicle paintwork. A screenwash additive should be added to the washer system in the quantities stated on the bottle.

2.0 litre engine – every 96 000 miles (160 000 km)

25 Timing belt renewal

Note: *Although the normal interval for timing belt renewal is 96 000 miles (160 000 km), it is strongly recommended that the interval is halved to 48 000 miles (80 000 km), especially on vehicles which are subjected to intensive use, ie. mainly short journeys or a lot of stop-start driving. The actual belt renewal interval is therefore very much up to the individual owner, but bear in mind that severe engine damage will result if the belt breaks.*

1 Refer to Chapter 2B.

Chapter 2 Part A:
Petrol engine in-car repair procedures

Contents

Degrees of difficulty

Easy, suitable for novice with little experience		**Fairly easy,** suitable for beginner with some experience		**Fairly difficult,** suitable for competent DIY mechanic		**Difficult,** suitable for experienced DIY mechanic		**Very difficult,** suitable for expert DIY or professional	

Specifications

Engine (general)

Capacity:
  1.1 litre engine .... 1124 cc
  1.4 litre engine .... 1360 cc
  1.6 litre engine .... 1587 cc

Designation:
  1.1 litre engine TU1
  1.4 litre engine TU3
  1.6 litre engine TU5

Engine codes*:
  1.1 litre engine .... HFZ and HFY (TU1JP)
  1.4 litre engine .... KFX (TU3JP)
  1.6 litre engine .... NFZ (TU5JP)

Bore:
  1.1 litre engine .... 72.00 mm
  1.4 litre engine .... 75.00 mm
  1.6 litre engine .... 78.50 mm

Stroke:
  1.1 litre engine .... 69.00 mm
  1.4 litre engine .... 77.00 mm
  1.6 litre engine .... 82.00 mm

Direction of crankshaft rotation .... Clockwise (viewed from right-hand side of vehicle)
No 1 cylinder location .... At transmission end of block

Compression ratio (typical):
  1.1 litre engine .... 9.7 : 1
  1.4 and 1.6 litre engine .... 10.2 : 1

The engine code is situated on front, left-hand end of the cylinder block. On cast-iron block engines, the code is stamped directly onto the cylinder block. On aluminium block engines the code can be stamped directly onto the block and/or stamped on a plate which is riveted to the block. The code given in brackets is the factory identification number.

Camshaft

Drive	Toothed belt
Number of bearings	5

Camshaft bearing journal diameter (outside diameter):

No 1	36.950 to 36.925 mm
No 2	40.650 to 40.625 mm
No 3	41.250 to 41.225 mm
No 4	41.850 to 41.825 mm
No 5	42.450 to 42.425 mm

Cylinder head bearing journal diameter (inside diameter):

No 1	37.000 to 37.039 mm
No 2	40.700 to 47.739 mm
No 3	41.300 to 41.339 mm
No 4	41.900 to 41.939 mm
No 5	42.500 to 42.539 mm

Valve clearances (engine cold)

Inlet	0.20 mm
Exhaust	0.40 mm

Lubrication system

Oil pump type	Gear-type, chain-driven off the crankshaft
Minimum oil pressure at 80°C	4 bars at 4000 rpm
Oil pressure warning switch operating pressure	0.8 bars

Torque wrench settings

	Nm	lbf ft
Big-end bearing cap nuts	38	28
Camshaft sprocket retaining bolt	80	59
Camshaft thrust fork retaining bolt	16	12
Crankshaft oil seal housing bolts – cast-iron block engine	8	6
Crankshaft pulley retaining bolts	8	6
Crankshaft sprocket retaining bolt	100	74
Cylinder head bolts (aluminium block engine):		
Stage 1	20	15
Stage 2	Angle-tighten a further 240°	
Cylinder head bolts (cast-iron block engine):		
Stage 1	20	15
Stage 2	Angle-tighten a further 120°	
Stage 3	Angle-tighten a further 120°	
Cylinder head cover nuts:		
M8 nuts	16	12
M6 nuts	7	5
Driveplate bolts	67	49
Engine-to-transmission bolts:		
Manual transmission models	40	30
Automatic transmission models	35	26
Engine/transmission left-hand mounting:		
Mounting centre nut	65	48
Mounting-to-bracket bolts	30	22
Mounting bracket-to-body bolts	19	14
Mounting bracket-to-manual transmission nuts	25	18
Mounting bracket-to-automatic transmission bolts	45	33
Mounting stud – automatic transmission	50	37
Engine/transmission rear mounting:		
Mounting-to-cylinder block bolts	40	30
Mounting link-to-mounting bolt	50	37
Mounting link-to-subframe bolt	39	29
Vibration damper-to-mounting bolt	32	24
Engine/transmission right-hand mounting:		
Mounting bracket nuts	45	33
Support bracket:		
Bracket to mounting bracket	45	33
Bracket to engine	26	19
Mounting to body	40	30
Mounting vibration damper	32	24
Flywheel bolts	67	49

Torque wrench settings (continued)

	Nm	lbf ft
Main bearing cap bolts (cast-iron block engine):		
Stage 1	20	15
Stage 2	Angle-tighten a further 49°	
Main bearing ladder casting (aluminium block engine):		
M11 bolts:		
Stage 1	20	15
Stage 2	Angle-tighten a further 44°	
M6 bolts	8	6
Oil pump retaining bolts	9	7
Piston oil jet spray tube bolts – cast-iron block engine	10	7
Roadwheel bolts	85	63
Sump drain plug	30	22
Sump retaining nuts and bolts	8	6
Timing belt cover bolts	8	6
Timing belt tensioner pulley nut	22	16

1 General information

How to use this Chapter

1 This Part of Chapter 2 describes those repair procedures that can reasonably be carried out on the petrol engine while it remains in the car. If the engine has been removed from the car and is being dismantled, as described in Part C, any preliminary dismantling procedures can be ignored.

2 Note that, while it may be possible physically to overhaul items such as the piston/connecting rod assemblies while the engine is in the car, such tasks are not normally carried out as separate operations. Usually, several additional procedures (not to mention the cleaning of components and of oilways) have to be carried out. For this reason, all such tasks are classed as major overhaul procedures, and are described in Part C of this Chapter.

3 Part C describes the removal of the engine/transmission from the vehicle, and the full overhaul procedures that can then be carried out.

Petrol engine description

4 All petrol engines are from the TU series of engines and are well-proven engines which has been fitted to many previous Peugeot and Citroën vehicles. The engine is of the in-line four-cylinder, overhead camshaft (OHC) type, mounted transversely at the front of the car with the transmission attached to its left-hand end. The 206 range was offered with a choice of 1.1 litre (1124 cc), 1.4 litre (1360 cc) and 1.6 litre (1587 cc) engines.

5 The crankshaft runs in five main bearings. Thrustwashers are fitted to No 2 main bearing (upper half) to control crankshaft endfloat.

6 The connecting rods rotate on horizontally-split bearing shells at their big-ends. The pistons are attached to the connecting rods by gudgeon pins, which are an interference fit in the connecting rod small-end eyes. The aluminium-alloy pistons are fitted with three piston rings – two compression rings and an oil control ring.

7 On 1.1 and 1.4 litre engines, the cylinder block is made of aluminium, and replaceable wet liners are fitted to the cylinder bores. Sealing O-rings are fitted at the base of each liner, to prevent the escape of coolant into the sump.

8 On 1.6 litre engines, the cylinder block is made from cast-iron, and the cylinder bores are an integral part of the cylinder block. On this type of engine, the cylinder bores are sometimes referred to as having dry liners.

9 The inlet and exhaust valves are each closed by coil springs, and operate in guides pressed into the cylinder head; the valve seat inserts are also pressed into the cylinder head, and can be renewed separately if worn.

10 The camshaft is driven by a toothed timing belt, and operates the eight valves via rocker arms. Valve clearances are adjusted by a screw-and-locknut arrangement. The camshaft rotates directly in the cylinder head. The timing belt also drives the coolant pump.

11 Lubrication is by means of an oil pump, which is driven (via a chain and sprocket) off the right-hand end of the crankshaft. It draws oil through a strainer located in the sump, and then forces it through an externally-mounted filter into galleries in the cylinder block/crankcase. From there, the oil is distributed to the crankshaft (main bearings) and camshaft. The big-end bearings are supplied with oil via internal drillings in the crankshaft, while the camshaft bearings also receive a pressurised supply. The camshaft lobes and valves are lubricated by splash, as are all other engine components.

Repair operations possible with the engine in the car

12 The following work can be carried out with the engine in the car:

a) *Compression pressure – testing.*

b) *Cylinder head cover – removal and refitting.*

c) *Timing belt covers – removal and refitting.*

d) *Timing belt – removal, refitting and adjustment.*

e) *Timing belt tensioner and sprockets – removal and refitting.*

f) *Camshaft oil seal – renewal.*

g) *Camshaft and rocker arms – removal, inspection and refitting.**

h) *Cylinder head – removal and refitting.*

i) *Cylinder head and pistons – decarbonising.*

j) *Sump – removal and refitting.*

k) *Oil pump – removal, overhaul and refitting.*

l) *Crankshaft oil seals – renewal.*

m) *Engine/transmission mountings – inspection and renewal.*

n) *Flywheel/driveplate – removal, inspection and refitting.*

The cylinder head must be removed for the successful completion of this work. Refer to Section 10 for details.

2 Compression test – description and interpretation

1 When engine performance is down, or if misfiring occurs which cannot be attributed to the ignition or fuel systems, a compression test can provide diagnostic clues as to the engine's condition. If the test is performed regularly, it can give warning of trouble before any other symptoms become apparent.

2 The engine must be fully warmed-up to normal operating temperature, the battery must be fully charged. The aid of an assistant will also be required.

3 Remove the ignition HT coil assembly (see Chapter 5B) then remove the spark plugs (see Chapter 1A).

4 Fit a compression tester to the No 1 cylinder spark plug hole – the type of tester which screws into the plug thread is to be preferred.

5 Have the assistant hold the throttle wide open, and crank the engine on the starter motor; after one or two revolutions, the compression pressure should build up to a maximum figure, and then stabilise. Record the highest reading obtained.

6 Repeat the test on the remaining cylinders, recording the pressure in each.

2A

3.4 Insert a 6 mm diameter bolt/pin (arrowed) into the hole in the cylinder block flange and locate it in the flywheel/driveplate hole

3.5 Lock the camshaft sprocket in position with a 10 mm diameter bolt/pin (arrowed)

7 All cylinders should produce very similar pressures; a difference of more than 2 bars between any two cylinders indicates a fault. Note that the compression should build up quickly in a healthy engine; low compression on the first stroke, followed by gradually-increasing pressure on successive strokes, indicates worn piston rings. A low compression reading on the first stroke, which does not build up during successive strokes, indicates leaking valves or a blown head gasket (a cracked head could also be the cause). Deposits on the undersides of the valve heads can also cause low compression.

8 Although Peugeot do not specify exact compression pressures, as a guide, any cylinder pressure of below 10 bars can be considered as less than healthy. Refer to a Peugeot dealer or other specialist if in doubt as to whether a particular pressure reading is acceptable.

9 If the pressure in any cylinder is low, carry out the following test to isolate the cause. Introduce a teaspoonful of clean oil into that cylinder through its spark plug hole, and repeat the test.

10 If the addition of oil temporarily improves the compression pressure, this indicates that bore or piston wear is responsible for the pressure loss. No improvement suggests that leaking or burnt valves, or a blown head gasket, may be to blame.

11 A low reading from two adjacent cylinders is almost certainly due to the head gasket having blown between them; the presence of coolant in the engine oil will confirm this.

12 If one cylinder is about 20 percent lower than the others and the engine has a slightly rough idle, a worn camshaft lobe could be the cause.

13 If the compression reading is unusually high, the combustion chambers are probably coated with carbon deposits. If this is the case, the cylinder head should be removed and decarbonised.

14 On completion of the test, refit the spark plugs and ignition HT coil (see Chapters 1A and 5B).

3 Engine assembly/ valve timing holes –
general information and usage

Note: *Do not attempt to rotate the engine whilst the crankshaft/camshaft are locked in position. If the engine is to be left in this state for a long period of time, it is a good idea to place warning notices inside the vehicle, and in the engine compartment. This will reduce the possibility of the engine being accidentally cranked on the starter motor, which is likely to cause damage with the locking pins in place.*

1 On all models, timing holes are drilled in the camshaft sprocket and in the rear of the flywheel/driveplate. The holes are used to ensure that the crankshaft and camshaft are correctly positioned when assembling the engine (to prevent the possibility of the valves contacting the pistons when refitting the cylinder head), or refitting the timing belt. When the timing holes are aligned with access holes in the cylinder head and the front of the cylinder block, suitable diameter bolts/pins can be inserted to lock both the camshaft and crankshaft in position, preventing them from rotating. Proceed as follows.

2 Remove the timing belt upper cover as described in Section 5.

3 The crankshaft must now be turned until the timing hole in the camshaft sprocket is aligned with the corresponding hole in the cylinder head. The holes are aligned when the camshaft sprocket hole is in the 2 o'clock position, when viewed from the right-hand end of the engine. The crankshaft can be turned by using a spanner on the crankshaft sprocket bolt, noting that it should always be rotated in a clockwise direction (viewed from the right-hand end of the engine).

4 With the camshaft sprocket hole correctly positioned, insert a 6 mm diameter bolt or pin through the hole in the front, left-hand flange of the cylinder block, and locate it in the timing hole in the rear of the flywheel/driveplate (see illustration). Note that it may be necessary to rotate the crankshaft slightly to get the holes to align.

5 With the flywheel correctly positioned, insert a 10 mm diameter bolt or a pin through the timing hole in the camshaft sprocket, and locate it in the hole in the cylinder head (see illustration).

6 The crankshaft and camshaft are now locked in position, preventing unnecessary rotation.

4 Cylinder head cover –
removal and refitting

Removal

1 Disconnect the battery negative lead.

2 Release the retaining clip and disconnect the breather hose from the cylinder head cover (see illustration).

3 Remove the ignition HT coil as described in Chapter 5B.

4.2 Disconnect the breather hose from the cylinder head cover

4.4a Unscrew the retaining nuts (arrowed) . . .

4.4b . . . then lift off the cylinder cover

4.5a Remove the spacers (arrowed) from the studs . . .

4.5b . . . then lift off the baffle plate

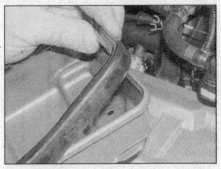
4.7 Ensure the rubber seal is correctly located on the cylinder head cover

2A

4 Undo the two retaining nuts and sealing washers (where fitted) then lift off the cylinder head cover, complete with its rubber seal **(see illustrations)**. Examine the seal for signs of damage and deterioration, and if necessary, renew it.
5 Remove the spacer from each cover stud then lift off the oil baffle plate **(see illustrations)**.

Refitting

6 Carefully clean the cylinder head and cover mating surfaces, and remove all traces of oil.
7 Fit the rubber seal over the edge of the cylinder head cover, ensuring that it is correctly located along its entire length **(see illustration)**.
8 Refit the oil baffle plate then fit the spacers to the cover studs.
9 Carefully refit the cylinder head cover to the engine, taking great care not to displace the rubber seal.
10 Fit the sealing washers (where fitted) and cover retaining nuts, tightening them to the specified torque. **Note:** *There are two possible sizes of cylinder head cover nut; some early engines have M8 cap nuts which are fitted with sealing washers whereas later engines have M6 cap nuts which are fitted without sealing washers. The torque wrench settings are different for each type of nut,*

ensure they are tightened to the correct torque (see Specifications).
11 Refit the ignition HT coil (see Chapter 5B) then reconnect the breather hose securely to the cylinder head cover. On completion reconnect the battery negative lead.

5 Timing belt covers – removal and refitting

Note: *On some early engines, a three-piece timing belt cover assembly is fitted (consisting of upper, centre and lower covers), on all later*

engines a two-piece cover is used (the centre and lower covers are integrated into one large lower cover).

Removal

Upper cover

1 Slacken and remove the two retaining bolts (one at the front and one at the rear), and remove the upper timing cover from the cylinder head **(see illustrations)**.

Centre cover – models with three-piece cover assembly

2 Remove the upper cover as described in paragraph 1.

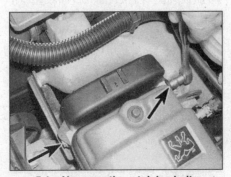
5.1a Unscrew the retaining bolts (arrowed) . . .

5.1b . . . and remove the timing belt upper cover

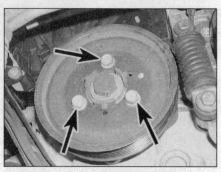

5.8a Unscrew the retaining bolts (arrowed) . . .

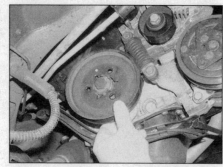

5.8b . . . then remove the crankshaft pulley

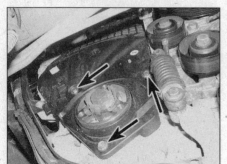

5.10a Unscrew the bolts (arrowed) . . .

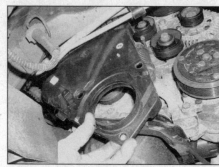

5.10b . . . and remove the timing belt lower cover from the engine

3 Firmly apply the handbrake then jack up the front of the vehicle and support it securely on axle stands (see *Jacking and vehicle support*). Remove the right-hand front roadwheel.
4 Undo the screws securing the front section of the right-hand wheelarch liner to the base of the bumper. Remove the fasteners (pull out the centre pin then remove the complete fastener) securing the liner section to the body then manoeuvre the front section of the liner out from underneath the wing.
5 Slacken and remove the retaining bolts and manoeuvre the centre cover out of position.

Lower cover

6 Remove the upper cover as described in paragraph 1.
7 Remove the auxiliary drivebelt as described in Chapter 1A.
8 Undo the three crankshaft pulley retaining bolts and remove the pulley, noting which way

round it is fitted **(see illustrations)**.
9 On models with a three-piece timing cover assembly, remove the centre cover as described above.
10 On all models, slacken and remove the retaining bolts then remove the lower cover from the engine **(see illustrations)**.

Refitting

Upper cover

11 Refitting is the reverse of removal.

Centre cover – models with three-piece cover assembly

12 Refitting is the reverse of removal, tightening the wheel bolts to the specified torque.

Lower cover

13 Locate the lower cover over the timing belt sprocket, and tighten its retaining bolts.

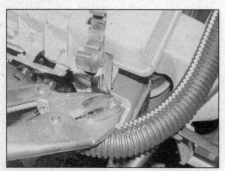

6.6a Unscrew the nut and lift off the bracket . . .

6.6b . . . then free the ECU mounting plate from the body and position it clear of the engine

14 Fit the pulley to the end of the crankshaft, ensuring it is fitted the correct way round, and tighten its bolts to the specified torque.
15 Refit the centre (where fitted) and upper covers as described above.
16 Refit and tension the auxiliary drivebelt as described in Chapter 1A.

6 Timing belt – general information, removal and refitting

Note: *Peugeot specify the use of a special electronic tool (SEEM C.TRONIC type 105.5 belt tensioning measuring tool) and the rocker arm contact plate (0132-AE) to correctly set the timing belt tension. If access to this equipment cannot be obtained, an approximate setting can be achieved using the method described below. If this method is used, the tension must be checked using the special electronic tool at the earliest possible opportunity. Do not drive the vehicle over large distances, or use high engine speeds, until the belt tension is known to be correct. Refer to a Peugeot dealer for advice.*

General information

1 The timing belt drives the camshaft and coolant pump from a toothed sprocket on the front of the crankshaft. If the belt breaks or slips in service, the pistons are likely to hit the valve heads, resulting in extensive (and expensive) damage.
2 The timing belt should be renewed at the specified intervals (see Chapter 1A), or earlier if it is contaminated with oil or if it is at all noisy in operation (a 'scraping' noise due to uneven wear).
3 If the timing belt is being removed, it is a wise precaution to check the condition of the coolant pump at the same time (check for signs of coolant leakage). This may avoid the need to remove the timing belt again at a later stage, should the coolant pump fail.

Removal

4 Disconnect the battery negative terminal.
5 Align the engine assembly/valve timing holes as described in Section 3, and lock both the camshaft sprocket and the flywheel/driveplate in position.
Caution: Do not attempt to rotate the engine whilst the locking tools are in position.
6 Unclip the wiring harness from the front of the engine management ECU to gain access to the mounting plate nut. Slacken and remove the nut using a pair of grips (the plate is secured in position with an anti-tamper nut) then remove the bracket. Free the ECU mounting plate from the body and position it clear of the engine **(see illustrations)**.
7 Remove the timing belt lower cover as described in Section 5.
8 Loosen the timing belt tensioner pulley retaining nut **(see illustration)**. Pivot the pulley

6.8 Slacken the nut then pivot the tensioner pulley clockwise to relieve the timing belt tension

in a clockwise direction, using a square-section key fitted to the hole in the pulley hub, then retighten the retaining nut **(see Tool Tip)**.
9 If the timing belt is to be re-used, use white paint or similar to mark the direction of rotation on the belt (if markings do not already exist). Slip the belt off the sprockets.
10 Check the timing belt carefully for any signs of uneven wear, splitting, or oil contamination. Pay particular attention to the roots of the teeth. Renew the belt if there is the slightest doubt about its condition. If the engine is undergoing an overhaul, and has covered more than 40 000 miles (60 000 km) with the existing belt fitted, renew the belt as a matter of course, regardless of its apparent condition. The cost of a new belt is nothing when compared to the cost of repairs, should the belt break in service. If signs of oil contamination are found, trace the source of the oil leak, and rectify it. Wash down the engine timing belt area and all related components, to remove all traces of oil.

Refitting

11 Prior to refitting, thoroughly clean the timing belt sprockets. Check that the tensioner pulley rotates freely, without any sign of roughness. If necessary, renew the tensioner pulley as described in Section 7. Make sure that the locking tools are still in place, as described in Section 3.
12 Manoeuvre the timing belt into position, ensuring that the arrows on the belt are pointing in the direction of rotation (clockwise, when viewed from the right-hand end of the engine).
13 Do not twist the timing belt sharply while refitting it. Fit the belt over the crankshaft and camshaft sprockets. Make sure that the 'front run' of the belt is taut – ie, ensure that any slack is on the tensioner pulley side of the belt. Fit the belt over the coolant pump sprocket and tensioner pulley. Ensure that the belt teeth are seated centrally in the sprockets.
14 Loosen the tensioner pulley retaining nut. Pivot the pulley anti-clockwise to remove all freeplay from the timing belt, then retighten the nut **(see illustration)**. Tension the timing belt as described under the relevant sub-heading.

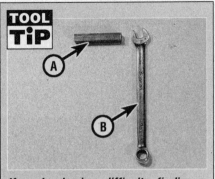

If you're having difficulty finding a square-section tool that will fit the tensioner pulley, obtain a length of standard 8 mm door handle rod from a DIY shop and cut it to length (A). Insert the rod into the pulley hub and rotate the pulley with an 8 mm spanner (B).

Tensioning without the special electronic measuring tool

Note: If this method is used, ensure that the belt tension is checked by a Peugeot dealer at the earliest possible opportunity.
15 If the special tool is not available, an approximate setting may be achieved by pivoting the tensioner pulley anti-clockwise until it is just possible to twist the timing belt through 90° by finger and thumb, midway between the crankshaft and camshaft sprockets. The deflection of the belt at the mid-point between the sprockets should be approximately 6.0 mm.
16 Remove the locking tools from the camshaft sprocket and flywheel/driveplate.
17 Using a suitable socket and extension bar on the crankshaft sprocket bolt, rotate the crankshaft through four complete rotations in a clockwise direction (viewed from the right-hand end of the engine). Refit the flywheel/driveplate locking tool and check that the camshaft timing hole is correctly aligned with the cylinder head hole.

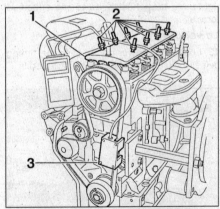

6.26 Fit the rocker arm plate (1) to the cylinder head and use the contact bolts (2) to lift the rocker arms clear of the camshaft (see text). Note the correct location for the measuring tool (3)

6.14 Pivot the tensioner pulley anti-clockwise to remove all freeplay from the timing belt then tighten the pulley nut

Caution: Do not at any time rotate the crankshaft anti-clockwise.
18 Slacken the tensioner pulley nut, re-tension the belt as described in paragraph 15, then tighten the tensioner pulley nut to the specified torque.
19 Remove the flywheel/driveplate locking tool then rotate the crankshaft through a further two turns clockwise. Check that both the camshaft sprocket and flywheel timing holes are still correctly aligned.
20 If all is well, refit the timing belt covers as described in Section 5.
21 Locate the engine management ECU bracket assembly on its mounting, refit the bracket and secure it in position with a new anti-tamper nut or standard nut.
22 Clip the wiring harness back into position then reconnect the battery negative terminal.

Tensioning using the special electronic measuring tool

23 Fit the special belt tensioning measuring equipment to the 'front run' of the timing belt, approximately midway between the camshaft and crankshaft sprockets. Position the tensioner pulley so that the belt is tensioned to a setting of 44 SEEM units, then retighten its retaining nut.
24 Remove the locking tools from the camshaft sprocket and flywheel/driveplate, and remove the measuring tool from the belt.
25 Using a suitable socket and extension bar on the crankshaft sprocket bolt, rotate the crankshaft through four complete rotations in a clockwise direction (viewed from the right-hand end of the engine). Refit the flywheel/driveplate locking tool and check that the camshaft timing hole is correctly aligned with the cylinder head hole.
Caution: Do not at any time rotate the crankshaft anti-clockwise.
26 To ensure an accurate reading, it is necessary to remove the valve spring load from the camshaft by fitting the rocker arm plate (0132-AE). Remove the cylinder head cover (see Section 4) then back off all the rocker arm contact bolts on the plate (0132-AE). Fit the plate to the cylinder head cover studs, ensuring it is fitted the correct way around then secure it in position with the cylinder head cover nuts **(see illustration)**.

2A

TOOL TIP

If the rocker arm plate is not available, slacken the locknuts and back off the adjusting screws on all the necessary rocker arms. It will be found that two of the rocker arms remain in contact with the camshaft, even with the adjusting screws backed fully off. To hold these arms clear of the camshaft, fix a stout metal bar to the cylinder head cover studs with the nuts and lift the arms using shorter lengths of metal bar pivoted on large sockets.

Tighten each rocker arm contact bolt until all rockers are lifted clear of the camshaft lobes. If the rocker arm plate is not available, obtain clearance between the rocker arms and camshaft by slackening the locknut and backing off the adjusting screws on all the necessary rocker arms. It will be found that two of the rocker arms remain in contact with the camshaft, even with the adjusting screws backed fully off. To hold these arms clear of the camshaft, use an arrangement similar to that shown **(see Tool Tip)**.
Caution: Do not overtighten the contact bolts any more than is necessary to obtain a small amount of clearance between the rocker arm roller and cam lobe. If the bolts are overtightened, there is a risk of the valves being forced into contact with the pistons, resulting in serious engine damage.
27 Refit the tensioning measuring equipment to the front run of the belt.
28 Slacken the tensioner pulley retaining nut whilst holding the pulley stationary. Gradually release the tensioner pulley until a tension

setting of between 29 and 33 SEEM units is indicated on the measuring equipment. With the belt correctly tensioned, hold the pulley stationary and tighten its retaining nut to the specified torque.
29 Remove the measuring tool from the belt then unscrew the nuts and remove the rocker arm contact plate (or home-made alternative) from the cylinder head.
30 Remove the flywheel/driveplate locking tool, then rotate the crankshaft through another four complete rotations in a clockwise direction. Refit the flywheel/driveplate locking tool and check that the camshaft timing hole is correctly aligned with the cylinder head hole.
31 If all is well, refit the timing belt covers and cylinder head cover as described in Sections 4 and 5. **Note:** *If the rocker arm adjusting screws were moved, adjust the valve clearances before refitting the cylinder head cover.*
32 Locate the engine management ECU bracket assembly on its mounting, refit the bracket and secure it in position with a new anti-tamper nut or standard nut. Clip the wiring harness back into position then reconnect the battery negative terminal.

7 Timing belt tensioner and sprockets – removal, inspection and refitting

Removal

1 Disconnect the battery negative terminal.
2 Position the engine assembly/valve timing holes as described in Section 3, and lock both the camshaft sprocket and flywheel/driveplate in position. *Do not* attempt to rotate the engine whilst the pins are in position.

Camshaft sprocket

3 Remove the timing belt as described in Section 6. **Note:** *On engines with a three-piece timing belt cover assembly, the sprocket can be removed without removing the belt completely. Referring to Sections 5 and 6, remove the centre timing belt cover then slacken the tensioner pulley retaining nut. Release the belt tension then disengage the timing belt from the camshaft sprocket, and*

move the belt clear, taking care not to bend or twist it sharply.
4 Remove the locking pin from the camshaft sprocket.
5 Slacken the camshaft sprocket retaining bolt and remove it, along with its washer. To prevent the camshaft rotating as the bolt is slackened, a sprocket-holding tool will be required. In the absence of the special Peugeot tool, an acceptable substitute can be fabricated as follows. Use two lengths of steel strip (one long, the other short), and three nuts and bolts; one nut and bolt forms the pivot of a forked tool, with the remaining two nuts and bolts at the tips of the 'forks' to engage with the sprocket spokes (see **Tool Tip** in *Refitting*).
Caution: Do not attempt to use the sprocket locking pin to prevent the sprocket from rotating whilst the bolt is slackened.
6 With the retaining bolt removed, slide the sprocket off the end of the camshaft. If the sprocket locating pin is a loose fit, remove it for safe-keeping. Examine the camshaft oil seal for signs of oil leakage and, if necessary, renew it as described in Section 8.

Crankshaft sprocket

7 Remove the timing belt as described in Section 6.
8 Slacken the crankshaft sprocket bolt. To prevent crankshaft rotation on manual transmission models, select top gear, and have an assistant apply the brakes firmly. If the engine has been removed from the vehicle or the vehicle is equipped with an automatic transmission unit, it will be necessary to lock the flywheel/driveplate (see Section 15).
Caution: Do not be tempted to use the flywheel/driveplate locking pin to prevent the crankshaft from rotating; temporarily remove the locking pin prior to slackening the pulley bolt, then refit it once the bolt has been slackened.
9 Unscrew the retaining bolt and washer, then slide the sprocket and off the end of crankshaft **(see illustrations)**.
10 If the Woodruff key is a loose fit in the crankshaft, remove it and store it with the sprocket for safe-keeping. If necessary, also slide the flanged spacer (where fitted) off the end of the crankshaft **(see illustration)**.

7.9b . . . then slide off the crankshaft sprocket

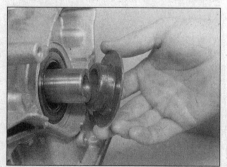

7.10 Remove the Woodruff key and flanged spacer (where fitted) from the crankshaft

7.9a Remove the retaining bolt and washer . . .

Examine the crankshaft oil seal for signs oil leakage and, if necessary, renew as described in Section 14.

Tensioner pulley

11 On models with a three-piece timing belt cover assembly, remove the centre timing belt cover; on models with a two-piece timing belt cover assembly, remove the lower cover (see Section 5).

12 Slacken and remove the timing belt tensioner pulley retaining nut, and slide the pulley off its mounting stud. Examine the mounting stud for signs of damage and, if necessary, renew it.

Inspection

13 Clean the sprockets thoroughly, and renew any that show signs of wear, damage or cracks.

14 Clean the tensioner assembly, but do not use any strong solvent which may enter the pulley bearing. Check that the pulley rotates freely about its hub, with no sign of stiffness or of free play. Renew the tensioner pulley if there is any doubt about its condition, or if there are any obvious signs of wear or damage.

15 Inspect the timing belt (see Section 6). Renew the belt is there is any doubt about its condition.

Refitting

Camshaft sprocket

16 Refit the locating pin (where removed) then locate the sprocket on the end of the camshaft. Ensure that the locating pin is correctly engaged with the sprocket and the cut-out in the camshaft end.

17 Refit the sprocket retaining bolt and washer. Tighten the bolt to the specified torque, whilst retaining the sprocket with the tool used on removal (**see Tool Tip**).

18 Realign the timing hole in the camshaft sprocket (see Section 3) with the corresponding hole in the cylinder head, and refit the locking pin.

19 Refit the timing belt as described in Section 6.

Crankshaft sprocket

20 Locate the Woodruff key in the crankshaft end, then slide on the flanged spacer (where fitted) aligning its slot with the Woodruff key.

21 Align the crankshaft sprocket slot with the Woodruff key, and slide it onto the end of the crankshaft.

22 Temporarily remove the locking pin from the rear of the flywheel/driveplate, then refit the crankshaft sprocket retaining bolt and washer. Tighten the bolt to the specified torque, whilst preventing crankshaft rotation using the method employed on removal. Refit the locking pin to the rear of the flywheel/driveplate.

23 Refit the timing belt as described in Section 6.

Using a home-made tool to hold the camshaft sprocket stationary whilst the bolt is tightened (shown with the cylinder head removed).

Tensioner pulley

24 Refit the tensioner pulley to its mounting stud, and fit the retaining nut.

25 Ensure that the 'front run' of the belt is taut – ie, ensure that any slack is on the pulley side of the belt. Check that the belt is centrally located on all its sprockets. Rotate the pulley anti-clockwise to remove all free play from the timing belt, then tighten the pulley retaining nut securely.

26 Tension the timing belt as described in Section 6.

27 Once the belt is correctly tensioned, refit the timing belt covers as described in Section 5.

8 Camshaft oil seal –
    renewal

Note: *If the camshaft oil seal has been leaking, check the timing belt for signs of oil contamination; the belt must be renewed if signs of oil contamination are found. Ensure that all traces of oil are removed from the sprockets and surrounding area before the new belt is fitted.*

1 Remove the camshaft sprocket as described in Section 7.

2 Punch or drill two small holes opposite each other in the oil seal. Screw a self-tapping screw into each, and pull on the screws with

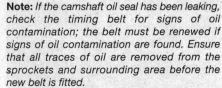

8.2 Carefully prise the camshaft oil seal out with a flat-bladed screwdriver

pliers to extract the seal. Alternatively, carefully prise the seal out using a flat-bladed screwdriver (**see illustration**).

3 Clean the seal housing, and polish off any burrs or raised edges, which may have caused the seal to fail in the first place.

4 Lubricate the lips of the new seal with clean engine oil, and drive it into position until it seats on its locating shoulder. Use a suitable tubular drift, such as a socket, which bears only on the hard outer edge of the seal. Take care not to damage the seal lips during fitting. Note that the seal lips should face inwards.

5 Refit the camshaft sprocket as described in Section 7.

9 Valve clearances –
    checking and adjustment

Note: *The valve clearances must be checked and adjusted only when the engine is cold.*

1 The importance of having the valve clearances correctly adjusted cannot be overstressed, as they vitally affect the performance of the engine. If the clearances are too big, the engine will be noisy (characteristic rattling or tapping noises) and engine efficiency will be reduced, as the valves open too late and close too early. A more serious problem arises if the clearances are too small, however. If this is the case, the valves may not close fully when the engine is hot, resulting in serious damage to the engine (eg, burnt valve seats and/or cylinder head warping/cracking). The clearances are checked and adjusted as follows.

2 Remove the cylinder head cover as described in Section 4.

3 The engine can now be turned using a suitable socket and extension bar fitted to the crankshaft sprocket bolt.

4 It is important that the clearance of each valve is checked and adjusted only when the valve is fully closed, with the rocker arm resting on the heel of the cam (directly opposite the peak). This can be ensured by carrying out the adjustments in the following sequence, noting that No 1 cylinder is at the transmission end of the engine. The correct valve clearances are given in the Specifications at the start of this Chapter. The valve locations can be determined from the position of the manifolds.

Valve fully open	Adjust valves
No 1 exhaust	*No 3 inlet and No 4 exhaust*
No 3 exhaust	*No 4 inlet and No 2 exhaust*
No 4 exhaust	*No 2 inlet and No 1 exhaust*
No 2 exhaust	*No 1 inlet and No 3 exhaust*

5 With the relevant valve fully open, check the clearances of the two valves specified. The clearances are checked by inserting a feeler blade of the correct thickness between the valve stem and the rocker arm adjusting screw. The feeler blade should be a light, sliding fit. If adjustment is necessary, slacken the adjusting screw locknut, and turn the

2A

screw as necessary **(see illustration)**. Once the correct clearance is obtained, hold the adjusting screw and tighten the locknut securely. Once the locknut has been tightened, recheck the valve clearance, and adjust again if necessary.

6 Rotate the crankshaft until the next valve in the sequence is fully open, and check the clearances of the next two specified valves.

7 Repeat the procedure until all eight valve clearances have been checked (and if necessary, adjusted), then refit the cylinder head cover as described in Section 4.

10 Camshaft and rocker arms – removal, inspection and refitting

General information

1 The rocker arm assembly is secured to the top of the cylinder head by the cylinder head bolts. Although in theory it is possible to undo the head bolts and remove the rocker arm assembly without removing the head, in practice, this is not recommended. Once the bolts have been removed, the head gasket will be disturbed, and the gasket will almost certainly leak or blow after refitting. For this reason, removal of the rocker arm assembly cannot be done without removing the cylinder head and renewing the head gasket.

2 The camshaft is slid out of the right-hand end of the cylinder head, and it therefore cannot be removed without first removing the cylinder head, due to a lack of clearance.

10.4 Remove the circlip and slide the components off the end of the rocker arm

10.9 Undo the retaining bolt and slide out the camshaft thrust fork

9.5 Adjusting a valve clearance

Removal

Rocker arm assembly

3 Remove the cylinder head as described in Section 11.

4 To dismantle the rocker arm assembly, carefully prise off the circlip from the right-hand end of the rocker shaft; retain the rocker pedestal, to prevent it being sprung off the end of the shaft. Slide the various components off the end of the shaft, keeping all components in their correct fitted order **(see illustration)**. Make a note of each component's correct fitted position and orientation as it is removed, to ensure it is fitted correctly on reassembly. **Note:** *Avoid touching the rocker arm roller bearing surfaces with your fingers.*

5 To separate the left-hand pedestal and shaft, first unscrew the cylinder head cover retaining stud from the top of the pedestal;

10.5 Lock two nuts together to enable the stud to be unscrewed from the left-hand end pedestal

10.10a Prise out the oil seal . . .

this can be achieved using a stud extractor, or two nuts locked together **(see illustration)**. With the stud removed, unscrew the grub screw from the top of the pedestal, and withdraw the rocker shaft.

Camshaft

6 Remove the cylinder head as described in Section 11.

7 With the head on a bench, remove the locking pin, then remove the camshaft sprocket as described in paragraphs 5 and 6 of Section 7.

8 Unbolt the coolant housing from the left-hand end of the cylinder head.

9 Undo the retaining bolt and slide out the camshaft thrust fork **(see illustration)**.

10 Using a large flat-bladed screwdriver, carefully prise the oil seal out of the right-hand end of the cylinder head, then slide out the camshaft **(see illustrations)**. **Note:** *On 1.4 litre engines equipped with air injection, take care not to damage the camshaft sensor lug as the camshaft is removed.* Discard the seal – a new one must be used on refitting.

Inspection

Rocker arm assembly

11 Examine the rocker arm roller surfaces which contact the camshaft lobes for wear ridges and scoring. Renew any rocker arms on which the rollers show signs of damage. If a rocker arm roller surface is badly scored, also examine the corresponding lobe on the camshaft for wear, as both will likely be worn. Renew worn components as necessary. The rocker arm assembly can be dismantled as described in paragraphs 4 and 5.

12 Inspect the ends of the (valve clearance) adjusting screws for signs of wear or damage, and renew as required.

13 If the rocker arm assembly has been dismantled, examine the rocker arm and shaft bearing surfaces for wear ridges and scoring. If there are obvious signs of wear, the relevant rocker arm(s) and/or the shaft must be renewed.

Camshaft

14 Examine the camshaft bearing surfaces and cam lobes for signs of wear ridges and scoring. Renew the camshaft if any of these conditions are apparent. Examine the

10.10b . . . then slide the camshaft out from the cylinder head

condition of the bearing surfaces, both on the camshaft journals and in the cylinder head. If the head bearing surfaces are worn excessively, the cylinder head will need to be renewed. If the necessary measuring equipment is available, camshaft bearing journal wear can be checked by direct measurement, noting that No 1 journal is at the transmission end of the head.

15 Examine the thrust fork for signs of wear or scoring, and renew as necessary.

Refitting

Rocker arm assembly

16 If the rocker arm assembly was dismantled, refit the rocker shaft to the left-hand pedestal, aligning its locating hole with the pedestal threaded hole. Refit the grub screw, and tighten it securely. With the grub screw in position, refit the cylinder head cover mounting stud to the pedestal, and tighten it securely. Apply a smear of clean engine oil to the shaft, then slide on all removed components, ensuring each is correctly fitted in its original position. **Note:** *Avoid touching the rocker arm roller bearing surfaces with your fingers.* Once all components are in position on the shaft, compress the right-hand pedestal and refit the circlip. Ensure that the circlip is correctly located in its groove on the shaft.

17 Refit the cylinder head and rocker arm assembly as described in Section 11.

Camshaft

18 Ensure that the cylinder head and camshaft bearing surfaces are clean, then liberally oil the camshaft bearings and lobes. Slide the camshaft back into position in the cylinder head. **Note:** *On 1.4 litre engines equipped with air injection, take care not to damage the camshaft sensor lug as the camshaft is refitted.*

19 Locate the thrust fork with the left-hand end of the camshaft. Refit the fork retaining bolt, tightening it to the specified torque setting.

20 Ensure that the coolant housing and cylinder head mating surfaces are clean and dry, then apply a smear of sealant to the housing mating surface. Refit the housing to the left-hand end of the head, and securely tighten its retaining bolts.

21 Lubricate the lips of the new seal with clean engine oil, then drive it into position until it seats on its locating shoulder. Use a suitable tubular drift, such as a socket, which bears only on the hard outer edge of the seal. Take care not to damage the seal lips during fitting. Note that the seal lips should face inwards.

22 Refit the camshaft sprocket as described in paragraphs 16 to 18 of Section 7.

23 Refit the cylinder head as described in Section 11.

---

11 Cylinder head – removal and refitting

Note: *Ensure the engine is cold before removing the cylinder head.*

Removal

1 Disconnect the battery negative lead.

2 Drain the cooling system as described in Chapter 1A.

3 Remove the ignition HT coil assembly (see Chapter 5B) then remove the spark plugs (see Chapter 1A).

4 Remove the cylinder head cover as described in Section 4.

5 Align the engine assembly/valve timing holes as described in Section 3, and lock both the camshaft sprocket and flywheel/driveplate in position.

Caution: Do not attempt to rotate the engine whilst the tools are in position.

6 Note that the following text assumes that the cylinder head will be removed with both inlet and exhaust manifolds attached; this is easier, but makes it a bulky and heavy assembly to handle. If it is wished to remove the manifolds first, proceed as described in Chapter 4A.

7 Carry out the following operations as described in Chapter 4A:

a) *Disconnect the exhaust system front pipe from the manifold. Disconnect or release the oxygen sensor wiring, so that it is not strained by the weight of the exhaust.*

b) *Remove the air cleaner housing inlet duct assembly.*

c) *Disconnect the fuel feed hose from the fuel*

11.9 Unscrew the bolts (arrowed) and free the wiring/power steering pipe bracket from the left-hand end of the cylinder head

rail (plug all openings, to prevent loss of fuel and entry of dirt into the fuel system).

d) *Disconnect the accelerator cable.*

e) *Disconnect the relevant electrical connectors and vacuum/breather hoses from the inlet manifold.*

f) *Where necessary unbolt the support bracket from the inlet manifold.*

g) *On 1.4 litre models with air injection, disconnect the hose from the injection valve which is fitted to the exhaust manifold.*

8 Remove the timing belt as described in Section 6. **Note:** *On engines with a three-piece timing belt cover assembly, the cylinder head can be removed without removing the belt completely. Referring to Sections 5 and 6, remove the centre timing belt cover then slacken the tensioner pulley retaining nut. Release the belt tension then disengage the timing belt from the camshaft sprocket, and move the belt clear, taking care not to bend or twist it sharply*

9 Unscrew the bolts and free the wiring/power steering pipe bracket from the coolant housing **(see illustration)**.

10 Slacken the retaining clips, and disconnect the coolant hoses from the housing on the left-hand end of the cylinder head. Disconnect the wiring connectors from the electrical sensors which are screwed into the coolant housing/cylinder head.

11 On models with power steering, referring to Chapter 10, unbolt the power steering pump from its mounting bracket. Undo the power steering pipe retaining clip screws and position the pump clear of the engine **(see illustrations)**. Support the weight of the pump

2A

11.11a Unscrew the front . . .

11.11b . . . and rear mounting bolts . . .

11.11c . . . then free the power steering pump from its mounting bracket and position it clear of the engine

11.12 Slacken and remove the cylinder head bolts as described in text . . .

11.13 . . . then lift off the rocker arm assembly

by tying it to the vehicle body to prevent any excess strain being placed on the hydraulic pipes/hoses. **Note:** *There is no need to disconnect the pipe/hose from the pump.*

12 Working in the *reverse* of the sequence shown in illustration 11.31a, progressively slacken the ten cylinder head bolts by half a turn at a time, until all bolts can be unscrewed by hand **(see illustration)**.

13 With all the cylinder head bolts removed, lift the rocker arm assembly off the cylinder head **(see illustration)**. **Note:** *Avoid touching the rocker arm roller bearing surfaces with your fingers.* Note the locating pins which are fitted to the base of each rocker arm pedestal. If any pin is a loose fit in the head or pedestal, remove it for safe-keeping.

14 On engines with a cast-iron cylinder block, lift the cylinder head away; seek assistance if possible, as it is a heavy assembly, especially if it is being removed complete with the manifolds.

15 On engines with an aluminium cylinder block, the joint between the cylinder head and gasket and the cylinder block/crankcase must now be broken without disturbing the wet liners. To break the joint, obtain two stout screwdrivers which fit into the cylinder head bolt holes. Gently 'rock' the cylinder head free towards the front of the car **(see illustration)**. Do not try to swivel the head on the cylinder block/crankcase; it is located by dowels, as well as by the tops of the liners. **Note:** *If care is not taken and the liners are moved, there is also a possibility of the bottom seals being disturbed, causing leakage after refitting the*

11.15 On aluminium block engines, use two stout screwdrivers to rock the cylinder head free from the block

head. When the joint is broken, lift the cylinder head away; seek assistance if possible, as it is a heavy assembly, especially if it is being removed complete with the manifolds.

16 On all models, remove the gasket from the top of the block, noting the two locating dowels. If the locating dowels are a loose fit, remove them and store them with the head for safe-keeping. Do not discard the gasket – on some models it will be needed for identification purposes (see paragraphs 21 and 22). Operations that require the rotation of the crankshaft (eg, cleaning the piston crowns), should only be carried out on aluminium block engines once the cylinder liners are firmly clamped in position **(see illustration)**. In the absence of the special Peugeot liner clamps, the liners can be clamped in position using large flat washers positioned underneath suitable-length bolts. Alternatively, the original head bolts could be temporarily refitted, with suitable spacers fitted to their shanks.

Caution: On aluminium block engines, do not attempt to rotate the crankshaft with the cylinder head removed, otherwise the wet liners may be displaced.

17 If the cylinder head is to be dismantled for overhaul, remove the camshaft as described in Section 10, then refer to Part C of this Chapter.

Preparation for refitting

18 The mating faces of the cylinder head and cylinder block/crankcase must be perfectly clean before refitting the head. Use a hard

11.16 On aluminium block engines clamp the cylinder liners in position before rotating the crankshaft (clamps arrowed)

plastic or wood scraper to remove all traces of gasket and carbon; also clean the piston crowns. **Note:** *On aluminium block engines, clamp the liners in position before turning the crankshaft (see paragraph 16).* Take particular care during the cleaning operations, as aluminium alloy is easily damaged. Also, make sure that the carbon is not allowed to enter the oil and water passages – this is particularly important for the lubrication system, as carbon could block the oil supply to the engine's components. Using adhesive tape and paper, seal the water, oil and bolt holes in the cylinder block/crankcase. To prevent carbon entering the gap between the pistons and bores, smear a little grease in the gap. After cleaning each piston, use a small brush to remove all traces of grease and carbon from the gap, then wipe away the remainder with a clean rag. Clean all the pistons in the same way.

19 Check the mating surfaces of the cylinder block/crankcase and the cylinder head for nicks, deep scratches and other damage. If slight, they may be removed carefully with a file, but if excessive, machining may be the only alternative to renewal.

20 If warpage of the cylinder head gasket surface is suspected, use a straight-edge to check it for distortion. Refer to Part C of this Chapter if necessary.

21 When purchasing a new cylinder head gasket, it is essential that a gasket of the correct thickness is obtained. On some models only one thickness of gasket is available, so this is not a problem. On other models, there are two different thicknesses available – the standard gasket, and a slightly thicker 'repair' gasket (+ 0.2 mm). The gaskets can be identified as described in the following paragraph, using the cut-outs on the left-hand end of the gasket.

22 With the gasket fitted the correct way up on the cylinder block, there will be a single or double cut-out, at the rear of the left-hand side of the gasket identifying the engine type (eg, TU3JP engine). In the centre of the gasket there will likely be another series of between 0 and 4 cut-outs, identifying the manufacturer of the gasket and whether or not it contains asbestos (these cut-outs are of little importance). The important cut-out location is at the front of the gasket; on the standard gasket there will be no cut-out in this position, whereas on the thicker 'repair' gasket there will be a single cut-out **(see illustration)**. Identify the gasket type, and ensure that the new gasket obtained is of the correct thickness. If there is any doubt as to which gasket is fitted, take the old gasket along to your Peugeot dealer, and have him confirm the gasket type.

23 Check the condition of the cylinder head bolts, and particularly their threads, whenever they are removed. Wash the bolts in suitable solvent, and wipe them dry. Check each for any sign of visible wear or damage, renewing any bolt if necessary. Measure the length of

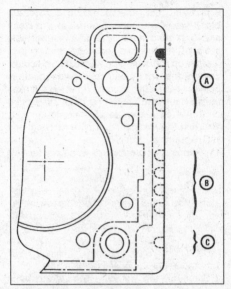

11.22 Cylinder head gasket identification markings

A *Engine type identification cutout locations*
B *Gasket manufacturer identification cutout locations*
C *Gasket thickness identification cutout location*

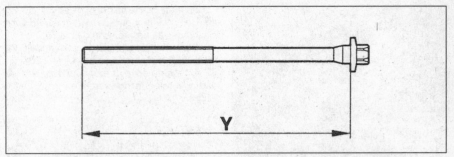

11.23 Measure the length of each cylinder head bolt (Y) to check for stretching – see text

11.25 Ensure the locating dowels (arrowed) are in position then fit the new head gasket

each bolt, from the underside of its head to the bolt end, to check for stretching **(see illustration)**. The bolts are 175.5 mm in length when new; if any bolt has stretched to more than 176.5 mm, renew all the cylinder head bolts as a set. Although Peugeot do not actually specify that the bolts must be renewed, it is strongly recommended that the bolts should be renewed as a complete set, regardless of their apparent condition, whenever they are disturbed.

24 On aluminium block engines, prior to refitting the cylinder head, check the cylinder liner protrusion as described Chapter 2C, Section 12.

Refitting

25 Wipe clean the mating surfaces of the cylinder head and cylinder block/crankcase. Check that the two locating dowels are in position at each end of the cylinder block/crankcase surface and, if necessary, remove the cylinder liner clamps **(see illustration)**.

26 Position a new gasket on the cylinder block/crankcase surface, ensuring that its identification cut-outs are at the left-hand end of the gasket.

27 Check that the flywheel/driveplate and camshaft sprocket are still correctly locked in position with their respective tools then, with the aid of an assistant, carefully refit the cylinder head assembly to the block, aligning it with the locating dowels.

28 Ensure that the locating pins are in position in the base of each rocker pedestal, then refit the rocker arm assembly to the cylinder head.

29 Lubricate the threads and underside of the heads of the cylinder head bolts lightly with clean engine oil.

30 Carefully enter each bolt into its relevant hole (*do not drop them in*) and screw in, by hand only, until finger-tight.

31 Working progressively and in the sequence shown, tighten the cylinder head bolts to their Stage 1 torque setting, using a torque wrench and suitable socket **(see illustrations)**.

32 Once all the bolts have been tightened to their Stage 1 setting, working again in the given sequence, angle-tighten the bolts through the specified Stage 2 angle, using a socket and extension bar. It is recommended that an angle-measuring gauge is used during this stage of the tightening, to ensure accuracy **(see illustration)**. If a gauge is not available, use white paint to make alignment marks between the bolt head and cylinder head prior to tightening; the marks can then

2A

11.31a Cylinder head bolt tightening sequence

11.31b Working in the specified sequence, tighten the cylinder head bolts to the specified stage 1 torque setting . . .

11.32 . . . and then through the specified stage 2 angle

be used to check that the bolt has been rotated through the correct angle during tightening.

33 On cast-iron block engines, it will then be necessary to tighten the bolts through the specified Stage 3 angle setting.

34 Refit and tension the timing belt as described in Section 6.

35 Reconnect the wiring connectors to the coolant temperature sensors on the coolant housing/cylinder head.

36 Reconnect the coolant hoses to the cylinder head coolant housing.

37 On models with power steering, ensure the mounting spacer (where fitted) is correctly fitted to the rear mounting then locate the pump on its mounting bracket Apply locking compound (Peugeot recommend the use of Loctite Frenetanch) to the pump lower front mounting bolt then install all the bolts; tighten the pump front (drivebelt pulley end) bolts to the specified torque first then tighten the rear bolts (see Chapter 10).

38 Secure the wiring/power steering pipe bracket to the cylinder head coolant housing, tightening its retaining bolts securely.

39 Working as described in the Chapter 4A, carry out the following tasks:

a) *Refit all disturbed wiring, hoses and control cable(s) to the inlet manifold and fuel system components.*

b) *Reconnect and adjust the accelerator cable.*

c) *Reconnect the exhaust system front pipe to the manifold and reconnect the oxygen sensor wiring connector.*

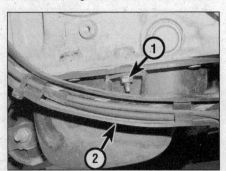

12.4 Unscrew the sump nut (1) and position the wiring harness guide (2) clear of the sump

d) *Refit the air cleaner and inlet duct.*

40 Check and, if necessary, adjust the valve clearances as described in Section 9.

41 Refit the spark plugs and install the ignition HT coil (see Chapters 1A and 5B).

42 On completion, reconnect the battery, and refill the cooling system as described in Chapter 1A.

12 Sump – removal and refitting

Removal

1 Firmly apply the handbrake, then jack up the front of the vehicle and support it on axle stands (see *Jacking and vehicle support*). Disconnect the battery negative lead.

2 Drain the engine oil, then clean and refit the engine oil drain plug, tightening it to the specified torque. If the engine is nearing its service interval when the oil and filter are due for renewal, it is recommended that the filter is also removed, and a new one fitted. After reassembly, the engine can then be refilled with fresh oil. Refer to Chapter 1A for further information.

3 Remove the exhaust system front pipe as described in Chapter 4A.

4 Progressively slacken and remove all the sump nuts and bolts and position the wiring harness guide clear of the sump **(see illustration)**. On cast-iron block engines, it may be necessary to unbolt the flywheel cover plate from the transmission to gain access to the left-hand sump fasteners.

5 Break the joint by striking the sump with the palm of your hand, then lower and withdraw the sump from under the car.

6 While the sump is removed, take the opportunity to check the oil pump pick-up/strainer for signs of clogging or splitting. If necessary, remove the pump as described in Section 13, and clean or renew the strainer.

Refitting

7 Clean all traces of sealant from the mating surfaces of the cylinder block/crankcase and sump, then use a clean rag to wipe out the sump and the engine's interior.

13.2 Unscrew the three bolts securing the oil pump in position

8 Ensure that the sump and cylinder block/crankcase mating surfaces are clean and dry, then apply a coating of suitable sealant to the sump mating surface.

9 Offer up the sump and locate it on its studs. Locate the wiring harness guide back in position then refit the sump retaining nuts and bolts. Tighten the nuts and bolts evenly and progressively to the specified torque.

10 Refit the exhaust front pipe as described in Chapter 4A.

11 Replenish the engine oil (see Chapter 1A).

13 Oil pump – removal, inspection and refitting

Removal

1 Remove the sump (see Section 12).

2 Slacken and remove the three bolts securing the oil pump in position **(see illustration)**. Disengage the pump sprocket from the chain, and remove the oil pump. If the pump locating dowel is a loose fit, remove and store it with the bolts for safe-keeping.

Inspection

3 Examine the oil pump sprocket for signs of damage and wear, such as chipped or missing teeth. If the sprocket is worn, the pump assembly must be renewed, as the sprocket is not available separately. It is also recommended that the chain and drive sprocket, fitted to the crankshaft, is renewed at the same time. On aluminium block engines, renewal of the chain and drive sprocket is an involved operation requiring the removal of the main bearing ladder, and therefore cannot be carried out with the engine still fitted to the vehicle. On cast-iron block engines, the oil pump drive sprocket and chain can be removed with the engine *in situ*, once the crankshaft sprocket has been removed and the crankshaft oil seal housing has been unbolted. See Part C for further information.

4 Slacken and remove the bolts securing the strainer cover to the pump body, then lift off the strainer cover. Remove the relief valve piston and spring (and guide pin – cast-iron block engines only), noting which way round they are fitted.

5 Examine the pump rotors and body for signs of wear ridges and scoring. If worn, the complete pump assembly must be renewed.

6 Examine the relief valve piston for signs of wear or damage, and renew if necessary. The condition of the relief valve spring can only be measured by comparing it with a new one; if there is any doubt about its condition, it should also be renewed. Both the piston and spring are available individually.

7 Thoroughly clean the oil pump strainer with a suitable solvent, and check it for signs of clogging or splitting. If the strainer is damaged, the strainer and cover assembly must be renewed.

8 Locate the relief valve spring, piston and (where fitted) the guide pin in the strainer cover, then refit the cover to the pump body. Align the relief valve piston with its bore in the pump. Refit the cover retaining bolts, tightening them securely.

Refitting

9 Ensure that the locating dowel is in position, then engage the pump sprocket with its drive chain. Locate the pump on its dowel, and refit the pump retaining bolts, tightening them to the specified torque setting.
10 Refit the sump as described in Section 12.

14 Crankshaft oil seals – renewal

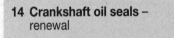

Right-hand (timing belt end) oil seal

1 Remove the crankshaft sprocket and flanged spacer (where fitted) as described in Section 7.
2 Make a note of the correct fitted depth of the seal in its housing then carefully punch or drill two small holes opposite each other in the seal. Screw a self-tapping screw into each, and pull on the screws with pliers to extract the seal. Alternatively, the seal can be levered out of position using a suitable flat-bladed screwdriver, taking great care not to damage the crankshaft/oil pump drive gear shoulder or seal housing (see illustration).
3 Clean the seal housing, and polish off any burrs or raised edges, which may have caused the seal to fail in the first place.
4 Lubricate the lips of the new seal with clean engine oil, and carefully locate the seal on the end of crankshaft. Note that its sealing lip must face inwards. Take care not to damage the seal lips during fitting.
5 Using a suitable tubular drift (such as a socket) which bears only on the hard outer edge of the seal, tap the seal into position, to the same depth in the housing as the original was prior to removal. The inner face of the seal must be flush with the inner wall of the crankcase.
6 Wash off any traces of oil, then refit the crankshaft sprocket as described in Section 7.

Left-hand (flywheel/driveplate end) oil seal

7 Remove the flywheel/driveplate (see Section 15).
8 Make a note of the correct fitted depth of the seal in its housing. Punch or drill two small holes opposite each other in the seal. Screw a self-tapping screw into each, and pull on the screws with pliers to extract the seal.
9 Clean the seal housing, and polish off any burrs or raised edges, which may have caused the seal to fail in the first place.
10 Lubricate the lips of the new seal with clean engine oil, and carefully locate the seal on the end of the crankshaft.

14.2 Using a screwdriver to lever the crankshaft right-hand oil seal out of position

11 Using a suitable tubular drift, which bears only on the hard outer edge of the seal, drive the seal into position, to the same depth in the housing as the original was prior to removal.
12 Wash off any traces of oil, then refit the flywheel/driveplate as described in Section 15.

15 Flywheel/driveplate – removal, inspection and refitting

Flywheel – manual transmission models

Removal

1 Remove the transmission as described in Chapter 7A, then remove the clutch assembly as described in Chapter 6.
2 Prevent the flywheel from turning by locking the ring gear teeth (see illustration). Alternatively, bolt a strap between the flywheel and the cylinder block/crankcase.
Caution: Do not attempt to lock the flywheel in position using the locking pin described in Section 3.
3 Slacken and remove the flywheel retaining bolts.
4 Remove the flywheel. Do not drop it, as it is very heavy. If the locating dowel is a loose fit in the crankshaft end, remove and store it with the flywheel for safe-keeping.

Inspection

5 If the flywheel's clutch mating surface is

15.2 Use a tool similar to that shown to lock the flywheel ring gear and prevent rotation

deeply scored, cracked or otherwise damaged, the flywheel must be renewed. However, it may be possible to have it surface-ground; seek the advice of a Peugeot dealer or engine reconditioning specialist.
6 If the ring gear is badly worn or has missing teeth, it must be renewed. This job is best left to a Peugeot dealer or engine reconditioning specialist. The temperature to which the new ring gear must be heated for installation is critical and, if not done accurately, the hardness of the teeth will be destroyed.

Refitting

7 Clean the mating surfaces of the flywheel and crankshaft.
8 Remove any traces of locking compound from the threads of the flywheel bolts and apply a small amount of fresh locking compound (Peugeot recommend Loctite Frenbloc) to the bolt threads.
9 Ensure that the locating dowel is in position. Offer up the flywheel, locating it on the dowel, and fit the retaining bolts.
10 Lock the flywheel using the method employed on dismantling, and tighten the retaining bolts evenly and progressively to the specified torque.
11 Refit the clutch as described in Chapter 6. Remove the locking tool, and refit the transmission as described in Chapter 7A.

Driveplate – automatic transmission models

Removal

12 Remove the transmission as described in Chapter 7B.
13 Prevent the driveplate from turning by locking the ring gear teeth with a similar arrangement to that shown in illustration 15.2. Alternatively, bolt a strap between the driveplate and the cylinder block/crankcase.
Caution: Do not attempt to lock the driveplate in position using the locking pin described in Section 3.
14 Slacken and remove the driveplate retaining bolts and remove the outer spacer plate and torque converter mounting plate.
15 Remove the driveplate and inner spacer plate from the end of the crankshaft. If the locating dowel is a loose fit in the crankshaft end, remove and store it with the driveplate for safe-keeping. **Note:** *The inner and outer spacer plates are different and are not interchangeable.*

Inspection

16 Inspect the driveplate and torque converter mounting plate for signs of wear or damage. If damage is found, the worn component must be renewed (it is not possible to renew the driveplate ring gear separately).

Refitting

17 Ensure all mating surfaces are clean and dry.
18 Remove any traces of locking compound from the threads of the driveplate bolts and

2A

16.8 Unscrew the mounting nut and bolts and remove the support bracket from the front of the right-hand mounting

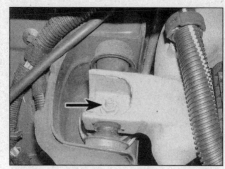

16.9 Unscrew the nut (arrowed) securing the mounting bracket to the mounting

apply a small amount of fresh locking compound (Peugeot recommend Loctite Frenbloc) to the bolt threads.

19 Ensure that the locating dowel is in position then refit the inner spacer plate, driveplate, torque converter mounting plate and outer spacer plate. Ensure all components are correctly located on the dowel then fit the retaining bolts.

20 Lock the driveplate using the method employed on dismantling, and tighten the retaining bolts evenly and progressively to the specified torque.

21 Refit the transmission as described in Chapter 7B.

16 Engine/transmission mountings – inspection and renewal

Inspection

1 If improved access is required, raise the front of the car and support it on axle stands (see *Jacking and vehicle support*).

2 Check the mounting rubber to see if it is cracked, hardened or separated from the metal at any point; renew the mounting if any such damage or deterioration is evident.

3 Check that all the mounting's fasteners are securely tightened; use a torque wrench to check if possible.

4 Using a large screwdriver or a crowbar, check for wear in the mounting by carefully levering against it to check for free play. Where this is not possible, enlist the aid of an assistant to move the engine/transmission back-and-forth, or from side-to-side, while you watch the mounting. While some free play is to be expected even from new components, excessive wear should be obvious. If excessive free play is found, check first that the fasteners are secure, then renew any worn components as described below.

Renewal

Right-hand mounting

5 Disconnect the battery negative lead.

6 Unclip the wiring harness from the front of the engine management ECU to gain access to the mounting plate nut. Slacken and remove the nut using a pair of grips (the plate is secured in position with an anti-tamper nut) then free the mounting plate from the body and position it clear of the engine mounting **(see illustrations 6.6a and 6.6b)**.

7 Place a jack beneath the engine, with a block of wood on the jack head. Raise the jack until it is supporting the weight of the engine.

8 Slacken and remove the mounting nut and bolts and remove the support bracket securing the mounting to the front of the engine unit **(see illustration)**.

9 Unscrew the vibration damper (where fitted) from the top of the mounting rubber then slacken and remove the nut and washer securing the mounting bracket to the mounting rubber **(see illustration)**.

10 Slacken and remove the three nuts securing the right-hand engine mounting bracket to the bracket/housing on the rear of the cylinder block **(see illustration)**.

11 Unclip the wiring harness then lift off the mounting bracket **(see illustration)**.

12 Make identification marks on the movement restrictors (the front and rear restrictors are different and are not interchangeable) then unscrew the nuts and remove both restrictors **(see illustration)**.

13 Using a strap wrench, unscrew the mounting rubber from the body **(see illustration)**.

14 Check for signs of wear or damage on all components, and renew as necessary.

15 On reassembly, screw the mounting rubber into the body, tightening it to the specified torque.

16 Refit the front and rear movement restrictors in their original locations. Ensure the restrictor pegs are correctly located in their holes then securely tighten their retaining nuts **(see illustration)**.

17 Install the mounting bracket and tighten its retaining nuts to the specified torque setting. Clip the wiring harness back into position then, where necessary, refit the vibration damper to the mounting, tightening it to the specified torque.

18 Remove the jack from under the engine. Refit the support bracket, tightening its fixings to the specified torque.

19 Locate the engine management ECU

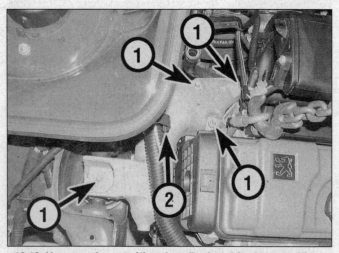

16.10 Unscrew the nuts (1) and unclip the wiring harness (2) . . .

16.11 . . . then lift off the right-hand mounting bracket

16.12 Unscrew the nuts and remove the front and rear movement restrictors

16.13 Use a strap wrench to unscrew the mounting rubber from the body

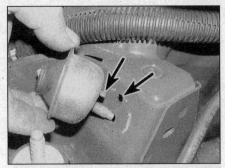

16.16 Ensure the movement restrictors are fitted in the correct locations with their pegs located in the body holes (arrowed)

assembly on its mounting and secure it in position with a new anti-tamper nut or standard nut. Clip the wiring harness back into position then reconnect the battery negative terminal.

Left-hand mounting

20 Remove the battery, battery tray and mounting plate as described in Chapter 5A.

21 Place a jack beneath the transmission, with a block of wood on the jack head. Raise the jack until it is supporting the weight of the transmission.

22 Slacken and remove the mounting rubber's centre nut and two retaining bolts and remove the mounting from the engine compartment **(see illustrations)**.

23 If necessary, undo the retaining bolts and remove the mounting bracket from the body **(see illustration)**.

24 On manual transmission models, to remove the transmission bracket, disconnect the clutch cable from the transmission (see Chapter 6) then unscrew the retaining nuts and remove the bracket from the top of the transmission **(see illustration)**.

25 On automatic transmission models, the mounting stud is a screw-fit into its mounting bracket and the bracket is secured to the

16.22a Unscrew the centre nut (1) and the mounting bolts (2) . . .

transmission by two bolts. If the mounting stud is tight, a universal stud extractor can be used to unscrew it.

26 Check carefully for signs of wear or damage on all components, and renew them where necessary.

27 On manual transmission models, refit the bracket to the transmission, tightening its mounting nuts to the specified torque. Reconnect the clutch cable as described in Chapter 6.

28 On automatic transmission models, ensure the transmission mounting bracket

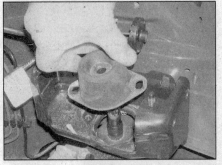

16.22b . . . then remove the left-hand mounting rubber

bolts and the stud are tightened to the specified torque. Slide the spacer onto the stud.

29 On all models, refit the mounting bracket to the vehicle body and tighten its bolts to the specified torque.

30 Fit the mounting rubber to the bracket and tighten its retaining bolts to the specified torque. Refit the mounting centre nut, and tighten it to the specified torque.

31 Remove the jack from underneath the transmission, then refit the battery as described in Chapter 5A.

2A

16.23 Unscrew the mounting bolts (locations arrowed) and remove the mounting bracket from the body

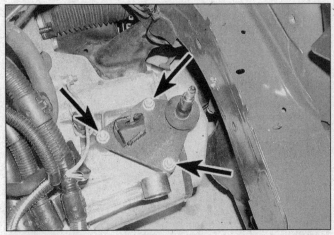

16.24 On manual transmission models disconnect the clutch cable then unscrew the nuts (arrowed) and remove the bracket from the transmission

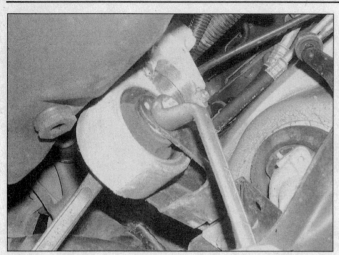

16.33 Slacken and remove the mounting nuts and bolts . . .

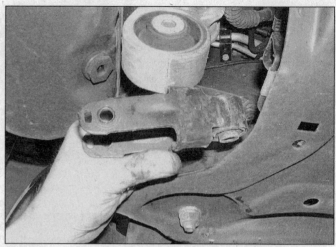

16.34 . . . then remove the rear mounting link from the vehicle

Rear mounting

32 If not already done, firmly apply the handbrake, then jack up the front of the vehicle and support it securely on axle stands (see *Jacking and vehicle support*).

33 Unscrew and remove the bolt securing the rear mounting link to the mounting on the rear of the cylinder block **(see illustration)**.

34 Remove the bolt securing the rear mounting link to the subframe and remove the mounting link **(see illustration)**.

35 To remove the mounting assembly it will first be necessary to remove the right-hand driveshaft as described in Chapter 8.

36 With the driveshaft removed, undo the retaining bolts and remove the mounting from the rear of the cylinder block.

37 Check carefully for signs of wear or damage on all components, and renew them where necessary.

38 On reassembly, fit the rear mounting assembly to the rear of the cylinder block, and tighten its retaining bolts to the specified torque. Refit the driveshaft as described in Chapter 8.

39 Refit the rear mounting link, and tighten both its bolts to their specified torque settings.

40 Lower the vehicle to the ground.

Chapter 2 Part B:
Diesel engine in-car repair procedures

Contents

Degrees of difficulty

Easy, suitable for novice with little experience	Fairly easy, suitable for beginner with some experience	Fairly difficult, suitable for competent DIY mechanic	Difficult, suitable for experienced DIY mechanic	Very difficult, suitable for expert DIY or professional 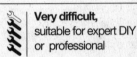

Specifications

General

Capacity:
  1.9 litre engine .... 1868 cc
  2.0 litre engine .... 1997 cc
Designation:
  1.9 litre engine DW8
  2.0 litre engine DW10
Engine codes*:
  1.9 litre engine:
    Engines with mechanical injection pump .... WJZ (DW8)
    Engines with electronically controlled injection pump .... WJY (DW8B)
  2.0 litre engine .... RHY (DW10TD)
Bore:
  1.9 litre engine .... 82.2 mm
  2.0 litre engine .... 85.0 mm
Stroke   88.00 mm
Direction of crankshaft rotation .... Clockwise (viewed from right-hand side of vehicle)
No 1 cylinder location .... At transmission end of block
Compression ratio (typical):
  1.9 litre engine .... 23 : 1
  2.0 litre engine .... 18 : 1

*The engine code is stamped on front of the cylinder block, just to the left of the oil filter/cooler.
The code given in brackets is the factory identification number.*

Compression pressures (engine hot, at cranking speed)

Normal .... 25 to 30 bars (363 to 435 psi)
Maximum difference between any two cylinders .... 5 bars (73 psi)

Camshaft

Drive .... Toothed belt
No of bearings:
  1.9 litre engine 3
  2.0 litre engine 5
Endfloat:
  1.9 litre engine .... 0.02 to 0.07 mm
  2.0 litre engine .... 0.07 to 0.38 mm

Valve clearances (engine cold)

1.9 litre engine:
Inlet .... 0.15 ± 0.07 mm
Exhaust .... 0.30 ± 0.07 mm
2.0 litre engine .... Automatically adjusted by hydraulic tappets

Lubrication system

Oil pump type .... Gear-type, chain-driven off the crankshaft right-hand end
Minimum oil pressure at 80°C:
1.9 litre engine .... 4.5 bar at 4000 rpm
2.0 litre engine .... 4 bar at 4000 rpm

Torque wrench settings

	Nm	lbf ft
Big-end bearing cap nuts:		
Stage 1	20	15
Stage 2	Tighten through a further 70°	
Camshaft:		
Bearing cap nuts – 1.9 litre engine	20	15
Bearing cap casting bolts – 2.0 litre engine	10	7
Camshaft sprocket		
Hub-to-camshaft bolt	43	32
Sprocket-to-hub bolts:		
1.9 litre engine	23	17
2.0 litre engine	20	15
Crankshaft right-hand (timing belt end) oil seal housing bolts	14	10
Crankshaft pulley bolt:		
1.9 litre engine	10	7
2.0 litre engine:		
Stage 1	40	30
Stage 2	Tighten through a further 50°	
Crankshaft sprocket bolt – 1.9 litre engine:		
Stage 1	40	30
Stage 2	Tighten through a further 55°	
Cylinder head bolts:		
1.9 litre engine:		
Stage 1	20	15
Stage 2	60	44
Stage 3	Tighten through a further 180°	
2.0 litre engine:		
Stage 1	20	15
Stage 2	60	44
Stage 3	Tighten through a further 220°	
Cylinder head cover bolts:		
1.9 litre engine:		
Upper cover bolts	10	7
Lower cover bolts	5	4
2.0 litre engines	10	7
Engine-to-transmission fixing bolts	55	41
Engine/transmission left-hand mounting:		
Mounting bracket-to-body bolts	19	14
Mounting stud to bracket	50	37
Mounting-to-bracket bolts	30	22
Mounting centre nut	65	48
Mounting bracket to transmission	60	44
Engine/transmission rear mounting:		
Mounting assembly-to-block bolts	45	33
Mounting link-to-mounting bolt	50	37
Mounting link-to-subframe bolt	35	26
Engine/transmission right-hand mounting:		
Vibration damper bracket-to-body bolts	22	16
Vibration damper	32	24
Mounting-to-engine bracket:		
Bracket-to-cylinder block bracket bolts	61	45
Bracket-to-mounting nut	45	33
Movement restrictors	20	15
Mounting to body	40	30

Torque wrench settings (continued)

	Nm	lbf ft
Engine/transmission right-hand mounting (continued):		
Cylinder block bracket bolts:		
M8 bolts	20	15
M10 bolts	45	33
Flywheel bolts	48	36
Fuel filter/thermostat housing bolts – 1.9 litre engine	15	11
Fuel filter plastic housing bolt – 1.9 litre engine	18	13
Injection pump sprocket:		
Sprocket-to-hub bolts – 1.9 litre engine	23	17
Sprocket nut – 2.0 litre engine	50	37
Main bearing cap bolts:		
1.9 litre engine	70	52
2.0 litre engine:		
Stage 1	25	18
Stage 2	Tighten through a further 60°	
Oil cooler centre bolt	50	37
Oil pump mounting bolts	16	12
Piston oil jet spray tube bolt	10	7
Roadwheel bolts	85	63
Sump bolts	16	12
Sump drain plug	34	25
Thermostat housing fixings – 2.0 litre engine:		
Housing studs	25	18
Retaining nuts and bolts	20	15
Timing belt cover bolts	8	6
Timing belt tensioner pulley bolt	23	17
Timing belt idler pulley bolt	43	32

1 General information

How to use this Chapter

1 This Part of Chapter 2 describes the repair procedures that can reasonably be carried out on the engine while it remains in the vehicle. If the engine has been removed from the vehicle and is being dismantled as described in Part C, any preliminary dismantling procedures can be ignored.

2 Note that, while it may be possible physically to overhaul items such as the piston/connecting rod assemblies while the engine is in the car, such tasks are not usually carried out as separate operations. Usually, several additional procedures are required (not to mention the cleaning of components and oilways); for this reason, all such tasks are classed as major overhaul procedures, and are described in Part C of this Chapter.

3 Part C describes the removal of the engine/transmission from the car, and the full overhaul procedures that can then be carried out.

Diesel engine description

4 The diesel engines are from the new DW series of diesel engines. The engines have been derived from the original XUD diesel engines which were well-proven units, having been fitted to many Peugeot and Citroën vehicles. The engine is of four-cylinder overhead camshaft design, mounted transversely, with the transmission mounted on the left-hand side. The 206 range was offered with a choice of 1.9 litre (1868 cc) normally-aspirated engine or the 2.0 litre (1997 cc) turbo engine.

5 The crankshaft runs in five main bearings of the usual shell type. Endfloat is controlled by thrustwashers either side of No 2 main bearing.

6 The connecting rods rotate on horizontally-split bearing shells at their big-ends. The pistons are attached to the connecting rods by gudgeon pins, which are secured in position with circlips. The aluminium-alloy pistons are fitted with three piston rings – two compression rings and an oil control ring.

7 The cylinder block is made from cast-iron, and the cylinder bores are an integral part of the cylinder block. On this type of engine, the cylinder bores are sometimes referred to as having dry liners.

8 The camshaft is driven by a toothed timing belt which also operates the coolant pump. On 1.9 litre engines, the camshaft operates the eight valves via bucket-type followers; valve clearances are adjusted by shims fitted between the valve stem and follower. On 2.0 litre engines, the camshaft operates the valves via followers and hydraulic tappets which automatically adjust the valve clearances. On all engines the camshaft runs in bearing caps which are bolted to the top of the cylinder head. The inlet and exhaust valves are each closed by coil springs, and operate in guides pressed into the cylinder head.

9 Lubrication is by means of an oil pump, which is driven (via a chain and sprocket) off the right-hand end of the crankshaft. It draws oil through a strainer located in the sump, and then forces it through an externally-mounted filter into galleries in the cylinder block/crankcase. From there, the oil is distributed to the crankshaft (main bearings) and camshaft. The big-end bearings are supplied with oil via internal drillings in the crankshaft, while the camshaft bearings also receive a pressurised supply. The camshaft lobes and valves are lubricated by splash, as are all other engine components. An oil cooler is mounted between the oil filter and cylinder block to keep the oil temperature stable under arduous operating temperatures.

Repair operations possible with the engine in the vehicle

10 The following work can be carried out with the engine in the car:

a) Compression and leakdown tests.
b) Cylinder head cover – removal and refitting.
c) Timing belt covers – removal and refitting.
d) Timing belt – removal, refitting and adjustment.
e) Timing belt sprockets and tensioner/idler pulleys – removal and refitting.
f) Camshaft oil seal – renewal.

2B

g) *Camshaft and followers – removal, inspection and refitting.*

h) *Cylinder head – removal and refitting.*

i) *Cylinder head and pistons – decarbonising.*

j) *Sump – removal and refitting.*

k) *Oil pump – removal, overhaul and refitting.*

l) *Crankshaft oil seals – renewal.*

m) *Engine/transmission mountings – inspection and renewal.*

n) *Flywheel – removal, inspection and refitting.*

2 Compression and leakdown tests – description and interpretation

Compression test

Note: *A compression tester specifically designed for diesel engines must be used for this test, because of the high pressures involved.*

1 When engine performance is down, or if misfiring occurs which cannot be attributed to the fuel system, a compression test can provide diagnostic clues as to the engine's condition. If the test is performed regularly, it can give warning of trouble before any other symptoms become apparent.

2 The tester is connected to an adapter which screws into the glow plug or injector hole. It is unlikely to be worthwhile buying such a tester for occasional use, but it may be possible to borrow or hire one – if not, have the test performed by a garage.

3 Unless specific instructions to the contrary are supplied with the tester, observe the following points:

a) *The battery must be in a good state of charge, the air filter must be clean, and the engine should be at normal operating temperature.*

b) *All the injectors or glow plugs should be removed before starting the test. If removing the injectors, also remove the flame shield washers, otherwise they may be blown out.*

c) *The injection pump (1.9 litre engine) or injectors (2.0 litre engine) must be disconnected, to prevent the engine from running or fuel from being discharged.*

4 Crank the engine on the starter motor; after one or two revolutions, the compression pressure should build up to a maximum figure, and then stabilise. Record the highest reading obtained.

5 Repeat the test on the remaining cylinders, recording the pressure in each.

6 All cylinders should produce very similar pressures; a difference of more than 5 bars between any two cylinders indicates a fault. Note that the compression should build up quickly in a healthy engine; low compression on the first stroke, followed by gradually-increasing pressure on successive strokes, indicates worn piston rings. A low

compression reading on the first stroke, which does not build up during successive strokes, indicates leaking valves or a blown head gasket (a cracked head could also be the cause). Deposits on the undersides of the valve heads can also cause low compression.

7 As a guide, any cylinder pressure of below 20 bars can be considered as less than healthy. Refer to a Peugeot dealer or other specialist if in doubt as to whether a particular pressure reading is acceptable.

8 The cause of poor compression is less easy to establish on a diesel engine than on a petrol one. The effect of introducing oil into the cylinders ('wet' testing) is not conclusive, because there is a risk that the oil will sit in the swirl chamber or in the recess on the piston crown instead of passing to the rings. A low reading from two adjacent cylinders is almost certainly due to the head gasket having blown between them; the presence of coolant in the engine oil will confirm this.

Leakdown test

9 A leakdown test measures the rate at which compressed air fed into the cylinder is lost. It is an alternative to a compression test, and in many ways it is better, since the escaping air provides easy identification of where pressure loss is occurring (piston rings, valves or head gasket).

10 The equipment needed for leakdown testing is unlikely to be available to the home mechanic. If poor compression is suspected, have the test performed by a suitably-equipped garage.

3 Engine assembly/ valve timing holes – general information and usage

Note: *Do not attempt to rotate the engine whilst the crankshaft/camshaft/injection pump (as applicable) are locked in position. If the engine is to be left in this state for a long*

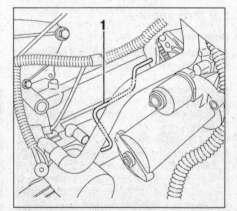

3.4 Insert the bolt/drill (Peugeot special tool shown – 1) in through the hole in the cylinder block flange (shown with the starter motor moved forwards for clarity) and locate it in the rear of the flywheel

period of time, it is a good idea to place suitable warning notices inside the vehicle, and in the engine compartment. This will reduce the possibility of the engine being accidentally cranked on the starter motor, which is likely to cause damage with the locking pins in place.

1.9 litre engine

1 Timing holes are drilled in the camshaft sprocket hub, injection pump sprocket hub and flywheel. The holes are used to align the crankshaft, camshaft and injection pump, and to prevent the possibility of the valves contacting the pistons when refitting the cylinder head, and to ensure the valve timing/injection pump timing is correct when refitting the timing belt. When the holes are aligned with their corresponding holes in the cylinder head and cylinder block (as appropriate), suitable diameter bolts/pins can be inserted to lock the camshaft, injection pump and crankshaft in position, preventing them from rotating unnecessarily. Proceed as follows.

2 Remove the injection pump sprocket and camshaft sprocket timing belt covers as described in Section 6 to gain access to the sprockets.

3 The crankshaft must now be rotated using a spanner on the crankshaft sprocket bolt. Note that the crankshaft must always be turned in a clockwise direction (viewed from the right-hand side of the vehicle). To improve access to the pulley, undo the screws securing the front section of the right-hand wheelarch liner to the base of the bumper. Remove the fasteners (pull out the centre pin then remove the complete fastener) securing the liner section to the body then manoeuvre the front section of the liner out from underneath the wing.

4 Rotate the crankshaft until the holes in the camshaft and injection pump sprocket hubs are aligned with the corresponding holes in the cylinder head/pump. With the camshaft sprocket hole correctly positioned, insert an 8 mm diameter bolt or drill through the hole in the front, left-hand flange of the cylinder block, located behind the starter motor, and locate it in the timing hole in the rear of the flywheel **(see illustration)**. Note that it may be necessary to rotate the crankshaft slightly, to get the holes to align.

5 With the flywheel correctly positioned, lock the camshaft sprocket in position by inserting an 8 mm diameter bolt or a drill through the timing hole in the sprocket hub, and locating it in the hole in the cylinder head **(see illustration)**.

6 Lock the injection pump sprocket in position by inserting a 6 mm diameter bolt or a drill through the timing hole in the sprocket hub and locating it in the hole in the pump.

7 The crankshaft, camshaft and injection pump are now locked in position, preventing unnecessary rotation.

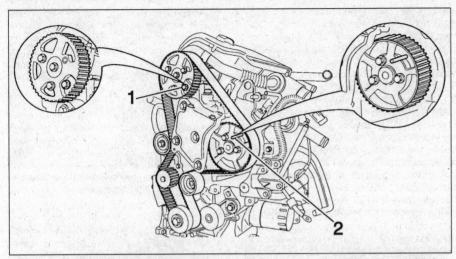

3.12 On 2.0 litre engines, peg the flywheel in position then insert a bolt/drill in through the hole in the camshaft sprocket hub and locate it in the cylinder head

3.5 On 1.9 litre engines, peg the camshaft and injection pump sprockets in position by inserting bolts/drills (1 and 2)

2.0 litre engine

8 Timing holes are drilled in the camshaft sprocket hub and flywheel. The holes are used to align the crankshaft and camshaft to prevent the possibility of the valves contacting the pistons when refitting the cylinder head, and to ensure the valve timing is correct when refitting the timing belt. When the holes are aligned with their corresponding holes in the cylinder head and cylinder block (as appropriate), suitable diameter bolts/pins can be inserted to lock both the camshaft and crankshaft in position, preventing them from rotating unnecessarily. Proceed as follows.

9 Remove the camshaft sprocket timing belt cover as described in Section 6 to gain access to the sprocket.

10 The crankshaft must now be rotated using a spanner on the crankshaft sprocket bolt. Note that the crankshaft must always be turned in a clockwise direction (viewed from the right-hand side of the vehicle). To improve access to the pulley, undo the bolts securing the right-hand inner cover to the wing valance and undercover and remove the cover from underneath the wing.

11 Rotate the crankshaft until the hole in the camshaft sprocket hub is aligned with the corresponding hole in the cylinder head. With

the camshaft sprocket hole correctly positioned, insert an 8 mm diameter bolt or drill through the hole in the front, left-hand flange of the cylinder block, located behind the starter motor, and locate it in the timing hole in the rear of the flywheel **(see illustration 3.4)**. Note that it may be necessary to rotate the crankshaft slightly, to get the holes to align.

12 With the flywheel correctly positioned, lock the camshaft sprocket in position by inserting a 6 mm diameter bolt or a drill through the timing hole in the sprocket hub, and locating it in the hole in the cylinder head **(see illustration)**.

13 The crankshaft and camshaft are now locked in position, preventing unnecessary rotation.

---

4   Cylinder head cover –
    removal and refitting

1.9 litre engine

Removal

1 Release the fasteners from the right-hand side and top of the engine cover then lift off

the cover, taking care not to lose its mounting rubbers **(see illustrations)**. Disconnect the battery negative lead.

2 Remove the upper section of the inlet manifold as described in Chapter 4B.

3 Unscrew the bolts securing the EGR pipe to the top of the exhaust manifold and the cylinder head cover. Free the pipe from the manifold and position it clear of the cylinder head cover. Recover the gasket and discard it; a new one should be used on refitting.

4 Slacken the retaining clips and disconnect the breather hoses from the upper section of the cylinder head cover.

5 Unscrew the eight retaining bolts then lift off the upper section of the cylinder head cover, complete with its rubber seal.

6 Unscrew the three retaining bolts and washers then remove the lower section of the cylinder head cover, complete with its rubber seal.

7 Inspect the cover seals for signs of damage or deterioration and, if necessary, renew.

Refitting

8 Carefully clean the cylinder head and cover mating surfaces, and remove all traces of oil.

9 Fit the rubber seals to both the cylinder head cover sections, ensuring they are correctly located along their entire length.

10 Fit the lower section of the cover the cylinder head. Ensure the rubber seal is still correctly located then refit the cover retaining bolts and washers, tightening them to the specified torque.

2B

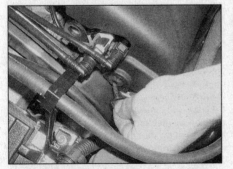

4.1a On 1.9 litre engines, remove the fasteners from the right-hand side . . .

4.1b . . . and top of the engine cover . . .

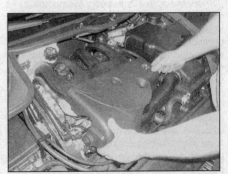

4.1c . . . then remove the cover from the engine

4.14a On 2.0 litre engines rotate each fastener 90° to release it . . .

4.14b . . . then lift off the engine cover

4.18 Removing the cylinder head cover – 2.0 litre engine

11 Refit the upper section of the cover to the lower section, ensuring its seal remains correctly seated, and tighten its retaining bolts to the specified torque.

12 Reconnect the breather hoses to the upper section of the cover.

13 Refit the EGR pipe and inlet manifold as described in Chapter 4B.

2.0 litre engine

Removal

14 Release the fasteners (rotate them 90° to release them) and remove the engine cover **(see illustrations)**.

15 Disconnect the battery negative lead then disconnect the wiring connector from the camshaft sensor.

16 Unscrew the bolts and free the engine cover right-hand mounting bracket from the cylinder head cover.

17 Release the retaining clips and disconnect the breather hoses from the cylinder head cover.

18 Working in a spiral pattern from the outside bolts inwards, slacken and remove the cylinder head cover retaining bolts and washers. Lift off the cylinder head cover, complete with its rubber seal **(see illustration)**. Inspect the cover seal for signs of damage or deterioration and, if necessary, renew.

Refitting

19 Carefully clean the cylinder head and cover mating surfaces, and remove all traces of oil.

20 Fit the rubber seal to the cylinder head cover, ensuring it is correctly located along its entire length **(see illustration)**.

21 Fit the cover the cylinder head, ensuring the rubber seal remains correctly located. Refit the cover retaining bolts and washers and tighten them to the specified torque, working in a spiral pattern from the centre bolts outwards.

22 Reconnect the breather hoses securely to the cover.

23 Reconnect the camshaft sensor wiring connector. It is recommended that the sensor air gap is checked (see Chapter 4B, Section 11).

24 Refit the engine cover mounting bracket, tightening its retaining bolts securely then refit the engine cover.

25 On completion reconnect the battery.

---

5 Crankshaft pulley – removal and refitting

1.9 litre engine

Removal

1 Remove the auxiliary drivebelt as described in Chapter 1B.

2 Undo the four crankshaft pulley retaining bolts and remove the pulley, noting which way round it is fitted.

Refitting

3 Fit the pulley to the end of the crankshaft, ensuring it is fitted the correct way round, and tighten its bolts to the specified torque.

4 Refit and tension the auxiliary drivebelt as described in Chapter 1B.

2.0 litre engine

Removal

5 Remove the auxiliary drivebelt as described in Chapter 1B.

6 Slacken the crankshaft pulley bolt. To prevent crankshaft rotation, select top gear, and have an assistant apply the brakes firmly. If the engine has been removed from the vehicle, it will be necessary to lock the flywheel (see Section 17).

Caution: Do not be tempted to use the flywheel locking pin to prevent the crankshaft from rotating; temporarily

5.7 On 2.0 litre engines, unscrew the bolt and washer and remove the crankshaft pulley

4.20 Ensure the rubber seal is correctly located in the cover groove

remove the locking pin (where fitted) prior to slackening the pulley bolt, then refit it once the bolt has been slackened.

7 Unscrew the retaining bolt and washer from the crankshaft and remove the pulley **(see illustration)**. If the pulley is a tight fit, it can be drawn off the crankshaft with a suitable puller.

8 If the Woodruff key is a loose fit in the crankshaft, remove it and store it with the pulley for safe-keeping. Examine the crankshaft oil seal for signs oil leakage and, if necessary, renew as described in Section 16.

Refitting

9 Where removed, locate the Woodruff key in the crankshaft end.

10 Align the crankshaft pulley slot with the Woodruff key, and slide it onto the end of the crankshaft.

11 Remove all traces of locking compound from the threads of the pulley bolt and crankshaft. Apply a drop of locking compound (Peugeot recommend the use of Loctite Frenetanch) to the threads of the bolt then refit the bolt and washer to the crankshaft.

12 Temporarily remove the locking pin (where fitted) from the rear of the flywheel, then tighten the bolt to the specified torque Stage 1 torque setting, whilst preventing crankshaft rotation using the method employed on removal.

13 Angle-tighten the pulley bolt through the specified Stage 2 angle, using a socket and extension bar. It is recommended that an angle-measuring gauge is used during this stage of the tightening, to ensure accuracy.

6.2 Unclip the fuel pipes from the top of the timing belt covers

Check the crankshaft pulley bolt is correctly tightened by applying a torque of 195 Nm (144 lbf ft) to it; the bolt should not move.
14 Refit the auxiliary drivebelt as described in Chapter 1B.

6 Timing belt covers – removal and refitting

Removal

Injection pump sprocket cover – 1.9 litre engine

1 Release the fasteners from the right-hand side and top of the engine cover then lift off the cover, taking care not to lose its mounting rubbers **(see illustrations 4.1a to 4.1c)**. Disconnect the battery negative lead.
2 Unclip the fuel pipes and position them clear of the timing belt covers **(see illustration)**.
3 Slacken and remove the cover upper and lower retaining bolts then manoeuvre the cover out of position.

Camshaft sprocket cover – 1.9 litre engine

Note: A small amount of coolant may weep from the coolant pump whilst the cover is removed. Do not worry about this, the leak will stop when the cover is refitted; ensure the coolant level is topped-up once the cover is refitted.

4 Remove the injection pump sprocket cover (see paragraphs 1 to 3).
5 Slacken and remove the two lower retaining bolts then manoeuvre the camshaft sprocket cover out of position.

Camshaft sprocket cover – 2.0 litre engine

Note: A small amount of coolant may weep from the coolant pump whilst the cover is removed. Do not worry about this, the leak will stop when the cover is refitted; ensure the coolant level is topped-up once the cover is refitted.

6 Release the fasteners (rotate the fasteners 90° to release them) and remove the engine cover **(see illustrations 4.14a and 4.14b)**. Disconnect the battery negative lead.

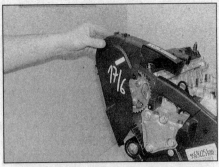

6.8 Removing the camshaft sprocket cover – 2.0 litre engine

7 Unclip the fuel pipes and position them clear of the timing belt covers
8 Unscrew the cover upper and lower retaining bolts (the cover lower bolt hole is slotted) then manoeuvre the cover out of position **(see illustration)**.

Injection pump sprocket cover – 2.0 litre engine

9 Remove the camshaft sprocket cover (see paragraphs 6 to 8).
10 Slacken and remove the two lower retaining bolts (the lower bolt hole is slotted) then manoeuvre the cover out of position **(see illustration)**.

Lower cover

11 Remove the crankshaft pulley as described in Section 5.
12 Remove the injection pump and camshaft sprocket covers as described earlier.
13 Unscrew the lower retaining bolts then manoeuvre the lower cover out of position **(see illustration)**.

Refitting

14 Refitting is the reverse of removal. Ensure that each cover section is correctly located, and that the cover retaining bolts are tightened to the specified torque.

7 Timing belt – general information, removal and refitting

Note: Peugeot specify the use of a special electronic tool (SEEM C.TRONIC type 105.5

6.13 Undo the retaining bolts (arrowed) and remove the timing belt lower cover – 2.0 litre engine

6.10 Removing the injection pump sprocket cover – 2.0 litre engine

belt tensioning measuring tool) to correctly set the timing belt tension. If access to this equipment cannot be obtained, an approximate setting can be achieved using the method described below. If this method is used, the tension must be checked using the special electronic tool at the earliest possible opportunity. Do not drive the vehicle over large distances, or use high engine speeds, until the belt tension is known to be correct. Refer to a Peugeot dealer for advice.

General information

1 The timing belt drives the camshaft, injection pump and coolant pump from a toothed sprocket on the front of the crankshaft. If the belt breaks or slips in service, the pistons are likely to hit the valve heads, resulting in extensive (and expensive) damage.
2 The timing belt should be renewed at the specified intervals (see Chapter 1B), or earlier if it is contaminated with oil or if it is at all noisy in operation (a 'scraping' noise due to uneven wear).
3 If the timing belt is being removed, it is a wise precaution to check the condition of the coolant pump at the same time (check for signs of coolant leakage). This may avoid the need to remove the timing belt again at a later stage, should the coolant pump fail.

Removal

4 Disconnect the battery negative terminal.
5 Remove the camshaft sprocket and injection pump sprocket timing belt covers as described in Section 6.
6 Align the engine assembly/valve timing holes as described in Section 3, and lock both the camshaft sprocket hub and the flywheel in position. On 1.9 litre engines also lock the injection pump sprocket hub.
Caution: Do not attempt to rotate the engine whilst the locking tools are in position.
7 Remove the crankshaft pulley as described in Section 5 then remove the timing belt lower cover (see Section 6).
8 Unscrew the mounting bolt and free the coolant expansion tank from its mounting on the bulkhead. Take care not to lose the mounting rubbers from the tank.

2B

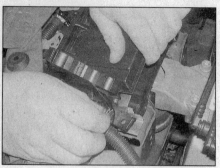

7.9 On 2.0 litre engines and later 1.9 litre (WJY) engines, unscrew the nut then remove the bracket and free the ECU mounting plate from the body

9 On 2.0 litre engines and later 1.9 litre (WJY) engines, unclip the wiring harness from the front of the injection system ECU. Slacken and remove the ECU mounting plate nut using a pair of grips (the plate is secured in position with an anti-tamper nut). Remove the cable/hose bracket then free the mounting plate from the body and position it clear of the engine **(see illustration)**.

10 Where necessary, remove the retaining bolts, screws and clips and remove the undercover (where fitted) from beneath the engine/transmission unit.

11 On all models, unscrew the nuts and bolts and remove the mounting link securing the rear engine/transmission mounting to the subframe.

12 Place a jack with a block of wood beneath the engine, to take the weight of the engine. Alternatively, attach a couple of lifting eyes to the engine, and fit a hoist or support bar to take the engine weight.

13 Unscrew the two bolts and remove the bracket from the right-hand engine/transmission mounting **(see illustration)**.

14 Unscrew the vibration damper (where fitted) from the mounting then unscrew the nut and bolts and lift off the right-hand mounting

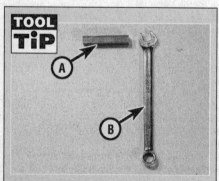

TOOL TIP

If you're having difficulty finding a square-section tool that will fit the tensioner pulley, obtain a length of standard 8 mm door handle rod from a DIY shop and cut it to length (A). Insert the rod into the pulley hub and rotate the pulley with an 8 mm spanner (B).

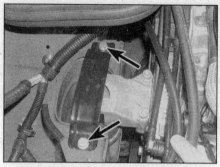

7.13 Undo the bolts and remove the bracket from the top of the right-hand engine/transmission mounting

bracket. Take care not to lose the bracket locating dowels.

15 Loosen the timing belt tensioner pulley retaining bolt. Pivot the pulley in a clockwise direction, using a square-section key fitted to the hole in the pulley hub, then retighten the retaining bolt **(see Tool Tip)**.

16 If the timing belt is to be re-used, use white paint or similar to mark the direction of rotation on the belt (if markings do not already exist). Slip the belt off the sprockets. If necessary, lower the engine slightly to enable the belt to be removed.

Caution: Take great care not to place any excess strain on the exhaust system or damage the radiator if the engine is moved. On models equipped with air conditioning, care must also be taken to ensure the auxiliary drivebelt pulleys do not damage the air conditioning pipes on the right-hand side of the engine compartment.

17 Check the timing belt carefully for any signs of uneven wear, splitting, or oil contamination. Pay particular attention to the roots of the teeth. Renew the belt if there is the slightest doubt about its condition. If the engine is undergoing an overhaul, and has covered more than 40 000 miles (60 000 km) on 1.9 litre engines or 48 000 miles (80 000 km) on 2.0 litre engines with the existing belt fitted, renew the belt as a matter of course, regardless of its apparent condition. The cost of a new belt is nothing when compared to the cost of repairs, should the belt break in service. If signs of oil contamination are found, trace the source of the oil leak, and rectify it. Wash down the engine timing belt area and all related components, to remove all traces of oil.

Refitting

1.9 litre engine

18 Prior to refitting, thoroughly clean the timing belt sprockets. Check that the tensioner and idler pulleys rotate freely, without any sign of roughness. If necessary, renew the pulleys as described in Section 8.

19 Ensure that the locking tools are still in place, as described in Section 3.

20 Slacken the bolts securing the camshaft and injection pump sprockets to their hubs.

Rotate both sprockets fully clockwise on their hubs then lightly tighten the sprocket bolts.

21 Manoeuvre the timing belt into position, ensuring that the arrows on the belt are pointing in the direction of rotation (clockwise, when viewed from the right-hand end of the engine).

22 Locate the belt on the crankshaft sprocket, taking care not to twist it sharply while refitting it, and route the belt round the idler pulley.

23 Ensure the 'front run' of the belt is taut then align the belt with the injection pump sprocket. Rotate the sprocket anti-clockwise on its hub until the belt and sprocket teeth are correctly aligned then engage the belt on the sprocket. **Note:** *Do not rotate the sprocket anti-clockwise any more than is necessary and never rotate it through more than one sprocket tooth of movement.*

24 Once the belt is correctly seated on the injection pump sprocket, ensure the belt 'front' and 'top' runs are taut then align the belt with the camshaft sprocket. Rotate the camshaft sprocket anti-clockwise on its hub until the belt and sprocket teeth are correctly aligned then engage the belt on the sprocket. **Note:** *Do not rotate the sprocket anti-clockwise any more than is necessary and never rotate it through more than one sprocket tooth of movement.*

25 Ensure that any slack is on the tensioner pulley side of the belt then locate the belt behind the tensioner pulley and over the coolant pump sprocket.

26 Ensure that the belt teeth are seated centrally in the sprockets then loosen the tensioner pulley retaining bolt. Pivot the pulley anti-clockwise to remove all freeplay from the timing belt, then retighten the bolt.

27 Remove one of the sprocket bolts from both the injection pump and camshaft sprockets and check that the sprockets are not at the end of their retaining bolt slots **(see illustration)**. If they are, the sprocket was rotated through more than one tooth of

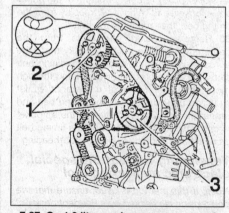

7.27 On 1.9 litre engines remove one of the bolts (1) from both the camshaft (2) and injection pump (3) sprockets and check that each sprocket is not at the end of its bolt slots (see inset)

movement whilst installing the belt; remove the timing belt and repeat the refitting procedure. If the sprockets are correctly positioned, tension the timing belt as described under the relevant sub-heading.

2.0 litre engine

28 Prior to refitting, thoroughly clean the timing belt sprockets. Check that the tensioner and idler pulleys rotate freely, without any sign of roughness. If necessary, renew the pulleys as described in Section 8.

29 Ensure that the locking tools are still in place, as described in Section 3.

30 Slacken the bolts securing the camshaft sprocket to its hub. Rotate the sprocket fully clockwise on its hub then lightly tighten the sprocket bolts **(see illustration)**.

31 Manoeuvre the timing belt into position, ensuring that the arrows on the belt are pointing in the direction of rotation (clockwise, when viewed from the right-hand end of the engine).

32 Locate the belt with the crankshaft sprocket, taking care not to twist the timing belt sharply while refitting it and route the belt round the idler pulley and engage it with the injection pump sprocket. **Note:** *It is not necessary to set the injection pump timing when refitting the belt due to the nature of the fuel system.*

33 Ensure the belt 'front' and 'top' runs are taut then align the belt with the camshaft sprocket. Rotate the sprocket anti-clockwise on its hub until the belt and sprocket teeth are correctly aligned then engage the belt on the sprocket. **Note:** *Do not rotate the sprocket anti-clockwise any more than is necessary and never rotate it through more than one sprocket tooth of movement.*

34 Ensure that any slack is on the tensioner pulley side of the belt then locate the belt behind the tensioner pulley and over the coolant pump sprocket.

35 Ensure that the belt teeth are seated centrally in the sprockets then loosen the tensioner pulley retaining bolt. Pivot the pulley anti-clockwise to remove all freeplay from the timing belt, then retighten the bolt.

36 Remove one of the bolts from the camshaft sprocket and check that the sprocket is not at the end of its retaining bolt slots. If it is, the sprocket was rotated through more than one tooth of movement whilst installing the belt; remove the timing belt and repeat the refitting procedure. If the sprocket is correctly positioned, tension the timing belt as described under the relevant sub-heading.

Tensioning without the special electronic measuring tool

Note: *If this method is used, ensure that the belt tension is checked by a Peugeot dealer at the earliest possible opportunity.*

37 Ensure the bolts securing the sprocket(s) to the hub(s) are loose, then slacken the tensioner pulley retaining bolt. Rotate the pulley anti-clockwise to adjust the timing belt

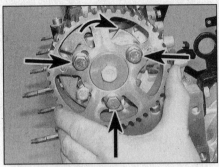

7.30 Slacken the bolts (arrowed) and rotate the camshaft sprocket fully clockwise on its hub

tension until it is just possible to twist the timing belt slightly, midway between the camshaft and injection pump sprockets. Hold the tensioner pulley stationary then securely tighten its retaining bolt.

38 Tighten all the sprocket bolts to the specified torque setting then remove the locking tools from the sprocket hub(s) and flywheel.

39 Using a suitable socket and extension bar on the crankshaft sprocket bolt, rotate the crankshaft through eight complete rotations in a clockwise direction (viewed from the right-hand end of the engine). Refit the flywheel locking tool and sprocket hub locking tool(s). **Caution: Do not at any time rotate the crankshaft anti-clockwise.**

40 Slacken the sprocket bolts and the tensioner pulley bolt. Re-tension the belt as described in paragraph 37, then tighten the tensioner pulley bolt to the specified torque.

41 Tighten the sprocket bolts to the specified torque then remove the locking tools again.

42 Rotate the crankshaft through a further two turns clockwise. Recheck the timing belt tension and ensure that the flywheel timing hole and the sprocket hub hole(s) are still correctly aligned.

43 If all is well, ensure the locating dowels (where fitted) are in position then refit the right-hand mounting bracket, tightening its nut and bolts to the specified torque. Tighten the vibration damper to the specified torque then refit the bracket to the body, tightening its bolts to the specified torque.

44 Refit the mounting link to the rear

7.49 The timing belt measuring tool should be fitted to the centre of the belt upper run

mounting, tightening its bolts to the specified torque. Where necessary, refit the undercover.

45 Seat the expansion tank back in position on the bulkhead, ensuring its mounting rubbers are in position, and securely tighten its retaining bolt.

46 Refit the timing belt covers and crankshaft pulley as described in Sections 6 and 5.

47 On 2.0 litre engines and later 1.9 litre (WJY) engines, locate the injection system ECU bracket assembly on its mounting and refit the hose/cable bracket. Secure the bracket/plate in position with a new anti-tamper nut or standard nut then clip the wiring harness back into position.

48 On all models, reconnect the battery negative terminal.

Tensioning using the special electronic measuring tool

49 Fit the special belt tensioning measuring equipment to the 'top run' of the timing belt, approximately midway between the camshaft and injection pump sprockets **(see illustration)**.

50 Ensure the bolts securing the sprocket(s) to the hub(s) are loose. Position the tensioner pulley so that the belt is tensioned to a setting of 106 SEEM units, then tighten the pulley retaining bolt to the specified torque.

51 Tighten all the sprocket bolts to the specified torque setting then remove the locking tools from the sprocket hub(s) and flywheel.

52 Remove the measuring tool from the belt then, using a suitable socket and extension bar on the crankshaft sprocket bolt, rotate the crankshaft through eight complete rotations in a clockwise direction (viewed from the right-hand end of the engine). Refit the flywheel locking tool and sprocket hub locking tool(s). **Caution: Do not at any time rotate the crankshaft anti-clockwise.**

53 Slacken the sprocket bolts and refit the tensioning measuring equipment to the top run of the belt.

54 Slacken the tensioner pulley retaining bolt whilst holding the pulley stationary. Gradually release the tensioner pulley until a tension setting of 41 ± 2 SEEM units is indicated on 1.9 litre engines, and a setting of 54 ± 2 SEEM units is indicated on 2.0 litre engines. With the belt correctly tensioned, hold the pulley stationary and tighten its retaining bolt to the specified torque.

55 Tighten all the sprocket bolts to the specified torque

56 Release the measuring equipment then refit it again to check the belt tension. The belt tension should be between 38 and 42 SEEM units on 1.9 litre engines and between 51 and 57 SEEM units on 2.0 litre engines. If the tension is incorrect, repeat the tensioning procedure described in paragraphs 49 to 55.

57 Once the belt is correctly tensioned, remove the measuring tool and the locking tools.

2B

8.7 Unscrew the bolt and remove the sprocket hub from the camshaft

58 Rotate the crankshaft through another two complete rotations in a clockwise direction. Refit the flywheel locking tool and check that the sprocket hub timing hole(s) are still correctly aligned.
59 If all is well, refit all disturbed components as described in paragraphs 43 to 48.

8 Timing belt sprockets and idler/tensioner pulleys – removal, inspection and refitting

Removal

1 Disconnect the battery negative terminal.
2 Position the engine assembly/valve timing holes as described in Section 3, and lock the sprocket hub(s) and flywheel in position.
Caution: Do not attempt to rotate the engine whilst the pins are in position.
3 Remove the timing belt as described in Section 7 then proceed under the relevant sub-heading. **Note:** *If the timing belt is not going to be renewed, there is no need to disturb the engine mounting.*

Camshaft sprocket

4 As a precaution, remove the flywheel locking pin then rotate the crankshaft **backwards** (anti-clockwise) through 90°; this will position the pistons mid-way up the bores and remove the risk of the valves contacting the pistons during the following operation.
5 If the sprocket hub is being removed, slacken the hub bolt. To prevent the camshaft

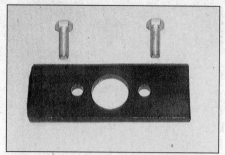

8.10 Home-made puller arrangement for removing the injection pump sprocket – 2.0 litre engine

rotating as the bolt is slackened, a sprocket-holding tool will be required. In the absence of the special Peugeot tool, an acceptable substitute can be fabricated as follows. Use two lengths of steel strip (one long, the other short); attach the short strip to the longer one with a nut a bolt to form a forked tool. Either fit a nut and bolt to the each of each of the strips to engage with the sprocket spokes or bend the ends of the strips at right-angles to engage with the sprocket spokes as shown in illustration 8.28.
6 Unscrew the three retaining bolts and remove the sprocket from its hub.
7 Unscrew the hub bolt and slide the hub off the end of the camshaft **(see illustration)**. If the Woodruff key is a loose fit, remove it for safe-keeping. Examine the camshaft oil seal for signs of oil leakage and, if necessary, renew it as described in Section 9.

Injection pump sprocket – 1.9 litre engine

8 Unscrew the three retaining bolts and remove the sprocket from its hub; The hub is an integral part of the injection pump.

Injection pump sprocket – 2.0 litre engine

9 Slacken the sprocket retaining nut whilst prevent rotation by retaining the sprocket with a holding tool (see paragraph 5).
10 The sprocket must then be freed from the injection pump shaft using a puller. In the absence of correct puller (Peugeot puller assembly 0188-R or a pattern substitute), a suitable alternative can be made out of a short

length of steel bar. Drill two holes in the bar to align with the threaded holes in the pump sprocket and larger hole in the centre of the bar which pass over the hexagonal section of the sprocket nut but not the nut flange **(see illustration)**.
11 Loosen the sprocket nut then bolt the steel bar to the sprocket by screwing two M7 bolts in the threaded holes provided. Evenly tighten the bolts, so the bar is forced into contact with nut, then unscrew the sprocket nut to draw the sprocket off the pump shaft. Once the sprocket has been released, unscrew the bolts and remove the bar then unscrew the nut and remove the sprocket **(see illustrations)**.

Crankshaft sprocket – 1.9 litre engine

12 As a precaution, remove the flywheel locking pin then rotate the crankshaft **backwards** (anti-clockwise) through 90°; this will position the pistons mid-way up the bores and remove the risk of the valves contacting the pistons during the following operation.
13 Slacken the crankshaft sprocket bolt. To prevent crankshaft rotation, select top gear, and have an assistant apply the brakes firmly. If the engine has been removed from the vehicle, it will be necessary to lock the flywheel (see Section 17).
14 Unscrew the retaining bolt and washer, then slide the sprocket off the end of the crankshaft. If the Woodruff key is a loose fit in the crankshaft, remove it and store it with the sprocket for safe-keeping. Examine the crankshaft oil seal for signs oil leakage and, if necessary, renew as described in Section 16.

Crankshaft sprocket – 2.0 litre engine

15 Slide the sprocket and off the end of the crankshaft. If the Woodruff key is a loose fit in the crankshaft, remove it and store it with the sprocket for safe-keeping **(see illustrations)**. Examine the crankshaft oil seal for signs oil leakage and, if necessary, renew as described in Section 16.

Tensioner pulley

16 Unscrew the bolt and remove the pulley from its mounting pin. Examine the mounting stud for signs of damage and, if necessary, renew it.

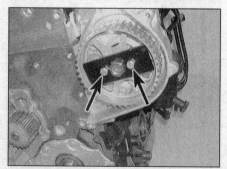

8.11a Fit the bar over the sprocket nut and screw in the two bolts (arrowed)

8.11b With the puller in position, retain the sprocket then unscrew the sprocket nut to release the sprocket from the pump shaft

8.11c Once the sprocket is free, remove the puller then unscrew the nut and lift off the sprocket

8.15a On 2.0 litre engines, slide the sprocket off the crankshaft . . .

8.15b . . . then remove the Woodruff key

8.17 Unscrew the mounting bolt and remove the idler pulley from the block

Idler pulley

17 Unscrew the mounting bolt and remove the idler pulley from the cylinder block **(see illustration)**.

Inspection

18 Clean the sprockets thoroughly, and renew any that show signs of wear, damage or cracks.
19 Clean the tensioner and idler pulleys, but do not use any strong solvent which may enter the pulley bearing. Check that each pulley rotates freely about its hub, with no sign of stiffness or of free play. Renew the pulley if there is any doubt about its condition, or if there are any obvious signs of wear or damage.
20 Inspect the timing belt (see Section 7). Renew the belt is there is any doubt about its condition.

Refitting

Camshaft sprocket

21 Where necessary, refit the Woodruff key to the camshaft then refit the sprocket hub, aligning its slot with the key.
22 Seat the camshaft sprocket on the hub and lightly tighten its bolts.
23 Refit the hub bolt and tighten it to the specified torque, using the holding tool to prevent rotation **(see illustration 8.28)**.
24 Align the hub timing hole with the cylinder head and insert the locking tool. Rotate the crankshaft 90° clockwise and lock the flywheel in position with the locking tool.
25 Refit the timing belt (see Section 7).

Injection pump sprocket – 1.9 litre engine

26 Seat the sprocket on the hub and lightly tighten its bolts.
27 Refit the timing belt (see Section 7).

Injection pump sprocket – 2.0 litre engine

28 Ensure the pump shaft and sprocket taper surfaces are clean and dry then fit the sprocket to the pump. Refit the sprocket nut and tighten it to the specified torque, using the holding tool to prevent rotation **(see illustration)**.
29 Refit the timing belt (see Section 7).

Crankshaft sprocket – 1.9 litre engine

30 Where removed, locate the Woodruff key in the crankshaft end.

31 Align the crankshaft pulley slot with the Woodruff key, and slide it onto the end of the crankshaft.
32 Remove all traces of locking compound from the threads of the pulley bolt and crankshaft. Apply a drop of locking compound (Peugeot recommend the use of Loctite Frenetanch) to the threads of the bolt then refit the bolt and washer to the crankshaft
33 Tighten the bolt to the specified torque Stage 1 torque setting, whilst preventing crankshaft rotation using the method employed on removal.
34 Angle-tighten the pulley bolt through the specified Stage 2 angle, using a socket and extension bar. It is recommended that an angle-measuring gauge is used during this stage of the tightening, to ensure accuracy.
35 Rotate the crankshaft 90° clockwise and lock the flywheel in position with the locking tool.
36 Refit the timing belt (see Section 7).

Crankshaft sprocket – 2.0 litre engine

37 Where removed, locate the Woodruff key in the crankshaft end.
38 Align the crankshaft pulley slot with the Woodruff key, and slide it onto the end of the crankshaft.
39 Refit the timing belt (see Section 7).

Tensioner pulley

40 Refit the tensioner pulley to its mounting pin, and fit the retaining bolt.
41 Refit the timing belt (see Section 7).

Idler pulley

42 Refit the idler pulley to the cylinder block and tighten its retaining bolt to the specified torque.
43 Refit the timing belt (see Section 7).

8.28 Retain the sprocket and tighten its retaining nut to the specified torque

sprockets and surrounding area before the new belt is fitted.
1 Remove the camshaft sprocket and hub as described in Section 8.
2 Punch or drill two small holes opposite each other in the oil seal. Screw a self-tapping screw into each, and pull on the screws with pliers to extract the seal.
3 Clean the seal housing, and polish off any burrs or raised edges, which may have caused the seal to fail in the first place.
4 Lubricate the lips of the new seal with clean engine oil, and drive/press it into position until it seats on its locating shoulder. Use a suitable tubular drift, such as a socket, which bears only on the hard outer edge of the seal **(see illustration)**. Take care not to damage the seal lips during fitting. Note that the seal lips should face inwards.
5 Refit the camshaft sprocket and hub as described in Section 8.

9 Camshaft oil seal – renewal

Note: *If the camshaft oil seal has been leaking, check the timing belt for signs of oil contamination; the belt must be renewed if signs of oil contamination are found. Ensure that all traces of oil are removed from the*

9.4 Using a socket, a length of stud and a nut to press the camshaft oil seal into position

2B

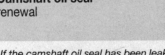

10.4 On 1.9 litre engines the camshaft bearing caps should be numbered (arrowed) for identification

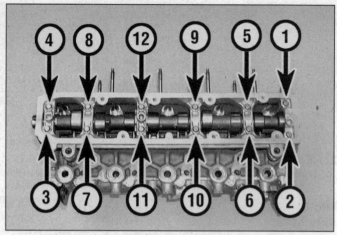

10.9 Camshaft bearing cap casting bolt slackening sequence – 2.0 litre engine

10 Camshaft and followers – removal, inspection and refitting

Note: *On 1.9 litre engines, valve clearance adjustment requires the removal of the camshaft. If the original camshaft is being refitted, it is worthwhile recording the valve clearances before it is removed, so any adjustments can be made before refitting it (see Section 11).*

Removal

1 Remove the cylinder head cover as described in Section 4.
2 Remove the braking system vacuum pump as described in Chapter 9.
3 Remove the camshaft sprocket and hub as described in Section 8. Proceed as described under the relevant sub-heading.

1.9 litre engine

4 The camshaft bearing caps should be numbered 1 to 3, number 1 being at the transmission end of the engine **(see illustration)**. If not, make identification marks on the caps, using white paint or a suitable marker pen. Also mark each cap in some way to indicate its correct fitted orientation. This will avoid the possibility of installing the caps the wrong way around on refitting.

5 Evenly and progressively slacken the camshaft bearing cap retaining nuts by one turn at a time. This will relieve the valve spring pressure on the bearing caps gradually and evenly. Once the pressure has been relieved, the nuts can be fully unscrewed and removed. **Caution: If the bearing cap nuts are carelessly slackened, the bearing caps may break. If any bearing cap breaks then the complete cylinder head assembly must be renewed; the bearing caps are matched to the head and are not available separately.**
6 Note the correct fitted orientation of the bearing caps, then remove them from the cylinder head.
7 Lift the camshaft away from the cylinder head, and slide the oil seal off the camshaft end.
8 Obtain eight small, clean plastic containers, and number them 1 to 8; alternatively, divide a larger container into eight compartments. Using a rubber sucker, withdraw each follower in turn, and place it in its respective container. Do not interchange the cam followers, or the rate of wear will be much-increased. If necessary, also remove the shim from the top of the valve stem, and store it with its respective follower. **Note:** *The shim may stick to the inside of the follower as it is withdrawn. If this happens, take care not to allow it to drop out as the follower is removed.*

2.0 litre engine

9 Working in the sequence shown, evenly and progressively slacken the camshaft bearing cap casting retaining bolts by one turn at a time **(see illustration)**. This will relieve the valve spring pressure on the bearing caps gradually and evenly. Once the pressure has been relieved, the bolts can be fully unscrewed and removed.
Caution: If the bearing cap casting bolt are carelessly slackened, the casting may break. If the casting breaks then the complete cylinder head assembly must be renewed; the casting is matched to the head and is not available separately.
10 Remove the camshaft bearing cap casting from the cylinder head **(see illustration)**. If the casting locating dowels are a loose fit in the head, remove them and store them with the casting for safe-keeping.
11 Lift the camshaft away from the cylinder head, and slide the oil seal off the camshaft end **(see illustration)**.
12 Obtain eight small, clean plastic containers, and number them 1 to 8; alternatively, divide a larger container into eight compartments. Lift each follower and hydraulic tappet out of position and place it in its respective container **(see illustrations)**. Do not interchange the cam followers or tappets, or the rate of wear will be much-increased.

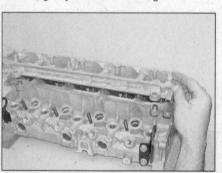

10.10 Remove the bearing cap casting . . .

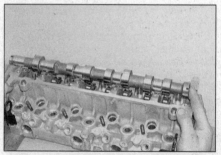

10.11 . . . then lift the camshaft out of position (shown with cylinder head removed)

10.12a Lift the camshaft followers . . .

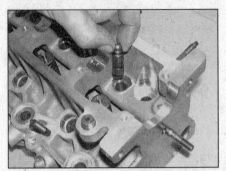

10.12b . . . and hydraulic tappets out from the cylinder head

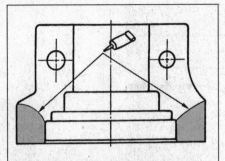

10.22 On 1.9 litre engines apply sealant to the areas shown on the camshaft end bearing caps

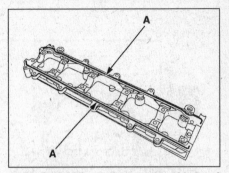

10.31 On 2.0 litre engines apply a thin bead of sealant (A) to the mating surface of the camshaft bearing cap casting as shown

Inspection

13 Examine the camshaft bearing surfaces and cam lobes for signs of wear ridges and scoring. Renew the camshaft if any of these conditions are apparent. Examine the condition of the bearing surfaces, both on the camshaft journals and in the cylinder head/bearing caps. If the head bearing surfaces are worn excessively, the cylinder head will need to be renewed.

14 Examine the cam follower bearing surfaces which contact the camshaft lobes for wear ridges and scoring. Renew any follower on which these conditions are apparent. If a follower bearing surface is badly scored, also examine the corresponding lobe on the camshaft for wear, as it is likely that both will be worn. Renew worn components as necessary.

15 On 2.0 litre engines, if the hydraulic tappets are thought to be faulty they should be renewed.

Refitting

1.9 litre engine

16 If the original camshaft is being refitted, and it is known that the valve clearances are correct, proceed to the next paragraph, otherwise, adjust the valves as described in Section 11 using the clearances noted before camshaft removal. If a new camshaft is used, fit it as described in paragraphs 17 to 23, and the adjust the valve clearances (Section 11).

Caution: Ensure the crankshaft is correctly positioned with the pistons mid-way up the bores before rotating the camshaft.

17 Fit each shim to the top of its valve stem.

Caution: Do not interchange the shims, as this will upset the valve clearances (see Section 11).

18 Liberally oil the cylinder head cam follower bores and the followers. Carefully refit the followers to the cylinder head, ensuring that each follower is refitted to its original bore. Some care will be required to enter the followers squarely into their bores.

19 Lubricate the cam lobes and bearing journals with clean engine oil of the specified grade. Then refit the camshaft back into position on the cylinder head.

20 Temporarily refit the sprocket hub to the end of the camshaft and position it so that the hub timing hole is aligned with the corresponding cut-out in the cylinder head. Ensure the crankshaft is still positioned 90° BTDC so the pistons are mid-way up the bores.

21 Fit the centre bearing cap the correct way round as previously noted, then screw on the nuts and tighten them two or three turns.

22 Apply sealing compound to the end bearing caps on the areas shown **(see illustration)**. Fit them in the correct positions, and tighten the nuts two or three turns.

23 Tighten all the nuts evenly and progressively to the specified torque, making sure that the camshaft remains correctly positioned.

Caution: If the bearing cap nuts are carelessly tightened, the bearing caps may break. If any bearing cap breaks then the complete cylinder head assembly must be renewed; the bearing caps are matched to the head and are not available separately.

24 Smear the lips of the new oil seal with clean engine oil and fit it onto the camshaft end, making sure its sealing lip is facing inwards. Press the oil seal in until it is flush with the end face of the camshaft bearing cap.

25 Refit the camshaft sprocket and hub as described in Section 8.

26 Refit the braking system vacuum pump as described in Chapter 9.

27 Refit the cylinder head cover as described in Section 4.

2.0 litre engine

28 Liberally oil the cylinder head tappet bores and the followers. Ensure the followers and hydraulic tappets are correctly clipped together then carefully refit them to the cylinder head, ensuring that each assembly is refitted in its original location.

29 Lubricate the cam bearing journals and followers with clean engine oil of the specified grade.

30 Ensure the crankshaft is still positioned 90° BTDC so the pistons are mid-way up the bores.

31 Ensure the mating surfaces of the camshaft bearing cap casting and cylinder head are clean and dry. Apply a thin bead of

sealant (Peugeot recommend the use of Autojoint OR) to the mating surface of the casting as shown **(see illustration)**.

32 Locate the camshaft correctly in the bearing cap casting then, ensuring the locating dowels are in position, refit the camshaft and bearing cap casting assembly to the head.

33 Install the bearing cap casting bolts, tightening all bolts by hand. Working in the sequence shown, evenly and progressively tighten the bolts to draw the casting squarely down onto the cylinder head **(see illustration)**. Once the casting is in contact with the head, go around in the specified sequence and tighten the bolts to the specified torque.

Caution: If the bearing cap casting bolt are carelessly tightened, the casting may break. If the casting breaks then the complete cylinder head assembly must be renewed; the casting is matched to the head and is not available separately.

34 Smear the lips of the new oil seal with clean engine oil and fit it onto the camshaft end, making sure its sealing lip is facing inwards. Press the oil seal in until it is flush with the end face of the camshaft bearing cap.

35 Refit the camshaft sprocket and hub as described in Section 8.

36 Refit the braking system vacuum pump as described in Chapter 9.

37 Refit the cylinder head cover as described in Section 4.

2B

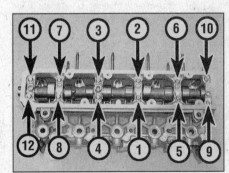

10.33 Camshaft bearing cap bolt tightening sequence – 2.0 litre engine

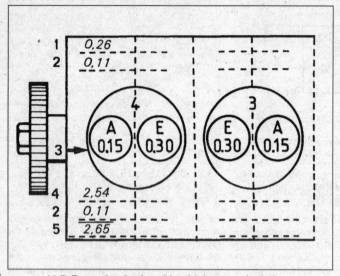

11.5 Example of valve shim thickness calculation – 1.9 litre engine

A Inlet valve
B Exhaust valve
1 Measured clearance
2 Difference from specified clearance (3)

3 Specified clearance
4 Thickness of shim fitted
5 Correct thickness of shim required

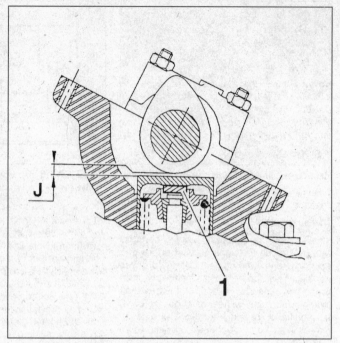

11.7 Valve clearance measurement (J). Clearance is altered by changing the shim (1)

11 Valve clearances – checking and adjustment

1.9 litre engine

Checking

1 The importance of having the valve clearances correctly adjusted cannot be overstressed, as they vitally affect the performance of the engine. Checking should not be regarded as a routine operation, however. It should only be necessary when the valve gear has become noisy, after engine overhaul, or when trying to trace the cause of power loss. The clearances are checked as follows. The engine must be cold for the check to be accurate.

2 To improve access to the crankshaft pulley, undo the screws securing the front section of the right-hand wheelarch liner to the base of the bumper. Remove the fasteners (pull out the centre pin then remove the complete fastener) securing the liner section to the body then manoeuvre the front section of the liner out from underneath the wing.

3 The engine can now be turned over using a suitable socket and extension bar fitted to the crankshaft pulley bolt. Note that the crankshaft must always be turned in a clockwise direction (viewed from the right-hand side of the vehicle).

4 Remove the cylinder head cover as described in Section 4.

5 On a piece of paper, draw the outline of the engine with the cylinders numbered from the flywheel end. Show the position of each valve, together with the specified valve clearance. Above each valve, draw lines for noting (1) the actual clearance and (2) the amount of adjustment required **(see illustration)**.

6 Turn the crankshaft until the inlet valve of No 1 cylinder (nearest the transmission) is fully closed, with the tip of the cam facing directly away from the bucket tappet.

7 Using feeler blades, measure the clearance between the base of the cam and the bucket tappet. Record the clearance on line (1) **(see illustration)**.

8 Repeat the measurement for the other seven valves, turning the crankshaft as necessary so that the cam lobe in question is always facing directly away from the relevant tappet.

9 Calculate the difference between each measured clearance and the desired value, and record it on line (2). Since the clearance is different for inlet and exhaust valves – make sure that you are aware which valve you are dealing with. The valve sequence from either end of the engine is:

In – Ex – Ex – In – In – Ex – Ex – In

10 If all the clearances are within tolerance, refit the cylinder head cover with reference to Section 4, and where applicable, lower the vehicle to the ground. If any clearance measured is outside the specified tolerance, adjustment must be carried out as described in the following paragraphs.

Adjustment

11 Remove the camshaft as described in Section 10.

12 Withdraw the first follower and its shim. Be careful that the shim does not fall out of the tappet. Clean the shim, and measure its thickness with a micrometer. The shims carry thickness markings, but wear may have reduced the original thickness, so be sure to check.

13 Refer to the clearance recorded for the valve concerned. If the clearance was more than that specified, the shim thickness must be increased by the difference recorded (2). If the clearance was less than that specified, the thickness of the shim must be decreased by the difference recorded (2).

14 Draw three more lines beneath each valve on the calculation paper as shown in illustration 11.5. On line (4) note the measured thickness of the shim, then add or deduct the difference from line (2) to give the final shim thickness required on line (5).

15 Repeat the procedure given in paragraphs 13 to 15 on the remaining valves, keeping each tappet identified for position.

16 When reassembling, oil the shim and fit it into the valve retainer, with the size marking face downwards. Oil the follower, and lower it onto the shim. Do not raise the follower after fitting, as the shim may become dislodged.

17 When all the followers are in position, complete with their shims, refit the camshaft as described in Section 10. Recheck the valve clearances before refitting the cylinder head cover, to make sure they are correct.

2.0 litre engine

18 The 2.0 litre engine is equipped with hydraulic tappets which automatically adjust the valve clearances. Therefore there is no need to check or adjust the valve clearances at any time.

12 Cylinder head –
removal and refitting

Note: *Ensure the engine is cold before removing the cylinder head.*
Caution: Be careful not to allow dirt into the fuel injection pump or injector pipes during this procedure.

1.9 litre engine

Removal

1 Remove the battery and battery tray as described in Chapter 5A.

2 Drain the cooling system as described in Chapter 1B.

3 Remove the braking system vacuum pump as described in Chapter 9.

4 Remove the timing belt as described in Section 7.

5 Once the timing belt has been removed, unscrew the single bolt securing the right-hand engine/transmission mounting bracket to the cylinder head. Leave all the bolts securing the bracket to the cylinder block then refit the upper bracket, securing the engine bracket to the mounting, and securely tighten its nuts and bolts. This will ensure the engine/transmission unit is securely supported through out the following procedure.

6 If the cylinder head is to be overhauled, remove the camshaft sprocket and camshaft (see Sections 8 and 10).

7 Referring to Chapter 4B, carry out the following operations.

  a) *Remove the air cleaner housing.*
  b) *Remove the inlet and exhaust manifolds.*
  c) *Disconnect and remove the fuel return hose from the end injector.*
  d) *Unscrew the union nuts and disconnect the fuel pipes from the fuel injectors and the fuel injection pump. Remove the pipes.*
  e) *If the cylinder head is being overhauled, remove the injectors.*

8 Remove the cylinder head cover as described in Section 4.

9 Remove the fuel filter as described in Chapter 1B.

10 Unscrew the retaining bolt and remove the filter plastic housing, complete with its sealing ring **(see illustration)**. Discard the sealing ring; a new one must be used on refitting.

11 Slacken and remove the three bolts, noting the correct fitted location of the sealing washer, securing the fuel filter/thermostat housing to the front of the cylinder head. Disconnect the coolant hose connecting the housing to the coolant pipe then free the housing from the cylinder head. Recover the housing gasket and discard it; a new one must be used on refitting.

12 Unscrew the securing nut and disconnect the feed wire from the relevant glow plug. Recover the washers.

13 Unscrew the bolt securing the coolant pipe to the left-hand end of the cylinder head.

14 Check that the wiring and hoses is released from all the relevant clips or guides on the cylinder head and positioned clear.

15 Working in the *reverse* of the sequence shown in illustration 12.33, progressively slacken the ten cylinder head bolts by half a turn at a time, until all bolts can be unscrewed by hand.

16 With all the cylinder head bolts removed, release the cylinder head from the cylinder block and locating dowel by rocking it. The Peugeot tool for doing this consists simply of two metal rods with 90-degree angled ends. Do not prise between the mating faces of the cylinder head and block, as this may damage the gasket faces. Lift the cylinder head away; seek assistance if possible.

17 Remove the gasket from the top of the block, noting the locating dowel. If the locating dowel is a loose fit, remove it and store it with the head for safe-keeping. Do not discard the gasket – it will be needed for identification purposes (see paragraphs 22 to 25).

18 If the cylinder head is to be dismantled for overhaul, remove the camshaft and followers as described in Section 10, then refer to Part C of this Chapter.

Preparation for refitting

19 The mating faces of the cylinder head and cylinder block must be perfectly clean before refitting the head. Use a hard plastic or wood scraper to remove all traces of gasket and carbon; also clean the piston crowns. Take particular care during the cleaning operations, as aluminium alloy is easily damaged. Also, make sure that the carbon is not allowed to enter the oil and water passages – this is particularly important for the lubrication system, as carbon could block the oil supply to the engine's components. Using adhesive tape and paper, seal the water, oil and bolt holes in the cylinder block/crankcase. To prevent carbon entering the gap between the pistons and bores, smear a little grease in the gap. After cleaning each piston, use a small brush to remove all traces of grease and carbon from the gap, then wipe away the remainder with a clean rag. Clean all the pistons in the same way.

20 Check the mating surfaces of the cylinder block and the cylinder head for nicks, deep scratches and other damage. If slight, they may be removed carefully with a file, but if excessive, machining may be the only alternative to renewal.

21 If warpage of the cylinder head gasket surface is suspected, use a straight-edge to check it for distortion. Refer to Part C of this Chapter if necessary.

22 When purchasing a new cylinder head gasket, it is essential that a gasket of the correct thickness is obtained. There are six different thicknesses of gasket available to enable the cylinder head-to-piston clearance to be accurately set. The gasket thickness can

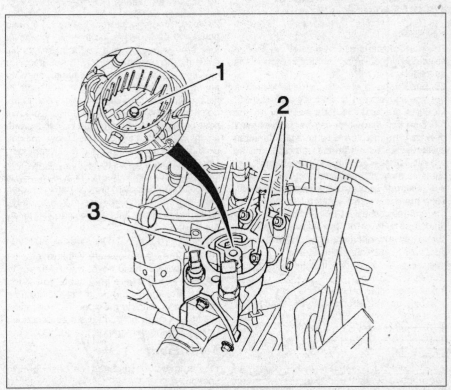

12.10 On 1.9 litre engines, unscrew the bolt (1) and remove fuel filter housing then undo the three bolts (2) and free the filter/thermostat housing (3) from the cylinder head

2B

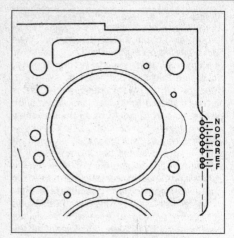

12.22 Cylinder head gasket thickness identification holes – 1.9 litre engine

12.23 Measuring piston protrusion

be determined by looking at the tab situated in front of No 1 cylinder (see illustration). There will be between 3 and 7 holes in the tab; the first two holes (in locations E and F) identify the engine type (D8W), these are present on all gaskets and are of no real significance. It is the last group of between 1 and 5 holes (in locations N to R) which identify the gasket thickness as follows.

Number of holes (hole locations)	Gasket thickness (when compressed)
1 (N)	1.26 mm
2 (N and O)	1.30 mm
3 (N, O and P)	1.34 mm
4 (N, O, P and Q)	1.38 mm
5 (N, O, P, Q and R)	1.42 mm
2 (N and R)	1.46 mm

The correct thickness of gasket required is selected by measuring the piston protrusions as follows.

23 Ensure the flywheel is correctly locked in position so pistons 1 and 4 are exactly at TDC. Mount a dial test indicator securely on the block so that its pointer can be easily pivoted between the piston crown and block mating surfaces. Zero the dial test indicator on the gasket surface of the cylinder block then carefully move the indicator over No 1 piston and measure its protrusion (see illustration). Take measurements at the front and rear of the piston, and take the average of the two measurements to be the piston protrusion. Repeat this procedure on No 4 piston.

24 Remove the locking tool then rotate the crankshaft half-a-turn (180°) clockwise to bring pistons 2 and 3 to TDC. Ensure the crank-shaft is accurately positioned then measure the protrusions of pistons No 2 and 3. Once all four pistons have been measured, rotate the crankshaft through a further half-a-turn (180°) clockwise to bring pistons 1 and 4 back to TDC then lock the flywheel in position again.

25 Using the largest protrusion measurement of the four pistons, select the correct thickness of gasket required using the following:

Piston protrusion measurement	Gasket thickness required
0.510 to 0.549 mm	1.26 mm
0.550 to 0.589 mm	1.30 mm
0.590 to 0.629 mm	1.34 mm
0.630 to 0.669 mm	1.38 mm
0.670 to 0.709 mm	1.42 mm
0.710 to 0.750 mm	1.46 mm

26 Check the condition of the cylinder head bolts, and particularly their threads, whenever they are removed. Wash the bolts in suitable solvent, and wipe them dry. Check each for any sign of visible wear or damage, renewing any bolt if necessary. Measure the length of each bolt, from the underside of its head to the bolt end, to check for stretching. There are two possible types of cylinder head bolt, those with a centring point at their end and those without. Bolts with a centring point are 124 mm long when new and must be renewed if any bolt has stretched to more than 125.5 mm. Bolts without a centring point are 120 mm long when new and must be renewed if they have stretched to more than 121.5 mm. Renew all the cylinder head bolts as a set if any bolt exceeds the maximum length. Although

Peugeot do not actually specify that the bolts must be renewed, it is strongly recommended that the bolts should be renewed as a complete set, regardless of their apparent condition, whenever they are disturbed.

Refitting

27 Wipe clean the mating surfaces of the cylinder head and cylinder block. Check that the locating dowel is in position in the cylinder block.

28 Position the correct thickness new gasket on the cylinder block surface, ensuring that its identification holes are at the front, left-hand end of the gasket.

29 Check that the flywheel and camshaft sprocket are still correctly locked in position with their respective tools. **Note:** *If the camshaft/camshaft sprocket are not installed, as a precaution, remove the flywheel locking pin then rotate the crankshaft **backwards** (anti-clockwise) through 90°; this will position the pistons mid-way up the bores and remove the risk of the valves contacting the pistons during the following operation.*

30 With the aid of an assistant, carefully refit the cylinder head assembly to the block, aligning it with the locating dowel.

31 Lubricate the threads and underside of the heads of the cylinder head bolts with a smear of grease (Peugeot recommend the use of Molykote G Rapid Plus grease).

32 Carefully enter each bolt into its relevant hole (do not drop them in) and screw in, by hand only, until finger-tight.

33 Working progressively and in the sequence shown, tighten the cylinder head bolts to their Stage 1 torque setting, using a torque wrench and suitable socket (see illustration).

34 Once all the bolts have been tightened to their Stage 1 setting, working again in the given sequence, tighten the cylinder head bolts to the specified Stage 2 torque setting.

35 Finally angle-tighten the bolts through the specified Stage 3 angle, using a socket and extension bar. It is recommended that an angle-measuring gauge is used during this stage of the tightening, to ensure accuracy. If a gauge is not available, use white paint to make alignment marks between the bolt head and cylinder head prior to tightening; the marks can then be used to check that the bolt has been rotated through the correct angle during tightening.

36 Where necessary, refit the camshaft and/or camshaft sprocket (see Sections 8 and 10). If the cylinder head has been overhauled, check the valve clearances before proceeding.

37 Ensure the engine/transmission unit is securely supported then remove the mounting bracket from the right-hand engine/transmission mounting. Refit the bolt securing the bracket to the cylinder head and tighten it to the specified torque.

38 Refit the timing belt as described in Section 7.

39 Refit the coolant pipe bolt and securely reconnect the glow plug wiring.

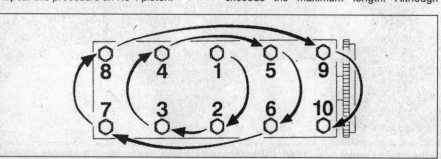

12.33 Cylinder head bolt tightening sequence

12.53 Disconnect the coolant temperature sensor wiring connector – 2.0 litre engine

40 Ensure the mating surfaces are clean and dry then refit the fuel filter/thermostat housing to the cylinder head, using a new gasket. Fit the housing retaining bolts, ensuring the sealing washer is fitted to the bolt located inside the filter housing, and tighten them to the specified torque. Reconnect the coolant hose securely to the housing.

41 Fit a new sealing ring to the base of the fuel filter plastic housing and refit the housing, tightening its bolt to the specified torque.

42 Refit the cylinder cover (see Section 4).

43 Referring to Chapter 4B, carry out the following.

a) *Refit the injectors (where removed).*

b) *Refit the fuel pipes connecting the injection pump to the injectors and reconnect the leak off hoses to the injectors.*

c) *Refit the manifolds and air cleaner housing.*

44 Refit the braking system vacuum pump as described in Chapter 9.

45 Fit a new fuel filter and refill the cooling system as described in Chapter 1B.

2.0 litre engine

Removal

46 Remove the battery and battery tray as described in Chapter 5A.

47 Drain the cooling system as described in Chapter 1B.

48 Remove the braking system vacuum pump as described in Chapter 9.

49 Unbolt the engine cover brackets and remove them from the cylinder head.

50 Remove the timing belt as described in Section 7. Once the timing belt has been removed, unscrew the two upper bolts securing the right-hand engine/transmission mounting bracket to the cylinder head. Leave the lower bolts securing the bracket to the cylinder block then refit the upper bracket, securing the engine bracket to the mounting, and securely tighten its nuts and bolts. This will ensure the engine/transmission unit is securely supported through out the following procedure.

51 Referring to Chapter 4B, carry out the following operations.

a) *Remove the air cleaner housing.*

b) *Remove the turbocharger.*

c) *Remove the high-pressure fuel pipe connecting the injection pump to the fuel rail and the fuel return pipe.*

d) *If the cylinder head is being overhauled, remove the fuel rail and injectors. If not disconnect the wiring connectors from the injectors and fuel rail sensor(s) then unbolt the wiring harness guide and position it clear of the head.*

52 Remove the camshaft as described in Section 10.

53 Disconnect the wiring connector from the coolant temperature sensor fitted to the thermostat housing **(see illustration)**.

54 Release the retaining clips and disconnect the coolant hoses from the coolant outlet housing on the left-hand end of the cylinder head **(see illustration)**.

55 Slacken and remove the engine oil dipstick tube retaining bolt.

56 Unscrew the nuts and bolts securing the coolant outlet housing to the end of cylinder head and remove the wiring bracket. Unscrew the two housing studs from the

12.54 On 2.0 litre engines disconnect the coolant hoses from the housing on the left-hand end of the cylinder head

cylinder head; to do this, screw two nuts onto the end of the stud then lock the nuts securely together and use the inner nut to unscrew the stud from the head **(see illustration)**.

57 Free the coolant outlet housing from the end of the cylinder head and recover its gasket. Discard the gasket, a new one must be used on refitting.

58 Working in the *reverse* of the sequence shown in illustration 12.33, progressively slacken the ten cylinder head bolts by half a turn at a time, until all bolts can be unscrewed by hand.

59 With all the cylinder head bolts removed, release the cylinder head from the cylinder block and locating dowels by rocking it. The Peugeot tool for doing this consists simply of two metal rods with 90-degree angled ends. Do not prise between the mating faces of the cylinder head and block, as this may damage the gasket faces. Lift the cylinder head away; seek assistance if possible.

60 Remove the gasket from the top of the block, noting the two locating dowels. If the locating dowels are a loose fit, remove them and store them with the head for safe-keeping. Do not discard the gasket – it will be needed for identification purposes (see paragraphs 63 to 66) **(see illustration)**.

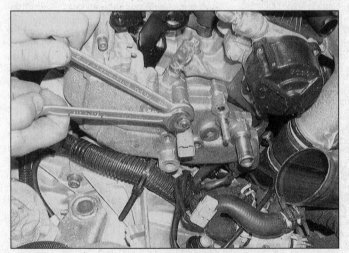

12.56 Lock two nuts together then unscrew the coolant outlet housing studs from the cylinder head

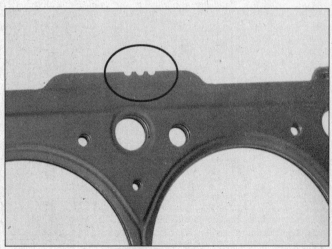

12.60 Cylinder head thickness can be identified by the cut-outs (circled)

2B

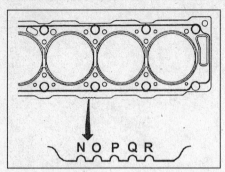

12.63 Cylinder head gasket identification notch location (1) – 2.0 litre engine

61 If the cylinder head is to be dismantled overhaul, refer to Part C of this Chapter.

Preparation for refitting

62 Clean and check the cylinder head and block mating surfaces as described in paragraphs 19 to 21.

63 When purchasing a new cylinder head gasket, it is essential that a gasket of the correct thickness is obtained. There are five different thicknesses of gasket available to enable the cylinder head-to-piston clearance to be accurately set. The gasket thickness can be determined by looking at the tab situated in front of No 2 and 3 cylinders. There will be between 1 and 5 notches on the tab **(see illustration)**. These notches identify the gasket thickness as follows.

Number of notches (notch locations)	Gasket thickness (when compressed)
1 (R)	1.30 mm
2 (Q and R)	1.35 mm
3 (P, Q and R)	1.40 mm
4 (O, P, Q and R)	1.45 mm
5 (N, O, P, Q and R)	1.50 mm

The correct thickness of gasket required is selected by measuring the piston protrusions as follows.

64 Rotate the crankshaft 90° clockwise to bring pistons No 1 and 4 to TDC then lock the flywheel in position with the locking tool. Mount a dial test indicator securely on the block so that its pointer cam be easily pivoted between the piston crown and block mating surfaces **(see illustration 12.23)**. Zero the dial test indicator on the gasket surface of the cylinder block then carefully move the indicator over No 1 piston and measure its protrusion. Take measurements at the front and rear of the piston, and take the average of the two measurements to be the piston protrusion. Repeat this procedure on No 4 piston.

65 Remove the locking tool then rotate the crankshaft half-a-turn (180°) clockwise to bring pistons 2 and 3 to TDC. Ensure the crankshaft is accurately positioned then measure the protrusions of pistons No 2 and 3. Once all four pistons have been measured, rotate the crankshaft through another 90° clockwise to position the pistons halfway up their bores.

66 Using the largest protrusion measurement of the four pistons, select the correct

12.74 Working in the specified sequence, tighten the cylinder head bolts to the specified Stage 1 and Stage 2 torque settings . . .

thickness of head required using the following table.

Piston protrusion measurement	Gasket thickness required
0.470 to 0.604 mm	1.30 mm
0.605 to 0.654 mm	1.35 mm
0.655 to 0.704 mm	1.40 mm
0.705 to 0.754 mm	1.45 mm
0.755 to 0.830 mm	1.50 mm

67 Check the condition of the cylinder head bolts, and particularly their threads, whenever they are removed. Wash the bolts in suitable solvent, and wipe them dry. Check each for any sign of visible wear or damage, renewing any bolt if necessary. Measure the length of each bolt, from the underside of its head to the bolt end, to check for stretching. The bolts are 131.5 mm long when new and must be renewed if any bolt has stretched to more than 133.4 mm. Renew all the cylinder head bolts as a set if any bolt exceeds the maximum length. Although Peugeot do not actually specify that the bolts must be renewed, it is strongly recommended that the bolts should be renewed as a complete set, regardless of their apparent condition, whenever they are disturbed.

Refitting

68 Bring pistons No 1 and 4 to TDC then rotate the crankshaft **backwards** (anti-clockwise) through 90°; this will position the pistons mid-way up the bores and remove the risk of the valves contacting the pistons during the following operation.

12.76 . . . then angle-tighten them through the specified Stage 3 angle

69 Wipe clean the mating surfaces of the cylinder head and cylinder block. Check that the locating dowels are in position in the cylinder block.

70 Position the correct thickness new gasket on the cylinder block surface, ensuring that its identification notches are at the front of the gasket and the gasket is the correct way up.

71 With the aid of an assistant, carefully refit the cylinder head assembly to the block, aligning it with the locating dowels.

72 Lubricate the threads and underside of the heads of the cylinder head bolts with a smear of grease (Peugeot recommend the use of Molykote G Rapid Plus grease).

73 Carefully enter each bolt into its relevant hole (do not drop them in) and screw in, by hand only, until finger-tight.

74 Working progressively and in the sequence shown in illustration 12.33, tighten the cylinder head bolts to their Stage 1 torque setting, using a torque wrench and suitable socket **(see illustration)**.

75 Once all the bolts have been tightened to their Stage 1 setting, working again in the given sequence, tighten the cylinder head bolts to the specified Stage 2 torque setting.

76 Finally angle-tighten the bolts through the specified Stage 3 angle, using a socket and extension bar. It is recommended that an angle-measuring gauge is used during this stage of the tightening, to ensure accuracy **(see illustration)**. If a gauge is not available, use white paint to make alignment marks between the bolt head and cylinder head prior to tightening; the marks can then be used to check that the bolt has been rotated through the correct angle during tightening.

77 Refit the camshaft and camshaft sprocket (see Sections 8 and 10).

78 Ensure the engine/transmission unit is securely supported then remove the mounting bracket from the right-hand engine/transmission mounting. Apply thread locking compound (Peugeot recommend the use of Loctite Frenetanch) to the M10 bolt then refit both bolts securing the bracket to the cylinder head, tightening them to the specified torque.

79 Refit the timing belt as described in Section 7.

80 Ensure the mating surfaces are clean and dry then refit the thermostat housing to the cylinder head, using a new gasket. Apply locking compound to the threads of the housing studs then screw the studs into the cylinder head, ensuring they pass through the gasket holes, and tighten them to the specified torque. Refit the wiring bracket and install the housing nuts and bolts, tightening them to the specified torque.

81 Reconnect the wiring connector to the coolant temperature sensor then securely reconnect the coolant hoses to the housing.

82 Refit the engine oil dipstick tube bolt and tighten securely.

83 Refit the cylinder cover (see Section 4) then refit the engine cover brackets to the cylinder head.

84 Referring to Chapter 4B, carry out the following.

a) *Refit the injectors and fuel rail (where removed) or reconnect the wiring connectors and secure the wiring harness guide in position (as applicable).*

b) *Refit the high-pressure fuel pipe connecting the injection pump to the fuel rail and reconnect the fuel return pipe.*

c) *Refit the turbocharger.*

d) *Refit the air cleaner housing.*

85 Refit the braking system vacuum pump as described in Chapter 9.

86 Refill the cooling system as described in Chapter 1B.

---

13 Sump – removal and refitting

Removal

1 Firmly apply the handbrake, then jack up the front of the vehicle and support it on axle stands (see *Jacking and vehicle support*). Disconnect the battery negative lead.

2 Where necessary, remove the retaining bolts, screws and clips and remove the undercover from beneath the engine/transmission unit.

3 Drain the engine oil, then clean and refit the engine oil drain plug, tightening it to the specified torque. If the engine is nearing its service interval when the oil and filter are due for renewal, it is recommended that the filter is also removed, and a new one fitted. After reassembly, the engine can then be refilled with fresh oil. Refer to Chapter 1B for further information.

4 On models with air conditioning, remove the auxiliary drivebelt as described in Chapter 1B. Unscrew the compressor mounting bolts and nuts. Free the compressor from the sump and support its weight by tying it to the vehicle, to prevent any excess strain being placed on the compressor lines. Take care not to lose the spacers from the compressor rear mountings (where fitted).

Caution: Do not disconnect the refrigerant lines from the compressor (refer to the warnings given in Chapter 3). Ensure the compressor is securely supported to prevent the refrigerant lines being damaged.

5 Progressively slacken and remove all the sump retaining bolts. On some models, it may be necessary to unbolt the flywheel cover plate from the transmission to gain access to the left-hand sump fasteners.

6 Break the joint by striking the sump with the palm of your hand. Lower the sump, and withdraw it from underneath the vehicle. On models with air conditioning, recover the sump locating dowel(s).

7 While the sump is removed, take the opportunity to check the oil pump pick-up/strainer for signs of clogging or splitting. If

necessary, remove the pump as described in Section 14, and clean or renew the strainer.

Refitting

8 Clean all traces of sealant from the mating surfaces of the cylinder block/crankcase and sump, then use a clean rag to wipe out the sump and the engine's interior.

9 Apply a thin coating of suitable sealant to the sump mating surface.

10 On models with air conditioning ensure the sump locating dowel(s) is/are correctly fitted (as applicable).

11 Offer up the sump to the cylinder block/crankcase and refit its retaining bolts. Tighten all bolts by hand then evenly and progressively tighten them to the specified torque setting.

12 Where necessary, ensure the spacers (where fitted) are correctly to the rear mountings then align the air conditioning compressor with the sump. Refit the mounting bolts and nuts; tighten compressor front (drivebelt pulley end) mounting bolts to the specified torque first, then tighten the rear mounting bolts to the specified torque (see Chapter 3). Refit the auxiliary drivebelt as described in Chapter 1B.

13 Refit the undercover (where fitted) then lower the vehicle to the ground and refill the engine with oil (see Chapter 1B).

---

14 Oil pump – removal, inspection and refitting

Removal

1 Remove the sump (see Section 13).

2 Unscrew the bolt securing the dipstick guide tube to the oil pump and remove the guide tube from the cylinder block **(see illustrations)**.

3 On 1.9 litre engines slacken and remove the three bolts securing the oil pump in position, noting the correct fitted location of the longer bolt. Disengage the pump sprocket from the chain, and remove the oil pump and spacer plate from the engine.

4 On 2.0 litre engines slacken and remove the three bolts securing the oil pump in position,

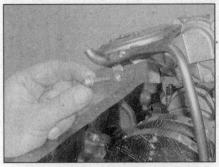

14.2a Unscrew the bolt securing the dipstick guide tube to the oil pump . . .

noting the correct fitted location of the each bolt (they are all different sizes) and the sealing washer **(see illustration)**. Disengage the pump sprocket from the chain, and remove the oil pump from the engine.

Inspection

5 Examine the oil pump sprocket for signs of damage and wear, such as chipped or missing teeth. If the sprocket is worn, the pump assembly must be renewed, as the sprocket is not available separately. It is also recommended that the chain and drive sprocket, fitted to the crankshaft, is renewed at the same time. The oil pump drive sprocket and chain can be removed with the engine *in situ*, once the crankshaft sprocket has been removed and the crankshaft oil seal housing has been unbolted. See Part C for further information.

6 Slacken and remove the bolts securing the strainer cover to the pump body, then lift off the strainer cover. Remove the relief valve piston and spring (and guide pin – 2.0 litre engine only), noting which way round they are fitted **(see illustrations overleaf)**.

7 Examine the pump rotors and body for signs of wear ridges and scoring. If worn, the complete pump assembly must be renewed.

8 Examine the relief valve piston for signs of wear or damage, and renew if necessary. The condition of the relief valve spring can only be measured by comparing it with a new one; if there is any doubt about its condition, it should also be renewed. Both the piston and spring are available individually.

14.2b . . . then remove the guide tube from the block (shown with engine removed)

14.4 Note the correct fitted location of each oil pump retaining bolt (arrowed) as it is removed

2B

14.6a Unscrew the retaining bolts . . .

14.6b . . . then lift off the cover and remove the spring . . .

14.6c . . . and relief valve piston, noting which way around it is fitted

9 Thoroughly clean the oil pump strainer with a suitable solvent, and check it for signs of clogging or splitting. If the strainer is damaged, the strainer and cover assembly must be renewed.

10 Locate the relief valve spring, piston and (where fitted) the guide pin in the strainer cover, then refit the cover to the pump body. Align the relief valve piston with its bore in the pump. Refit the cover retaining bolts, tightening them securely.

Refitting

11 On 1.9 litre engines, fit the spacer plate then offer up the pump, engaging the pump sprocket with its drive chain. Refit the pump retaining bolts, ensuring the longer bolt is fitted to the rear hole, and tighten them to the specified torque setting.

12 On 2.0 litre engines, engage the pump sprocket with the drive chain then install the retaining bolts. Fit the sealing washer to the rear bolt then install the pump retaining bolts, ensuring they are fitted in their original locations. Tighten the bolts to the specified torque.

13 On all models, refit the dipstick guide tube to the cylinder block and securely tighten its retaining bolt.

14 Refit the sump as described in Section 13.

15 Oil cooler –
removal and refitting

Removal

1 The oil cooler is mounted on the front of the cylinder block. To gain access to the cooler, firmly apply the handbrake, then jack up the front of the vehicle and support it on axle stands (see *Jacking and vehicle support*). Disconnect the battery negative lead.

2 Where necessary, remove the retaining bolts, screws and clips and remove the undercover from beneath the engine/transmission unit.

3 Position a suitable container beneath the oil filter. Unscrew the filter using an oil filter removal tool if necessary, and drain the oil into the container (see Chapter 1B). If the oil

filter is damaged or distorted during removal, it must be renewed. Given the low cost of a new oil filter relative to the cost of repairing the damage which could result if a re-used filter springs a leak, it is probably a good idea to renew the filter in any case.

4 Using a hose clamp or similar, clamp both the oil cooler coolant hoses to minimise coolant loss during subsequent operations.

5 Slacken the retaining clips, and disconnect both coolant hoses from the oil cooler – be prepared for some coolant spillage. Wash off any spilt coolant immediately with cold water, and dry the surrounding area before proceeding further.

6 Slacken and remove the oil cooler centre bolt, and remove the cooler from the cylinder block **(see illustration)**. Remove the sealing ring (where fitted) from the rear of the cooler, and discard it; a new one must be used on refitting.

Caution: Ensure no dirt is allowed to enter the engine whilst the oil cooler is removed.

Refitting

7 Where a sealing ring was fitted to the oil cooler, fit a new sealing ring to the oil cooler. Where no sealing ring was fitted, ensure the oil cooler mating surface is clean and dry then apply a bead of suitable sealant to the cooler.

8 Clean the oil cooler centre bolt and apply a smear of fresh sealant to its threads.

9 Locate the fluid cooler on the front of the cylinder block, ensuring its locating notch its correctly located with the lug on the block. Refit the cooler centre bolt and tighten it to the specified torque.

15.6 Oil cooler centre bolt (A) and locating notch (B)

10 Reconnect the coolant hoses to the oil cooler, and securely tighten their retaining clips. Remove the hose clamp(s).

11 Fit the oil filter (see Chapter 1B), then refit the undercover (where fitted) and lower the vehicle to the ground.

12 Top-up the engine oil level and the cooling system as described in *Weekly checks*. Start the engine, and check the oil cooler for signs of leakage.

16 Crankshaft oil seals –
renewal

Right-hand (timing belt end) oil seal

1 Remove the crankshaft sprocket as described in Section 8.

2 Make a note of the correct fitted depth of the seal in its housing then carefully punch or drill two small holes opposite each other in the seal. Screw a self-tapping screw into each, and pull on the screws with pliers to extract the seal **(see illustration)**. Alternatively, the seal can be levered out of position using a suitable flat-bladed screwdriver, taking great care not to damage the oil pump drive gear shoulder or seal housing.

3 Clean the seal housing, and polish off any burrs or raised edges, which may have caused the seal to fail in the first place.

4 Lubricate the lips of the new seal with clean engine oil, and carefully locate the seal on the end of crankshaft. Note that its sealing lip

16.2 Using a self-tapping screw and pliers to remove the crankshaft right-hand oil seal

must face inwards. Take care not to damage the seal lips during fitting.

5 Using a suitable tubular drift (such as a socket) which bears only on the hard outer edge of the seal, tap the seal into position to the same depth in the housing as the original was prior to removal. The inner face of the seal must be flush with the inner wall of the crankcase.

6 Wash off any traces of oil, then refit the crankshaft sprocket as described in Section 8.

Left-hand (flywheel end) oil seal

7 Remove the flywheel (see Section 17).

8 Make a note of the correct fitted depth of the seal in its housing. Punch or drill two small holes opposite each other in the seal. Screw a self-tapping screw into each, and pull on the screws with pliers to extract the seal.

9 Clean the seal housing, and polish off any burrs or raised edges, which may have caused the seal to fail in the first place.

10 Lubricate the lips of the new seal with clean engine oil, and carefully locate the seal on the end of the crankshaft.

11 Using a suitable tubular drift, which bears only on the hard outer edge of the seal, drive the seal into position, to the same depth in the housing as the original was prior to removal.

12 Wash off any traces of oil, then refit the flywheel as described in Section 17.

17 Flywheel – removal, inspection and refitting

Removal

Note: *New flywheel retaining bolts must be used on refitting.*

1 Remove the transmission as described in Chapter 7A, then remove the clutch assembly as described in Chapter 6.

2 Prevent the flywheel from turning by locking the ring gear teeth with a similar arrangement to that shown **(see illustration)**. Alternatively, bolt a strap between the flywheel and the cylinder block/crankcase.

Caution: Do not attempt to lock the flywheel in position using the locking pin described in Section 3.

3 Slacken and remove the flywheel retaining bolts. Discard the bolts; new ones must be used on refitting.

4 Remove the flywheel. Do not drop it, as it is very heavy. If the locating dowel is a loose fit in the crankshaft end, remove and store it with the flywheel for safe-keeping.

Inspection

5 If the flywheel's clutch mating surface is deeply scored, cracked or otherwise damaged, the flywheel must be renewed. However, it may be possible to have it surface-ground; seek the advice of a Peugeot dealer or engine reconditioning specialist.

6 If the ring gear is badly worn or has missing teeth, it must be renewed. This job is best left to a Peugeot dealer or engine reconditioning specialist. The temperature to which the new ring gear must be heated for installation is critical and, if not done accurately, the hardness of the teeth will be destroyed.

Refitting

7 Clean the mating surfaces of the flywheel and crankshaft. Remove any remaining locking compound from the threads of the crankshaft holes, using the correct size of tap, if available.

 HAYNES HiNT *If a suitable tap is not available, cut two slots along the threads of one of the original flywheel bolts and use the bolt to remove the locking compound from the threads.*

8 Ensure that the locating dowel is in position. Offer up the flywheel, locating it on the dowel, and fit the new retaining bolts **(see illustration)**.

9 Lock the flywheel using the method employed on dismantling, and tighten the retaining bolts evenly and progressively to the specified torque **(see illustration)**.

10 Refit the clutch as described in Chapter 6. Remove the locking tool, and refit the transmission as described in Chapter 7A.

18 Engine/transmission mountings – inspection and renewal

Inspection

1 If improved access is required, raise the front of the car and support it on axle stands (see *Jacking and vehicle support*).

2 Check the mounting rubber to see if it is cracked, hardened or separated from the metal at any point; renew the mounting if any such damage or deterioration is evident.

3 Check that all the mounting's fasteners are securely tightened; use a torque wrench to check if possible.

4 Using a large screwdriver or a crowbar, check for wear in the mounting by carefully

17.2 Lock the flywheel ring gear

levering against it to check for free play. Where this is not possible, enlist the aid of an assistant to move the engine/transmission back-and-forth, or from side-to-side, while you watch the mounting. While some free play is to be expected even from new components, excessive wear should be obvious. If excessive free play is found, check first that the fasteners are secure, then renew any worn components as described below.

Renewal

Right-hand mounting

5 Disconnect the battery negative lead then remove the engine cover. On 1.9 litre engines, remove the fasteners from the right-hand side and top of the cover then lift off the cover, taking care not to lose its mounting rubbers **(see illustrations 4.1a to 4.1c)**, on 2.0 litre engines remove the fasteners (rotate them 90º to release them) then lift off the engine cover **(see illustrations 4.14a and 4.14b)**.

6 Remove the undercover (where fitted) then place a jack beneath the engine, with a block of wood on the jack head. Raise the jack until it is supporting the weight of the engine.

7 On 2.0 litre engines and later 1.9 litre (WJY) engines, unclip the wiring harness from the front of the injection system ECU. Slacken and remove the ECU mounting plate nut using a pair of grips (the plate is secured in position with an anti-tamper nut). Remove the cable/hose bracket then free the mounting plate from the body and position it clear of the engine.

17.8 Locate the flywheel on the crankshaft then fit the new retaining bolts

17.9 Lock the flywheel (tool arrowed) then tighten the retaining bolts evenly and progressively to the specified torque

2B

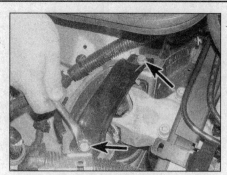

18.8 Unscrew the bolts and remove the bracket from the top of the right-hand mounting

18.9 Unscrew the vibration damper (where fitted) from the top of the mounting to gain access to the mounting nut

8 Slacken and remove the mounting bolts and remove the bracket from the top of the mounting **(see illustration)**.

9 Unscrew the vibration damper (where fitted) from the top of the mounting rubber then slacken and remove the nut securing the mounting bracket to the mounting rubber **(see illustration)**.

10 Slacken and remove the three bolts securing the right-hand engine mounting bracket to the bracket on the side of the cylinder block then lift off the mounting bracket, taking care not to lose the locating dowels (where fitted).

11 Make identification marks on the movement restrictors (the front and rear restrictors are different and are not interchangeable) then unscrew the nuts and remove both restrictors.

12 Using a strap wrench, unscrew the mounting rubber from the body

13 Check for signs of wear or damage on all components, and renew as necessary.

14 On reassembly, screw the mounting rubber into the body, tightening it to the specified torque.

15 Refit the front and rear movement restrictors in their original locations. Ensure the restrictor pegs are correctly located in their holes then securely tighten their retaining nuts.

16 Ensure the dowels (where fitted) are in position then install the mounting bracket, tightening its retaining bolts and nut to their specified torque settings

17 Refit the vibration damper (where fitted) to the mounting, tightening it to the specified torque.

18 Fit the bracket over the vibration damper, tightening its bolts to the specified torque.

19 Remove the jack from under the engine then refit the undercover (where fitted). Reconnect the battery negative lead then refit the engine cover.

Left-hand mounting

20 Remove the battery, battery tray and mounting plate as described in Chapter 5A.

21 Remove the undercover (where fitted) and place a jack beneath the transmission, with a block of wood on the jack head. Raise the jack until it is supporting the weight of the transmission.

22 Slacken and remove the mounting rubber's centre nut and two retaining bolts and remove the mounting from the engine compartment.

23 If necessary, undo the retaining bolts and remove the mounting bracket from the body.

24 The mounting stud is a screw-fit into its mounting bracket and the bracket is secured to the transmission by two bolts. If the mounting stud is tight, a universal stud extractor can be used to unscrew it.

25 Check carefully for signs of wear or damage on all components, and renew them where necessary.

26 Where necessary, refit the mounting bracket to the top of the transmission unit and tighten its bolts to the specified torque. Apply locking compound (Peugeot recommend the use of Loctite Frenetanch) to the stud threads then refit the stud to the bracket, tightening it to the specified torque. Slide the spacer onto the stud.

27 Refit the mounting bracket to the vehicle body and tighten its bolts to the specified torque.

28 Fit the mounting rubber to the bracket and tighten its retaining bolts to the specified

torque. Refit the mounting centre nut, and tighten it to the specified torque.

29 Remove the jack from underneath the transmission and refit the undercover (where fitted).

30 Refit the battery as described in Chapter 5A.

Rear mounting

31 If not already done, firmly apply the handbrake, then jack up the front of the vehicle and support it securely on axle stands (see *Jacking and vehicle support*).

32 Where necessary, remove the retaining bolts, screws and clips and remove the undercover from beneath the engine/transmission unit.

33 Unscrew and remove the bolt securing the rear mounting link to the mounting on the rear of the cylinder block.

34 Remove the bolt securing the rear mounting link to the subframe.

35 To remove the mounting assembly it will first be necessary to remove the right-hand driveshaft as described in Chapter 8.

36 With the driveshaft removed, undo the retaining bolts and remove the mounting from the rear of the cylinder block.

37 Check carefully for signs of wear or damage on all components, and renew them where necessary.

38 On reassembly, fit the rear mounting assembly to the rear of the cylinder block, and tighten its retaining bolts to the specified torque. Refit the driveshaft as described in Chapter 8.

39 Refit the rear mounting link, and tighten both its bolts to their specified torque settings.

40 Refit the undercover (where fitted) then lower the vehicle to the ground.

Chapter 2 Part C:
Engine removal and overhaul procedures

Contents

Degrees of difficulty

| Easy, suitable for novice with little experience | | Fairly easy, suitable for beginner with some experience | | Fairly difficult, suitable for competent DIY mechanic | | Difficult, suitable for experienced DIY mechanic | | Very difficult, suitable for expert DIY or professional | |

Specifications

Note: *At the time of writing, some specifications for certain engines were not available. Where the relevant specifications are not given here, refer to your Peugeot dealer for further information.*

Cylinder head

Maximum gasket face distortion:
   Petrol engine .... 0.05 mm
   Diesel engine .... 0.03 mm
Cylinder head height:
   Petrol engine .... 111.2 ± 0.08 mm
   Diesel engine:
      1.9 litre engine (from centre of camshaft to head mating surface) .. 139.95 to 140.25 mm
      2.0 litre engine .... 133.0 mm
Swirl chamber protrusion – 1.9 litre diesel engine .... 0 to 0.03 mm
Valve head-to-cylinder head measurement – diesel engine:
   1.9 litre engine:
      Inlet .... 0.775 ± 0.275 mm recessed
      Exhaust .... 1.175 ± 0.275 mm recessed
   2.0 litre engine .... Less than 0.2 mm protrusion

Valves

	Inlet	Exhaust
Valve head diameter:		
Petrol engines:		
1.1 and 1.4 litre engine	36.7 ± 0.01 mm	29.4 mm
1.6 litre engine	39.35 mm	31.4 mm
Diesel engines:		
1.9 litre engine	38.5 ± 0.2 mm	33.0 ± 0.2 mm
2.0 litre engine	35.6 mm	33.8 mm
Valve stem diameter:		
Petrol engines:		
1.1 and 1.4 litre engine	6.965 to 6.980 mm	6.945 to 6.960 mm
1.6 litre engine	6.956 to 6.970 mm	6.955 to 6.970 mm
Diesel engines:		
1.9 litre engine	7.970 to 7.985 mm	7.970 to 7.985 mm
2.0 litre engine	5.978 ± 0.007 mm	5.968 ± 0.007 mm
Valve overall length:		
Petrol engines:		
1.1 and 1.4 litre engine	112.76 mm	112.56 mm
1.6 litre engine	111.50 mm	111.50 mm
Diesel engines:		
1.9 litre engines (minimum)	112.40 mm	111.85 mm
2.0 litre engines:		
Standard	107.18 mm	107.18 mm
Minimum	106.78 mm	106.78 mm

Cylinder block

Cylinder bore diameter:	
Petrol engines:	
1.1 litre engine:	
Size group A	72.000 to 72.010 mm
Size group B	72.010 to 72.020 mm
Size group C	72.020 to 72.030 mm
1.4 litre engine:	
Size group A	75.000 to 75.010 mm
Size group B	75.010 to 75.020 mm
Size group C	75.020 to 75.030 mm
1.6 litre engine	78.5 mm (nominal)
Diesel engines:	
1.9 litre engine:	
Standard	82.200 to 82.218 mm
Oversize	82.800 to 82.818 mm
2.0 litre engines:	
Standard	85.000 to 85.018 mm
Oversize	85.600 to 85.618 mm
Liner protrusion – aluminium block petrol engine:	
Standard	0.03 to 0.10 mm
Maximum difference between any two liners	0.05 mm

Pistons

Piston diameter:	
Petrol engines:	
1.1 litre engine:	
Size group A	71.950 to 71.959 mm
Size group B	71.960 to 71.969 mm
Size group C	71.970 to 71.980 mm
1.4 litre engine:	
Size group A	74.950 to 74.959 mm
Size group B	74.960 to 74.969 mm
Size group C	74.970 to 74.980 mm
1.6 litre engine	
Standard	78.455 to 78.470 mm
Oversize	78.840 to 78.855 mm
Diesel engines:	
1.9 litre engine:	
Standard	82.121 to 82.139 mm
Oversize	82.721 to 82.739 mm
2.0 litre engine	Not available

Crankshaft

Endfloat:
  Petrol engine . . . .   0.07 to 0.27 mm
  Diesel engine . . . .   0.07 to 0.32 mm
Main bearing journal diameter:
  Petrol engines:
    Standard . . . .   49.965 to 49.981 mm
    Undersize . . . .   49.665 to 49.681 mm
  Diesel engines:
    Standard . . . .   59.977 to 60.000 mm
    Undersize . . . .   59.677 to 59.700 mm
Big-end bearing journal diameter:
  Petrol engines:
    Standard . . . .   44.975 to 44.991 mm
    Undersize . . . .   44.675 to 44.691 mm
  Diesel models:
    Standard . . . .   49.980 to 50.000 mm
    Undersize . . . .   49.680 to 49.700 mm
Maximum bearing journal out-of-round (all models) . . . .   0.007 mm
Main bearing running clearance:
  Petrol engines . . . .   0.010 to 0.036 mm
  Diesel engines* . . . .   0.025 to 0.050 mm
Big-end bearing running clearance – all models* . . . .   0.025 to 0.050 mm
*These are suggested figures, typical for this type of engine – no exact values are stated by Peugeot.

Piston rings

End gaps:
  Petrol engines*:
    Top compression ring . . . .   0.2 to 0.4 mm
    Second compression ring . . . .   0.3 to 0.5 mm
    Oil control ring . . . .   0.3 to 0.5 mm
  Diesel engines:
    1.9 litre engine:
      Top compression ring . . . .   0.20 to 0.35 mm
      Second compression ring . . . .   0.40 to 0.60 mm
      Oil control ring . . . .   0.25 to 0.50 mm
    2.0 litre engine*:
      Top compression ring . . . .   0.20 to 0.35 mm
      Second compression ring . . . .   0.40 to 0.60 mm
      Oil control ring . . . .   0.25 to 0.50 mm
*These are suggested figures, typical for this type of engine – no exact values are stated by Peugeot.

Lubrication system

Petrol engines:
  Minimum oil pressure at 80°C . . . .   4 bars at 4000 rpm
  Oil pressure warning switch operating pressure . . . .   0.8 bars
Diesel engines:
  Minimum oil pressure at 80°C:
    1.9 litre engine . . . .   4.5 bar at 4000 rpm
    2.0 litre engine . . . .   4 bar at 4000 rpm

Torque wrench settings

Petrol engines
Refer to Chapter 2A Specifications.

Diesel engines
Refer to Chapter 2B Specifications.

---

1 General information

1 Included in this Part of Chapter 2 are details of removing the engine/transmission from the car and general overhaul procedures for the cylinder head, cylinder block/crankcase and all other engine internal components.

2 The information given ranges from advice concerning preparation for an overhaul and the purchase of replacement parts, to detailed step-by-step procedures covering removal, inspection, renovation and refitting of engine internal components.

3 After Section 6, all instructions are based on the assumption that the engine has been removed from the car. For information concerning in-car engine repair, as well as the removal and refitting of those external components necessary for full overhaul, refer to Part A or B of this Chapter (as applicable) and to Section 6. Ignore any preliminary dismantling operations described in Part A or B that are no longer relevant once the engine has been removed from the car.

4 Apart from torque wrench settings, which are given at the beginning of Part A or B (as applicable), all specifications relating to engine overhaul are at the beginning of this Part of Chapter 2.

2C

2 Engine overhaul – general information

1 It is not always easy to determine when, or if, an engine should be completely overhauled, as a number of factors must be considered.

2 High mileage is not necessarily an indication that an overhaul is needed, while low mileage does not preclude the need for an overhaul. Frequency of servicing is probably the most important consideration. An engine which has had regular and frequent oil and filter changes, as well as other required maintenance, should give many thousands of miles of reliable service. Conversely, a neglected engine may require an overhaul very early in its life.

3 Excessive oil consumption is an indication that piston rings, valve seals and/or valve guides are in need of attention. Make sure that oil leaks are not responsible before deciding that the rings and/or guides are worn. Perform a compression test, as described in Part A (petrol engines) or B (diesel engines) of this Chapter, to determine the likely cause of the problem.

4 Check the oil pressure with a gauge fitted in place of the oil pressure switch, and compare it with that specified. If it is extremely low, the main and big-end bearings, and/or the oil pump, are probably worn out.

5 Loss of power, rough running, knocking or metallic engine noises, excessive valve gear noise, and high fuel consumption may also point to the need for an overhaul, especially if they are all present at the same time. If a complete service does not remedy the situation, major mechanical work is the only solution.

6 An engine overhaul involves restoring all internal parts to the specification of a new engine. During an overhaul, the cylinder liners (where applicable), the pistons and the piston rings are renewed. New main and big-end bearings are generally fitted; if necessary, the crankshaft may be reground, to restore the journals. The valves are also serviced as well, since they are usually in less-than-perfect condition at this point. While the engine is being overhauled, other components, such as the starter and alternator, can be overhauled as well. The end result should be an as-new engine that will give many trouble-free miles.
Note: *Critical cooling system components such as the hoses, thermostat and water pump should be renewed when an engine is overhauled. The radiator should be checked carefully, to ensure that it is not clogged or leaking. Also, it is a good idea to renew the oil pump whenever the engine is overhauled.*

7 Before beginning the engine overhaul, read through the entire procedure, to familiarise yourself with the scope and requirements of the job. Overhauling an engine is not difficult if you carefully follow all of the instructions, have the necessary tools and equipment, and pay close attention to all specifications. It can, however, be time-consuming.

8 Plan on the car being off the road for a minimum of two weeks, especially if parts must be taken to an engineering works for repair or reconditioning. Check on the availability of parts and make sure that any necessary special tools and equipment are obtained in advance. Most work can be done with typical hand tools, although a number of precision measuring tools are required for inspecting parts to determine if they must be renewed. Often the engineering works will handle the inspection of parts and offer advice concerning reconditioning and renewal.
Note: *Always wait until the engine has been completely dismantled, and until all components (especially the cylinder block/crankcase and the crankshaft) have been inspected, before deciding what service and repair operations must be performed by an engineering works. The condition of these components will be the major factor to consider when determining whether to overhaul the original engine, or to buy a reconditioned unit. Do not, therefore, purchase parts or have overhaul work done on other components until they have been thoroughly inspected.*

9 As a general rule, time is the primary cost of an overhaul, so it does not pay to fit worn or sub-standard parts.

10 As a final note, to ensure maximum life and minimum trouble from a reconditioned engine, everything must be assembled with care, in a spotlessly-clean environment.

3 Engine/transmission removal – methods and precautions

1 If you have decided that the engine must be removed for overhaul or major repair work, several preliminary steps should be taken.

2 Locating a suitable place to work is extremely important. Adequate work space, along with storage space for the car, will be needed. If a workshop or garage is not available, at the very least, a flat, level, clean work surface is required.

3 Cleaning the engine compartment and engine/transmission before beginning the removal procedure will help keep tools clean and organised.

4 An engine hoist or A-frame will also be necessary. Make sure the equipment is rated in excess of the combined weight of the engine and transmission. Safety is of primary importance, considering the potential hazards involved in lifting the engine/transmission out of the car.

5 If this is the first time you have removed an engine, an assistant should ideally be available. Advice and aid from someone more experienced would also be helpful. There are many instances when one person cannot simultaneously perform all of the operations required when lifting the engine out of the vehicle.

6 Plan the operation ahead of time. Before starting work, arrange for the hire of or obtain all of the tools and equipment you will need. Some of the equipment necessary to perform engine/transmission removal and installation safely and with relative ease (in addition to an engine hoist) is as follows: a heavy duty trolley jack, complete sets of spanners and sockets as described in the rear of this manual, wooden blocks, and plenty of rags and cleaning solvent for mopping up spilled oil, coolant and fuel. If the hoist must be hired, make sure that you arrange for it in advance, and perform all of the operations possible without it beforehand. This will save you money and time.

7 Plan for the car to be out of use for quite a while. An engineering works will be required to perform some of the work which the do-it-yourselfer cannot accomplish without special equipment. These places often have a busy schedule, so it would be a good idea to consult them before removing the engine, in order to accurately estimate the amount of time required to rebuild or repair components that may need work.

8 Always be extremely careful when removing and refitting the engine/transmission. Serious injury can result from careless actions. Plan ahead and take your time, and a job of this nature, although major, can be accomplished successfully.

4 Petrol engine and transmission – removal, separation and refitting

Removal

Note: *The engine can be removed from the car only as a complete unit with the transmission; the two are then separated for overhaul.*

1 Park the vehicle on firm, level ground. Chock the rear wheels, then firmly apply the handbrake. Jack up the front of the vehicle, and securely support it on axle stands (see *Jacking and vehicle support*). Remove both front roadwheels.

2 Remove the battery, battery tray and mounting plate as described in Chapter 5A.

3 Remove the complete air cleaner housing and duct assembly, as described in Chapter 4A.

4 If the engine is to be dismantled, working as described in Chapter 1A, first drain the oil and remove the oil filter. Clean and refit the drain plug, tightening it securely.

5 Remove the auxiliary drivebelt as described in Chapter 1A.

6 Remove the radiator and coolant expansion tank as described in Chapter 3.

4.7a Unscrew the power steering pipe clip screws and the pump mounting bolts . . .

4.7b . . . then free the pump from its mounting bracket and position it clear of the engine

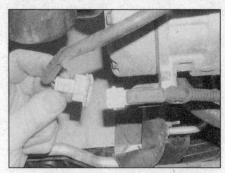

4.8a Disconnect the wiring connector . . .

7 On models with power steering, referring to Chapter 10, unbolt the power steering pump from its mounting bracket. Undo the power steering pipe retaining clip screws then position the pump clear of the engine **(see illustrations)**. Support the weight of the pump by tying it to the vehicle body to prevent any excess strain being placed on the hydraulic pipes/hoses. **Note:** *There is no need to disconnect the pipe/hose from the pump.*

8 On models with air conditioning, disconnect the compressor wiring connector then unscrew the compressor mounting bolts and nuts **(see illustrations)**. Free the compressor from the engine and support its weight by tying it to the vehicle, to prevent any excess strain being placed on the compressor lines. Take care not to lose the spacers from the compressor rear mountings (where fitted).

Caution: Do not disconnect the refrigerant lines from the compressor (refer to the warnings given in Chapter 3). Ensure the compressor is securely supported to prevent the refrigerant lines being damaged.

9 Remove the alternator as described in Chapter 5A.

10 Working as described in Chapter 4A, carry out the following operations.

a) *Depressurise the fuel system and disconnect the fuel hose from the fuel rail.*

b) *Disconnect the accelerator cable.*

c) *Disconnect the purge valve and braking system servo vacuum hoses from the inlet manifold.*

d) *Remove the exhaust system front pipe.*

11 Unclip the wiring harness then slacken and remove the ECU mounting plate nut (the

plate is secured in position with an anti-tamper nut, unscrew the nut using a pair of grips). Free the mounting plate from the body then disconnect the wiring connectors from the ECU and relay. Rotate the locking ring anti-clockwise and disconnect the engine harness connector then unscrew the locking nut and free the harness from the bracket. Remove the bracket assembly and secure the harness to the engine unit **(see illustrations)**.

12 Release the retaining clips and disconnect the heater matrix hoses from their connection on the engine compartment bulkhead **(see illustrations)**.

13 On manual transmission models, carry out the following operations using the information in Chapters 6 and 7A.

a) *Disconnect the clutch cable from the transmission.*

2C

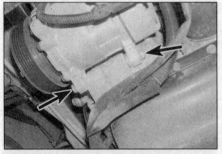

4.8b . . . unscrew the mounting bolts and nuts (lower fixings arrowed) and free the air conditioning compressor from the engine

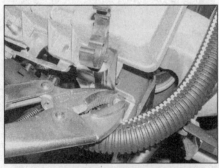

4.11a Unscrew the mounting nut and remove the bracket . . .

4.11b . . . then free the ECU mounting plate from the body and disconnect the engine harness connector

4.11c Disconnect the ECU wiring connector . . .

4.11d . . . and the relay wiring connector then unscrew the locking nut (arrowed) and free the harness from the mounting plate

4.12a Release the retaining clips . . .

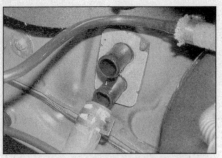

4.12b . . . and disconnect the coolant hoses from the heater matrix unions on the bulkhead

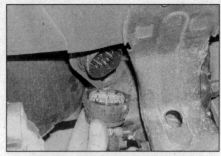

4.16 Rotate the locking ring anti-clockwise and disconnect the engine wiring harness connector

4.17a Unscrew the nuts (arrowed) . . .

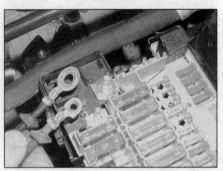

4.17b . . . and disconnect the engine wiring harness leads from the fuse/relay box

4.19a Unscrew the nuts and bolts . . .

4.19b . . . and remove the rear mounting link

b) Drain the transmission oil or be prepared for some spillage as the engine/transmission unit is removed.
c) Disconnect the gearchange mechanism link rods from the transmission.
d) Unbolt the body earth lead from the transmission.

14 On automatic transmission models, carry out the following operations using the information in Chapter 7B.

a) Disconnect the selector cable from the transmission.
b) Drain the transmission fluid or be prepared for some fluid spillage as the engine/transmission unit is removed.
c) Disconnect the main transmission wiring

connector and unbolt the earth lead(s) from the transmission.

15 Remove both driveshafts as described in Chapter 8.

16 Trace the wiring harness back from the engine to the wiring connector in the front, left-hand corner of the engine compartment. Rotate the locking ring anti-clockwise and disconnect the connector (see illustration).

17 Remove the fuse/relay box lid then undo the nuts and disconnect the engine wiring harness leads from the terminals (see illustrations). Release the wiring harness from its clips so that it is free to be removed with the engine/transmission.

18 Manoeuvre the engine hoist into position,

and attach it to the lifting brackets bolted onto the cylinder head. Raise the hoist until it is supporting the weight of the engine.

19 From underneath the vehicle, slacken and remove the nuts and bolts securing the rear mounting link to the mounting assembly and subframe, and remove the link (see illustrations).

20 Slacken and remove the centre nut and washer from the engine/transmission left-hand mounting. Undo the two bolts securing the mounting to its bracket, and remove the mounting from the engine compartment. Undo the retaining bolts and remove the mounting bracket from the body (see illustrations).

4.20a Unscrew the centre nut (1) and bolts (2) . . .

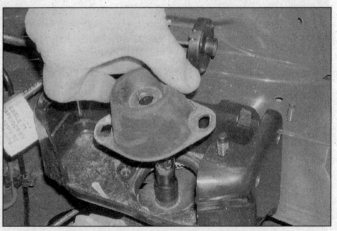

4.20b . . . and remove the rubber mounting from the left-hand mounting

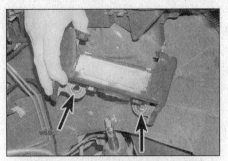

4.20c Unscrew the mounting bolts (locations arrowed) and remove the left-hand mounting bracket from the body

21 Working on the right-hand engine/transmission mounting, slacken and remove the mounting nut/bolts and remove the support bracket securing the mounting to the front of the engine unit (see illustration).
22 Unscrew the vibration damper (where fitted) from the top of the right-hand mounting rubber. Slacken and remove the nut and washer securing the mounting bracket to the mounting rubber and the three nuts securing the right-hand engine mounting bracket to the bracket/housing on the rear of the cylinder block. Unclip the wiring harness then lift off the bracket (see illustrations).
23 Make a final check that any components

which would prevent the removal of the engine/transmission from the car have been removed or disconnected. Ensure that components such as the gearchange selector link rods are secured so that they cannot be damaged on removal.
24 Lift the engine/transmission out of the car, ensuring that nothing is trapped or damaged (see illustration). Enlist the help of an assistant during this procedure, as it will be necessary to tilt the assembly slightly to clear the body panels
Caution: On models equipped with air conditioning, care must be taken to ensure the auxiliary drivebelt pulleys do not damage the air conditioning pipes on the right-hand side of the engine compartment. As a precaution, cover the condenser with a stout piece of cardboard to ensure it is not damaged.
25 Once the engine is high enough, lift it out over the front of the body, and lower the unit to the ground.

Separation

Engine and manual transmission unit

26 With the engine/transmission assembly removed, support the assembly on suitable blocks of wood, on a workbench (or failing that, on a clean area of the workshop floor).

27 Undo the retaining bolts and remove the lower cover plate (where fitted) from the transmission.
28 Slacken and remove the retaining bolts and remove the starter motor from the transmission, taking care not to lose the locating dowel (see illustration).
29 Ensure that both engine and transmission are adequately supported, then slacken and remove the remaining bolts securing the transmission housing to the engine. Note the correct fitted positions of each bolt (and the relevant brackets) as they are removed, to use as a reference on refitting.
30 Carefully withdraw the transmission from the engine, ensuring that the weight of the transmission is not allowed to hang on the input shaft while it is engaged with the clutch friction disc.
31 If they are loose, remove the locating dowels from the engine or transmission, and keep them in a safe place.

Engine and automatic transmission unit

Note: *New torque converter nuts will be required on refitting.*

32 With the engine/transmission assembly removed, support the assembly on suitable blocks of wood, on a workbench (or failing that, on a clean area of the workshop floor).

4.21 Unscrew the nut and bolts and remove the support bracket from the right-hand mounting

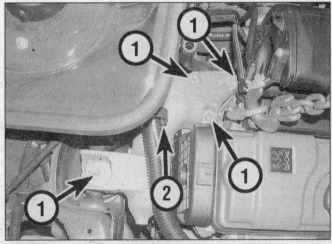

4.22a Unscrew the nuts (1) and unclip the wiring harness (2) . . .

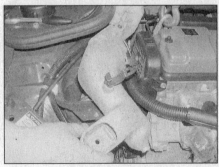

4.22b . . . then lift off the right-hand engine mounting bracket

4.24 Lifting the engine/transmission unit out of position

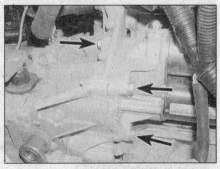

4.28 Unscrew the mounting bolts (arrowed) and remove the starter motor

33 Undo the retaining bolts, and remove the lower cover plate (where fitted) from the transmission.

34 Slacken and remove the retaining bolts and remove the starter motor from the transmission, taking care not to lose the locating dowel **(see illustration 4.28)**.

35 Access to the torque converter retaining nuts is gained via the starter motor aperture. Use a socket and extension bar to rotate the crankshaft pulley to align the first nut with the aperture **(see illustration)**. Unscrew the nut then rotate the crankshaft 120°. Remove the second nut then rotate the crankshaft another 120° Unscrew the third and final nut and discard all three nuts; new ones must be used on refitting.

36 To ensure that the torque converter does not fall out as the transmission is removed, secure it in position using a length of metal strip bolted to one of the starter motor bolt holes.

37 Ensure that both engine and transmission are adequately supported, then slacken and remove the remaining bolts securing the transmission housing to the engine. Note the correct fitted positions of each bolt (and the relevant brackets) as they are removed, to use as a reference on refitting.

38 Carefully withdraw the transmission from the engine, ensuring that the weight of the transmission is not allowed to hang on the torque converter while it is engaged with the driveplate.

39 If they are loose, remove the locating dowels from the engine or transmission, and keep them in a safe place.

Refitting

Engine and manual transmission unit

40 If the engine and transmission have been separated, perform the operations described below in paragraphs 41 to 46. If not, proceed as described from paragraph 47 onwards.

41 Check the clutch release mechanism components are correctly assembled (see Chapter 6)

42 Ensure that the locating dowels are correctly positioned in the engine or transmission.

43 Carefully offer the transmission to the engine, until the locating dowels are engaged. Ensure that the weight of the transmission is not allowed to hang on the input shaft as it is engaged with the clutch friction disc.

44 Refit the transmission housing-to-engine bolts, ensuring that all the necessary brackets are correctly positioned, and tighten them to the specified torque.

45 Ensure the locating dowel is in position then refit the starter motor, tightening its retaining bolts securely.

46 Refit the flywheel cover plate (where fitted) to the transmission, and securely tighten its retaining bolts.

47 Reconnect the hoist and lifting tackle to the engine lifting brackets. With the aid of an assistant, lift the assembly over the engine compartment.

48 The assembly should be tilted as necessary to clear the surrounding components, as during removal; lower the assembly into position in the engine compartment, manipulating the hoist and lifting tackle as necessary.

49 With the engine/transmission in position, refit the right-hand engine/transmission mounting bracket, tightening the nuts by hand only at this stage.

50 Working on the left-hand mounting, refit the mounting bracket to the body and tighten its retaining bolts to the specified torque. Refit the mounting rubber and refit the mounting retaining bolts and washers and the centre nut and washer, tightening them lightly only.

51 From underneath the vehicle, refit the rear mounting link and install both its bolts.

52 Rock the engine to settle it on its mountings. Ensure the left-hand mounting is centralised on its bracket then go around and tighten all the mounting nuts and bolts to their specified torque settings. The hoist can then be detached from the engine and removed.

53 Refit the vibration damper (where fitted) to the right-hand mounting and tighten it to the specified torque.

54 The remainder of the refitting procedure is a direct reversal of the removal sequence, noting the following points:

a) *Ensure that the wiring loom is correctly routed and retained by all the relevant retaining clips; all connectors should be correctly and securely reconnected.*

b) *Ensure all disturbed hoses are correctly and securely reconnected.*

c) *On models with air conditioning, ensure the mounting spacers (where fitted) are correctly fitted to the rear mountings. Tighten the compressor front (drivebelt pulley end) mounting bolts to the specified torque first then tighten the rear bolts (see Chapter 3).*

d) *On models with power steering, ensure the mounting spacer (where fitted) is correctly fitted to the rear mounting. Apply locking compound (Peugeot recommend the use of Loctite Frenetanch) to the pump lower front mounting bolt then install all the bolts; tighten the pump front (drivebelt pulley end) bolts to the specified torque first then tighten the rear bolts (see Chapter 10).*

e) *Tighten all fixings to the specified torque (where given).*

f) *Prior to refitting the driveshafts to the transmission, renew the driveshaft oil seals as described in Chapter 7A.*

g) *Reconnect the clutch cable and gear-change linkage link rods to the transmission and refill/top-up the transmission unit with oil (see Chapters 6 and 7A).*

h) *Adjust the accelerator cable as described in Chapter 4A.*

i) *Refill the cooling system and engine oil as described in Chapter 1A.*

Engine and automatic transmission unit

55 If the engine and transmission have been separated, perform the operations described below in paragraphs 56 to 62. If not, proceed as described from paragraph 63 onwards.

56 Ensure that the bush fitted to the centre of the crankshaft is in good condition, and apply

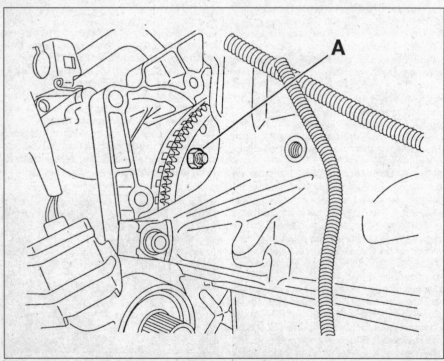

4.35 Working through the starter motor aperture, unscrew the torque converter nuts (1), rotating the crankshaft as necessary

a little Molykote BR2 grease to the torque converter centring pin.

Caution: Do not apply too much, otherwise there is a possibility of the grease contaminating the torque converter.

57 Ensure that the engine/transmission locating dowels are correctly positioned.

58 Carefully offer up transmission, aligning the torque converter studs with the driveplate holes, then engage the transmission unit with the engine.

Caution: Do not allow the weight of the transmission unit to hang on the torque converter as the unit is installed.

59 With the transmission and engine correctly joined, refit the transmission-to-engine unit bolts, ensuring that all the necessary brackets are correctly positioned, and tighten them to the specified torque.

60 Screw the new nuts onto the torque converter studs, tightening them lightly only, rotating the crankshaft as necessary. Tighten all three nuts to the specified stage 1 torque setting. Once all have been tightened to the stage 1 torque, go around and tighten them to the specified stage 2 torque setting.

61 Ensure the locating dowel is in position then refit the starter motor, tightening its retaining bolts securely.

62 Refit the cover plate (where fitted) to the transmission, and securely tighten its retaining bolts.

63 Install the engine/transmission unit as described in paragraphs 47 to 53.

64 The remainder of the refitting procedure is a direct reversal of the removal sequence, noting the following points:

a) *Ensure that the wiring loom is correctly routed and retained by all the relevant retaining clips; all connectors should be correctly and securely reconnected.*

b) *Ensure all disturbed hoses are correctly and securely reconnected.*

c) *On models with air conditioning, ensure the mounting spacers (where fitted) are correctly fitted to the rear mountings. Tighten the compressor front (drivebelt pulley end) mounting bolts to the specified torque first then tighten the rear bolts (see Chapter 3).*

d) *On models with power steering, ensure the mounting spacer (where fitted) is correctly fitted to the rear mounting. Apply locking compound (Peugeot recommend the use of Loctite Frenetanch) to the pump lower front mounting bolt then install all the bolts; tighten the pump front (drivebelt pulley end) bolts to the specified torque first then tighten the rear bolts (see Chapter 10).*

e) *Tighten all fixings to the specified torque (where given).*

f) *Prior to refitting the driveshafts to the transmission, renew the driveshaft oil seals as described in Chapter 7B.*

g) *Reconnect and adjust the selector cable refill/top-up the transmission unit with oil as described in Chapter 7B.*

h) *Adjust the accelerator cable as described in Chapter 4A.*

i) *Refill the cooling system and engine oil as described in Chapter 1A.*

5 Diesel engine and transmission – removal, separation and refitting

Removal

Note: *The engine can be removed from the car only as a complete unit with the transmission; the two are then separated for overhaul.*

1 Park the vehicle on firm, level ground. Chock the rear wheels, then firmly apply the handbrake. Jack up the front of the vehicle, and securely support it on axle stands (see *Jacking and vehicle support*). Remove both front roadwheels.

2 Where necessary, remove the retaining bolts, screws and clips and remove the undercover (where fitted) from beneath the engine/transmission unit. Also unbolt the plastic covers (where fitted) from the left- and right-hand wing valances.

3 Remove the battery, battery tray and mounting plate as described in Chapter 5A.

4 Remove the air cleaner housing and duct assembly, as described in the Chapter 4B.

5 If the engine is to be dismantled, working as described in Chapter 1B, first drain the oil and remove the oil filter. Clean and refit the drain plug, tightening it securely.

6 Remove the auxiliary drivebelt as described in Chapter 1B.

7 Remove the radiator, coolant expansion tank and the cooling fan and front panel assembly as described in Chapter 3.

8 On models with power steering, referring to Chapter 10, unbolt the power steering pump from its mounting bracket. Undo the power steering pipe retaining clip screws then position the pump clear of the engine **(see illustrations 4.7a and 4.7b).** Support the weight of the pump by tying it to the vehicle body to prevent any excess strain being placed on the hydraulic pipes/hoses. **Note:** *There is no need to disconnect the pipe/hose from the pump.*

9 On models with air conditioning, disconnect the compressor wiring connector then unscrew the compressor mounting bolts and nuts. Free the compressor from the engine and support its weight by tying it to the vehicle, to prevent any excess strain being placed on the compressor lines. Take care not to lose the spacers from the compressor rear mountings (where fitted).

Caution: Do not disconnect the refrigerant lines from the compressor (refer to the warnings given in Chapter 3). Ensure the compressor is securely supported to prevent the refrigerant lines being damaged.

10 Remove the alternator as described in Chapter 5A.

11 Remove the crankshaft pulley from the engine as described in Chapter 2B.

12 On models with a manually-adjusted auxiliary drivebelt tensioner, unscrew the tensioner mounting bolts and remove the tensioner assembly from the engine bracket.

13 On models with a spring-loaded auxiliary drivebelt tensioner, unscrew the bolt(s) and remove the adjustment pulley and (where fitted) idler pulley from the engine bracket.

14 On 1.9 litre (WJY) engines and all 2.0 litre engines, unclip the wiring harness then slacken and remove the ECU mounting plate nut (the plate is secured in position with an anti-tamper nut, unscrew the nut using a pair of grips). Free the mounting plate from the body then disconnect the wiring connectors from the ECU and relay. Rotate the locking ring anti-clockwise and disconnect the engine harness connector then unscrew the locking nut and free the harness from the bracket. Remove the bracket assembly and secure the harness to the engine unit.

15 Working as described in Chapter 4B and 4C; carry out the following operations.

a) *Remove the exhaust front pipe.*

b) *Disconnect the fuel feed and return pipes at the unions on the top of the engine. Plug the hose/pipe ends and unions to prevent the entry of dirt into the fuel system and free the pipes from the timing belt covers*

c) *On 1.9 litre engines disconnect the accelerator cable from the injection pump.*

d) *On 2.0 litre engines, remove the EGR solenoid valves from the bulkhead (mark the hoses to avoid confusion on refitting).*

e) *On 1.9 litre (WJZ) engines remove the EGR system ECU.*

16 Release the retaining clips and disconnect the heater matrix hoses from their connections on the bulkhead **(see illustrations 4.12a and 4.12b).**

17 On 2.0 litre engines, remove the rubber insulation covers from the terminals on the top of the coolant heater, located on the top of the transmission unit. Unscrew the nuts and disconnect the wiring from the heater.

18 On all engines, disconnect the braking system servo vacuum hose from the vacuum pump on the left-hand end of the cylinder head **(see illustration).**

5.18 Disconnect the servo unit vacuum hose from the vacuum pump

2C

5.32 Remove the starter motor taking care not to lose the locating dowel (arrowed)

19 Carry out the following operations using the information in Chapters 6 and 7A.

a) On right-hand drive models, unbolt the clutch slave cylinder from the transmission then free the hydraulic pipe/hose from its retaining clips and position it clear of the transmission.

b) On left-hand drive models, disconnect the clutch cable from the transmission.

c) Drain the transmission oil or be prepared for some spillage as the engine/transmission unit is removed.

d) Disconnect the gearchange mechanism link rods from the transmission.

e) Disconnect the wiring connectors from the reversing light switch and speedometer drive and unbolt the earth lead(s) from the transmission.

20 Remove both driveshafts as described in Chapter 8.

21 Trace the wiring harness back from the engine to the wiring connector in the front, left-hand corner of the engine compartment. Rotate the locking ring anti-clockwise and disconnect the connector **(see illustration 4.16)**. Remove the fuse/relay box lid then undo the nuts and disconnect the engine wiring harness leads from the terminals **(see illustrations 4.17a and 4.17b)**. Release the wiring harness from its clips so that it is free to be removed with the engine/transmission.

22 Manoeuvre the engine hoist into position, and attach it to the lifting brackets bolted onto the cylinder head. Raise the hoist until it is supporting the weight of the engine.

23 Slacken and remove the centre nut and washer from the engine/transmission left-hand mounting. Undo the two bolts securing the mounting to its bracket, and remove the mounting from the engine compartment. Undo the retaining bolts and remove the mounting bracket from the body **(see illustrations 4.20a to 4.20c)**.

24 From underneath the vehicle, slacken and remove the nuts and bolts securing the rear mounting link to the mounting assembly and subframe, and remove the link **(see illustrations 4.19a and 4.19b)**.

25 Slacken and remove the mounting bolts and remove the bracket from the top of the right-hand mounting. Unscrew the vibration damper (where fitted) from the top of the mounting rubber then slacken and remove the

nut securing the mounting bracket to the mounting rubber.

26 Slacken and remove the three bolts securing the right-hand engine mounting bracket to the bracket on the side of the cylinder block then lift off the bracket, taking care not to lose the locating dowels (where fitted).

27 Make a final check that any components which would prevent the removal of the engine/transmission from the car have been removed or disconnected. Ensure that components such as the gearchange selector link rods are secured so that they cannot be damaged on removal.

28 Lift the engine/transmission out of the car, ensuring that nothing is trapped or damaged. Enlist the help of an assistant during this procedure, as it will be necessary to tilt the assembly slightly to clear the body panels **Caution: On models equipped with air conditioning, care must be taken to ensure air conditioning system condenser is not damaged.**

29 Once the engine is high enough, lift it out over the front of the body, and lower the unit to the ground.

Separation

30 With the engine/transmission assembly removed, support the assembly on suitable blocks of wood, on a workbench (or failing that, on a clean area of the workshop floor).

31 Undo the retaining bolts and remove the lower cover plate from the transmission.

32 Slacken and remove the retaining bolts and remove the starter motor from the transmission, taking care not to lose the locating dowel **(see illustration)**.

33 Ensure that both engine and transmission are adequately supported, then slacken and remove the remaining bolts securing the transmission housing to the engine. Note the correct fitted positions of each bolt (and the relevant brackets) as they are removed, to use as a reference on refitting.

34 Carefully withdraw the transmission from the engine, ensuring that the weight of the transmission is not allowed to hang on the input shaft while it is engaged with the clutch friction disc.

35 If they are loose, remove the locating dowels from the engine or transmission, and keep them in a safe place.

Refitting

36 If the engine and transmission have been separated, perform the operations described below in paragraphs 37 to 42. If not, proceed as described from paragraph 43 onwards.

37 Check the clutch release mechanism components are correctly assembled (see Chapter 6)

38 Ensure that the locating dowels are correctly positioned in the engine or transmission.

39 Carefully offer the transmission to the engine, until the locating dowels are engaged.

Ensure that the weight of the transmission is not allowed to hang on the input shaft as it is engaged with the clutch friction disc.

40 Refit the transmission housing-to-engine bolts, ensuring that all the necessary brackets are correctly positioned, and tighten them to the specified torque.

41 Ensure the locating dowels is in position then refit the starter motor, tighten its retaining bolts securely.

42 Refit the flywheel cover plate to the transmission, and securely tighten its retaining bolts.

43 Reconnect the hoist and lifting tackle to the engine lifting brackets. With the aid of an assistant, lift the assembly over the engine compartment.

44 The assembly should be tilted as necessary to clear the surrounding components, as during removal; lower the assembly into position in the engine compartment, manipulating the hoist and lifting tackle as necessary.

45 With the engine/transmission in position, refit the right-hand engine/transmission mounting bracket, ensuring the locating dowels are in position. Refit the bracket bolts and nut, tightening them lightly only.

46 Working on the left-hand mounting, refit the mounting bracket to the body and tighten its retaining bolts to the specified torque. Refit the mounting rubber and refit the mounting retaining bolts and washers and the centre nut and washer, tightening them lightly only.

47 From underneath the vehicle, refit the rear mounting link and install both its bolts.

48 Rock the engine to settle it on its mountings. Ensure the left-hand mounting is centralised on its bracket then go around and tighten all the mounting nuts and bolts to their specified torque settings. The hoist can then be detached from the engine and removed.

49 Refit the vibration damper to the right-hand mounting and tighten it to the specified torque. Fit the bracket over the vibration damper, tightening its bolts to the specified torque.

50 The remainder of the refitting procedure is a direct reversal of the removal sequence, noting the following points:

a) Ensure that the wiring loom is correctly routed and retained by all the relevant retaining clips; all connectors should be correctly and securely reconnected.

b) Ensure all disturbed hoses are correctly and securely reconnected.

c) On models with air conditioning, ensure the mounting spacers are correctly fitted to the rear mountings (where fitted). Tighten the compressor front (drivebelt pulley end) mounting bolts to the specified torque first then tighten the rear bolts (see Chapter 3).

d) On models with power steering, ensure the mounting spacer (where fitted) is correctly fitted to the rear mounting. Apply locking compound (Peugeot recommend the use of Loctite Frenetanch) to the pump lower front mounting bolt then install all the bolts; tighten the pump front (drivebelt pulley end) bolts to the specified torque first then tighten the rear bolts (see Chapter 10).

e) Tighten all fixings to the specified torque (where given).

f) Prior to refitting the driveshafts to the transmission, renew the driveshaft oil seals as described in Chapter 7A.

g) Reconnect the clutch cable/slave cylinder (as applicable) and gearchange linkage link rods to the transmission and refill/top-up the transmission unit with oil (see Chapters 6 and 7A).

h) Adjust the accelerator cable as described in Chapter 4B.

i) Refill the cooling system and engine oil as described in Chapter 1B.

6 Engine overhaul – dismantling sequence

1 It is much easier to dismantle and work on the engine if it is mounted on a portable engine stand. These stands can often be hired from a tool hire shop. Before the engine is mounted on a stand, the flywheel/driveplate should be removed, so that the stand bolts can be tightened into the end of the cylinder block/crankcase.

2 If a stand is not available, it is possible to dismantle the engine with it blocked up on a sturdy workbench, or on the floor. Be extra-careful not to tip or drop the engine when working without a stand.

3 If you are going to obtain a reconditioned engine, all the external components must be removed first, to be transferred to the replacement engine (just as they will if you are doing a complete engine overhaul yourself). These components include the following:

a) Inlet and exhaust manifolds (Chapter 4A or 4B).

b) Injection pump and mounting bracket – diesel engine (Chapter 4B).

c) Alternator/power steering pump/air conditioning compressor brackets (as applicable).

d) Wiring harness, coolant hoses/pipes and all electrical switches and sensors.

e) Oil filter.

f) Flywheel/driveplate (Chapter 2A or 2B).

Note: When removing the external components from the engine, pay close attention to details that may be helpful or important during refitting. Note the fitted position of gaskets, seals, spacers, pins, washers, bolts, and other small items.

4 If you are obtaining a 'short' engine (cylinder block/crankcase, crankshaft, pistons and connecting rods all assembled), then the cylinder head, sump, oil pump, and timing belt will have to be removed also.

5 If you are planning a complete overhaul, the engine can be dismantled, and the internal components removed, in the order given below, referring to Part A or B of this Chapter unless otherwise stated.

a) Inlet and exhaust manifolds (Chapter 4A or 4B).

b) Timing belt, sprockets and tensioner pulley(s).

c) Injection pump and mounting bracket – diesel engine (Chapter 4B).

d) Cylinder head.

e) Flywheel/driveplate.

f) Sump.

g) Oil pump.

h) Pistons/connecting rods (Section 10).

i) Crankshaft (Section 11).

6 Before beginning the dismantling and overhaul procedures, make sure that you have all of the tools necessary. Refer to *Tools and working facilities* for further information.

7 Cylinder head – dismantling

Note: New and reconditioned cylinder heads are available from the manufacturer, and from engine overhaul specialists. Some specialist tools are required for dismantling and inspection, and new components may not be readily available. It may therefore be more practical and economical for the home mechanic to purchase a reconditioned head, rather than dismantle, inspect and recondition the original head.

1 Remove the cylinder head as described in Part A or B of this Chapter (as applicable).

2 On petrol engines, remove the following from the cylinder head.

a) Inlet and exhaust manifolds (Chapter 4A)

b) Spark plugs.

c) Camshaft (Chapter 2A).

3 On diesel engines, remove the following from the cylinder head.

a) Inlet and exhaust manifolds (Chapter 4B).

b) Injectors (Chapter 4B).

c) Glow plugs (Chapter 5C)

d) Camshaft, followers and shims/tappets (Chapter 2B).

4 On all engines, using a valve spring compressor, compress each valve spring in turn until the split collets can be removed.

7.4a Compress the valve spring with a spring compressor until the collets are released from the retainer

7.4b Pull the oil seal off the top of the valve guide and discard it

components removed, in the order given below, referring to Part A or B of this Chapter unless otherwise stated.

Release the compressor, and lift off the spring retainer, spring. On 1.9 litre diesel engines remove the spring cup and thrust washer from the cylinder head, on all other engines remove the spring seat. Using a pair of pliers, carefully extract the valve stem oil seal from the top of the guide **(see illustrations)**.

5 If, when the valve spring compressor is screwed down, the spring retainer refuses to free and expose the split collets, gently tap the top of the tool, directly over the retainer, with a light hammer. This will free the retainer.

6 Withdraw the valve through the combustion chamber.

7 It is essential that each valve is stored together with its collets, retainer, spring, and spring cup/thrust washer/spring seat. The valves should also be kept in their correct sequence, unless they are so badly worn that they are to be renewed. If they are going to be kept and used again, place each valve assembly in a labelled polythene bag or similar small container **(see illustration)**. Note that No 1 valve is nearest to the transmission (flywheel/driveplate) end of the engine.

8 Cylinder head and valves – cleaning and inspection

1 Thorough cleaning of the cylinder head and valve components, followed by a detailed inspection, will enable you to decide how much valve service work must be carried out during the engine overhaul. **Note:** If the

7.7 Place each valve and its associated components in a labelled polythene bag

2C

8.6 Checking the cylinder head gasket surface for distortion

8.11 Checking a swirl chamber protrusion – 1.9 litre diesel engine

8.13 Measuring a valve stem diameter

engine has been severely overheated, it is best to assume that the cylinder head is warped – check carefully for signs of this.

Cleaning

2 Scrape away all traces of old gasket material from the cylinder head.

3 Scrape away the carbon from the combustion chambers and ports, then wash the cylinder head thoroughly with paraffin or a suitable solvent.

4 Scrape off any heavy carbon deposits that may have formed on the valves, then use a power-operated wire brush to remove deposits from the valve heads and stems.

Inspection

Note: *Be sure to perform all the following inspection procedures before concluding that the services of a machine shop or engine overhaul specialist are required. Make a list of all items that require attention.*

Cylinder head

5 Inspect the head very carefully for cracks, evidence of coolant leakage, and other damage. If cracks are found, a new cylinder head should be obtained.

6 Use a straight-edge and feeler blade to check that the cylinder head gasket surface is not distorted **(see illustration)**. If it is, it may be possible to have it machined, provided that the cylinder head is not reduced to less than the specified height. **Note:** *On diesel engines, it may be necessary to re-cut the valve seats if the cylinder head is machined. This is necessary in order to maintain the correct dimensions between the valve heads and cylinder head gasket face (see paragraph 10). On 1.9 litre engines it may also be necessary to re-cut the swirl chamber seats to ensure the swirl chamber protrusion remains within the specified limits (see paragraph 11).*

7 Examine the valve seats in each of the combustion chambers. If they are severely pitted, cracked, or burned, they will need to be renewed or re-cut by an engine overhaul specialist. If they are only slightly pitted, this can be removed by grinding-in the valve heads and seats with fine valve-grinding compound, as described below.

8 Check the valve guides for wear by inserting the relevant valve, and checking for

side-to-side motion of the valve. A very small amount of movement is acceptable. If the movement seems excessive, remove the valve. Measure the valve stem diameter (see below), and renew the valve if it is worn. If the valve stem is not worn, the wear must be in the valve guide, and the guide must be renewed. The renewal of valve guides is best carried out by a Peugeot dealer or engine overhaul specialist, who will have the necessary tools available. Where no valve stem diameter is specified, seek the advice of a Peugeot dealer on the best course of action.

9 If renewing the valve guides, the valve seats should be re-cut or re-ground only *after* the guides have been fitted.

10 On diesel engines, insert all the valves in their original locations. Using a dial test indicator, check that the valve head-to-cylinder head measurement of each valve is within the limits given in the Specifications. Zero the dial test indicator on the gasket surface of the cylinder head, then measure the recess/protrusion of each valve. If any valve is not within the specified limits, the valve seat will have to be renewed (where possible) or re-cut.

11 On 1.9 litre diesel engines, inspect the swirl chambers for burning or damage such as cracking. Small cracks in the chambers are acceptable; renewal of the chambers will only be required if chamber tracts are badly burned and disfigured, or if they are no longer a tight fit in the cylinder head. If there is any doubt as to the swirl chamber condition, seek the advice of a Peugeot dealer or a suitable repairer who specialises in diesel engines. Swirl chamber renewal should be entrusted to a specialist. Using a dial test indicator, check that the swirl chamber protrusion is within the limits given in the Specifications **(see illustration)**. Zero the dial test indicator on the gasket surface of the cylinder head, then measure the protrusion of the swirl chamber. If the protrusion is not within the specified limits, the advice of a Peugeot dealer or suitable repairer who specialises in diesel engines should be sought.

Valves

12 Examine the head of each valve for pitting, burning, cracks, and general wear.

Check the valve stem for scoring and wear ridges. Rotate the valve, and check for any obvious indication that it is bent. Look for pits or excessive wear on the tip of each valve stem. Renew any valve that shows any such signs of wear or damage.

13 If the valve appears satisfactory at this stage, measure the valve stem diameter at several points using a micrometer **(see illustration)**. Any significant difference in the readings obtained indicates wear of the valve stem. Should any of these conditions be apparent, the valve(s) must be renewed.

14 If the valves are in satisfactory condition, they should be ground (lapped) into their respective seats, to ensure a smooth, gas-tight seal. If the seat is only lightly pitted, or if it has been re-cut, fine grinding compound *only* should be used to produce the required finish. Coarse valve-grinding compound should *not* be used, unless a seat is badly burned or deeply pitted. If this is the case, the cylinder head and valves should be inspected by an expert, to decide whether seat re-cutting, or even the renewal of the valve or seat insert (where possible) is required.

15 Valve grinding is carried out as follows. Place the head upside-down on a bench.

16 Smear a trace of (the appropriate grade of) valve-grinding compound on the seat face, and press a suction grinding tool onto the valve head **(see illustration)**. With a semi-rotary action, grind the valve head to its seat, lifting the valve occasionally to redistribute the grinding compound. A light spring placed under the valve head will greatly ease this operation.

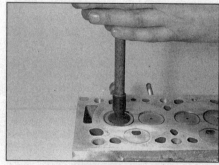

8.16 Grinding-in a valve

9.1 Lubricate the valve stem with clean engine oil and insert the valve into its guide

9.3 Press the new oil seal squarely onto the valve guide with a socket

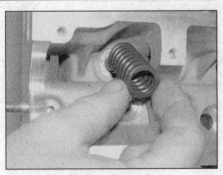

9.4a Fit the valve spring . . .

17 If coarse grinding compound is being used, work only until a dull, matt even surface is produced on both the valve seat and the valve, then wipe off the used compound, and repeat the process with fine compound. When a smooth unbroken ring of light grey matt finish is produced on both the valve and seat, the grinding operation is complete. *Do not* grind-in the valves any further than absolutely necessary, or the seat will be prematurely sunk into the cylinder head.

18 When all the valves have been ground-in, carefully wash off *all* traces of grinding compound using paraffin or a suitable solvent, before reassembling the cylinder head.

Valve components

19 Examine the valve springs for signs of damage and discoloration. No minimum free length is specified by Peugeot, so the only way of judging valve spring wear is by comparison with a new component.

20 Stand each spring on a flat surface, and check it for squareness. If any of the springs are damaged, distorted or have lost their tension, obtain a complete new set of springs. It is normal to fit new springs as a matter of course if a major overhaul is being carried out.

21 Renew the valve stem oil seals regardless of their apparent condition.

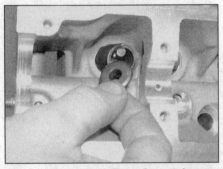

9.4b . . . then locate the spring retainer on the spring upper end

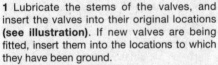

9 Cylinder head – reassembly

1 Lubricate the stems of the valves, and insert the valves into their original locations **(see illustration)**. If new valves are being fitted, insert them into the locations to which they have been ground.

2 On 1.9 litre diesel engines, refit the thrustwasher then install the spring cup, ensuring the flat surface faces downwards. On all other engines refit the spring seat.

3 On all engines, dip the new valve stem seal in fresh engine oil. Carefully locate it over the valve and onto the guide. Take care not to damage the seal as it is passed over the valve stem. Use a suitable socket or tube to press the seal firmly onto the guide **(see illustration)**.

4 Locate the valve spring on top of its seat, then refit the spring retainer **(see illustrations)**.

5 Compress the valve spring, and locate the split collets in the recess in the valve stem **(see illustration)**. Release the compressor, then repeat the procedure on the remaining valves **(see Haynes Hint)**.

6 With all the valves installed, support the cylinder head on blocks of wood and, using a hammer and interposed block of wood, tap the end of each valve stem to settle the components.

7 The cylinder head can then be refitted as described in Part A or B of this Chapter.

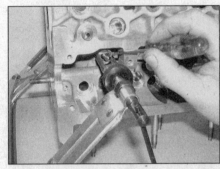

9.5 Compress the valve spring and locate the collets in the recess on the valve stem

10 Piston/connecting rod assembly – removal

1 Remove the cylinder head, sump and oil pump as described in Part A or B of this Chapter (as applicable).

2 If there is a pronounced wear ridge at the top of any bore, it may be necessary to remove it with a scraper or ridge reamer to avoid piston damage during removal. Such a ridge indicates excess bore wear.

3 Using a hammer and centre-punch, paint or similar, mark each connecting rod and big-end bearing cap with its respective cylinder number on the flat machined surface provided; if the engine has been dismantled before, note carefully any identifying marks made previously **(see illustration)**. Note that

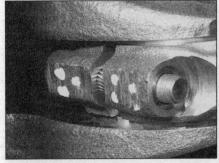

10.3 Make identification marks on the connecting rod and bearing cap to avoid confusion on refitting (No 3 shown)

2C

Use a little dab of grease to hold the collets in position on the valve stem while the spring compressor is released.

No 1 cylinder is at the transmission (flywheel) end of the engine.

4 Turn the crankshaft to bring pistons 1 and 4 to BDC (bottom dead centre).

5 Unscrew the nuts from No 1 piston big-end bearing cap. Take off the cap, and recover the bottom half bearing shell **(see illustration)**. If the bearing shells are to be re-used, tape the cap and the shell together.

6 To prevent the possibility of damage to the crankshaft bearing journals, tape over the connecting rod bolt threads **(see illustration)**.

7 Using a hammer handle, push the piston up through the bore, and remove it from the top of the cylinder block. Recover the bearing shell, and tape it to the connecting rod for safe-keeping.

8 Loosely refit the big-end cap to the connecting rod, and secure with the nuts – this will help to keep the components in their correct order. **Note:** *New big-end cap nuts will be required on refitting.*

9 Remove No 4 assembly in the same way.

10 Turn the crankshaft through 180° to bring pistons 2 and 3 to BDC (bottom dead centre), and remove them in the same way.

11 Crankshaft – removal

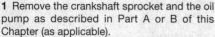

1 Remove the crankshaft sprocket and the oil pump as described in Part A or B of this Chapter (as applicable).

2 Remove the pistons and connecting rods, as described in Section 10. If no work is to be done on the pistons and connecting rods, there is no need to remove the cylinder head, or to push the pistons out of the cylinder bores. The pistons should just be pushed far enough up the bores so that they are positioned clear of the crankshaft journals.

3 Check the crankshaft endfloat as described in Section 14, then proceed as follows.

Aluminium block petrol engine

4 Work around the outside of the cylinder block, and unscrew all the small (M6) bolts securing the main bearing ladder to the base of the cylinder block. Note the correct fitted

10.5 Removing a big-end bearing cap and shell

depth of both the left- and right-hand crankshaft oil seals in the cylinder block/main bearing ladder.

5 Working in a diagonal sequence, evenly and progressively slacken the ten large (M11) main bearing ladder retaining bolts by a turn at a time. Once all the bolts are loose, remove them from the ladder.

6 With all the retaining bolts removed, carefully lift the main bearing ladder casting away from the base of the cylinder block. Recover the lower main bearing shells, and tape them to their respective locations in the casting. If the two locating dowels are a loose fit, remove them and store them with the casting for safe-keeping.

7 Lift out the crankshaft, and discard both the oil seals. Remove the oil pump drive chain from the end of the crankshaft. Where necessary, slide off the drive sprocket, and recover the Woodruff key.

8 Recover the upper main bearing shells, and store them along with the relevant lower bearing shell. Also recover the two thrustwashers (one fitted either side of No 2 main bearing) from the cylinder block.

Cast-iron block petrol engine

9 Unbolt and remove the crankshaft left- and right-hand oil seal housings from each end of the cylinder block, noting the correct fitted locations of the locating dowels. If the locating dowels are a loose fit, remove them and store them with the housings for safe-keeping.

10 Remove the oil pump drive chain, and

10.6 To protect the crankshaft journals, tape over the connecting rod bolt threads

slide the drive sprocket off the end of the crankshaft. Remove the Woodruff key, and store it with the sprocket for safe-keeping.

11 The main bearing caps should be numbered 1 to 5 from the transmission (flywheel/driveplate) end of the engine. If not, mark them accordingly using a centre-punch or paint.

12 Unscrew and remove the main bearing cap retaining bolts, and withdraw the caps. Recover the lower main bearing shells, and tape them to their respective caps for safe-keeping.

13 Carefully lift out the crankshaft, taking care not to displace the upper main bearing shell.

14 Recover the upper bearing shells from the cylinder block, and tape them to their respective caps for safe-keeping. Remove the thrustwasher halves from the side of No 2 main bearing, and store them with the bearing cap.

Diesel engine

15 Slacken and remove the retaining bolts, and remove the oil housing from the right-hand (timing belt) end of the cylinder block **(see illustration)**.

16 Remove the oil pump drive chain, and slide the drive sprocket off from the crankshaft. Remove the Woodruff key, and store it with the sprocket for safe-keeping then remove the sealing ring (where fitted) from the crankshaft **(see illustrations)**.

17 The main bearing caps should be numbered 1 to 5, starting from the trans-

11.15 Removing the oil seal housing – diesel engine

11.16a Slide the oil pump drive sprocket off the crankshaft and remove the Woodruff key . . .

11.16b . . . then remove the sealing ring (where fitted)

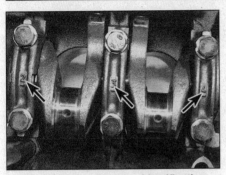

11.17 Main bearing cap identification markings (arrowed)

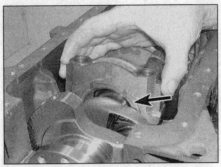

11.18 Removing No 2 main bearing cap and thrustwasher (arrowed)

11.19 Lift out the crankshaft and discard the left-hand end oil seal

mission (flywheel) end of the engine **(see illustration)**. If not, mark them accordingly using a centre-punch. Also note the correct fitted depth of the rear crankshaft oil seal in the bearing cap.

18 Slacken and remove the main bearing cap retaining bolts, and lift off each bearing cap. Recover the lower bearing shells, and tape them to their respective caps for safe-keeping. Also recover the lower thrustwasher halves from the side of No 2 main bearing cap **(see illustration)**. Remove the sealing strips from the sides of No 1 main bearing cap, and discard them.

19 Lift out the crankshaft, and discard the left-hand (flywheel end) oil seal **(see illustration)**.

20 Recover the upper bearing shells from the cylinder block, and tape them to their respective caps for safe-keeping. Remove the upper thrustwasher halves from the side of No 2 main bearing, and store them with the lower halves.

12 Cylinder block/crankcase – cleaning and inspection

Cleaning

1 Remove all external components and electrical switches/sensors from the block. For complete cleaning, the core plugs should ideally be removed **(see illustration)**. Drill a small hole in the plugs, then insert a self-tapping screw into the hole. Pull out the plugs

by pulling on the screw with a pair of grips, or by using a slide hammer.

2 On aluminium block petrol engines with wet liners, remove the liners – see paragraph 18.

3 On 1.6 litre petrol engines and all diesel engines, undo the retaining bolts and remove the piston oil jet spray tubes (there is one for each piston) from inside the cylinder block **(see illustration)**.

4 Scrape all traces of gasket from the cylinder block/crankcase, and from the main bearing ladder/caps (as applicable), taking care not to damage the gasket/sealing surfaces.

5 Remove all oil gallery plugs (where fitted). The plugs are usually very tight – they may have to be drilled out, and the holes re-tapped. Use new plugs when the engine is reassembled.

6 If any of the castings are extremely dirty, all should be steam-cleaned.

7 After the castings are returned, clean all oil holes and oil galleries one more time. Flush all internal passages with warm water until the water runs clear. Dry thoroughly, and apply a light film of oil to all mating surfaces, to prevent rusting. On cast-iron block engines, also oil the cylinder bores. If you have access to compressed air, use it to speed up the drying process, and to blow out all the oil holes and galleries.

⚠ **Warning: Wear eye protection when using compressed air.**

8 If the castings are not very dirty, you can do an adequate cleaning job with hot (as hot as you can stand), soapy water and a stiff brush. Take plenty of time, and do a thorough job.

Regardless of the cleaning method used, be sure to clean all oil holes and galleries very thoroughly, and to dry all components well. On cast-iron block engines, protect the cylinder bores as described above, to prevent rusting.

9 All threaded holes must be clean, to ensure accurate torque readings during reassembly. To clean the threads, run the correct-size tap into each of the holes to remove rust, corrosion, thread sealant or sludge, and to restore damaged threads **(see illustration)**. If possible, use compressed air to clear the holes of debris produced by this operation.

10 Apply suitable sealant to the new oil gallery plugs, and insert them into the holes in the block. Tighten them securely.

11 On 1.6 litre petrol engines and all diesel engines, clean the threads of the piston oil jet retaining bolts, and apply a drop of thread-locking compound (Peugeot recommend Loctite Frenetanch) to each bolt threads. Refit the piston oil jet spray tubes to the cylinder block, and tighten the retaining bolts to the specified torque setting.

12 If the engine is not going to be reassembled right away, cover it with a large plastic bag to keep it clean; protect all mating surfaces and the cylinder bores as described above, to prevent rusting.

Inspection

Cast-iron cylinder block

13 Visually check the castings for cracks and corrosion. Look for stripped threads in the threaded holes. If there has been any history

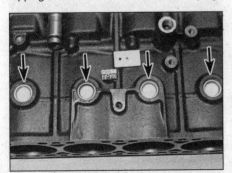

12.1 Cylinder block core plugs (arrowed)

12.3 Unscrew the retaining bolts and remove the piston oil spray tubes from the block

12.9 Clean out cylinder block threads using correct size taps

2C

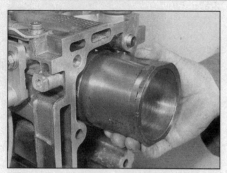

12.18a On aluminium block petrol engines, remove each cylinder liner . . .

12.18b . . . and remove the sealing ring (arrowed) from the liner base

of internal water leakage, it may be worthwhile having an engine overhaul specialist check the cylinder block/crankcase with special equipment. If defects are found, have them repaired if possible, or renew the assembly.

14 Check each cylinder bore for scuffing and scoring. Check for signs of a wear ridge at the top of the cylinder, indicating that the bore is excessively worn.

15 If the necessary measuring equipment is available, measure the bore diameter of each cylinder liner at the top (just under the wear ridge), centre, and bottom of the cylinder bore, parallel to the crankshaft axis.

16 Next, measure the bore diameter at the same three locations, at right-angles to the crankshaft axis. Compare the results with the figures given in the Specifications. Where no figures are stated by Peugeot, or if there is any doubt about the condition of the cylinder bores, seek the advice of a Peugeot dealer or suitable engine reconditioning specialist.

17 At the time of writing, it was not clear whether oversize pistons were available for all models. Consult your Peugeot dealer for the latest information on piston availability. If oversize pistons are available, then it may be possible to have the cylinder bores rebored and fit the oversize pistons. If oversize pistons are not available, and the bores are worn, renewal of the block seems to be the only option.

Aluminium cylinder block

18 Remove the liner clamps (where used), then use a hard wood drift to tap out each liner from the inside of the cylinder block. When all the liners are released, tip the cylinder block/crankcase on its side and remove each liner from the top of the block. As each liner is removed, stick masking tape on its left-hand (transmission side) face, and write the cylinder number on the tape. No 1 cylinder is at the transmission (flywheel/driveplate) end of the engine. Remove the sealing ring from the base of each liner, and discard **(see illustrations)**.

19 Check each cylinder liner for scuffing and scoring. Check for signs of a wear ridge at the top of the liner, indicating that the bore is excessively worn.

20 If the necessary measuring equipment is available, measure the bore diameter of each

cylinder liner at the top (just under the wear ridge), centre, and bottom of the cylinder bore, parallel to the crankshaft axis.

21 Next, measure the bore diameter at the same three locations, at right-angles to the crankshaft axis. Compare the results with the figures given in the Specifications.

22 Repeat the procedure for the remaining cylinder liners.

23 If the liner wear exceeds the permitted tolerances at any point, or if the cylinder liner walls are badly scored or scuffed, then renewal of the relevant liner assembly will be necessary. If there is any doubt about the condition of the cylinder bores, seek the advice of a Peugeot dealer or engine reconditioning specialist.

24 If renewal is necessary, new liners, complete with pistons and piston rings, can be purchased from a Peugeot dealer. Note that it is not possible to buy liners individually – they are supplied only as a matched assembly complete with piston and rings.

25 To allow for manufacturing tolerances, pistons and liners are separated into three size groups. The size group of each piston is indicated by a letter (A, B or C) stamped onto its crown, and the size group of each liner is indicated by a series of 1 to 3 notches and/or an ink mark on the upper lip of the liner; a single notch/A' mark for group A, two notches/B'' mark for group B, and three notches/C''' mark for group C. Ensure that each piston and its respective liner are both of the same size group. It is permissible to have different size group piston and liner assemblies fitted to the same engine, but

13.2 Removing a piston ring with the aid of a feeler blade

never fit a piston of one size group to a liner in a different group.

26 Prior to installing the liners, check the liner protrusion as follows. Thoroughly clean the mating surfaces of the liner and cylinder block. Insert the liners into the block ensuring each one is correctly seated; if the original liners are being refitted, ensure the liners are fitted in their original locations. With all four liners correctly installed, use a dial gauge (or a straight-edge and feeler blade) to check that the protrusion of each liner above the upper surface of the cylinder block is within the limits given in the Specifications. The maximum difference between any two liners must not be exceeded. **Note:** *If new liners are being fitted, it is permissible to interchange them to bring the difference in protrusion within limits. Remember to keep each piston with its respective liner.* If liner protrusion is not within the specified limits, seek the advice of a Peugeot dealer or engine reconditioning specialist before proceeding with the engine rebuild.

27 Once the protrusions have been checked, remove the liners from the block and fit a new sealing ring carefully to the base of each liner. Lubricate the base of each liner with a smear of oil to aid installation.

28 Insert each liner into the cylinder block, taking care not to damage the O-ring, and press it home as far as possible by hand. Using a hammer and a block of wood, tap each liner lightly but fully onto its locating shoulder. If the original liners are being refitted, use the marks made on removal to ensure that each is refitted the correct way round, and is inserted into its original bore.

29 Wipe clean, then lightly oil, all exposed liner surfaces, to prevent rusting. Where necessary, clamp the liners back in position.

13 Piston/connecting rod assembly – inspection

1 Before the inspection process can begin, the piston/connecting rod assemblies must be cleaned, and the original piston rings removed from the pistons.

2 Carefully expand the old rings over the top of the pistons. The use of two or three old feeler blades will be helpful in preventing the rings dropping into empty grooves **(see illustration)**. Be careful not to scratch the piston with the ends of the ring. The rings are brittle, and will snap if they are spread too far. They are also very sharp – protect your hands and fingers. Note that the third ring incorporates an expander. Always remove the rings from the top of the piston. Keep each set of rings with its piston if the old rings are to be re-used.

3 Scrape away all traces of carbon from the top of the piston. A hand-held wire brush (or a piece of fine emery cloth) can be used, once the majority of the deposits have been scraped away.

4 Remove the carbon from the ring grooves in the piston, using an old ring. Break the ring in half to do this (be careful not to cut your fingers – piston rings are sharp). Be careful to remove only the carbon deposits – do not remove any metal, and do not nick or scratch the sides of the ring grooves.

5 Once the deposits have been removed, clean the piston/connecting rod assembly with paraffin or a suitable solvent, and dry thoroughly. Make sure that the oil return holes in the ring grooves are clear.

6 If the pistons and cylinder bores are not damaged or worn excessively, and if the cylinder block does not need to be rebored (where possible), the original pistons can be refitted. Normal piston wear shows up as even vertical wear on the piston thrust surfaces, and slight looseness of the top ring in its groove. New piston rings should always be used when the engine is reassembled.

7 Carefully inspect each piston for cracks around the skirt, around the gudgeon pin holes, and at the piston ring 'lands' (between the ring grooves).

8 Look for scoring and scuffing on the piston skirt, holes in the piston crown, and burned areas at the edge of the crown. If the skirt is scored or scuffed, the engine may have been suffering from overheating, and/or abnormal combustion which caused excessively high operating temperatures. The cooling and lubrication systems should be checked thoroughly. Scorch marks on the sides of the pistons show that blow-by has occurred. A hole in the piston crown, or burned areas at the edge of the piston crown, indicates that abnormal combustion (pre-ignition, knocking, or detonation) has been occurring. If any of the above problems exist, the causes must be investigated and corrected, or the damage will occur again. The causes may include incorrect ignition/injection pump timing, or a faulty injector (as applicable).

9 Corrosion of the piston, in the form of pitting, indicates that coolant has been leaking into the combustion chamber and/or the crankcase. Again, the cause must be corrected, or the problem may persist in the rebuilt engine.

10 On aluminium block engines with wet liners, it is not possible to renew the pistons separately; pistons are only supplied with piston rings and a liner, as a part of a matched assembly (see Section 12). On iron-block engines, pistons can be purchased from a Peugeot dealer.

11 Examine each connecting rod carefully for signs of damage, such as cracks around the big-end and small-end bearings. Check that the rod is not bent or distorted. Damage is highly unlikely, unless the engine has been seized or badly overheated. Detailed checking of the connecting rod assembly can only be carried out by a Peugeot dealer or engine specialist with the necessary equipment.

12 The connecting rod big-end cap nuts must be renewed whenever they are

13.15a On diesel engines, prise out the circlip . . .

disturbed. Although Peugeot do not specify that the bolts must also renewed, it is recommended that the nuts and bolts are replaced as a complete set.

13 On petrol engines, the gudgeon pins are an interference fit in the connecting rod small-end bearing. Therefore, piston and/or connecting rod renewal should be entrusted to a Peugeot dealer or engine repair specialist, who will have the necessary tooling to remove and install the gudgeon pins.

14 On diesel engines, the gudgeon pins are of the floating type, secured in position by two circlips. On these engines, the pistons and connecting rods can be separated as follows.

15 Using a small flat-bladed screwdriver,

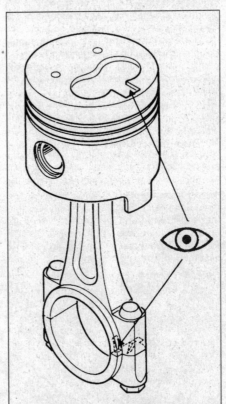
13.19 On 1.9 litre diesel engines ensure the piston cut-out is positioned on the same side as the connecting rod bearing shell locating cut-out

13.15b . . . then withdraw the gudgeon pin and separate the piston and connecting rod

prise out the circlips, and push out the gudgeon pin (see illustrations). Hand pressure should be sufficient to remove the pin. Identify the piston and rod to ensure correct reassembly. Discard the circlips – new ones *must* be used on refitting.

16 Examine the gudgeon pin and connecting rod small-end bearing for signs of wear or damage. Wear can be cured by renewing both the pin and bush (where possible) or connecting rod. Bush renewal, however, is a specialist job – press facilities are required, and the new bush must be reamed accurately.

17 The connecting rods themselves should not be in need of renewal, unless seizure or some other major mechanical failure has occurred. Check the alignment of the connecting rods visually, and if the rods are not straight, take them to an engine overhaul specialist for a more detailed check.

18 Examine all components, and obtain any new parts from your Peugeot dealer. If new pistons are purchased, they will be supplied complete with gudgeon pins and circlips. Circlips can also be purchased individually.

19 On 1.9 litre diesel engines, position the piston so that the cut-out on the piston crown is positioned on the same side as the connecting rod big-end bearing shell cut-out (see illustration).

20 On 2.0 litre diesel engines, position the piston so that the valve recesses on the piston crown are on the opposite side to the connecting rod big-end bearing shell cut-outs (see illustration).

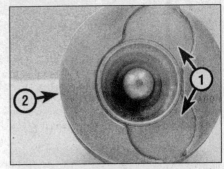
13.20 On 2.0 litre diesel engines position the valve recesses (1) on the piston crown on the opposite side to the connecting rod bearing shell locating cut-out (2 – not visible)

2C

14.2 Checking crankshaft endfloat using a dial gauge

21 Ensure the piston and connecting rod are correctly positioned then apply a smear of clean engine oil to the gudgeon pin. Slide it into the piston and through the connecting rod small-end. Check that the piston pivots freely on the rod, then secure the gudgeon pin in position with two new circlips. Ensure that each circlip is correctly located in its groove in the piston.

14 Crankshaft – inspection

Checking crankshaft endfloat

1 If the crankshaft endfloat is to be checked, this must be done when the crankshaft is still installed in the cylinder block/crankcase, but is free to move (see Section 11).

2 Check the endfloat using a dial gauge in contact with the end of the crankshaft. Push the crankshaft fully one way, and then zero the gauge. Push the crankshaft fully the other way, and check the endfloat. The result can be compared with the specified amount, and will give an indication as to whether new thrustwashers are required (see illustration).

3 If a dial gauge is not available, feeler blades can be used. First push the crankshaft fully

towards the flywheel end of the engine, then use feeler blades to measure the gap between the web of No 2 crankpin and the thrust-washer (see illustration).

Inspection

4 Clean the crankshaft using paraffin or a suitable solvent, and dry it, preferably with compressed air if available. Be sure to clean the oil holes with a pipe cleaner or similar probe, to ensure that they are not obstructed.

⚠️ **Warning: Wear eye protection when using compressed air.**

5 Check the main and big-end bearing journals for uneven wear, scoring, pitting and cracking.

6 Big-end bearing wear is accompanied by distinct metallic knocking when the engine is running (particularly noticeable when the engine is pulling from low speed) and some loss of oil pressure.

7 Main bearing wear is accompanied by severe engine vibration and rumble – getting progressively worse as engine speed increases – and again by loss of oil pressure.

8 Check the bearing journal for roughness by running a finger lightly over the bearing surface. Any roughness (which will be accompanied by obvious bearing wear) indicates that the crankshaft requires regrinding (where possible) or renewal.

9 If the crankshaft has been reground, check for burrs around the crankshaft oil holes (the holes are usually chamfered, so burrs should not be a problem unless regrinding has been carried out carelessly). Remove any burrs with a fine file or scraper, and thoroughly clean the oil holes as described previously.

10 Using a micrometer, measure the diameter of the main and big-end bearing journals, and compare the results with the Specifications **(see illustration)**. By measuring the diameter at a number of points around each journal's circumference, you will be able to determine whether or not the

journal is out-of-round. Take the measurement at each end of the journal, near the webs, to determine if the journal is tapered. Compare the results obtained with those given in the Specifications. Where no specified journal measurements are quoted, seek the advice of a Peugeot dealer.

11 Check the oil seal contact surfaces at each end of the crankshaft for wear and damage. If the seal has worn a deep groove in the surface of the crankshaft, consult an engine overhaul specialist; repair may be possible, but otherwise a new crankshaft will be required.

12 At the time of writing, it was not clear whether Peugeot produce oversize bearing shells for all of these engines. On some engines, if the crankshaft journals have not already been reground, it may be possible to have the crankshaft reconditioned, and to fit oversize shells (see Section 18 and 19). If no oversize shells are available and the crankshaft has worn beyond the specified limits, it will have to be renewed. Consult your Peugeot dealer or engine specialist for further information on parts availability.

15 Main and big-end bearings – inspection

1 Even though the main and big-end bearings should be renewed during the engine overhaul, the old bearings should be retained for close examination, as they may reveal valuable information about the condition of the engine. The bearing shells are graded by thickness, the grade of each shell being indicated by the colour code marked on it.

2 Bearing failure can occur due to lack of lubrication, the presence of dirt or other foreign particles, overloading the engine, or corrosion **(see illustration)**. Regardless of the cause of bearing failure, the cause must be corrected (where applicable) before the

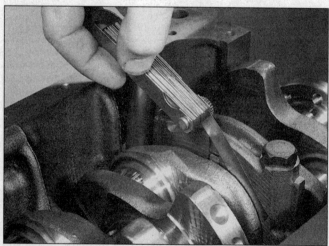

14.3 Checking crankshaft endfloat using feeler blades

14.10 Measuring a crankshaft big-end journal diameter using a micrometer

engine is reassembled, to prevent it from happening again.

3 When examining the bearing shells, remove them from the cylinder block/crankcase, the main bearing ladder/caps (as appropriate), the connecting rods and the connecting rod big-end bearing caps. Lay them out on a clean surface in the same general position as their location in the engine. This will enable you to match any bearing problems with the corresponding crankshaft journal.

Caution: Do not touch any shell's bearing surface with your fingers while checking it; there is a risk of scratching the delicate surface, or of depositing particles of dirt on it.

4 Dirt and other foreign matter gets into the engine in a variety of ways. It may be left in the engine during assembly, or it may pass through filters or the crankcase ventilation system. It may get into the oil, and from there into the bearings. Metal chips from machining operations and normal engine wear are often present. Abrasives are sometimes left in engine components after reconditioning, especially when parts are not thoroughly cleaned using the proper cleaning methods. Whatever the source, these foreign objects often end up embedded in the soft bearing material, and are easily recognised. Large particles will not embed in the bearing, and will score or gouge the bearing and journal. The best prevention for this cause of bearing failure is to clean all parts thoroughly, and keep everything spotlessly-clean during engine assembly. Frequent and regular engine oil and filter changes are also recommended.

5 Lack of lubrication (or lubrication breakdown) has a number of interrelated causes. Excessive heat (which thins the oil), overloading (which squeezes the oil from the bearing face) and oil leakage (from excessive bearing clearances, worn oil pump or high engine speeds) all contribute to lubrication breakdown. Blocked oil passages, which usually are the result of misaligned oil holes in a bearing shell, will also oil-starve a bearing, and destroy it. When lack of lubrication is the cause of bearing failure, the bearing material is wiped or extruded from the steel backing of the bearing. Temperatures may increase to the point where the steel backing turns blue from overheating.

6 Driving habits can have a definite effect on bearing life. Full-throttle, low-speed operation (labouring the engine) puts very high loads on bearings, tending to squeeze out the oil film. These loads cause the bearings to flex, which produces fine cracks in the bearing face (fatigue failure). Eventually, the bearing material will loosen in pieces, and tear away from the steel backing.

7 Short-distance driving leads to corrosion of bearings, because insufficient engine heat is produced to drive off the condensed water and corrosive gases. These products collect in the engine oil, forming acid and sludge. As the oil is carried to the engine bearings, the

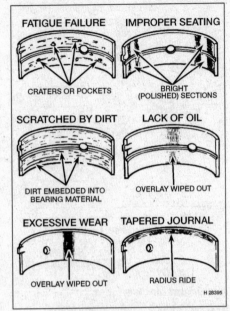

15.2 Typical bearing failures

acid attacks and corrodes the bearing material.

8 Incorrect bearing installation during engine assembly will lead to bearing failure as well. Tight-fitting bearings leave insufficient bearing running clearance, and will result in oil starvation. Dirt or foreign particles trapped behind a bearing shell result in high spots on the bearing, which lead to failure.

9 As mentioned at the beginning of this Section, the bearing shells should be renewed as a matter of course during engine overhaul; to do otherwise is false economy. Refer to Section 18 and 19 for details of bearing shell selection.

16 Engine overhaul – reassembly sequence

1 Before reassembly begins, ensure that all new parts have been obtained, and that all necessary tools are available. Read through the entire procedure to familiarise yourself

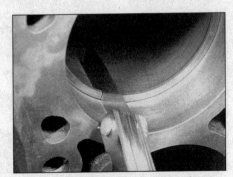

17.5 Measuring a piston ring end gap using feeler blades

with the work involved, and to ensure that all items necessary for reassembly of the engine are at hand. In addition to all normal tools and materials, thread-locking compound will be needed. A tube of suitable liquid sealant will also be required for the joint faces that are fitted without gaskets. It is recommended that Peugeot's own product(s) are used, which are specially formulated for this purpose; the relevant product names are quoted in the text of each Section where they are required.

2 In order to save time and avoid problems, engine reassembly can be carried out in the following order, referring to Part A or B of this Chapter unless otherwise stated.:

  a) *Crankshaft (See Section 18).*
  b) *Piston/connecting rod assemblies (See Section 19).*
  c) *Oil pump.*
  d) *Sump.*
  e) *Flywheel/driveplate.*
  f) *Cylinder head.*
  g) *Injection pump and mounting bracket – diesel engine (Chapter 4B).*
  h) *Timing belt tensioner pulley(s) and sprockets, and timing belt.*
  i) *Engine external components.*

3 At this stage, all engine components should be absolutely clean and dry, with all faults repaired. The components should be laid out (or in individual containers) on a completely clean work surface.

17 Piston rings – refitting

2C

1 Before fitting new piston rings, the ring end gaps must be checked as follows.

2 Lay out the piston/connecting rod assemblies and the new piston ring sets, so that the ring sets will be matched with the same piston and cylinder during the end gap measurement and subsequent engine reassembly.

3 Insert the top ring into the first cylinder, and push it down the bore using the top of the piston. This will ensure that the ring remains square with the cylinder walls. Position the ring near the bottom of the cylinder bore, at the lower limit of ring travel. Note that the top and second compression rings are different. The second ring can be identified by its taper; on petrol engines it also has a step on its lower surface.

4 Measure the end gap using feeler blades.

5 Repeat the procedure with the ring at the top of the cylinder bore, at the upper limit of its travel **(see illustration)**, and compare the measurements with the figures given in the Specifications. Where no figures are given, seek the advice of a Peugeot dealer or engine reconditioning specialist. If the end gaps are incorrect, check that you have the correct rings for your engine and for the cylinder bore size.

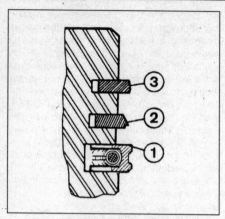

**17.9a Piston ring fitting diagram –
petrol engine**

1 Oil control ring
2 Second compression ring
3 Top compression ring

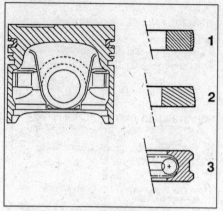

**17.9b Piston ring fitting diagram –
1.9 litre diesel engine**

1 Top compression ring
2 Second compression ring
3 Oil control ring

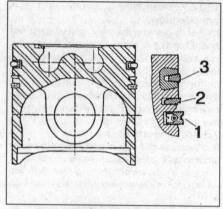

**17.9c Piston ring fitting diagram –
2.0 litre diesel engine**

1 Oil control ring
2 Second compression ring
3 Top compression ring

6 Repeat the checking procedure for each ring in the first cylinder, and then for the rings in the remaining cylinders. Remember to keep rings, pistons and cylinders matched up.

7 Once the ring end gaps have been checked and if necessary corrected, the rings can be fitted to the pistons.

8 Fit the oil control ring expander (where fitted) then install the ring.

9 The second and top rings are different and can be identified from their cross-sections; the top ring is symmetrical whilst the second ring is tapered. Fit the second ring, ensuring its identification (TOP) marking is facing upwards, then install the top ring **(see illustrations)**. Arrange the oil control, second and top ring end gaps so they are equally spaced 120° apart. **Note:** *Always follow any instructions supplied with the new piston ring sets – different manufacturers may specify different procedures. Do not mix up the top and second compression rings, as they have different cross-sections.*

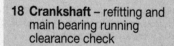

18 Crankshaft – refitting and main bearing running clearance check

Selection of new bearing shells

Petrol engine

1 To ensure that the main bearing running clearance can be accurately set, there are different grades of bearing shell; there are six different grades of bearing shell on aluminium block engines and three different grades on cast-iron block engines. The grades are indicated by a colour-coding marked on the edge of each shell, which denotes the shell's thickness, as listed in the following table. The upper shell on all bearings is of the same size (colour code black), and the running clearance is controlled by fitting a lower bearing shell of the required thickness.

Aluminium block engine

Bearing colour code	Thickness (mm)	
	Standard	Undersize
Blue (class A)	1.823	1.973
Orange (class B)	1.829	1.979
Black (class C)	1.835	1.985
Yellow (class D)	1.841	1.991
Green (class E)	1.847	1.998
White (class G)	1.853	2.003

Cast-iron block engine

Bearing colour code	Thickness (mm)	
	Standard	Undersize
Blue (class A)	1.844	1.994
Black (class B)	1.858	2.008
Green (class C)	1.869	2.019

2 New bearing shells can be selected using the reference marks on the cylinder block/crankcase. The cylinder block marks identify the diameter of the bearing bores and the crankshaft marks, the diameter of the crankshaft journals.

3 The cylinder block reference marks are on the right-hand (timing belt) end of the block, and the crankshaft reference marks are on the right-hand (timing belt) end of the crankshaft, on the right-hand web of No 4 crankpin **(see illustration)**. These marks can be used to select bearing shells of the required thickness as follows.

4 On both the crankshaft and block there are two lines of identification: a bar code, which is used by Peugeot during production, and a row of five letters. The first letter in the sequence refers to the size of No 1 bearing (at the flywheel/driveplate end). The last letter in the sequence (which is followed by an arrow) refers to the size of No 5 main bearing. These marks can be used to select the required bearing shell grade as follows.

5 Obtain the identification letter of both the relevant crankshaft journal and the cylinder block bearing bore. Referring to the correct selection chart (there are different charts for aluminium and cast-iron block engines), noting that the cylinder block letters are listed across the top of the chart, and the crankshaft letters down the side **(see illustrations)**.

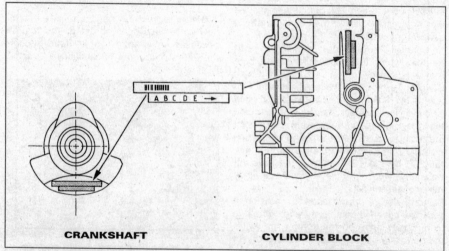

CRANKSHAFT　　　　**CYLINDER BLOCK**

18.3 Cylinder block and crankshaft identification markings – petrol engine

Trace a vertical line down from the relevant cylinder block letter, and a horizontal line across from the relevant crankshaft letter, and find the point at which both lines cross. This crossover point will indicate the grade of lower bearing shell required to give the correct main bearing running clearance.

6 Repeat this procedure so that the required bearing shell grade is obtained for each of the five main bearing journals.

7 Seek the advice of your Peugeot dealer for the latest information on parts availability when ordering new bearing shells.

Diesel engine

8 On all diesel engines both the upper and lower bearing shells are of the same thickness. Peugeot produce both a standard set of shells and an undersize shells.

Main bearing running clearance check

Petrol engine

9 The running clearance check can be carried out using the original bearing shells. However, it is preferable to use a new set, since the results obtained will be more conclusive.

10 Clean the backs of the bearing shells, and the bearing locations in both the cylinder block/crankcase and the main bearing ladder/bearing caps (as applicable).

11 Press the bearing shells into their locations, ensuring that the tab on each shell engages in the notch in the cylinder block/crankcase or main bearing ladder/bearing cap. Take care not to touch any shell's bearing surface with your fingers. Note that the grooved bearing shells, both upper and lower, are fitted to Nos 2 and 4 main bearings **(see illustration)**. If the original bearing shells are being used for the check, ensure that they are refitted in their original locations. The clearance can be checked in either of two ways.

12 One method (which will be difficult to achieve without a range of internal micrometers or internal/external expanding calipers) is to refit the main bearing ladder casting/bearing caps to the cylinder block/crankcase, with the bearing shells in place. With the casting/cap retaining bolts correctly tightened (see paragraphs 34 or 47 – as applicable), measure the internal diameter of each assembled pair of bearing shells. If the diameter of each corresponding crankshaft journal is measured and then subtracted from the bearing internal diameter, the result will be the main bearing running clearance.

13 The second (and more accurate) method is to use an American product known as Plastigauge. This consists of a fine thread of perfectly-round plastic, which is compressed between the bearing shell and the journal. When the shell is removed, the plastic is deformed, and can be measured with a special card gauge supplied with the kit. The running clearance is determined from this gauge. Plastigauge should be available from your Peugeot dealer; otherwise, enquiries at one of the larger specialist motor factors should produce the name of a stockist in your area. The procedure for using Plastigauge is as follows.

14 With the main bearing upper shells in place, carefully lay the crankshaft in position. Do not use any lubricant; the crankshaft journals and bearing shells must be perfectly clean and dry.

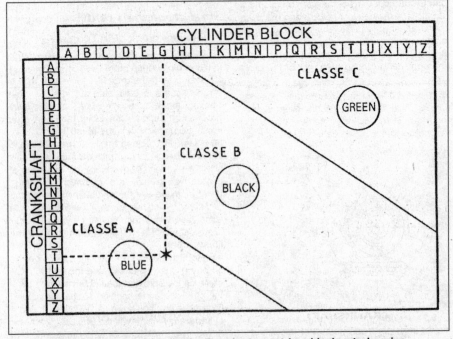

18.5a Main bearing shell selection chart – aluminium block petrol engine

18.11 On petrol engines ensure the grooved bearing shells are fitted to No 2 and 4 main bearings

2C

18.5b Main bearing shell selection chart – cast-iron block petrol engine

18.15 Plastigauge in place on a crankshaft main bearing journal

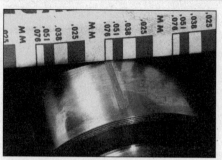

18.18 Measure the width of the deformed Plastigauge using the scale on the card supplied

18.29 Fit the thrustwashers to each side of No 2 main bearing ensuring their oilway grooves are facing outwards

15 Cut several lengths of the appropriate-size Plastigauge (they should be slightly shorter than the width of the main bearings), and place one length on each crankshaft journal axis **(see illustration)**.

16 On aluminium block engines, ensure the lower bearing shells are correctly fitted then refit the main bearing ladder casting, tightening its retaining bolts as described in paragraph 34. Take care not to disturb the Plastigauge, and *do not* rotate the crankshaft at any time during this operation. Remove the main bearing ladder casting, again taking great care not to disturb the Plastigauge or rotate the crankshaft.

17 On cast-iron block engines, ensure the lower bearing shells are correctly fitted then refit the main bearing caps, tightening the retaining bolts as described in paragraph 47. Take care not to disturb the Plastigauge, and *do not* rotate the crankshaft at any time during this operation. Remove the main bearing caps, again taking great care not to disturb the Plastigauge or rotate the crankshaft.

18 On all engines, compare the width of the crushed Plastigauge on each journal to the scale printed on the Plastigauge envelope, to obtain the main bearing running clearance **(see illustration)**. Compare the clearance measured with that in the Specifications at the start of this Chapter.

19 If the clearance is significantly different from that expected, the bearing shells may be the wrong size (or excessively worn, if the original shells are being re-used). Before deciding that different-size shells are required,

make sure that no dirt or oil was trapped between the bearing shells and the caps or block when the clearance was measured. If the Plastigauge was wider at one end than at the other, the crankshaft journal may be tapered.

20 If the clearance is not as specified, use the reading obtained, along with the shell thicknesses quoted above, to calculate the necessary grade of bearing shells required. When calculating the bearing clearance required, bear in mind that it is always better to have the running clearance towards the lower end of the specified range, to allow for wear in use.

21 Where necessary, obtain the required grades of bearing shell, and repeat the running clearance checking process described above.

22 On completion, carefully scrape away all traces of the Plastigauge material from the crankshaft and bearing shells. Use your fingernail, or a wooden or plastic scraper which is unlikely to score the bearing surfaces.

Diesel engine

23 The running clearance check can be carried out using the original bearing shells. However, it is preferable to use a new set, since the results obtained will be more conclusive.

24 Clean the backs of the bearing shells, and the bearing locations in both the cylinder block/crankcase and the main bearing caps.

25 Press the bearing shells into their locations, ensuring that the tab on each shell engages in the notch in the cylinder block/crankcase or main bearing cap. Take care not to touch any

shell's bearing surface with your fingers. Note that all the upper bearing shells are grooved and all the lower bearing shells are plain. If the original bearing shells are being used for the check, ensure that they are refitted in their original locations. The clearance can be checked in either of two ways.

26 One method (which will be difficult to achieve without a range of internal micrometers or internal/external expanding calipers) is to refit the main bearing caps to the cylinder block/crankcase, with the bearing shells in place. With the cap retaining bolts correctly tightened (see paragraphs 67 or 68 – as applicable), measure the internal diameter of each assembled pair of bearing shells. If the diameter of each corresponding crankshaft journal is measured and then subtracted from the bearing internal diameter, the result will be the main bearing running clearance.

27 The second (and more accurate) method is to use an Plastigauge to check the clearances as described in paragraphs 14 to 22, tightening the main bearing cap bolts as described in paragraphs 67 or 68 (as applicable).

Final crankshaft refitting

Aluminium block petrol engine

28 Carefully lift the crankshaft out of the cylinder block once more.

29 Using a little grease, stick the upper thrustwashers to each side of the No 2 main bearing upper location; ensure that the oilway grooves on each thrustwasher face outwards (away from the block) **(see illustration)**.

30 Place the bearing shells in their locations as described in paragraphs 10 and 11. If new shells are being fitted, ensure that all traces of protective grease are cleaned off using paraffin. Wipe dry the shells and connecting rods with a lint-free cloth. Liberally lubricate each bearing shell in the cylinder block/crankcase with clean engine oil **(see illustration)**.

31 Refit the Woodruff key, then slide on the oil pump drive sprocket, and locate the drive chain on the sprocket **(see illustration)**. Lower the crankshaft into position so that Nos 2 and 3 cylinder crankpins are at TDC; Nos 1 and 4 cylinder crankpins will be at BDC, ready for fitting No 1 piston. Check the crankshaft endfloat as described in Section 14.

18.30 Ensure each bearing shell tab (arrowed) is correctly located then lubricate the shell with clean engine oil

18.31 Refitting the oil pump drive chain and sprocket – aluminium block petrol engine

18.32 Apply a thin film of sealant to the cylinder block mating surface . . .

18.33 . . . then lower the main bearing ladder casting into position

18.34a Tighten the ten main M11 bearing bolts to the specified Stage 1 torque setting . . .

32 Thoroughly degrease the mating surfaces of the cylinder block/crankcase and the main bearing ladder. Apply a thin bead of suitable sealant to the cylinder block mating surface of the main bearing ladder casting, then spread to an even film **(see illustration)**.

33 Ensure the locating dowels are in position then lubricate the lower bearing shells with clean engine oil. Refit the main bearing ladder to the cylinder block, ensuring that the lower bearings remain correctly fitted **(see illustration)**.

34 Install the ten M11 main bearing ladder retaining bolts, and tighten them all by hand only. Working in a spiral pattern from the centre bolts outwards, evenly and progressively tighten the ten bolts to the specified Stage 1 torque wrench setting. Once all the bolts have been tightened to the Stage 1 setting, working in the same sequence, angle-tighten the bolts through the specified Stage 2 angle using a socket and extension bar. It is recommended that an angle-measuring gauge is used during this stage of the tightening, to ensure accuracy **(see illustrations)**. If a gauge is not available, use a dab of white paint to make alignment marks between the bolt head and casting prior to tightening; the marks can then be used to check that the bolt has been rotated sufficiently during tightening.

35 Refit all the M6 bolts securing the main bearing ladder to the base of the cylinder block, and tighten them to the specified torque. Check that the crankshaft rotates freely.

36 Refit the piston/connecting rod assemblies

to the crankshaft as described in Section 19.

37 Ensuring that the drive chain is correctly located on the sprocket, refit the oil pump and sump as described in Part A of this Chapter.

38 Fit two new crankshaft oil seals as described in Part A.

39 Refit the flywheel/driveplate as described in Part A of this Chapter.

40 Refit the cylinder head (where removed) as described in Part A. Also refit the crankshaft sprocket and timing belt (see Part A).

Cast-iron block petrol engine

41 Carefully lift the crankshaft out of the cylinder block once more.

42 Using a little grease, stick the upper thrustwashers to each side of the No 2 main bearing upper location. Ensure that the oilway grooves on each thrustwasher face outwards (away from the cylinder block) **(see illustration)**.

43 Place the bearing shells in their locations as described in paragraphs 10 and 11 **(see illustration)**. If new shells are being fitted, ensure that all traces of protective grease are cleaned off using paraffin. Wipe dry the shells and connecting rods with a lint-free cloth. Liberally lubricate each bearing shell in the cylinder block/crankcase and cap with clean engine oil.

44 Lower the crankshaft into position so that Nos 2 and 3 cylinder crankpins are at TDC; Nos 1 and 4 cylinder crankpins will be at BDC, ready for fitting No 1 piston. Check the crankshaft endfloat as described in Section 14.

45 Lubricate the lower bearing shells in the

main bearing caps with clean engine oil. Make sure that the locating lugs on the shells engage with the corresponding recesses in the caps.

46 Fit the main bearing caps to their correct locations, ensuring that they are fitted the correct way round (the bearing shell lug recesses in the block and caps must be on the same side).

47 Lightly lubricate the threads and the underside of the heads of the main bearing cap bolts with engine oil then refit the bolts. Working in a spiral sequence from the centre bolts outwards, tighten the main bearing cap bolts evenly and progressively to the specified Stage 1 torque wrench setting. Once all the bolts have been tightened to the Stage 1 setting, working in the same sequence, angle-tighten the bolts through the specified Stage 2 angle, using a socket and extension bar. It is recommended that an angle-measuring gauge is used during this stage of the tightening, to ensure accuracy. If a gauge is not available, use a dab of white paint to make alignment marks between the bolt head and casting prior to tightening; the marks can then be used to check that the bolt has been rotated sufficiently during tightening.

48 Check that the crankshaft rotates freely.

49 Refit the piston/connecting rod assemblies to the crankshaft as described in Section 19.

50 Refit the Woodruff key to the crankshaft groove, and slide on the oil pump drive sprocket. Locate the drive chain on the sprocket.

18.34b . . . then angle-tighten them through the specified Stage 2 angle

18.42 Fit the thrustwashers to the sides of No 2 main bearing, ensuring their oilway grooves face outwards

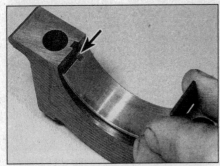

18.43 Ensure the tab (arrowed) is locates in the cut-out when fitting the bearing shells

2C

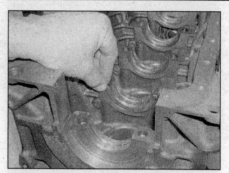

18.59 Fit the thrustwashers to the sides of No 2 main bearing, ensuring their oilway grooves face outwards

18.60a On diesel engine ensure the grooved bearing shells are fitted to the cylinder block . . .

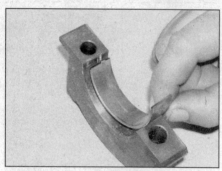

18.60b . . . and the plain bearing shells to the main bearing caps

51 Ensure that the mating surfaces of right-hand (timing belt end) oil seal housing and cylinder block are clean and dry. Note the correct fitted depth of the front oil seal then, using a large flat-bladed screwdriver, lever the seal out of the housing.

52 Apply a smear of suitable sealant to the oil seal housing mating surface, and make sure that the locating dowels are in position. Slide the housing over the end of the crankshaft, and into position on the cylinder block. Tighten the housing retaining bolts securely.

53 Repeat the operations in paragraphs 51 and 52, and fit the left-hand (flywheel/driveplate end) oil seal housing.

54 Fit new crankshaft oil seals as described in Part A of this Chapter.

55 Ensuring that the chain is correctly located on the drive sprocket, refit the oil pump and sump as described in Part A of this Chapter.

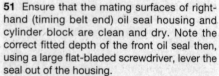

18.63 Fit No 2 to 5 bearing caps and install the bearing cap bolts

56 Refit the flywheel/driveplate as described in Part A of this Chapter.

57 Refit the cylinder head (where removed) and install the crankshaft sprocket and timing belt as described in the relevant Sections of Part A.

Diesel engine

58 Carefully lift the crankshaft out of the cylinder block once more.

59 Using a little grease, stick the thrustwashers to each side of No 2 main bearing upper location and bearing cap (see illustration). Ensure that the oilway grooves on each thrustwasher face outwards (away from the cylinder block).

60 Place the bearing shells in their locations as described in paragraphs 24 and 25 (see illustrations). If new shells are being fitted, ensure that all traces of protective grease are cleaned off using paraffin. Wipe dry the shells and connecting rods with a lint-free cloth. Liberally lubricate each bearing shell in the cylinder block/crankcase and cap with clean engine oil.

61 Lower the crankshaft into position so that Nos 2 and 3 cylinder crankpins are at TDC; Nos 1 and 4 cylinder crankpins will be at BDC, ready for fitting No 1 piston.

62 Lubricate the lower bearing shells in the main bearing caps with clean engine oil. Make sure that the locating lugs on the shells engage with the corresponding recesses in the caps.

63 Fit main bearing caps Nos 2 to 5 to their correct locations, ensuring that they are fitted

the correct way round (the bearing shell tab recesses in the block and caps must be on the same side) (see illustration). Ensure the thrustwashers remain correctly fitted to No 2 bearing cap then refit the bearing cap bolts, tightening them only lightly at this stage. Check the crankshaft endfloat as described in Section 14.

64 Apply a small amount of sealant to the No 1 main bearing cap mating face on the cylinder block, around the sealing strip holes (see illustration).

65 Locate the tab of each sealing strip over the pins on the base of No 1 bearing cap, and press the strips into the bearing cap grooves. It is now necessary to obtain two thin metal strips, of 0.25 mm thickness or less, in order to prevent the strips moving when the cap is being fitted. Peugeot garages use the tool shown, which acts as a clamp. Metal strips (such as old feeler blades) can be used, provided all burrs which may damage the sealing strips are first removed (see illustrations).

66 Where applicable, oil both sides of the metal strips, and hold them on the sealing strips. Fit the No 1 main bearing cap, insert the bolts loosely, then carefully pull out the metal strips in a horizontal direction, using a pair of pliers (see illustration).

67 On 1.9 litre engines, working in the specified sequence, evenly and progressively tighten the main bearing cap bolts to the specified torque (see illustration).

68 On 2.0 litre engines, working in the

18.64 Apply sealant to the No 1 main bearing cap mating surface of the cylinder block

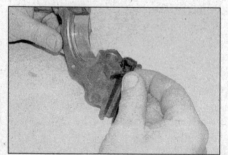

18.65a Fit the sealing strips to each side of No 1 main bearing cap, ensuring they are correctly engaged with the pins

18.65b Using the Peugeot special tool to fit No 1 main bearing cap

18.66 Fitting No 1 main bearing caps using metal strips to retain the sealing strips

sequence shown in illustration 18.67, tighten the main bearing cap bolts evenly and progressively to the specified Stage 1 torque wrench setting. Once all the bolts have been tightened to the Stage 1 setting, working in the specified sequence, angle-tighten the bolts through the specified Stage 2 angle, using a socket and extension bar. It is recommended that an angle-measuring gauge is used during this stage of the tightening, to ensure accuracy **(see illustrations)**. If a gauge is not available, use a

dab of white paint to make alignment marks between the bolt head and casting prior to tightening; the marks can then be used to check that the bolt has been rotated sufficiently during tightening.

69 On all engines, check that the sealing strips protrude slightly from above the cylinder block/crankcase mating surface by approximately 1 mm. If not, remove the bearing cap again and refit; the seals are supplied the correct length and should not be cut. Also check that the crankshaft rotates freely.

70 Fit a new crankshaft left-hand (flywheel end) oil seal as described in Part B.

71 Refit the piston/connecting rod assemblies to the crankshaft as described in Section 19.

72 Fit a new sealing ring (where fitted) the crankshaft then refit the Woodruff key and slide on the oil pump drive sprocket and spacer. Locate the drive chain on the sprocket.

73 Ensure that the mating surfaces of the right-hand (timing belt end) oil seal housing and cylinder block are clean and dry. Note the correct fitted depth of the oil seal then, using a large flat-bladed screwdriver, lever the old seal out of the housing.

74 Apply a smear of suitable sealant to the oil seal housing mating surface. Ensure that the locating dowels are in position, then slide the housing over the end of the crankshaft and into position on the cylinder block. Tighten the housing retaining bolts to the specified torque.

75 Fit a new crankshaft right-hand (timing belt end) oil seal as described in Part B.

76 Ensuring that the drive chain is correctly located on the sprocket, refit the oil pump and sump as described in Part B.

77 Refit the flywheel as described in Part B of this Chapter.

78 Refit the cylinder head (where removed) as described in Part B. Also refit the crankshaft sprocket and timing belt (see Part B).

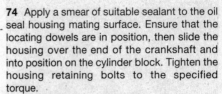

19 Piston/connecting rod assembly – refitting and big-end bearing running clearance check

Selection of bearing shells

1 On most engines, there are two sizes of big-end bearing shell produced by Peugeot; a standard size for use with the standard crankshaft, and an oversize for use once the crankshaft journals have been reground.

2 Consult your Peugeot dealer for the latest information on parts availability. Always quote the diameter of the crankshaft big-end crankpins when ordering bearing shells.

3 Before refitting the piston/connecting rod assemblies, we recommend that the big-end bearing running clearance is checked as follows.

Big-end bearing running clearance check

Note: *Use the original connecting rod cap nuts for the check, not the new ones.*

4 Clean the backs of the bearing shells, and the bearing locations in both the connecting rod and bearing cap.

5 Press the bearing shells into their locations, ensuring that the tab on each shell engages in the notch in the connecting rod and cap. Take care not to touch any shell's bearing surface with your fingers **(see illustration)**. If the original bearing shells are being used for the

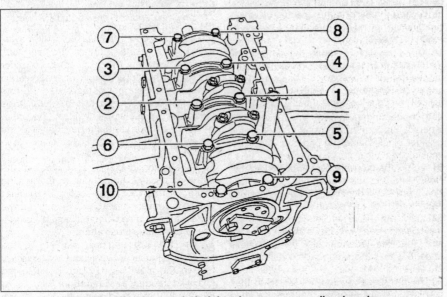

18.67 Main bearing cap bolt tightening sequence – diesel engine

18.68a On 2.0 litre diesel engines, tighten the main bearing cap bolts to the specified Stage 1 torque setting . . .

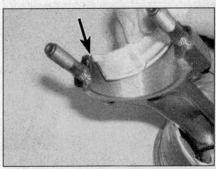

18.68b . . . then angle-tighten them through the specified Stage 2 angle

19.5 Ensure the bearing shell tab (arrowed) locates correctly in the cut-out

2C

19.20 Tap the piston into the bore using a hammer handle

19.21 Fit the big-end bearing cap, ensuring it is the right way around, and screw on the new nuts

19.22 On petrol engines tighten the big-end bearing cap nuts to the specified torque

check, ensure that they are refitted in their original locations. The clearance can be checked in either of two ways.

6 One method is to refit the big-end bearing cap to the connecting rod, ensuring that they are fitted the correct way around, with the bearing shells in place. With the cap retaining nuts correctly tightened (see paragraph 22 or 23 – as applicable), use an internal micrometer or vernier caliper to measure the internal diameter of each assembled pair of bearing shells. If the diameter of each corresponding crankshaft journal is measured and then subtracted from the bearing internal diameter, the result will be the big-end bearing running clearance.

7 The second, and more accurate method is to use Plastigauge (see Section 18).

8 Ensure that the bearing shells are correctly fitted. Place a strand of Plastigauge on each (cleaned) crankpin journal.

9 Refit the (clean) piston/connecting rod assemblies to the crankshaft, and refit the big-end bearing caps, using the marks made or noted on removal to ensure that they are fitted the correct way around.

10 Tighten the bearing cap nuts as described below in paragraph 22 or 23 (as applicable). Take care not to disturb the Plastigauge, nor rotate the connecting rod during the tightening sequence.

11 Dismantle the assemblies without rotating the connecting rods. Use the scale printed on the Plastigauge envelope to obtain the big-end bearing running clearance.

12 If the clearance is significantly different from that expected, the bearing shells may be the wrong size (or excessively worn, if the

original shells are being re-used). Make sure that no dirt or oil was trapped between the bearing shells and the caps or block when the clearance was measured. If the Plastigauge was wider at one end than at the other, the crankshaft journal may be tapered.

13 Note that Peugeot do not specify a recommended big-end bearing running clearance. The figure given in the Specifications is a guide figure, which is typical for this type of engine. Before condemning the components concerned, refer to your Peugeot dealer or engine reconditioning specialist for further information on the specified running clearance. Their advice on the best course of action to be taken can then also be obtained.

14 On completion, carefully scrape away all traces of the Plastigauge material from the crankshaft and bearing shells. Use your fingernail, or some other object which is unlikely to score the bearing surfaces.

Final piston/connecting rod refitting

Note: *New big-end cap nuts must be used on refitting.*

15 Note that the following procedure assumes that the cylinder liners (aluminium block petrol engines) are in position in the cylinder block/crankcase as described in Section 12, and that the crankshaft and main bearing ladder/caps are in place (see Section 18).

16 Ensure that the bearing shells are correctly fitted as described earlier. If new shells are being fitted, ensure that all traces of the protective grease are cleaned off using

paraffin. Wipe dry the shells and connecting rods with a lint-free cloth.

17 Lubricate the cylinder bores, the pistons, and piston rings, then lay out each piston/connecting rod assembly in its respective position.

18 Start with assembly No 1. Make sure that the piston rings are still spaced as described in Section 17, then clamp them in position with a piston ring compressor.

19 Insert the piston/connecting rod assembly into the top of cylinder/liner No 1, ensuring the piston is correctly positioned as follows.

a) *On petrol engines, ensure that the arrow on the piston crown is pointing towards the timing belt end of the engine.*

b) *On 1.9 litre diesel engines, ensure that the cloverleaf-shaped cut-out on the piston crown is towards the front (oil filter side) of the cylinder block.*

c) *On 2.0 litre diesel engines, ensure that the valve recesses on the piston crown are towards the rear of the cylinder block.*

20 Once the piston is correctly positioned, using a block of wood or hammer handle against the piston crown, tap the assembly into the cylinder/liner until the piston crown is flush with the top of the cylinder/liner **(see illustration)**.

21 Ensure that the bearing shell is still correctly installed. Liberally lubricate the crankpin and both bearing shells. Taking care not to mark the cylinder/liner bores, pull the piston/connecting rod assembly down the bore and onto the crankpin. Refit the big-end bearing cap and fit the new nuts, tightening them finger-tight at first **(see illustration)**. Note that the faces with the identification marks must match (which means that the bearing shell locating tabs abut each other).

22 On petrol engines, tighten the bearing cap retaining nuts evenly and progressively to the specified torque setting **(see illustration)**.

23 On diesel engines, tighten the bearing cap retaining nuts evenly and progressively to the Stage 1 torque setting. Once both nuts have been tightened to the Stage 1 setting, angle-tighten them through the specified Stage 2 angle, using a socket and extension bar. It is recommended that an angle-measuring gauge is used during this stage of the tightening, to ensure accuracy **(see illustrations)**. If a gauge

19.23a On diesel engines, tighten the big-end bearing cap nuts to the specified Stage 1 torque setting . . .

19.23b . . . then angle-tighten them through the specified Stage 2 angle

is not available, use a dab of white paint to make alignment marks between the nut and bearing cap prior to tightening; the marks can then be used to check that the nut has been rotated sufficiently during tightening.

24 On all engines, once the bearing cap retaining nuts have been correctly tightened, rotate the crankshaft. Check that it turns freely; some stiffness is to be expected if new components have been fitted, but there should be no signs of binding or tight spots.

25 Refit the other three piston/connecting rod assemblies in the same way.

26 Refit the cylinder head and oil pump as described in Part A or B of this Chapter (as applicable).

20 Engine – initial start-up after overhaul

1 With the engine refitted in the vehicle, double-check the engine oil and coolant levels. Make a final check that everything has been reconnected, and that there are no tools or rags left in the engine compartment.

2 Switch on the ignition and immediately turn the engine on the starter (do not allow the glow plugs to heat up on diesel engines) until the oil pressure warning light goes out.

3 Pressurise/prime the fuel system as described in Chapter 4A, Section 7, or Chapter 4B, Section 5, then start the engine, noting that this may take a little longer than usual, due to the fuel system components having been disturbed.

4 While the engine is idling, check for fuel, water and oil leaks. Don't be alarmed if there are some odd smells and smoke from parts getting hot and burning off oil deposits.

5 Assuming all is well, keep the engine idling until hot water is felt circulating through the top hose, then switch off the engine.

6 Allow the engine to cool then recheck the oil and coolant levels as described in *Weekly checks*, and top-up as necessary.

7 If new pistons, rings or crankshaft bearings have been fitted, the engine must be treated as new, and run-in for the first 500 miles (800 km). *Do not* operate the engine at full-throttle, or allow it to labour at low engine speeds in any gear. It is recommended that the oil and filter be changed at the end of this period.

2C

Chapter 3
Cooling, heating and ventilation systems

Contents

Degrees of difficulty

Easy, suitable for novice with little experience	**Fairly easy,** suitable for beginner with some experience	**Fairly difficult,** suitable for competent DIY mechanic 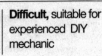	**Difficult,** suitable for experienced DIY mechanic	**Very difficult,** suitable for expert DIY or professional

Specifications

General
Maximum system pressure .... 1.4 bars

Thermostat
Start of opening temperature:
  Petrol engine models .... 89°C
  Diesel engine models .... 83°C

Torque wrench settings

	Nm	lbf ft
Air conditioning compressor mounting bolts:		
Petrol engine	25	18
Diesel engine:		
Front (drivebelt pulley end) bolts	40	30
Rear bolts	30	22

1 General information and precautions

General information

1 The cooling system is of pressurised type, comprising a coolant pump driven by the timing belt, an aluminium radiator, an expansion tank, an electric cooling fan, a thermostat, a heater matrix, and all associated hoses and switches.

2 The system functions as follows. Cold coolant in the bottom of the radiator passes through the bottom hose to the coolant pump, where it is pumped around the cylinder block and head passages. After cooling the cylinder bores, combustion surfaces and valve seats, the coolant reaches the underside of the thermostat, which is initially closed. The coolant passes through the heater, and is returned via the cylinder block to the coolant pump.

3 When the engine is cold, the coolant circulates only through the cylinder block, cylinder head, and heater. When the coolant reaches a predetermined temperature, the thermostat opens, and the coolant passes through the top hose to the radiator. As the coolant passes down through the radiator, it is cooled by the inrush of air when the car is in forward motion. The airflow is supplemented by the action of the electric cooling fan when necessary. Upon reaching the bottom of the radiator, the coolant has now cooled, and the cycle is repeated.

4 On models with automatic transmission, a proportion of the coolant is recirculated through the transmission fluid cooler mounted on the transmission. On models fitted with an engine oil cooler, the coolant is also passed through the oil cooler.

5 On models without air conditioning a single-speed cooling fan is fitted. This is controlled by a thermostatic sensor on petrol and WJZ diesel engines, and by the injection system electronic control unit on all other diesel engines (see Section 7).

6 Models with air conditioning have a two-speed cooling fan which is controlled by a "Bitron" control unit on petrol and WJZ diesel engines. On all other diesel engines the fan is controlled by the injection system electronic control unit (see Section 7)

Precautions

⚠️ *Warning: Do not attempt to remove the expansion tank filler cap, or to disturb any part of the cooling system, while the engine is hot, as there is a high risk of scalding. If the expansion tank filler cap must be removed before the engine and radiator have fully cooled (even though this is not recommended), the pressure in the cooling system must first be relieved. Cover the cap with a thick layer of cloth to avoid scalding, and slowly unscrew the filler cap until a hissing sound is heard. When the hissing has stopped, indicating that the pressure has reduced, slowly unscrew the filler cap until it can be removed; if more*

2.5 Disconnecting the expansion tank hose from the radiator

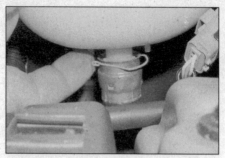

2.12 Where click-fit hose connectors are used, remove the circlip then disconnect the hose

2.13 Ensure the sealing ring and circlip (arrowed) are correctly fitted to the hose union before reconnecting a click-fit connector

hissing sounds are heard, wait until they have stopped before unscrewing the cap. At all times keep well away from the filler cap opening, and protect your hands.

⚠️ **Warning: Do not allow antifreeze to come into contact with your skin, or with the painted surfaces of the vehicle. Rinse off spills immediately, with plenty of water. Never leave antifreeze lying around in an open container, or in a puddle in the driveway or on the garage floor. Children and pets are attracted by its sweet smell, but antifreeze can be fatal if ingested.**

⚠️ **Warning: If the engine is hot, the electric cooling fan(s) may start rotating even if the engine is not running. Be careful to keep your hands, hair, and any loose clothing well clear when working in the engine compartment.**

⚠️ **Warning: Refer to Section 11 for precautions to be observed when working on models equipped with air conditioning.**

2 Cooling system hoses – disconnection and renewal

Note: *Refer to the warnings given in Section 1 of this Chapter before proceeding. Hoses should only be disconnected once the engine has cooled sufficiently to avoid scalding.*

1 If the checks described in the *Hose and fluid leak check* Section in Chapter 1A or 1B reveal a faulty hose, it must be renewed as follows.

3.3 On petrol engine models, unhook the retaining strap and free the expansion tank from its bracket

2 First drain the cooling system (see Chapter 1A or 1B). If the coolant is not due for renewal, it may be re-used, providing it is collected in a clean container.

3 To disconnect a hose, proceed as follows, according to the type of hose connection.

Conventional hose connections

4 On conventional connections, the clips used to secure the hoses in position may be either standard worm-drive clips, spring clips or disposable crimped types. The crimped type of clip is not designed to be re-used and should be replaced with a worm drive type on reassembly.

5 To disconnect a hose, release the retaining clips and move them along the hose, clear of the relevant inlet/outlet. Carefully work the hose free. The hoses can be removed with relative ease when new – on an older car, they may have stuck **(see illustration)**.

6 If a hose proves to be difficult to remove, try to release it by rotating its ends before attempting to free it. Gently prise the end of the hose with a blunt instrument (such as a flat-bladed screwdriver), but do not apply too much force, and take care not to damage the pipe stubs or hoses. Note in particular that the radiator inlet stub is fragile; do not use excessive force when attempting to remove the hose. If all else fails, cut the hose with a sharp knife, then slit it so that it can be peeled off in two pieces. Although this may prove expensive if the hose is otherwise undamaged, it is preferable to buying a new radiator. Check first, however, that a new hose is readily available.

7 When fitting a hose, first slide the clips onto the hose, then work the hose into position. If crimped-type clips were originally fitted, use standard worm-drive clips when refitting the hose.

8 Work the hose into position, checking that it is correctly routed, then slide each clip back along the hose until it passes over the flared end of the relevant inlet/outlet, before tightening the clip securely.

 HAYNES HINT *If the hose is stiff, use a little soapy water as a lubricant or soften the hose by soaking it in hot water. Do not use oil or grease as these may attack the rubber.*

9 Refill the cooling system (see Chapter 1A or 1B).

10 Check thoroughly for leaks as soon as possible after disturbing any part of the cooling system.

Click-fit connections

Note: *New sealing ring should be used when reconnecting the hose.*

Removal

11 On certain models, some cooling system hoses are secured in position with click-fit connectors where the hose is retained by a large circlip.

12 To disconnect this type of hose fitting, carefully prise the circlip out of position then disconnect the hose connection **(see illustration)**. Once the hose has been disconnected, refit the circlip to the hose union. Inspect the hose unit sealing ring for signs of damage or deterioration and renew if necessary.

13 On refitting, ensure that the sealing ring is in position and circlip is correctly located in the groove in the union **(see illustration)**. Lubricate the sealing ring with a smear of soapy water, to ease installation, then push the hose into its union until it is heard to click into position.

14 Ensure the hose is securely retained by the circlip then refill the cooling system as described in Chapter 1A or 1B.

15 Check thoroughly for leaks as soon as possible after disturbing any part of the cooling system.

3 Coolant expansion tank – removal and refitting

Removal

1 Referring to Chapter 1A or 1B, drain the cooling system sufficiently to empty the contents of the expansion tank. Do not drain any more coolant than is necessary.

2 Release the retaining clip(s) and disconnect the hose(s) from the top of the expansion tank.

3 On petrol engine models, unhook the retaining strap and free the expansion tank from its mounting bracket **(see illustration)**.

4 On diesel engine models, unscrew the mounting bolt from the left-hand side of the tank then free the tank from its mounting bracket. Take care not to lose the mounting rubbers from the tank lower mountings.

5 On all models, prise out the circlip from the coolant hose end fitting then free expansion tank from the lower hose and remove it from the engine compartment. Refit the circlip correctly to the groove in the hose end fitting **(see illustrations 2.12 and 2.13)**.

6 If necessary, slacken and remove the mounting nuts/bolts and remove the mounting bracket from the vehicle **(see illustration)**.

Refitting

7 Refitting is the reverse of removal, ensuring the hoses are securely reconnected. On completion, top-up the coolant level as described in *Weekly checks*.

4 Radiator – removal, inspection and refitting

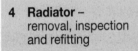

Note: *If leakage is the reason for removing the radiator, bear in mind that minor leaks can often be cured using a radiator sealant with the radiator in situ.*

Removal

1 Disconnect the battery negative lead.
2 Drain the cooling system (see Chapter 1A or 1B).

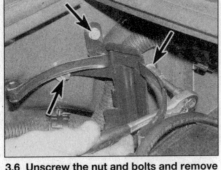

3.6 Unscrew the nut and bolts and remove the expansion tank mounting bracket (petrol engine model shown)

3 Where necessary, disconnect the wiring connector from the cooling fan switch fitted to the top of the radiator.
4 Release the retaining clips and disconnect the expansion tank hose and the upper and lower coolant hoses from the radiator **(see illustrations)**.
5 Slacken and remove the retaining screws securing the radiator upper mounting brackets to the front panel. Unclip both brackets from the panel and remove them from the radiator **(see illustrations)**.
6 Carefully lift the radiator out of position, taking care not to damage the radiator fins. Recover the radiator lower mounting rubbers **(see illustrations)**.

Inspection

7 If the radiator has been removed due to

suspected blockage, reverse-flush it as described in Chapter 1A or 1B. Clean dirt and debris from the radiator fins, using an air line (in which case, wear eye protection) or a soft brush. Be careful, as the fins are sharp, and easily damaged.

8 If necessary, a radiator specialist can perform a 'flow test' on the radiator, to establish whether an internal blockage exists.
9 A leaking radiator must be referred to a specialist for permanent repair. Do not attempt to weld or solder a leaking radiator, as damage to the plastic components may result.
10 In an emergency, minor leaks from the radiator can be cured by using a suitable radiator sealant, in accordance with its manufacturer's instructions, with the radiator *in situ*.
11 Inspect the condition of the radiator mounting rubbers, and renew them if necessary.

Refitting

12 Refitting is a reversal of removal, bearing in mind the following points:
 a) *Ensure that the lower lugs on the radiator are correctly engaged with the mounting rubbers in the body panel.*
 b) *Reconnect the hoses with reference to Section 2, using new sealing rings where applicable.*
 c) *On completion, refill the cooling system as described in Chapter 1A or 1B.*

3

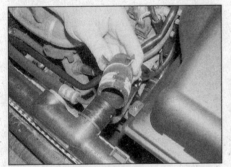

4.4a Release the retaining clips and disconnect the upper . . .

4.4b . . . and lower hoses from the radiator

4.5a Undo the retaining screws (arrowed) . . .

4.5b . . . and remove the upper mounting brackets from the radiator

4.6a Lift the radiator out of position . . .

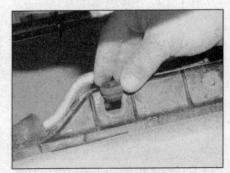

4.6b . . . and recover the lower mounting rubbers from the front panel

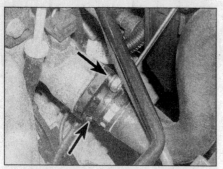

5.4 On petrol engines, unscrew the retaining bolts (locations arrowed) and free the outlet union from the coolant housing

5.5 On early models remove the thermostat and sealing ring from the coolant housing

5.7a On 1.9 litre diesel engines remove the fasteners from the right-hand side . . .

5 Thermostat – removal, testing and refitting

Removal

1 Disconnect the battery negative lead.
2 Drain the cooling system (see Chapter 1A or 1B).

Petrol engine

3 The thermostat is fitted to the coolant housing on the left-hand end of the cylinder head.
4 Unscrew the retaining bolts and free outlet union from the coolant housing **(see illustration)**.
5 On early models with a separate thermostat, recover the thermostat and sealing ring from the coolant housing, noting which

way around it is fitted **(see illustration)**.
6 On later models where the thermostat is an integral part of the outlet union. Recover the sealing ring then release the retaining clip and remove the union from the coolant hose.

Diesel engine

7 On 1.9 litre engines, release the fasteners from the right-hand side and top of the engine cover then lift off the cover, taking care not to lose its mounting rubbers **(see illustrations)**. The thermostat is fitted to the front of the fuel filter/thermostat housing on the front of the cylinder head.
8 On 2.0 litre engines remove the fasteners (rotate them 90° to release them) and lift off the engine cover **(see illustrations)**. The thermostat is fitted to the top of the coolant outlet housing on the left-hand end of the cylinder head.

9 On all engines, unscrew the retaining bolts and free the outlet union from the housing to expose the thermostat, taking care not to strain the hose.
10 Remove the thermostat from the housing, noting which way around it is fitted, and recover the sealing ring **(see illustrations)**.

Testing

11 A rough test of the thermostat may be made by suspending it with a piece of string in a container full of water. Heat the water to bring it to the boil – the thermostat must open by the time the water boils. If not, renew it.
12 If a thermometer is available, the precise opening temperature of the thermostat may be determined; compare with the figures given in the Specifications. The opening temperature is also marked on the thermostat.
13 A thermostat which fails to close as the water cools must also be renewed.

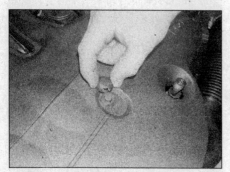

5.7b . . . and top of the engine cover . . .

5.7c . . . then remove the cover from the engine

5.8a On 2.0 litre diesel engines, rotate each fastener 90° to release it . . .

5.8b . . . then lift off the engine cover

5.10a Lift the thermostat out from its housing . . .

5.10b . . . and remove the sealing ring (2.0 litre diesel engine shown)

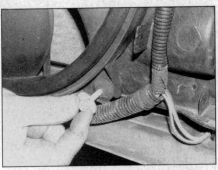

6.3a Unscrew the fan mounting bolts and washers . . .

6.3b . . . and recover the collar from the rear of each mounting rubber

6.4a Disconnect the fan wiring connector (arrowed) . . .

Refitting

Petrol engine

14 Refitting is a reversal of removal, bearing in mind the following points.

a) Examine the sealing ring for damage or deterioration, and if necessary, renew.

b) Where a separate thermostat is fitted, ensure it is installed the correct way round, with the spring(s) facing into the housing.

c) On completion, refill the cooling system as described in Chapter 1A.

Diesel engine

15 Refitting is a reversal of removal, bearing in mind the following points.

a) Examine the sealing ring for damage or deterioration, and if necessary, renew.

b) Ensure that the thermostat is fitted the correct way round, with the spring(s) facing into the housing.

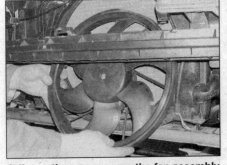

6.4b . . . then manoeuvre the fan assembly out of position

6.7a Undo the retaining screws (arrowed) . . .

c) On completion, refill the cooling system as described in Chapter 1B.

6 Electric cooling fan – removal and refitting

Removal

1 The cooling fan can be removed on its own or complete with the front panel assembly. Proceed as described under the relevant sub-heading.

Cooling fan

2 Remove the front bumper as described in Chapter 11.

3 Slacken and remove the three bolts and washers securing the cooling fan to the front

6.6 Remove the retaining clips (arrowed) and free the bonnet release cable from the front panel

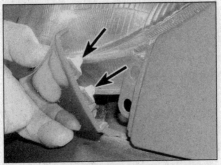

6.7b . . . then unclip the ends of the panel from the wings (clips arrowed) . . .

panel. Recover the collar from the rear of each mounting rubber **(see illustrations)**.

4 Free the fan assembly from the front panel to gain access to the wiring connector. Lift the retaining clip then disconnect the wiring connector and manoeuvre the fan assembly out of position **(see illustrations)**.

Cooling fan and front panel assembly

5 Remove the radiator as described in Section 4.

6 Remove the bonnet lock as described in Chapter 11. Remove the retaining clips and free the bonnet release cable from the front panel **(see illustration)**.

7 Slacken and remove the retaining screws securing the front trim panel in position. Carefully unclip the trim panel from the inner edge of each headlight then unclip the ends of the panel from each wing and remove the panel from the vehicle **(see illustrations)**.

8 Remove the air filter housing as described in Chapter 4A or 4B (as applicable).

9 Unclip and remove the cooling duct (where fitted) connecting the battery box to the front panel. Rotate the cooling duct elbow to free it from the left-hand end of the front panel and remove it from the vehicle **(see illustrations)**.

10 Unscrew the bolt and detach the cooling fan earth lead, located at the base of the fan/radiator mounting panel, from the body **(see illustration)**.

11 On models with air conditioning, unscrew the bolts securing the dehydrator reservoir to

3

6.7c . . . and remove the front trim panel from the vehicle

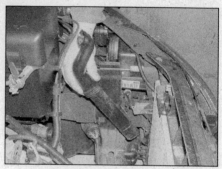

6.9a Remove the battery box cooling duct . . .

6.9b . . . and unclip the elbow from the front panel

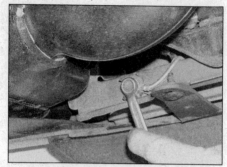

6.10 Unscrew the bolt and detach the cooling fan earth lead from the body

6.11a Unscrew the bolts (arrowed) securing the dehydrator . . .

6.11b . . . and the refrigerant pipe to the front panel . . .

6.11c . . . then position the condenser clear, taking care not to lose its mounting rubbers

the fan/radiator mounting panel and the bolt securing the refrigerant pipe to the base of the panel. Free the dehydrator and condenser,

6.13 Disconnect the cooling fan wiring connector from the left-hand side of the panel

and position them clear of the front panel, taking care not to strain the refrigerant pipes/hoses. Also take care not to lose the condenser upper and lower mounting rubbers (see illustrations).

Caution: Do not disconnect the refrigerant lines from the dehydrator/condenser (refer to the warnings given in Section 11). Ensure the compressor is securely supported to prevent the refrigerant lines being damaged.

12 On models with air conditioning, remove both headlights as described in Chapter 12, Section 7.

13 On all models, disconnect the cooling fan wiring connector located on the left-hand side of the panel (see illustration).

14 Trace the fan wiring back to the fuse/relay box, releasing its retaining clips from the body. Remove the fuse/relay box cover and

pull out the large cooling fan fuse. Carefully prise out the locking clip then unclip the fan wiring connector from the fuse/relay box so it is free to be removed with the front panel assembly (see illustrations).

15 Unclip the wiring harness from the right-hand side of the front panel.

16 Unscrew the four bolts securing the top of the front panel to the body then carefully manoeuvre the assembly upwards and out of position (see illustrations). On models with air conditioning, take great care not to damage the condenser as the panel is removed.

17 With the mounting panel removed, disconnect the wiring connector then unscrew the mounting bolts and remove the fan assembly (see illustrations). Recover the spacers and washers from the fan mounting rubbers.

6.14a Remove the cooling fan fuse . . .

6.14b . . . then prise out the locking clip . . .

6.14c . . . and free the fan connector from the fuse/relay box

6.16a Unscrew the mounting bolts
(arrowed) . . .

6.16b . . . then lift the front panel assembly
out of position

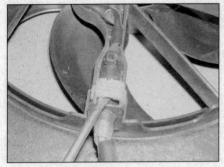

6.17a Disconnect the wiring connector . . .

6.17b . . . then undo the retaining bolts
(arrowed) and remove the fan assembly

6.21a Remove the fasteners (arrowed –
pull out the centre pins then remove the
complete fastener) . . .

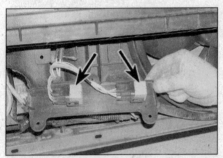

6.21b . . . and free the cover from the front
panel to gain access to the cooling fan
relays (arrowed)

Refitting

18 Refitting is a reversal of removal.

Cooling fan relays

19 The relays are fitted to the front panel and are located behind the cover on the right-hand side of the cooling fan.
20 To gain access to the relays, remove the front bumper as described in Chapter 11.
21 Release the fasteners and remove the cover from the front panel. The relays can then be removed (see illustrations).

Cooling fan resistor – models with air conditioning

22 The cooling fan resistor is fitted to the front panel and is also located on the right-hand side of the cooling fan.
23 To gain access to the resistor, remove the

front bumper as described in Chapter 11.
24 Disconnect the wiring connector then undo the retaining screws and remove the resistor from the front panel (see illustration).

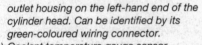

7 Cooling system electrical sensors – general information, removal and refitting

General information

Petrol engine models

1 Petrol engine models are fitted with the following temperature sensors (see illustrations).
 a) Engine management system coolant temperature sensor – fitted to the coolant

outlet housing on the left-hand end of the cylinder head. Can be identified by its green-coloured wiring connector.
 b) Coolant temperature gauge sensor – fitted to the left-hand end of the cylinder head. Can be identified by its blue-coloured wiring connector.
 c) Cooling fan temperature sensor (models not equipped with air conditioning) – fitted to the top of the radiator. **Note:** On models with air conditioning, the cooling fan is operated by the air conditioning system control unit (see below).
 d) Air conditioning control system (Bitron) temperature sensor – also fitted to the coolant outlet housing on the left-hand end of the cylinder head. Can be identified by its brown-coloured wiring connector.

3

6.24 Disconnect the cooling fan resistor
wiring connector

7.1a Engine management system coolant
temperature sensor (1) and air conditioning
control system (Bitron) temperature
sensor (2) locations – petrol engine

7.1b On petrol engines the coolant
temperature gauge temperature sensor
(arrowed) is screwed into the left-hand end
of the cylinder head

7.6 On 2.0 litre diesel engines with a plastic housing, prise out the retaining clip (arrowed) to release the coolant temperature sensor

1.9 litre diesel engine models

2 1.9 litre diesel engine models are fitted with the following sensors.
a) *Coolant temperature gauge sensor unit – fitted to the fuel filter/thermostat housing.*
b) *Cooling fan temperature sensor (WJZ engine) – fitted to the top of the radiator.* **Note:** *On later WJY engines, the cooling fan is operated by the fuel injection system control unit (see below).*
c) *Fuel injection/preheating system coolant temperature sensor – fitted to the coolant outlet housing on the left-hand end of the cylinder head.*

2.0 litre diesel engine models

3 On these models there is only one coolant temperature sensor which is fitted to the coolant outlet housing on the left-hand end of the cylinder head. The coolant temperature gauge and the cooling fan are all operated by the fuel injection ECU using the signal supplied by this sensor.

Removal

Note: *Ensure the engine is cold before removing a temperature sensor.*
4 Partially drain the cooling system to just below the level of the sensor (as described in Chapter 1A or 1B). Alternatively, have ready a suitable bung to plug the sensor aperture whilst the sensor is removed. If this method is used, take great care not to damage the

8.3a Remove the coolant pump . . .

switch aperture or use anything which will allow foreign matter to enter the cooling system.
5 Disconnect the battery negative terminal then disconnect the wiring connector from the sensor.
6 On 2.0 litre diesel engines fitted with a plastic coolant outlet housing, prise out the sensor retaining circlip then remove the sensor and sealing ring from the housing **(see illustration)**. If the system has not been drained, plug the sensor aperture to prevent further coolant loss.
7 On all other engines, unscrew the sensor and recover the sealing washer (where applicable). If the system has not been drained, plug the sensor aperture to prevent further coolant loss.

Refitting

8 On 2.0 litre diesel engines with a plastic coolant outlet housing, fit a new sealing ring to the sensor. Push the sensor firmly into the housing and secure it in position with the circlip, ensuring it is correctly located in the housing groove.
9 On all other engines, if the sensor was originally fitted using sealing compound, clean the sensor threads thoroughly, and coat them with fresh sealing compound. If the sensor was originally fitted using a sealing washer, use a new sealing washer. Fit the sensor and tighten securely.
10 Reconnect the wiring connector then refit any components removed from access
11 Top-up the cooling system as described in *Weekly checks*.

8 Coolant pump – removal and refitting

Removal

1 Drain the cooling system (see Chapter 1A or 1B).
2 Remove the timing belt as described in Chapter 2A or 2B as applicable.
3 Slacken and remove the retaining bolts and withdraw the pump assembly from the engine.

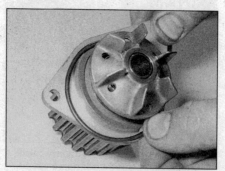

8.3b . . . and recover the sealing ring/gasket (1.4 litre petrol engine shown)

Recover the pump sealing ring/gasket (as applicable) and discard it; a new one must be used on refitting **(see illustrations)**.

Refitting

4 Ensure that the pump and cylinder block/housing mating surfaces are clean and dry.
5 Fit the new sealing ring/gasket (as applicable) to the pump then refit the pump assembly, tightening its retaining bolts securely.
6 Refit the timing belt as described in Chapter 2A or 2B (as applicable).
7 Refill the cooling system as described in Chapter 1A or 1B (as applicable).

9 Heating and ventilation system – general information

Note: *Refer to Section 11 for information on the air conditioning side of the system.*

Manually-controlled heating/ventilation system

1 The heating/ventilation system consists of a four-speed blower motor (housed behind the facia), face level vents in the centre and at each end of the facia, and air ducts to the front footwells.
2 The control unit is located in the facia, and the controls operate flap valves to deflect and mix the air flowing through the various parts of the heating/ventilation system. The flap valves are contained in the air distribution housing, which acts as a central distribution unit, passing air to the various ducts and vents.
3 Cold air enters the system through the grille on the right-hand side of the bonnet. If required, the airflow is boosted by the blower, and then flows through the various ducts, according to the settings of the controls. Stale air is expelled through ducts at the rear of the vehicle. If warm air is required, the cold air is passed over the heater matrix, which is heated by the engine coolant.
4 A recirculation lever enables the outside air supply to be closed off, while the air inside the vehicle is recirculated. This can be useful to prevent unpleasant odours entering from outside the vehicle, but should only be used briefly, as the recirculated air inside the vehicle will soon become stale.
5 On 2.0 litre diesel engine models an electric coolant heater is fitted to the feed hose to the heater matrix. When the coolant temperature is cold, the heater warms the coolant before it enters the heater matrix. This quickly increases the temperature of the heater matrix on cold starts, resulting in warm air being available to heat the vehicle interior soon after start-up.

Automatic climate control system

6 A fully automatic electronic climate control system was offered as an option on some

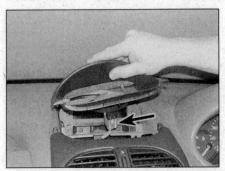

10.2 Unclip the clock/multi-function unit surround from the facia and disconnect the wiring connector (arrowed)

10.3a Undo the retaining screws (arrowed) . . .

10.3b . . . then unclip the centre vent panel from the facia

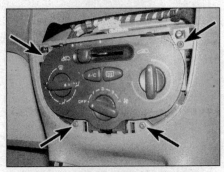

10.4a Undo the retaining screws (arrowed) . . .

10.4b . . . then unclip the control panel and manoeuvre it out from the facia

models. The main components of the system are exactly the same as those described for the manual system, the only major difference being that the temperature and distribution flaps in the heating/ventilation housing are operated by electric motors rather than cables.

7 The operation of the system is controlled by the electronic control module (which is incorporated in the blower motor assembly) along with the following sensors.
  a) *The passenger compartment sensor – informs the control module of the temperature of the air inside the passenger compartment.*
  b) *Evaporator temperature sensor – informs the control module of the evaporator temperature.*
  c) *Heater matrix temperature sensor – informs the control module of the heater matrix temperature.*

8 Using the information from the above sensors, the control module determines the appropriate settings for the heating/ventilation system housing flaps to maintain the passenger compartment at the desired setting on the control panel.

9 If the system develops a fault, the vehicle should be taken to a Peugeot dealer. A complete test of the system can then be carried out, using a special electronic diagnostic test unit which is simply plugged into the system's diagnostic connector (located next to the fusebox).

10 Heater/ventilation components – removal and refitting

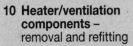

Heating/ventilation control panel

Removal

1 Remove the audio unit as described in Chapter 12.
2 Carefully unclip the clock/multi-function unit surround from the top of the facia and remove it, disconnecting the wiring connector from the hazard warning light switch **(see illustration)**.
3 Slacken and remove the retaining screws

securing the top of the centre vent panel to the facia. Carefully unclip the panel and remove it from the facia **(see illustrations)**.
4 Slacken and remove the four screws then release the upper retaining clip(s) and free the heating/ventilation control unit from the facia **(see illustrations)**.
5 On models with a manual control panel, disconnect the wiring connector from the rear of the control panel. Note the correct fitted location of each control cables (the end fittings are colour-coded) then unhook the cable retaining clips. Detach the cables and remove the control panel from the vehicle **(see illustration)**.
6 On models with an automatic climate control system, disconnect the wiring connectors and remove the control panel from the vehicle.

Refitting

7 Refitting is the reverse of removal. On models with a manual control panel ensure the control cables are correctly reconnected and securely held by the retaining clips; check the operation of the control knobs before securing the control panel to the facia **(see illustration)**.

Heater/ventilation control cables

Removal

8 Remove the facia as described in Chapter 11.
9 Release the retaining clip and detach the relevant cable from the rear of the control panel and the heating/ventilation housing. Remove the cable, noting its correct routing.

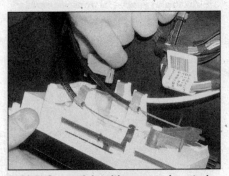

10.5 On models with a manual control panel, disconnect the wiring connector then release the retaining clips and detach the cables

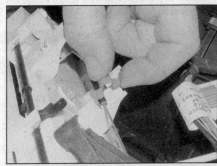

10.7 Ensure the control cables are correctly reconnected and securely held by the retaining clips

3

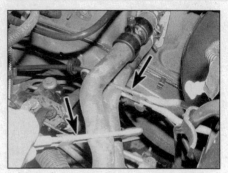

10.12 Clamp the heater matrix coolant hoses to minimise coolant loss

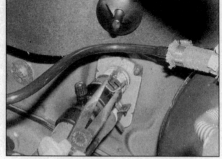

10.13a Release the retaining clips . . .

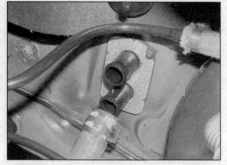

10.13b . . . and disconnect both coolant hoses from the heater matrix pipe unions

Refitting

10 Refitting is the reverse of removal, ensuring the cable is securely retained by its clips. Check the operation of the control panel and cables before refitting the facia (see Chapter 11).

Heater matrix

Note: *New matrix pipe sealing rings must be used on refitting. Suitable screws/bolts will also be required to secure the matrix/pipe unions in position.*

Removal

11 To improve access to the matrix unions on the bulkhead, remove the battery and battery tray as described in Chapter 5A. Where necessary also remove the air cleaner housing intake duct (see Chapter 4A or 4B).
12 Drain the cooling system (see Chapter 1A or 1B). Alternatively, clamp the heater matrix

coolant hoses to minimise coolant loss **(see illustration)**.
13 Release the retaining clips and disconnect the coolant hoses from the heater matrix pipe unions on the engine compartment bulkhead **(see illustrations)**.
14 Slacken and remove the screw securing the heater matrix pipes to the bulkhead and remove the retaining plate and seal **(see illustrations)**.
15 Remove the facia assembly as described in Chapter 11.
16 Position a container beneath the heater matrix pipe union on the left-hand side of the heating/ventilation housing to catch any spilt coolant.
17 Slacken and remove the screws securing the matrix pipes to the housing and release the clips securing the pipes to the matrix. **Note:** *The clips are designed to be snapped off and replaced with bolts on refitting.*

18 Free the pipes from the matrix, catching the coolant in the container, then free them from the bulkhead and remove them from the vehicle. Recover the sealing rings fitted to the pipe unions and discard them; new ones should be used on refitting. Take care not to lose the bulkhead seal or retaining plate from the pipes **(see illustrations)**.
19 Release the retaining clips then slide the matrix out from the housing. **Note:** *The clips are designed to be snapped off and replaced with bolts on refitting. Keep the matrix unions uppermost as the matrix is removed to prevent coolant spillage* **(see illustrations)**.

Refitting

20 Ease the matrix into the housing and clip it into position. If the retaining clips where broken on removal, secure the matrix in position using self-tapping screws fitted to the holes provided **(see illustration)**.

10.14a Undo the retaining screw (location arrowed) and remove the retaining plate . . .

10.14b . . . and seal from the pipes

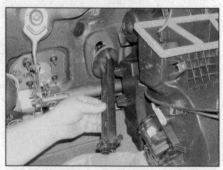

10.18a Manoeuvre the heater matrix pipes out of position . . .

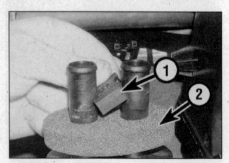

10.18b . . . taking care not to lose the retaining plate (1) or seal (2) from the bulkhead end of the pipes

10.19a Release the retaining clips (arrowed) . . .

10.19b . . . then slide the heater matrix out from the housing

10.20 Secure the heater matrix in position with self-tapping screws (arrowed) if the retaining clips are no longer any use

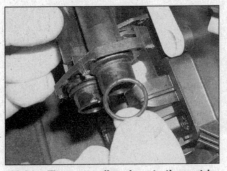

10.21a Fit new sealing rings to the matrix pipe unions . . .

10.21b . . . and secure the pipes in position using screws and nuts (arrowed) in the holes provided

21 Ensure the bulkhead seal and retaining plate are correctly fitted to the matrix pipes and fit a new sealing ring to each of the pipe unions. Manoeuvre the pipe assembly into position and secure it to the matrix using screws/nuts and bolts fitted to the three holes provided **(see illustrations)**.

22 Working in the engine compartment, refit the seal and retaining plate to the heater matrix pipes and securely tighten the retaining screw. Remove the clamps (where fitted) then reconnect the coolant hoses, securing them in position with the retaining clips.

23 Refit the facia assembly (see Chapter 11).

24 Refit the battery (see Chapter 5A).

25 Refill the cooling system (see Chapter 1A or 1B).

Heater blower motor

Removal

26 The blower motor is fitted to the top of the heating/ventilation housing, on the left-hand side.

27 On right-hand drive models, remove the glovebox as described in Section 27 of Chapter 11. Access to the motor can then be gained through the glovebox aperture.

28 On left-hand drive models, remove the steering column as described in Chapter 10 to gain access to the motor.

29 Where necessary, slacken and remove the retaining screw securing the motor to the housing (this screw may not be fitted).

30 Disconnect the wiring connector(s) from the blower motor **(see illustration)**.

31 Rotate the motor clockwise to free it from the housing then manoeuvre it out of position **(see illustration)**.

Refitting

32 Refitting is the reverse of removal. If the motor is not a secure fit in the housing, fix it in position by fitting a self-tapping screw to the hole provided.

Heater blower motor resistor

Removal

33 On left-hand drive models, remove the glovebox as described in Section 27 of Chapter 11.

34 On all models, set the air recirculation flap

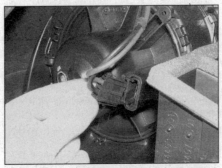

10.30 Disconnect the wiring connector from the blower motor . . .

lever to the recirculation position. Access to the resistor can then be gained via recirculation intake aperture on the underside of the heating/ventilation housing duct.

35 Rotate the resistor to free it from the duct and pull it into the duct. Disconnect the wiring connector and remove the resistor from the housing **(see illustrations)**. **Note:** *If access proves difficult, remove the blower motor and remove the resistor through the blower motor aperture.*

Refitting

36 Manoeuvre the resistor into position and securely connect it to the wiring connector. Once the connector is securely fitted located the resistor in the duct and clip it in position. Refit any components removed for access.

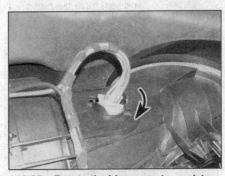

10.35a Rotate the blower motor resistor and pull it into the duct . . .

10.31 . . . then rotate the motor clockwise to free it from the housing (arrow indicates hole provided for retaining screw – if fitted)

Heating/ventilation housing assembly

Models not fitted with air conditioning – removal

37 To improve access to the matrix unions on the bulkhead, remove the battery and battery tray as described in Chapter 5A. Where necessary also remove the air cleaner housing intake duct (see Chapter 4A or 4B).

38 Drain the cooling system (see Chapter 1A or 1B). Alternatively, working in the engine compartment, clamp the heater matrix coolant hoses to minimise coolant loss **(see illustration 10.12)**.

39 Release the retaining clips and disconnect the coolant hoses from the heater matrix pipe

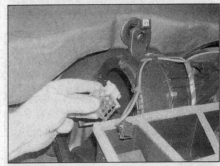

10.35b . . . then disconnect it from the wiring connector and manoeuvre it out of position (shown being removed through blower motor aperture – facia removed for clarity)

3

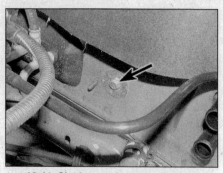

10.41 Slacken and remove the bolt (arrowed) securing the heating/ventilation housing to the bulkhead

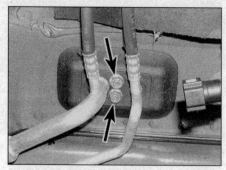

10.48 Air conditioning pipe union retaining nuts (arrowed)

unions on the engine compartment bulkhead **(see illustrations 10.13a and 10.13b)**.

40 Slacken and remove the screw securing the heater matrix pipes to the bulkhead and remove the retaining plate and seal **(see illustrations 10.14a and 10.14b)**.

41 Slacken and remove the bolt securing the heating/ventilation housing to the bulkhead **(see illustration)**.

42 Remove the facia assembly as described in Chapter 11.

43 Disconnect the wiring connectors from the heating/ventilation housing components then remove the housing and control panel assembly from the vehicle. Keep the heater matrix pipe unions uppermost as the assembly is removed to prevent coolant spillage.

44 Recover the seal and retaining plate from the heater matrix pipes **(see illustration 10.18b)** and the seal from the housing mounting. Renew the seals if they show signs of damage or deterioration.

Models not fitted with air conditioning – refitting

45 Refitting is the reverse of removal ensuring the seals are in position on the pipes and housing mounting. On completion, refill the cooling system (see Chapter 1A or 1B).

Models with air conditioning – removal

⚠️ *Warning: Refer to Section 11 for precautions to be observed when working on models equipped with air conditioning. Do not attempt the following procedure unless the system has been professionally discharged.*

46 Have the air conditioning system discharged by an air conditioning specialist and obtain some plugs to seal the air conditioning pipe unions whilst the system is disconnected.

47 Carry out the operations described in paragraphs 37 to 41.

48 Unscrew the two nuts securing the air conditioning pipe union to the bulkhead **(see illustration)**. Separate the pipes from the evaporator and quickly seal the pipe and evaporator unions to prevent the entry of moisture into the refrigerant circuit. Discard the sealing rings, new ones must be used on refitting.

⚠️ *Warning: Failure to seal the refrigerant pipe unions will result in the dehydrator reservoir become saturated, necessitating its renewal.*

49 Remove the heating/ventilation housing assembly as described in paragraphs 42 to 44 and recover the seal from the evaporator.

Models with air conditioning – refitting

50 Ensure the bulkhead seals are correctly fitted to the evaporator, matrix pipes and housing mounting. Manoeuvre the housing assembly into position, locating the housing drain hose correctly in its hole in the floor.

51 Loosely refit the housing mounting bolt then refit the retaining plate to the heater matrix pipe and loosely install the retaining screw.

52 Lubricate the new evaporator union sealing rings with compressor oil. Remove the plugs and install the sealing rings then quickly fit the refrigerant pipe union to the evaporator. Ensure the refrigerant pipes and evaporator are correctly joined then refit the retaining nuts, tighten them securely.

53 Tighten the matrix pipe retaining screw securely and securely tighten the housing mounting bolt.

54 The remainder of refitting is the reverse of removal. On completion, refill the cooling system (see Chapter 1A or 1B).

Automatic climate control system

55 The automatic climate control system sensors and motors are all fitted to the heating/ventilation housing. At the time of writing it was unclear whether they were available separately or were an integral part of the housing assembly. Refer to your Peugeot dealer for the latest information on parts availability.

Coolant heater

Removal

56 Remove the battery and battery tray as described in Chapter 5A to gain access to the heater which is mounted on the top of the transmission unit.

57 Remove the rubber insulation covers then unscrew the nuts and disconnect the wiring

connectors from the heater terminals **(see illustration)**.

58 Drain the cooling system (see Chapter 1B). Alternatively, clamp the coolant hoses on each side of the heater to minimise coolant loss.

59 Release the retaining clips and disconnect the coolant hoses from the heater.

60 Unscrew the bolts securing the heater bracket to the transmission unit and remove the heater from the engine compartment.

Refitting

61 Refitting is the reverse of removal. On completion, refill the cooling system (see Chapter 1B).

11 Air conditioning system – general information and precautions

General information

1 An air conditioning system is available on certain models. It enables the temperature of incoming air to be lowered, and also dehumidifies the air, which makes for rapid demisting and increased comfort.

2 The cooling side of the system works in the same way as a domestic refrigerator. Refrigerant gas is drawn into a belt-driven compressor, and passes into a condenser mounted on the front of the radiator, where it loses heat and becomes liquid. The liquid passes through an expansion valve to an evaporator, where it changes from liquid under high pressure to gas under low pressure. This change is accompanied by a drop in temperature, which cools the evaporator. The refrigerant returns to the compressor, and the cycle begins again.

3 Air blown through the evaporator passes to the heating/ventilation housing, where it is mixed with hot air blown through the heater matrix to achieve the desired temperature in the passenger compartment.

4 The heating side of the system works in the same way as on models without air conditioning (see Section 9).

5 The operation of the system is controlled electronically by the 'Bitron' control unit,

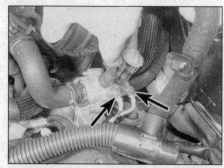

10.57 Remove the rubber insulation covers then unscrew the nuts (arrowed) and disconnect the wiring from the coolant heater terminals – 2.0 litre diesel engine

which controls the electric cooling fan, the compressor and the facia-mounted warning light. Any problems with the system should be referred to a Peugeot dealer.

Precautions

6 When an air conditioning system is fitted, it is necessary to observe special precautions whenever dealing with any part of the system, or its associated components. The refrigerant is potentially dangerous, and should only be handled by qualified persons. Uncontrolled discharging of the refrigerant is dangerous and damaging to the environment for the following reasons.

a) *If it is splashed onto the skin, it can cause frostbite.*

b) *The refrigerant is heavier then air and so displaces oxygen. In a confined space which is not adequately ventilated this could lead to a risk of suffocation. The gas is odourless and colourless so there is no warning of its presence in the atmosphere.*

c) *Although not poisonous, in the presence of a naked flame (including a cigarette) it forms a noxious gas which causes headaches, nausea, etc.*

⚠️ *Warning: Never attempt to open any air conditioning system refrigerant pipe/hose union without first having the system fully discharged by an air conditioning specialist. On completion of work, have the system recharged with the correct type and amount of fresh refrigerant.*

⚠️ *Warning: Always seal disconnected refrigerant pipe/ hose unions as soon as they are disconnected. Failure to form an air-tight seal on any union will result in the dehydrator reservoir become saturated, necessitating its renewal. Also renew all sealing rings disturbed.*

Caution: Do not operated the air conditioning system if it is known to be short of refrigerant as this could damage the compressor.

---

12 Air conditioning system components – removal and refitting

⚠️ *Warning: Refer to the precautions given in Section 11 and have the system discharged by an air conditioning specialist before carrying out any work on the air conditioning system*

Compressor

Removal

1 Have the air conditioning system fully discharged by an air conditioning specialist.

2 Remove the auxiliary drivebelt as described in Chapter 1A or 1B (as applicable).

3 Disconnect the compressor wiring connector from the engine harness (see illustration).

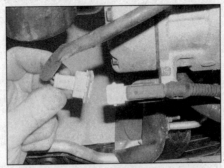

12.3 Disconnect the wiring connector from the air conditioning compressor

4 Unscrew the bolt securing the refrigerant pipe retaining plate to the compressor (**see illustration**). Separate the pipes from the compressor and quickly seal the pipe and compressor unions to prevent the entry of moisture into the refrigerant circuit. Discard the sealing rings, new ones must be used on refitting.

⚠️ *Warning: Failure to seal the refrigerant pipe unions will result in the dehydrator reservoir become saturated, necessitating its renewal.*

5 Unscrew the compressor mounting bolts and nuts then free the compressor from its mounting bracket and remove it from the engine (**see illustrations**). Take care not to lose the spacers from the compressor rear mountings (where fitted).

Refitting

6 Ensure the spacers are correctly fitted to the rear mountings then manoeuvre the compressor into position and fit the mounting bolts and nuts. Tighten the compressor front (drivebelt pulley) end mounting bolts to the specified torque first then tighten the rear bolts.

7 Lubricate the new refrigerant pipe sealing rings with compressor oil. Remove the plugs and install the sealing rings then quickly fit the refrigerant pipes to the compressor. Ensure the refrigerant pipes are correctly joined then refit the retaining bolt, tighten it securely.

8 Reconnect the wiring connector then refit the auxiliary drivebelt (see Chapter 1A or 1B).

12.5a Compressor front and rear lower mounting bolts (arrowed) – petrol engine

12.4 Refrigerant pipe retaining plate bolt (arrowed)

9 Have the air conditioning system recharged with the correct type and amount of refrigerant by a specialist before using the system.

Condenser

Removal

10 Have the air conditioning system fully discharged by an air conditioning specialist.

11 Remove the radiator as described in Section 4.

12 Unscrew the nut/bolt and disconnect the dehydrator pipe from the right-hand side of the condenser then release the retaining clip and detach the compressor pipe from the condenser. Quickly seal the pipe and condenser unions to prevent the entry of moisture into the refrigerant circuit. Discard the sealing ring(s); new one(s) must be used on refitting.

⚠️ *Warning: Failure to seal the refrigerant pipe unions will result in the dehydrator reservoir become saturated, necessitating its renewal.*

13 Free the condenser from the front panel and remove it from the vehicle, taking care not to lose the condenser upper and lower mounting rubbers.

Refitting

14 Ensure the upper and lower mounting rubbers are correctly fitted then seat the condenser in position in the front panel.

15 Lubricate the sealing rings with compressor oil. Remove the plugs and install

12.5b Compressor front and rear lower mounting bolts and nuts (arrowed) – diesel engine

3

the sealing rings then quickly fit the refrigerant pipes to the condenser. Securely tighten the dehydrator pipe union nut/bolt and ensure the compressor pipe is correctly joined.

16 Refit the radiator as described in Section 4.

17 Have the air conditioning system recharged with the correct type and amount of refrigerant by a specialist before using the system.

Dehydrator reservoir

Removal

18 The dehydrator reservoir is located on the right-hand side of the condenser where it is mounted onto the front panel.

19 Have the air conditioning system fully discharged by an air conditioning specialist.

20 Unscrew the nuts and disconnect the pipes from the dehydrator reservoir. Quickly seal the pipe and dehydrator unions to prevent the entry of moisture into the refrigerant circuit. Discard the sealing rings, new ones must be used on refitting.

⚠️ **Warning: Failure to seal the refrigerant pipe unions will result in the dehydrator reservoir become saturated, necessitating its renewal.**

21 Unscrew the mounting bolts and remove the dehydrator reservoir from the vehicle.

Refitting

22 Fit the dehydrator reservoir to the front panel and securely tighten its mounting bolts.

23 Lubricate the new sealing rings with compressor oil. Remove the plugs and install the sealing rings then quickly fit the refrigerant pipes to the dehydrator, tightening their retaining nuts securely.

24 Have the air conditioning system recharged with the correct type and amount of refrigerant by a specialist before using the system.

Evaporator

Removal

25 Have the air conditioning system fully discharged by an air conditioning specialist.

26 Remove the heating/ventilation housing as described in Section 9.

27 Release the retaining clips and slide the evaporator out from the front of the housing.

Refitting

28 Install the evaporator in the housing then refit the housing as described in Section 9.

Chapter 4 Part A:
Fuel/exhaust systems – petrol engine

Contents

Degrees of difficulty

Easy, suitable for novice with little experience		**Fairly easy,** suitable for beginner with some experience		**Fairly difficult,** suitable for competent DIY mechanic		**Difficult,** suitable for experienced DIY mechanic		**Very difficult,** suitable for expert DIY or professional	

Specifications

System type
1.1 litre models	Magneti Marelli 1AP
1.4 litre models:	
Later models with pulse air injection	Bosch Motronic MP7.3
All other models	Magneti Marelli 1AP
1.6 litre models	Bosch Motronic MP7.2

Fuel system data
Fuel pump type	Electric, immersed in tank
Fuel pump regulated constant pressure	3.5 ± 0.2 bars
Specified idle speed	850 ± 100 rpm (not adjustable – controlled by ECU)
Idle mixture CO content	Less than 1.0 % (not adjustable- controlled by ECU)

Recommended fuel
Minimum octane rating	95 RON unleaded (UK unleaded premium). Leaded/lead replacement fuel (LRP) must **not** be used

Torque wrench settings
	Nm	lbf ft
Exhaust manifold nuts:		
Long nuts	16	12
Short nuts	25	18
Inlet manifold nuts	8	6
Knock sensor	20	15
Roadwheel bolts	85	63

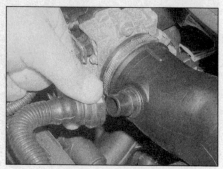

2.1 Disconnect the breather hose(s) . . .

2.2 . . . then slacken the retaining clips and remove the duct connecting the air cleaner housing to the manifold (1.4 litre engine shown)

2.3a Lift the air cleaner housing to free it from its mounting bracket (arrowed) . . .

1 General information and precautions

1 The fuel supply system consists of a fuel tank (which is mounted under the rear of the car, with an electric fuel pump immersed in it), a fuel filter, fuel feed and return lines. The fuel pump supplies fuel to the fuel rail, which acts as a reservoir for the four fuel injectors which inject fuel into the inlet tracts. The fuel filter incorporated in the feed line from the pump to the fuel rail ensures that the fuel supplied to the injectors is clean.

2 Refer to Section 6 for further information on the operation of the engine management system, and to Section 16 for information on the exhaust system.

⚠ **Warning: Many of the procedures in this Chapter require the removal of fuel lines and connections, which may result in some fuel spillage. Before carrying out any operation on the fuel system, refer to the precautions given in 'Safety first!' at the beginning of this manual, and follow them implicitly. Petrol is a highly dangerous and volatile liquid, and the precautions necessary when handling it cannot be overstressed.**
Note: Residual pressure will remain in the fuel lines long after the vehicle was last used. When disconnecting any fuel line, first depressurise the fuel system as described in Section 7.

2 Air cleaner assembly and intake ducts – removal and refitting

Removal

1 Unclip and disconnect the breather hose(s) from the manifold end of the duct connecting the air cleaner housing to the inlet manifold **(see illustration)**.

2 Slacken the retaining clips then free the duct from the manifold and air cleaner housing, and remove it from the engine compartment **(see illustration)**.

3 Lift the air cleaner housing assembly off of

its mounting bracket and remove it from the engine compartment. Recover the mounting rubber fitted to the housing lower locating peg and the sealing ring from the housing intake duct **(see illustrations)**.

4 To remove the intake duct, firmly apply the handbrake then jack up the front of the car and support it on axle stands (see *Jacking and vehicle support*). Undo the screws securing the front section of the left-hand wheelarch liner to the base of the bumper then remove the fasteners (pull out the centre pin then remove the complete fastener) securing the liner to the body and manoeuvre it out from underneath the wing. Remove the retaining bolts and remove the duct assembly from the vehicle (on 1.4 and 1.6 litre engines a resonator chamber is incorporated into the duct to reduce intake noise).

Refitting

5 Refitting is a reversal of the removal procedure, ensuring that all hoses and ducts are properly reconnected and correctly seated and, where necessary, securely held by their retaining clips.

3 Accelerator cable – removal, refitting and adjustment

Removal

1 Working in the engine compartment, free

2.3b . . . then recover the lower mounting rubber (1) and rubber sealing ring (2)

the accelerator inner cable from the throttle housing cam, then pull the outer cable out from its mounting bracket rubber grommet. Recover the spring clip from the outer cable **(see illustration)**.

2 Working back along the length of the cable, free it from any retaining clips or ties, noting its correct routing.

3 Working inside the vehicle, reach up behind the facia then release the retaining clip and detach the inner cable from the top of the accelerator pedal **(see illustration)**.

4 Remove the retaining clip which secure the outer cable end fitting to the bulkhead then tie a length of string to the end of the cable.

5 Return to the engine compartment, release the cable grommet from the bulkhead and withdraw the cable. When the end of the cable appears, untie the string and leave it in position – it can then be used to draw the cable back into position on refitting.

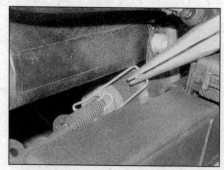

3.1 Remove the spring clip from the accelerator outer cable

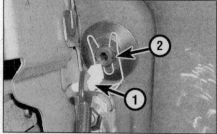

3.3 Free the inner cable end fitting (1) from the accelerator pedal and remove the retaining clip (2) from the outer cable (shown with facia removed)

Refitting

6 Tie the string to the end of the cable, then use the string to draw the cable into position through the bulkhead. Once the cable end is visible, untie the string, then secure the outer cable in position with the retaining clip and attach the inner cable into the pedal end.

7 From within the engine compartment, ensure the outer cable is correctly seated in the bulkhead grommet, then work along the cable, securing it in position with the retaining clips and ties, and ensuring that the cable is correctly routed.

8 Pass the outer cable through its mounting bracket grommet, and reconnect the inner cable to the throttle cam. Adjust the cable as described below.

Adjustment

9 Remove the spring clip from the accelerator outer cable **(see illustration 3.1)**. Ensuring that the throttle cam is fully against its stop, gently pull the cable out of its grommet until all free play is removed from the inner cable.

10 With the cable held in this position, refit the spring clip to the last exposed outer cable groove in front of the rubber grommet. When the clip is refitted and the outer cable is released, there should be only a small amount of free play in the inner cable.

11 Have an assistant depress the accelerator pedal, and check that the throttle cam opens fully and returns smoothly to its stop.

Note: *On models with an automatic transmission unit, Peugeot specify that the automatic transmission electronic control unit (ECU) should be reprogrammed every time the accelerator cable is adjusted. If the transmission performance has been adversely affected by accelerator cable adjustment, take the vehicle to a Peugeot dealer to have the transmission ECU reprogrammed with the necessary diagnostic equipment.*

4 Accelerator pedal –
removal and refitting

Removal

1 Working inside the vehicle, reach up behind the facia then release the retaining clip and detach the inner cable from the top of the accelerator pedal.

2 On right-hand drive models, remove the retaining clip then slide out the pivot pin and remove the accelerator pedal from the pedal mounting bracket.

3 On left-hand drive models, remove the retaining clip then slide the pedal off its pivot shaft. The pivot shaft is a screw fit in the body.

Refitting

4 Refitting is a reversal of the removal procedure, applying a little multi-purpose grease to the pedal pivot point. On completion, adjust the accelerator cable as described in Section 3.

5 Unleaded petrol –
general information and usage

Note: *The information given in this Chapter is correct at the time of writing. If updated information is thought to be required, check with a Peugeot dealer. If travelling abroad, consult one of the motoring organisations (or a similar authority) for advice on the fuel available.*

1 The fuel recommended by Peugeot is given in the Specifications Section of this Chapter, followed by the equivalent petrol currently on sale in the UK.

2 All models are designed to run on fuel with a minimum octane rating of 95 (RON). All models have a catalytic converter, and so must be run on unleaded fuel only. Under no circumstances should leaded/lead replacement fuel (UK 4-star/LRP) be used, as this may damage the converter.

3 Super unleaded petrol (98 octane) can also be used in all models if wished, though there is no advantage in doing so.

6 Engine management system
– general information

Note: *The engine management ECU is of the 'auto-adaptive' type, meaning that as it operates, it also monitors and stores the settings which give optimum engine performance under all operating conditions. When the battery is disconnected, these settings are lost and the ECU reverts to the base settings programmed into its memory at the factory. On restarting, this may lead to the engine running/idling roughly for a short while, until the ECU has re-learned the optimum settings during the first few miles of driving. To aid this re-learning process, initialise the ECU as follows once the battery has been reconnected.*

a) Turn on the ignition switch then turn it off for 10 seconds. Turn the ignition on and wait for 10 seconds before starting the engine without touching the accelerator pedal.

b) On engines with a Bosch system, warm the engine up to to normal operating temperature. When the cooling fan cuts in, switch off the engine. Restart the engine, allow it to idle for a few minutes, then take it on a short road test driving at varying engine speeds/loads. At least once during the road test, decelerate from an engine speed of above 4000 rpm for at least 5 seconds.

c) On engines with a Magneti Marelli system, warm the engine up to normal operating temperature. When the cooling fan cuts in, take the vehicle on a short road test driving at varying engine speeds/loads. At least once during the road test, when it is

safe to do so, fully depress the accelerator pedal and accelerate for at least 2 seconds.

Bosch Motronic MP7.2 system

1 The Bosch Motronic MP7.2 engine management (fuel injection/ignition) system is fitted to all 1.6 litre models. The system incorporates a closed-loop catalytic converter and an evaporative emission control system, and complies with the very latest emission control standards. Refer to Chapter 5B for information on the ignition side of the system; the fuel side of the system operates as follows.

2 The fuel pump (which is immersed in the fuel tank) supplies fuel from the tank to the fuel rail, via a filter mounted on the front of the fuel tank. Fuel supply pressure is controlled by the pressure regulator which is incorporated in the fuel pump assembly. The outlet of the fuel filter is connected to a T-piece, one end of which is connected to the pressure regulator and the other to the fuel rail. When the optimum operating pressure of the fuel system is exceeded, the regulator allows excess fuel to return directly from the filter to the fuel tank. This system means that there is only a single fuel pipe running from the fuel tank to the fuel rail.

3 The electrical control system consists of the ECU, along with the following sensors:

a) Throttle potentiometer – informs the ECU of the throttle position, and the rate of throttle opening/closing.

b) Coolant temperature sensor – informs the ECU of engine temperature.

c) Intake air temperature sensor – informs the ECU of the temperature of the air passing through the throttle housing.

d) Oxygen sensor – informs the ECU of the oxygen content of the exhaust gases (explained in greater detail in Part C of this Chapter).

e) Crankshaft sensor – informs the ECU of the crankshaft position and speed of rotation.

f) Manifold absolute pressure (MAP) sensor – informs the ECU of the load on the engine (expressed in terms of inlet manifold vacuum).

g) Knock sensor – informs the ECU when pre-ignition ('pinking') is occurring.

h) Vehicle speed sensor – informs the ECU of the vehicle speed.

i) Power steering pressure switch – informs the ECU when the power steering pump is under load.

j) Air conditioning system pressure switch – informs ECU when the air conditioning compressor is under load.

4 All the above signals are analysed by the ECU which selects the fuelling response appropriate to those values. The ECU controls the fuel injectors (varying the pulse width – the length of time the injectors are held open – to provide a richer or weaker mixture, as appropriate). The mixture is constantly varied

4A

by the ECU, to provide the best setting for cranking, starting (with either a hot or cold engine), warm-up, idle, cruising and acceleration. The injectors are operated 'semi-sequentially', injectors No 1 and 4 being operated as one pair and injectors No 2 and 3 as the other.

5 The ECU also has full control over the engine idle speed, via a stepper motor fitted to the throttle housing. When the throttle valve is closed, the ECU controls the opening of the valve, which in turn regulates the amount of air entering the manifold, and so controls the idle speed.

6 The ECU also controls the exhaust and evaporative emission control systems, which are described in detail in Part C of this Chapter.

7 On early models, an electric heating element is fitted to the aluminium throttle housing; the heater is supplied with current by the ECU, and warms the throttle housing on cold starts to prevent possible icing of the throttle valve. Later models have a plastic throttle valve housing and no longer require a heating element.

8 If there is an abnormality in any of the readings obtained from the various sensors, the ECU enters its back-up mode. In this event, it ignores the abnormal sensor signal and assumes a pre-programmed value which will allow the engine to continue running (albeit at reduced efficiency). If the ECU enters this back-up mode, the warning light on the instrument panel will come on, and the relevant fault code will be stored in the ECU memory.

9 If the warning light comes on, the vehicle should be taken to a Peugeot dealer at the earliest opportunity. A complete test of the engine management system can then be carried out, using a special electronic diagnostic test unit which is simply plugged into the system's diagnostic connector (located next to the fusebox).

Magneti Marelli 1AP system

10 The Magneti Marelli 1AP engine management (fuel injection/ignition) system is fitted to all 1.1 litre models and all 1.4 litre models not equipped with pulse air injection. Refer to Chapter 5B for information on the ignition side of the system.

11 The system is very similar in operation to the Bosch MP7.2 system described above, apart from the idle speed control system.

12 On the Magneti Marelli system, the idle speed is controlled by the ECU via a stepper motor fitted to the throttle housing. The motor has a pushrod controlling the opening of an air passage which bypasses the throttle valve. When the throttle valve is closed, the ECU controls the movement of the motor pushrod, which regulates the amount of air which flows through the throttle housing passage, so controlling the idle speed. The bypass passage is also used as an additional air supply during cold starting.

Bosch Motronic MP7.3 system

13 Some later 1.4 litre engines are fitted with a Bosch Motronic MP7.3 engine management system which incorporates a pulse air injection system. The system is a development of the MP7.2 system designed to meet the next level of emission standards. The changes include the following.

a) *The system is fully 'sequential' with all injectors being controlled individually.*

b) *A body accelerometer sensor is fitted to measure the vertical movement of the vehicle body. The sensor informs the ECU of the quality of the road surface on which the vehicle is being driven. This ensures the ECU does not diagnose variations in engine speed due to an uneven road surface as an ignition misfire.*

c) *A camshaft sensor is fitted to inform the ECU of the position of No 1 piston.*

d) *An additional oxygen sensor is fitted down stream of the catalytic converter (see Part C for further information).*

e) *Pulse air system is fitted to improve exhaust emissions during warm-up (see Part C for further information).*

f) *The idle speed is controlled by a stepper motor fitted to the throttle housing (see paragraph 12).*

---

7 Fuel system – depressurisation and pressurising

Note: *Refer to the warning note in Section 1 before proceeding.*

Depressurisation

⚠️ **Warning: The following procedure will merely relieve the pressure in the fuel system – remember that fuel will still be present in the system components and take precautions accordingly before disconnecting any of them.**

1 The fuel system referred to in this Section is defined as the tank-mounted fuel pump, the fuel filter, the fuel injectors, the fuel rail and the pipes of the fuel lines between these components. All these contain fuel which will be under pressure while the engine is running, and/or while the ignition is switched on. The pressure will remain for some time after the ignition has been switched off, and must be relieved in a controlled fashion when any of these components are disturbed for servicing work.

2 Disconnect the battery negative terminal.

3 Some models are equipped with a pressure relief valve on the fuel rail. On these models, unscrew the cap from the valve and position a container beneath the valve. Hold a wad of rag over the valve and relieve the pressure in the system by depressing the valve core with a suitable screwdriver. Be prepared for the squirt of fuel as the valve core is depressed and catch it with the rag. Hold the valve core

---

down until no more fuel is expelled from the valve. Once the pressure is relieved, securely refit the valve cap.

4 Where no valve is fitted to the fuel rail, it will be necessary to release the pressure as the fuel pipe is disconnected. Place a container beneath the union and position a large rag around the union to catch any fuel spray which may be expelled. Slowly release and disconnect the fuel pipe and catch any spilt fuel in the container. Plug the pipe/union to minimise fuel loss and prevent the entry of dirt into the fuel system.

Pressurising

5 After any work is carried out on the fuel system, the system should be pressurised as follows.

6 Depress the accelerator pedal fully then switch on the ignition. Hold the pedal depressed for approximately 1 second then release it. The ECU should then operate the fuel pump for between 20 and 30 seconds to refill the fuel system. Once the fuel pump stops the ignition can be switched off.

---

8 Fuel pump – removal and refitting

Removal

Note: *A pop rivet gun and new rivets will be required on refitting.*

1 Disconnect the battery negative lead.

2 For access to the fuel pump, tilt or remove the right-hand rear seat cushion (see Chapter 11).

3 Carefully drill the heads off the three rivets securing the fuel pump cover plate to the floor, taking care not to damage the plate/vehicle body **(see illustration)**. Remove the plate from the vehicle.

4 Using a screwdriver, carefully prise the plastic access cover from the floor to expose the fuel pump **(see illustration)**.

5 Disconnect the wiring connector from the fuel pump, and tape the connector to the vehicle body, to prevent it from disappearing behind the tank **(see illustration)**.

6 Depress the retaining clips and detach both fuel pipes from the top of the pump, bearing in

8.3 Drill the heads off the rivets (arrowed) then remove the cover plate from the floor

8.4 Remove the plastic cover to gain access to the fuel pump

8.5 Disconnect the wiring connector . . .

8.6 . . . then unclip the fuel feed and return pipes from the pump

mind the information given in Section 7 on depressurising the fuel system (the hose end fittings are colour-coded for identification) **(see illustration)**. Plug the pipe ends to minimise fuel loss and prevent the entry of dirt.

7 Noting the alignment marks on the tank, pump cover and the locking ring, unscrew the ring and remove it from the tank. This is best accomplished by using a screwdriver on the raised ribs of the locking ring. Carefully tap the screwdriver to turn the ring anti-clockwise until it can be unscrewed by hand.

8 Carefully lift the fuel pump assembly out of the fuel tank, taking great care not to damage the fuel gauge sender unit float arm, or to spill fuel onto the interior of the vehicle **(see illustration)**. Recover the rubber sealing ring and discard it – a new one must be used on refitting.

9 Note that the fuel pump is only available as a complete assembly – no components are available separately.

Refitting

10 Ensure the fuel pump pick-up filter is clean and free of debris. Fit the new sealing ring to the top of the fuel tank **(see illustration)**.

11 Carefully manoeuvre the pump assembly into the fuel tank, taking care not to damage the float arm.

8.8 Manoeuvre the fuel pump assembly out of position taking care not to bend the float arm (arrowed)

12 Align the arrow on the fuel pump cover with the arrow on the fuel tank and clip the pump assembly into position.

13 Refit the locking ring and tighten it securely until its alignment mark aligns with the pump cover and tank arrows **(see illustration)**.

14 Securely reconnect the feed and return pipes to the pump cover then reconnect the pump wiring connector.

15 Reconnect the battery negative terminal and pressurise the fuel system (see Section 7). Start the engine and check the fuel pump feed and return hoses unions for signs of leakage.

16 If all is well, refit the plastic access cover

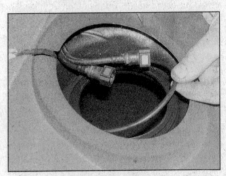

8.10 On refitting fit a new sealing ring to the fuel tank

ensuring its locating tab is at the front.

17 Refit the cover plate and secure it in position with new pop rivets **(see illustration)**. Refit the rear seat cushion (see Chapter 11).

9 Fuel gauge sender unit – removal and refitting

The fuel gauge sender unit is an integral part of the fuel pump assembly and is not available separately. Refer to Section 8 for removal and refitting details.

 4A

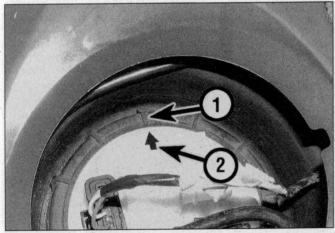

8.13 Tighten the locking ring until its alignment mark (1) is correctly aligned with the pump cover mark (2) and the fuel tank mark (not shown)

8.17 Secure the cover plate in position with new pop rivets

10.3 Removing the right-hand rear wheelarch liner front section

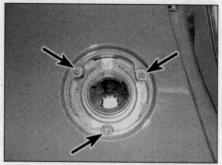

10.4 Undo the screws (arrowed) securing the fuel filler neck to the body

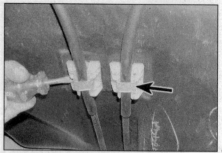

10.7 Prise off the retaining clips (arrowed) and free the handbrake cables from the fuel tank

10 Fuel tank – removal and refitting

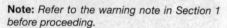

Note: *Refer to the warning note in Section 1 before proceeding.*

Removal

1 Before removing the fuel tank, all fuel must be drained from the tank. Since a fuel tank drain plug is not provided, it is therefore preferable to carry out the removal operation when the tank is nearly empty. Before proceeding, disconnect the battery negative lead and syphon or hand-pump the remaining fuel from the tank.

2 Chock the front wheels then jack up the rear of the vehicle and support it on axle stands (*see Jacking and vehicle support*). Remove the right-hand rear roadwheel.

3 Remove the retaining screws and fasteners (pull out the centre pin then remove the complete fasteners) and remove the front section of the right-hand rear wheelarch liner to gain access to the fuel tank filler neck (**see illustration**).

4 Remove the fuel filler cap then slacken and remove the three screws securing the filler neck to the body (**see illustration**).

5 Remove the exhaust system and relevant heatshield(s) as described in Section 16.

6 Disconnect the two handbrake cables from the handbrake lever – see Chapter 9.

7 From underneath the vehicle, remove the retaining clips, and release each handbrake cable from its clip on the underside of the fuel tank (**see illustration**). Position both cables clear of the tank, so that they will not hinder the removal procedure.

8 Depress the retaining clips and detach the fuel pipe and vent pipe from their unions located next to the fuel filter; bear in mind the information given in Section 7 on depressurising the fuel system when disconnecting the fuel pipe (**see illustration**). Plug the pipe ends to minimise fuel loss and prevent the entry of dirt.

9 Place a trolley jack with an interposed block of wood beneath the tank, then raise the jack until it is supporting the weight of the tank.

10 Slacken and remove the four nuts securing the fuel tank to the body and remove the support strap from the right-hand mountings (**see illustration**).

11 Slowly lower the fuel tank out of position until access can be gained to the top of the tank. Disconnect the wiring connector from the fuel pump then manoeuvre the tank and filler neck assembly out from underneath the vehicle.

12 If the tank is contaminated with sediment or water, remove the fuel pump (Section 8), and swill the tank out with clean fuel. The tank

is injection-moulded from a synthetic material – if seriously damaged, it should be renewed. However, in certain cases, it may be possible to have small leaks or minor damage repaired. Seek the advice of a specialist before attempting to repair the fuel tank.

13 To separate the filler neck from the tank, it will be necessary to cut the hard plastic vent/breather pipes. Remove the retaining clips securing the flexible connectors to the tank/filler neck then cut both pipes at the locations shown (**see illustration**). Mark the pipes to ensure they are correctly reconnected then remove the filler neck. **Note:** *The filler neck can be removed without disturbing the fuel tank.*

Refitting

14 Refitting is the reverse of the removal procedure, noting the following points:
  a) If necessary, refit the filler neck to the tank. Reconnect the vent/breather pipes with quick-release couplings (available from your Peugeot dealer) and secure the flexible connector to the filler neck/tank with new retaining clips.
  b) Ensure wiring connector and fuel/vent pipes are securely reconnected and retained by all the relevant clips. When lifting the tank back into position, take care to ensure that the pipes/wiring do

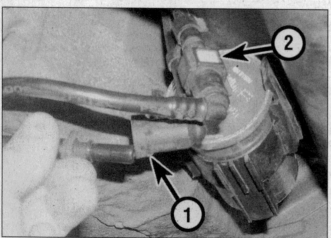

10.8 Disconnect the vent pipe (1) and fuel pipe (2) from their unions near the fuel filter

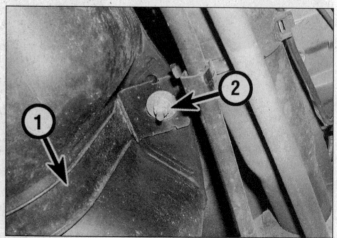

10.10 Unscrew the mounting nuts (2) and remove the support strap (1) from the fuel tank right-hand mountings

not become trapped between the tank and vehicle body.

c) Reconnect the handbrake cables and adjust the handbrake as described in Chapter 9.

d) Refit the exhaust as described in Section 16.

e) On completion, refill the tank with a small amount of fuel and pressurise the fuel system as described in Section 7. Check for signs of leakage prior to taking the vehicle out on the road.

11 Engine management system – testing and adjustment

Testing

1 If a fault appears in the engine management system, first ensure that all the system wiring connectors are securely connected and free of corrosion. Ensure that the fault is not due to poor maintenance; ie, check that the air cleaner filter element is clean, the spark plugs are in good condition and correctly gapped, the cylinder compression pressures are correct and that the engine breather hoses are clear and undamaged, referring to Chapters 1A, 2A and 5B for further information.

2 If these checks fail to reveal the cause of the problem, the vehicle should be taken to a suitably-equipped Peugeot dealer for testing using a diagnostic tester which is connected into the diagnostic socket next to the fusebox. The tester will locate the fault quickly and simply, alleviating the need to test all the system components individually, which is a time-consuming operation that carries a risk of damaging the ECU.

Adjustment

3 Whilst it is possible to check the exhaust CO level and the idle speed, if these are found to be in need of adjustment, the car *must* be taken to a suitably-equipped Peugeot dealer for further testing. Neither the mixture adjustment (exhaust gas CO level) nor the idle speed are adjustable, and should either be incorrect, a fault must be present in the engine management system.

12 Throttle housing – removal and refitting

Removal

1 Disconnect the battery negative terminal.

2 Unclip and disconnect the breather hose(s) from the manifold end of the duct connecting the air cleaner housing to the inlet manifold. Slacken the retaining clips then free the duct from the manifold and air cleaner housing and remove it from the engine compartment.

3 Free the accelerator inner cable from the throttle cam.

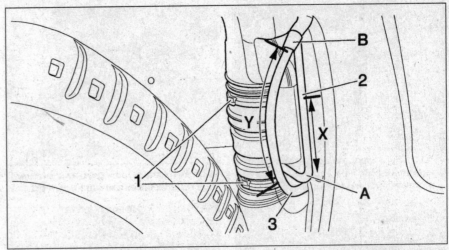

10.13 Cut the vent/breather pipes at the points shown when separating the fuel tank and filler neck

1 Retaining clips
2 Vent/breather pipe – cut at X (55 mm up from bend A)

3 Vent/breather pipe – cut at Y (150 mm down from union B)

4 Depress the retaining clip and disconnect the wiring connectors from the throttle potentiometer, intake air temperature sensor and, where necessary, from the idle speed stepper motor and electric heating element (as applicable) **(see illustration)**.

5 Slacken and remove the three retaining screws and remove the throttle housing from the inlet manifold **(see illustrations)**. Recover the sealing ring from manifold and discard it; a new one must be used on refitting.

Refitting

6 Refitting is a reversal of the removal procedure, noting the following points:

a) Fit a new sealing ring to the manifold, then refit the throttle housing and securely tighten its retaining screws **(see illustration)**.

b) Ensure all wiring is correctly routed, and that the connectors are securely reconnected.

c) On completion, adjust the accelerator cable as described in Section 3.

12.4 Disconnect the wiring connectors from all the throttle housing components

12.5a Undo the three retaining screws (arrowed) . . .

12.5b . . . then remove the throttle housing from the manifold and recover the sealing ring (1.4 litre engine shown)

12.6 On refitting ensure the new sealing ring is correctly fitted to the manifold

4A

13.3 Disconnect the accelerator cable from the throttle cam and free it from the mounting bracket (spring clip arrowed)

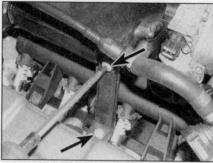

13.4 Undo the retaining screws (arrowed) and remove the accelerator cable bracket

13.5 Depress the retaining clip (arrowed) and disconnect the fuel hose from the fuel rail

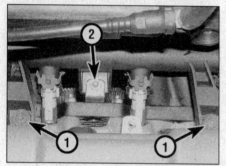

13.6a Unscrew the fuel rail mounting bolts (1) and the nut (2) . . .

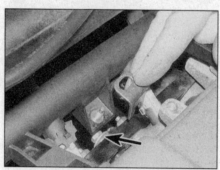

13.6b . . . then loosen the bolt (arrowed) and lift off the centre bracket

13.8a Free the injectors from the cylinder head then manoeuvre the fuel rail assembly out of position (1.4 litre engine shown)

13 Engine management system components – removal and refitting

Fuel rail and injectors

Note: *Refer to the warning note in Section 1 before proceeding.*

Note: *If a faulty injector is suspected, before condemning the injector, it is worth trying the effect of one of the proprietary injector-cleaning treatments which are available from car accessory shops.*

1 Unclip and disconnect the breather hose(s) from the manifold end of the duct connecting the air cleaner housing to the inlet manifold. Slacken the retaining clips then free the duct from the manifold and air cleaner housing and remove it from the engine compartment.

2 Remove the ignition HT coil as described in Chapter 5B.

3 Free the accelerator inner cable from the throttle housing cam, then pull the outer cable out from its mounting bracket rubber grommet, complete with its spring clip **(see illustration)**.

4 Unscrew the bolts and remove the accelerator cable bracket from the manifold/cylinder head **(see illustration)**.

5 Depress the retaining clip and disconnect the fuel pipe from the right-hand end of the fuel rail, bearing in mind the information given in Section 7 on depressurising the fuel system **(see illustration)**.

6 Slacken and remove the two bolts securing the fuel rail to the cylinder head, and the nut securing the rail to the manifold. Loosen the bolt securing the fuel rail centre bracket to the inlet manifold, then lift off the bracket (the bracket is slotted to ease removal) **(see illustrations)**.

7 Disconnect the injector wiring harness connector then unclip the connector from the rear of the inlet manifold. Also disconnect the wiring connectors from the throttle housing and power steering switch and position the wiring harness clear of the manifold so that it does not hinder fuel rail removal.

8 Carefully ease the fuel rail and injector assembly out from the cylinder head and manoeuvre it out of position. Remove the seals from the end of each injector and discard them; they must be renewed whenever they are disturbed **(see illustrations)**.

9 Disconnect the wiring connector(s) then slide out the retaining clip(s) and remove the relevant injector(s) from the fuel rail. Remove the upper seal from each disturbed injector and discard; all disturbed seals must be renewed **(see illustrations)**.

13.8b Remove the seal from the end of each injector

13.9a Disconnect the wiring connector . . .

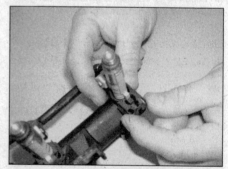

13.9b . . . then slide off the retaining clip and remove the injector from the fuel rail

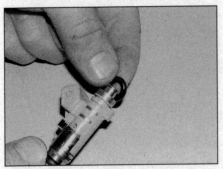

13.10 Renew all injector seals disturbed on removal

13.14 Disconnect the wiring connector from the throttle potentiometer . . .

13.15 . . . then undo the retaining screws (arrowed) and remove it from the throttle housing (1.4 litre engine shown)

10 Refitting is a reversal of the removal procedure, noting the following points.

a) Fit new seals to all disturbed injector unions **(see illustration)**.

b) Apply a smear of engine oil to the seals to aid installation, then ease the injectors and fuel rail into position ensuring that none of the seals are displaced.

c) On completion, reconnect the battery and pressurise the fuel system as described in Section 7. Start the engine and check for fuel leaks.

Fuel pressure regulator

11 The fuel pressure regulator is an integral part of the fuel pump assembly and is not available separately.
12 Refer to Section 8 for removal and refitting details.

Throttle potentiometer

13 Disconnect the battery negative terminal.
14 Depress the retaining clip and disconnect the wiring connector from the throttle potentiometer **(see illustration)**.
15 Slacken and remove the two retaining screws, then disengage the potentiometer from the throttle valve spindle and remove it from the vehicle **(see illustration)**.
16 Refit in the reverse order of removal.
17 Ensure that the potentiometer is correctly engaged with the throttle valve spindle.

Electronic Control Unit (ECU)

18 The ECU is located on the right-hand side of the engine compartment.
19 To remove the ECU, first disconnect the battery.
20 Unclip the wiring harness then slacken and remove the ECU mounting plate nut.
21 The plate is secured in position with an anti-tamper nut, unscrew the nut using a pair of grips then lift off the wiring bracket **(see illustration)**.
22 Free the mounting plate from the body

then lift the retaining clip and disconnect the ECU wiring connector **(see illustration)**.
23 Unscrew the ECU mounting nuts (these are also anti-tamper nuts) then remove the ECU from the mounting plate.
24 Refitting is a reverse of the removal procedure ensuring the wiring connector is securely reconnected.
25 Secure the ECU and mounting plate in position with new anti-tamper nuts or standard nuts.

Idle speed stepper motor

26 The idle speed stepper motor is fitted to the rear of the throttle housing.
27 Disconnect the battery negative terminal

13.21 Using a pair of grips to unscrew the ECU mounting plate nut

13.27 Disconnect the wiring connector from the idle speed stepper motor (arrowed) . . .

then disconnect the wiring connector from the motor **(see illustration)**.
28 Slacken and remove the retaining screws then remove the motor from the throttle housing **(see illustration)**. If necessary, remove the throttle potentiometer to improve access to the motor lower screw.
29 Refitting is a reversal of the removal procedure ensuring the seal is in good condition.

Manifold absolute pressure (MAP) sensor

30 The MAP sensor is mounted on the inlet manifold. To remove it, first disconnect the battery negative terminal.

13.22 Lift the retaining clip and carefully disconnect the wiring connector from the ECU

13.28 . . . then undo the retaining screws (arrowed) and remove the motor from the throttle housing

4A

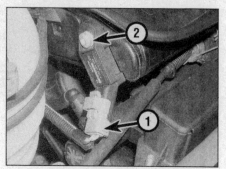

13.31 Disconnect the wiring connector (1) then undo the retaining screw (2) and remove the MAP sensor (1.4 litre engine shown)

13.35 Disconnect the wiring connector . . .

13.36 . . . then unclip the intake air temperature sensor from the throttle housing (1.4 litre engine shown)

31 Disconnect the wiring connector then undo the screw and remove the sensor from the manifold **(see illustration)**.
32 Refitting is a reversal of the removal procedure ensuring the sensor seal is in good condition.

Coolant temperature sensor

33 The coolant temperature sensor is screwed into the coolant outlet housing on the left-hand end of the cylinder head. Refer to Chapter 3, Section 7, for removal and refitting information.

Intake air temperature sensor

34 The intake air temperature sensor is fitted to the base of the throttle housing. To remove the sensor first disconnect the battery negative terminal.
35 Disconnect the wiring connector from the sensor **(see illustration)**.

13.39a Disconnect the wiring connector then undo the retaining screw (arrowed) . . .

36 Release the retaining clips **(see Tool Tip)** and ease the sensor out from the throttle housing **(see illustration)**.
37 Refitting is the reverse of removal ensuring the sensor seal is in good condition.

Crankshaft sensor

38 The crankshaft sensor is situated on the front face of the transmission clutch housing. To remove the sensor, first disconnect the battery negative terminal.
39 Disconnect the sensor wiring connector and unclip the wiring. Undo the retaining bolt and remove the sensor and bracket assembly from the transmission unit **(see illustrations)**.
40 Refitting is reverse of the removal procedure.

Engine management system relay unit

41 The relay unit is mounted onto the underside of the ECU mounting plate. To remove the sensor, first disconnect the battery negative terminal.
42 Unclip the wiring harness then slacken and remove the ECU mounting plate nut. The plate is secured in position with an anti-tamper nut, unscrew the nut using a pair of grips and lift off the wiring bracket **(see illustration 13.18)**.
43 Free the mounting plate assembly from the body. Disconnect the wiring connector from the relay then unscrew the nut and remove the relay from the plate **(see illustration)**.
44 Refitting is a reverse of the removal

The intake air temperature sensor clips can be released by passing a close-fitting ring spanner over the end of the sensor.

procedure ensuring the wiring connector is securely reconnected. Secure the ECU mounting plate in position with a new anti-tamper nut or a standard nut.

Throttle housing heating element

Note: *The heating element is only fitted to aluminium throttle housings. Plastic housings do not need a heater.*
45 The heating element is fitted to the top of the throttle housing. To remove it, first disconnect the battery negative terminal.
46 Disconnect the wiring connector then unscrew the retaining screw and remove the heating element from the throttle housing **(see illustrations)**.
47 Refitting is the reverse of removal.

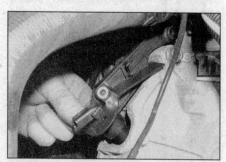

13.39b . . . then remove the crankshaft sensor from the front of the transmission clutch housing

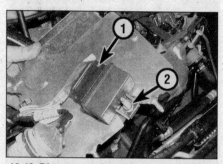

13.43 Disconnect the wiring connector (1) then undo the nut (2) and remove the relay from the ECU plate

13.46a Disconnect the wiring connector then undo the retaining screw (arrowed) . . .

13.46b . . . and remove the heating element from the throttle housing (1.4 litre engine shown)

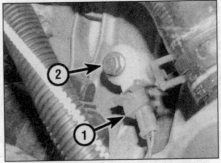

13.51 Disconnect the wiring connector (1) then undo the bolt (2) and remove the knock sensor from the cylinder block

13.53 Fuel cut-off inertia switch is located in the rear, left-hand corner of the engine compartment

Vehicle speed sensor

48 The vehicle speed sensor is an integral part of the speedometer drive. Refer to Chapter 7A or 7B (as applicable) for removal and refitting details.

Knock sensor

49 The knock sensor is screwed onto the rear of the cylinder block. To remove it, first disconnect the battery negative terminal.
50 To gain access to the sensor, firmly apply the handbrake then jack up the front of the vehicle and support it on axle stands (see *Jacking and vehicle support*).
51 Disconnect the wiring connector from the sensor then unscrew the retaining bolt and remove the sensor from underneath the vehicle (see illustration).
52 Refitting is the reverse of removal. Ensure the sensor and cylinder block mating surfaces are clean and dry and tighten the sensor mounting bolt to the specified torque.

Fuel cut-off inertia switch

53 The fuel cut-off inertia switch is located in the left-hand rear corner of the engine compartment (see illustration). To remove it, first disconnect the battery negative terminal.
54 Cut the retaining clip (where fitted) then unscrew the retaining nuts and remove the switch from the vehicle, disconnecting it from the wiring connector.
55 Refitting is the reverse of removal. On completion, reset the switch by firmly depressing its button.

Power steering pressure switch

Caution: Ensure no dirt is allowed to enter into the hydraulic system during the following procedure.
56 The power steering pressure switch is fitted to the power steering pipe located on the left-hand end of the cylinder head. To remove it, first disconnect the battery negative terminal.
57 Disconnect the wiring connector from the switch then wipe the area around the switch clean (see illustration). Unscrew the switch and remove it from the pipe, along with its sealing washer. Plug the pipe whilst the switch is removed to minimise fluid loss and prevent the entry of dirt into the hydraulic system.
58 Refitting is the reverse of removal, using a new sealing washer. On completion, check the power steering fluid level and, if necessary, bleed the hydraulic system (see Chapter 10).

Air conditioning system pressure switch

59 The air conditioning pressure switch is fitted to the refrigerant pipe located on the right-hand end of the radiator. Switch renewal requires the air conditioning system to be discharged and drained (see Chapter 3).

Camshaft position sensor

Note: *1.4 litre engine with pulse air injection*
60 The camshaft position sensor is fitted to the rear of the coolant outlet housing on the left-hand end of the cylinder head. To remove it, first disconnect the battery negative terminal.

61 Disconnect the wiring connector then unscrew the retaining bolt and remove the sensor from the housing.
62 Refitting is the reverse of removal ensuring the sensor seal is in good condition.

Body accelerometer

Note: *1.4 litre engines with pulse air injection*
63 The body accelerometer is located in the engine compartment. To remove it, first disconnect the battery negative terminal.
64 Disconnect the wiring connector then unscrew the mounting bolt and remove the sensor from the vehicle.
65 Refitting is the reverse of removal.

14 Inlet manifold – removal and refitting

Removal

Note: *Refer to the warning note in Section 1 before proceeding.*
1 Disconnect the battery negative terminal.
2 Remove the fuel rail and injectors as described in Section 13.
3 If not already having done so, disconnect the wiring connectors from the throttle housing components then unclip the harness and position it clear of the manifold
4 Release the retaining clips and disconnect the vacuum servo unit pipe and purge valve pipe from the inlet manifold (see illustrations).

4A

13.57 Disconnecting the wiring connector from the power steering pressure switch

14.4a Disconnect the braking system servo vacuum pipe . . .

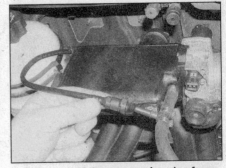

14.4b . . . and the purge valve pipe from the inlet manifold (1.4 litre engine shown)

14.8a Unscrew the retaining nuts (upper nuts arrowed) . . .

14.8b . . . then manoeuvre the inlet manifold assembly out of position (1.4 litre engine shown)

14.9 Ensure the new sealing rings are correctly fitted to the manifold prior to refitting

5 Disconnect the wiring connector from the manifold absolute pressure (MAP) sensor and unclip the wiring from the manifold.

6 Unclip the fuel pipe and position it clear of the manifold.

7 Where necessary, undo the retaining bolts and remove the support bracket from the underside of the manifold.

8 Undo the manifold retaining nuts and withdraw the manifold from the engine compartment. Recover the four manifold seals and discard them; new ones must be used on refitting **(see illustrations)**.

Refitting

9 Refitting is a reverse of the relevant removal procedure, noting the following points:
a) *Ensure that the manifold and cylinder head mating surfaces are clean and dry, then locate the new seals in their recesses in the manifold* **(see illustration)**. *Refit the manifold and tighten its retaining nuts to the specified torque.*
b) *Ensure that all relevant hoses are reconnected to their original positions and are securely held (where necessary) by the retaining clips.*
c) *Ensure the wiring is correctly routed and all connectors are securely reconnected.*
d) *Adjust the accelerator cable as described in Section 3.*

15 Exhaust manifold – removal and refitting

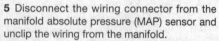

Removal

1 On 1.4 litre engines with pulse air injection, remove the pulse air injection valve as described in Part C, Section 2.

2 On all models, slacken and remove the retaining screws and remove the shroud from the top of the exhaust manifold.

3 Firmly apply the handbrake, then jack up the front of the vehicle and support it on axle stands (see *Jacking and vehicle support*).

4 Undo the nuts securing the exhaust front pipe to the manifold, then remove the bolt securing the front pipe to its mounting

bracket. Disconnect the front pipe from the manifold, and recover the gasket.

5 Undo the eight retaining nuts securing the manifold to the head. Manoeuvre the manifold out of the engine compartment, and discard the manifold gasket(s).

Refitting

6 Refitting is the reverse of the removal procedure, noting the following points:
a) *Examine all the exhaust manifold studs for signs of damage and corrosion; remove all traces of corrosion, and repair or renew any damaged studs.*
b) *Ensure that the manifold and cylinder head sealing faces are clean and flat, and fit the new manifold gasket(s). Tighten the manifold retaining nuts to the specified torque.*
c) *Reconnect the front pipe to the manifold using the information given in Section 16.*
d) *On 1.4 litre models with pulse air injection, refit the air injection valve as described in Part C.*

16 Exhaust system – general information, removal and refitting

General information

1 The exhaust system consists of four sections; the front pipe, the intermediate pipe, the catalytic converter and the tailpipe. All

exhaust sections are joined by flanged joints. The front pipe joints are secured by nuts and bolts, the intermediate pipe joint being of the spring-loaded ball type, to allow for movement in the exhaust system, and the other joints are secured by clamping rings.

2 The system is suspended throughout its entire length by rubber mountings.

Removal

3 Each exhaust section can be removed individually, or alternatively, the complete system can be removed as a unit. Even if only one part of the system needs attention, it is often easier to remove the whole system and separate the sections on the bench.

4 To remove the system or part of the system, first jack up the front or rear of the car and support it on axle stands (see *Jacking and vehicle support*). Alternatively, position the car over an inspection pit or on car ramps.

Front pipe

5 Trace the wiring back from oxygen sensor to its wiring connector. Disconnect the connector and free the wiring from all its clips an ties so the sensor is free to be removed with the front pipe **(see illustration)**.

6 Undo the nuts securing the front pipe flange joint to the manifold, and the single bolt securing the front pipe to its mounting bracket **(see illustration)**. Separate the flange joint and collect the gasket.

7 Slacken and remove the two nuts securing the front pipe flange joint to the intermediate pipe, and recover the spring cups and springs

16.5 Disconnect the oxygen sensor wiring connector and free it from its bracket

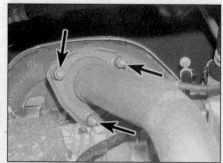

16.6 Front pipe-to-manifold nuts (arrowed)

16.7 Front pipe-to-intermediate pipe spring-loaded joint

16.9 Slacken and remove the nut, washer and bolt then free the clamping ring from the flange joint

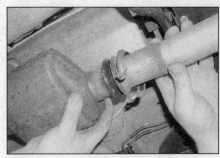

16.10 Free the intermediate pipe from the catalytic converter and remove it from the vehicle

(see illustration). Remove the bolts and collars, then withdraw the front pipe from underneath the vehicle. Recover the wire-mesh gasket.

Intermediate pipe

8 Undo the two nuts securing the front pipe flange joint to the intermediate pipe **(see illustration 16.7)**. Recover the springs and spring cups, and withdraw the bolts and collars.
9 Slacken and remove the nut, washer and bolt from the catalytic converter clamping ring and disengage the clamp from the flange joint **(see illustration)**.
10 Free the intermediate pipe and withdraw it from underneath the vehicle **(see illustration)**. Recover the wire-mesh gasket from the front pipe joint.

Catalytic converter

11 On 1.4 litre engine models with pulse air injection, trace the wiring back from catalytic converter oxygen sensor to its wiring connector. Disconnect the connector and free the wiring from all its clips and ties so the sensor is free to be removed with the converter.
12 On all engines, slacken and remove the nut, washer and bolt from each of the clamping rings and disengage the clamps from the flange joints.
13 Free the catalytic converter from its mounting rubber and withdraw it from underneath the vehicle **(see illustration)**.

Tailpipe

14 Slacken and remove the nut, washer and bolt from the tailpipe clamping ring and disengage the clamp from the flange joint **(see illustration)**.
15 Unhook the tailpipe from its mounting rubbers and remove it from the vehicle.

Complete system (minus front pipe)

16 On 1.4 litre engine models with pulse air injection, trace the wiring back from catalytic converter oxygen sensor to its wiring connector. Disconnect the connector and free the wiring from all its clips and ties so the sensor is free to be removed with the converter.
17 On all engines, undo the two nuts securing the front pipe flange joint to the intermediate pipe. Recover the springs and spring cups, and withdraw the bolts and collars.

18 Free the system from all its mounting rubbers and lower it from under the vehicle. Recover the wire-mesh gasket from the front pipe joint.

Heat shield(s)

19 The heat shields are secured to the underside of the body by various nuts and fasteners. If a shield is being removed to gain access to a component located behind it, remove the retaining nuts and/or fastener (unscrew the centre screw then pull out the complete fastener), and manoeuvre the shield out of position **(see illustrations)**. On some models it may be necessary to free the exhaust system from its mountings to gain clearance necessary to remove the larger heat shield.

Refitting

20 Each section is refitted by reversing the removal sequence, noting the following points:
  a) *Ensure that all traces of corrosion have been removed from the flanges and renew all necessary gaskets.*
  b) *Inspect the rubber mountings for signs of damage or deterioration, and renew as necessary.*
  c) *Where joints are secured together by a clamping ring, apply a smear of exhaust system jointing paste to the flange joint to ensure a gas-tight seal. Insert the bolt through the clamping ring and fit the washer. Ensure the bolt and washer cut-outs are correctly engaged with the clamping ring then securely tighten the nut.*
  d) *Prior to tightening the exhaust system fasteners, ensure that all rubber mountings are correctly located, and that there is adequate clearance between the exhaust system and vehicle underbody.*

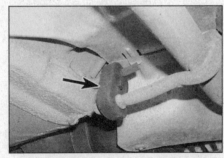

16.13 Free the catalytic converter pipe from its rear mounting (arrowed) and remove it from the vehicle

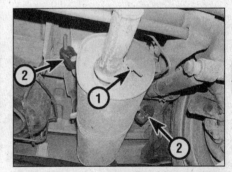

16.14 Tailpipe clamping ring (1) and rubber mountings (2)

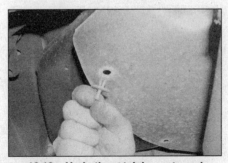

16.19a Undo the retaining nuts and fasteners (slacken the centre screws then pull out the complete fastener) . . .

16.19b . . . and manoeuvre the various heat shields away from the vehicle

4A

Chapter 4 Part B:
Fuel/exhaust systems – diesel engine

Contents

Degrees of difficulty

Easy, suitable for novice with little experience	**Fairly easy,** suitable for beginner with some experience	**Fairly difficult,** suitable for competent DIY mechanic	**Difficult,** suitable for experienced DIY mechanic	**Very difficult,** suitable for expert DIY or professional

Specifications

General

System type:
  1.9 litre engine:
    WJZ engine . . . . Indirect injection system incorporating a distributor fuel injection pump
    WJY engine . . . . Indirect injection system incorporating a semi-electronically controlled distributor fuel injection pump
  2.0 litre engine . . . . High-pressure direct injection (HDI) 'common-rail' system incorporating an electronically controlled fuel injection pump and injectors

Injection pump type:
  1.9 litre engine:
    WJZ engine . . . . Lucas DWLP11
    WJY engine . . . . Lucas DWLP12
  2.0 litre engine . . . . Bosch EDC 15C2

Adjustment data

Idle speed:
  1.9 litre engine . . . . 875 ± 25 rpm
  2.0 litre engine . . . . 800 ± 20 rpm – controlled by ECU
Maximum speed:
  1.9 litre engine . . . . Not available
  2.0 litre engine . . . . 5000 rpm – controlled by ECU

Injectors

Opening pressure:
1.9 litre engine	135 ± 5 bars
2.0 litre engine	Controlled by ECU

Turbocharger

Type	KKK K03
Boost pressure (approximate)	1 bar at 3000 rpm

Torque wrench settings

	Nm	lbf ft
1.9 litre engine		
Exhaust manifold nuts	30	22
Fuel pipe union nuts	25	18
Inlet manifold:		
Lower section nuts/bolts	20	15
Upper section:		
M6 bolts	8	6
M8 bolts	18	13
Injection pump:		
Front mounting bolts	20	15
Rear mounting bolt	23	17
Mounting bracket-to-cylinder head bolts	20	15
Injection pump sprocket-to-hub bolts	23	17
Injectors to cylinder head	90	66
Roadwheel bolts	85	63
2.0 litre engine		
EGR valve bolts	10	7
Exhaust manifold nuts	20	15
Fuel filter bracket bolts	18	13
Fuel pipe union nuts	20	15
Fuel pressure sensor	35	26
Fuel rail mounting bolts	23	17
Inlet manifold nuts and bolts	23	17
Injection pump:		
Front mounting bolts/nut	23	17
Rear bracket bolts	20	15
Mounting bracket-to-cylinder head bolts	20	15
Injection pump sprocket nut	50	37
Injector retaining clamp nut	30	22
Roadwheel bolts	85	63
Turbocharger:		
Mounting nuts	25	18
Exhaust flange bolts	23	17
Support bracket:		
Bracket-to-cylinder block bolts	23	17
Bracket-to-turbo bolt	30	22
Oil feed pipe:		
Pipe-to-turbo union bolt	22	16
Pipe-to-cylinder block union nut	48	35
Oil return hose union bolts	12	9

1 General information

1.9 litre (WJZ) engine

1 The fuel system consists of a fuel tank (which is mounted under the rear of the car), a fuel filter with integral water separator, a fuel injection pump, injectors and associated components.

2 The injection pump draws fuel from the tank through the fuel filter, which is mounted on the thermostat housing on the left-hand end of the cylinder head. The fuel filter removes all foreign matter and water, and ensures that the fuel supplied to the injection pump is clean. Excess fuel is returned from the bleed outlet on the filter housing lid to the tank. The filter housing incorporates a thermostat. When the temperature of the fuel in the filter housing is below 15°C, the filter housing thermostat opens and allows the fuel to circulate between the filter housing and thermostat housing which effectively warms the fuel. When the fuel in the filter housing reaches 35°C, the thermostat closes.

3 The fuel injection pump is driven at half-crankshaft speed by the timing belt. The high pressure required to inject the fuel into the compressed air in the swirl chambers is achieved by two opposed pistons forced together by rollers running in a cam ring. The fuel passes through a central rotor with a single outlet drilling which aligns with ports leading to the injector pipes.

4 Fuel metering is controlled by a centrifugal governor, which reacts to accelerator pedal position and engine speed. The governor is linked to a metering valve, which increases or decreases the amount of fuel delivered at each pumping stroke.

5 Basic injection timing is determined when the timing belt is fitted. When the engine is running, it is varied automatically to suit the prevailing engine speed by a mechanism which turns the cam plate or ring.

6 The four fuel injectors produce a homogeneous spray of fuel into the swirl chambers located in the cylinder head. The injectors are calibrated to open and close at critical pressures to provide efficient and even combustion. Each injector needle is lubricated by fuel, which accumulates in the spring chamber and is channelled to the injection pump return hose by leak-off pipes.

7 Cold starting is assisted by preheater or 'glow' plugs fitted to each swirl chamber. A thermostatic sensor in the cooling system operates a fast idle lever on the injection pump to increase the idling speed when the engine is cold.

8 A stop solenoid cuts the fuel supply to the injection pump rotor when the ignition is switched off, and there is also a hand-operated stop lever for use in an emergency **(see illustration)**.

9 Provided that the specified maintenance is carried out, the fuel injection equipment will give long and trouble-free service. The injection pump itself may well outlast the engine. The main potential cause of damage to the injection pump and injectors is dirt or water in the fuel.

10 A catalytic converter and exhaust gas recirculation (EGR) system are fitted to the engine to reduce exhaust emissions. Refer to Part C for further information.

11 Servicing of the injection pump and injectors is very limited for the home mechanic, and any dismantling or adjustment other than that described in this Chapter must be entrusted to a Peugeot dealer or fuel injection specialist.

⚠ *Warning: It is necessary to take certain precautions when working on the fuel system components, particularly the fuel injectors. Before carrying out any operations on the fuel system, refer to the precautions given in 'Safety first!' at the beginning of this manual, and to any additional warning notes at the start of the relevant Sections.*

1.9 litre (WJY) engine

12 Later 1.9 litre (WJY) engines are fitted with an electronically-controlled fuel injection

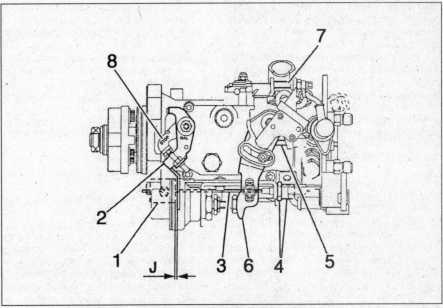

1.8 Injection pump details – 1.9 litre engine

1	Fast idle cable end fitting	5	Maximum speed adjustment screw	8	Manual stop lever
2	Fast idle lever	6	Accelerator lever	J	Fast idle cable end fitting clearance
3	Fast idle cable	7	Anti-stall speed adjustment screw		
4	Fast idle cable adjustment screw and locknut				

pump to improve emissions in order to meet the next level of emission standards being introduced. The fuel system is very similar to that described in paragraphs 1 to 11, with the following changes to the injection pump.

13 The fuel injection pump electrical control system consists of the ECU, along with the following sensors:

a) *Throttle potentiometer – informs the injection pump accelerator lever position, and the rate of throttle opening/closing.*

b) *Coolant temperature sensor – informs the ECU of engine temperature.*

c) *Crankshaft sensor – informs the ECU of the crankshaft position and speed of rotation.*

d) *Vehicle speed sensor – informs the ECU of the vehicle speed.*

e) *Injector needle lift sensor – informs the ECU when the start of injection occurs at No 1 injector.*

f) *Atmospheric pressure sensor (incorporated in the ECU) – measures the atmospheric pressure to prevent problems when driving at high-altitude.*

14 All the above signals are analysed by the ECU which controls the injection timing via the advance solenoid valve which is fitted to the injection pump. By opening and closing the solenoid valve, the ECU can advance and retard the injection timing as necessary. When the advance solenoid is open, the hydraulic pressure on the pump piston is reduced which results in the injection timing being retarded. To advance the injection timing, the ECU closes the solenoid valve which increases the pressure on the piston.

15 The ECU also controls the exhaust gas recirculation (EGR) system, described in detail in Part C of this Chapter, and the engine cooling fan.

16 If there is an abnormality in any of the readings obtained from the various sensors, the ECU enters its back-up mode. In this event, it ignores the abnormal sensor signal and assumes a pre-programmed value which will allow the engine to continue running (albeit at reduced efficiency). If the ECU enters this back-up mode, the warning light on the instrument panel will come on, and the relevant fault code will be stored in the ECU memory.

17 If the warning light comes on, the vehicle should be taken to a Peugeot dealer at the earliest opportunity. A complete test of the engine management system can then be carried out, using a special electronic diagnostic test unit which is simply plugged into the system's diagnostic connector (located next to the fusebox).

⚠ *Warning: It is necessary to take certain precautions when working on the fuel system components, particularly the fuel injectors. Before carrying out any operations on the fuel system, refer to the precautions given in 'Safety first!' at the beginning of this manual, and to any additional warning notes at the start of the relevant Sections.*

2.0 litre engine

18 All 2.0 litre engines are fitted with a high-pressure direct injection (HDI) system which incorporates the very latest in diesel injection

4B

technology. On the HDI system, the injection pump is used purely to provide the pressure required for the injection system and has no control over the injection timing (unlike conventional diesel injection systems). The injection timing is controlled by the electronic control unit (ECU) via the electrically-operated injectors. The system operates as follows.

19 The fuel system consists of a fuel tank (which is mounted under the rear of the car, with an electric fuel pump immersed in it), a fuel filter with integral water separator, a fuel injection pump, injectors and associated components.

20 The fuel pump supplies fuel to the fuel filter housing which is located at the front of the engine. The fuel filter removes all foreign matter and water and ensures that the fuel supplied to the injection pump is clean. Excess fuel is returned from the outlet on the filter housing lid to the tank via the fuel cooler. The fuel cooler is fitted to the underside of the vehicle and is cooled by the passing airflow to ensure the fuel is cool before it enters the fuel tank.

21 The fuel is heated to ensure no problems occur when the ambient temperature is very low. On early models the filter housing is connected to the coolant outlet housing on the left-hand end of the cylinder head and is fitted with a thermostat. When the temperature of the fuel in the filter housing is below 15°C, the filter housing thermostat opens and allows the fuel to circulate around the coolant outlet housing which effectively warms the fuel. When the fuel in the filter housing reaches 25°C, the thermostat closes. On later models an electrically-operated fuel heater is fitted to the fuel feed pipe to the filter housing, the heater is controlled by the ECU.

21 The fuel injection pump is driven at half-crankshaft speed by the timing belt. The high pressure required in the system (up to 1350 bar) is produced by the three pistons in the pump. The injection pump supplies high pressure fuel to the fuel rail, which acts as a reservoir for the four injectors. Since the injection pump has no control over the injection timing (unlike conventional diesel injection systems), this means that there is no need to time the injection pump when installing the timing belt.

22 The electrical control system consists of the ECU, along with the following sensors:

a) *Accelerator pedal position sensor – informs the ECU of the accelerator pedal position, and the rate of throttle opening/closing.*

b) *Coolant temperature sensor – informs the ECU of engine temperature.*

c) *Airflow meter (incorporating the intake air temperature sensor – informs the ECU of the amount and temperature of air passing through the intake duct.*

d) *Crankshaft sensor – informs the ECU of the crankshaft position and speed of rotation.*

e) *Camshaft position sensor – informs the*

ECU of the positions of the pistons.

f) *Fuel temperature sensor (where fitted) – informs the ECU of the temperature of the fuel in the fuel rail.*

g) *Fuel pressure sensor – informs the ECU of the fuel pressure present in the fuel rail.*

h) *Atmospheric pressure sensor (incorporated in the ECU) – measures the atmospheric pressure to prevent problems when driving at high-altitude.*

i) *Vehicle speed sensor – informs the ECU of the vehicle speed.*

j) *Power steering pressure switch – informs the ECU when the power steering pump is under load.*

k) *Air conditioning system relay – informs ECU when the air conditioning compressor is under load.*

23 All the above signals are analysed by the ECU which selects the fuelling response appropriate to those values. The ECU controls the fuel injectors (varying the pulse width – the length of time the injectors are held open – to provide a richer or weaker mixture, as appropriate). The mixture is constantly varied by the ECU, to provide the best setting for cranking, starting (with either a hot or cold engine), warm-up, idle, cruising and acceleration. The injectors are operated 'semi-sequentially', injectors No 1 and 4 being operated as one pair and injectors No 2 and 3 as the other.

24 The ECU also has full control over the fuel pressure present in the fuel rail via the high-pressure fuel regulator and third piston deactivator solenoid valve which are fitted to the injection pump. To reduce the pressure, the ECU opens the high-pressure fuel regulator which allows the excess fuel to return direct to the tank from the pump. The third piston deactivator is used mainly to reduce the load on the engine, but can also be used to lower the fuel pressure. The deactivator solenoid valve relieves the fuel pressure from the third piston of the pump which results in only two of the pistons pressurising the fuel system.

25 The ECU also controls the exhaust gas recirculation (EGR) system, described in detail in Part C of this Chapter, and the engine cooling fan.

26 A turbocharger is fitted to increases engine efficiency. It does this by raising the pressure in the inlet manifold above atmospheric pressure. Instead of the air simply being sucked into the cylinders, it is forced in.

27 Energy for the operation of the turbocharger comes from the exhaust gas. The gas flows through a specially-shaped housing (the turbine housing) and in so doing, spins the turbine wheel. The turbine wheel is attached to a shaft, at the end of which is another vaned wheel known as the compressor wheel. The compressor wheel spins in its own housing, and compresses the inlet air on the way to the inlet manifold. The turbo shaft is pressure-lubricated by an oil

feed pipe from the main oil gallery. The shaft 'floats' on a cushion of oil. A drain pipe returns the oil to the sump. Boost pressure (the pressure in the inlet manifold) is limited by a wastegate, which diverts the exhaust gas away from the turbine wheel in response to a pressure-sensitive actuator.

28 If there is an abnormality in any of the readings obtained from the various sensors, the ECU enters its back-up mode. In this event, it ignores the abnormal sensor signal and assumes a pre-programmed value which will allow the engine to continue running (albeit at reduced efficiency). If the ECU enters this back-up mode, the warning light on the instrument panel will come on, and the relevant fault code will be stored in the ECU memory.

29 If the warning light comes on, the vehicle should be taken to a Peugeot dealer at the earliest opportunity. A complete test of the engine management system can then be carried out, using a special electronic diagnostic test unit which is simply plugged into the system's diagnostic connector (located next to the fusebox).

⚠ *Warning: It is necessary to take certain precautions when working on the fuel system components, particularly the fuel injectors. Before carrying out any operations on the fuel system, refer to the precautions given in 'Safety first!' at the beginning of this manual, and to any additional warning notes at the start of the relevant Sections.*

⚠ *Warning: Always wait at least 30 seconds after switching off the engine before disconnecting any fuel hoses/pipes. This will allow the pressure in the system to return to atmospheric pressure.*

Caution: Due to the high operating pressure of the injection system, Peugeot recommend that the high-pressure system metal pipes must be renewed whenever a union nut is slackened. Failure to renew a pipe could result in a fuel leak.

Caution: Do not operated the engine if any of the air intake ducts are disconnected or the filter element is removed. Any debris entering the engine will cause sever damage to the turbocharger.

Caution: To prevent damage to the turbocharger, do not race the engine immediately after start-up. Allow it to idle to give the oil a few seconds to circulate around the turbocharger bearings. Always allow the engine to return to idle speed before switching it off – do not blip the throttle and switch off, as this will leave the turbo spinning without lubrication.

Caution: Observe the recommended intervals for oil and filter changing, and use a reputable oil of the specified quality. Neglect of oil changing, or use of inferior oil, can cause carbon formation on the turbo shaft, leading to subsequent failure.

2.1a On 1.9 litre engines, remove the fasteners from the right-hand side . . .

2.1b . . . and top of the engine cover . . .

2.1c . . . and remove the cover from the engine

2.2a Slacken the retaining clips securing the intake duct to the air cleaner housing and manifold . . .

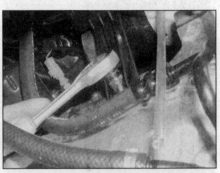

2.2b . . . then unscrew the mounting bolt securing it to the cylinder block . . .

2.2c . . . and remove the duct from the engine compartment

| 2 | Air cleaner assembly and intake ducts – removal and refitting |

Removal

1.9 litre engine

1 Release the fasteners from the right-hand side and top of the engine cover then lift off the cover, taking care not to lose its mounting rubbers **(see illustrations)**.

2 Slacken the retaining clips securing the intake duct to the manifold and air cleaner housing. Unscrew the bolt securing the intake duct resonator chamber bolt to the front of the cylinder block then remove the duct assembly from the engine compartment **(see illustrations)**.

3 Lift the air cleaner housing assembly off of its mounting bracket and remove it from the engine compartment. Recover the mounting rubber fitted to the housing lower locating peg and the sealing ring from the housing intake duct **(see illustrations)**.

4 To remove the intake duct, firmly apply the handbrake then jack up the front of the car and support it on axle stands (see *Jacking and vehicle support*). Undo the screws securing the front section of the left-hand wheelarch liner to the base of the bumper then remove the fasteners (pull out the centre pin then

4B

2.3a Lift out the air cleaner housing . . .

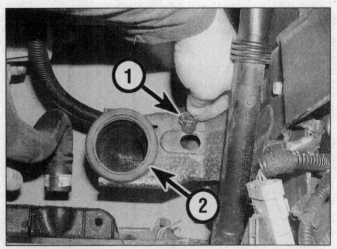

2.3b . . . and recover the mounting rubber (1) and intake duct sealing ring (2)

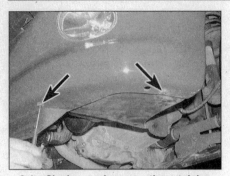

2.4a Slacken and remove the retaining screws (arrowed) . . .

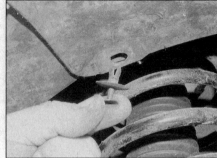

2.4b . . . and fasteners . . .

2.4c . . . and remove the front section of the left-hand wheelarch liner

2.5a On 2.0 litre engines, rotate each fastener 90° to release it . . .

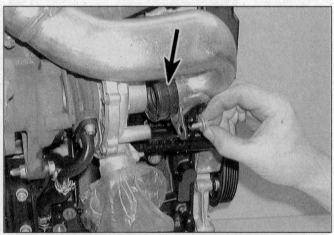

2.5b . . . then lift off the engine cover

remove the complete fastener) securing the liner to the body and manoeuvre it out from underneath the wing **(see illustrations)**. Remove the retaining bolts and remove the duct assembly from the vehicle.

2.0 litre engine

5 Remove the fasteners (rotate them 90° to release them) and remove the engine cover **(see illustrations)**.
6 Unscrew the retaining clip and free the flexible duct from the air cleaner housing.

Caution: Never touch the air temperature sensor or metallic plate of the airflow meter as they are easily damaged.
7 Unscrew the two bolts and free the accelerator pedal position sensor bracket from the side of the air cleaner housing.
8 Lift the air cleaner housing assembly off of its mounting bracket and remove it from the engine compartment. Recover the mounting rubber fitted to the housing lower locating peg and the sealing ring from the housing intake duct **(see illustrations 2.3a and 2.3b)**. If

necessary, also remove the intake duct as described in paragraph 4.
9 If necessary, disconnect the wiring connector from the airflow meter then slacken the retaining clip securing the airflow meter duct to the intake pipe, and remove the airflow meter and duct as an assembly.
10 To remove the pipe linking the airflow meter duct to the turbocharger, release the retaining clips and free the flexible duct and breather hose from the top of the pipe and unscrew the pipe upper mounting bolt. Firmly apply the handbrake then jack up the front of the car and support it on axle stands (see *Jacking and vehicle support*). Unscrew the bolt securing the pipe to the side of the turbocharger then manoeuvre the pipe out of position. Recover the sealing ring fitted between the pipe and turbocharger **(see illustrations)**.

Refitting

11 Refitting is a reversal of the removal procedure, ensuring that all hoses and ducts are properly reconnected and correctly seated and are securely held by their retaining clips/bolts.

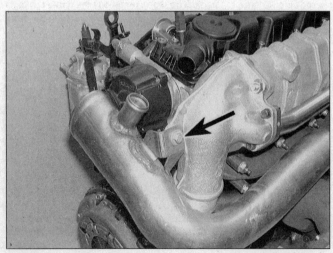

2.10a On 2.0 litre engines, unscrew the upper mounting bolt . . .

2.10b . . . and the bolt securing the pipe to the turbocharger. Remove the pipe and recover the sealing ring (arrowed – shown with the engine removed)

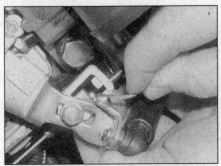

3.1a On 1.9 litre engines, free the accelerator inner cable from the lever . . .

3.1b . . . then withdraw the outer cable from the pump bracket, complete with spring clip

3.1c Remove the cable locating collar from the pump whilst the cable is removed

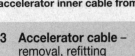

3 Accelerator cable –
removal, refitting and adjustment

Removal

1 On 1.9 litre engines, release the fasteners from the right-hand side and top of the engine cover then lift off the cover, taking care not to lose its mounting rubbers **(see illustrations 2.1a to 2.1c)**. Free the accelerator inner cable from the injection pump accelerator lever, then pull the outer cable out from the mounting bracket, complete with its spring clip. Whilst the cable is disconnected, remove the cable locating collar from the mounting bracket for safe-keeping **(see illustrations)**.

2 On 2.0 litre engines, working in the engine compartment, unscrew the two bolts and free the accelerator pedal position sensor bracket from the side of the air cleaner housing. Detach the accelerator inner cable from the sensor, then pull the outer cable out from sensor bracket, complete with the spring clip **(see illustrations)**.

3 On all engines, working back along the length of the cable, free it from any retaining clips or ties, noting its correct routing.

4 Working inside the vehicle, reach up behind the facia then release the retaining clip and detach the inner cable from the top of the accelerator pedal **(see illustration)**.

5 Remove the retaining clip which secures the outer cable end fitting to the bulkhead then tie a length of string to the end of the cable.

6 Return to the engine compartment, release the cable grommet from the bulkhead and withdraw the cable. When the end of the cable appears, untie the string and leave it in position – it can then be used to draw the cable back into position on refitting.

Refitting

7 Tie the string to the end of the cable, then use the string to draw the cable into position through the bulkhead. Once the cable end is visible, untie the string, then secure the outer cable in position with the retaining clip and fit the inner cable into the pedal end.

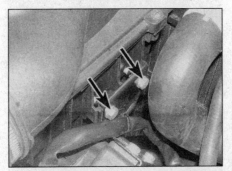

3.2a On 2.0 litre engines, undo the two bolts (arrowed) and free the accelerator pedal sensor from the air cleaner housing . . .

3.2b . . . then detach the cable from the sensor

8 From within the engine compartment, ensure the outer cable is correctly seated in the bulkhead grommet, then work along the cable, securing it in position with the retaining clips and ties, and ensuring that the cable is correctly routed.

9 On 1.9 litre engines, fit the locating collar to the mounting bracket then pass the cable through the collar and reconnect the inner cable to the accelerator lever. Adjust the cable as described below.

10 On 2.0 litre engines, pass the outer cable through the sensor bracket grommet and reconnect the inner cable to the accelerator pedal position sensor. Refit the sensor bracket to the side of the air cleaner housing,

tightening its retaining bolts securely, then adjust the cable as described below.

Adjustment

11 On 1.9 litre engines, release the fasteners from the right-hand side and top of the engine cover then lift off the cover, taking care not to lose its mounting rubbers **(see illustrations 2.1a to 2.1c)**.

12 On all engines, remove the spring clip from the accelerator outer cable **(see illustration)**. Ensuring that the injection pump lever/accelerator pedal position sensor is fully against its stop, gently pull the cable out of its grommet until all free play is removed from the inner cable.

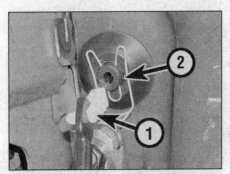

3.4 Unclip the inner cable end fitting (1) from the top of the pedal then remove the retaining clip (2) securing the outer cable to the bulkhead

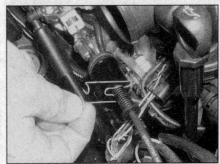

3.12 Slide off the spring clip and adjust the accelerator cable as described in text (1.9 litre engine shown)

4B

3.13 Remove all freeplay from the cable then fit the spring clip to the last exposed groove on the outer cable (2.0 litre engine shown)

13 With the cable held in this position, refit the spring clip to the last exposed outer cable groove in front of the rubber grommet and washer **(see illustration)**. When the clip is refitted and the outer cable is released, there should be only a small amount of free play in the inner cable.

14 Have an assistant depress the accelerator pedal, and check that the accelerator lever/pedal position sensor opens fully and returns smoothly to its stop.

15 On 1.9 litre engines, ensure the mounting rubbers are all correctly fitted then install the engine cover, securing it in position with the fasteners.

4 Accelerator pedal – removal and refitting

Removal

1 Working inside the vehicle, reach up behind the facia then release the retaining clip and detach the inner cable from the top of the accelerator pedal.

2 On right-hand drive models, remove the retaining clip then slide out the pivot pin and remove the accelerator pedal from the pedal mounting bracket.

3 On left-hand drive models, remove the retaining clip then slide the pedal off its pivot shaft. The pivot shaft is a screw fit in the body.

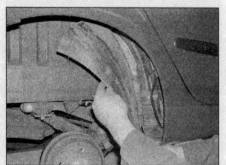

8.3 Remove the front section of the right-hand rear wheelarch liner to gain access to the fuel tank filler neck

Refitting

4 Refitting is a reversal of the removal procedure, applying a little multi-purpose grease to the pedal pivot point. On completion, adjust the accelerator cable as described in Section 3.

5 Fuel system – priming

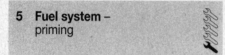

1 After disconnecting part of the fuel supply system or running out of fuel, it is necessary to prime the fuel system as follows.

1.9 litre engine

2 All models are fitted with a hand-operated priming pump which is built into the fuel filter housing. To gain access to the pump, release the fasteners from the right-hand side and top of the engine cover then lift off the cover, taking care not to lose its mounting rubbers **(see illustrations 2.1a to 2.1c)**.

3 Pump the priming pump until resistance is felt then pump a few more times **(see illustration)**. This will prime the fuel system components and remove all air from the system.

4 Start the engine as normal. If difficulty is encountered, pump the priming pump a few times with the ignition switched on.

5 Once the engine has started, ensure the mounting rubbers are all correctly fitted then install the engine cover, securing it in position with the fasteners.

2.0 litre engine

6 On completion of work on the fuel system slacken, or leave loose (as appropriate), the **new** fuel filter drain screw. Operate the low pressure pump 4 or 5 times by switching on the ignition each time for a period of 5 seconds. Switch off the ignition and wait for a period of 5 to 10 seconds to allow the pressure to fall in the fuel supply circuit. Tighten the drain screw and wipe away all spilt fuel. Start the engine and check that there is no sign whatever of fuel seepage from the filter drain screw once the engine is running.

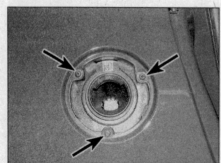

8.4 Undo the three screws (arrowed) securing the filler neck to the body

5.3 Priming the fuel system – 1.9 litre engine

6 Fuel supply pump (2.0 litre engine) – removal and refitting

Refer to Chapter 4A, Section 8.

7 Fuel gauge sender – removal and refitting

The fuel gauge sender unit can be removed as described in Chapter 4A, Section 8. **Note:** *On 1.9 litre engines the fuel gauge sender unit does not have the fuel pump as part of the assembly. On 2.0 litre engines the fuel gauge sender unit is an integral part of the fuel pump and is not available separately.*

8 Fuel tank – removal and refitting

Caution: Be careful not to allow dirt into the fuel system during this procedure.

Removal

1 Before removing the fuel tank, all fuel must be drained from the tank. Since a fuel tank drain plug is not provided, it is therefore preferable to carry out the removal operation when the tank is nearly empty. Before proceeding, disconnect the battery negative lead and syphon or hand-pump the remaining fuel from the tank.

2 Chock the front wheels then jack up the rear of the vehicle and support it on axle stands (*see Jacking and vehicle support*). Remove the right-hand rear roadwheel.

3 Remove the retaining screws and fasteners (pull out the centre pin then remove the complete fasteners) and remove the front section of the right-hand wheelarch liner to gain access to the fuel tank filler neck **(see illustration)**.

4 Remove the fuel filler cap then slacken and remove the three screws securing the filler neck to the body **(see illustration)**.

5 Remove the exhaust system and relevant heat shield(s) as described in Section 20.

6 Disconnect the two handbrake cables from the handbrake lever – see Chapter 9.

7 From underneath the vehicle, remove the retaining clips, and release each handbrake cable from its guides on the underside of the fuel tank **(see illustration)**. Position both cables clear of the tank, so that they will not hinder the removal procedure.

8 Place a trolley jack with an interposed block of wood beneath the tank, then raise the jack until it is supporting the weight of the tank.

9 Slacken and remove the four nuts securing the fuel tank to the body and remove the support strap from the right-hand mountings **(see illustration)**.

10 Slowly lower the fuel tank out of position until access can be gained to the top of the tank. Disconnect the fuel pipes and the wiring connectors then free the pipes from all the relevant retaining clips and manoeuvre the tank and filler neck assembly out from underneath the vehicle. Plug the pipe ends to prevent the entry of dirt into the fuel system.

11 If the tank is contaminated with sediment or water, remove the fuel pump and/or fuel gauge sender (Section 6 or 7), and swill the tank out with clean fuel. The tank is injection-moulded from a synthetic material – if seriously damaged, it should be renewed. However, in certain cases, it may be possible to have small leaks or minor damage repaired. Seek the advice of a specialist before attempting to repair the fuel tank.

12 To separate the filler neck from the tank, it will be necessary to cut the hard plastic vent/breather pipes. Remove the retaining clips securing the flexible connectors to the tank/filler neck then cut both pipes at the locations shown **(see illustration)**. Mark the pipes to ensure they are correctly reconnected then remove the filler neck. **Note:** *The filler neck can be removed without disturbing the fuel tank.*

Refitting

13 Refitting is the reverse of the removal procedure, noting the following points:
  a) *If necessary, refit the filler neck to the tank. Reconnect the vent/breather pipes with quick-release couplings (available from your Peugeot dealer) and secure the flexible connectors to the filler neck/tank with new retaining clips.*
  b) *Ensure wiring connector and fuel pipes are securely reconnected and retained by all the relevant clips. When lifting the tank back into position, take care to ensure that the pipes/wiring do not become trapped between the tank and vehicle body.*
  c) *Reconnect the handbrake cables and adjust the handbrake as described in Chapter 9.*
  d) *Refit the exhaust as described in Section 20.*
  e) *On completion, refill the tank with a small amount of fuel and prime the fuel system as described in Section 5. Check for signs of leakage prior to taking the vehicle out on the road.*

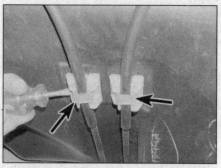

8.7 Prise off the retaining clips and free the handbrake cables from the fuel tank

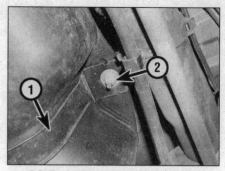

8.9 Fuel tank mounting nut (2) and support strap (1)

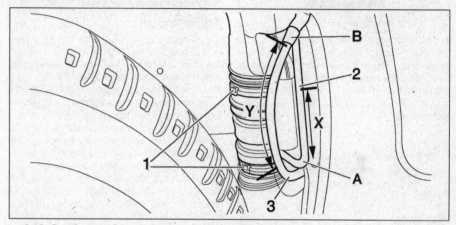

8.12 Cut the vent/breather pipes at the points shown when separating the fuel tank and filler neck

1 Retaining clips
2 Vent/breather pipe – cut at X (55 mm up from bend A)

3 Vent/breather pipe – cut at Y (150 mm down from union B)

9 Maximum speed – checking and adjustment

Caution: The maximum speed adjustment screw is sealed by the manufacturers at the factory, using paint or an anti-tamper cap. There is no reason why it should require adjustment. Do not disturb the screw if the vehicle is still within the warranty period, otherwise the warranty will be invalidated. This adjustment requires the use of a tachometer suitable for use on diesel engines.

1.9 litre engine

Note: *At the time of writing, Peugeot did not specify a maximum speed for the 1.9 litre engine. Refer to your Peugeot dealer for the latest available information.*

1 Run the engine to normal operating temperature.

2 Have an assistant fully depress the accelerator pedal, and check that the maximum engine speed is as specified by the dealer. Do not keep the engine at maximum speed for more than two or three seconds.

3 If adjustment is necessary, stop the engine, release the fasteners from the right-hand side and top of the engine cover then lift off the cover, taking care not to lose its mounting rubbers **(see illustration 2.1a to 2.1c)**.

4 Loosen the locknut, turn the maximum speed adjustment screw as necessary, and retighten the locknut **(see illustration)**.

5 Repeat the procedure in paragraph 2 to check the adjustment.

6 Stop the engine and disconnect the tachometer.

7 Where necessary, ensure the mounting rubbers are all correctly fitted then install the engine cover, securing it in position with the fasteners.

9.4 Maximum speed adjustment screw fitted with tamperproof cap (arrowed) – 1.9 litre engine

4B

10.4 Slacken the retaining screw (arrowed) then slide the end fitting off the fast idle cable

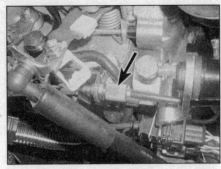

10.13 Fast idle cable adjustment screw and locknut

2.0 litre engine

8 The maximum speed is controlled by the ECU and cannot be adjusted by the home mechanic. The speed can be checked as described above (see paragraphs 1 and 2) but if adjustment is needed, the vehicle will have to be taken to a Peugeot dealer for testing (see Section 1).

---

10 Fast idle thermostatic sensor (1.9 litre engine) – removal, refitting and adjustment

Removal

Note: *A new sealing washer must be used when refitting the sensor.*

1 The thermostatic sensor is located in the side of the thermostat/fuel filter housing.
2 To gain access to the sensor, remove the intake duct connecting the air cleaner housing to the inlet manifold as described in Section 2.
3 Drain the cooling system as described in Chapter 1B.
4 Loosen the clamp screw or nut (as applicable), and disconnect the fast idle cable end fitting from the inner cable at the fuel injection pump fast idle lever **(see illustration)**.
5 Slide the cable from the adjustment screw located in the bracket on the fuel injection pump.
6 Using a suitable open-ended spanner, unscrew the thermostatic sensor from the fuel filter/thermostat housing, and withdraw the sensor complete with the cable. Recover the sealing washer and discard it; a new one should be used on refitting.

Refitting

7 Fit the sensor, complete with a new sealing washer, and tighten it securely.
8 Ensure the cable is correctly routed then pass it through the adjustment screw on the bracket.
9 Insert the inner cable through the fast idle lever, and position the end fitting on the cable, but do not tighten the clamp screw or nut (as applicable).
10 Adjust the cable as described in the following paragraphs.

Adjustment

11 Release the fasteners from the right-hand side and top of the engine cover then lift off the cover, taking care not to lose its mounting rubbers **(see illustrations 2.1a to 2.1c)**.
12 With the engine cold, slacken the fast idle cable end fitting clamp screw/nut. Push the fast idle lever fully towards the flywheel end of the engine then remove all slack from the cable. With the fast idle lever against its stop and the end fitting firmly against the lever, securely tighten the clamp screw or nut.
13 Check the fast idle lever is firmly against its stop. If necessary, adjust the cable using the screw and locknut arrangement fitted to the injection pump bracket **(see illustration)**.
14 Ensure the end fitting clamp screw/nut and adjuster locknut are securely tightened then measure the exposed length of the fast idle inner cable.
15 Refit the intake duct assembly (where removed – see Section 2).
16 Refill the cooling system as described in Chapter 1B, and run the engine to its normal operating temperature.
17 With the engine at its normal operating temperature, the thermostatic sensor cable should be slack with approximately 0.5 to 1.0 mm of freeplay present. If no freeplay is present in the cable, it is likely that the sensor is faulty. If the thermostatic sensor is functioning correctly, the cable travel should be at least 6 mm from cold to hot.
18 Check that the engine speed increases

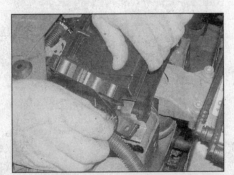

11.9 Unscrew the anti-tamperproof nut and remove the bracket then free the ECU mounting plate from the body

when the fast idle lever is pushed towards the flywheel end of the engine.
19 If all is well, stop the engine.
20 Ensure the mounting rubbers are all correctly fitted then install the engine cover, securing it in position with the fasteners.

---

11 Injection system electrical components – removal and refitting

1.9 litre (WJZ) engine

Stop solenoid

1 The stop solenoid is part of the immobiliser unit which is located on the top of the fuel injection pump, its purpose being to cut the fuel supply when the ignition is switched off. Renewal of the immobiliser/solenoid unit is a complex operation which should be entrusted to a Peugeot dealer or Lucas injection specialist. The immobiliser unit is secured in position with shear bolts which have to drilled out (a high-risk operation which could lead to damage if carried out carelessly) and the new unit will have to be initialised on refitting.

Fuel cut-off inertia switch

Note: *A fuel cut-off inertia switch is not fitted to all models.*

2 The fuel cut-off inertia switch is located in the left-hand rear corner of the engine compartment. To remove it, first disconnect the battery negative terminal.
3 Unscrew the retaining bolts then disconnect the wiring connector and remove the switch from the vehicle.
4 Refitting is the reverse of removal. On completion, reset the switch by firmly depressing its button.

1.9 litre (WJY) engine

Stop solenoid

5 See paragraph 1.

Electronic control unit

6 The ECU is located on the right-hand side of the engine compartment.
7 To remove the ECU, first disconnect the battery.
8 Unclip the wiring harness then slacken and remove the ECU mounting plate nut. The plate is secured in position with an anti-tamper nut, unscrew the nut using a pair of grips.
9 Remove the cable/hose guide bracket then free the mounting plate from the body **(see illustration)**.
10 Lift the retaining clips and disconnect the ECU wiring connectors then unscrew the mounting nuts (these are also anti-tamper nuts) and remove the ECU from the mounting plate.
11 Refitting is a reverse of the removal procedure, ensuring the wiring connectors are securely reconnected. Secure the ECU and mounting plate in position with new anti-tamper nuts or standard nuts.

11.14a Slacken the mounting bolt . . .

11.14b . . . then free the crankshaft sensor from the bolt and manoeuvre it out of position

Crankshaft sensor

12 The crankshaft sensor is situated on the top of the transmission unit.

13 To remove the sensor, first disconnect the battery negative terminal.

14 Disconnect the wiring connector from the sensor then slacken the mounting bolt and remove the sensor from the transmission unit (the sensor is slotted to ease removal) **(see illustrations)**.

15 Refitting is reverse of the removal procedure.

11.21 Lift the retaining clip (1) and disconnect the wiring connector then undo the retaining nut (2) and remove the injection system relay

Vehicle speed sensor

16 The vehicle speed sensor is an integral part of the speedometer drive. Refer to Chapter 7A for removal and refitting details.

Injector needle lift sensor

17 The needle lift sensor is an integral part of No 1 cylinder injector. See Section 14 for removal and refitting details.

Injection system relay unit

18 The relay unit is mounted onto the underside of the ECU mounting plate. To remove the sensor, first disconnect the battery negative terminal.

19 Unclip the wiring harness then slacken and remove the ECU mounting plate nut. The plate is secured in position with an anti-tamper nut, unscrew the nut using a pair of grips.

20 Remove the cable/hose guide bracket then free the mounting plate from the body.

21 Lift the retaining clip and disconnect the wiring connector from the relay unit **(see illustration)**. Unscrew the mounting nut and remove the relay from the mounting plate.

22 Refitting is a reverse of the removal procedure, ensuring the wiring connector is securely reconnected. Secure the mounting plate in position with new anti-tamper nuts or standard nuts.

Coolant temperature sensor

23 The coolant temperature sensor is screwed into the fuel filter/thermostat housing. Refer to Chapter 3 for removal and refitting information.

Throttle potentiometer and advance solenoid

24 These components are both fitted to the injection pump. If either of the above are faulty, replacement should be entrusted to a Peugeot dealer who will have the necessary special equipment to adjust and calibrate the replacements on refitting.

Fuel cut-off inertia switch

Note: *A fuel cut-off inertia switch is not fitted to all models.*

25 Refer to paragraphs 2 to 4.

2.0 litre engine

Electronic control unit

26 The ECU is located on the right-hand side of the engine compartment.

27 To remove the ECU, first disconnect the battery.

28 Unclip the wiring harness then slacken and remove the ECU mounting plate nut. The plate is secured in position with an anti-tamper nut, unscrew the nut using a pair of grips.

29 Remove the bracket then free the mounting plate from the body **(see illustration)**.

30 Lift the retaining clip and disconnect the ECU wiring connector then unscrew the mounting nuts (these are also anti-tamper nuts) and remove the ECU from the mounting plate **(see illustration)**.

31 Refitting is a reverse of the removal procedure, ensuring the wiring connector is securely reconnected. Secure the ECU and mounting plate in position with new anti-tamper nuts or standard nuts.

4B

11.29 Unscrew the mounting nut (see text) and remove the bracket . . .

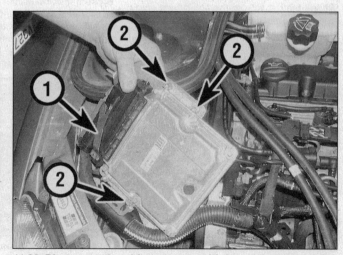

11.30 Disconnect the wiring connector (1) then undo the retaining nuts (2) and remove the ECU from the mounting plate

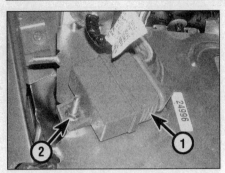

11.37 Injection relay wiring connector and retaining nut (2)

Crankshaft sensor

32 Refer to paragraphs 12 to 15. Access to the sensor is poor; remove the battery and battery tray to improve access (see Chapter 5A)

Vehicle speed sensor

33 The vehicle speed sensor is an integral part of the speedometer drive. Refer to Chapter 7A for removal and refitting details.

Injection system relay unit

34 The relay unit is mounted onto the underside of the ECU mounting plate. To remove the sensor, first disconnect the battery negative terminal.

35 Unclip the wiring harness then slacken and remove the ECU mounting plate nut. The plate is secured in position with an anti-tamper nut, unscrew the nut using a pair of grips.

36 Free the mounting plate from the body.

37 Release the retaining clip and disconnect the wiring connector from the relay unit. Unscrew the mounting nut and remove the relay from the mounting plate **(see illustration)**.

38 Refitting is a reverse of the removal procedure, ensuring the wiring connector is securely reconnected. Secure the mounting plate in position with a new anti-tamper nut or standard nut.

Coolant temperature sensor

39 The coolant temperature sensor is fitted to the side of the coolant outlet housing on the left-hand end of the cylinder **(see**

11.39 Coolant temperature sensor (arrowed) is fitted to the coolant outlet housing on the left-hand end of the cylinder head

illustration). Refer to Chapter 3 for removal and refitting information.

Airflow meter

40 The airflow meter is fitted to intake duct connecting the air cleaner housing to the turbocharger intake pipe. Disconnect the battery negative terminal prior to removal.

41 Slacken the retaining clips and remove the intake duct connecting the airflow meter to the intake pipe **(see illustration)**.

42 Slacken the retaining clip and free the airflow meter from the air cleaner housing. Disconnect the wiring connector and remove the airflow meter from the vehicle, noting which way around it is fitted **(see illustration)**. *Caution: Never touch the air temperature sensor or metallic plate of the airflow meter as they are easily damaged.*

43 Refitting is the reverse of removal, ensuring the airflow meter is fitted the correct way around with the arrow moulded on its body pointing in the direction of airflow (towards the turbocharger pipe).

Camshaft position sensor

44 The camshaft position sensor is fitted to the top of the cylinder head cover right-hand end.

45 Remove the fasteners (rotate them 90° to release them) and remove the engine cover **(see illustrations 2.5a and 2.5b)**.

46 Remove the camshaft sprocket timing belt cover (see Chapter 2B).

47 Disconnect the battery negative terminal

11.41 Slacken the retaining clips and remove the duct linking the airflow meter to the intake pipe

then disconnect the camshaft sensor wiring connector.

48 Unscrew the retaining bolt and remove the sensor from the engine.

49 On refitting, align the camshaft hub timing hole with the cylinder head hole (see Chapter 2B, Section 3). Insert the flywheel locking tool to ensure the camshaft is correctly positioned.

50 Fit the sensor to its mounting bracket and lightly tighten its bolt.

51 If a new sensor is being fitted, position the sensor so its fitting lug is in contact with the rear of the camshaft hub then securely tighten the sensor bolt. The lug automatically sets the sensor air gap to the correct distance and will be knocked off the first time the engine is started.

52 If the original sensor is being refitted, using feeler gauges, set the gap between the sensor tip and camshaft hub to 1.2 mm. Ensure the sensor is correctly positioned then securely tighten its retaining bolt **(see illustration)**. Check the air gap and, if necessary, readjust.

53 Once the sensor is correctly positioned, refit the timing belt cover and remove the flywheel locking tool (where fitted).

54 Reconnect the sensor wiring connector then securely refit the engine cover.

Fuel temperature sensor

55 The fuel temperature sensor (where fitted) is fitted to the fuel rail.

56 Disconnect the battery negative terminal then remove the fasteners (rotate them 90° to release them) and remove the engine cover **(see illustrations 2.5a and 2.5b)**.

57 Disconnect the wiring connector then unscrew the retaining bolt and remove the sensor from the fuel rail **(see illustration)**.

58 Refitting is the reverse of removal.

Fuel pressure sensor

⚠️ *Warning: Always wait at least 30 seconds after switching off the engine before disconnecting any fuel hoses/pipes. This will allow the pressure in the system to return to atmospheric pressure.*

Caution: Be careful not to allow dirt into the fuel rail/sensor during this procedure.

11.42 Free the airflow meter from the air cleaner housing and disconnect its wiring connector

11.52 On 2.0 litre engines, adjust the camshaft sensor air gap as described in text

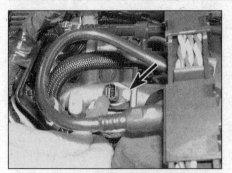

11.57 Disconnect the wiring connector then unscrew the mounting bolt (arrowed) and remove the fuel temperature sensor from the fuel rail

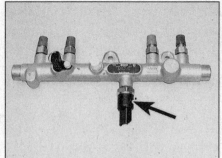

11.59 Fuel pressure sensor (arrowed) is screwed into the base of the fuel rail (shown with fuel rail removed)

11.67 The fuel cut-off inertia switch is located in the left-hand rear corner of the engine compartment

59 The fuel pressure sensor is fitted to the fuel rail **(see illustration)**.
60 Disconnect the battery negative terminal then release the fasteners (rotate them 90° to release them) and remove the engine cover **(see illustrations 2.5a and 2.5b)**.
61 Disconnect the wiring connector from the pressure sensor.
62 Remove all traces of dirt from around the sensor; the sensor and its surrounding area must be clean and dry before proceeding. Position a wad of rag beneath the sensor to catch any spilt fuel.
63 Unscrew the sensor from the fuel rail and remove it along with its sealing washer. Discard the washer; a new one must be used on refitting. Plug the fuel rail to prevent the entry of dirt into the fuel system.

64 Refitting is the reverse of removal, using a new sealing washer and tightening the sensor to the specified torque. On completion, prime the fuel system as described in Section 5.

Third piston deactivator solenoid valve

65 The solenoid valve is mounted on the top of the injection pump; it is an integral part of the pump and cannot be renewed. If the valve is faulty the injection pump will have to be renewed or repaired. Never attempt to remove the solenoid from the pump.

High-pressure fuel regulator

66 The high-pressure fuel regulator is mounted on the rear of the injection pump; it is an integral part of the pump and cannot be renewed. If the regulator is faulty the injection pump will have to be renewed or repaired. Never attempt to remove the regulator from the pump.

Fuel cut-off inertia switch

67 Refer to paragraphs 2 to 4 **(see illustration)**.

Fuel heater – later models with electrically-operated fuel heater

⚠️ *Warning: Always wait at least 30 seconds after switching off the engine before disconnecting any fuel hoses/pipes. This will allow the pressure in the system to return to atmospheric pressure.*

Caution: Be careful not to allow dirt into the fuel pipes/heater during this procedure.
68 The fuel heater is fitted to the fuel feed pipe to the filter housing **(see illustration)**.
69 Disconnect the battery negative terminal then release the fasteners (rotate them 90° to release them) and remove the engine cover **(see illustrations 2.5a and 2.5b)**.
70 Disconnect the wiring connector from the heater.
71 Remove all traces of dirt from around the heater; the heater and its surrounding area must be clean and dry before proceeding. Position a wad of rag beneath the heater to catch any spilt fuel.
72 Release the clips and disconnect the fuel pipes from the heater. Plug the fuel pipes to prevent the entry of dirt into the fuel system.
73 Unscrew the retaining bolt and remove the fuel heater from the engine.
74 Refitting is the reverse of removal. On completion, prime the fuel system as described in Section 5.

Accelerator pedal position sensor

75 Working in the engine compartment, unscrew the two bolts and free the accelerator pedal position sensor bracket from the side of the air cleaner housing **(see illustrations)**.
76 Disconnect the sensor wiring connector **(see illustration)**.
77 Free the accelerator inner cable from the

4B

11.68 Fuel heater assembly – later models

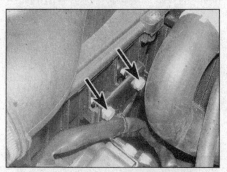

11.75a Undo the two bolts (arrowed) . . .

11.75b . . . and free the accelerator pedal sensor from the side of the air cleaner housing

11.76 Disconnect the wiring connector (arrowed) . . .

sensor then free the outer cable from sensor bracket, complete with the spring clip, and remove the sensor from the vehicle **(see illustration)**

78 Refitting is the reverse of removal, adjusting the accelerator cable as described in Section 3.

12 Fuel injection pump – removal and refitting

Caution: Be careful not to allow dirt into the injection pump or injector pipes during this procedure.

1.9 litre engine

Removal

Note: *If the injection pump is being taken to a injection specialist for repair, unlock the immobiliser module as follows before disconnecting the battery. Switch on the ignition and lower the driver's door window. Get out of the vehicle and close all the doors then switch off the ignition. Reach in through the window and switch on the ignition again, wait at least ten seconds then switch the ignition off. Immediately disconnect the battery negative lead then disconnect the wiring connectors from the injection pump (the pump must be disconnected within ten minutes of the ignition being switched off). If the immobiliser module is not unlocked it will not be possible for the pump repairers to test the pump.*

1 Disconnect the battery negative lead.

2 Release the fasteners from the right-hand side and top of the engine cover then lift off the cover, taking care not to lose its mounting rubbers **(see illustrations 2.1a to 2.1c)**.

3 Remove the intake duct connecting the air cleaner housing to the manifold (see Section 2).

4 Cover the alternator with a plastic bag, as a precaution against fuel.

5 Remove the injection pump sprocket and hub as described in Chapter 2B, Section 8.

6 Remove the upper section of the inlet manifold (see Section 18).

7 Disconnect the accelerator cable from the fuel injection pump (see Section 3).

8 Disconnect the fast idle cable from the fuel injection pump (see Section 10).

9 Trace the injection pump fuel feed pipe back to the filter. Wipe clean the pipe end fitting then release and disconnect the pipe from the filter. Plug the pipe end and filter housing union to minimise fuel loss and prevent the entry of dirt into the system.

10 Wipe clean the area around the injection pump fuel return metal pipe unions. Disconnect the return pipe and hose from the metal pipe and plug the pipe and union ends to minimise fuel loss and prevent the entry of dirt into the system.

11 Disconnect the wiring connectors from the injection pump **(see illustration)**.

11.77 . . . then detach the cable and remove the accelerator pedal position sensor from the vehicle

12 Remove all traces of dirt from all the injector pipe unions. Unscrew the union nuts securing the injector pipes to the fuel injection pump and injectors. Counterhold the adaptors on the pump, while unscrewing the pipe-to-pump union nuts. Remove the pipes as a set. Plug the injection pump/injector unions to prevent the entry of dirt.

13 Slacken the pump rear mounting bolt.

14 Unscrew the three front mounting bolts securing to the mounting bracket then manoeuvre the pump out of position.

15 If necessary, unbolt the pump mounting bracket and remove it from the cylinder head, taking care not to lose its locating dowels.

Refitting

16 If necessary, ensure the locating dowels are in position, then refit the mounting bracket to the cylinder head. Tighten the bracket bolts to the specified torque

17 Ensure the pump rear mounting bolt, spacer, washer and nut are correctly fitted to the mounting bracket.

18 Manoeuvre the pump into position and seat it correctly in the mounting bracket.

19 Refit the pump front mounting bolts, tightening them to the specified torque. Once the front mounting bolts have been tightened, tighten the rear mounting bolt to the specified torque.

20 Refit and reconnect the injector fuel pipes. Loosely tighten all the union nuts to ensure all pipes are correctly seated then go around and tighten them to the specified torque.

12.11 On 1.9 litre engines, disconnect the wiring connectors (arrowed) from the rear of the injection pump

Counterhold the injection pump adaptors whilst tightening the injection pump end nuts.

21 Reconnect all relevant wiring to the pump.

22 Securely reconnect the feed and return pipes to the injection pump and fuel filter housing.

23 Reconnect and adjust the accelerator cable as described in Section 3.

24 Reconnect and adjust the fast idle cable as described in Section 10.

25 Refit the injection pump sprocket and timing belt as described in Chapter 2B, Section 8.

26 Refit the inlet manifold as described in Section 18.

27 Prime the fuel system as described in Section 5. Start the engine and check for signs of fuel leaks before refitting the engine cover.

2.0 litre engine

Warning: Always wait at least 30 seconds after switching off the engine before disconnecting any fuel hoses/pipes. This will allow the pressure in the system to return to atmospheric pressure.

Removal

Note: *A new high-pressure fuel pipe will be required on refitting. The pipe should be renewed whenever a union nut is slackened.*

28 Disconnect the battery negative lead.

29 Remove the injection pump sprocket as described in Chapter 2B, Section 8.

30 Cover the alternator with a plastic bag, as a precaution against fuel.

31 Drain the fuel filter housing (see Chapter 1B).

32 Wipe clean the area around the fuel outlet unions on the top of the fuel filter housing. Disconnect the pipes from the housing and plug the pipe and union ends to minimise fuel loss and prevent the entry of dirt into the system.

33 Free the fuel filter housing from its mounting bracket and position it clear of the injection pump. Slacken and remove the bolts and remove the filter housing mounting bracket.

34 Remove all traces of dirt from the injection pump feed and return hose unions, and the high-pressure fuel pipe unions; the pump and its surrounding area must be clean and dry before proceeding. Position a wad of rag beneath the pipe to catch any spilt fuel.

35 Counterhold the adaptors then slacken the union nuts securing the high-pressure fuel pipe to the injection pump/fuel rail. Remove the fuel pipe and plug the pump/fuel rail unions to prevent the entry of dirt into the fuel system **(see illustration)**. Discard the pipe; a new one should be used on refitting.

Caution: Never unscrew the adaptors from the fuel rail or injection pump.

36 Release the retaining clips and disconnect the fuel feed and return hoses from the pump **(see illustration)**. Plug the hoses ends and pump unions to prevent the entry of dirt.

12.35 On 2.0 litre engines, counterhold the adapters while slackening the union nuts to remove the high-pressure pipe linking the pump and the fuel rail

37 Disconnect the wiring connectors from the injection pump third piston deactivator solenoid and the high-pressure fuel regulator.

38 Unscrew the two bolts securing the rear bracket to the injection pump. Slacken the bolt securing the bracket to the mounting bracket and pivot the bracket away from the pump.

39 Slacken and remove the three front mounting nut/bolts securing the pump to the mounting bracket. Remove the injection pump and recover the spacers fitted between the pump and bracket.

40 If necessary, unbolt the pump mounting bracket and remove it from the cylinder head, taking care not to lose its locating dowels.

Refitting

41 If necessary, ensure the locating dowels are in position, then refit the mounting bracket to the cylinder head. Tighten the bracket bolts to the specified torque.

42 Ensure the rear bracket, spacer, captive nut and bolt are correctly fitted to the pump mounting bracket.

43 Manoeuvre the pump into position and engage it with the mounting stud. Align the rear mounting bracket with the pump and fit the bolts, tightening them lightly only at this stage.

44 Ensure the spacers are correctly positioned between the pump and bracket then refit the front mounting bolts. Fit the nut to the mounting stud then tighten the pump front mounting nut and bolts to the specified torque.

45 Tighten the bolts securing the rear bracket to the pump to the specified torque then tighten the bolt securing the bracket to the pump mounting bracket to the specified torque.

46 Reconnect the wiring connectors to the injection pump.

47 Fit the new high-pressure fuel pipe to the injection pump/fuel rail. Tighten both its union nuts by hand to ensure the pipe is correctly positioned then tighten the union nuts to the specified torque whilst counterholding the pump/fuel rail adaptor **(see illustration)**.

48 Reconnect the feed and return hoses to the pump, tightening the retaining clips securely.

49 Refit the fuel filter mounting bracket and tighten its retaining bolts to the specified torque. Securely refit the filter housing to the bracket then reconnect the fuel pipes.

50 Refit the injection pump sprocket and timing belt as described in Chapter 2B, Section 8.

51 Prime the fuel system as described in Section 5. Start the engine and check for signs of fuel leaks before refitting the engine cover.

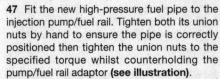

13 Injection timing – checking and adjustment

1.9 litre engine

1 The injection timing is set when the timing belt is installed. If at any time a fault is suspected, referring to Chapter 2B, Section 3, remove the timing belt covers and check that the flywheel, camshaft and injection pump timing holes are all correctly aligned so the locking tools can be inserted. If the timing holes are correctly aligned, the injection pump timing is correct (Peugeot do not specify any static or dynamic timing figures for this engine – on the WJY engine the timing is being constantly altered by the ECU anyway). If not, remove and refit the timing belt as described in Chapter 2B.

2.0 litre engine

2 On the 2.0 litre engine the injection timing is determined by the ECU using the information from its various sensors. Checking and adjustment can only be carried out using specialist diagnostic equipment (see Section 1).

4B

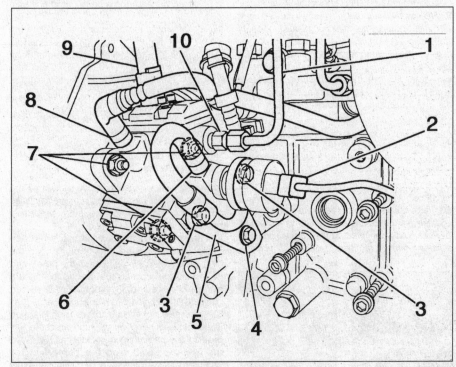

12.36 Injection pump details – 2.0 litre engine

1 *High-pressure pipe*
2 *High-pressure fuel regulator wiring connector*
3 *Rear bracket-to-pump bolts*
4 *Rear bracket-to-mounting bracket bolt*
5 *Rear bracket*
6 *Fuel return hose*
7 *Pump front mounting nut/bolts*
8 *Fuel feed hose*
9 *Third piston deactivator solenoid valve wiring connector*
10 *Fuel pipe adaptor*

12.47 On 2.0 litre engines, when refitting the new high-pressure pipe to the pump and fuel rail, counterhold their adapters to tighten the union nuts to the specified torque wrench setting

14 Fuel injectors –
removal and refitting

⚠ *Warning: Exercise extreme caution when working on the fuel injectors. Never expose the hands or any part of the body to injector spray, as the high working pressure can cause the fuel to penetrate the skin, with possibly fatal results. You are strongly advised to have any work which involves testing the injectors under pressure carried out by a dealer or fuel injection specialist.*

1.9 litre engine

Caution: Be careful not to allow dirt into the injection pump or injectors during this procedure.

Removal

1 Remove the upper section of the inlet manifold as described in Section 18.
2 Disconnect the leak-off pipe(s) from the injector to be removed **(see illustration)**.
3 Remove all traces of dirt from all the injector pipe unions. Unscrew the union nuts securing the injector pipes to the fuel injection pump and injectors **(see illustration)**. Counterhold the adaptors on the pump, while unscrewing the pipe-to-pump union nuts. Remove the pipes as a set. Plug the injection pump/injector unions to prevent the entry of dirt.
4 On WJY engines, if No 1 injector is being removed trace the needle lift sensor wiring back from the injector and disconnect its wiring connector from the main harness.
5 Remove all traces of dirt from around the injector then unscrew the injector from the cylinder head. Recover the injector fire seal washer from the cylinder head and discard it; a new one must be used on refitting.
Caution: Take care not to drop the

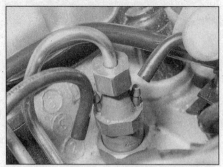

14.2 Disconnecting the leak-off pipe from the injector – 1.9 litre engine

injectors, or allow the needles at their tips to become damaged. The injectors are precision-made to fine limits, and must not be handled roughly. In particular, never mount them in a bench vice.

Refitting

6 Fit the new fire seal washer ensuring its convex surface is facing upwards (towards the injector).
7 Carefully refit the injector to the cylinder head, tightening it to the specified torque.
8 Reconnect the leak-off pipe(s) to the injector. Where necessary, reconnect the needle lift sensor wiring connector.
9 With all the injectors correctly installed, refit and reconnect the injector pipes. Loosely tighten all the union nuts to ensure all pipes are correctly seated then go around and tighten them to the specified torque. Counterhold the injection pump adaptors whilst tightening the injection pump end nuts.
10 Refit the inlet manifold as described in Section 18.
11 Prime the fuel system as described in Section 5. Start the engine and check for signs of fuel leaks before refitting the engine cover.

2.0 litre engine

⚠ *Warning: Always wait at least 30 seconds after switching off the engine before disconnecting any fuel hoses/pipes. This will allow the pressure in the system to return to atmospheric pressure.*

Removal

Caution: Be careful not to allow dirt into the fuel rail or injectors during this procedure.

Note: *A new high-pressure fuel pipe will be required for each injector on refitting. They should be renewed whenever a union nut is slackened.*

12 Remove the fasteners (rotate them 90° to release them) and remove the engine cover **(see illustrations 2.5a and 2.5b)**.
13 Disconnect the battery negative terminal. Each injector can then be removed as follows; if necessary unbolt the engine cover bracket/ wiring harness guide and/or disconnect the breather hose to improve access.
14 Disconnect the wiring connector from the injector.
15 Remove all traces of dirt from the injector and high-pressure fuel pipe unions, the injector and its surrounding area must be clean and dry before proceeding. Position a wad of rag beneath the pipe to catch any spilt fuel.
16 Counterhold the adaptor then slacken the union nuts securing the high-pressure fuel pipe to the injector/fuel rail **(see illustration)**. Remove the fuel pipe and plug the injector/fuel rail unions to prevent the entry of dirt into the fuel system. Discard the pipe; a new one should be used on refitting.
Caution: Never unscrew the adaptors from the fuel rail or injector.
17 Remove the retaining clip and disconnect the leak-off pipe connector from the injector **(see illustration)**.

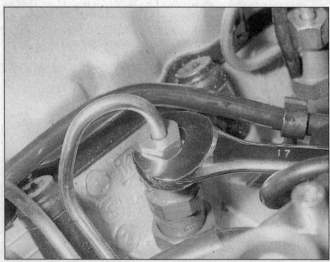

14.3 Unscrewing an injector pipe nut – 1.9 litre engine

14.16 On 2.0 litre engines, retain the adaptors whilst slackening the union nuts then remove and discard the high-pressure pipe linking the injector to the fuel rail

14.17 Remove the retaining clip and disconnect the leak-off pipe connector from the injector

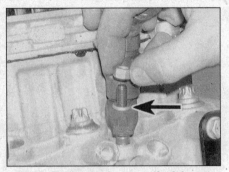

14.18 Slacken and remove the injector retaining nut and lift off the domed washer (arrowed)

14.19a Remove the injector and retaining clamp from the cylinder head . . .

18 Slacken and remove the injector retaining nut and domed washer **(see illustration)**.

19 Carefully remove the injector and retaining clamp from the cylinder head, noting which way up the clamp is fitted. If the retaining clamp pin is a loose fit, remove it and store it with the clamp for safe-keeping **(see illustrations)**.

 If the injector is a tight fit, remove the retaining clamp stud (using two nuts locked together) and free the injector by rotating it with an open-ended spanner located on the retaining clamp flats. Never rotate the injector using a spanner on the large nut on the upper end of the injector as this will seriously damage the injector.

Caution: Take care not to knock or drop the injector. The injectors are precision-made to fine limits, and must not be handled roughly. In particular, never mount them in a bench vice.

20 Recover the injector sealing washer and collar and discard them; new ones must be used on refitting.

Refitting

21 Where necessary, refit the injector retaining clamp stud to the cylinder head. Ensure the stud is fitted the correctly way around (shorter length of thread screwed into the head) then tighten it securely.

22 Fit a new sealing collar and washer to the injector **(see illustrations)**.

23 Engage the retaining clamp with the injector flats, ensuring the flat surface of the clamp is facing downwards.

24 Ensure the clamp pin is correctly fitted to the cylinder head then manoeuvre the injector and retaining clamp into position.

25 Ensure the injector and clamp are correctly located then fit the domed washer with its convex surface facing downwards. Refit the retaining clamp nut, tighten it lightly only at this stage.

26 Fit the new high-pressure fuel pipe and lightly tighten its union nuts.

27 Ensure the high-pressure pipe is correctly seated then tighten the injector retaining clamp nut to the specified torque.

28 Tighten the high-pressure fuel pipe union nuts to the specified torque whilst counterholding the injector/fuel rail adaptor.

29 Reconnect the wiring connector and leak-off pipe connector securely to the injector.

30 Reconnect the battery then prime the fuel system as described in Section 5.

31 Start the engine and check for fuel leaks before refitting the engine cover.

15 Fuel rail (2.0 litre engine) – removal and refitting

⚠ *Warning: Always wait at least 30 seconds after switching off the engine before disconnecting any fuel hoses/pipes. This will allow the*

pressure in the system to return to atmospheric pressure.
Caution: Be careful not to allow dirt into the injection pump or injectors during this procedure.

Removal

Note: *New high-pressure fuel pipes will be required on refitting. They should be renewed whenever a union nut is slackened.*

1 Disconnect the battery negative terminal then release the fasteners (rotate them 90° to release them) and remove the engine cover **(see illustrations 2.5 and 2.5b)**.

2 Disconnect the breather hose from the cylinder head cover and position it clear of the fuel rail.

3 Unscrew the bolts and remove the engine cover mounting bracket from the right-hand side of the cylinder head. Undo the nuts and free the injector wiring harness guide from the cylinder head.

4 Remove all traces of dirt from the injector and high-pressure fuel pipe unions, the fuel rail and its surrounding area must be clean and dry before proceeding. Position a wad of rag beneath the fuel rail to catch any spilt fuel.

5 Wipe clean the area around the fuel outlet unions on the top of the fuel filter housing. Disconnect the pipes from the housing and plug the pipe and union ends to minimise fuel loss and prevent the entry of dirt into the system. Free the fuel filter housing from its mounting bracket and position it clear of the injection pump.

4B

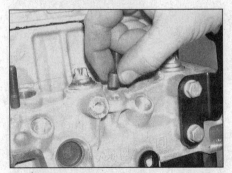

14.19b . . . and remove the clamp pin

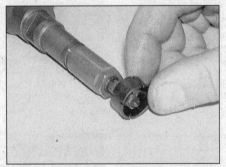

14.22a Slide the new sealing collar onto the injector . . .

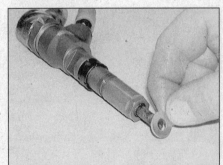

14.22b . . . then fit the new sealing washer

15.6a Retain the adaptors whilst slackening the union nuts then remove and discard the high-pressure pipes linking the pump and injectors to the fuel rail

15.6b Plug/cap all unions to prevent the entry of dirt into the fuel system

6 Counterhold the adaptors then slacken the union nuts securing the high-pressure fuel pipes to the fuel rail/injection pump/injectors. Remove the fuel pipes and plug all the fuel unions to prevent the entry of dirt into the fuel system (see illustrations). Discard the pipes; new ones should be used on refitting.

Caution: Never unscrew the adaptors from the fuel rail, injection pump or injectors.

7 Disconnect the wiring connectors from the fuel temperature sensor (where fitted) and pressure sensor which are fitted to the fuel rail.

8 Unscrew the three mounting bolts then remove the fuel rail from the cylinder head (see illustrations).

Refitting

9 Manoeuvre the fuel rail into position and lightly tighten its mounting bolts. Reconnect the wiring connectors to the fuel temperature and pressure sensors.

10 Fit the new high-pressure fuel pipes and lightly tighten all the union nuts to seat the pipes in position. Ensure all pipes are correctly seated then go around and tighten all the unions nuts to the specified torque, counterholding each adaptor as the nut is

tightened. **Note:** *If it is not possible to connect the pipes to the injectors. Remove the injectors and refit them, connecting the pipe to the injectors before tightening the retaining clamp nuts (see Section 14).*

11 Once all pipe union nuts are correctly tightened, tighten the fuel rail mounting bolts to the specified torque.

12 Refit the fuel filter housing to its bracket then reconnect the fuel hoses.

13 Refit the engine cover bracket to the cylinder head and reconnect the breather hose.

14 Reconnect the battery then prime the fuel system as described in Section 5.

15 Start the engine and check for fuel leaks before refitting the engine cover.

16 Fuel cooler (2.0 litre engine) – removal and refitting

Caution: Be careful not to allow dirt into the fuel system during this procedure.

Removal

1 Chock the rear wheels, firmly apply the

handbrake then jack up the front of the vehicle and support it on axle stands (see *Jacking and vehicle support*).

2 Remove all traces of dirt from fuel cooler and its surrounding area on the vehicle underbody. Position a container underneath the cooler to catch any spilt fuel.

3 Release the retaining clips and disconnect the fuel pipes from the cooler (see illustration). Plug the pipe ends to minimise fuel loss and prevent the entry of dirt into the fuel system.

4 Unscrew the mounting nuts and remove the fuel cooler from the vehicle. Inspect the cooler mounting rubber for signs of damage or deterioration and renew if necessary.

Refitting

5 Ensure the mounting rubber is correctly fitted to the body then engage the fuel cooler peg in the rubber. Locate the cooler on its mounting studs and refit the mounting nuts, tightening them securely.

6 Reconnect the fuel pipes securely to the cooler then lower the vehicle to the ground.

7 Prime the fuel system (see Section 5) then start the engine and check for signs of fuel leaks.

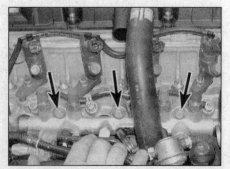

15.8a Undo the mounting bolts (arrowed) . . .

15.8b . . . and manoeuvre the fuel rail out of position

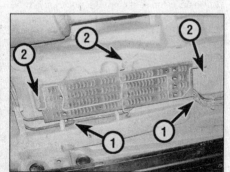

16.3 Fuel cooler fuel pipe unions (1) and mounting nuts (2) – 2.0 litre engine

17 Turbocharger –
removal and refitting

Removal

1 Firmly apply the handbrake then jack up the front of the vehicle and support it on axle sands (see *Jacking and vehicle support*).
2 Remove the right-hand driveshaft as described in Chapter 8.
3 Unscrew the nuts and bolts and remove the mounting link securing the rear engine/transmission mounting to the subframe. Undo the retaining bolts and remove the rear mounting assembly from the rear of the cylinder block.
4 Remove the exhaust front pipe as described in Section 20.
5 Unscrew the bolts and remove the exhaust outlet flange from the turbocharger.
6 Slacken the retaining clip and free the flexible duct from the top of the turbocharger intake pipe. Also unscrew the pipe upper mounting bolt. Unscrew the bolt securing the intake pipe to the side of the turbocharger then manoeuvre the pipe out of position. Recover the sealing ring fitted between the pipe and turbocharger.
7 Slacken the retaining clips securing the outlet pipe to its connecting sleeves on the turbocharger and inlet manifold then unclip and remove the pipe.
8 Slacken the retaining clip and remove the connecting sleeve from the turbocharger **(see illustration)**.
9 Remove the EGR valve (see Chapter 4C, Section 3).
10 Unscrew the retaining bolts and remove the support bracket from the base of the turbocharger.
11 Wipe clean the area around the oil feed and return unions on the cylinder block **(see illustration)**. Where the feed pipe is secured by a union nut, unscrew the nut then free the pipe from the block and recover the filter (where fitted) from inside the pipe. Where the feed pipe is secured in position with a union bolt, unscrew the bolt and recover the sealing washers; discard the sealing washers, new ones should be used on refitting.
12 Release the retaining clip and detach the oil return hose from the block.
13 Undo the power steering pipe clip screws and free the pipes from the underside of the engine/transmission unit **(see illustration)**. Unscrew the retaining bolts and remove the flywheel lower cover plate from the transmission unit.
14 Unscrew the nuts securing the turbocharger to the exhaust manifold then manoeuvre the turbocharger downwards and out of position. If necessary, tilt the engine slightly forwards to gain the necessary clearance required to remove the turbocharger. Discard the nuts; new ones should be used on refitting.

17.8 Removing the connecting sleeve from the turbocharger

15 Do not attempt to dismantle the turbocharger any further. If the unit is thought to be faulty take it to a turbo specialist for testing and examination. They will be able to inform you if the unit can be overhauled or will need renewing.

Refitting

16 Refitting is the reverse of removal, noting the following.
a) Ensure all mating surfaces are clean and dry.
b) Secure the turbocharger to the exhaust manifold with new nuts.
c) Tighten all fixings to the specified torque (where given).
d) Refit the driveshaft as described in Chapter 8 and check the transmission oil level as described in Chapter 1B).
e) Ensure all turbocharger ducts are correctly and securely reconnected.
f) When starting the engine for the first time, disconnect the injection pump wiring connector(s) then turn the engine over on the starter motor until the oil pressure warning light goes out; this will allow oil to be circulated around the turbocharger bearings before the engine is started. Reconnect the injection pump then start the engine as normal.

18 Inlet manifold –
removal and refitting

1.9 litre engine

Removal

1 Disconnect the battery negative terminal.
2 Release the fasteners from the right-hand side and top of the engine cover then lift off the cover, taking care not to lose its mounting rubbers **(see illustrations 2.1a to 2.1c)**.
3 Slacken the retaining clip and detach the intake duct from the EGR valve. Release the retaining clip and detach the EGR pipe from the side of the EGR valve. **Note:** *If the pipe is secured in position with a crimped-type clip, discard the clip and obtain a new one for use on refitting*

17.11 Turbocharger oil feed pipe union and return hose union

4 Disconnect the breather hose from the left-hand end of the manifold upper section.
5 Unscrew the bolts securing the manifold upper section to the cylinder head and lower section. **Note:** *Unscrew the mounting bolt and free the coolant expansion tank from its mounting bracket, taking care not to lose its mounting rubbers, to improve access to the rear right-hand manifold bolt.*
6 Remove the manifold upper section, complete with EGR valve, disconnecting the wiring connector and vacuum hose from the EGR valve solenoid. Recover the four seals fitted between the upper and lower sections.
7 To remove the lower section of the manifold, unscrew the bolts securing the EGR pipe to the top of the exhaust manifold and the cylinder head cover. Free the pipe from the manifold and recover its gasket. Discard the gasket; a new one should be used on refitting.
8 Slacken and remove the nuts and bolt securing the inlet manifold to the cylinder head. Remove the manifold and EGR pipe as an assembly. Recover the manifold gaskets and discard them; new ones must be used on refitting.

Refitting

9 Examine all the manifold studs for signs of damage and corrosion; remove all traces of corrosion, and repair or renew any damaged studs.
10 Ensure that the mating surfaces are clean and flat, and fit the new manifold gaskets.

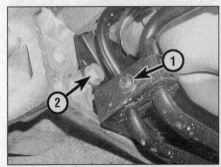

17.13 Undo the power steering pipe clip screw (1) then undo the bolts (2) and remove the flywheel lower cover plate from the transmission unit

4B

11 Route the EGR pipe correct through the lower section of the manifold then install both as an assembly. Tighten the manifold retaining nuts and bolt to the specified torque.
12 Fit a new gasket to the exhaust manifold then reconnect the EGR pipe, tightening its retaining bolts securely.
13 Fit a new seal to each of the upper manifold section joints then refit the upper section of the manifold, reconnecting the wiring connector and vacuum hose to the EGR solenoid valve. Refit the retaining bolts, tightening them to the specified torque, and reconnect the breather hose.
14 Where necessary, ensure the mounting rubbers are in position then seat the coolant expansion tank in its mounting bracket. Secure the tank in position with the retaining bolt.
15 Reconnect the intake duct and EGR pipe to the manifold upper section, secure them in position with their retaining clips.
16 Ensure the mounting rubbers are all correctly fitted then install the engine cover, securing it in position with the fasteners. Reconnect the battery.

2.0 litre engine

Removal

17 Remove the exhaust manifold as described in Section 19.
18 Slacken and remove the nuts and bolt securing the inlet manifold to the cylinder head. Remove the manifold and recover the manifold gasket. Discard the gasket; a new one must be used on refitting.

Refitting

19 Examine all the manifold studs for signs of damage and corrosion; remove all traces of corrosion, and repair or renew any damaged studs.
20 Ensure that the mating surfaces are clean and flat, and fit the new manifold gasket.
21 Refit the manifold and tighten its retaining nuts and bolt to the specified torque.
22 Refit the exhaust manifold as described in Section 19.

---

19 Exhaust manifold –
removal and refitting

1.9 litre engine

Removal

1 Disconnect the battery negative terminal.
2 Release the fasteners from the right-hand side and top of the engine cover then lift off the cover, taking care not to lose its mounting rubbers **(see illustrations 2.1a to 2.1c)**.
3 Release the retaining clip and detach the EGR pipe from the side of the EGR valve.
Note: *If the pipe is secured in position with a crimped-type clip, discard the clip and obtain a new one for use on refitting*

4 Unscrew the bolts securing the EGR pipe to the top of the exhaust manifold and the cylinder head cover. Free the pipe from the manifold and recover its gasket. Discard the gasket; a new one should be used on refitting.
5 Disconnect the exhaust pipe from the manifold as described in Section 20.
6 Unscrew the exhaust manifold retaining nuts and remove the spacers from the manifold studs.
7 Remove the exhaust manifold and recover the manifold gaskets. Discard the gaskets; new ones must be used on refitting.

Refitting

8 Examine all the manifold studs for signs of damage and corrosion; remove all traces of corrosion, and repair or renew any damaged studs.
9 Ensure that the mating surfaces are clean and flat, and fit the new manifold gaskets.
10 Refit the manifold then fit the spacers to the mounting studs and screw on the retaining nuts. Tighten the nuts evenly and progressively to the specified torque.
11 Fit a new gasket then reconnect the EGR pipe to the manifold, tightening its retaining bolts securely. Reconnect the pipe to the EGR valve, securing it in position with the retaining clip, and refit the bolt securing the pipe to the cylinder head cover.
12 Reconnect the exhaust front pipe as described in Section 20.
13 Refit the engine cover then reconnect the battery.

2.0 litre engine

Removal

14 Remove the turbocharger as described in Section 17.
15 Unscrew the exhaust manifold retaining nuts and remove the spacers from the manifold studs.
16 Remove the exhaust manifold and recover the manifold gasket. Discard the gasket; a new one must be used on refitting.

Refitting

17 Examine all the manifold studs for signs of damage and corrosion; remove all traces of corrosion, and repair or renew any damaged studs.

**20.6 Front pipe to manifold joint –
1.9 litre engine (retaining bolt and spring
arrangement arrowed)**

18 Ensure that the mating surfaces are clean and flat, and fit the new manifold gaskets.
19 Refit the manifold then fit the spacers to the mounting studs and screw on the retaining nuts. Tighten the nuts evenly and progressively to the specified torque.
20 Refit the turbocharger as described in Section 17.

---

20 Exhaust system –
general information,
removal and refitting

General information

1 The exhaust system consists of two sections; the front pipe (which incorporates the catalytic converter) and the tailpipe.
2 On 1.9 litre engines, the front pipe is secured to the manifold by nuts and bolts, the joint being of the spring-loaded ball type, to allow for movement in the exhaust system. The front pipe is secured to the tailpipe by a clamping ring. The system is suspended throughout its entire length by rubber mountings.
3 On 2.0 litre engines, the front pipe incorporates a flexible section at its front end to allow for movement in the exhaust system. Both the exhaust joints are joined by clamping rings and the system is suspended throughout its entire length by rubber mountings.

Removal

4 Each exhaust section can be removed individually or, alternatively, the complete system can be removed as a unit. Even if only one part of the system needs attention, it is often easier to remove the whole system and separate the sections on the bench.
5 To remove the system or part of the system, first jack up the front or rear of the car and support it on axle stands (see *Jacking and vehicle support*). Alternatively, position the car over an inspection pit or on car ramps.

Front pipe – 1.9 litre engine

6 Undo the nuts securing the front pipe flange joint to the manifold, and recover the spring cups and spring **(see illustration)**. Remove the bolts and recover the wire-mesh gasket.
7 Have an assistant support the front end of the pipe, then slacken and remove the nut, washer and bolt from the tailpipe clamping ring and disengage the clamp from the flange joint **(see illustration)**.
8 Free the front pipe from its mounting rubber(s) and remove it from underneath the vehicle.

Front pipe – 2.0 litre engine

9 Slacken and remove the nut, washer and bolt from the clamping rings securing the front pipe to the tailpipe and turbocharger flange. Disengage both clamps from the flange joints **(see illustration)**.

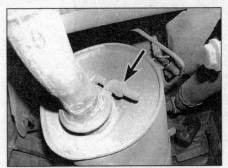

20.7 Slacken and remove the nut (arrowed), washer and bolt then free the clamping ring from the flange joint

20.9 Front pipe-to-manifold clamping ring – 2.0 litre engine (viewed from underneath)

10 Unscrew the three nuts securing the front pipe mounting plate to the rear of the subframe **(see illustration)**.

11 Free the front pipe from its rear mounting and manoeuvre it out of position, complete with its front mounting plate. If necessary the mounting plate and front mounting rubbers can then be separated from the front pipe.

Tailpipe

12 Slacken and remove the nut, washer and bolt from the tailpipe clamping ring and disengage the clamp from the flange joint **(see illustration)**.

13 Unhook the tailpipe from its mounting rubbers and remove it from the vehicle.

Complete system – 1.9 litre engine

14 Undo the nuts securing the front pipe flange joint to the manifold, and recover the spring cups, springs and bolts.

15 With the aid of an assistant, free the system from all its mounting rubbers and lower it from under the vehicle. Recover the wire-mesh gasket from the front pipe joint.

Complete system – 2.0 litre engine

16 Slacken and remove the nut, washer and bolt from the clamping ring securing the front pipe to the turbocharger flange. Disengage the clamp from the flange joint.

17 Unscrew the three nuts securing the front pipe mounting plate to the rear of the subframe **(see illustration 20.10)**.

18 With the aid of an assistant, free the system from its mounting rubbers and lower it from under the vehicle, complete with its front mounting plate. If necessary the mounting plate and front mounting rubbers can then be separated from the front pipe.

Heatshield(s)

19 The heat shields are secured to the underside of the body by various nuts and fasteners. If a shield is being removed to gain access to a component located behind it, remove the retaining nuts and/or fastener (unscrew the centre screw then pull out the complete fastener), and manoeuvre the shield out of position. On some models it may be necessary to free the exhaust system from its

mountings to gain the clearance necessary to remove the larger heat shield.

Refitting

20 Each section is refitted by reversing the removal sequence, noting the following points:

a) *Ensure that all traces of corrosion have been removed from the flanges and renew all necessary gaskets.*

b) *Inspect the rubber mountings for signs of damage or deterioration, and renew as necessary.*

c) *Where joints are secured together by a clamping ring, apply a smear of exhaust system jointing paste to the flange joint to ensure a gas-tight seal.*

d) *Prior to tightening the exhaust system fasteners, ensure that all rubber mountings are correctly located, and that there is adequate clearance between the exhaust system and vehicle underbody. On 2.0 litre engines ensure no excess strain is being placed on the flexible section of the front pipe.*

4B

20.10 On 2.0 litre engines, unscrew the three nuts (arrowed) securing the front pipe mounting plate to the subframe

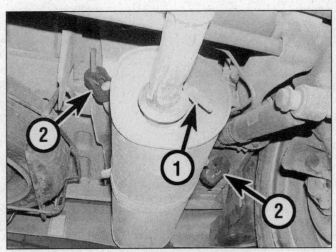

20.12 Tailpipe clamping ring (1) and rubber mountings (2)

Chapter 4 Part C:
Emission control systems

Contents

Degrees of difficulty

Easy, suitable for novice with little experience		Fairly easy, suitable for beginner with some experience		Fairly difficult, suitable for competent DIY mechanic		Difficult, suitable for experienced DIY mechanic		Very difficult, suitable for expert DIY or professional	

Specifications

Torque wrench settings	Nm	lbf ft
Air injection valve – 1.4 litre engine with pulse air injection:		
Valve-to-cylinder head bolts	8	6
Valve-to-adaptor nuts	7	5
Valve adaptor-to-exhaust manifold bolts	7	5
EGR valve and adaptor nuts and bolts – 2.0 litre engine	10	7
Roadwheel bolts	85	63

1 General information

1 All petrol engine models have the ability to use unleaded petrol, and also have various other features built into the fuel system to help minimise harmful emissions. On top of this, all models are equipped with the crankcase emission control system, a catalytic converter and an evaporative emission control system. Some 1.4 litre engines are also fitted with a pulse air injection system to further reduce exhaust emissions.

2 All diesel engine models are also designed to meet the strict emission requirements. All models are equipped with a crankcase emission control system, a catalytic converter and an exhaust gas recirculation (EGR) system.

3 The emission control systems function as follows.

Petrol models

Crankcase emission control

4 To reduce the emission of unburned hydrocarbons from the crankcase into the atmosphere, the engine is sealed and the blow-by gases and oil vapour are removed from inside the crankcase, through a wire mesh oil separator, into the inlet tract to be burned by the engine during normal combustion.

5 Crankcase pressure is always relatively higher than manifold pressure, so the gases tend to move into the inlet tract.

Exhaust emission control

6 To minimise the amount of pollutants which escape into the atmosphere, all models are fitted with a catalytic converter in the exhaust system. The system is of the closed-loop type in which an oxygen sensor (situated upstream of the catalytic converter) in the exhaust system provides the engine management system ECU with constant feedback, enabling the ECU to adjust the mixture to provide the best possible conditions for the converter to operate. On 1.4 litre models with pulse air injection, there are actually two oxygen sensors to allow for greater control of the emissions; in addition to the sensor located upstream of the catalytic converter, a second sensor is also fitted downstream of the converter.

7 The oxygen sensor has a heating element built-in that is controlled by the ECU through the engine management system relay to quickly bring the sensor's tip to an efficient operating temperature. The sensor's tip is sensitive to oxygen and sends the ECU a varying voltage depending on the amount of oxygen in the exhaust gases; if the intake air/fuel mixture is too rich, the exhaust gases are low in oxygen so the sensor sends a low-voltage signal, the voltage rising as the mixture weakens and the amount of oxygen rises in the exhaust gases. Peak conversion efficiency of all major pollutants occurs if the intake air/fuel mixture is maintained at the chemically-correct ratio for the complete combustion of petrol of 14.7 parts (by weight) of air to 1 part of fuel (the 'stoichiometric' ratio). The sensor output voltage alters in a large step at this point, the ECU using the signal change as a reference point and correcting the intake air/fuel mixture accordingly by altering the fuel injector pulse width.

Evaporative emission control

8 To minimise the escape into the atmosphere of unburned hydrocarbons, an evaporative emission control system is fitted to all models. The fuel tank filler cap is sealed and a charcoal canister is mounted underneath the right-hand wing to collect the petrol vapours generated in the tank when the car is parked. It stores them until they can be cleared from the canister (under the control of the engine management system ECU) via the purge valve into the inlet tract to be burned by the engine during normal combustion.

9 To ensure that the engine runs correctly when it is cold and/or idling, and to protect the catalytic converter from the effects of an over-rich mixture, the purge control valve is not opened by the ECU until the engine has warmed up, and the engine is under load; the valve solenoid is then modulated on and off to allow the stored vapour to pass into the inlet tract.

4C

2.6a Undo the retaining screws . . .

2.6b . . . and fasteners . . .

2.6c . . . and remove the front and rear sections of the right-hand wheelarch liner

Pulse air injection system – later 1.4 litre models

10 Some later 1.4 litre models are fitted with a pulse air injection system. The purpose of the system is to decrease exhaust gas emissions whilst the engine is warming up. The system achieves this by raising the temperature of the exhaust gases which has the effect of quickly warming the catalytic converter to its normal operating temperature. Once the catalytic converter is up to temperature, the system switches off.

11 The system consists of the pump and the air injection valve and is controlled by the engine management ECU. When the engine is cold, the ECU switches on the pump which injects a controlled amount of air into the cylinder head exhaust ports via the air injection valve which is fitted to the top of the exhaust manifold. The air flows through the valve and internal passages in the manifold and cylinder head and mixes with the exhaust gases in the cylinder head ports. This air causes any unburnt particles of fuel in the mixture to burn in the exhaust port/manifold which effectively raises the temperature of the exhaust gases. Once the catalytic converter is up to temperature, the ECU switches off the air pump. The air injection valve then acts as a non-return valve, preventing the exhaust gases from passing through the valve to the pump.

Diesel models

Crankcase emission control

12 Refer to paragraphs 4 and 5.

Exhaust emission control

13 To minimise the level of exhaust pollutants released into the atmosphere, a catalytic converter is fitted in the exhaust system.

14 The catalytic converter consists of a canister containing a fine mesh impregnated with a catalyst material, over which the hot exhaust gases pass. The catalyst speeds up the oxidation of harmful carbon monoxide, unburnt hydrocarbons and soot, effectively reducing the quantity of harmful products released into the atmosphere via the exhaust gases.

Exhaust gas recirculation system

15 This system is designed to recirculate small quantities of exhaust gas into the inlet tract, and

therefore into the combustion process. This process reduces the level of nitrogen oxide (NOx) present in the final exhaust gas which is released into the atmosphere.

16 On 1.9 litre (WJZ) engines, the system is controlled by the EGR system electronic control unit using the signals received from the accelerator lever switch (on the injection pump), the coolant temperature sensor and crankshaft sensor. The EGR valve is mounted onto the front of the inlet manifold and is joined to the exhaust manifold by a metal pipe. The valve incorporates a vacuum diaphragm unit and an electrical solenoid valve. When the solenoid valve is opened, the vacuum created by the braking system vacuum pump is allowed to act on the diaphragm unit. The diaphragm then opens the EGR valve, allowing the exhaust gases to pass through the valve and into the inlet tract. To ensure that the engine runs correctly when it is warmed up and/or under load, the EGR valve is modulated on and off as necessary.

17 On 1.9 litre (WJY) engines, the system is controlled by the injection system ECU (see Chapter 4B). The EGR valve is the same as that fitted to earlier (WJZ) engines and operates as described in paragraph 16.

18 On 2.0 litre engine, the system is controlled by the injection ECU (see Chapter 4B) and consists of the EGR valve and the regulator valve. The EGR valve is mounted on the top of the exhaust manifold and the regulator valve is fitted to the inlet manifold intake elbow. Both the EGR valve and regulator incorporate vacuum diaphragms and are controlled via electric solenoid valves which are connected to

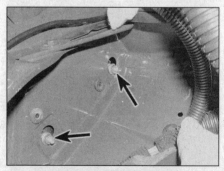

2.7 Loosen the retaining nuts (arrowed) . . .

the braking system vacuum pump. When the solenoid valves are opened, vacuum is allowed to act on the diaphragms which causes the EGR valve to open (allowing exhaust gases to pass from the exhaust manifold to the inlet manifold) and the regulator valve to close (restricting the inlet manifold intake). The ECU modulates the EGR valve and regulator as necessary, to ensure optimum performance under all operating conditions.

2 Petrol engine emission control systems – testing and component renewal

Crankcase emission control

1 The components of this system require no attention other than to check that the hose(s) are clear and undamaged at regular intervals.

Evaporative emission control system

Testing

2 If the system is thought to be faulty, disconnect the hoses from the charcoal canister and purge control valve and check that they are clear by blowing through them. If the purge control valve or charcoal canister are thought to be faulty, they must be renewed.

Charcoal canister – renewal

3 The charcoal canister is located behind the right-hand front wing.

4 To gain access to the canister, firmly apply the handbrake then jack up the front of the vehicle and support it on axle stands (see *Jacking and vehicle support*). Remove the right-hand front roadwheel.

5 Undo the screws securing the front section of the right-hand wheelarch liner to the base of the bumper. Remove the fasteners (pull out the centre pin then remove the complete fastener) securing the liner to the body then manoeuvre the liner out from underneath the wing.

6 Remove the rear section of the wheelarch liner in the same way (**see illustrations**).

7 Working in the engine compartment, slacken the nuts securing the canister to the body (the nuts do not need to be removed) (**see illustration**).

2.8 ... then free the charcoal canister from the body and disconnect its hoses, noting their correct fitted locations

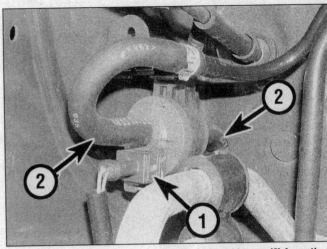

2.12 Disconnect the wiring connector (1) and hoses (2) from the purge valve which is located at the left-hand rear corner of the engine compartment

8 Free the canister from the body and mark the hoses for identification purposes. Disconnect both hoses and remove the canister from the vehicle **(see illustration)**.

9 Refitting is a reverse of the removal procedure ensuring the hoses are correctly reconnected. Lower the vehicle to the ground and tighten the wheel bolts to the specified torque.

Purge valve – renewal

10 The purge valve is located in the right-hand rear corner of the engine compartment.

11 To gain access to the valve, remove the coolant expansion tank as described in Chapter 3.

12 Disconnect the battery negative terminal then disconnect the wiring connector from the valve **(see illustration)**.

13 Disconnect the hoses from either end of the valve then release the valve from its retaining clip and remove it from the engine compartment, noting which way around it is fitted.

14 Refitting is a reversal of the removal procedure, ensuring the valve is fitted the correct way around and the hoses are securely connected. Refit the coolant expansion tank as described in Chapter 3.

Exhaust emission control

Testing

15 The performance of the catalytic converter can be checked only by measuring the exhaust gases using a good-quality, carefully-calibrated exhaust gas analyser.

16 If the CO level at the tailpipe is too high, the vehicle should be taken to a Peugeot dealer so that the complete engine management system, including the oxygen sensor(s), can be thoroughly checked using the special diagnostic equipment (see Chapter 4A). Once these have been checked and are known to be free from faults, the fault must be in the catalytic converter, which must be renewed as described in Chapter 4A.

Catalytic converter – renewal

17 Refer to Chapter 4A.

Oxygen sensor – renewal

Note: *The oxygen sensor is delicate and will not work if it is dropped or knocked, if its power supply is disrupted, or if any cleaning materials are used on it.*

18 Trace the wiring back from the oxygen sensor (screwed into the top of the exhaust front pipe – on 1.4 litre models with pulse air injection the downstream sensor is screwed into the catalytic converter) to its wiring connector. Disconnect the wiring and free it from any relevant retaining clips or ties **(see illustration)**.

19 Unscrew the sensor and remove it from the exhaust system **(see illustration)**.

20 Refitting is a reverse of the removal procedure. Prior to installing the sensor apply a smear of high temperature grease to the sensor threads. Ensure the sensor is securely tightened and that the wiring is correctly routed and in no danger of contacting either the exhaust system or engine.

Pulse air injection system

Testing

21 If the air injection pump is thought not to be operating correctly, the vehicle should be taken to a Peugeot dealer so that the complete engine management system, including the pump, can be thoroughly checked using the special diagnostic equipment (see Chapter 4A).

22 The air injection valve can be checked once it has been removed. The valve should flow air only in one direction; when blown through from the valve (pump) union. If not, it is faulty and should be renewed.

Air pump – renewal

23 The air pump is located on the left-hand side of the engine compartment.

24 To gain access to the pump, remove the air cleaner housing as described in Chapter 4A.

25 Unscrew the mounting bolts then disconnect the vacuum hoses and wiring connector and remove the pump from the vehicle.

26 Refitting is the reverse of removal.

Air injection valve – renewal

27 The air injection valve is mounted on the front of the cylinder head.

28 Disconnect the air hose from the valve.

2.18 Disconnect the wiring connector and unclip the connector ...

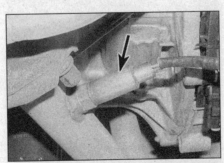

2.19 ... then unscrew the oxygen sensor (arrowed) and remove it from the exhaust system

4C

29 Unscrew the bolts securing the valve adaptor to the top of the exhaust manifold **(see illustration)**.

30 Unscrew the bolts securing the valve to the front of the cylinder head then remove the valve and adaptor assembly from the engine.

31 If necessary, unscrew the retaining nuts and separate the valve and adaptor. Recover the gasket and discard it; a new one should be used on refitting.

32 Refitting is the reverse of removal, using a new gasket (where necessary) and tighten the fixings to the specified torque.

 3 Diesel engine emission control systems – testing and component renewal

Crankcase emission control

1 The components of this system require no attention other than to check that the hose(s) are clear and undamaged at regular intervals.

Exhaust emission control

Testing

2 The performance of the catalytic converter can be checked only by measuring the exhaust gases using a good-quality, carefully-calibrated exhaust gas analyser.

3 If the catalytic converter is thought to be faulty, before assuming the catalytic converter is faulty, it is worth checking the problem is not due to a faulty injector(s). Refer to your Peugeot dealer for further information.

Catalytic converter – renewal

4 Refer to Chapter 4B.

EGR system – 1.9 litre (WJZ) engine

Testing

5 If the EGR system is thought not to be operating correctly, the vehicle should be taken to a Peugeot dealer for testing.

EGR valve – renewal

6 Remove the upper section of the inlet manifold as described in Chapter 4B. The EGR valve can then be removed from the manifold.

7 Refitting is the reverse of removal.

Coolant temperature sensor – renewal

8 The coolant temperature sensor is screwed into the fuel filter/thermostat housing. Refer to Chapter 3 for removal and refitting information.

Crankshaft sensor – renewal

9 The crankshaft sensor is situated on the top of the transmission clutch housing. To remove the sensor, first disconnect the battery negative terminal.

10 Disconnect the sensor wiring connector then undo the retaining bolt and remove the sensor from the transmission unit.

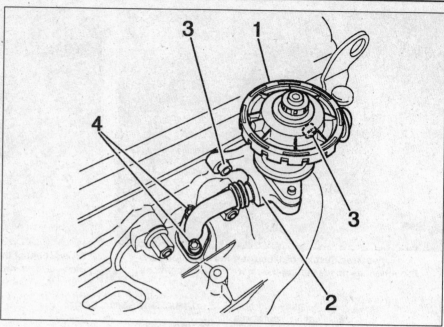

2.29 Pulse air injection valve – later 1.4 litre engine

1 Air injection valve
2 Valve adaptor
3 Valve-to-cylinder head bolts
4 Adaptor-to-manifold bolts

11 Refitting is reverse of the removal procedure.

Electronic control unit (ECU) – renewal

12 The ECU is located on the right-hand side of the engine compartment.

13 To remove the ECU, first disconnect the battery.

14 Undo the retaining nuts/bolts then disconnect the wiring connector and remove the ECU.

15 Refitting is a reverse of the removal procedure ensuring the wiring connector is securely reconnected.

Accelerator lever switch – renewal

16 The switch is fitted to the top of the injection pump. If the switch is faulty, replacement should be entrusted to a Peugeot dealer who will have the necessary special equipment to adjust the replacement on refitting.

3.21a On 2.0 litre diesel engines, rotate each fastener 90° to release it . . .

EGR system – 1.9 litre (WJY) engine

Testing

17 If the EGR system is thought not to be operating correctly, the vehicle should be taken to a Peugeot dealer for testing using the special diagnostic equipment (see Chapter 4B).

EGR valve – renewal

18 Remove the upper section of the inlet manifold as described in Chapter 4B. The EGR valve can then be removed from the manifold.

19 Refitting is the reverse of removal.

EGR system – 2.0 litre engine

Testing

20 If the EGR system is thought not to be operating correctly, the vehicle should be taken to a Peugeot dealer for testing using the special diagnostic equipment (see Chapter 4B).

EGR valve – renewal

21 Disconnect the battery negative terminal then release the fasteners (rotate them 90° to release them) and remove the engine cover **(see illustrations)**.

22 Disconnect the vacuum hose from the EGR valve which is fitted to the top of the exhaust manifold.

23 Unscrew the nuts securing the valve to the exhaust manifold and the valve adaptor to the inlet manifold intake flange. Recover the valve gasket and discard it; a new one should be used on refitting.

3.21b . . . then lift off the engine cover

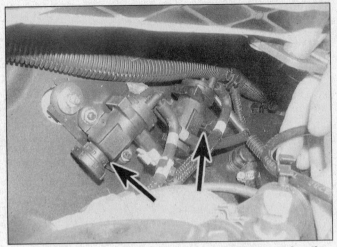

3.32 EGR system solenoid valves (arrowed) are mounted on the
bulkhead – 2.0 litre diesel engine

24 Refitting is the reverse of removal, using a new gasket and tighten the valve nuts to the specified torque.

EGR regulator – renewal

25 Firmly apply the handbrake then jack up the front of the vehicle and support it on axle stands (see *Jacking and vehicle support*).
26 To improve access, remove the battery and battery tray (see Chapter 5A).
27 Slacken the retaining clips and remove the flexible duct connecting the airflow meter to the turbocharger intake pipe. Unscrew the intake pipe upper mounting bolt. Unscrew the bolt securing the intake pipe to the side of the turbocharger then manoeuvre the pipe out of position. Recover the sealing ring fitted between the pipe and turbocharger.
28 Slacken the retaining clips securing the outlet pipe to its connecting sleeves on the turbocharger and EGR regulator and remove the pipe.
29 Slacken the retaining clip and remove the connecting sleeve from the EGR regulator.
30 Disconnect the vacuum hose then unscrew the retaining nuts and remove the EGR regulator from the inlet manifold elbow.
31 Refitting is the reverse of removal, ensuring all the intake ducts are correctly and securely refitted.

EGR solenoid valves – renewal

32 The solenoid valves are mounted on the engine compartment bulkhead, directly behind the intake duct **(see illustration)**. One valve operates the EGR valve and the other the regulator; trace the vacuum hose back from the regulator and EGR valve to identify the valves.
33 Make a note of the correct fitted positions of each hose (mark the hoses to avoid confusion on refitting) then disconnect the vacuum hoses from each valve.
34 Unscrew the mounting bolts and remove the valve bracket assembly from the bulkhead. The valves can then be removed from the bracket.
35 Refitting is the reverse of removal, ensuring the vacuum hoses are securely reconnected to their original valve unions.

---

4 Catalytic converter – general information and precautions

1 The catalytic converter is a reliable and simple device which needs no maintenance in itself, but there are some facts of which an owner should be aware if the converter is to function properly for its full service life.

Petrol models

a) DO NOT use leaded/lead-replacement petrol in a car equipped with a catalytic converter – the lead will coat the precious metals, reducing their converting efficiency and will eventually destroy the converter.
b) Always keep the ignition and fuel systems well-maintained in accordance with the manufacturer's schedule.
c) If the engine develops a misfire, do not drive the car at all (or at least as little as possible) until the fault is cured.
d) DO NOT push- or tow-start the car – this will soak the catalytic converter in unburned fuel, causing it to overheat when the engine does start.
e) DO NOT switch off the ignition at high engine speeds.
f) DO NOT use fuel or engine oil additives – these may contain substances harmful to the catalytic converter.
g) DO NOT continue to use the car if the engine burns oil to the extent of leaving a visible trail of blue smoke.
h) Remember that the catalytic converter operates at very high temperatures. DO NOT, therefore, park the car in dry undergrowth, over long grass or piles of dead leaves after a long run.
i) Remember that the catalytic converter is FRAGILE – do not strike it with tools during servicing work.
j) In some cases a sulphurous smell (like that of rotten eggs) may be noticed from the exhaust. This is common to many catalytic converter-equipped cars and once the car has covered a few thousand miles the problem should disappear.
k) The catalytic converter, used on a well-maintained and well-driven car, should last for between 50 000 and 100 000 miles – if the converter is no longer effective it must be renewed.

Diesel models

2 Refer to the information given in parts f, g, h and i of the petrol models information given above.

4C

Chapter 5 Part A:
Starting and charging systems

Contents

Degrees of difficulty

Easy, suitable for novice with little experience	**Fairly easy,** suitable for beginner with some experience	**Fairly difficult,** suitable for competent DIY mechanic	**Difficult,** suitable for experienced DIY mechanic	**Very difficult,** suitable for expert DIY or professional

Specifications

System type	12-volt, negative earth

Battery

Type	Fulmen, Delco or Steco
Charge condition:	
Poor	12.5 volts
Normal	12.6 volts
Good	12.7 volts

Alternator

Type	Valeo or Bosch (depending on model)

Starter motor

Type	Valeo or Bosch (depending on model)

Torque wrench settings	Nm	lbf ft
Alternator mounting bolts:		
Petrol engine	37	27
Diesel engine:		
1.9 litre engine:		
Front (drivebelt pulley end) bolts	43	32
Rear bolts	30	22
2.0 litre engine:		
Front (drivebelt pulley end) bolts	41	30
Rear bolts	39	29
Oil pressure switch:		
Petrol engine	25	18
Diesel engine	30	22

1 General information and precautions

General information

1 The engine electrical system consists mainly of the charging and starting systems. Because of their engine-related functions, these components are covered separately from the body electrical devices such as the lights, instruments, etc (which are covered in Chapter 12). On petrol engine models refer to Part B for information on the ignition system, and on diesel models refer to Part C for information on the preheating system.

2 The electrical system is of the 12-volt negative earth type.

3 The battery is of the low maintenance or 'maintenance-free' (sealed for life) type and is charged by the alternator, which is belt-driven from the crankshaft pulley.

4 The starter motor is of the pre-engaged type incorporating an integral solenoid. On starting, the solenoid moves the drive pinion into engagement with the flywheel ring gear before the starter motor is energised. Once the engine has started, a one-way clutch prevents the motor armature being driven by the engine while the pinion is disengaging from the flywheel.

Precautions

5 Further details of the various systems are given in the relevant Sections of this Chapter. While some repair procedures are given, the usual course of action is to renew the component concerned. The owner whose interest extends beyond mere component renewal should obtain a copy of the *Automobile Electrical & Electronic Systems Manual*, available from the publishers of this manual.

6 It is necessary to take extra care when working on the electrical system to avoid damage to semi-conductor devices (diodes and transistors), and to avoid the risk of personal injury. In addition to the precautions given in *Safety first!* at the beginning of this manual, observe the following when working on the system:

7 *Always remove rings, watches, etc, before working on the electrical system.* Even with the battery disconnected, capacitive discharge could occur if a component's live terminal is earthed through a metal object. This could cause a shock or nasty burn.

8 *Do not reverse the battery connections.* Components such as the alternator, electronic control units, or any other components having semi-conductor circuitry could be irreparably damaged.

9 If the engine is being started using jump leads and a slave battery, connect the batteries *positive-to-positive* and *negative-to-negative* (see *Jump starting*). This also applies when connecting a battery charger.

10 Never disconnect the battery terminals, the alternator, any electrical wiring or any test instruments when the ignition is switched on/the engine is running.

11 Do not allow the engine to turn the alternator when the alternator is not connected.

12 Never 'test' for alternator output by 'flashing' the output lead to earth.

13 Never use an ohmmeter of the type incorporating a hand-cranked generator for circuit or continuity testing.

14 Always ensure that the battery negative lead is disconnected when working on the electrical system.

15 Before using electric-arc welding equipment on the car, disconnect the battery, alternator and components such as the engine management electronic control unit to protect them from the risk of damage.

16 The radio/cassette unit fitted as standard equipment by Peugeot is equipped with a built-in security code to deter thieves. If the power source to the unit is cut, the anti-theft system will activate. Even if the power source is immediately reconnected, the radio/cassette unit will not function until the correct security code has been entered. Therefore, if you do not know the correct security code for the radio/cassette unit **do not** disconnect the battery negative terminal of the battery or remove the radio/cassette unit from the vehicle. Refer to *Audio unit anti-theft system* in the Reference Section for further information.

2 Electrical fault finding – general information

Refer to Chapter 12.

3 Battery – testing and charging

Standard and low maintenance battery – testing

1 If the vehicle covers a small annual mileage, it is worthwhile checking the specific gravity of the electrolyte every three months to determine the state of charge of the battery. Use a hydrometer to make the check and compare the results with the following table. Note that the specific gravity readings assume an electrolyte temperature of 15°C (60°F); for every 10°C (18°F) below 15°C (60°F) subtract 0.007. For every 10°C (18°F) above 15°C (60°F) add 0.007.

	Above 25°C (77°F)	Below 25°C (77°F)
Fully-charged	1.210 to 1.230	1.270 to 1.290
70% charged	1.170 to 1.190	1.230 to 1.250
Discharged	1.050 to 1.070	1.110 to 1.130

2 If the battery condition is suspect, first check the specific gravity of electrolyte in each cell. A variation of 0.040 or more between any cells indicates loss of electrolyte or deterioration of the internal plates.

3 If the specific gravity variation is 0.040 or more, the battery should be renewed. If the cell variation is satisfactory but the battery is discharged, it should be charged as described later in this Section.

Maintenance-free battery – testing

4 In cases where a 'sealed for life' maintenance-free battery is fitted, topping-up and testing of the electrolyte in each cell is not possible. The condition of the battery can therefore only be tested using a battery condition indicator or a voltmeter.

5 Certain models may be fitted with a 'Delco' type maintenance-free battery, with a built-in charge condition indicator. The indicator is located in the top of the battery casing, and indicates the condition of the battery from its colour. If the indicator shows green, then the battery is in a good state of charge. If the indicator turns darker, eventually to black, then the battery requires charging, as described later in this Section. If the indicator shows clear/yellow, then the electrolyte level in the battery is too low to allow further use, and the battery should be renewed. **Do not** attempt to charge, load or jump start a battery when the indicator shows clear/yellow.

6 If testing the battery using a voltmeter, connect the voltmeter across the battery and compare the result with those given in the Specifications under 'Charge condition'. The test is only accurate if the battery has not been subjected to any kind of charge for the previous six hours. If this is not the case, switch on the headlights for 30 seconds, then wait four to five minutes before testing the battery after switching off the headlights. All other electrical circuits must be switched off, so check that the doors and tailgate are fully shut when making the test.

7 If the voltage reading is less than 12.2 volts, then the battery is discharged, whilst a reading of 12.2 to 12.4 volts indicates a partially discharged condition.

8 If the battery is to be charged, remove it from the vehicle (Section 4) and charge it as described later in this Section.

Standard and low maintenance battery – charging

Note: *The following is intended as a guide only. Always refer to the manufacturer's recommendations (often printed on a label attached to the battery) before charging a battery.*

9 Charge the battery at a rate of 3.5 to 4 amps and continue to charge the battery at this rate until no further rise in specific gravity is noted over a four hour period.

10 Alternatively, a trickle charger charging at the rate of 1.5 amps can safely be used overnight.

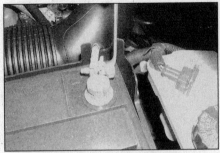

4.2 Remove the cover from the battery tray to gain access to the battery

4.3 Slacken the bolt and disconnect the clamp from the battery negative (–) terminal first . . .

4.4 . . . then lift the quick-release lever and disconnect the clamp from the positive (+) terminal

11 Specially rapid 'boost' charges which are claimed to restore the power of the battery in 1 to 2 hours are not recommended, as they can cause serious damage to the battery plates through overheating.

12 While charging the battery, note that the temperature of the electrolyte should never exceed 37.8°C (100°F).

Maintenance-free battery – charging

Note: *The following is intended as a guide only. Always refer to the manufacturer's recommendations (often printed on a label attached to the battery) before charging a battery.*

13 This battery type takes considerably longer to fully recharge than the standard type, the time taken being dependent on the extent of discharge, but it can take anything up to three days.

14 A constant voltage type charger is required,

to be set, when connected, to 13.9 to 14.9 volts with a charger current below 25 amps. Using this method, the battery should be usable within three hours, giving a voltage reading of 12.5 volts, but this is for a partially discharged battery and, as mentioned, full charging can take considerably longer.

15 If the battery is to be charged from a fully discharged state (condition reading less than 12.2 volts), have it recharged by your Peugeot dealer or local automotive electrician, as the charge rate is higher and constant supervision during charging is necessary.

4 Battery – removal and refitting

Note: *On models equipped with a Peugeot anti-theft alarm system, disable the alarm before*

disconnecting the battery (see Chapter 12). If a Peugeot audio unit is fitted, refer to 'Audio unit anti-theft system' in the Reference Section.

Removal (typical procedure)

1 The battery is located on the left-hand side of the engine compartment.

2 Remove the cover from the battery tray to gain access to the battery terminals **(see illustration)**.

3 Slacken the clamp bolt and disconnect the clamp from the battery negative (–) terminal **(see illustration)**.

4 Release the quick-release lever and disconnect the clamp from the battery positive (+) terminal **(see illustration)**.

5 Unscrew the bolts and remove the battery retaining clamp then lift the battery out of its tray **(see illustration)**.

6 To remove the battery tray, undo the retaining bolts then unclip wiring from the tray. The battery tray can then be lifted out of position, freeing it from its cooling duct **(see illustrations)**. On diesel engine models it will be necessary to undo the nut and free the preheating unit from the rear of the tray (see Chapter 5C). On automatic transmission models it will be necessary to unclip and remove the transmission electronic control unit (ECU) mounting plate from the battery tray, disconnect the earth lead from the plate (see Chapter 7B, Section 9).

7 If necessary, with the tray removed, undo the retaining nut and bolts and remove the mounting plate from the top of the left-hand engine/transmission mounting **(see illustrations)**.

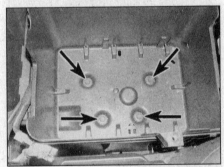

4.5 Undo the retaining bolts (arrowed) and remove the battery retaining clamp

4.6a Unscrew the retaining bolts (arrowed) . . .

4.6b . . . and lift out the battery tray, freeing the wiring from the clips on the side of the tray

4.7a Unscrew the retaining nut and bolts (arrowed) . . .

4.7b . . . then remove the mounting plate from the top of the left-hand engine/transmission mounting

5A

7.3a On 1.9 litre diesel engines remove the fasteners from the right-hand side . . .

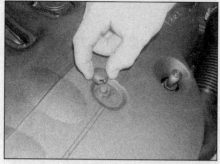

7.3b . . . and top of the engine cover . . .

7.3c . . . then remove the cover from the engine

Refitting

8 Refitting is a reversal of removal, but smear petroleum jelly on the terminals when reconnecting the leads, and always reconnect the positive lead first, negative lead last. If the battery tray has been removed ensure the cooling duct is securely connected to the front of the tray and all the wiring is clipped in position. Before starting the engine for the first time, turn on the ignition and wait for ten seconds to initialise the various electronic control units.

7.3d On 2.0 litre diesel engines, rotate each fastener 90° to release it . . .

7.3e . . . then lift off the engine cover

5 Charging system – testing

Note: *Refer to the warnings given in 'Safety first!' and in Section 1 of this Chapter before starting work.*

1 If the ignition warning light fails to illuminate when the ignition is switched on, first check the alternator wiring connections for security. If satisfactory, check that the warning light bulb has not blown, and that the bulbholder is secure in its location in the instrument panel. If the light still fails to illuminate, check the continuity of the warning light feed wire from the alternator to the bulbholder. If all is satisfactory, the alternator is at fault and should be renewed or taken to an auto-electrician for testing and repair.

2 If the ignition warning light illuminates when the engine is running, stop the engine and check that the drivebelt is correctly tensioned (see the relevant part of Chapter 1) and that the alternator connections are secure. If all is so far satisfactory, have the alternator checked by an auto-electrician for testing and repair.

3 If the alternator output is suspect even though the warning light works correctly, the regulated voltage may be checked as follows.

4 Connect a voltmeter across the battery terminals and start the engine.

5 Increase the engine speed until the voltmeter reading remains steady; the reading should be approximately 12 to 13 volts, and no more than 14 volts.

6 Switch on as many electrical accessories (eg, the headlights, heated rear window and

heater blower) as possible, and check that the alternator maintains the regulated voltage at around 13 to 14 volts.

7 If the regulated voltage is not as stated, the fault may be due to worn brushes, weak brush springs, a faulty voltage regulator, a faulty diode, a severed phase winding or worn or damaged slip rings. The alternator should be renewed or taken to an auto-electrician for testing and repair.

6 Auxiliary drivebelt – removal, refitting and tensioning

Refer to the procedure given for the auxiliary drivebelt in Chapter 1A or 1B (as applicable).

7 Alternator – removal and refitting

Removal

1 Disconnect the battery negative lead.

2 Slacken the auxiliary drivebelt tension and release the belt from the alternator pulley (refer to Chapter 1A or 1B – as applicable). Where necessary, remove the retaining bolts, screws and clips and remove the undercover from the engine/transmission unit to improve access.

3 On diesel engines remove the engine cover. On 1.9 litre engines remove the fasteners from the right-hand side and top of the cover then lift off the cover; on 2.0 litre engines remove the four fasteners (rotate them 90° to release them) then lift off the cover **(see illustrations)**.

4 On models with power steering, referring to Chapter 10, unbolt the power steering pump and position it clear of the engine taking care not to lose the spacer (where fitted) from the rear mounting **(see illustrations)**. Support the weight of the pump by tying it to the vehicle body/engine to prevent any excess strain being placed on the hydraulic pipes/hoses. **Note:** *There is no need to disconnect the pipe/hose from the pump. Release the pipes/hoses from any necessary clips to prevent them being strained.*

7.4a Slacken and remove the power steering pump front mounting bolts . . .

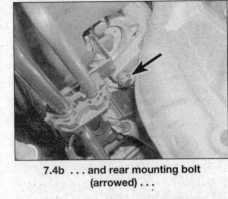

7.4b ... and rear mounting bolt (arrowed) ...

7.4c ... then position the power steering pump clear of the engine (petrol engine shown)

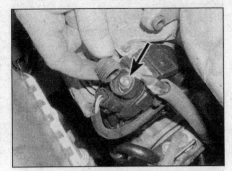

7.5a Remove the rubber cap then unscrew the nut (arrowed) ...

5 Remove the rubber cover(s) from the alternator terminals, then unscrew the retaining nut(s) and disconnect the wiring from the rear of the alternator **(see illustrations)**.

6 Where necessary, unscrew the mounting nut/bolt (as applicable) and remove the auxiliary drivebelt tensioner/idler pulley to gain access to the alternator lower mounting bolt **(see illustration)**.

7 Unscrew the mounting bolts, noting each correct fitted location, and manoeuvre the alternator out of position **(see illustrations)**. On diesel engines, recover the spacer/spacer and collar arrangement from each of the rear mountings.

Refitting

8 Refitting is a reversal of removal, noting the following.

a) On diesel engines, ensure the spacer/spacer and collar arrangement is correctly fitted to each rear mounting.

Tighten the alternator front (drivebelt pulley end) mounting bolts to the specified torque first then tighten the rear mounting bolts to the specified torque.

b) On models with power steering, ensure the mounting spacer (where fitted) is correctly fitted to the rear mounting. Apply locking compound (Peugeot recommend the use of Loctite Frenetanch) to the pump mounting bolts; tighten the pump front (drivebelt pulley end) bolts to the specified torque first then tighten the rear bolts.

c) Refit the auxiliary drivebelt as described in Chapter 1A or 1B (as applicable).

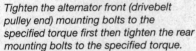

8 Alternator – testing and overhaul

If the alternator is thought to be suspect, it should be removed from the vehicle and taken to an auto-electrician for testing. Most auto-electricians will be able to supply and fit brushes at a reasonable cost. However, check on the cost of repairs before proceeding as it may prove more economical to obtain a new or exchange alternator.

5A

7.5b ... and disconnect the wiring from the alternator (petrol engine shown)

7.6 On some engines it will be necessary to unbolt the auxiliary drivebelt idler pulley to gain access to the alternator lower mounting bolt

7.7a Unscrew the mounting bolts (front bolts arrowed) ...

7.7b ... and remove the alternator from the engine (petrol engine shown)

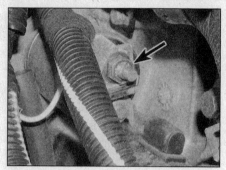

10.4 Unscrew the nuts and disconnect the wiring from the starter motor solenoid

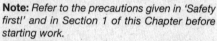

9 Starting system – testing

Note: *Refer to the precautions given in 'Safety first!' and in Section 1 of this Chapter before starting work.*

1 If the starter motor fails to operate when the ignition key is turned to the appropriate position, the following possible causes may be to blame.

   a) *The battery is faulty.*
   b) *The electrical connections between the switch, solenoid, battery and starter motor are somewhere failing to pass the necessary current from the battery through the starter to earth.*
   c) *The solenoid is faulty.*
   d) *The starter motor is mechanically or electrically defective.*

2 To check the battery, switch on the headlights. If they dim after a few seconds, this indicates that the battery is discharged – recharge (see Section 3) or renew the battery. If the headlights glow brightly, operate the ignition switch and observe the lights. If they dim, then this indicates that current is reaching the starter motor, therefore the fault must lie in the starter motor. If the lights continue to glow brightly (and no clicking sound can be heard from the starter motor solenoid), this indicates that there is a fault in the circuit or solenoid – see following paragraphs. If the starter motor turns slowly when operated, but the battery is in good condition, then this shows that either the starter motor is faulty, or there is considerable resistance in the circuit.

3 If a fault in the circuit is suspected, disconnect the battery leads (including the earth connection to the body), the starter/solenoid wiring and the engine/transmission earth strap. Thoroughly clean the connections, and reconnect the leads and wiring, then use a voltmeter or test lamp to check that full battery voltage is available at the battery positive lead connection to the solenoid, and that the earth is sound. Smear petroleum jelly around the battery terminals to prevent corrosion – corroded connections are amongst the most frequent causes of electrical system faults.

4 If the battery and all connections are in good condition, check the circuit by disconnecting the wire from the solenoid blade terminal. Connect a voltmeter or test lamp between the wire end and a good earth (such as the battery negative terminal), and check that the wire is live when the ignition switch is turned to the 'start' position. If it is, then the circuit is sound – if not the circuit wiring can be checked as described in Chapter 12.

5 The solenoid contacts can be checked by connecting a voltmeter or test lamp between the battery positive feed connection on the starter side of the solenoid, and earth. When the ignition switch is turned to the 'start' position, there should be a reading or lighted bulb, as applicable. If there is no reading or lighted bulb, the solenoid is faulty and should be renewed.

6 If the circuit and solenoid are proved sound, the fault must lie in the starter motor.

In this event, it may be possible to have the starter motor overhauled by a specialist, but check on the cost of spares before proceeding, as it may prove more economical to obtain a new or exchange motor.

10 Starter motor – removal and refitting

Removal

1 Disconnect the battery negative lead.

2 On diesel engines remove the engine cover. On 1.9 litre engines remove the fasteners from the right-hand side and top of the cover then lift off the cover; on 2.0 litre engines remove the four fasteners (rotate them 90° to release them) then lift off the cover (see illustrations 7.3a to 7.3e). On 1.9 litre engines, remove the intake duct linking the air cleaner housing to the inlet manifold as described in Chapter 4B.

3 So that access to the motor can be gained both from above and below, firmly apply the handbrake then jack up the front of the vehicle and support it on axle stands (see *Jacking and vehicle support*). Where necessary, remove the retaining bolts, screws and clips and remove the undercover (where fitted) from the engine/transmission unit to improve access.

4 On all engines, slacken and remove the two retaining nuts and disconnect the wiring from the starter motor solenoid. Recover the washers under the nuts (see illustration).

5 Undo the three mounting bolts, supporting the motor as the bolts are withdrawn (see illustration). Recover the washers from under the bolt heads and note the locations of any wiring or hose brackets secured by the bolts.

6 Manoeuvre the starter motor out from underneath the engine and recover the locating dowel(s) from the motor/transmission (as applicable) (see illustration).

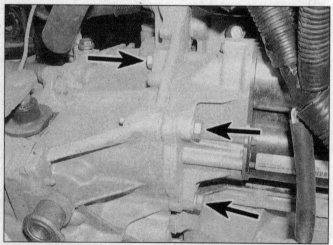

10.5 Starter motor mounting bolts – petrol engine

10.6 Remove the starter motor and recover the locating dowel (arrowed – diesel engine shown)

Refitting

7 Refitting is a reversal of removal, ensuring that the locating dowel(s) are correctly positioned. Also make sure that any wiring or hose brackets are in place under the bolt heads as noted prior to removal.

11 Starter motor – testing and overhaul

If the starter motor is thought to be suspect, it should be removed from the vehicle and taken to an auto-electrician for testing. Most auto-electricians will be able to supply and fit brushes at a reasonable cost. However, check on the cost of repairs before proceeding as it may prove more economical to obtain a new or exchange motor.

12 Ignition switch – removal and refitting

The ignition switch is integral with the steering column lock, and can be removed as described in Chapter 10.

13 Oil pressure warning light switch – removal and refitting

Removal

1 The switch is located at the front of the cylinder block, above the oil filter mounting. Note that on some models access to the switch may be improved if the vehicle is jacked up and supported on axle stands so that the switch can be reached from underneath (see *Jacking and vehicle support*).
2 Disconnect the battery negative lead.
3 Remove the protective sleeve from the

13.3 Disconnect the wiring connector (arrowed) from the oil pressure switch

wiring plug (where applicable), then disconnect the wiring from the switch **(see illustration)**.
4 Wipe clean the area around the switch then unscrew the switch from the cylinder block, and recover the sealing washer. Be prepared for oil spillage, and if the switch is to be left removed from the engine for any length of time, plug the hole in the cylinder block.

Refitting

5 Examine the sealing washer for signs of damage or deterioration and if necessary renew.
6 Refit the switch, complete with washer, and tighten it to the specified torque. Reconnect the wiring connector.
7 Lower the vehicle to the ground then check and, if necessary, top up the engine oil as described in *Weekly checks*.

14 Oil level/temperature sensor – removal and refitting

Removal

1 On petrol engines, the sensor is located on the front side of the cylinder block, just to the right of the oil filter. On diesel engines it is

14.1 Oil level/temperature sensor location – diesel engine

fitted to the rear of the cylinder block, at its left-hand end **(see illustration)**. Note that on some models access to the switch may be improved if the vehicle is jacked up and supported on axle stands so that the switch can be reached from underneath (see *Jacking and vehicle support*).
2 Disconnect the battery negative lead.
3 Trace the wiring back from the sensor and disconnect its connector from the main harness. Note the correct routing of the wiring and release it from all the relevant clips and ties.
4 Wipe clean the area around the sensor then unscrew it from the cylinder block, and recover the sealing washer. If the sensor is to be left removed from the engine for any length of time, plug the hole in the cylinder block.

Refitting

5 Examine the sealing washer for signs of damage or deterioration and if necessary renew.
6 Refit the sensor, complete with washer, and tighten it securely. Ensure the sensor wiring is correctly routed and retained by all the necessary clips and ties then reconnect it to the main harness.
7 Lower the vehicle to the ground then check and, if necessary, top up the engine oil as described in *Weekly checks*.

5A

Chapter 5 Part B:
Ignition system – petrol engine

Contents

Degrees of difficulty

Easy, suitable for novice with little experience	Fairly easy, suitable for beginner with some experience	Fairly difficult, suitable for competent DIY mechanic	Difficult, suitable for experienced DIY mechanic	Very difficult, suitable for expert DIY or professional 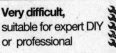

Specifications

System type	Static (distributorless) ignition system controlled by engine management ECU
Firing order	1-3-4-2 (No 1 cylinder at transmission end)
Spark plugs	See Chapter 1A Specifications

Ignition HT coil
Resistances:
Primary windings	0.50 to 0.66 ohms (approximate)
Secondary windings	Not available

Torque wrench setting	**Nm**	**lbf ft**
Ignition HT coil bolts	8	6

1 General information

1 The ignition system is integrated with the fuel injection system to form a combined engine management system under the control of one ECU (see Chapter 4A for further information). The ignition side of the system is distributorless and consists of the ignition HT coil and the knock sensor.

2 The ignition HT coil has four outputs and is mounted directly onto the spark plugs. The coil assembly actually consists of two separate HT coils which supply two cylinders each (one coil supplies cylinders 1 and 4, and the other cylinders 2 and 3). Under the control of the ECU, the ignition coil operates on the 'wasted spark' principle; ie, each spark plug sparks twice for every cycle of the engine, once on the compression stroke and once on the exhaust stroke. The ECU uses its inputs from the various sensors to calculate the required ignition advance setting and coil charging time.

3 The knock sensor is mounted onto the rear of the cylinder block and prevents the engine 'pinking' under load. The sensor is sensitive to vibration and detects the knocking which occurs when the engine starts to 'pink' (pre-ignite). The knock sensor sends an electrical signal to the ECU which in turn retards the ignition advance setting until the 'pinking' ceases.

2 Ignition system – testing

⚠ Warning: Voltages produced by an electronic ignition system are considerably higher than those produced by conventional ignition systems. Extreme care must be taken when working on the system with the ignition switched on. Persons with surgically-implanted cardiac pacemaker devices should keep well clear of the ignition circuits, components and test equipment.

1 If a fault appears in the engine management (fuel injection/ignition) system first ensure that the fault is not due to a poor electrical connection or poor maintenance; ie, check that the air cleaner filter element is clean, the spark plugs are in good condition and correctly gapped, that the engine breather hoses are clear and undamaged, referring to Chapter 1A for further information. Also check that the accelerator cable is correctly adjusted as described in Chapter 4A. If the engine is running very roughly, check the compression pressures and the valve clearances as described in Chapter 2A.

2 If these checks fail to reveal the cause of the problem the vehicle should be taken to a suitably-equipped Peugeot dealer for testing. A wiring block connector is incorporated in the engine management circuit into which a special electronic diagnostic tester can be plugged (see Chapter 4A). The tester will locate the fault quickly and simply alleviating the need to test all the system components individually which is a time consuming operation that carries a high risk of damaging the ECU.

3 The only ignition system checks which can be carried out by the home mechanic are those described in Chapter 1A, relating to the spark plugs. If necessary, the system wiring and wiring connectors can be checked as described in Chapter 12 ensuring that the ECU wiring connector(s) have first been disconnected.

3.2 Disconnect the breather hose from the cylinder head cover

3.3 Disconnecting the wiring connector from the ignition HT coil

3.4a Undo the retaining bolts (arrowed) . . .

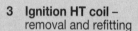

3 Ignition HT coil – removal and refitting

Removal

1 Disconnect the battery negative terminal. The ignition HT coil is mounted on the rear of the cylinder head is connected directly to the spark plugs.
2 Release the retaining clips and disconnect the breather hose from the cylinder head cover (see illustration).
3 Disconnect the wiring connector from the HT coil (see illustration).
4 Unscrew the retaining bolts securing the HT coil to the cylinder head. Carefully pull the coil assembly squarely off the spark plugs and remove it from the engine compartment (see illustrations). Note that the spark plug caps can be detached from the HT coil and renewed separately, if necessary.

Refitting

5 Ensure the plug caps are all securely fitted to the coil.

6 Ease the coil assembly onto the top of the spark plugs. Ensure the coil is correctly seated then refit its retaining bolts, tightening them to the specified torque.
7 Reconnect the wiring connector to the coil then reconnect the breather hose to the cylinder head cover.
8 On completion, reconnect the battery.

4 Ignition timing – checking and adjustment

1 There are no timing marks on the flywheel or crankshaft pulley, therefore, it is not possible for the home mechanic to check the ignition timing. The timing is constantly being monitored and adjusted by the engine management ECU so nominal values cannot be given anyway. The only way the ignition timing can be checked is using special electronic test equipment, connected to the engine management system diagnostic connector (see Chapter 4A for further information).

3.4b . . . then ease the ignition HT coil assembly off from the spark plugs and remove it from the engine

2 On engine with a Magneti Marelli engine management system, adjustment of the ignition timing is possible. However, adjustments can be made only by re-programming the ECU using the special test equipment.
3 On all engines with Bosch engine management systems, no adjustment of the ignition timing is possible. Should the ignition timing be incorrect, then a fault must be present in the engine management system.

Chapter 5 Part C:
Preheating system – diesel engine

Contents

Degrees of difficulty

Easy, suitable for novice with little experience	**Fairly easy,** suitable for beginner with some experience	**Fairly difficult,** suitable for competent DIY mechanic	**Difficult,** suitable for experienced DIY mechanic	**Very difficult,** suitable for expert DIY or professional

Specifications

Glow plugs
Resistance (typical) .... Less than 1 ohm

Torque wrench setting	**Nm**	**lbf ft**
Glow plugs	22	16

1 General information

1 Each cylinder has a heater plug (commonly called a glow plug). The plugs are fitted to the cylinder head and electrically-operated before and during start-up when the engine is cold.
2 The electrical feed to the glow plugs is controlled by the preheating system control unit. On 1.9 litre (WJZ) engines the control unit operates using the signals received from the coolant temperature sensor and accelerator switch on the injection pump (like the EGR system – see Chapter 4C). On later 1.9 litre (WJY) engines and all 2.0 litre engines the control unit is operated by the injection system ECU (see Chapter 4B).
3 The glow plugs also provide a 'post-heating' function, whereby the glow plugs remain switched on for a period after the engine has started. Once the starter has been switched off, the glow plugs begin a timed 'post-heating' cycle. Post-heating only takes place if the engine is cold (coolant temperature below 60°C on 1.9 litre engines and below 20°C on 2.0 litre engines) and the supply to the plugs will be interrupted if the engine is placed under load.
4 A warning light in the instrument panel tells the driver that preheating is taking place. When the light goes out, the engine is ready to be started. The voltage supply to the glow plugs continues for several seconds after the light goes out. If no attempt is made to start,

the timer then cuts off the supply, in order to avoid draining the battery and overheating the glow plugs.

2 Preheating system – testing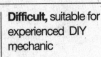

1.9 litre engine

1 If the system malfunctions, testing is ultimately by substitution of known good units, but some preliminary checks may be made as follows.
2 Release the fasteners from the right-hand side and top of the engine cover then lift off the cover, taking care not to lose its mounting rubbers.
3 Connect a voltmeter or 12-volt test lamp between the glow plug supply cable and earth (engine or vehicle metal). Make sure that the live connection is kept clear of the engine and bodywork.
4 Have an assistant switch on the ignition, and check that voltage is applied to the glow plugs. Note the time for which the warning light is lit, and the total time for which voltage is applied before the system cuts out. Switch off the ignition.
5 At a coolant temperature of 20°C, typical times noted should be 5 or 6 seconds for warning light operation, followed by a further 10 seconds supply after the light goes out. Warning light time will increase with lower temperatures and decrease with higher temperatures.

6 If there is no supply at all, the control unit or associated wiring is at fault.
7 To locate a defective glow plug, disconnect the main supply cable and the interconnecting wire or strap from the top of the glow plugs. Be careful not to drop the nuts and washers.
8 Use a continuity tester, or a 12-volt test lamp connected to the battery positive terminal, to check for continuity between each glow plug terminal and earth. The resistance of a glow plug in good condition is very low (less than 1 ohm), so if the test lamp does not light or the continuity tester shows a high resistance, the glow plug is certainly defective.
9 If an ammeter is available, the current draw of each glow plug can be checked. After an initial surge, each plug should draw approximately 12 amps. Any plug which draws much more or less than this is probably defective.
10 As a final check, the glow plugs can be removed and inspected as described in the following Section.

2.0 litre engines

11 The system can be checked as described in paragraphs 3 to 10. However testing will be difficult due to the temperatures at which the preheating system functions; at coolant temperatures above 0°C preheating is virtually unnecessary. Approximate times for preheating duration are as follows.

Coolant temperature	Preheating time
–30°C	20 seconds
–10°C	5 seconds
0°C	0.5 seconds
18°C	No preheating necessary

5C

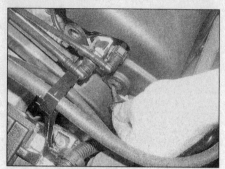

3.2a On 1.9 litre engines, remove the fasteners from the right-hand side . . .

3.2b . . . and top of the engine cover . . .

3.2c . . . then remove the cover from the engine

3 Glow plugs – removal, inspection and refitting

Removal

Caution: If the preheating system has just been energised, or if the engine has been running, the glow plugs will be very hot.

1 Disconnect the battery negative lead

2 On 1.9 litre engines, release the fasteners from the right-hand side and top of the engine cover then lift off the cover, taking care not to lose its mounting rubbers **(see illustrations)**.

3 On 2.0 litre engines, release the fasteners (rotate them 90° to release them) and remove the engine cover.

4 Unscrew the nut from the relevant plug terminal and recover the washer (where fitted) **(see illustration)**.

3.4 Unscrew the nut (arrowed) and disconnect the wiring from the glow plug terminal (1.9 litre engine shown)

3.5 Unscrew the glow plug and remove it from the cylinder head (2.0 litre engine shown with fuel rail removed)

5 Free the wire(s) from the glow plug then unscrew the plug and remove it from the cylinder head **(see illustration)**.

Inspection

6 Inspect each glow plug for physical damage. Burnt or eroded glow plug tips can be caused by a bad injector spray pattern. Have the injectors checked if this sort of damage is found.

7 If the glow plugs are in good physical condition, check them electrically using a 12-volt test lamp or continuity tester as described in the previous Section.

8 The glow plugs can be energised by applying 12 volts to them to verify that they heat up evenly and in the required time. Observe the following precautions.

 a) Support the glow plug by clamping it carefully in a vice or self-locking pliers. Remember it will become red-hot.

 b) Make sure that the power supply or test lead incorporates a fuse or overload trip to protect against damage from a short-circuit.

 c) After testing, allow the glow plug to cool for several minutes before attempting to handle it.

9 A glow plug in good condition will start to glow red at the tip shortly after drawing current. Any plug which takes a long time to start glowing, or which starts glowing in the middle instead of at the tip, is defective.

Refitting

10 Apply a smear of copper-based anti-seize compound to the plug threads refit the plug to

4.3 Unscrew the retaining nut (arrowed) and free the preheating control unit from the rear of the battery tray

the cylinder head, tightening it to the specified torque. Do not overtighten, as this can damage the glow plug element.

11 Reconnect the wiring to the glow plug and secure it in position with the washer (where fitted) and retaining nut.

12 Securely refit the engine cover then reconnect the battery.

4 Preheating system control unit – removal and refitting

Removal

1 The unit is located on the left-hand side of the engine compartment where it is mounted onto the rear of the battery tray.

2 Disconnect the battery negative lead.

3 Unscrew the retaining nut and free the control unit from the battery tray **(see illustration)**. Take care not to lose the bolt from the battery tray.

4 Disconnect the wiring connector from the base of the unit **(see illustration)**.

5 Note the correct fitted locations of the main feed and supply wires then unscrew the retaining nuts and washers. Free the wires from the unit terminals and remove the unit from the engine compartment.

Refitting

6 Refitting is a reversal of removal, ensuring that the wiring connectors are correctly connected.

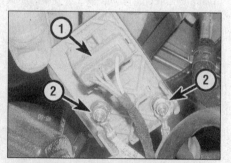

4.4 Disconnect the wiring connector (1) then unscrew the nuts (2) and disconnect the feed and supply wires from the unit

Chapter 6
Clutch

Contents

Degrees of difficulty

| Easy, suitable for novice with little experience | | Fairly easy, suitable for beginner with some experience | | Fairly difficult, suitable for competent DIY mechanic | | Difficult, suitable for experienced DIY mechanic | | Very difficult, suitable for expert DIY or professional | |

Specifications

Type . . . . Single dry plate with diaphragm spring. Hydraulically-operated release mechanism on right-hand drive diesel engine models and cable-operated release mechanism on all others

Friction plate diameter
Petrol models:
  1.1 and 1.4 litre models . . . . 180 mm
  1.6 litre models . . . . 200 mm
Diesel models:
  1.9 litre models . . . . 200 mm
  2.0 litre models . . . . 228 mm

Torque wrench settings

	Nm	lbf ft
Cable upper end fitting nuts – right-hand drive models	10	7
Hydraulic system components:		
Master cylinder mounting nuts	20	15
Slave cylinder mounting bolts	20	15
Slave cylinder bleed screw	7	5
Pressure plate retaining bolts:		
Petrol engine models	15	11
Diesel engine models	20	15

6

1 General information

The clutch consists of a friction plate, a pressure plate assembly, a release bearing and the release mechanism; all of these components are contained in the large cast-aluminium alloy bellhousing, sandwiched between the engine and the transmission.

The friction plate is fitted between the engine flywheel and the clutch pressure plate, and is allowed to slide on the transmission input shaft splines.

The pressure plate assembly is bolted to the engine flywheel. When the engine is running, drive is transmitted from the crankshaft, via the flywheel, to the friction plate (these components being clamped securely together by the pressure plate assembly) and from the friction plate to the transmission input shaft.

To interrupt the drive, the spring pressure must be relaxed. On the models covered in this manual, two different types of clutch release mechanism are used; right-hand drive diesel engine models have a hydraulically-operated clutch release mechanism where as all other models have a cable-operated clutch release mechanism.

On the hydraulically–operated release mechanism, the clutch pedal is connected to the master cylinder pushrod. The master cylinder is mounted on the engine compartment bulkhead and is connected to the slave cylinder mounted on the front of the transmission unit. The hydraulic fluid for the system is taken from the braking system master cylinder fluid reservoir which is linked to the clutch master cylinder via the pipe on the side of the reservoir. Depressing the clutch pedal moves the piston in the master cylinder forwards. Hydraulic pressure in the pipe/hose forces the piston in the slave cylinder forwards which in turn moves the clutch release fork.

On the cable-operated clutch, the clutch pedal is linked to the clutch release fork lever by a cable. Depressing the clutch pedal pulls the control cable inner wire, and this moves the release fork.

On all clutches, as the clutch release fork moves it presses the release bearing against the pressure plate spring fingers. This causes the springs to deform and releases the clamping force on the pressure plate.

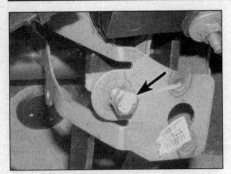

2.2 Clutch pedal stop bolt (shown with facia removed)

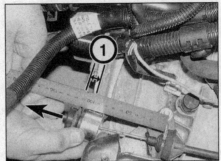

2.4a Pull back on the release lever fork and measure the amount of movement (1) . . .

2.4b . . . then measure the release lever travel (2) during a full pedal stroke to check the cable self-adjust mechanism – see text (petrol engine shown)

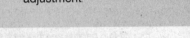

2 Clutch – adjustment

Cable-operated clutch

1 The clutch cable incorporates an automatic adjustment mechanism and therefore requires no regular adjustment. If the automatic adjustment mechanism is thought to be faulty it can be checked as follows.

2 Reach up behind the facia and locate the clutch pedal stop bolt. Back off the stop bolt until a small amount of freeplay is present then screw the bolt in until all freeplay is removed from the cable, without tensioning the cable at all (see illustration).

3 To gain access to the transmission end of the cable, remove the air cleaner housing as

described in the relevant part of Chapter 4. To further improve access, also remove the battery and battery tray as described in Chapter 5A.

4 Pull back on the clutch release fork lever and check that the fork moves at least 5 mm. Have an assistant operate the clutch pedal a few times to operated the clutch adjustment mechanism then measure the release lever travel during a full pedal stroke (ensure there are no obstructions beneath the clutch pedal); this should be at least 24 mm (see illustration). If the release lever will not move backwards when pulled, or the lever travel is less than specified, the automatic adjustment mechanism is faulty and the cable should be renewed.

5 On completion of the check, refit all components removed for access.

Hydraulically-operated clutch

6 The hydraulic circuit is self-adjusting and requires no regular adjustment. Should there be any problems with the clutch, bleed the hydraulic circuit. If this fails to solve the problem; renew the hydraulic system components.

3 Clutch cable – removal and refitting

Removal

1 To gain access to the transmission end of the cable remove the air cleaner housing as described in the relevant part of Chapter 4.

Where necessary, also remove the battery, battery tray and mounting plate (see Chapter 5A).

2 Working in the engine compartment, free the inner cable fitting from the end of the release fork lever then unclip the outer cable end fitting and grommet from the bracket on the transmission unit (see illustrations). Work back along the cable, releasing it from any relevant clips and guides whilst noting its correct routing.

3 Working inside the vehicle, reach up and unhook the cable from the upper end of the clutch pedal (see illustration). Note that access to the upper end of the pedal is very poor and can only be improved by removing the steering column (see Chapter 10).

4 On right-hand drive models, remove the coolant expansion tank as described in Chapter 3. Unscrew the cable end fitting retaining nuts then free the cable end fitting and grommet from the bulkhead and remove the cable from the vehicle (see illustration).

5 On left-hand drive models, return to the engine compartment, then release the outer cable end fitting and grommet from the bulkhead. Withdraw the cable forwards and remove it from the vehicle.

6 Examine the cable, looking for worn end fittings or a damaged outer casing, and for signs of fraying of the inner wire. Check the cable's operation; the inner wire should move smoothly and easily through the outer casing. Remember that a cable that appears

3.2a Free the inner cable fitting from the release lever . . .

3.2b . . . then unclip the outer cable from the transmission bracket (petrol engine shown)

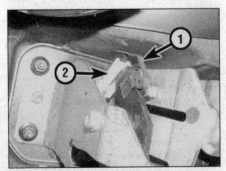

3.3 Release the clip (1) and unhook the cable end fitting (2) from the top of the clutch pedal (shown with facia removed)

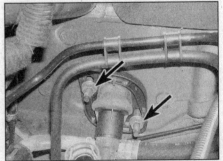

3.4 On right-hand drive models undo the nuts (arrowed) and free the cable end fitting from the bulkhead

serviceable when tested off the car may well be much heavier in operation when in its working position. Renew the cable if it shows signs of excessive wear or any damage or the automatic adjustment mechanism is faulty.

Refitting

7 Apply a thin smear of multi-purpose grease to the inner cable end fittings and lubricate the outer cable grommets with a silicone-based lubricant spray to ease installation.

8 Route the cable correctly around the engine compartment then pass the cable through the engine compartment bulkhead.

9 On right-hand drive models, locate the outer cable end fitting on the studs and tighten its retaining nuts to the specified torque.

10 On left-hand drive models, push firmly on the outer cable end fitting to ensure its grommet is correctly seated in the bulkhead.

11 On all models, from inside the vehicle, hook the inner cable onto the clutch pedal, and check that it is correctly located.

12 Ensuring that the cable is correctly routed and retained by all the relevant retaining clips and guides, engage the inner cable with the release fork lever then locate the outer cable in the transmission bracket, ensuring its grommet is correctly seated.

13 Operate the clutch pedal several times to operate the automatic adjustment mechanism.

14 Check the operation of the adjustment mechanism as described in Section 2 then refit all components removed for access. On right-hand drive models refit the coolant expansion tank as described in Chapter 3 and top-up the cooling system.

---

4 Clutch pedal – removal and refitting

Removal

Cable-operated clutch

1 To improve access to the transmission end of the clutch cable remove the air cleaner housing as described in the relevant part of Chapter 4. Where necessary, also remove the battery, battery tray and mounting plate (see Chapter 5A).

2 Free the inner cable fitting from the end of the release fork lever then unclip the outer cable end fitting and grommet from the bracket on the transmission unit **(see illustrations 3.2a and 3.2b)**.

3 To improve access to the clutch pedal, remove the steering column as described in Chapter 10.

4 Unhook the clutch cable from the upper end of the pedal **(see illustration 3.3)**.

5 Where necessary, carefully unhook and remove the assistance spring assembly from the side of the pedal.

6 Unhook the return spring (where fitted) from the pedal then slacken and remove the pivot bolt and nut **(see illustration)**. Manoeuvre the clutch pedal and (where fitted) return spring out of position and slide the spacer out from the pedal pivot.

7 Examine all components for signs of wear or damage and renew as necessary.

Hydraulically-operated clutch

8 To improve access to the clutch pedal, remove the steering column as described in Chapter 10.

9 Remove the pivot clip securing the master cylinder pushrod to the clutch pedal. To remove the pivot clip, unhook its lower retaining tang then pivot it upwards slightly before sliding it out of position.

10 Remove the pedal as described in paragraphs 5 to 7.

Refitting

Cable-operated clutch

11 Apply a smear of multi-purpose grease to the spacer and insert it into the pedal pivot bore. Where necessary, refit the return spring to the pedal pivot.

12 Refit the pedal assembly and insert the pivot bolt, tightening its nut securely. Ensure the return spring (where fitted) is correctly located.

13 Refit the assistance spring assembly (where fitted), ensuring it is correctly located on both the pedal and bracket.

14 Hook the cable end fitting back onto the upper end of the pedal.

15 Working in the engine compartment, engage the inner cable with the release fork lever then locate the outer cable in the transmission bracket, ensuring its grommet is correctly seated (lubricate the grommet with a silicone-based spray to ease installation).

16 Operate the clutch pedal several times to operates the automatic adjustment mechanism.

17 Check the operation of the adjustment mechanism as described in Section 2 then refit all components removed for access (see the relevant parts of Chapters 4, 5 and 10 – as applicable).

Hydraulically-operated clutch

18 Install the pedal as described in paragraphs 11 to 13.

19 Align the pedal with the master cylinder pushrod and securely refit the pivot clip.

20 Refit the steering column (where removed) as described in Chapter 10.

---

5 Clutch hydraulic system components – removal and refitting

 Warning: Hydraulic fluid is poisonous; wash off immediately and thoroughly in the case of skin contact, and seek immediate medical advice if any fluid is swallowed or gets into the eyes. Certain types of hydraulic fluid

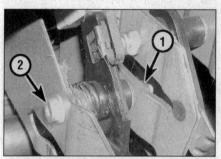

4.6 Unscrew the nut (1) and withdraw the clutch pedal pivot bolt (2) (shown with facia removed)

are inflammable, and may ignite when allowed into contact with hot components; when servicing any hydraulic system, it is safest to assume that the fluid is inflammable, and to take precautions against the risk of fire as though it is petrol that is being handled. Hydraulic fluid is also an effective paint stripper, and will attack plastics; if any is spilt, it should be washed off immediately, using copious quantities of fresh water. Finally, it is hygroscopic (it absorbs moisture from the air) – old fluid may be contaminated and unfit for further use. When topping-up or renewing the fluid, always use the recommended type, and ensure that it comes from a freshly-opened sealed container.

Master cylinder

Removal

1 From inside the vehicle, remove the pivot clip securing the master cylinder pushrod to the clutch pedal. To remove the pivot clip, unhook its lower retaining tang then pivot it upwards slightly before sliding it out of position.

2 Remove the coolant expansion tank as described in Chapter 3.

3 Remove all traces of dirt from the exterior of the master cylinder.

4 Disconnect the fluid supply hose union on the side of the master cylinder then prise out the circlip from the master cylinder union and disconnect the clutch pipe. Plug the master cylinder unions and pipe ends to minimise fluid loss and prevent the entry of dirt. Refit the circlip correctly to the groove in the master cylinder.

5 Unscrew the mounting nuts securing the master cylinder to the bulkhead. Manoeuvre the master cylinder out of position and recover the seal fitted between the cylinder and bulkhead.

6 At the time of writing it was unclear whether it was possible to overhaul the master cylinder. Refer to your Peugeot dealer for the latest information on parts availability.

Refitting

7 Prior to refitting, ensure the circlip is correctly fitted to the master cylinder union.

8 Fit the seal to the rear of the master cylinder then locate the master cylinder on its studs.

6

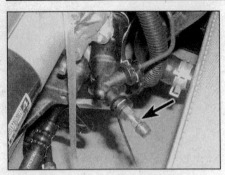

6.6 Clutch slave cylinder bleed screw (arrowed – viewed from above)

Refit the mounting nuts, tightening them to the specified torque.

9 Reconnect the hydraulic pipe to the master cylinder, making sure it is securely retained by the circlip, then securely reconnect the fluid supply hose.

10 Align the pedal with the master cylinder pushrod and securely refit the pivot clip.

11 Bleed the hydraulic system as described in Section 6.

12 Once the clutch is functioning correctly, refit the coolant expansion tank (see Chapter 3) and top-up the cooling system.

Slave cylinder

Removal

13 To improve access to the slave cylinder, remove the air cleaner housing as described in Chapter 4B.

14 Prise out the circlip from the slave cylinder union and disconnect the clutch pipe. Plug the slave cylinder union and pipe end to minimise fluid loss and prevent the entry of dirt. Refit the circlip correctly to the groove in the cylinder.

15 Release the wiring harness from its retaining clips and position it clear of the slave cylinder.

16 Slacken and remove the bolts securing the slave cylinder to the front of the transmission housing then manoeuvre the cylinder out of position.

17 At the time of writing it was unclear

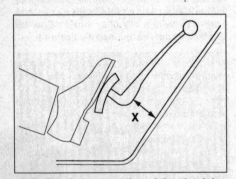

6.14 Check the operation of the clutch by measuring the distance (X) between the clutch pedal and bulkhead at the point where the clutch engages/disengages – see text

whether it was possible to overhaul the slave cylinder. Refer to your Peugeot dealer for the latest information on parts availability.

Refitting

18 Prior to refitting, ensure the circlip is correctly fitted to the slave cylinder union.

19 Engage the slave cylinder with the release fork lever and seat it correctly on the transmission unit. Refit the slave cylinder retaining bolts, tightening them to the specified torque.

20 Reconnect the clutch pipe to the cylinder, ensuring it is securely retained by the circlip. Clip the wiring harness back into position.

21 Bleed the hydraulic system as described in Section 6.

22 Once the clutch is functioning correctly, refit the air cleaner housing (see Chapter 4B).

6 Clutch hydraulic system – bleeding

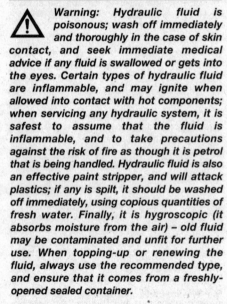

⚠ **Warning: Hydraulic fluid is poisonous; wash off immediately and thoroughly in the case of skin contact, and seek immediate medical advice if any fluid is swallowed or gets into the eyes. Certain types of hydraulic fluid are inflammable, and may ignite when allowed into contact with hot components; when servicing any hydraulic system, it is safest to assume that the fluid is inflammable, and to take precautions against the risk of fire as though it is petrol that is being handled. Hydraulic fluid is also an effective paint stripper, and will attack plastics; if any is spilt, it should be washed off immediately, using copious quantities of fresh water. Finally, it is hygroscopic (it absorbs moisture from the air) – old fluid may be contaminated and unfit for further use. When topping-up or renewing the fluid, always use the recommended type, and ensure that it comes from a freshly-opened sealed container.**

1 The correct operation of any hydraulic system is only possible after removing all air from the components and circuit; this is achieved by bleeding the system. During the bleeding procedure, add only clean, unused hydraulic fluid of the recommended type; never re-use fluid that has already been bled from the system. Ensure that sufficient fluid is available before starting work.

2 If hydraulic fluid has been lost from the system, or air has entered because of a leak, ensure that the fault is cured before proceeding further.

3 Park the vehicle on level ground.

4 Collect a clean glass jar, a suitable length of plastic or rubber tubing which is a tight fit over the bleed screw, and a ring spanner to fit the screw. The aid of an assistant will also help, although clutch bleeding can be performed by an individual since the pedal will stay

depressed and will not automatically spring back to the fully raised position.

5 Unscrew the master cylinder reservoir cap (the clutch master cylinder shares the same reservoir as the braking system) and fill the reservoir right up to the base of the filler neck. Refit the cap loosely, and remember to maintain the fluid level at least above the DANGER level line throughout the procedure, or there is a risk of further air entering the system.

6 Remove the dust cap from the slave cylinder bleed screw located on the front of the transmission unit **(see illustration)**. Remove all traces of dirt then fit the spanner and tube to the screw, place the other end of the tube in the jar, and pour in sufficient fluid to cover the end of the tube.

7 Slacken the bleed screw approximately one complete turn.

8 Operate the clutch pedal by hand rapidly through twelve complete downward and upward strokes, at the rate of approximately one stroke a second; on the twelfth stroke leave the pedal fully depressed.

9 Return to the engine compartment and securely tighten the bleed screw.

10 Raise the clutch pedal fully.

11 Fill the master cylinder reservoir back up to the base of the filler neck then loosely refit the cap.

12 Repeat the operations described in paragraphs 7 to 10.

13 Top-up the master cylinder fluid level to the MAXI mark then refit the reservoir cap.

14 Operate the clutch pedal through approximately 40 strokes and check the operation of the clutch pedal. There should be a distance of at least 35 mm between the pedal and bulkhead at the point where the clutch disengages/engages **(see illustration)**. If the pedal feels at all spongy, air must still be present in the system, and further bleeding is required. Failure to bleed properly after a reasonable repetition of the bleeding procedure may be due to worn master cylinder seals.

15 When bleeding is complete, wash off any spilt fluid then tighten the bleed screw to the specified torque and refit the dust cap.

16 Check the hydraulic fluid level in the master cylinder reservoir, and top-up if necessary (*Weekly checks*). Discard any fluid that has been bled from the system; it will not be fit for re-use.

7 Clutch assembly – removal, inspection and refitting

Note: *Although some friction materials no longer contain asbestos, it is safest to assume they do, and to take precautions accordingly.*

Removal

⚠ **Warning: Dust created by clutch wear and deposited on the clutch components may contain asbestos, which is a health hazard. DON'T**

blow it out with compressed air, nor inhale any of it. DO NOT use petrol or petroleum-based solvents to clean off the dust. Brake system cleaner or methylated spirit should be used to flush the dust into a suitable receptacle. After the clutch components are wiped clean with rags, dispose of the contaminated rags and cleaner in a sealed, marked container.

1 Unless the complete engine/transmission unit is to be removed from the car and separated for major overhaul (see Chapter 2C), the clutch can be reached by removing the transmission as described in Chapter 7A.

2 Before disturbing the clutch, use chalk or a marker pen to mark the relationship of the pressure plate assembly to the flywheel.

3 Working in a diagonal sequence, slacken the pressure plate bolts by half a turn at a time, until spring pressure is released and the bolts can be unscrewed by hand.

4 Prise the pressure plate assembly off its locating dowels, and collect the friction plate, noting which way round the plate is fitted **(see illustrations)**.

Inspection

Note: *Due to the amount of work necessary to remove and refit clutch components, it is considered good practice to renew the clutch friction plate, pressure plate assembly and release bearing as a matched set, even if only one of these is worn enough to require renewal. It is worth considering the renewal of the clutch components on a preventive basis if the engine and/or transmission have been removed for some other reason.*

5 Remove the clutch assembly.

6 When cleaning clutch components, read first the warning at the beginning of this Section; remove dust using a clean, dry cloth, and working in a well-ventilated atmosphere.

7 Check the friction plate facings for signs of wear, damage or oil contamination. If the friction material is cracked, burnt, scored or damaged, or if it is contaminated with oil or grease (shown by shiny black patches), the friction plate must be renewed.

8 If the friction material is still serviceable, check that the centre boss splines are unworn, that the torsion springs are in good condition and securely fastened, and that all

7.4a Free the pressure plate from its locating dowels . . .

the rivets are tight. If any wear or damage is found, the friction plate must be renewed.

9 If the friction material is fouled with oil, this must be due to an oil leak from the crankshaft left-hand oil seal, from the sump-to-cylinder block joint, or from the transmission input shaft. Renew the seal or repair the joint, as appropriate, as described in Chapter 2A, 2B or 7A, before installing the new friction plate.

10 Check the pressure plate assembly for obvious signs of wear or damage; shake it to check for loose rivets or worn or damaged fulcrum rings, and check that the drive straps securing the pressure plate to the cover do not show signs (such as a deep yellow or blue discoloration) of overheating. If the diaphragm spring is worn or damaged, or if its pressure is in any way suspect, the pressure plate assembly should be renewed.

11 Examine the machined bearing surfaces of the pressure plate and of the flywheel; they should be clean, completely flat, and free from scratches or scoring. If either is discoloured from excessive heat, or shows signs of cracks, it should be renewed – although minor damage of this nature can sometimes be polished away using emery paper.

12 Check that the release bearing contact surface rotates smoothly and easily, with no sign of noise or roughness. Also check that the surface itself is smooth and unworn, with no signs of cracks, pitting or scoring. If there is any doubt about its condition, the bearing must be renewed (see Section 8).

Refitting

13 On reassembly, ensure that the bearing

7.4b . . . and remove the friction plate, noting which way around it is fitted

surfaces of the flywheel and pressure plate are completely clean, smooth, and free from oil or grease. Use solvent to remove any protective grease from new components.

14 Fit the friction plate so that its spring hub assembly faces away from the flywheel; there may be a marking showing which way round the plate is to be refitted **(see illustration)**.

15 Refit the pressure plate assembly, aligning the marks made on dismantling (if the original pressure plate is re-used), and locating the pressure plate on its three locating dowels. Fit the pressure plate bolts, but tighten them only finger-tight, so that the friction plate can still be moved.

16 The friction plate must now be centralised, so that when the transmission is refitted, its input shaft will pass through the splines at the centre of the friction plate.

17 Centralisation can be achieved by passing a screwdriver or other long bar through the friction plate and into the hole in the crankshaft; the friction plate can then be moved around until it is centred on the crankshaft hole. Alternatively, a clutch-aligning-tool can be used to eliminate the guesswork; these can be obtained from most accessory shops **(see illustration)**. A home-made aligning tool can be fabricated from a length of metal rod or wooden dowel which fits closely inside the crankshaft hole, and has insulating tape wound around it to match the diameter of the friction plate splined hole.

18 When the friction plate is centralised, tighten the pressure plate bolts evenly and progressively in a diagonal sequence to the specified torque setting **(see illustration)**.

6

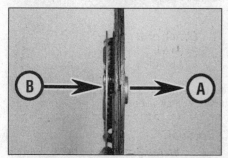

7.14 Ensure the friction plate is fitted the correct way around with its spring hub (B) facing away from the flywheel side (A)

7.17 Align the friction plate centrally inside the pressure plate . . .

7.18 . . . then tighten the pressure plate bolts evenly and progressively to the specified torque

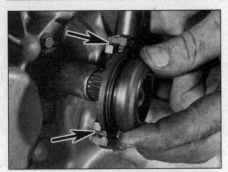

8.2 On petrol engine models, free the release bearing from the fork and slide it off the guide sleeve

8.3a Tap out the roll pin . . .

8.3b . . . then remove the release lever from the top of the fork shaft

19 Check the clutch release mechanism (see Section 8) then refit the transmission as described in Chapter 7A.

8 Clutch release mechanism – removal, inspection and refitting

Note: *Refer to the warning concerning the dangers of asbestos dust at the beginning of Section 7.*

Removal

1 Unless the complete engine/transmission unit is to be removed from the car and separated for major overhaul (see Chapter 2C), the clutch release mechanism can be reached by removing the transmission only, as described in Chapter 7A.

Petrol engine models

2 Unhook the release bearing from the fork, and slide it off its guide sleeve **(see illustration)**.
3 Drive out the roll pin, and remove the release lever from the top of the release fork shaft **(see illustrations)**. Discard the roll pin – a new one must be used on refitting.
4 Depress the retaining tabs, then free the upper bush from the housing and slide it off the release fork shaft. Disengage the shaft from its lower bush, and manoeuvre it out from the transmission **(see illustrations)**. The lower pivot bush can then be removed from the transmission housing.

Diesel engine models

5 Free the rubber gaiter from the transmission housing and remove it from the release fork.
6 Unclip the fork balljoint from its pivot stud then remove the fork and bearing assembly from the transmission unit.

Inspection

7 Check the release mechanism, renewing any component which is worn or damaged. Carefully check all bearing surfaces and points of contact.
8 When checking the release bearing itself, note that it is often considered worthwhile to renew it as a matter of course. Check that the contact surface rotates smoothly and easily, with no sign of noise or roughness, and that the surface itself is smooth and unworn, with no signs of cracks, pitting or scoring. If there is any doubt about its condition, the bearing must be renewed.

Refitting

Petrol engine models

9 Apply a smear of molybdenum disulphide grease (Peugeot recommend the use of Molykote BR2 Plus) to the shaft pivot bushes and the contact surfaces of the release fork, bearing and guide tube. **Note:** *Ensure no grease is applied to the input shaft splines.*
10 Locate the lower pivot bush in the transmission, ensuring it is securely retained by its locating tangs, and insert the release fork **(see illustration)**. Slide the upper bush down the release fork shaft, and clip it into position in the transmission housing.
11 Refit the release lever to the shaft, aligning it with the shaft hole, and secure it in position by tapping a new roll pin fully into position.
12 Slide the release bearing onto the its guide shaft and engage its tabs correctly with the release fork.
13 Check the operation of the release mechanism then refit the transmission as described in Chapter 7A.

Diesel engine models

14 Apply a smear of molybdenum disulphide grease (Peugeot recommend the use of Molykote BR2 Plus) to the contact surfaces of the release fork, bearing and guide tube. **Note:** *Ensure no grease is applied to the input shaft splines.*
15 Ensure the pivot stud is securely fitted to the transmission housing.
16 Engage the release bearing tabs with the end of the release fork then manoeuvre the assembly into position. Locate the bearing on its guide sleeve then press the fork firmly onto its pivot stud. Check the operation of the release mechanism, ensuring the fork is a secure fit on the stud.
17 Fit the gaiter to the fork and seat it correctly in the transmission housing.
18 Refit the transmission as described in Chapter 7A.

8.4a Unclip the upper pivot bush from the transmission housing and slide it off the shaft . . .

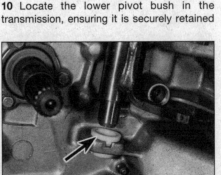

8.4b . . . then free the shaft from its lower bush (arrowed) and manoeuvre it out of position

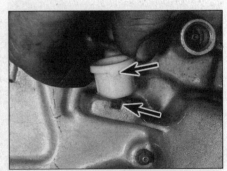

8.10 On refitting ensure the lower bush lug is correctly located in the transmission housing

Chapter 7 Part A:
Manual transmission

Contents

Degrees of difficulty

| Easy, suitable for novice with little experience | | Fairly easy, suitable for beginner with some experience | | Fairly difficult, suitable for competent DIY mechanic | | Difficult, suitable for experienced DIY mechanic | | Very difficult, suitable for expert DIY or professional | |

Specifications

General

Type . . . . Manual, five forward speeds and reverse. Synchromesh on all forward speeds

Designation:
Petrol engine models MA5
Diesel engine models BE4/5
Transmission code:
Petrol models:
1.1 litre models . . . . 20 CE 43, 20 CE 44 or 20 CE 47
1.4 litre models . . . . 20 CE 44 or 20 CE 45
1.6 litre models . . . . 20 CD 32S or 20 CD 38N
Diesel models:
1.9 litre models . . . . 20DL02, 20DL03, 20DL12, 20DL13, 20DL22, 20DL23, 20DL24 or 20DL25
2.0 litre models . . . . 20DL06 or 20DL07

Note: *Transmission code is stamped on the front of the clutch housing on petrol engine modes, and on the front face of the transmission housing on diesel engine models.*

Lubrication

Capacity:
Petrol engine models . . . . 2.0 litres
Diesel engine models . . . . 1.9 litres
Recommended oil type . . . . See *Lubricants and fluids*
Recommended gearchange linkage grease:
Relay lever pivot ball . . . . Esso 3106 Grease
Relay lever pivot and link rod balljoints . . . . Esso Norva 275 Grease

7A

Torque wrench settings

	Nm	lbf ft
Petrol engine models – MA5 transmission		
Clutch release bearing guide sleeve bolts	12	9
Engine-to-transmission fixing bolts	40	30
Gearchange linkage fixings:		
Relay lever pivot bolt	30	22
Linkage rod-to-lever pivot bolt	8	6
Gearchange lever mounting nuts	8	6
Left-hand engine/transmission mounting:		
Mounting bracket-to-transmission nuts	25	18
Mounting bracket-to-body bolts	19	14
Mounting-to-bracket bolts	30	22
Mounting centre nut	65	48
Oil drain plug	25	18
Oil filler/level plug	25	18
Rear mounting link:		
Link-to-mounting bolt	50	37
Link-to-subframe bolt	39	29
Reversing light switch	25	18
Roadwheel bolts	85	63
Diesel engine models – BE4/5 transmission		
Clutch release bearing guide sleeve bolts	12	9
Engine-to-transmission fixing bolts	55	41
Gearchange linkage fixings:		
Relay lever pivot bolt	30	22
Linkage rod-to-lever pivot bolt	8	6
Gearchange lever mounting nuts	8	6
Left-hand engine/transmission mounting:		
Mounting bracket-to-body bolts	19	14
Mounting stud to bracket	50	37
Mounting-to-bracket bolts	30	22
Mounting centre nut	65	48
Mounting bracket to transmission	60	44
Oil drain plug	35	26
Oil filler/level plug	22	16
Rear mounting link:		
Link-to-mounting bolt	50	37
Link-to-subframe bolt	35	26
Reversing light switch	25	18
Roadwheel bolts	85	63
Speedometer drive housing bolts	15	11

1 General information

1 The transmission is contained in a cast-aluminium alloy casing bolted to the engine's left-hand end, and consists of the gearbox and final drive differential – often called a transaxle.
2 Drive is transmitted from the crankshaft via the clutch to the input shaft, which has a splined extension to accept the clutch friction plate, and rotates in sealed ball-bearings. From the input shaft, drive is transmitted to the output shaft, which rotates in a roller bearing at its right-hand end, and a sealed ball-bearing at its left-hand end. From the output shaft, the drive is transmitted to the differential crownwheel, which rotates with the differential case and planetary gears, thus driving the sun gears and driveshafts. The rotation of the planetary gears on their shaft allows the inner roadwheel to rotate at a slower speed than the outer roadwheel when the car is cornering.
3 The input and output shafts are arranged side by side, parallel to the crankshaft and driveshafts, so that their gear pinion teeth are in constant mesh. In the neutral position, the output shaft gear pinions rotate freely, so that drive cannot be transmitted to the crownwheel.
4 Gear selection is via a floor-mounted lever and selector rod mechanism. The selector rod causes the appropriate selector fork to move its respective synchro-sleeve along the shaft, to lock the gear pinion to the synchro-hub. Since the synchro-hubs are splined to the output shaft, this locks the pinion to the shaft, so that drive can be transmitted. To ensure that gear-changing can be made quickly and quietly, a synchro-mesh system is fitted to all forward gears, consisting of baulk rings and spring-loaded fingers, as well as the gear pinions and synchro-hubs. The synchro-mesh cones are formed on the mating faces of the baulk rings and gear pinions.
5 Two different manual transmissions are used on the models covered in this manual; petrol engine models have the MA5 transmission, whereas diesel engine models are fitted with the BE4/5 unit.

2 Manual transmission – draining and refilling

Note: *A suitable square section wrench may be required to undo the transmission filler/level and drain plugs on some models. These wrenches can be obtained from most motor factors or your Peugeot dealer.*
1 This operation is much quicker and more efficient if the car is first taken on a journey of sufficient length to warm the engine/transmission up to normal operating temperature.

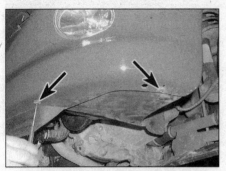

2.3a Slacken and remove the retaining screws (arrowed) . . .

2.3b . . . and fasteners . . .

2.3c . . . and remove the front section of the left-hand wheelarch liner

2 Park the car on level ground, switch off the ignition and apply the handbrake firmly. For improved access, jack up the front of the car and support it securely on axle stands (see *Jacking and vehicle support*). Note that the car must be level to ensure accuracy when refilling and checking the oil level.

3 On 2.0 litre diesel engines, undo the bolts securing the left-hand inner cover to the wing valance and undercover and remove the cover to gain access to the transmission filler/level plug. On all other engines, to improve access to the filler/level plug, remove the retaining screws and fasteners (pull out the centre pin then remove the complete fasteners) and remove the front section of the left-hand wheelarch liner **(see illustrations)**.

4 Wipe clean the area around the filler/level plug, which is situated on the left-hand end of the transmission, next to the end cover.

Unscrew the filler/level plug from the transmission and recover the sealing washer **(see illustrations)**.

5 Position a suitable container under the drain plug (situated at the rear of the transmission) and unscrew the plug. On petrol engine models, the plug is on the left-hand side of the differential housing; on diesel engine models, it is on the base of the differential housing **(see illustrations)**. Where necessary, remove the retaining bolts, screws and clips and remove the undercover from the engine/transmission unit to gain access to the drain plug.

6 Allow the oil to drain completely into the container. If the oil is hot, take precautions against scalding. Clean both the filler/level and the drain plugs, being especially careful to wipe any metallic particles off the magnetic inserts. Discard the original sealing washers; they should be renewed whenever they are disturbed.

7 When the oil has finished draining, clean the drain plug threads and those of the transmission casing, fit a new sealing washer and refit the drain plug, tightening it to the specified torque wrench setting. Refit the undercover (where fitted) then lower the vehicle to the ground.

8 Refilling the transmission is an extremely awkward operation. Above all, allow plenty of time for the oil level to settle properly before checking it. Note that the car must be parked on flat level ground when checking the oil level.

9 Refill the transmission with the exact amount of the specified type of oil then check the oil level as described in the relevant part of Chapter 1; if the correct amount was poured into the transmission and a large amount flows out on checking the level, refit the filler/level plug and take the car on a short journey so that the new oil is distributed fully around the transmission components, then check the level again on your return. Once the oil level is correct, securely refit the inner cover/wheelarch liner (as applicable).

3 Gearchange linkage – removal and refitting

1 Firmly apply the handbrake, then jack up the front of the vehicle and support it on axle stands (see *Jacking and vehicle support*).

2 To improve access to the transmission end of the linkage, remove the battery and battery tray (see Chapter 5A).

3 To gain access to the gearchange lever end of the linkage, remove the exhaust system heatshields (where fitted). Remove the retaining nuts and/or fasteners (unscrew the centre screw then pull out the complete fastener), and manoeuvre the shields out of position. On some models it may be necessary to free the exhaust system from its mountings to gain the clearance necessary to remove the larger heat shield (see the relevant part of Chapter 4).

7A

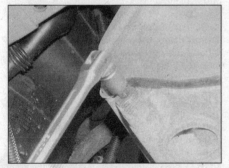

2.4a Unscrewing the transmission unit filler/level plug – petrol engine

2.4b Unscrewing the transmission filler/level plug – diesel engine

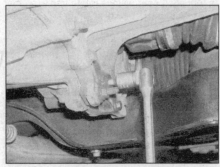

2.5a Unscrewing the transmission drain plug – petrol engine

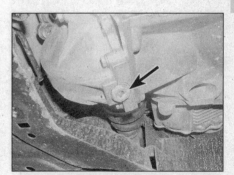

2.5b Transmission drain plug location – diesel engine

3.4 Unscrew the nut and withdraw the pivot bolt securing the linkage rod to the gearchange lever

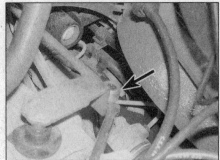

3.5 Carefully lever the link rods off their balljoints on the transmission unit

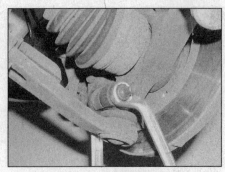

4.3 Unscrew the nut and remove the lower arm balljoint clamp bolt

4 Slacken and remove the nut, and withdraw the pivot bolt securing the linkage rod to the base of the gearchange lever **(see illustration)**.

5 Using a flat-bladed screwdriver, carefully lever the three link rods off their balljoints on the transmission **(see illustration)**. Disengage the linkage rod from the relay lever, and remove it from underneath the vehicle, complete with its link rods.

6 Slacken and remove the relay lever pivot bolt, then manoeuvre the relay lever and link rod out of position, noting the correct fitted locations of the spacer, pivot bushes and washers fitted to the centre of the lever.

7 Inspect all the linkage components for

signs of wear or damage, paying particular attention to the pivot bushes and link rod balljoints, and renew worn components as necessary. If necessary, the gearchange lever can be removed as follows.

8 Unclip the gearchange lever gaiter from the centre console then pull off the knob from the gearchange lever and remove the gaiter. Slacken and remove the gearchange lever retaining nuts and lift off the retaining plate (where fitted) then lower the lever out from underneath the vehicle.

9 Peel back the lower gaiter from the base of the gearchange lever, then disengage the lever mounting plate, and slide the upper gaiter up the lever to gain access to the gearchange lever pivot ball. Examine the lever components for signs of wear or damage, paying particular attention to the rubber gaiters, and renew components as necessary. The lever can be separated from its baseplate after the retaining ring has been unclipped.

Refitting

10 Refitting is a reversal of the removal procedure, noting the following points:
 a) Apply a smear of the special grease (see Specifications) to the relay lever pivot ball, the link rod balljoints and the relay lever pivot bushes.
 b) Ensure that the gearchange lever rubber gaiters are correctly seated before refitting the lever assembly to the vehicle.
 c) Apply a drop of locking compound (Peugeot recommend Loctite Frenetanch) to the threads of the relay lever pivot bolt prior to refitting.

 d) Tighten all fixings to their specified torques (where given) and ensure that the link rods are securely pressed onto their balljoints.

4 Oil seals – renewal

Driveshaft oil seals

1 Chock the rear wheels, apply the handbrake, then jack up the front of the car and support it on axle stands (see Jacking and vehicle support). Remove the appropriate front roadwheel.

2 Drain the transmission oil as described in Section 2.

3 Slacken and remove the suspension lower arm balljoint clamp bolt and nut **(see illustration)**. Discard the nut – a new one must be used on refitting.

4 Pull down on the lower arm to free its balljoint from the swivel hub **(see Tool Tip)**. Once the balljoint is freed from the swivel hub, peg the lower arm in position by inserting a suitable socket in between the top of the arm inner end and the subframe **(see illustration)**.

5 Recover the protector plate from lower arm balljoint **(see illustration)**.

Right-hand seal

6 Loosen the two intermediate bearing retaining bolt nuts, then rotate the bolts through 90° so that their offset heads are clear of the bearing outer race **(see illustrations)**.

To free the lower arm, attach a long bar (such as a jack handle) securely to the lower arm. Fit a block of wood to the inner end of the bar, to act as a pivot, then use the bar to pull the lower arm out from the swivel hub.

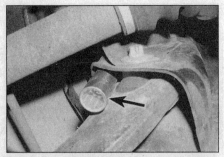

4.4 Secure the lower arm clear of the swivel hub by inserting a socket in between the top of the arm and the subframe

4.5 Remove the protector plate from the lower arm balljoint

4.6a On the right-hand driveshaft, slacken the two intermediate bearing retaining bolt nuts . . .

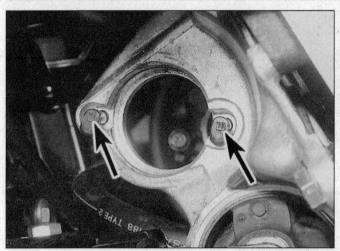

4.6b ... then rotate the bolts through 90° to disengage their offset heads (arrowed) from the bearing (shown with driveshaft removed for clarity)

4.8 Free the right-hand driveshaft from the transmission and slide off the dust seal

7 Carefully pull the swivel hub assembly outwards, and pull on the inner end of the driveshaft to free the intermediate bearing from its mounting bracket.

8 Once the driveshaft end is free from the transmission, slide the dust seal/plate off the inner end of the shaft, noting which way around it is fitted, and support the inner end of the driveshaft to avoid damaging the constant velocity joints or gaiters (see illustration).

9 Carefully prise the oil seal out of the transmission, using a large flat-bladed screwdriver (see illustration).

10 Remove all traces of dirt from the area around the oil seal aperture, then apply a smear of grease to the outer lip of the new oil seal. Fit the new seal into its aperture, and drive it squarely into position using a suitable tubular drift (such as a socket) which bears only on the hard outer edge of the seal, until it abuts its locating shoulder. If the seal was supplied with a plastic protector sleeve, leave this in position until the driveshaft has been refitted.

11 Thoroughly clean the driveshaft splines, then apply a thin film of grease to the oil seal lip.

12 Slide the dust seal/plate into position on the end of the shaft, ensuring that its flat surface is facing the transmission.

13 Carefully locate the inner driveshaft splines with those of the differential sun gear, taking care not to damage the oil seal, then align the intermediate bearing with its mounting bracket, and push the driveshaft fully into position. If necessary, use a soft-faced mallet to tap the outer race of the bearing into position in the mounting bracket.

14 Fit the protector plate to the lower arm balljoint.

15 Align the lower arm balljoint with the swivel hub. Remove the socket (used to peg the arm in position) and seat the balljoint shank correctly in the swivel hub. Insert the clamp bolt then fit the new nut and tighten to the specified torque (see Chapter 10).

16 Ensure that the intermediate bearing is correctly seated, then rotate its retaining bolts back through 90°, so that their offset heads are resting against the bearing outer race. Evenly and progressively tighten the retaining bolt nuts to the specified torque (see Chapter 10). Ensure that the dust seal/plate is tight against the driveshaft oil seal (see illustration).

17 Refit the roadwheel, then lower the vehicle to the ground and tighten the roadwheel bolts to the specified torque.

18 Refill the transmission with the specified type and amount of oil, and check the level using the information given in the relevant part of Chapter 1.

Left-hand seal

19 Pull the swivel hub assembly outwards and withdraw the driveshaft inner constant velocity joint from the transmission, taking care not to damage the driveshaft oil seal. Support the driveshaft, to avoid damaging the constant velocity joints or gaiters.

20 Renew the oil seal as described above in paragraphs 9 to 11 (see illustration).

21 Carefully locate the inner constant velocity joint splines with those of the differential sun gear, taking care not to damage the oil seal, and push the driveshaft fully into position. Where fitted, remove the plastic protector from the oil seal.

22 Fit the protector plate to the lower arm balljoint.

23 Align the lower arm balljoint with the swivel hub. Remove the socket (used to peg the arm in position) and seat the balljoint

7A

4.9 Use a large flat-bladed screwdriver to lever the right-hand oil seal out of position

4.16 On refitting ensure the dust seal is tight against the oil seal

4.20 Removing the left-hand oil seal (petrol engine model shown)

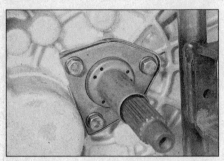

4.27 Unscrew the retaining bolts and slide the clutch bearing guide sleeve off the input shaft

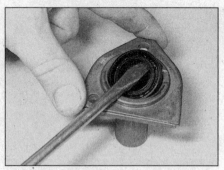

4.28 Carefully lever the seal out of the housing, noting which way around it is fitted

shank correctly in the swivel hub. Insert the clamp bolt then fit the new nut and tighten to the specified torque (see Chapter 10).

24 Refit the roadwheel, then lower the vehicle to the ground and tighten the roadwheel bolts to the specified torque.

25 Refill the transmission with the specified type and amount of oil, and check the level using the information given in the relevant part of Chapter 1.

Input shaft oil seal

26 Remove the transmission as described in Section 7.

27 Undo the three bolts securing the clutch release bearing guide sleeve in position, and slide the guide off the input shaft, along with its sealing ring or gasket (as applicable) **(see illustration)**. Recover any shims or thrustwashers which have stuck to the rear of the guide sleeve, and refit them to the input shaft.

28 Carefully lever the oil seal out of the guide using a suitable flat-bladed screwdriver **(see illustration)**.

29 Before fitting a new seal, check the input shaft's seal rubbing surface for signs of burrs, scratches or other damage, which may have caused the seal to fail in the first place. It may be possible to polish away minor faults of this

sort using fine abrasive paper; however, more serious defects will require the renewal of the input shaft. Ensure that the input shaft is clean and greased, to protect the seal lips on refitting.

30 Dip the new seal in clean oil, and fit it to the guide sleeve.

31 Fit a new sealing ring or gasket (as applicable) to the rear of the guide sleeve, then carefully slide the sleeve into position over the input shaft. Refit the retaining bolts and tighten them to the specified torque setting **(see illustrations)**.

32 Take the opportunity to inspect the clutch components if not already done (Chapter 6). Finally, refit the transmission as described in Section 7.

Selector shaft oil seal

Petrol engine models

33 On these models, to renew the selector shaft seal, the transmission must be dismantled. This task should therefore be entrusted to a Peugeot dealer or transmission specialist.

Diesel engine models

34 Park the car on level ground, apply the handbrake, then jack up the front of the vehicle and support it on axle stands (see

Jacking and vehicle support). Remove the left-hand front roadwheel.

35 Using a large flat-bladed screwdriver, lever the link rod balljoint off the transmission selector shaft, and disconnect the link rod.

36 Using a large flat-bladed screwdriver, carefully prise the selector shaft seal out of the housing, and slide it off the end of the shaft.

37 Before fitting a new seal, check the selector shaft's seal rubbing surface for signs of burrs, scratches or other damage, which may have caused the seal to fail in the first place. It may be possible to polish away minor faults of this sort using fine abrasive paper; however, more serious defects will require the renewal of the selector shaft.

38 Apply a smear of grease to the new seal's outer edge and sealing lip, then carefully slide the seal along the selector rod. Press the seal fully into position in the transmission housing.

39 Refit the link rod to the selector shaft, ensuring that its balljoint is pressed firmly onto the shaft. Lower the car to the ground.

---

5 Reversing light switch – testing, removal and refitting

Testing

1 The reversing light circuit is controlled by a plunger-type switch screwed into the top of the transmission casing. If a fault develops, first ensure that the circuit fuse has not blown.

2 To test the switch, disconnect the wiring connector, and use a multimeter (set to the resistance function) or a battery-and-bulb test circuit to check that there is continuity between the switch terminals only when reverse gear is selected. If this is not the case, and there are no obvious breaks or other damage to the wires, the switch is faulty, and must be renewed.

4.31a Fit a new sealing ring/gasket (as applicable) . . .

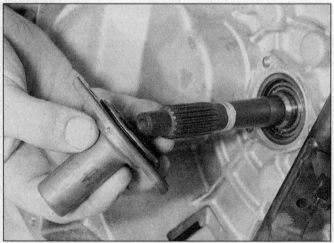

4.31b . . . then slide the housing assembly back onto the input shaft

Removal

3 Where necessary, to improve access to the switch, remove the air cleaner housing intake duct assembly/battery and battery tray (as applicable – see the relevant part of Chapter 4 and 5A).

4 Disconnect the wiring connector, then unscrew the switch from the transmission casing along with its sealing washer **(see illustrations)**.

Refitting

5 Fit a new sealing washer to the switch, then screw it back into position in the top of the transmission housing and tighten it to the specified torque setting. Refit the wiring plug, and test the operation of the circuit. Refit any components removed for access.

6 Speedometer drive –
removal and refitting

Removal

1 Chock the rear wheels, firmly apply the handbrake, then jack up the front of the car and support it on axle stands (see *Jacking and vehicle support*). The speedometer drive is on the rear of the transmission housing, next to the inner end of the right-hand driveshaft.

2 Disconnect the wiring connector from the speedometer drive **(see illustration)**.

3 Slacken and remove the retaining bolt and remove the heatshield (where fitted). Withdraw the speedometer drive and driven pinion assembly from the transmission housing, along with its sealing ring.

4 If necessary, the pinion can be slid out of the housing, and the oil seal can be removed from the top of the housing. Examine the pinion for signs of damage, and renew if necessary. Renew the housing sealing ring as a matter of course.

5 If the driven pinion is worn or damaged,

also examine the drive pinion in the transmission housing for similar signs.

6 On petrol engine models, to renew the drive pinion, the transmission must be dismantled and the differential gear removed. This task should therefore be entrusted to a Peugeot dealer or a transmission specialist.

7 On diesel engine models, to remove the drive pinion, first disengage the right-hand driveshaft from the transmission, as described in paragraphs 1 to 7 of Section 4. Undo the three retaining bolts, and remove the speedometer drive housing from the

transmission, along with its sealing ring. Remove the drive pinion from the differential gear, and recover any adjustment shims from the gear **(see illustrations)**.

Refitting

8 On diesel engine models, where the drive pinion has been removed, refit the adjustment shims to the differential gear, then locate the speedometer drive on the gear, ensuring it is correctly engaged in the gear slots **(see illustration)**. Fit a new sealing ring to the rear of the speedometer drive housing, then refit

5.4a Disconnecting the wiring connector from the reversing light switch – petrol engine

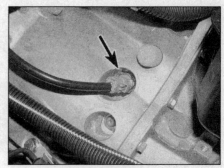

5.4b Reversing light switch – diesel engine

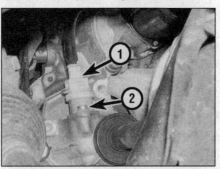

6.2 Disconnect the wiring connector (1) then undo the retaining bolt (2) and withdraw the speedometer drive assembly

6.7a On diesel engines, unscrew the retaining bolts ...

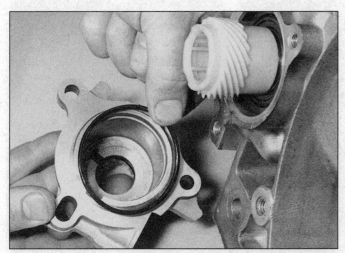

6.7b ... and remove the housing, sealing ring and drive pinion from the transmission unit (shown with transmission removed)

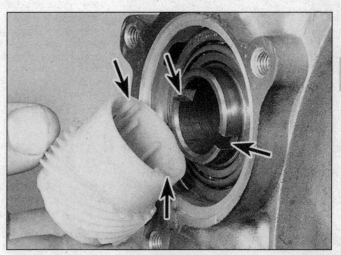

6.8 On diesel engines ensure the drive pinion dogs are correctly engaged with the gear slots (arrowed) on refitting

7A

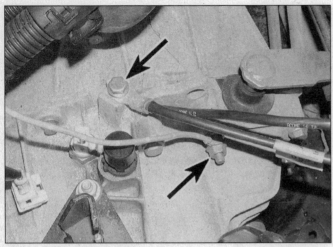

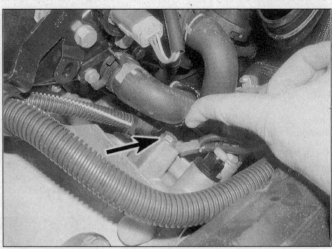

7.9a Unscrew the nut and bolt and detach the earth leads from the transmission unit – petrol engine

7.9b Unscrew the bolt (arrowed) and disconnect the earth lead from the transmission unit – diesel engine

the housing to the transmission and tighten its retaining bolts to the specified torque. Inspect the driveshaft oil seal for signs of wear, and renew if necessary. Refit the driveshaft to the transmission, with reference to Section 4.

9 On all models, apply a smear of grease to the lips of the seal and to the driven pinion shaft, and slide the pinion into position in the speedometer drive.

10 Fit a new sealing ring to the speedometer drive and refit it to the transmission, ensuring that the drive and driven pinions are correctly engaged. Refit the drive retaining bolt, complete with heatshield (where fitted), and tighten securely.

11 Reconnect the wiring connector to the speedometer drive then lower the vehicle to the ground.

7 Manual transmission –
removal and refitting

Removal

1 Chock the rear wheels, then firmly apply the handbrake. Jack up the front of the vehicle, and securely support it on axle stands (see

Jacking and vehicle support). Remove both front roadwheels.

2 Drain the transmission oil as described in Section 2, then refit the drain and filler plugs, and tighten to their specified torque settings.

3 Remove both driveshafts as described in Chapter 8.

4 Remove the battery, battery tray and mounting plate (see Chapter 5A).

5 Remove the air cleaner housing and intake duct and (where fitted) the crankshaft sensor as described in the relevant part of Chapter 4.

6 Remove the starter motor (Chapter 5A).

7 On petrol engine models and left-hand drive diesel engine models, detach the clutch cable from the transmission unit as described in Chapter 6.

8 On right-hand drive diesel engine models, unscrew the mounting bolts and free the clutch slave cylinder and hydraulic hose from transmission unit (see Chapter 6).

9 Disconnect the wiring connectors from the reversing light switch and the speedometer drive. Undo the retaining nut/bolt(s), and disconnect the earth straps from the top of the transmission housing **(see illustrations)**. Free the wiring from any relevant retaining clips, and position it clear of the transmission.

10 Using a flat-bladed screwdriver, carefully lever the three gearchange mechanism link rods off their respective balljoints on the transmission. Position the rods clear of the transmission.

11 Undo the retaining bolt(s), and remove the flywheel lower cover plate (where fitted) from the transmission.

12 On diesel engine models, remove the speedometer drive gear housing and gear assembly from the transmission as described in Section 6. On 2.0 litre engines also unscrew the bolts securing the coolant heater bracket to the top of the transmission unit.

13 Place a jack with a block of wood beneath the engine, to take the weight of the engine. Alternatively, attach a couple of lifting eyes to the engine, and fit a hoist or support bar to take the engine weight.

14 Place a jack and block of wood beneath the transmission, and raise the jack to take the weight of the transmission.

15 Slacken and remove the centre nut and washer from the left-hand engine/transmission mounting then undo the mounting bolts and remove the mounting. Unscrew the bolts securing the mounting bracket to the body and remove the bracket **(see illustrations)**.

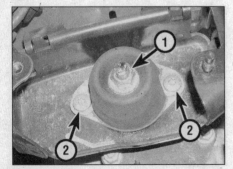

7.15a Slacken and remove the centre nut and washer (1) then undo the mounting bolts (2) . . .

7.15b . . . and lift off the mounting rubber

7.15c Unscrew the mounting bolts (locations arrowed) and remove the left-hand mounting bracket from the body

7.16 On petrol engine models undo the nuts (arrowed) and remove the mounting bracket from the top of the transmission unit

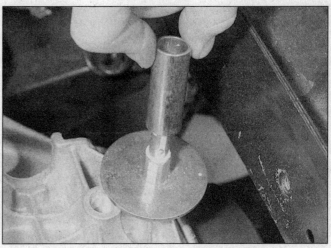

7.17a On diesel engine models slide off the spacer . . .

16 On petrol engine models, undo the three retaining nuts and remove the mounting plate from the top of the transmission **(see illustration)**.

17 On diesel engine models, slide the spacer off the mounting stud, then unscrew the stud from the top of the transmission housing and remove it along with its washer. If the mounting stud is tight, a universal stud extractor can be used to unscrew it **(see illustrations)**.

18 On all models, unscrew the nuts and bolts and remove the mounting link securing the rear engine/transmission mounting to the subframe **(see illustration)**.

19 With the jack positioned beneath the transmission taking the weight, slacken and remove the remaining bolts securing the transmission housing to the engine. Note the correct fitted positions of each bolt, and the necessary brackets, as they are removed, to use as a reference on refitting. Make a final check that all components have been disconnected, and are positioned clear of the transmission so that they will not hinder the removal procedure.

20 With the bolts removed, move the trolley jack and transmission to the left, to free it from its locating dowels. If necessary, lower the engine slightly to enable the transmission to be freed.

Caution: Take great care not to place any excess strain on the exhaust system or damage the radiator if the engine is moved. On models equipped with air conditioning, care must also be taken to ensure the auxiliary drivebelt pulleys do not damage the air conditioning pipes on the right-hand side of the engine compartment.

21 Once the transmission is free, lower the jack and manoeuvre the unit out from under the car. Remove the locating dowels from the transmission or engine if they are loose, and keep them in a safe place.

Refitting

22 The transmission is refitted by a reversal of the removal procedure, bearing in mind the following points:

a) *Prior to refitting, check the clutch assembly and release mechanism components (see Chapter 6). Lubricate the release bearing guide with a little high-melting-point grease (Peugeot recommend the use of Molykote BR2 plus). Do not apply too much grease, otherwise there is a possibility of the grease contaminating the clutch friction plate, and ensure no grease is applied to the input shaft/friction plate splines.*

b) *Ensure that the locating dowels are correctly positioned prior to installation.*

c) *On diesel engine models, apply thread-locking fluid to the left-hand engine/transmission mounting stud threads, prior to refitting it to the transmission. Tighten the stud to the specified torque.*

d) *Tighten all nuts and bolts to the specified torque (where given).*

e) *Renew the driveshaft oil seals, then refit the driveshafts (see Chapter 8).*

f) *Reconnect the clutch cable/refit the slave cylinder (see Chapter 6).*

g) *On completion, refill the transmission with the specified type and quantity of lubricant, as described in the relevant part of Chapter 1.*

8 Manual transmission overhaul – general information

1 Overhauling a manual transmission is a difficult and involved job for the DIY home mechanic. In addition to dismantling and reassembling many small parts, clearances must be precisely measured and, if necessary, changed by selecting shims and spacers. Internal transmission components are also often difficult to obtain, and in many instances, extremely expensive. Because of this, if the transmission develops a fault or becomes noisy, the best course of action is to have the unit overhauled by a specialist repairer, or to obtain an exchange reconditioned unit.

2 Nevertheless, it is not impossible for the more experienced mechanic to overhaul the transmission, provided the special tools are available, and the job is done in a deliberate step-by-step manner, so that nothing is overlooked.

7A

7.17b . . . and unscrew the left-hand mounting stud from the top of the transmission unit

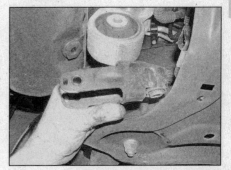

7.18 Unscrew the mounting nuts and bolts and remove the mounting link securing the rear mounting to the subframe

3 The tools necessary for an overhaul include internal and external circlip pliers, bearing pullers, a slide hammer, a set of pin punches, a dial test indicator, and possibly a hydraulic press. In addition, a large, sturdy workbench and a vice will be required.

4 During dismantling of the transmission, make careful notes of how each component is fitted, to make reassembly easier and more accurate.

5 Before dismantling the transmission, it will help if you have some idea what area is malfunctioning. Certain problems can be closely related to specific areas in the transmission, which can make component examination and replacement easier. Refer to the *Fault Finding* Section for more information.

Chapter 7 Part B:
Automatic transmission

Contents

Degrees of difficulty

Easy, suitable for novice with little experience	Fairly easy, suitable for beginner with some experience	Fairly difficult, suitable for competent DIY mechanic	Difficult, suitable for experienced DIY mechanic	Very difficult, suitable for expert DIY or professional

Specifications

General
Type .... Auto-adaptive four-speed electronically controlled automatic with three (normal, sport and snow) driving modes
Designation AL4

Lubrication
Recommended fluid .... See *Lubricants and fluids*
Capacity:
  Refilling after draining .... 3.0 litres*
  From dry .... 6.0 litres
*If the torque converter is also removed and drained, add a further 2 litres

Torque wrench settings

	Nm	lbf ft
Engine-to-transmission fixing bolts	35	26
Fluid cooler centre bolt	50	37
Fluid drain plug	33	24
Fluid filler plug	24	18
Fluid level plug	24	18
Fluid pressure sensor bolts	9	7
Input shaft speed sensor bolt	10	7
Left-hand engine/transmission mounting:		
Mounting bracket-to-body bolts	19	14
Mounting stud	50	37
Mounting-to-bracket bolts	30	22
Mounting centre nut	65	48
Bracket-to-transmission bolts	45	33
Multi-function switch retaining bolts	10	7
Output shaft speed sensor bolt	10	7
Rear mounting link:		
Link-to-mounting bolt	50	37
Link-to-subframe bolt	39	29
Roadwheel bolts	85	63
Torque converter-to-driveplate nuts:		
Stage 1	10	7
Stage 2	30	22

1 General information

1 Some petrol engine models were offered with the option of a four-speed electronically-controlled automatic transmission, consisting of a torque converter, an epicyclic geartrain, and hydraulically-operated clutches and brakes. The unit is controlled by the electronic control unit (ECU) via the electrically-operated solenoid valves in the hydraulic block within the transmission unit. The transmission has three driving modes; normal, sport and snow modes; the mode buttons are situated on the right-hand side of the selector lever and the mode indicator lights are incorporated in the instrument panel.

2 The normal mode is the standard mode for driving in which the transmission shifts up at relatively low engine speeds to combine reasonable performance with economy. If the transmission unit is switched into sport mode, the transmission will shift up only at high engine speeds, giving improved acceleration and overtaking performance. In snow mode, the transmission will select 2nd gear when the vehicle pulls away from a standing start; this helps maintain traction on slippery surfaces.

3 The torque converter provides a fluid coupling between the engine and transmission, which acts as an automatic clutch, and also provides a degree of torque multiplication when accelerating.

4 The epicyclic geartrain provides either of the four forward or one reverse gear ratios, according to which of its component parts are held stationary or allowed to turn. The components of the geartrain are held or released by brakes and clutches which are controlled by the ECU via the electrically-operated solenoid valves in the hydraulic unit. A fluid pump within the transmission provides the necessary hydraulic pressure to operate the brakes and clutches.

5 Driver control of the transmission is by a six-position selector lever. The transmission has a 'drive' position, and a 'hold' facility on the first three gear ratios. The 'drive' position D provides automatic changing throughout the range of all four gear ratios, and is the one to select for normal driving. An automatic kickdown facility shifts the transmission down a gear if the accelerator pedal is fully depressed. The 'hold' facility is very similar, but limits the number of gear ratios available – ie, when the selector lever is in the 3 position, only the first three ratios can be selected; in the 2 position, only the first two can be selected. When the lever is in the 2 position, the transmission can be locked in first gear using the button on the right-hand side of the selector lever. These lower ratio 'hold' settings are useful for providing engine braking when travelling down steep gradients, or for preventing unwanted selection of top gear on twisty roads. Note, however, that the

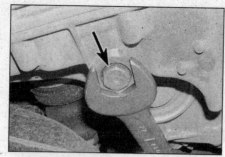

2.3 Unscrewing the transmission drain plug. The smaller plug (arrowed) in the centre of the drain plug is the level plug

transmission should *never* be shifted down at high engine speeds.

6 On some models, the selector lever is equipped with a shift-lock function. This prevents the selector lever being moved from the P position unless the brake pedal is depressed.

7 Due to the complexity of the automatic transmission, any repair or overhaul work must be left to a Peugeot dealer with the necessary special equipment for fault diagnosis and repair. The contents of the following Sections are therefore confined to supplying general information, and any service information and instructions that can be used by the owner.

Note: *The automatic transmission unit is of the 'auto-adaptive' type. This means that it takes into account your driving style and modifies the transmission shift points to provide optimum performance and economy to suit. When the battery is disconnected, the transmission will lose its memory and will resort to one of its many base shift programs. The transmission will then relearn the optimum shift points when the vehicle is driven a few miles. During these first few miles of driving, there maybe a noticeable difference in performance whilst the transmission adapts to your individual style.*

2 Automatic transmission fluid – draining and refilling

Note: *A suitable square section wrench may*

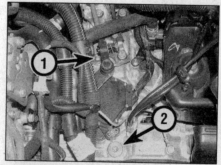

2.7 Transmission filler plug (1) location. DO NOT remove the selector shaft bolt (2)

be required to undo the transmission filler plug. These wrenches can be obtained from most motor factors or your Peugeot dealer.
Note: *The transmission unit is equipped with a fluid wear sensor to inform the driver when the fluid needs replacing (the ECU flashes the Sport and Snow mode indicator lights when fluid replacement is necessary). If the transmission unit is drained and refilled with new fluid, this sensor should be reset. This can only be done using the Peugeot diagnostic test box.*

Draining

1 This operation is much quicker and more efficient if the car is first taken on a journey of sufficient length to warm the engine/transmission up to normal operating temperature.

2 Park the car on level ground, switch off the ignition and apply the handbrake firmly. For improved access, jack up the front of the car and support it securely on axle stands (see *Jacking and vehicle support*).

3 Position a suitable container under the drain plug, situated on the base of the transmission. Unscrew the drain plug (the smaller plug in the centre of the drain plug is the level plug – see Chapter 1A) and recover the sealing washer **(see illustration)**. Allow the fluid to drain completely into the container.

⚠ **Warning: If the fluid is hot, take precautions against scalding.**

4 Clean the drain plug, being especially careful to wipe off any metallic particles. Discard the sealing washer; it should be renewed whenever it is disturbed.

5 When the fluid has finished draining, clean the drain plug threads and those of the transmission casing, fit a new sealing washer and refit the drain plug, tightening it to the specified torque wrench setting. If the car was raised for the draining operation, now lower it to the ground.

Refilling

6 To improve access to the filler plug, remove the battery and battery tray as described in Chapter 5A. If necessary, also unclip the selector cable end fitting from its balljoint on the transmission lever.

7 Wipe clean the area around the filler plug which is situated directly behind the transmission selector lever **(see illustration)**. Unscrew the filler plug from the transmission and recover the sealing washer.
Caution: Do not unscrew the selector shaft bolt (located in front of the selector lever).

8 Carefully refill the transmission with the correct amount of the specified type of fluid. Fit the new sealing washer to the filler plug then refit the plug, tightening it to the specified torque. Reconnect the selector cable to the lever (where disconnected – support the lever when pressing the cable onto its balljoint to prevent the lever being bent) then refit the battery (see Chapter 5A).

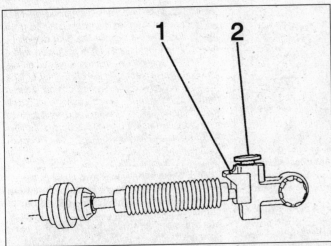

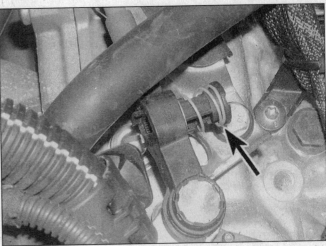

3.3 On selector cables where the locking plunger spring is not visible, release the retaining clip (1) to extend the plunger (2) and unlock the adjustment mechanism

3.4 On selector cables where the spring (arrowed) is visible, depress the plunger to release the adjustment mechanism

9 Take the vehicle on a short journey to warm the transmission up to normal operating temperature.

10 On your return, check the transmission fluid level as described in Chapter 1A.

3 Selector cable – adjustment

1 To gain access to the transmission end of the selector cable, remove the battery and battery tray as described in Chapter 5A.

2 Position the selector lever firmly against its detent in the P (park) position. There are two possible types of adjustment mechanism on the selector cable end fitting; identify which type is present and proceed as follows.

3 Where the locking plunger spring is not visible, release the plunger retaining clip and allow the plunger to extend fully from the end fitting **(see illustration)**. Ensure the transmission unit selector lever is pushed fully towards the rear then lock up the adjustment mechanism by depressing the plunger back into the end fitting.

4 If the locking plunger spring is visible, push

the plunger fully into the end fitting and hold it in position **(see illustration)**. Ensure the transmission unit selector lever is pushed fully towards the rear then lock up the adjustment mechanism by releasing the plunger.

5 Check the operation of the selector lever before refitting the battery tray and battery (see Chapter 5A).

4 Selector cable – removal and refitting

Removal

1 Firmly apply the handbrake, then jack up the front of the vehicle and support it on axle stands (see *Jacking and vehicle support*). Position the selector lever in the P position.

2 To gain access to the transmission end of the selector cable, remove the battery and battery tray as described in Chapter 5A.

3 Unclip the selector cable end fitting from the balljoint on the transmission lever. Remove the retaining clip and free the cable from the transmission bracket **(see illustrations)**.

4 To gain access to the base of the selector lever, remove the exhaust system heat shield(s). Remove the retaining nuts and/or fasteners (unscrew the centre screw then pull out the complete fastener), and manoeuvre the shields out of position. On some models it may be necessary to free the exhaust system from its mountings to gain the clearance necessary to remove the larger heat shield.

5 Unclip the cover plate from the base of the selector lever housing and recover its seal.

6 Lever the selector cable off the selector lever balljoint then free the outer cable from the front of the housing and manoeuvre it out of position. Recover the seal fitted between the outer cable and housing.

Refitting

7 Refitting is the reverse of removal, noting the following points.

a) Renew the cable and selector cover plate seals if they show signs of damage or deterioration.

b) Support the transmission selector lever when pressing the cable onto its balljoint to prevent the lever being bent.

c) Ensure the cable end fitting and cover plate and correctly seated on the selector lever housing to ensure a water-tight seal.

d) Adjust the cable as described in Section 3 before refitting all components removed for access.

5 Selector lever assembly – removal and refitting

Removal

1 Carry out the operations described in paragraphs 1 to 4 of Section 4.

2 Remove the centre console as described in Chapter 11.

3 Disconnect the wiring connector(s) from the

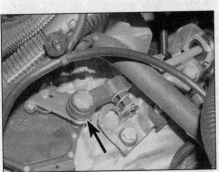

4.3a Unclip the selector cable end fitting (arrowed) from its balljoint . . .

4.3b . . . then remove the retaining clip (arrowed) and free the cable from the transmission unit

7B

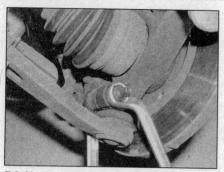

7.2 Unscrew the nut and remove the lower arm balljoint clamp bolt

To free the lower arm, attach a long bar (such as a jack handle) securely to the lower arm. Fit a block of wood to the inner end of the bar, to act as a pivot, then use the bar to pull the lower arm out from the swivel hub.

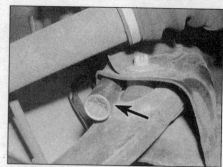

7.3 Secure the lower arm clear of the swivel hub by inserting a socket in between the top of the arm and the subframe

lever assembly then remove the connector bracket from the rear of the selector lever.

4 Free the mode switch from the selector lever gate panel then unclip and remove the panel.

5 Slacken and remove the selector lever mounting nuts and bolts then remove the upper section of the selector lever housing.

6 Working underneath the vehicle, free the selector lever housing from the underbody then manoeuvre the lever and cable assembly out of position. If necessary, separate the cable from the lever as described in paragraphs 5 and 6 of Section 4.

Refitting

7 Refitting is the reverse of removal, noting the following points.

a) If the lever and cable have been separated, renew the cable and selector cover plate seals if they show signs of damage or deterioration.

b) Ensure the cable end fitting and cover plate and correctly seated on the selector lever housing to ensure a water-tight seal.

c) Adjust the cable as described in Section 3 before refitting all components removed for access.

---

6 Speedometer drive –
removal and refitting

Refer to Chapter 7A, Section 6.

---

7 Oil seals –
renewal

Driveshaft oil seals

1 Chock the rear wheels, apply the handbrake, then jack up the front of the car and support it on axle stands (see *Jacking and vehicle support*). Remove the appropriate front roadwheel.

2 Slacken and remove the suspension lower arm balljoint clamp bolt and nut **(see illustration)**. Discard the nut – a new one must be used on refitting.

3 Pull down on the lower arm to free its balljoint from the swivel hub **(see Tool Tip)**.

7.4 Remove the protector plate from the lower arm balljoint

Once the balljoint is freed from the swivel hub, peg the lower arm in position by inserting a suitable socket in between the top of the arm inner end and the subframe **(see illustration)**.

4 Recover the protector plate from lower arm balljoint **(see illustration)**.

Right-hand seal

5 Loosen the two intermediate bearing retaining bolt nuts, then rotate the bolts through 90° so that their offset heads are clear of the bearing outer race **(see illustrations)**.

6 Carefully pull the swivel hub assembly outwards, and pull on the inner end of the

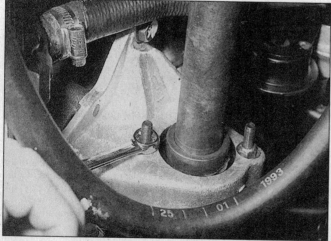

7.5a On the right-hand driveshaft, slacken the two intermediate bearing retaining bolt nuts . . .

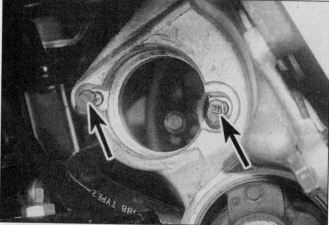

7.5b . . . then rotate the bolts through 90° to disengage their offset heads (arrowed) from the bearing (shown with driveshaft removed for clarity)

driveshaft to free the intermediate bearing from its mounting bracket.

7 Once the driveshaft end is free from the transmission, remove the dust seal/plate (as applicable) off the inner end of the shaft, noting which way around it is fitted, and support the inner end of the driveshaft to avoid damaging the constant velocity joints or gaiters.

8 Remove the O-ring from the differential sun gear shaft then carefully remove the oil seal from of the transmission, taking care not to damage the shaft or housing. To remove the seal, carefully punch or drill two small holes opposite each other into the seal. Screw a self-tapping screw into each hole and pull on the screws to extract the seal.

9 Remove all traces of dirt from the area around the oil seal aperture, then apply a smear of grease to the outer edge and sealing lip of the new oil seal. Ease the new seal onto the shaft, taking care not to damage its lip, and into its aperture. Drive the seal squarely into position using a suitable tubular drift (such as a socket) which bears only on the hard outer edge of the seal.

10 Once the seal is correctly installed, fit a new O-ring to the sun gear shaft and slide along until it abuts the seal.

11 Fit the dust seal/plate onto the end of the driveshaft, ensuring that its flat surface is facing the transmission.

12 Carefully locate the inner driveshaft splines with those of the differential sun gear, then align the intermediate bearing with its mounting bracket, and push the driveshaft fully into position. If necessary, use a soft-faced mallet to tap the outer race of the bearing into position in the mounting bracket.

13 Fit the protector plate to the lower arm balljoint.

14 Align the lower arm balljoint with the swivel hub. Remove the socket (used to peg the arm in position) and seat the balljoint shank correctly in the swivel hub. Insert the clamp bolt then fit the new nut and tighten to the specified torque (see Chapter 10).

15 Ensure that the intermediate bearing is correctly seated, then rotate its retaining bolts back through 90°, so that their offset heads are resting against the bearing outer race. Evenly and progressively tighten the retaining bolt nuts to the specified torque (see Chapter 8). Ensure that the dust seal/plate is tight against the driveshaft oil seal.

16 Refit the roadwheel, then lower the vehicle to the ground and tighten the roadwheel bolts to the specified torque.

Left-hand seal

17 Pull the swivel hub assembly outwards and withdraw the driveshaft inner constant velocity joint from the transmission, taking care not to damage the driveshaft oil seal. Support the driveshaft, to avoid damaging the constant velocity joints or gaiters.

18 Carefully prise the oil seal out of the

transmission, using a large flat-bladed screwdriver.

19 Remove all traces of dirt from the area around the oil seal aperture, then apply a smear of grease to the outer lip of the new oil seal. Fit the new seal into its aperture, and drive it squarely into position using a suitable tubular drift (such as a socket) which bears only on the hard outer edge of the seal, until it abuts its locating shoulder. If the seal was supplied with a plastic protector sleeve, leave this in position until the driveshaft has been refitted.

20 Thoroughly clean the driveshaft splines, then apply a thin film of grease to the oil seal lip.

21 Carefully locate the inner constant velocity joint splines with those of the differential sun gear, taking care not to damage the oil seal, and push the driveshaft fully into position. Where fitted, remove the plastic protector from the oil seal.

22 Fit the protector plate to the lower arm balljoint.

23 Align the lower arm balljoint with the swivel hub. Remove the socket (used to peg the arm in position) and seat the balljoint shank correctly in the swivel hub. Insert the clamp bolt then fit the new nut and tighten to the specified torque (see Chapter 10).

24 Refit the roadwheel, then lower the vehicle to the ground and tighten the roadwheel bolts to the specified torque.

Selector shaft oil seal

25 To gain access to the transmission selector shaft, remove the battery and battery tray as described in Chapter 5A.

26 Position the selector lever firmly against its detent mechanism in the P position.

27 Slacken and remove the nut and clamp bolt securing the selector lever to the transmission shaft **(see illustration)**. Make alignment marks between the shaft and lever then free the lever from the shaft.

28 Remove the retaining clip and free the selector cable from transmission bracket **(see illustration 4.3b)**. Position the cable clear of the selector shaft.

29 Make alignment marks between the multi-function switch and transmission unit then unscrew the retaining bolts and remove the switch.

30 Carefully remove the oil seal from of the transmission, taking care not to damage the shaft or housing. To remove the seal, carefully punch or drill two small holes opposite each other into the seal. Screw a self-tapping screw into each hole and pull on the screws to extract the seal.

31 Remove all traces of dirt from the area around the oil seal aperture, then apply a smear of grease to the outer edge and sealing lip of the new oil seal. Ease the new seal onto the shaft, taking care not to damage its lip, and press it squarely into its aperture.

32 Locate the multi-function switch back on the selector shaft. Align the marks made prior

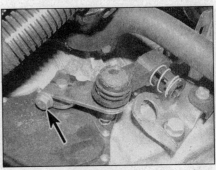

7.27 Unscrew the nut and clamp bolt (arrowed) and free the selector lever from the transmission shaft

to removal then refit the switch bolts, tightening them to the specified torque.

33 Seat the selector cable in the transmission bracket and engage the selector lever with the transmission shaft. Ensure the marks made on removal are correctly aligned then refit the lever clamp bolt and nut and tighten securely.

34 Secure the selector cable in position with the retaining clip then adjust the cable as described in Section 3.

35 Refit all components removed for access.

Torque converter seal

36 Remove the transmission unit as described in Section 10.

37 Carefully slide the torque converter off the transmission shaft whilst being prepared for fluid spillage.

38 Note the correct fitted position of the seal in the housing then carefully lever it out of position, taking care not to mark the housing or shaft.

39 Remove all traces of dirt from the area around the oil seal aperture. Ease the new seal into its aperture, ensuring its sealing lip is facing inwards, then press it squarely into position.

40 Engage the torque converter with the transmission shaft splines and slide it into position, taking care not to damage the oil seal.

41 Refit the transmission unit as described in Section 10.

8 Fluid cooler – removal and refitting

7B

Caution: Be careful not to allow dirt into the transmission unit during this procedure.

Removal

1 The fluid cooler is mounted on the rear of the transmission housing. To gain access to the cooler, remove the battery, battery tray and mounting plate as described in Chapter 5A.

2 Remove all traces of dirt from around the fluid cooler before proceeding.

3 Using a hose clamp or similar, clamp both the fluid cooler coolant hoses to minimise coolant loss during subsequent operations.

8.4 Release the retaining clips and disconnect the coolant hoses (arrowed) from the fluid cooler (viewed from above)

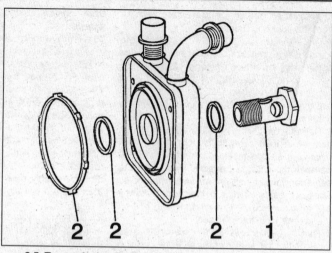

8.5 Transmission fluid cooler centre bolt (1) and seals (2)

4 Release the retaining clips, and disconnect both coolant hoses from the fluid cooler – be prepared for some coolant spillage **(see illustration)**. Wash off any spilt coolant immediately with cold water, and dry the surrounding area before proceeding further.

5 Slacken and remove the fluid cooler centre bolt, and remove the cooler from the transmission. Remove the seal from the centre bolt, and the two seals fitted to the rear of the cooler, and discard them; new ones must be used on refitting **(see illustration)**.

Refitting

6 Lubricate the new seals with clean automatic transmission fluid, then fit the two new seals to the rear of the fluid cooler, and a new seal to the centre bolt.

7 Locate the fluid cooler on the rear of transmission housing then refit the centre bolt. Ensure the cooler is correctly positioned then tighten the centre bolt to the specified torque setting.

8 Reconnect the coolant hoses to the fluid cooler, and secure them in position with their retaining clips. Remove the hose clamps then refit the battery (see Chapter 5A).

9 Top-up the cooling system as described in *Weekly checks* and check the transmission unit fluid level as described in Chapter 1A.

---

9 Transmission control system components – removal and refitting

Electronic control unit (ECU)

Note: *The automatic transmission electronic control system relies on accurate communication between the engine management ECU and the automatic transmission ECU. If the accelerator cable is removed and/or adjusted, or if either ECU is renewed, then both ECUs must be 'initialised'. The initialisation procedure requires access to specialised electronic test equipment and so it is recommended that this operation is entrusted to a suitably-equipped Peugeot dealer.*

Removal

1 Remove the battery (see Chapter 5A).

2 Disconnect the earth lead from the ECU mounting plate then release the plate tabs from the battery tray slots and lift the assembly out of position **(see illustrations)**.

3 Lift the retaining clip and disconnect the wiring connector from the ECU then remove the ECU and mounting plate from the vehicle

(see illustration). If necessary, undo the retaining nuts and separate the ECU and mounting plate.

Refitting

4 Refitting is the reverse of removal, ensuring the wiring connector is securely reconnected.

Output shaft speed sensor

Caution: Be careful not to allow dirt into the transmission unit during this procedure.

Removal

5 The output shaft sensor is fitted to the rear of the transmission unit.

6 To gain access to the sensor, remove the battery and battery tray as described in Chapter 5A.

7 Trace the sensor wiring back to its connector, located next to the transmission main wiring harness connector. Unclip the connector from its bracket then disconnect it **(see illustration)**.

8 Wipe clean the area around the sensor then slacken and remove the sensor retaining bolt. Remove the sensor along with its sealing ring; discard the sealing ring, a new one must be used on refitting.

9.2a Disconnect the earth lead from the ECU mounting plate . . .

9.2b . . . then unclip the plate from the battery tray

9.3 Release the retaining clip and disconnect the wiring connector from the ECU

9.7 Disconnecting the output shaft speed sensor wiring connector

9.13 Release the retaining clip (arrowed) then disconnect the main wiring connector from the transmission unit

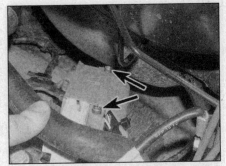

9.14a Unscrew the two bolts (arrowed) and free the connector from the transmission unit

Refitting

9 Refitting is the reverse of removal, noting the following points.

a) Fit a new sealing ring to the sensor and tighten the sensor bolt to the specified torque.

b) On completion, check the transmission fluid level as described in Chapter 1A.

Input shaft speed sensor

Caution: Be careful not to allow dirt into the transmission unit during this procedure.

10 The input shaft speed sensor is located on the left-hand end of the transmission unit.

11 To gain access to the sensor, chock the rear wheels, firmly apply the handbrake then jack up the front of the vehicle and securely support it on axle stands (see *Jacking and vehicle support*). Remove the left-hand front roadwheel.

12 To gain access to the main wiring connector, remove the battery and battery tray (see Chapter 5A).

13 Lift the retaining clip and disconnect the main wiring connector from the top of the transmission unit (**see illustration**).

14 Unscrew the two bolts and free the main wiring connector from the transmission unit. Cut the cable tie securing the wiring to the connector cover then release the clips and slide the cover off the connector (**see illustrations**).

15 Trace the wiring back from the sensor being removed, freeing it from all the relevant retaining clips and ties, to the main wiring connector. Carefully release the retaining clips then slide the sensor connector out from the rear of the main connector, noting which way around it is fitted (**see illustration**).

16 Wipe clean the area around the sensor. Slacken and remove the retaining bolt then remove the sensor along with its sealing ring (**see illustration**). Discard the sealing ring, a new one must be used on refitting.

Refitting

17 Refitting is the reverse of removal, noting the following points.

a) Fit a new sealing ring to the sensor and tighten the sensor bolt to the specified torque.

9.14b Cut the cable tie . . .

b) Ensure the sensor wiring is correctly routed and retained by all the necessary clips and ties.

c) Clip the sensor wiring back into the main wiring connector, ensuring it is fitted the right way around. Slide the cover back onto the main connector, ensuring it is clipped securely in position, and secure the wiring to the cover with a new cable tie. Secure the connector to the transmission unit with the retaining bolts.

d) On completion, check the transmission fluid level as described in Chapter 1A.

Fluid pressure sensor

Caution: Be careful not to allow dirt into the transmission unit during this procedure.

Removal

18 The fluid pressure sensor is located on the

9.15 Release the retaining clips and free the relevant wiring connector from the main connector

9.14c . . . then slide the cover off the rear of the connector

base of the transmission unit.

19 To gain access to the sensor, chock the rear wheels, firmly apply the handbrake then jack up the front of the vehicle and securely support it on axle stands (see *Jacking and vehicle support*). Remove the left-hand front roadwheel.

20 Drain the transmission fluid as described in Section 2.

21 Disconnect the sensor connector from the main wiring connector as described in paragraphs 12 to 15.

22 Wipe clean the area around the sensor then slacken and remove the sensor retaining bolts (**see illustration**). Remove the sensor along with its sealing ring; discard the sealing ring, a new one must be used on refitting.

Refitting

23 Refitting is the reverse of removal, noting

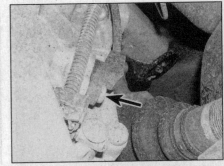

9.16 Input shaft sensor retaining bolt (arrowed)

7B

9.22 Fluid pressure sensor is secured to the base of the transmission unit by two bolts (arrowed)

the following points.

a) *Fit a new sealing ring to the sensor and tighten the sensor bolts to the specified torque.*

b) *Ensure the sensor wiring is correctly routed and retained by all the necessary clips and ties.*

c) *Clip the sensor wiring back into the main wiring connector, ensuring it is fitted the right way around. Slide the cover back onto the main connector, ensuring it is clipped securely in position, and secure the wiring to the cover with a new cable tie.*

d) *On completion, refill the transmission with fluid as described in Section 2.*

Multi-function switch

Note: *The multi-function switch is slotted to allow for adjustment. Accurate adjustment requires the use of the special Peugeot electronic test equipment and so must be entrusted to a suitably-equipped Peugeot dealer. If the original switch is to be refitted, ensure accurate alignment marks are made prior to removal.*

Removal

24 Remove the battery and battery tray (see Chapter 5A).

25 Position the selector lever firmly against its detent mechanism in the P position.

26 Slacken and remove the nut and clamp bolt securing the selector lever to the transmission shaft **(see illustration 7.27)**. Make alignment marks between the shaft and lever then free the lever from the shaft.

27 Remove the retaining clip and free the selector cable from transmission bracket. Position the cable clear of the selector shaft.

28 Disconnect the switch connector from the main wiring connector as described in paragraphs 12 to 15.

29 Make accurate alignment marks between the multi-function switch and transmission unit then unscrew the retaining bolts and remove the switch.

Refitting

30 Locate the multi-function switch back on the selector shaft. Align the marks made prior to removal then refit the switch bolts, tightening them to the specified torque.

31 Clip the sensor wiring back into the main wiring connector, ensuring it is fitted the right way around. Slide the cover back onto the main connector, ensuring it is clipped securely in position, and secure the wiring to the cover with a new cable tie. Locate the connector on the transmission unit and securely tighten its retaining bolts.

32 Reconnect the main wiring connector to the transmission unit.

33 Seat the selector cable in the transmission bracket and engage the selector lever with the transmission shaft. Ensure the marks made on removal are correctly aligned then refit the lever clamp bolt and nut and tighten securely.

34 Secure the selector cable in position with the retaining clip then adjust the cable as described in Section 3.

35 Refit the battery and battery tray (see Chapter 5A).

10 Automatic transmission – removal and refitting

Removal

1 Chock the rear wheels, then firmly apply the handbrake. Jack up the front of the vehicle, and securely support it on axle stands (see *Jacking and vehicle support*). Remove both front roadwheels.

2 Undo the screws securing the front section of the left-hand wheelarch liner to the base of the bumper. Remove the fasteners (pull out

the centre pin then remove the complete fastener) securing the liner section to the body then manoeuvre the front section of the liner out from underneath the wing **(see illustrations)**.

3 Remove both driveshafts as described in Chapter 8.

4 Remove the automatic transmission ECU as described in Section 9.

5 Remove the battery tray and mounting plate (see Chapter 5A).

6 Remove the air cleaner housing and intake duct as described in Chapter 4A. With the housing removed, undo the bolt and remove the housing mounting bracket from the left-hand side of the engine compartment. Also remove the crankshaft sensor.

7 Remove the starter motor (Chapter 5A).

8 Unclip the selector cable end fitting off the balljoint on the transmission lever. Remove the retaining clip then free the outer cable from its bracket and position it clear of the transmission unit **(see illustrations 4.3a and 4.3b)**.

9 Using a hose clamp or similar, clamp both the fluid cooler coolant hoses to minimise coolant loss. Release the retaining clips and disconnect both coolant hoses from the fluid cooler – be prepared for some coolant spillage **(see illustration 8.4)**. Wash off any spilt coolant immediately with cold water, and dry the surrounding area before proceeding further.

10 Lift the retaining clip and disconnect the main wiring connector from the transmission wiring block, located at the rear of the unit. Also disconnect the output shaft speed sensor wiring connector (located next to the main connector) then position the wiring harness clear of the transmission unit **(see illustrations 9.13 and 9.7)**.

11 Disconnect the wiring connector from the speedometer drive. Undo the retaining nut/bolt(s), and disconnect the earth straps from the top of the transmission housing **(see illustration)**. Free the wiring from any relevant retaining clips, and position it clear of the transmission.

12 Undo the retaining bolts and remove the lower driveplate cover plate (where fitted) from the transmission.

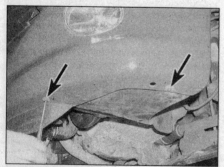

10.2a Slacken and remove the retaining screws (arrowed) . . .

10.2b . . . and fasteners . . .

10.2c . . . and remove the front section of the left-hand wheelarch liner

10.11 Unscrew the bolts (arrowed) and disconnect the earth leads from the transmission unit

13 Access to the torque converter retaining nuts is gained via the starter motor aperture. Use a socket and extension bar to rotate the crankshaft pulley to align the first nut with the aperture **(see illustration)**. Unscrew the nut then rotate the crankshaft 120°. Remove the second nut then rotate the crankshaft another 120° Unscrew the third and final nut and discard all three nuts; new ones must be used on refitting.

14 To ensure that the torque converter does not fall out as the transmission is removed, secure it in position using a length of metal strip bolted to one of the starter motor bolt holes.

15 Place a jack with a block of wood beneath the engine, to take the weight of the engine. Alternatively, attach a couple of lifting eyes to the engine, and fit a hoist or support bar to take the engine weight.

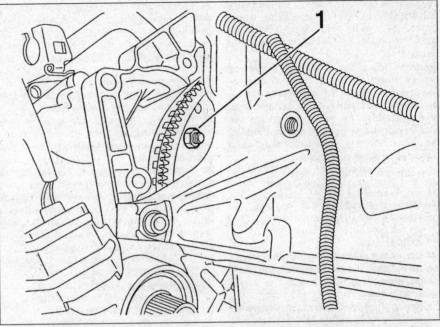

10.13 Access to the torque converter nuts (1) is gained via the starter motor aperture

16 Place a jack and block of wood beneath the transmission, and raise the jack to take the weight of the transmission.

17 Slacken and remove the centre nut and washer from the left-hand engine/ transmission mounting then undo the mounting bolts and remove the mounting. Unscrew the bolts securing the mounting bracket to the body and remove the bracket **(see illustrations)**.

18 Slide the spacer off the mounting stud, then unscrew the stud from the top of the transmission housing and remove it along with its washer. If the mounting stud is tight, a universal stud extractor can be used to unscrew it.

19 Unscrew the nuts and bolts and remove the mounting link securing the rear engine/transmission mounting to the subframe **(see illustrations)**.

20 With the jack positioned beneath the transmission taking the weight, slacken and remove the remaining bolts securing the transmission housing to the engine. Note the correct fitted positions of each bolt and the necessary brackets, as they are removed, to use as a reference on refitting. Make a final check that all components have been disconnected, and are positioned clear of the transmission so that they will not hinder the removal procedure.

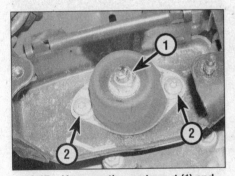

10.17a Unscrew the centre nut (1) and mounting bolts (2) . . .

10.17b . . . then lift off the left-hand mounting

10.17c Unscrew the bolts (locations arrowed) and remove the mounting bracket from the body

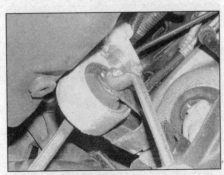

10.19a Unscrew the mounting nuts and bolts . . .

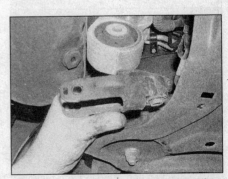

10.19b . . . and remove the rear mounting link

7B

21 With the bolts removed, move the trolley jack and transmission to the left, to free it from its locating dowels. If necessary, lower the engine slightly to enable the transmission to be freed.

Caution: Take great care not to place any excess strain on the exhaust system or damage the radiator if the engine is moved. On models equipped with air conditioning, care must also be taken to ensure the auxiliary drivebelt pulleys do not damage the air conditioning pipes on the right-hand side of the engine compartment.

22 Once the transmission is free, lower the jack and manoeuvre the unit out from under the car. Remove the locating dowels from the transmission or engine if they are loose, and keep them in a safe place.

Refitting

23 Ensure that the bush fitted to the centre of the crankshaft is in good condition, and apply a little Molykote BR2 grease to the torque converter centring pin.

Caution: Do not apply too much, otherwise there is a possibility of the grease contaminating the torque converter.

24 Ensure that the engine/transmission locating dowels are correctly positioned then raise the transmission unit into position. Align the torque converter studs with the driveplate holes then engage the transmission unit with the engine.

Caution: Do not allow the weight of the transmission unit to hang on the torque converter as the unit is installed.

25 With the transmission and engine correctly joined, refit the transmission-to-engine unit bolts and tighten them to the specified torque.

26 Screw the new nuts onto the torque converter studs, tightening them lightly only, rotating the crankshaft as necessary. Tighten all three nuts to the specified Stage 1 torque setting. Once all have been tightened to the Stage 1 torque, go around and tighten them to the specified Stage 2 torque setting.

27 The remainder of refitting is the reverse of removal, noting the following.

a) Apply thread-locking fluid to the left-hand engine/transmission mounting stud threads, prior to refitting it to the transmission. Tighten the stud to the specified torque.

b) Tighten all nuts and bolts to the specified torque (where given).

c) Renew the driveshaft oil seals, then refit the driveshafts (see Chapter 8).

d) Reconnect the selector cable and adjust as described in Section 3.

e) On completion, check the transmission fluid level as described in Chapter 1A.

11 Automatic transmission overhaul – general information

1 In the event of a fault occurring with the transmission, it is first necessary to determine whether it is of an electrical, mechanical or hydraulic nature and, to do this, special test equipment is required. It is therefore essential to have the work carried out by a Peugeot dealer if a transmission fault is suspected.

2 Do not remove the transmission from the car for possible repair before professional fault diagnosis has been carried out, since most tests require the transmission to be in the vehicle.

Chapter 8
Driveshafts

Contents

Degrees of difficulty

Easy, suitable for novice with little experience	**Fairly easy,** suitable for beginner with some experience	**Fairly difficult,** suitable for competent DIY mechanic 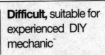	**Difficult,** suitable for experienced DIY mechanic	**Very difficult,** suitable for expert DIY or professional

Specifications

Lubrication (overhaul only – see text)

Lubricant type/specification .... Use only special grease supplied in sachets with gaiter kits – joints are otherwise pre-packed with grease and sealed

Torque wrench settings

	Nm	lbf ft
Driveshaft retaining nut:		
Staked nut	245	181
Nut retained with locking cap and R-clip	325	240
Right-hand driveshaft intermediate bearing retaining bolt nuts		
Petrol engine models	10	7
Diesel engine models	13	10
Roadwheel bolts	85	63
Suspension lower arm balljoint clamp bolt nut	40	30

1 General information

1 Drive is transmitted from the differential to the front wheels by means of two solid-steel driveshafts of unequal length.

2 Both driveshafts are splined at their outer ends, to accept the wheel hubs, and are threaded so that each hub can be fastened by a large nut. The inner end of each driveshaft is splined, to accept the differential sun gear.

3 Constant velocity (CV) joints are fitted to each end of the driveshafts, to ensure that the smooth and efficient transmission of power at all suspension and steering angles. On petrol engine models, the outer constant velocity joints are of the spider-and-yoke type; on diesel engine models, they are of the ball-and-cage type. The inner constant velocity joints are of the tripod type on all models.

4 On the right-hand side, due to the length of the driveshaft, the inner constant velocity joint is situated approximately halfway along the shaft's length, and an intermediate support bearing is mounted in the engine/transmission rear mounting bracket. The inner end of the driveshaft passes through the bearing (which prevents any lateral movement of the driveshaft inner end) and the inner constant velocity joint outer member.

2 Driveshafts – removal and refitting

Removal

Note: *Do not allow the vehicle to rest on its wheels with one or both driveshafts removed, as damage to the wheel bearing(s) may result. If moving the vehicle is unavoidable, temporarily insert the outer end of the driveshaft(s) in the hub(s) and tighten the hub nut(s): in this case, the inner end(s) of the driveshaft(s) must be supported, for example by suspending with string from the vehicle underbody. Do not allow the driveshaft to hang down under its own weight.*

1 If necessary, slacken the driveshaft nut (see paragraphs 4 to 6).

2 Chock the rear wheels of the car and firmly apply the handbrake. Jack up the front of the car and support it on axle stands (see *Jacking and vehicle support*). Remove the appropriate front roadwheel. Where necessary, remove the retaining bolts, screws and clips and remove the undercover (where fitted) from beneath the engine/transmission unit.

3 Drain the transmission oil or fluid as described in Chapter 7A or 7B (as applicable) or be prepared for some fluid loss as the shafts are removed.

4 On models where the driveshaft nut is staked, using a hammer and a chisel or similar tool, tap up the staking securing the driveshaft retaining nut in position **(see illustration)**. Note that a new retaining nut must be used on refitting.

2.4 Where the driveshaft nut is staked in position, relieve the staking with a suitable chisel-nosed tool

8

2.5a Where the driveshaft nut is secured with an R-clip, withdraw the R-clip ...

2.5b ... then remove the locking cap

2.6 Have an assistant firmly depress the brake pedal whilst you slacken the driveshaft nut (note wheelbolts – arrowed)

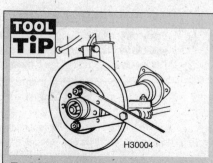

Tool Tip 1: Using a fabricated tool to hold the front hub stationary whilst the driveshaft nut is slackened.

2.7 Unscrew the nut and withdraw the lower arm balljoint clamp bolt

Tool Tip 2: To free the lower arm, attach a long bar (such as a jack handle) securely to the lower arm. Fit a block of wood to the inner end of the bar, to act as a pivot, then use the bar to pull the lower arm out from the swivel hub.

5 On models where the driveshaft nut is secured by an R-clip, withdraw the R-clip and remove the locking cap from the driveshaft retaining nut (see illustrations).

6 Refit at least two roadwheel bolts to the front hub, and tighten them securely. Have an assistant firmly depress the brake pedal to prevent the front hub from rotating, then using a socket and a long extension bar, slacken and remove the driveshaft retaining nut (see illustration). Alternatively, a tool can be fabricated from two lengths of steel strip (one long, one short) and a nut and bolt; the nut and bolt forming the pivot of a forked tool. Bolt the tool to the hub using two wheel bolts, and hold the tool to prevent the hub from rotating as the driveshaft retaining nut is undone (see Tool Tip 1). This nut is very tight; make sure that there is no risk of pulling the car off the axle stands (see Jacking and vehicle support). Note: If the roadwheel trim allows access to the driveshaft nut, the initial slackening can be done with the vehicle resting on its wheels on the ground.

7 Slacken and remove the suspension lower arm balljoint clamp bolt and nut (see illustration). Discard the nut – a new one must be used on refitting.

Left-hand driveshaft

8 Turn the steering onto full right-hand lock.

9 Pull down on the lower arm to free its balljoint from the swivel hub (see Tool Tip 2). Once the balljoint is freed from the swivel hub, peg the lower arm in position by inserting a suitable socket in between the top of the arm inner end and the subframe (see illustration 2.15).

10 Recover the protector plate from lower arm balljoint (see illustration).

11 Carefully pull the swivel hub assembly outwards, and withdraw the driveshaft outer constant velocity joint from the hub assembly (see illustration). If necessary, the shaft can be tapped out of the hub using a soft-faced mallet.

12 Support the driveshaft, then withdraw the inner constant velocity joint from the transmission, taking care not to damage the driveshaft oil seal. Remove the driveshaft from the vehicle (see illustration).

2.10 Free the lower arm balljoint from the swivel hub and remove the protector plate (arrowed)

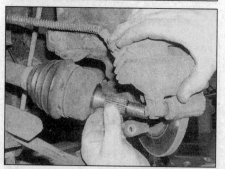

2.11 Free the driveshaft outer joint from the swivel hub ...

2.12 ... then free the inner joint from the transmission and remove the driveshaft from the vehicle

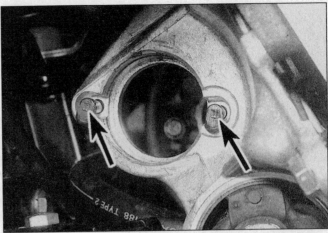

2.13a On the right-hand driveshaft, slacken the two intermediate bearing retaining bolt nuts . . .

2.13b . . . then rotate the bolts through 90° to disengage their offset heads (arrowed) from the bearing (shown with driveshaft removed for clarity)

Right-hand driveshaft

13 Loosen the two intermediate bearing retaining bolt nuts, then rotate the bolts through 90°, so that their offset heads are clear of the bearing outer race **(see illustrations)**.
14 Turn the steering onto full left-hand lock.
15 Pull down on the lower arm to free its balljoint from the swivel hub **(see Tool Tip 2)** Once the balljoint is freed from the swivel hub, peg the lower arm in position by inserting a suitable socket in between the top of the arm inner end and the subframe **(see illustration)**.
16 Recover the protector plate from lower arm balljoint **(see illustration)**.

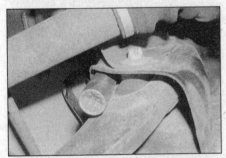

2.15 Secure the lower arm clear of the swivel hub by inserting a socket in between the top of the arm and the subframe

17 Carefully pull the swivel hub assembly outwards, and withdraw the driveshaft outer constant velocity joint from the hub assembly **(see illustration)**. If necessary, the shaft can be tapped out of the hub using a soft-faced mallet.
18 Support the outer end of the driveshaft, then pull on the inner end of the shaft to free the intermediate bearing from its mounting bracket.
19 Once the driveshaft end is free from the transmission, slide the dust seal/plate off the inner end of the shaft, noting which way around it is fitted, and remove the driveshaft **(see illustration)**.

Refitting

20 Before installing the driveshaft, examine the driveshaft oil seal in the transmission for signs of damage or deterioration and, if necessary, renew it, referring to Chapter 7A or 7B for further information. (Having got this far it is worth renewing the seal as a matter of course.)
21 Thoroughly clean the driveshaft splines, and the apertures in the transmission and hub assembly. Apply a thin film of multi-purpose grease (Peugeot recommend the use of Total 3945) to the oil seal lips, and to the driveshaft outer joint splines and shoulders. Check that all gaiter clips are securely fastened.

Left-hand driveshaft

22 Offer up the driveshaft, and locate the joint splines with those of the differential sun gear, taking great care not to damage the oil seal. Push the joint fully into position.
23 Locate the outer constant velocity joint splines with those of the swivel hub, and slide the joint back into position in the hub.
24 Fit the protector plate to the lower arm balljoint.
25 Align the lower arm balljoint with the swivel hub. Remove the socket (used to peg the arm in position) and seat the balljoint shank correctly in the swivel hub, aligning the protector plate tang with the hub slot. Insert the clamp bolt then fit the new nut and tighten to the specified torque.
26 Lubricate the inner face and threads of the driveshaft retaining nut with clean engine oil (Peugeot recommend the use of Molykote D321R) and fit it to the end of the driveshaft (a new nut must be used on models with a staked nut). Use the method employed on removal to prevent the hub from rotating, and tighten the driveshaft retaining nut to the specified torque. Check that the hub rotates freely.
27 On models where the driveshaft nut is staked, stake the new nut into the driveshaft

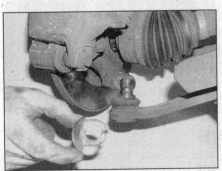

2.16 Recover the protector plate from the lower arm balljoint

2.17 Free the driveshaft outer joint from the swivel hub . . .

2.19 . . . then free the intermediate bearing from its bracket and recover the dust seal from the shaft inner end

8

2.27 Where the driveshaft nut is staked in position, tighten the new nut then stake it firmly into the driveshaft groove

2.39 Secure the right-hand driveshaft intermediate bearing in position then slide the dust seal tight up against the oil seal

groove using a hammer and punch **(see illustration)**.

28 On models where the driveshaft nut is secured by an R-clip, engage the locking cap with the driveshaft nut so that one of its cut-outs is aligned with the driveshaft hole. Secure the cap in position with the R-clip **(see illustrations 2.5a and 2.5b)**.

29 Refit the roadwheel and undercover (where fitted), then lower the vehicle to the ground and tighten the roadwheel bolts to the specified torque.

30 Top-up/refill the transmission with the specified type and amount of fluid/oil, and check the level using the information given in Chapter 7A or 7B.

Right-hand driveshaft

31 Check that the intermediate bearing rotates smoothly, without any sign of roughness or undue free play between its inner and outer races. If necessary, renew the bearing as described in Section 5. Examine the dust seal for signs of damage or deterioration, and renew if necessary.

32 Apply a smear of grease to the outer race of the intermediate bearing, and to the inner lip of the dust seal.

33 On models with an automatic transmission unit, check the condition of the O-ring fitted to the differential sun gear shaft. Renew the O-ring if it shows signs of damage or deterioration.

34 On all models, pass the inner end of the

shaft through the bearing mounting bracket, then carefully slide the dust seal/plate into position on the driveshaft, ensuring that its flat surface is facing the transmission.

35 Carefully locate the inner driveshaft splines with those of the differential sun gear, taking care not to damage the oil seal. Align the intermediate bearing with its mounting bracket, and push the driveshaft fully into position. If necessary, use a soft-faced mallet to tap the outer race of the bearing into position in the mounting bracket.

36 Locate the outer constant velocity joint splines with those of the swivel hub, and slide the joint back into position in the hub.

37 Fit the protector plate to the lower arm balljoint.

38 Align the lower arm balljoint with the swivel hub. Remove the socket (used to peg the arm in position) and seat the balljoint shank correctly in the swivel hub, aligning the protector plate tang with the hub slot. Insert the clamp bolt then fit the new nut and tighten to the specified torque.

39 Ensure that the intermediate bearing is correctly seated, then rotate its retaining bolts back through 90°, so that their offset heads are resting against the bearing outer race. Evenly and progressively tighten the retaining bolt nuts to the specified torque. Ensure that the dust seal/plate is tight against the driveshaft oil seal **(see illustration)**.

40 Carry out the operations described above in paragraphs 26 to 30.

3 Driveshaft rubber gaiters – renewal

1 Remove the driveshaft from the car as described in Section 2 and proceed as described under the relevant sub-heading.

Outer joint

2 Secure the driveshaft in a vice equipped with soft jaws. Mark the position of the gaiter on the driveshaft then release the two gaiter retaining clips. If necessary, the gaiter retaining clips can be cut to release them.

3 Slide the gaiter down the shaft, to expose the outer constant velocity joint. Scoop out the excess grease.

4 Using a hammer and suitable soft metal drift, sharply strike the inner member of the outer joint to drive it off the end of the shaft. The joint is retained on the driveshaft by a circlip, and striking the joint in this manner forces the circlip into its groove, so allowing the joint to slide off.

5 Once the joint assembly has been removed, remove the circlip from the groove in the driveshaft splines, and discard it. A new circlip must be fitted on reassembly.

6 Withdraw the gaiter from the driveshaft.

7 With the constant velocity joint removed from the driveshaft, thoroughly clean the joint and dry it thoroughly. Carry out a visual inspection of the joint.

8 Move the inner splined driving member from side-to-side, to expose each ball in turn at the top of its track. Examine the balls for cracks, flat spots, or signs of surface pitting.

9 Inspect the ball tracks on the inner and outer members. If the tracks have widened, the balls will no longer be a tight fit. At the same time, check the ball cage windows for wear or cracking between the windows.

10 If on inspection, any of the constant velocity joint components are found to be worn or damaged, it will be necessary to renew the complete joint assembly (where available), or even the complete driveshaft (where no joint components are available separately). Refer to your Peugeot dealer for further information on parts availability. If the joint is in satisfactory condition, obtain a repair kit consisting of a new gaiter, circlip, retaining clips, and the correct type and quantity of grease.

11 Tape over the splines on the end of the driveshaft, to protect the new gaiter. Slide the gaiter onto the shaft and locate it correctly on the driveshaft.

12 Remove the tape and fit the new circlip to the driveshaft, ensuring it is correctly located in the driveshaft groove **(see illustration)**.

13 Locate the outer joint on the driveshaft splines and slide it on until the inner member abuts the circlip **(see illustration)**. Tap the joint outer member sharply with a hammer and soft-metal drift to force the inner member over the circlip and fully onto the driveshaft.

3.12 Fit the new circlip to the groove in the driveshaft splines . . .

3.13 . . . then locate the joint outer member on the splines and slide it over the circlip. Ensure that the joint is firmly retained by the circlip . . .

Pull on the joint assembly to make sure it is securely retained by the circlip.

14 Work the grease well into the ball tracks of the joint and fill the gaiter with any excess **(see illustration)**.

15 Locate the outer lip of the gaiter in the groove(s) on the joint outer member and ensure the gaiter inner end is correctly seated in the driveshaft groove. Where there is no groove, align the gaiter with the marks made prior to removal.

16 Ensure the gaiter is correctly located then lift the inner lip of the gaiter to equalise the air pressure inside.

17 Ensure the gaiter is correctly located then secure it in position with the retaining clips. Note that there are two possible types of retaining clip which are secured as follows.

18 The most frequently used type of clip simply clips around the gaiter and is secured in position by crimping its raised section. In the absence of the special tool, carefully compress the clip raised section using a pair of side cutters, taking great care not to cut through the clip.

19 The other type of clip is in the form of a metal strap with a buckle at one end. Pass the end of the strap through the buckle slot the seat the clip on the gaiter; if sufficient clip is available wrap the clip twice around the gaiter. In the absence of the special tool, use a hook fabricated out of welding rod and a pair of pliers, to pull the clip tightly to remove all slack then bend the strap back over the buckle. Cut off the excess then bend the strap end behind the buckle before folding the

3.14 . . . then pack the joint and gaiter with the grease supplied

buckle firmly down onto the strap to secure the clip in position **(see illustrations)**.

20 Check the joint moves smoothly in all directions then refit the driveshaft as described in Section 2.

Inner joint

21 Remove the outer constant velocity joint as described in paragraphs 2 to 5.

22 Tape over the splines on the driveshaft and carefully remove the outer joint gaiter. It is recommended that the outer gaiter is also renewed, regardless of its apparent condition.

23 Mark the position of the inner joint gaiter on the driveshaft then cut/release the two gaiter retaining clips **(see illustration)**.

24 Free the gaiter from the inner joint outer member then remove the outer member and spring from the shaft **(see illustrations)**. Slide the gaiter off and remove it from the shaft.

25 Thoroughly clean the joint. Check the

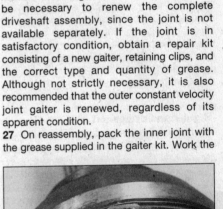

3.19a Wrap the retaining clip around the gaiter (twice if possible) and pull it tight using a pair of pliers and a hook fabricated out of welding rod

tripod joint bearings and joint outer member for signs of wear, pitting or scuffing on their bearing surfaces. Check that the bearing rollers rotate smoothly and easily around the tripod joint, with no traces of roughness.

26 If on inspection, the tripod joint or outer member reveal signs of wear or damage, it will be necessary to renew the complete driveshaft assembly, since the joint is not available separately. If the joint is in satisfactory condition, obtain a repair kit consisting of a new gaiter, retaining clips, and the correct type and quantity of grease. Although not strictly necessary, it is also recommended that the outer constant velocity joint gaiter is renewed, regardless of its apparent condition.

27 On reassembly, pack the inner joint with the grease supplied in the gaiter kit. Work the

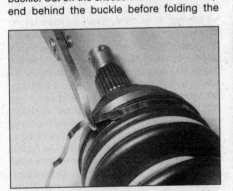

3.19b Bend the clip back over the buckle then cut off the excess

3.19c Fold the clip end underneath the buckle . . .

3.19d . . . then fold the buckle firmly down onto the clip to secure it in position

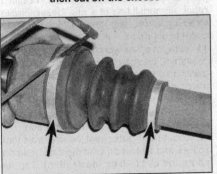

3.23 Cut the inner and outer clips (arrowed) to release them

3.24a Free the inner joint outer member from the gaiter . . .

3.24b . . . and recover the spring

8

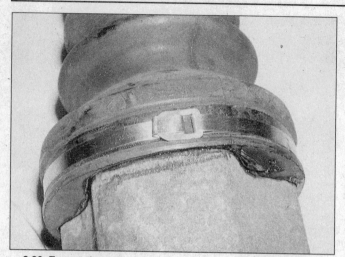

3.30 Ensure the gaiter retaining clips are both securely fitted

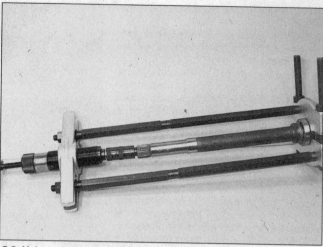

5.3 Using a long-reach bearing puller to remove the intermediate bearing from the right-hand driveshaft

grease well into the bearing tracks and rollers, while twisting the joint.

28 Clean the shaft, using emery cloth to remove any rust or sharp edges which may damage the gaiter. Slide the gaiter inner end plastic bush (where fitted) onto the shaft and locate it in the groove. Slide the gaiter onto the shaft and locate it correctly in the driveshaft groove.

29 Fit the spring to the end of the driveshaft then refit the outer member, engaging it correctly with the gaiter.

30 Ensure the gaiter is correctly located then lift the inner lip of the gaiter to equalise the air pressure inside. Fit both the inner and outer retaining clips, securing them in position using the information given in paragraphs 17 to 19 **(see illustration)**. Ensure that the gaiter retaining clips are securely tightened, then check that the joint moves freely in all directions.

31 Refit the outer constant velocity joint components using the information given in paragraph 12 to 20.

32 Check the joints move smoothly in all directions then refit the driveshaft as described in Section 2.

4 Driveshaft overhaul – general information

1 If any of the checks described in Chapter 1A or 1B reveal wear in any driveshaft joint, first remove the roadwheel trim or centre cap (as appropriate).

2 On models with a staked driveshaft nut, if the staking is still effective, the driveshaft nut should be correctly tightened; if in doubt, relieve the staking, then tighten the nut to the specified torque and restake it into the driveshaft grooves. Refit the roadwheel trim or centre cap (as applicable), and repeat the check on the remaining driveshaft nut.

3 On models where the driveshaft nut is secured by an R-clip, if the R-clip is fitted, the driveshaft nut should be correctly tightened; if in doubt, remove the R-clip and locking cap, and use a torque wrench to check that the nut is securely fastened. Once tightened, refit the locking cap and R-clip, then refit the centre cap or trim. Repeat this check on the remaining driveshaft nut.

4 Road test the vehicle, and listen for a metallic clicking from the front as the vehicle is driven slowly in a circle on full-lock. If a clicking noise is heard, this indicates wear in the outer constant velocity joint. This means that the joint must be renewed; reconditioning is not possible.

5 If vibration, consistent with road speed, is felt through the car when accelerating, there is a possibility of wear in the inner constant velocity joints.

6 To check the joints for wear, remove the driveshafts, then dismantle them as described in Section 3; if any wear or free play is found, the affected joint must be renewed. In the case of the inner joints (and on some models,

the outer joints), this means that the complete driveshaft assembly must be renewed, as the joints are not available separately. Refer to your Peugeot dealer for information on the availability of driveshaft components.

5 Right-hand driveshaft intermediate bearing – renewal

Note: *A suitable bearing puller will be required, to draw the bearing and collar off the driveshaft end.*

1 Remove the right-hand driveshaft as described in Section 2 of this Chapter.

2 Check that the bearing outer race rotates smoothly and easily, without any signs of roughness or undue free play between the inner and outer races. If necessary, renew the bearing as follows.

3 Using a long-reach universal bearing puller, carefully draw the collar and intermediate bearing off the driveshaft inner end **(see illustration)**. Apply a smear of grease to the inner race of the new bearing, then fit the bearing over the end of the driveshaft. Using a hammer and suitable piece of tubing which bears only on the bearing inner race, tap the new bearing into position on the driveshaft, until it abuts the constant velocity joint outer member. Once the bearing is correctly positioned, tap the bearing collar onto the shaft until it contacts the bearing inner race.

4 Check that the bearing rotates freely, then refit the driveshaft.

Chapter 9
Braking system

Contents

Degrees of difficulty

| Easy, suitable for novice with little experience | | Fairly easy, suitable for beginner with some experience | | Fairly difficult, suitable for competent DIY mechanic | | Difficult, suitable for experienced DIY mechanic | | Very difficult, suitable for expert DIY or professional | |

Specifications

Front brakes

Type	Disc, with single-piston sliding caliper
Disc diameter:	
2.0 litre diesel engine models	266.0 mm
All other models	247.0 mm
Disc thickness:	
New:	
Solid disc:	
Early (pre 1999) 1.1 litre petrol engine models without ABS	10.0 mm
All other models	13.0 mm
Ventilated disc	20.4 mm
Minimum thickness:	
Solid disc:	
Early (pre 1999) 1.1 litre petrol engine models without ABS	8.0 mm
All other models	11.0 mm
Ventilated disc	18.4 mm
Maximum disc run-out	0.05 mm
Brake pad friction material minimum thickness	2.0 mm

Rear brakes

Drum internal diameter:	
2.0 litre diesel engine models and all models fitted with ABS:	
New	203.0 mm
Maximum	205.0 mm
All other models*:	
New	180.0 mm
Maximum	183.0 mm
Brake shoe friction material minimum thickness	1.5 mm

*Some models fitted with an automatic transmission unit maybe equipped with the larger drums

9

Torque wrench settings

	Nm	lbf ft
ABS wheel sensor retaining bolt	9	7
Brake pedal pivot shaft nut	15	11
Brake pipe union nuts	15	11
Front brake caliper:		
Guide pin bolts	30	22
Mounting bracket bolts	105	77
Front brake disc screws	10	7
Handbrake lever mounting nuts	15	11
Load-sensitive pressure regulating valve bolt	18	13
Master cylinder-to-servo unit nuts	20	15
Rear hub nut:	200	148
Rear wheel cylinder retaining bolts	8	6
Roadwheel bolts	85	63
Vacuum pump retaining nut and bolts – diesel engine	20	15
Vacuum servo unit/pedal bracket/crossover linkage mounting nuts	20	15

1 General information

1 The braking system is of the servo-assisted, dual-circuit hydraulic type. The arrangement of the hydraulic system is such that each circuit operates one front and one rear brake from a tandem master cylinder. Under normal circumstances, both circuits operate in unison. However, in the event of hydraulic failure in one circuit, full braking force will still be available at two wheels. An Anti-lock Braking System (ABS) was available as an optional extra on most models (refer to Section 19 for further information on ABS operation).

2 The front disc brakes are actuated by single-piston sliding type calipers, which ensure that equal pressure is applied to each disc pad.

3 The rear drum brakes incorporate leading and trailing shoes, which are actuated by twin-piston wheel cylinders. A self-adjust mechanism is incorporated, to automatically compensate for brake shoe wear. As the brake shoe linings wear, the footbrake operation automatically operates the adjuster mechanism, which effectively lengthens the shoe strut and repositions the brake shoes, to maintain the lining-to-drum clearance. The hydraulic pressure applied to the rear brakes is regulated by the pressure control valve(s) to help prevent rear wheel lock-up during emergency braking

4 The handbrake provides an independent mechanical means of rear brake application.

5 On diesel engines, there is insufficient vacuum in the inlet manifold to operate the braking system servo effectively at all times. To overcome this problem, a vacuum pump is fitted to the engine to provide sufficient vacuum to operate the servo unit. The vacuum pump is mounted on the end of the cylinder head, and driven directly off the end of the camshaft.

Note: *When servicing any part of the system, work carefully and methodically; also observe scrupulous cleanliness when overhauling any part of the hydraulic system. Always renew components (in axle sets, where applicable) if in doubt about their condition, and use only genuine Peugeot replacement parts, or at least those of known good quality. Note the warnings given in 'Safety first' and at relevant points in this Chapter concerning the dangers of asbestos dust and hydraulic fluid.*

2 Hydraulic system – bleeding

⚠️ *Warning: Hydraulic fluid is poisonous; wash off immediately and thoroughly in the case of skin contact, and seek immediate medical advice if any fluid is swallowed or gets into the eyes. Certain types of hydraulic fluid are inflammable, and may ignite when allowed into contact with hot components; when servicing any hydraulic system, it is safest to assume that the fluid is inflammable, and to take precautions against the risk of fire as though it is petrol that is being handled. Hydraulic fluid is also an effective paint stripper, and will attack plastics; if any is spilt, it should be washed off immediately, using copious quantities of fresh water. Finally, it is hygroscopic (it absorbs moisture from the air) – old fluid may be contaminated and unfit for further use. When topping-up or renewing the fluid, always use the recommended type, and ensure that it comes from a freshly-opened sealed container.*

General

Note: *If difficulty is experienced in bleeding the braking circuit on models with ABS, this maybe due to air being trapped in the ABS hydraulic unit. If this is the case then the vehicle should be taken to a Peugeot dealer so that the system can be bled using special equipment.*

1 The correct operation of any hydraulic system is only possible after removing all air from the components and circuit; this is achieved by bleeding the system.

2 During the bleeding procedure, add only clean, unused hydraulic fluid of the recommended type; never re-use fluid that has already been bled from the system. Ensure that sufficient fluid is available before starting work.

3 If there is any possibility of incorrect fluid being already in the system, the brake components and circuit must be flushed completely with uncontaminated, correct fluid, and new seals should be fitted to the various components.

4 If hydraulic fluid has been lost from the system, or air has entered because of a leak, ensure that the fault is cured before proceeding further.

5 Park the vehicle on level ground, then chock the wheels and release the handbrake.

6 Check that all pipes and hoses are secure, unions tight and bleed screws closed. Clean any dirt from around the bleed screws.

7 Unscrew the master cylinder reservoir cap, and top the master cylinder reservoir up to the MAX level line; refit the cap loosely, and remember to maintain the fluid level at least above the DANGER level line throughout the procedure, or there is a risk of further air entering the system.

8 There are a number of one-man, do-it-yourself brake bleeding kits currently available from motor accessory shops. It is recommended that one of these kits is used whenever possible, as they greatly simplify the bleeding operation, and also reduce the risk of expelled air and fluid being drawn back into the system. If such a kit is not available, the basic (two-man) method must be used, which is described in detail below.

9 If a kit is to be used, prepare the vehicle as described previously, and follow the kit manufacturer's instructions, as the procedure may vary slightly according to the type being used; generally, they are as outlined below in the relevant sub-section.

10 Whichever method is used, the same sequence must be followed (paragraphs 11 and 12) to ensure the removal of all air from the system.

Bleeding sequence

11 If the system has been only partially disconnected, and suitable precautions were taken to minimise fluid loss, it should be necessary only to bleed that part of the system (ie, the primary or secondary circuit).

12 If the complete system is to be bled, then it should be done working in the following sequence:

 a) *Left-hand front brake.*
 b) *Right-hand front brake.*
 c) *Left-hand rear brake.*
 d) *Right-hand rear brake.*

Bleeding – basic (two-man) method

13 Collect a clean glass jar, a suitable length of plastic or rubber tubing which is a tight fit over the bleed screw, and a ring spanner to fit the screw. The help of an assistant will also be required.

14 Remove the dust cap from the first screw in the sequence. Fit the spanner and tube to the screw, place the other end of the tube in the jar, and pour in sufficient fluid to cover the end of the tube.

15 Ensure that the master cylinder reservoir fluid level is maintained at least above the DANGER level line throughout the procedure.

16 Have the assistant fully depress the brake pedal several times to build up pressure, then maintain it on the final downstroke.

17 While pedal pressure is maintained, unscrew the bleed screw (approximately one turn) and allow the compressed fluid and air to flow into the jar. The assistant should maintain pedal pressure, following it down to the floor if necessary, and should not release it until instructed to do so. When the flow stops, tighten the bleed screw again, have the assistant release the pedal slowly, and recheck the reservoir fluid level.

18 Repeat the steps given in paragraphs 16 and 17 until the fluid emerging from the bleed screw is free from air bubbles. If the master cylinder has been drained and refilled, and air is being bled from the first screw in the sequence, allow approximately five seconds between cycles for the master cylinder passages to refill.

19 When no more air bubbles appear, tighten the bleed screw securely, remove the tube and spanner, and refit the dust cap. Do not overtighten the bleed screw.

20 Repeat the procedure on the remaining screws in the sequence, until all air is removed from the system and the brake pedal feels firm again.

Bleeding – using a one-way valve kit

21 As their name implies, these kits consist of a length of tubing with a one-way valve fitted, to prevent expelled air and fluid being drawn back into the system; some kits include a translucent container, which can be positioned so that the air bubbles can be more easily seen flowing from the end of the tube.

22 The kit is connected to the bleed screw, which is then opened **(see illustration)**. The user returns to the driver's seat, depresses the brake pedal with a smooth, steady stroke, and slowly releases it; this is repeated until the expelled fluid is clear of air bubbles.

23 Note that these kits simplify work so much that it is easy to forget the master cylinder reservoir fluid level; ensure that this is maintained at least above the DANGER level line at all times.

Bleeding – using a pressure-bleeding kit

24 These kits are usually operated by the reservoir of pressurised air contained in the spare tyre. However, note that it will probably be necessary to reduce the pressure to a lower level than normal; refer to the instructions supplied with the kit.

25 By connecting a pressurised, fluid-filled container to the master cylinder reservoir, bleeding can be carried out simply by opening each screw in turn (in the specified sequence), and allowing the fluid to flow out until no more air bubbles can be seen in the expelled fluid.

26 This method has the advantage that the large reservoir of fluid provides an additional safeguard against air being drawn into the system during bleeding.

27 Pressure-bleeding is particularly effective when bleeding 'difficult' systems, or when bleeding the complete system at the time of routine fluid renewal.

All methods

28 When bleeding is complete, and firm pedal feel is restored, wash off any spilt fluid, tighten the bleed screws, and refit their dust caps.

29 Check the hydraulic fluid level in the master cylinder reservoir, and top-up if necessary (*Weekly checks*).

30 Discard any fluid that has been bled from the system; it will not be fit for re-use.

31 Check the feel of the brake pedal. If it feels at all spongy, air must still be present in the system, and further bleeding is required. Failure to bleed properly after a reasonable repetition of the bleeding procedure may be due to worn master cylinder seals.

2.22 Using a one-way valve kit to bleed a front brake caliper

3 Hydraulic pipes and hoses – renewal

Note: Before starting work, refer to the note at the beginning of Section 2 concerning the dangers of hydraulic fluid.

1 If any pipe or hose is to be renewed, minimise fluid loss by first removing the master cylinder reservoir cap, then tightening it down onto a piece of polythene to obtain an airtight seal. Alternatively, flexible hoses can be sealed, if required, using a proprietary brake hose clamp; metal brake pipe unions can be plugged (if care is taken not to allow dirt into the system) or capped immediately they are disconnected. Place a wad of rag under any union that is to be disconnected, to catch any spilt fluid.

2 If a flexible hose is to be disconnected, unscrew the brake pipe union nut before removing the spring clip which secures the hose to its mounting bracket **(see illustration)**.

3 To unscrew the union nuts, it is preferable to obtain a brake pipe spanner of the correct size; these are available from most large motor accessory shops **(see illustration)**. Failing this, a close-fitting open-ended spanner will be required, though if the nuts are tight or corroded, their flats may be rounded-off if the spanner slips. In such a case, a self-locking wrench is often the only way to unscrew a stubborn union, but it follows that the pipe and the damaged nuts must be

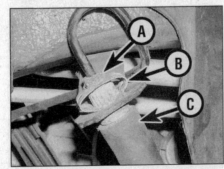

3.2 Unscrew the brake pipe union nut (A) then remove the retaining clip (B) and free the flexible hose (C) from its bracket

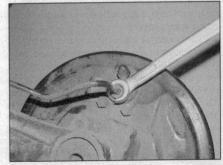

3.3 Using a brake pipe spanner to slacken a brake pipe union nut

4.3 Slacken and remove the caliper lower guide pin bolt . . .

4.4 . . . then pivot the caliper upwards . . .

4.5 . . . and withdraw the brake pads from the caliper bracket

renewed on reassembly. Always clean a union and surrounding area before disconnecting it. If disconnecting a component with more than one union, make a careful note of the connections before disturbing any of them.

4 If a brake pipe is to be renewed, it can be obtained, cut to length and with the union nuts and end flares in place, from Peugeot dealers. All that is then necessary is to bend it to shape, following the line of the original, before fitting it to the car. Alternatively, most motor accessory shops can make up brake pipes from kits, but this requires very careful measurement of the original, to ensure that the replacement is of the correct length. The safest answer is usually to take the original to the shop as a pattern.

5 On refitting, do not overtighten the union nuts. It is not necessary to exercise brute force to obtain a sound joint.

6 Ensure that the pipes and hoses are correctly routed, with no kinks, and that they are secured in the clips or brackets provided. After fitting, remove the polythene from the reservoir, and bleed the hydraulic system as described in Section 2. Wash off any spilt fluid, and check carefully for fluid leaks.

4 Front brake pads – renewal

> ⚠ **Warning: Renew both sets of front brake pads at the same time – never renew the pads on only one wheel,**

as uneven braking may result. Note that the dust created by wear of the pads may contain asbestos, which is a health hazard. Never blow it out with compressed air, and don't inhale any of it. An approved filtering mask should be worn when working on the brakes. DO NOT use petrol or petroleum-based solvents to clean brake parts; use brake cleaner or methylated spirit only.

Note: *New guide pin bolts must be used on refitting.*

1 Apply the handbrake, then jack up the front of the vehicle and support it on axle stands (see *Jacking and vehicle support*). Remove the front roadwheels.

2 Push the piston into its bore by pulling the caliper outwards.

3 Slacken and remove the caliper lower guide pin bolt; discard the bolt – a new bolt must be used on refitting **(see illustration)**.

4 Pivot the caliper upwards to gain access to the brake pads **(see illustration)**.

5 Withdraw the two brake pads from the caliper mounting bracket **(see illustration)**.

6 First measure the thickness of each brake pad's friction material. If either pad is worn at any point to the specified minimum thickness or less, all four pads must be renewed **(see illustration)**. Also, the pads should be renewed if any are fouled with oil or grease; there is no proper way of degreasing friction material, once contaminated. If any of the brake pads are worn unevenly, or are fouled with oil or grease, trace and rectify the cause before reassembly. New brake pads are available from Peugeot dealers.

7 If the brake pads are still serviceable, carefully clean them using a clean, fine wire brush or similar, paying particular attention to the sides and back of the metal backing. Clean out the grooves (where present) in the friction material, and pick out any large embedded particles of dirt or debris. Carefully clean the pad locations in the caliper body/mounting bracket.

8 Prior to fitting the pads, check that the guide pins are free to slide easily in the caliper mounting bracket, and check that the rubber guide pin gaiters are undamaged. Brush the dust and dirt from the caliper and piston, but **do not** inhale it, as it is injurious to health. Inspect the dust seal around the piston for damage, and the piston for evidence of fluid leaks, corrosion or damage. If attention to any of these components is necessary, refer to Section 8.

9 If new brake pads are to be fitted, the caliper piston must be pushed back into the cylinder to make room for them. Either use a G-clamp or similar tool, or use suitable pieces of wood as levers. Provided that the master cylinder reservoir has not been overfilled with hydraulic fluid, there should be no spillage, but keep a careful watch on the fluid level while retracting the piston. If the fluid level rises above the MAX level line at any time, the surplus should be siphoned off or ejected via a plastic tube connected to the bleed screw (see Section 2). **Note:** *Do not syphon the fluid by mouth, as it is poisonous; use a syringe or an old poultry baster.*

10 Install the pads in the caliper mounting bracket, ensuring that the friction material of each pad is against the brake disc. Ensure the pad anti-rattle springs are correctly located in the bracket then pivot the caliper down into position.

11 Align the cut-outs in the guide pin with the caliper slot then fit the new guide pin bolt **(see illustration)**. Ensure the bolt plate is correctly located in the guide pin cut-outs (the plate prevents the guide pin rotating as the bolt is tightened) then tighten the bolt to the specified torque.

12 Depress the brake pedal repeatedly, until the pads are pressed into firm contact with the brake disc, and normal (non-assisted) pedal pressure is restored.

4.6 Measuring brake pad friction material thickness

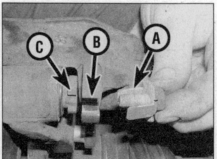

4.11 Ensure the bolt plate (A) engages correctly with the caliper slot (B) and guide pin slots (C) when fitting the guide pin bolt

13 Repeat the above procedure on the remaining front brake caliper.

14 Refit the roadwheels, then lower the vehicle to the ground and tighten the roadwheel bolts to the specified torque.

15 Finally, check the fluid level (*Weekly checks*).

 HAYNES HiNT *New pads will not give full braking efficiency until they have bedded-in. Be prepared for this, and avoid hard braking as far as possible for the first hundred miles or so after pad renewal.*

5 Rear brake shoes – renewal

⚠️ **Warning: Brake shoes must be renewed on both rear wheels at the same time – never renew the shoes on only one wheel, as uneven braking may result. Also, the dust created by wear of the shoes may contain asbestos, which is a health hazard. Never blow it out with compressed air, and don't inhale any of it. An approved filtering mask should be worn when working on the brakes. DO NOT use petrol or petroleum-based solvents to clean brake parts; use brake cleaner or methylated spirit only.**

1 Remove the brake drum (see Section 7).

2 Working carefully, and taking the necessary precautions, remove all traces of brake dust from the brake drum, backplate and shoes.

3 Measure the thickness of the friction material of each brake shoe at several points; if either shoe is worn at any point to the specified minimum thickness or less, all four shoes must be renewed as a set. The shoes should also be renewed if any are fouled with oil or grease; there is no proper way of degreasing friction material, once contaminated.

4 If any of the brake shoes are worn unevenly, or fouled with oil or grease, trace and rectify the cause before reassembly.

5 To renew the brake shoes, proceed as described under the relevant sub-heading. Prior to removing the shoes, take careful note of the correct fitted positions of the springs and adjuster strut, to use as a guide on reassembly.

Bosch brake shoes

6 Using a pair of pliers, remove the shoe retainer spring cups by depressing and turning them through 90°. With the cups removed, lift off the springs and withdraw the retainer pins **(see illustrations)**.

7 Ease the shoes out one at a time from the lower pivot point, to release the tension of the return spring, then disconnect the lower return spring from both shoes **(see illustrations)**.

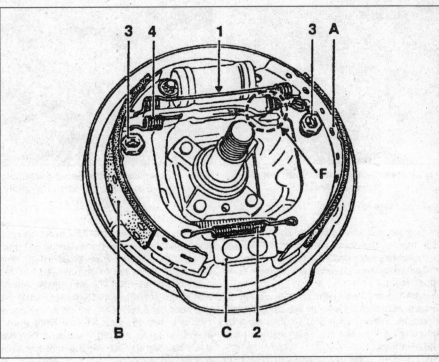

5.6a Bosch rear brake shoe components

A Leading shoe
B Trailing shoe
C Lower pivot point
F Adjuster strut mechanism
1 Upper return spring
2 Lower return spring
3 Retainer pin, spring and cup
4 Adjuster strut-to-trailing shoe spring

8 Ease the upper end of both shoes out from their wheel cylinder locations, taking care not to damage the wheel cylinder seals, and disconnect the handbrake cable from the trailing shoe. The brake shoe and adjuster strut assembly can then be manoeuvred out

5.6b Remove the spring cup . . .

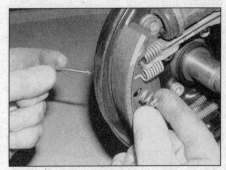

5.6c . . . and recover the spring and retainer pin

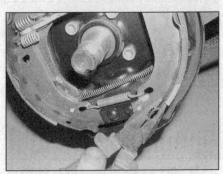

5.7a Ease the shoes out from the lower pivot point . . .

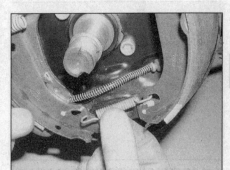

5.7b . . . then unhook and remove the lower return spring

9

5.8a Free the both shoes from the wheel cylinder . . .

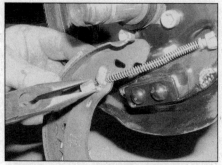

5.8b . . . then detach the handbrake cable and remove the shoe and strut assembly from the vehicle

5.8c Whilst the shoe assembly is removed, wrap a stout elastic band around the wheel cylinder to prevent the pistons being accidentally expelled

of position and away from the backplate. Do not depress the brake pedal until the brakes are reassembled; wrap an elastic band around the wheel cylinder pistons to retain them **(see illustrations)**.

9 With the shoe and adjuster strut assembly on a bench, make a note of the correct fitted positions of the springs and adjuster strut, to use as a guide on reassembly **(see illustrations)**.

10 Carefully unhook the adjuster strut bolt retaining spring from the leading shoe. Pivot the leading shoe out from the adjuster strut bolt then detach the leading shoe and return spring from the trailing shoe. Unhook the adjuster strut from the trailing shoe and recover the spring **(see illustrations)**.

11 Withdraw the adjuster bolt from the strut, and carefully examine the assembly for signs of wear or damage **(see illustration)**. Pay particular attention to the threads of the adjuster bolt and the knurled adjuster wheel, and renew if necessary. Note that left-hand and right-hand struts are not interchangeable. Also note that the strut adjuster bolts are not interchangeable; **the left-hand strut bolt has a left-handed thread**, and the right-hand bolt a right-handed thread.

12 All return springs should be renewed, regardless of their apparent condition; spring kits are available from Peugeot dealers.

13 Ensure that the components on the end of the strut are correctly positioned, then apply a little high-melting-point grease to the threads

of the adjuster bolt (Peugeot recommend the use of Lubritherm G200). Screw the adjuster wheel onto the bolt until only a small gap exists between the wheel and the head of the bolt, then fit the bolt in the strut.

14 Fit the adjuster strut retaining spring to the trailing shoe, ensuring that the shorter hook of the spring is engaged with the shoe. Attach the adjuster strut to the spring end, then ease the strut into its slot in the trailing shoe **(see illustration)**.

15 Engage the upper return spring with the trailing shoe, then hook the leading shoe onto the other end of the spring. Lever the leading shoe down until the adjuster bolt head is correctly located in its groove. Once the bolt is correctly located, hook its retaining spring

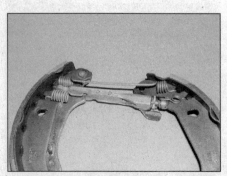

5.9a Note the correct fitted locations of the springs . . .

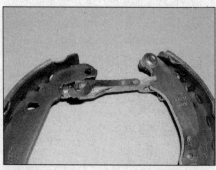

5.9b . . . and strut components before separating the shoe and strut assembly

5.10a Unhook the adjuster strut bolt spring . . .

5.10b . . . then pivot the leading shoe off the bolt and remove the shoe and upper return spring

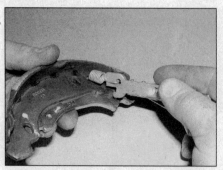

5.10c Unhook the adjuster strut from the trailing shoe, noting which way around its spring is fitted

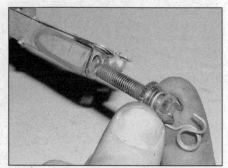

5.11 Check the adjuster strut bolt for signs of wear or damage

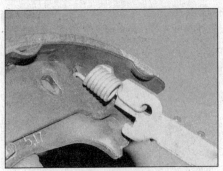

5.14 Hook the shorter end of the spring onto the trailing shoe, then attach the adjuster strut and locate it on the shoe, ensuring it is correctly engaged with the handbrake lever

into the slot on the leading shoe **(see illustration)**.

16 Peel back the rubber protective caps, and check the wheel cylinder for fluid leaks or other damage; check that both cylinder pistons are free to move easily. Refer to Section 9, if necessary, for information on wheel cylinder renewal.

17 Prior to installation, clean the backplate, and apply a thin smear of high-temperature brake grease or anti-seize compound (Peugeot recommend the use of Lubritherm G200) to all those surfaces of the backplate which bear on the shoes, particularly the wheel cylinder pistons and lower pivot point **(see illustration)**. Do not allow the lubricant to foul the friction material.

18 Remove the elastic band fitted to the wheel cylinder then manoeuvre the shoe and strut assembly into position. Attach the handbrake cable to the trailing shoe then locate the upper end of both shoes correctly with the wheel cylinder pistons. Fit the lower return spring to both shoes then ease the shoes into position on the lower pivot point.

19 Tap the shoes to centralise them with the backplate, then refit the shoe retainer pins and springs, and secure them in position with the spring cups.

20 Using a screwdriver, turn the strut adjuster wheel to expand the shoes until the brake drum just slides over the shoes.

21 Refit the brake drum (see Section 7).

22 Repeat the above procedure on the remaining rear brake.

23 Once both sets of rear shoes have been renewed, adjust the lining-to-drum clearance by repeatedly depressing the brake pedal with the handbrake fully released. Whilst depressing the pedal, have an assistant listen to the rear drums, to check that the adjuster strut is functioning correctly; if so, a clicking sound will be emitted by the strut as the pedal is depressed.

24 Check and, if necessary, adjust the handbrake as described in Section 15.

25 On completion, check the hydraulic fluid level as described in *Weekly checks*.

> **HAYNES HINT** *New shoes will not give full braking efficiency until they have bedded-in. Be prepared for this, and avoid hard braking as far as possible for the first hundred miles or so after pad renewal.*

Lucas brake shoes

26 Make a note of the correct fitted positions of the springs and adjuster strut, to use as a guide on reassembly **(see illustration overleaf)**.

27 On models with ABS, as a precaution, unbolt the rear wheel sensor and position it clear of the backplate (see Section 20).

28 Carefully unhook the upper return spring and remove it from the brake shoes.

29 Unhook the adjusting lever spring then remove the retaining hook and strut adjusting lever from the leading shoe.

30 Using a pair of pliers, remove the leading shoe retainer spring cup by depressing it and turning through 90°. Lift off the spring, then withdraw the retainer pin (see illustrations 5.6b and 5.6c). Free the leading shoe from the lower pivot point and adjuster strut then remove the shoe and lower return spring.

31 Remove the adjuster strut assembly from the trailing shoe.

32 Remove the trailing shoe retainer spring cup, spring and pin as described above, then detach the handbrake cable and remove the shoe from the vehicle. Do not depress the brake pedal until the brakes are reassembled; wrap a strong elastic band around the wheel cylinder pistons to retain them **(see illustration 5.8c)**.

33 Withdraw the forked end from the strut, and carefully examine the assembly for signs of wear or damage. Pay particular attention to the threads and the knurled adjuster wheel, and renew if necessary. Note that left-hand and right-hand struts are not interchangeable; the left-hand fork has a right-handed thread, and **the right-hand fork a left-handed thread**.

34 All return springs should be renewed, regardless of their apparent condition; spring kits are available from Peugeot dealers.

35 Peel back the rubber protective caps, and check the wheel cylinder for fluid leaks or other damage; check that both cylinder pistons are free to move easily. Refer to Section 9, if necessary, for information on wheel cylinder renewal.

36 Prior to installation, clean the backplate, and apply a thin smear of high-temperature brake grease or anti-seize compound (Peugeot recommend the use of Lubritherm G200) to all those surfaces of the backplate which bear on the shoes, particularly the wheel cylinder pistons and lower pivot point. Do not allow the lubricant to foul the friction material. Also lubricate the adjuster strut threads.

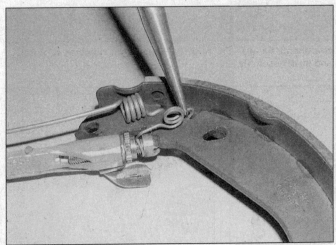

5.15 Fit the upper return spring and leading shoe. Ensure the shoe is correctly located in the bolt slot then hook the bolt spring into position

5.17 Lubricate the shoe contact surfaces of the rear backplate with a smear of high-melting point grease

9

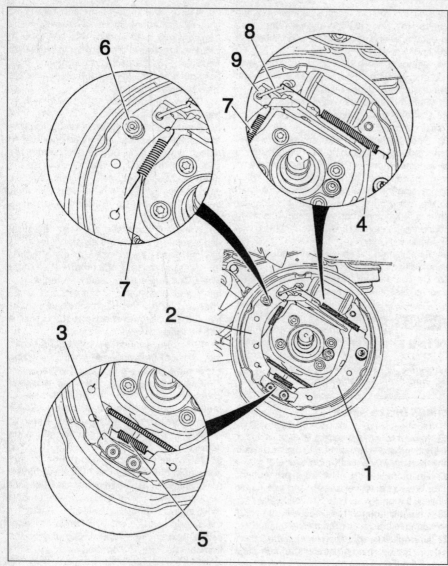

5.26 Lucas rear brake shoe components

1 Leading shoe
2 Trailing shoe
3 Lower pivot point
4 Upper return spring
5 Lower return spring
6 Retainer pin, spring and cup
7 Adjusting lever spring
8 Retaining hook
9 Strut adjusting lever

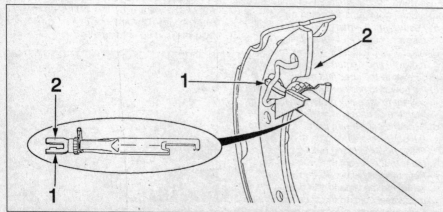

5.39 Ensure the adjuster strut forked end is positioned so its notched side (1) faces outwards and its flat side (2) inwards

37 Ensure that the handbrake lever stop-peg is correctly located against the edge of the trailing shoe, and remove the elastic band fitted to the wheel cylinder.

38 Connect the handbrake cable to the trailing shoe lever then locate the upper end of the shoe in the wheel cylinder piston. Refit the retainer pin and spring, and secure it in position with the spring cup.

39 Screw in the adjuster wheel until the minimum strut length is obtained, then hook the strut into position on the trailing shoe. Position the adjuster strut forked end, so that the notched side of its cut-out faces outwards **(see illustration)**.

40 Hook the lower return spring onto the trailing shoe then fit the leading shoe to the spring. Locate the leading shoe in position, ensuring that it is correctly engaged with the adjuster strut fork, then secure it in position with the retainer pin, spring and spring cup.

41 Fit the strut adjusting lever to the leading shoe pin. Ensure the lever is correctly engaged with the adjuster strut forked end and wheel then secure it in position with the retaining hook.

42 Fit the adjusting lever spring to the leading shoe ensuring the shorter hook of the spring is engaged with the lever.

43 Install the upper return spring, then tap the shoes to centralise them with the backplate.

44 On models with ABS, clean the rear wheel sensor body and its location in the backplate. Also clean the threads of the sensor retaining bolt. Lubricate the sensor body with multi-purpose grease (Peugeot recommend Esso Norva 275). Ensure the sensor tip is clean then seat the sensor in position in the backplate. Apply a drop of thread locking compound to the threads of the sensor bolt then install the bolt, tightening it to the specified torque.

45 Using a screwdriver, turn the strut adjuster wheel to expand the shoes until the brake drum just slides over the shoes.

46 Refit the brake drum as described in Section 7.

47 Repeat the above procedure on the remaining rear brake.

48 Once both sets of rear shoes have been renewed, adjust the lining-to-drum clearance by repeatedly depressing the brake pedal with the handbrake fully released. Whilst depressing the pedal, have an assistant listen to the rear drums, to check that the adjuster strut is functioning correctly; if so, a clicking sound will be emitted by the strut as the pedal is depressed.

49 Check and, if necessary, adjust the handbrake as described in Section 15.

50 On completion, check the hydraulic fluid level as described in *Weekly checks*.

HAYNES HINT *New shoes will not give full braking efficiency until they have bedded-in. Be prepared for this, and avoid hard braking as far as possible for the first hundred miles or so after pad renewal.*

6.3 Measuring front brake disc thickness using a micrometer

6.4 Checking front brake disc run-out using a dial gauge

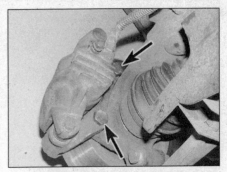

6.6a Unscrew the caliper bracket mounting bolts (arrowed) . . .

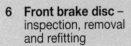

6 Front brake disc –
inspection, removal and refitting

Note: *Before starting work, refer to the note at the beginning of Section 4 concerning the dangers of asbestos dust.*

Inspection

Note: *If either disc requires renewal, BOTH should be renewed at the same time, to ensure even and consistent braking. New brake pads should also be fitted.*

1 Apply the handbrake, then jack up the front of the car and support it on axle stands (see *Jacking and vehicle support*). Remove the appropriate front roadwheel.

2 Slowly rotate the brake disc so that the full area of both sides can be checked; remove the brake pads if better access is required to the inboard surface. Light scoring is normal in the area swept by the brake pads, but if heavy scoring or cracks are found, the disc must be renewed.

3 It is normal to find a lip of rust and brake dust around the disc's perimeter; this can be scraped off if required. If, however, a lip has formed due to excessive wear of the brake pad swept area, then the disc's thickness must be measured using a micrometer. Take measurements at several places around the disc, at the inside and outside of the pad swept area; if the disc has worn at any point to the specified minimum thickness or less, the disc must be renewed **(see illustration)**.

4 If the disc is thought to be warped, it can be checked for run-out. Either use a dial gauge mounted on any convenient fixed point, while the disc is slowly rotated, or use feeler blades to measure (at several points all around the disc) the clearance between the disc and a fixed point, such as the caliper mounting bracket **(see illustration)**. If the measurements obtained are at the specified maximum or beyond, the disc is excessively warped, and must be renewed; however, it is worth checking first that the hub bearing is in good condition (*Steering and suspension check* in the relevant part of Chapter 1 and/or Chapter 10).

5 Check the disc for cracks, especially around the wheel bolt holes, and any other wear or damage, and renew if necessary.

6.6b . . . then slide the caliper assembly off the brake disc

Removal

Note: *New caliper mounting bolts will be needed on refitting.*

6 Slacken and remove the two bolts securing the brake caliper mounting bracket to the swivel hub. Slide the caliper assembly off the disc and tie it to the front strut spring, to avoid placing any strain on the hydraulic brake hose **(see illustrations)**.

7 Use chalk or paint to mark the relationship of the disc to the hub, then remove the screws securing the brake disc to the hub, and remove the disc **(see illustration)**. If it is tight, lightly tap its rear face with a hide or plastic mallet.

Refitting

8 Refitting is the reverse of the removal procedure, noting the following points:

a) *Ensure that the mating surfaces of the disc and hub are clean and flat.*

b) *Align (if applicable) the marks made on removal, and tighten the disc retaining screws to the specified torque.*

c) *If a new disc has been fitted, use a suitable solvent to wipe any preservative coating from the disc, before refitting the caliper.*

d) *Slide the caliper into position, ensuring the pads pass either side of the disc, then fit the new mounting bolts and tighten them to the specified torque.*

e) *Refit the roadwheel, then lower the vehicle to the ground and tighten the roadwheel bolts to the specified torque. On completion, repeatedly depress the brake pedal until normal (non-assisted) pedal pressure returns.*

6.7 Undo the retaining screws (arrowed) and remove the brake disc from the hub

7 Rear brake drum –
removal, inspection and refitting

Note: *Before starting work, refer to the note at the beginning of Section 5 concerning the dangers of asbestos dust.*

Removal

Note: *A new rear hub nut, cap and seal must be used on refitting.*

1 Chock the front wheels, then jack up the rear of the vehicle and support it on axle stands (see *Jacking and vehicle support*). Remove the appropriate rear wheel.

2 Using a hammer and a large flat-bladed screwdriver, carefully tap and prise the cap out of the centre of the brake drum **(see illustration)**. Discard the cap – a new one must be used on refitting.

7.2 Tap the cap out from the centre of the brake drum

7.3 Relieve the hub nut staking using a hammer and pointed-nose chisel

7.4 Remove the hub nut and thrustwasher . . .

7.5 . . . and slide off the brake drum

3 Using a hammer and chisel, tap up the staking securing the hub retaining nut to the groove in the stub axle (see illustration).
4 Using a socket and long bar, slacken and remove the rear hub nut, and withdraw the thrustwasher (see illustration). Discard the hub nut – a new nut must used on refitting.
5 It should now be possible to withdraw the brake drum and hub bearing assembly from the stub axle by hand (see illustration). It may be difficult to remove the drum due to the tightness of the hub bearing on the stub axle, or due to the brake shoes binding on the inner circumference of the drum. If the bearing is tight, tap the periphery of the drum using a hide or plastic mallet, or use a universal puller, secured to the drum with the wheel bolts, to pull it off. If the brake shoes are binding, first check that the handbrake is fully released. If necessary, fully slacken the handbrake cable adjuster nut, to obtain maximum freeplay in the cable to enable the drum to be removed.
6 Once the drum has been removed, slide the seal off the stub axle noting which way around it is fitted (see illustration). Discard the seal – a new one must be used on refitting. If the stub axle spacer is loose, remove it and store it with the brake drum.

Inspection

Note: *If either drum requires renewal, BOTH should be renewed at the same time, to ensure even and consistent braking. New brake shoes should also be fitted.*
7 Working carefully, remove all traces of brake dust from the drum, but *avoid inhaling the dust, as it is injurious to health.*

8 Clean the outside of the drum, and check it for obvious signs of wear or damage, such as cracks around the roadwheel bolt holes; renew the drum if necessary.
9 Examine carefully the inside of the drum. Light scoring of the friction surface is normal, but if heavy scoring is found, the drum must be renewed. It is usual to find a lip on the drum's inboard edge which consists of a mixture of rust and brake dust; this should be scraped away, to leave a smooth surface which can be polished with fine (120- to 150-grade) emery paper. If, however, the lip is due to the friction surface being recessed by excessive wear, then the drum must be renewed.
10 If the drum is thought to be excessively worn, or oval, its internal diameter must be measured at several points using an internal micrometer. Take measurements in pairs, the second at right-angles to the first, and compare the two, to check for signs of ovality. Provided that it does not enlarge the drum to beyond the specified maximum diameter, it may be possible to have the drum refinished by skimming or grinding; if this is not possible, the drums on both sides must be renewed. Note that if the drum is to be skimmed, BOTH drums must be refinished, to maintain a consistent internal diameter on both sides.

Refitting

11 If a new brake drum is to be installed, install the new shoes (see Section 5) and use a suitable solvent to remove any preservative coating that may have been applied to the drum interior.

12 Lubricate the lip of the new seal with a smear of multi-purpose grease. Ensure the spacer is in position then slide the seal onto the stub axle, ensuring its sealing lip is facing outwards (towards the hub).
13 Slide the brake drum assembly into position then refit the thrustwasher.
14 Fit the new hub nut and tighten it to the specified torque. Secure the nut in position by staking it firmly into the groove on the stub axle then tap the new hub cap into place in the centre of the brake drum (see illustration).
15 Depress the footbrake several times to operate the self-adjusting mechanism.
16 Repeat the above procedure on the remaining rear brake assembly (where necessary), then check and, if necessary, adjust the handbrake cable as described in Section 15.
17 On completion, refit the roadwheel(s), then lower the vehicle to the ground and tighten the wheel bolts to the specified torque.

8 Front brake caliper – removal, overhaul and refitting

Note: *Before starting work, refer to the note at the beginning of Section 2 concerning the dangers of hydraulic fluid, and to the warning at the beginning of Section 4 concerning the dangers of asbestos dust.*

Removal

Note: *New guide pin bolts must be used on refitting.*
1 Apply the handbrake, then jack up the front of the vehicle and support it on axle stands (see *Jacking and vehicle support*). Remove the appropriate roadwheel.
2 Minimise fluid loss by first removing the master cylinder reservoir cap, and then tightening it down onto a piece of polythene, to obtain an airtight seal. Alternatively, use a brake hose clamp, a G-clamp or a similar tool to clamp the flexible hose.
3 Clean the area around the brake caliper hose union, then loosen the union.
4 Slacken and remove the upper and lower caliper guide pin bolts; discard both bolts – new ones must be used on refitting.

7.6 Remove the seal from the stub axle

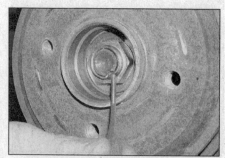

7.14 Tighten the new hub nut correctly then stake it securely into the stub axle groove

5 Lift the caliper away from the brake disc, then unscrew the caliper from the end of the brake hose. Note that the brake pads need not be disturbed, and can be left in position in the caliper mounting bracket.

Overhaul

6 With the caliper on the bench, wipe away all traces of dust and dirt, but *avoid inhaling the dust, as it is a health hazard.*

7 Where necessary, use a small flat-bladed screwdriver to carefully prise the dust seal retaining clip out of the caliper bore.

8 Withdraw the partially-ejected piston from the caliper body, and remove the dust seal.

 HAYNES HINT *If the piston cannot be withdrawn by hand, it can be pushed out by applying compressed air to the brake hose union hole. Only low pressure should be required, such as is generated by a foot pump. As the piston is expelled take great care not to trap your fingers between the piston and caliper.*

9 Using a small screwdriver, extract the piston hydraulic seal, taking great care not to damage the caliper bore.

10 Thoroughly clean all components, using only methylated spirit, isopropyl alcohol or clean hydraulic fluid as a cleaning medium. Never use mineral-based solvents such as petrol or paraffin, as they will attack the hydraulic system's rubber components. Dry the components immediately, using compressed air or a clean, lint-free cloth. Use compressed air to blow clear the fluid passages.

 Warning: Wear eye protection when using compressed air.

11 Check all components, and renew any that are worn or damaged. Check particularly the cylinder bore and piston; these should be renewed (note that this means the renewal of the complete body assembly) if they are scratched, worn or corroded in any way. Similarly check the condition of the guide pins and their bores in the caliper mounting bracket; both pins should be undamaged and (when cleaned) a reasonably tight sliding fit in the mounting bracket bores. If there is any doubt about the condition of any component, renew it.

12 If the assembly is fit for further use, obtain the appropriate repair kit; the components are available from Peugeot dealers in various combinations.

13 Renew all rubber seals and gaiters disturbed on dismantling as a matter of course; these should never be re-used.

14 On reassembly, ensure that all components are absolutely clean and dry.

15 Soak the piston and the new piston (fluid) seal in clean hydraulic fluid. Smear clean fluid on the cylinder bore surface.

16 Fit the new piston (fluid) seal, using only your fingers (no tools) to manipulate it into the cylinder bore groove.

17 Fit the new dust seal to the rear of the piston and seat the outer lip of the seal in the caliper body. Carefully ease the piston squarely into the caliper bore using a twisting motion. Press the piston fully into the bore, then seat the inner lip of the dust seal in the piston groove.

18 Where fitted, install the dust seal retaining clip, ensuring that it is correctly seated in the caliper groove.

19 If the guide pins are being renewed, lubricate the pin shafts with the special grease supplied in the repair kit, or a copper-based high-temperature brake grease or anti-seize compound (eg, Duckhams Copper 10). Locate the new gaiters in the pin grooves then insert the pins into the caliper bracket. Seat the gaiters correctly in the mounting bracket grooves then check both guide pins slide smoothly and easily.

Refitting

20 Screw the caliper body fully onto the flexible hose union

21 Ensure the brake pads are still correctly fitted to the caliper mounting bracket then fit the caliper over the pads.

22 Align the cut-out of each guide pin with the caliper slot then fit the new guide pin bolts **(see illustration)**. Ensure each bolt plate is correctly located in the guide pin cut-outs (the plate prevents the guide pin rotating as bolt is tightened) then tighten both bolts to the specified torque.

23 Tighten the brake hose union nut to the specified torque then remove the brake hose clamp or polythene (as applicable).

24 Bleed the hydraulic system (see Section 2). Providing the precautions described were taken to minimise brake fluid loss, it should only be necessary to bleed the relevant front brake.

25 Depress the brake pedal repeatedly, until the pads are pressed into firm contact with the brake disc, and normal (non-assisted) pedal pressure is restored.

26 Refit the roadwheel, then lower the vehicle to the ground and tighten the roadwheel bolts to the specified torque.

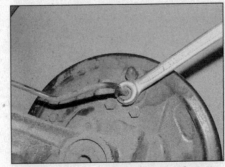

9.4 Unscrew the union nut and detach the brake pipe from the rear of the wheel cylinder

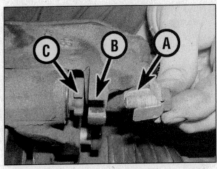

8.22 Ensure the bolt plate (A) engages correctly with the caliper slot (B) and guide pin slots (C) when fitting the guide pin bolt

27 On completion check the front brake hose is in no danger of contacting the tyre when the steering is on full lock. If necessary, adjust the hose position by slackening the union nut securing the pipe to the caliper hose and remove the hose clip. Position the hose end correctly in the bracket then secure it in position with the clip. Tighten the pipe union nut to the specified torque then bleed the front brake again (see Section 2).

9 Rear wheel cylinder – removal and refitting

Note: *Before starting work, refer to the note at the beginning of Section 2 concerning the dangers of hydraulic fluid, and to the warning at the beginning of Section 5 concerning the dangers of asbestos dust.*

Removal

Note: *New wheel cylinder retaining bolts will be needed on refitting.*

1 Remove the brake drum (see Section 7).

2 Using pliers, carefully unhook the upper brake shoe return spring, and remove it from both brake shoes. Pull the upper ends of the shoes away from the wheel cylinder to disengage them from the pistons.

3 Minimise fluid loss by first removing the master cylinder reservoir cap, and then tightening it down onto a piece of polythene, to obtain an airtight seal. Alternatively, use a brake hose clamp, a G-clamp or a similar tool to clamp the flexible hose at the nearest convenient point to the wheel cylinder.

4 Wipe away all traces of dirt around the brake pipe union at the rear of the wheel cylinder, and unscrew the union nut **(see illustration)**. Carefully ease the pipe out of the wheel cylinder, and plug or tape over its end to prevent dirt entry. Wipe off any spilt fluid immediately.

5 Unscrew the two wheel cylinder retaining bolts from the rear of the backplate, and remove the cylinder, taking great care not to allow surplus hydraulic fluid to contaminate the brake shoe linings. Discard the bolts – new ones must be used on refitting.

9

6 Note that it is not possible to overhaul the cylinder, since no components are available separately. If faulty, the complete wheel cylinder assembly must be renewed.

Refitting

7 Ensure that the backplate and wheel cylinder mating surfaces are clean, then spread the brake shoes and manoeuvre the wheel cylinder into position.

8 Engage the brake pipe, and screw in the union nut two or three turns to ensure that the thread has started.

9 Fit the new retaining bolts to the wheel cylinder and tighten them to the specified torque.

10 Tighten the brake pipe union nut to the specified torque then remove the clamp from the flexible brake hose, or the polythene from the master cylinder reservoir (as applicable).

11 Ensure that the brake shoes are correctly located in the cylinder pistons, then carefully refit the brake shoe upper return spring. Use a screwdriver to stretch the spring into position.

12 Refit the brake drum (see Section 7).

13 Bleed the brake hydraulic system as described in Section 2. Providing suitable precautions were taken to minimise loss of fluid, it should only be necessary to bleed the relevant rear brake.

10 Master cylinder –
removal, overhaul and refitting

Note: *Before starting, refer to the warning in Section 2 on the dangers of hydraulic fluid.*

Removal

Note: *A new O-ring must be used when refitting the master cylinder.*

1 Remove the master cylinder reservoir cap and filter and syphon the hydraulic fluid from the reservoir. **Note:** *Do not syphon the fluid by mouth, as it is poisonous; use a syringe or an old poultry baster.* Alternatively, open any convenient bleed screw in the system, and gently pump the brake pedal to expel the fluid through a plastic tube connected to the screw (see Section 2).

2 Disconnect the wiring connector from the brake fluid level sender unit.

3 On right-hand drive diesel engine models, disconnect the clutch master cylinder fluid supply hose from the side of the master cylinder reservoir. Plug the hose end to minimise fluid loss and prevent the entry of dirt into the system.

4 Remove the R-clip then free the fluid reservoir clip from the master cylinder pin. Carefully ease the reservoir out of from the top of the master cylinder and remove it from the vehicle.

5 Wipe clean the area around the brake pipe unions on the side of the master cylinder, and place absorbent rags beneath the pipe unions to catch any surplus fluid. Make a note of the correct fitted positions of the unions, then unscrew the union nuts and carefully withdraw the pipes. Plug or tape over the pipe ends and master cylinder orifices, to minimise the loss of brake fluid, and to prevent the entry of dirt into the system. Wash off any spilt fluid immediately with cold water.

6 Slacken and remove the two nuts securing the master cylinder to the vacuum servo unit, then withdraw the unit from the engine compartment. Remove the O-ring from the rear of the master cylinder, and discard it.

Overhaul

7 At the time of writing it was unclear whether it was possible to overhaul the master cylinder. Refer to your Peugeot dealer for the latest information on parts availability.

Refitting

8 Prior to refitting, measure the distance from the tip of the vacuum servo unit pushrod to the master cylinder mating surface of the unit. This should be 22.3 mm ± 0.1 mm. If not inspect the servo unit/brake pedal for signs of a problem. If nothing obvious is found, seek the advice of a Peugeot dealer before installing the master cylinder.

9 Remove all traces of dirt from the master cylinder and servo unit mating surfaces, and fit a new O-ring to the groove on the master cylinder body. Inspect the fluid reservoir seals and renew them if they show signs of damage or deterioration.

10 Fit the master cylinder to the servo unit, ensuring that the servo unit pushrod enters the master cylinder bore centrally. Refit the master cylinder mounting nuts, and tighten them to the specified torque.

11 Wipe clean the brake pipe unions, then refit them to the master cylinder ports and tighten them to the specified torque.

12 Lubricate the seals with a smear of brake fluid then ease the fluid reservoir back into position on the reservoir. Engage the reservoir clip with the master cylinder pin and secure it in position with the R-clip.

13 On right-hand drive diesel engine models, securely reconnect the clutch fluid hose to the reservoir.

14 On all models, reconnect the wiring connector to the fluid level sender.

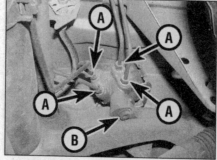

11.6 Load-sensitive pressure regulating valve brake pipe unions (A) and retaining bolt (B)

15 Refill the master cylinder reservoir with new fluid, and bleed the complete hydraulic system (see Section 2).

16 Bleed the clutch hydraulic system, where necessary (Chapter 6).

11 Rear brake pressure-regulating valve(s) –
testing, removal and refitting

Note: *Before starting work, refer to the warning at the beginning of Section 2 concerning the dangers of hydraulic fluid.*

1 On most models, a load-sensitive pressure regulating valve is fitted to the hydraulic circuit to each rear brake. The valve is mounted onto the underside of the rear of the vehicle, and is attached to the rear suspension by a spring. The valve measures the load on the rear axle, via the movement of the suspension, and regulates the hydraulic pressure being applied to the rear brakes to help prevent the rear wheels locking up under heavy braking.

2 On some models the valves are incorporated into the rear wheel cylinders; on these models the valves are pressure-sensitive only and are not affected by the load being carried by the vehicle.

3 Specialist equipment is required to check the performance of the valve(s), so if the valve is thought to be faulty, the car should be taken to a suitably-equipped Peugeot dealer for testing. Repairs are not possible and, if faulty, the valve must be renewed; on models with a load-sensitive valve, adjustment is possible but, again, specialist equipment is needed to carry out this procedure.

Removal

Note: *Before starting, refer to the warning in Section 2 on the dangers of hydraulic fluid.*

Load-sensitive valve

4 Firmly chock the front wheels, then jack up the rear of the vehicle and support it on axle stands (see *Jacking and vehicle support*).

5 Minimise fluid loss by first removing the master cylinder reservoir cap, and then tightening it down onto a piece of polythene, to obtain an airtight seal.

6 Wipe clean the area around the brake pipe unions on the valve, and place absorbent rags beneath the pipe unions to catch any surplus fluid **(see illustration)**. To avoid confusion on refitting, make alignment marks between the pipes and valve.

7 Slacken the union nuts and disconnect the brake pipes from the valve. Plug or tape over the pipe ends and valve orifices, to minimise the loss of brake fluid, and to prevent the entry of dirt into the system. Wash off any spilt fluid immediately with cold water.

8 Slacken and remove the valve retaining bolt then unhook the valve spring from its bolt and remove the valve assembly from underneath the vehicle.

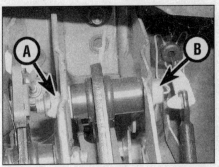

Pressure-sensitive valve

9 The valve is an integral part of the rear wheel cylinder. Refer to Section 9 for removal details.

Refitting

Load-sensitive valve

10 Prior to refitting, clean the valve retaining bolt threads and apply a few drops of thread-locking compound (Peugeot recommend the use of Loctite Frenetanch) to the bolt.
11 Manoeuvre the valve assembly into position, and hook the spring onto its suspension bolt. Align the valve correctly with its mounting bracket and secure it in position with the retaining bolt, tightening it to the specified torque.
12 Reconnect the brake pipes to their specific unions on the valve and tighten their union nuts to the specified torque.
13 Remove the polythene from the master cylinder reservoir and bleed the complete hydraulic system as described in Section 2. If a new valve assembly has been fitted, it is recommended that the vehicle is taken to a Peugeot dealer so the valve operation can be checked and, if necessary, adjusted using their special test equipment.

Pressure-sensitive valve

14 Refit the wheel cylinder as described in Section 9.

12 Brake pedal – removal and refitting

Removal

1 Access to the pedal is poor with the facia in position. The only way access can be significantly improved is to remove the facia as described in Chapter 11.
2 On left-hand drive models, remove the stop-light switch (see Section 18).
3 On all models, remove the pivot clip securing the servo unit pushrod (left-hand drive models) or crossover linkage (right-hand drive models) to the brake pedal. To remove the pivot clip, unhook its lower retaining tang then pivot it

upwards slightly before sliding it out of position **(see illustrations 13.9a and 13.9b)**.
4 Slacken and remove the pivot bolt and nut then manoeuvre the brake pedal out of position **(see illustration)**. Slide the spacer out from the pedal pivot.
5 Examine all components for signs of wear or damage and renew as necessary.

Refitting

6 Apply a smear of multi-purpose grease to the spacer and insert it into the pedal pivot bore.
7 Manoeuvre the pedal into position, making sure it is correctly engaged with the servo unit/crossover linkage (as applicable). Insert the pivot bolt and nut, tightening it to the specified torque.
8 Align the pedal with the pushrod/linkage (as applicable) and insert the pivot clip, ensuring it is securely clipped in position.
9 On left-hand drive models, install the stop-light switch (see Section 18)
10 Where necessary, refit the facia (see Chapter 11).

13 Vacuum servo unit – testing, removal and refitting

Testing

1 To test the operation of the servo unit, depress the footbrake several times to exhaust the vacuum, then start the engine whilst keeping the pedal firmly depressed. As the engine starts, there should be a noticeable 'give' in the brake pedal as the vacuum builds up. Allow the engine to run for at least two minutes, then switch it off. If the brake pedal is now depressed it should feel normal, but further applications should result in the pedal feeling firmer, with the pedal stroke decreasing with each application.
2 If the servo does not operate as described, first inspect the servo unit check valve as described in Section 14. On diesel engine models, also check the operation of the vacuum pump as described in Section 22.
3 If the servo unit still fails to operate satisfactorily, the fault lies within the unit itself.

12.4 Unscrew the nut (A) and withdraw the brake pedal bolt (B) pivot (shown with facia removed)

Repairs to the unit are not possible – if faulty, the servo unit must be renewed.

Removal

Note: *A new servo mounting gasket will be required on refitting.*

Right-hand drive models

4 Remove the battery and battery tray as described in Chapter 5A.
5 Remove the master cylinder as described in Section 10.
6 Disconnect the vacuum hose from servo unit check valve.
7 On petrol engine models with manual transmission, detach the clutch cable from the transmission unit (see Chapter 6).
8 On all models, remove the glovebox as described in Chapter 11, Section 27.
9 Remove the pivot clip securing the crossover linkage to the servo unit pushrod. To remove the pivot clip, unhook its lower retaining tang then pivot it upwards slightly before sliding it out of position **(see illustrations)**.
10 Unscrew the nuts securing the crossover linkage plate to the servo unit studs and the bolt securing the plate to the upper mounting bracket **(see illustration)**.
11 Release the retaining clips on the servo unit bore then ease the servo unit end of the crossover linkage slightly away from the bulkhead to gain access to the servo retaining clips (where fitted). Slide the clips off the servo unit studs.

13.9a Unhook the base of the pivot clip then pivot it upwards ...

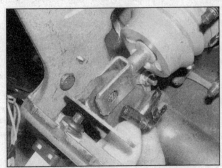

13.9b ... and slide it out from the servo unit pushrod

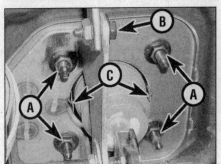

13.10 Unscrew the mounting nuts (A) and bracket bolt (B) then release the servo unit retaining clips (C)

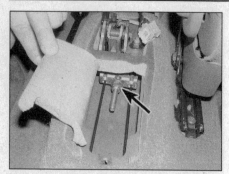

15.5 Remove the rear section of the centre console to gain access to the handbrake cable adjuster nut (arrowed)

12 Return to the engine compartment and remove the servo unit. Recover the seal which is fitted between the servo unit and bulkhead and discard it – a new one must be used on refitting.

Left-hand drive models

13 Remove the battery and battery tray as described in Chapter 5A.
14 Remove the master cylinder as described in Section 10.
15 Disconnect the vacuum hose from servo unit check valve.
16 On models with manual transmission, detach the clutch cable from the transmission unit (see Chapter 6).
17 Remove the pivot clip securing the brake pedal to the servo unit pushrod. To remove the pivot clip, unhook its lower retaining tang then pivot it upwards slightly before sliding it out of position.
18 Disconnect the wiring connector from the stop-light switch.
19 Unscrew the nuts securing the pedal mounting bracket to the servo unit studs and the bolt securing the bracket assembly to the upper mounting bracket.
20 Release the retaining clips located at the top and bottom of the servo unit bore then ease the pedal bracket assembly away from the bulkhead to gain access to the servo retaining clips (where fitted). **Note:** *If necessary, disconnect the steering column from the steering gear pinion to gain the necessary clearance required to position the pedal bracket assembly clear (see Chapter 10).*
21 Slide the retaining clips off the servo unit studs.
22 Return to the engine compartment and remove the servo unit. Recover the seal which is fitted between the servo unit and bulkhead and discard it – a new one must be used on refitting.

Refitting

23 Refitting is the reverse of removal, noting the following points.
  a) *Prior to refitting measure the distance from the end of the vacuum servo unit pushrod to the servo unit master cylinder mating surface. This should be 22.3 ± 0.1 mm; if not seek the advice of a Peugeot dealer.*

  b) *Ensure the servo unit and bulkhead mating surfaces are clean and dry and fit a new seal to the rear of the servo.*
  c) *Secure the servo in position with the retaining clips and tighten the servo unit/pedal bracket nuts to the specified torque.*
  d) *Refit the master cylinder (Section 10) and bleed the complete hydraulic system (Section 2).*

14 Vacuum servo unit check valve – removal, testing and refitting

Removal

1 Slacken the retaining clip (where fitted), and disconnect the vacuum hose from the servo unit check valve.
2 Withdraw the valve from its rubber sealing grommet, using a pulling and twisting motion. Remove the grommet from the servo.

Testing

3 Examine the check valve for signs of damage, and renew if necessary. The valve may be tested by blowing through it in both directions. Air should flow through the valve in one direction only – when blown through from the servo unit end of the valve. Renew the valve if this is not the case.
4 Examine the rubber sealing grommet and flexible vacuum hose for signs of damage or deterioration, and renew as necessary.

Refitting

5 Fit the sealing grommet into the servo unit.
6 Ease the check valve into position, taking care not to displace or damage the grommet. Reconnect the vacuum hose to the valve, and tighten its retaining clip (as applicable).
7 On completion, start the engine and check the check valve-to-servo unit connection for signs of air leaks.

15 Handbrake – adjustment

1 To check the handbrake adjustment, first apply the footbrake firmly several times with the handbrake released to establish correct shoe-to-drum clearance, then apply and release the handbrake several times to ensure that the self-adjust mechanism is fully adjusted. Applying normal moderate pressure, pull the handbrake lever to the fully-applied position, counting the number of clicks emitted from the handbrake ratchet mechanism. If adjustment is correct, there should be 4 to 7 clicks before the handbrake is fully applied. If this is not the case, adjust as follows.
2 Chock the front wheels, then jack up the rear of the vehicle and support it on axle stands (see *Jacking and vehicle support*).
3 For access to the handbrake adjuster nut,

remove the rear section of the centre console (Chapter 11).
4 Apply and release the handbrake a few times whilst observing the handbrake lever equaliser plate. The plate must remain square to the handbrake lever as the lever is applied and released. If not, there is a fault with the cables which must be rectified before adjustment can be carried out.
5 If the cables are operating freely, fully release the handbrake lever then slacken the adjuster nut **(see illustration)**.
6 Start the engine and apply the footbrake approximately forty times; this will ensure the self-adjusting mechanism is correctly adjusted.
7 Switch the engine off then tighten the adjuster nut until all the freeplay is removed from both handbrake cables. Fully apply and release the handbrake at least ten times to settle the cables in position.
8 With the handbrake lever set on the second notch of the ratchet mechanism, rotate the adjuster nut so that only a slight drag can be felt when the rear wheels/hubs are turned. Once this is so, fully release the handbrake lever, and check that the wheels/hubs rotate freely. Check the adjustment by applying the handbrake fully, counting the clicks from the handbrake ratchet and, if necessary, re-adjust.
9 Check the operation of the handbrake warning light (the light should illuminate when the lever is set on the first notch of the ratchet mechanism) then refit the centre console, then lower the vehicle to the ground.

16 Handbrake lever – removal and refitting

Removal

1 Remove the rear section of the centre console (Chapter 11).
2 Slacken the handbrake adjuster nut to obtain maximum freeplay in the cables, and disengage the inner cables from the handbrake lever equaliser plate.
3 Slacken and remove the three handbrake lever retaining nuts, and remove the lever from the vehicle **(see illustration)**.

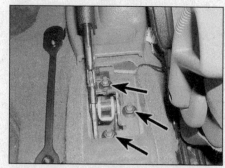

16.3 Handbrake lever is secured to the floor by three nuts (arrowed)

Refitting

4 Refitting is a reversal of removal, tightening the handbrake lever nuts to the specified torque. Prior to refitting the centre console, adjust the handbrake (see Section 15).

17 Handbrake cables –
removal and refitting

Removal

1 Remove the rear section of the centre console (Chapter 11). The handbrake cable consists of two sections, a right and a left-hand section, which are linked to the lever by an equaliser plate. Each section can be removed as follows.
2 Slacken the handbrake lever adjuster nut **(see illustration 15.5)** to obtain maximum freeplay in the cable(s), and disengage the inner cables from the handbrake lever plate.
3 Firmly chock the front wheels, then jack up the rear of the vehicle and support it on axle stands (see *Jacking and vehicle support*).
4 Referring to the relevant part of Chapter 4, remove the exhaust system heatshield(s) to gain access to the front end of the handbrake cables.
5 Prise off the retaining clip and free the cable from its guide on the underside of the fuel tank **(see illustration)**.
6 Free the front end of the outer cable from the body, then work back along the length of the cable, freeing it from all its retaining clips and guides.
7 Remove the rear brake shoes from the relevant side as described in Section 5.
8 Release the retaining clips **(see Tool Tip)** then free the handbrake outer cable out from the brake backplate, and remove it from underneath the vehicle **(see illustration)**.

Refitting

9 Refitting is a reversal of the removal procedure, adjusting the handbrake as described in Section 15.

18 Stop-light switch –
removal, refitting
and adjustment

Removal

1 On left-hand drive models, the stop-light switch is located on the pedal bracket behind the facia. On right-hand drive models the switch is fitted to the left-hand end of the pedal crossover linkage.
2 Reach up behind the facia and disconnect the wiring connector then pull the switch out from the pedal bracket **(see illustrations)**.

Refitting and adjustment

3 Hold the brake pedal down then press the switch fully into the mounting bracket (this will

17.5 Prise off the retaining clip and free the handbrake cable from the underside of the fuel tank

require the aid of an assistant on right-hand drive models).
4 Slowly release the brake pedal and pull it back up to its stop; the pedal will automatically adjust the position of the switch in the mounting bracket.
5 Reconnect the wiring connector, and check the operation of the stop-lights.

19 Anti-lock Braking System
(ABS) – general information

1 ABS is available as an option on certain models covered by this manual. The system comprises of a hydraulic unit and the four roadwheel sensors. The hydraulic unit contains the electronic control unit (ECU), the eight solenoid valves (two for each brake – one inlet and one outlet) and the electrically-driven return pump. The purpose of the system is to prevent the wheel(s) locking during heavy braking. This is achieved by automatic release of the brake on the relevant wheel, followed by re-application of the brake.
2 The solenoid valves are controlled by the ECU, which receives signals from the four wheel sensors (front sensors are fitted to the swivel hubs, and the rear wheel sensors are fitted to the rear of the backplates) which monitor the speed of rotation of each wheel. By comparing these signals, the ECU can determine the speed at which the vehicle is travelling. It can then use this speed to determine when a wheel is decelerating at an

18.2a Disconnect the wiring connector . . .

TOOL TIP

Release the handbrake cable end fitting clips by passing a close-fitting ring spanner over the end fitting.

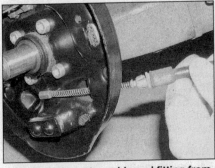

17.8 Free the outer cable end fitting from the backplate and remove the cable from the vehicle

abnormal rate, compared to the speed of the vehicle, and therefore predicts when a wheel is about to lock. During normal operation, the ABS system has no effect on braking and the hydraulic system functions in the same way as a non-ABS system.
3 If the ECU senses that a wheel is about to lock, it closes the relevant outlet solenoid valve in the hydraulic unit, which then isolates the brake on the relevant wheel, effectively sealing-in hydraulic pressure.
4 If the speed of rotation of the wheel continues to decrease at an abnormal rate, the ECU opens the relevant inlet solenoid valve and operates the return pump which returns the hydraulic fluid back to the master cylinder, releasing the brake. Once the speed of rotation of the wheel returns to an acceptable rate, the

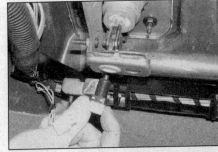

18.2b . . . then pull the stop-light switch out of its mounting bracket (shown with facia removed for clarity)

9

pump stops and the solenoid valves switch again. This allows hydraulic master cylinder pressure to return to the caliper/wheel cylinder (as applicable), which reapplies the brake. This cycle can be carried out many times a second.

5 The action of the solenoid valves and return pump creates pulses in the hydraulic circuit. When the ABS system is functioning, these pulses can be felt through the brake pedal.

6 The operation of the ABS is dependent on electrical signals. To prevent the system responding to any inaccurate signals, a built-in safety circuit monitors all signals received by the ECU. If an inaccurate signal or low battery voltage is detected, the system is automatically shut down and the warning light in the instrument panel is illuminated to inform the driver that the ABS system is not operational. Normal braking should still be available, however.

7 If a fault does develop in the ABS system, the vehicle must be taken to a Peugeot dealer for fault diagnosis and repair.

20 Anti-lock Braking System (ABS) components – removal and refitting

Hydraulic unit

Caution: Disconnect the battery before disconnecting the hydraulic unions from the hydraulic unit and do not reconnect the battery until after the hydraulic system has been bled. Plug the hydraulic unions of the unit and ensure it is stored upright (in the same position as it is fitted to the vehicle) and is not tipped onto its side, or upside down. Failure to do this could lead to air entering the unit, requiring the unit to be bled using special Peugeot test equipment on refitting (see Section 2).

Note: *Before starting work, refer to the note at the beginning of Section 2 concerning the dangers of hydraulic fluid.*

Removal

1 Disconnect the battery negative lead.

2 Apply the handbrake, then jack up the front of the vehicle and support it on axle stands (see *Jacking and vehicle support*). Remove the front roadwheels.

3 Remove all traces if dirt from the exterior of the hydraulic unit then disconnect the wiring connector.

4 Mark the locations of the hydraulic fluid pipes to ensure correct refitting, then unscrew the union nuts, and disconnect the pipes from the hydraulic unit. Be prepared for fluid spillage, and plug the open ends of the pipes and the hydraulic unit, to prevent dirt ingress and further fluid loss.

5 Slacken and remove the three mounting bolts and remove the hydraulic unit from the vehicle, keeping the unit upright.

Refitting

6 Manoeuvre the unit into position and securely tighten its mounting bolts.

7 Reconnect the hydraulic pipes to the correct unions on the unit and tighten the union nuts to the specified torque.

8 Securely reconnect the hydraulic unit wiring connector.

9 Bleed the complete hydraulic system as described in Section 2. Once the system is correctly bled, reconnect the battery.

Front wheel sensor

Removal

10 Disconnect the battery negative lead.

11 Apply the handbrake, then jack up the front of the vehicle and support securely on axle stands (see *Jacking and vehicle support*). To improve access, remove the front roadwheel.

12 Slacken and remove the bolts and remove the protective shield (where fitted) from the sensor.

13 Trace the wiring back from the sensor and separate the two halves of the wiring connector. Release the wiring from the all the relevant clips and ties, noting its routing.

14 Slacken and remove the retaining bolt and withdraw the sensor from the swivel hub.

Refitting

15 Ensure the mating surfaces of the sensor and swivel hub are clean and apply a little grease to the sensor body (Peugeot recommend Esso Norva 275) before refitting.

16 Make sure the sensor tip is clean then ease it into position in the swivel hub.

17 Clean the threads of the sensor bolt and

apply a few drops of thread locking compound. Refit the bolt and tighten it to the specified torque.

18 Work along the sensor wiring, making sure it is correctly routed, securing it in position with all the relevant clips and ties. Reconnect the wiring connector.

19 Refit the protective shield (where fitted) and securely tighten its bolts. Lower the vehicle and (where necessary) tighten the wheel bolts to the specified torque.

Rear wheel sensor

Removal

20 Chock the front wheels, then jack up the rear of the vehicle and support it on axle stands (see *Jacking and vehicle support*).

21 Trace the wiring back from the sensor and separate the two halves of the wiring connector. Release the wiring from the all the relevant clips and ties, noting its routing.

22 Slacken and remove the retaining bolt and withdraw the sensor from the swivel hub.

Refitting

23 Ensure the mating surfaces of the sensor and swivel hub are clean and apply a little grease (Peugeot recommend Esso Norva 275) to the sensor body before refitting.

24 Make sure the sensor tip is clean then ease it into position in the backplate.

25 Clean the threads of the sensor bolt and apply a few drops of thread locking compound. Refit the bolt and tighten it to the specified torque.

26 Work along the sensor wiring, making sure it is correctly routed, securing it in position with all the relevant clips and ties. Reconnect the wiring connector then lower the vehicle.

21 Vacuum pump (diesel engine models) – removal and refitting

Removal

1 On 1.9 litre engines, release the fasteners from the right-hand side and top of the engine cover then lift off the cover, taking care not to lose its mounting rubbers (see illustrations).

21.1a On 1.9 litre engines remove the fasteners from the right-hand side . . .

21.1b . . . and top of the engine cover . . .

21.1c . . . then lift the cover off the engine

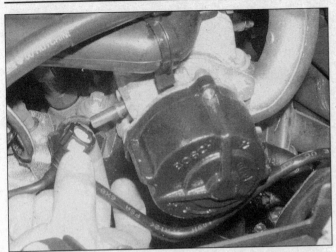

21.3 Disconnect the vacuum hose from the pump . . .

21.4 . . . then unscrew the mounting nut and bolts
(arrowed – 1.9 litre engine shown)

2 On 2.0 litre engines, remove the fasteners (rotate them 90° to release them) and lift off the engine cover.

3 Release the retaining clip and disconnect the vacuum hose from the pump **(see illustration)**.

4 Slacken and remove the retaining nut and bolts securing the pump to the left-hand end of the cylinder head **(see illustration)**.

5 Remove the pump, along with its two sealing rings. Discard the sealing rings – new ones must be used on refitting.

Refitting

6 Fit new sealing rings to the pump recesses **(see illustration)**.

7 Align the pump drive dog with the slot in the end of the camshaft then seat the pump on the cylinder head, ensuring that the O-rings remain correctly seated **(see illustration)**.

8 Refit the pump retaining nut and bolts and tighten them to the specified torque.

9 Reconnect the vacuum hose to the pump, and tighten its securing clip, then refit the engine cover.

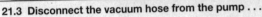

22 Vacuum pump (diesel engine models) – testing and overhaul

1 The operation of the braking system vacuum pump can be checked using a vacuum gauge.

2 Disconnect the vacuum pipe from the pump, and connect the gauge to the pump union using a suitable length of hose.

3 Start the engine and allow it to idle, then measure the vacuum created by the pump. As a guide, after one minute, a minimum of approximately 800 mm Hg should be recorded. If the vacuum registered is significantly less than this, it is likely that the pump is faulty. However, seek the advice of a Peugeot dealer before condemning the pump.

4 Overhaul of the vacuum pump is not possible, since no components are available separately for it. If faulty, the complete pump assembly must be renewed.

21.6 Ensure the sealing rings (arrowed) are correctly installed . . .

21.7 . . . then refit the pump aligning its drive dog with the camshaft slot (arrows – 2.0 litre engine shown)

9

Chapter 10
Suspension and steering

Contents

Degrees of difficulty

Easy, suitable for novice with little experience	**Fairly easy,** suitable for beginner with some experience	**Fairly difficult,** suitable for competent DIY mechanic	**Difficult,** suitable for experienced DIY mechanic	**Very difficult,** suitable for expert DIY or professional

Specifications

Steering
Power steering fluid type .... See *Lubricants and fluids*

Wheel alignment and steering angles
Camber .... 0° ± 30'
Castor:
  Manual steering .... 2° ± 30'
  Power steering .... 3° ± 30'
Front wheel toe setting .... 0° 7' ± 4' (0.75 ± 0.5 mm) toe-in

Roadwheels
Type .... Pressed-steel or aluminium alloy (depending on model)
Size .... 5B x 13 or 5.5J x 14 (depending on model)
Maximum run-out at rim .... 1.2 mm
Maximum eccentricity on tyre bead locating surface .... 0.8 mm

10

Torque wrench settings

	Nm	lbf ft

Front suspension

Anti-roll bar:
Mounting clamp bolts	104	77
Connecting link nuts	36	27
Lower arm balljoint clamp bolt	40	30
Lower arm mounting bolts	141	104
Strut upper mounting bolts	20	15
Strut upper mounting retaining nut	45	33
Strut-to-swivel hub bolt	54	40
Subframe mounting bolts	110	81

Rear suspension

Rear axle mounting bolts	110	81
Shock absorber lower mounting bolt	150	111
Shock absorber upper mounting bolt	70	52

Steering

Power steering pump:
Mounting bolts	25	18
Feed pipe union nut	20	15
Feed pipe clip bolt	20	15
Steering column mounting nuts and bolts	40	30
Steering column universal joint clamp bolt nut	25	18

Steering gear:
Mounting studs	10	7
Mounting nuts	80	59
Power steering feed and return pipe clamp bolt	20	15
Power steering pipe union nuts	8	6
Steering wheel bolt	35	26
Track rod balljoint (to swivel hub) nut	35	26
Track rod balljoint locknut	45	33
Track rod inner balljoint to steering rack	70	52

Roadwheels

Wheel bolts	85	63

1 General information

1 The independent front suspension is of the MacPherson strut type, incorporating coil springs and integral telescopic shock absorbers. The MacPherson struts are located by transverse lower suspension arms, which utilise rubber inner mounting bushes, and incorporate a balljoint at the outer ends. The front swivel hubs, which carry the wheel bearings, brake calipers and the hub/disc assemblies, are bolted to the MacPherson struts, and connected to the lower arms via the balljoints. A front anti-roll bar is fitted to most models. The anti-roll bar is rubber-mounted onto the subframe, and is connected directly to the front suspension struts.

2 The rear suspension is of the independent trailing arm type, which consists of two trailing arms, linked by a tubular crossmember. Torsion bars linking the trailing arms are situated in front of and behind the crossmember. On most models an anti-roll bar linking the arms passes through the centre of the crossmember.

3 The complete rear axle assembly is mounted onto the vehicle underbody by four 'Pay Free' rubber mountings. These mountings are designed to move slightly under extreme cornering forces. This movement of the rear axle assembly has the effect of actually turning the rear wheels slightly, to help steer the vehicle in the required direction. This improves the handling of the vehicle when cornering at high speeds.

4 The steering column has a universal joint fitted in the centre of its length, which is connected to an intermediate shaft having a second universal joint at its lower end. The lower universal joint is clamped to the steering gear pinion by means of a clamp bolt.

5 The steering gear is mounted onto the front subframe, and is connected by two track rods, with balljoints at their outer ends, to the steering arms projecting rearwards from the swivel hubs. The track rod ends are threaded, to facilitate adjustment.

6 Power-assisted steering is fitted as standard on some models, and is available as an option on most others. The hydraulic steering system is powered by a belt-driven pump, which is driven off the crankshaft pulley.

2 Front swivel hub assembly – removal and refitting

Removal

Note: *All self-locking nuts disturbed on removal must be renewed as a matter of course. These include the track rod balljoint nut, lower suspension arm balljoint clamp bolt nut, and the swivel hub clamp bolt nut. New brake caliper mounting bolts must also be used on refitting.*

1 If necessary, slacken the driveshaft nut (see paragraphs 3 to 5).

2 Chock the rear wheels of the car and firmly apply the handbrake. Jack up the front of the car and support it on axle stands (see *Jacking and vehicle support*). Remove the appropriate front roadwheel.

3 On models where the driveshaft nut is staked, using a hammer and a chisel or similar tool, tap up the staking securing the driveshaft retaining nut in position **(see illustration)**. Note that a new retaining nut must be used on refitting.

4 On models where the driveshaft nut is

2.3 Where the driveshaft nut is staked in position, relieve the staking with a suitable chisel-nosed tool

2.4a Where the driveshaft nut is secured with an R-clip, withdraw the R-clip . . .

2.4b . . . then remove the locking cap

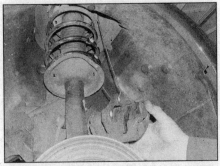

2.5 Have an assistant firmly depress the brake pedal whilst you slacken the driveshaft nut (note wheelbolts – arrowed)

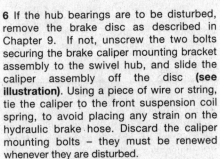

2.6 Tie the brake caliper to the coil spring to prevent the brake hose being strained

2.9 Releasing a track rod balljoint using a balljoint separator

secured by an R-clip, withdraw the R-clip and remove the locking cap from the driveshaft retaining nut **(see illustrations)**.

5 Refit at least two roadwheel bolts to the front hub, and tighten them securely. Have an assistant firmly depress the brake pedal to prevent the front hub from rotating, then using a socket and a long extension bar, slacken and remove the driveshaft retaining nut **(see illustration)**. Alternatively, a tool can be fabricated from two lengths of steel strip (one long, one short) and a nut and bolt; the nut and bolt forming the pivot of a forked tool. Bolt the tool to the hub using two wheel bolts, and hold the tool to prevent the hub from rotating as the driveshaft retaining nut is undone (see Chapter 8, Section 2). **Note:** *If the roadwheel trim allows access to the driveshaft nut, the initial slackening can be done with the vehicle resting on its wheels on the ground.*

6 If the hub bearings are to be disturbed, remove the brake disc as described in Chapter 9. If not, unscrew the two bolts securing the brake caliper mounting bracket assembly to the swivel hub, and slide the caliper assembly off the disc **(see illustration)**. Using a piece of wire or string, tie the caliper to the front suspension coil spring, to avoid placing any strain on the hydraulic brake hose. Discard the caliper mounting bolts – they must be renewed whenever they are disturbed.

7 Slacken and remove the bolt securing the support bracket (where fitted) to the top of the swivel hub.

8 On models with ABS, remove the wheel sensor from the swivel hub as described in Chapter 9.

9 On all models, slacken and remove the nut securing the steering gear track rod balljoint

to the swivel hub, and release the balljoint tapered shank using a balljoint separator **(see illustration)**.

10 Slacken and remove the suspension lower arm balljoint clamp bolt and nut **(see illustration)**. Discard the nut – a new one must be used on refitting.

11 Undo the nut and withdraw the swivel hub-to-suspension strut clamp bolt **(see illustration)**. Discard the nut – a new one must be used on refitting.

12 Pull down on the lower arm to free its balljoint from the swivel hub **(see Tool Tip)**. Once the balljoint is freed from the swivel hub,

2.10 Unscrew the nut and remove the balljoint clamp bolt from the swivel hub

2.11 Undo the nut and withdraw the strut clamp bolt from the swivel hub

TOOL TiP

To free the lower arm, attach a long bar (such as a jack handle) securely to the lower arm. Attach a block of wood to the inner end of the bar, to act as a pivot, then use the bar to pull the lower arm out from the swivel hub.

10

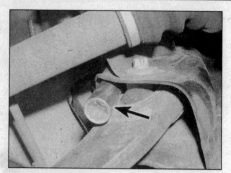

2.12 Pull the lower arm down and hold it in position by inserting a socket (arrowed) inbetween the arm and subframe

2.13 Remove the protector plate from the lower arm balljoint

2.19 Tighten the track rod balljoint nut to the specified torque

peg the lower arm in position by inserting a suitable socket in between the top of the arm inner end and the subframe **(see illustration)**.
13 Recover the protector plate from lower arm balljoint **(see illustration)**.
14 Free the swivel hub assembly from the end of the strut, then release it from the outer constant velocity joint splines, and remove it from the vehicle. If the swivel hub is a tight fit on the strut, use a large flat-bladed screwdriver to carefully open up the clamp a little.

Refitting

15 Ensure that the driveshaft outer constant velocity joint and hub splines are clean and dry. Apply a thin film of multi-purpose grease (Peugeot recommend the use of Total 3945) to the driveshaft outer joint splines then slide the hub fully onto the driveshaft splines.
16 Slide the hub assembly fully onto the suspension strut, aligning the split in the hub clamp with the lug on the base of the strut. Also ensure that the stop bosses on the strut are in contact with the top surface of the swivel hub. Insert the swivel hub-to-suspension strut clamp bolt then fit a new nut and tighten it to the specified torque.
17 Fit the protector plate to the lower arm balljoint.
18 Align the lower arm balljoint with the swivel hub. Remove the socket (used to peg the arm in position) and seat the balljoint shank correctly in the swivel hub, aligning the protector plate tang with the hub slot. Insert the clamp bolt then fit the new nut and tighten to the specified torque.

19 Locate the track rod balljoint in the swivel hub, then fit a new retaining nut and tighten it to the specified torque **(see illustration)**.
20 Referring to Chapter 9, refit the brake disc (where removed) to the hub and tighten its retaining screws to the specified torque. Slide the brake caliper assembly into position, ensuring the pads pass either side of the disc, then fit the new mounting bolts and tighten them to the specified torque (see Chapter 9).
21 Where necessary, refit the ABS wheel sensor as described in Chapter 9.
22 Refit the wiring support bracket (where fitted) to the top of the swivel hub, and tighten its retaining bolt securely.
23 Lubricate the inner face and threads of the driveshaft retaining nut with a smear of oil (Peugeot recommend the use of Molykote D321R) and fit it to the end of the driveshaft (a new nut must be used on models with a staked nut). Use the method employed on removal to prevent the hub from rotating, and tighten the driveshaft retaining nut to the specified torque (see Chapter 8). Check that the hub rotates freely.
24 On models where the driveshaft nut is staked, stake the new nut into the driveshaft groove using a hammer and punch **(see illustration)**.
25 On models where the driveshaft nut is secured by an R-clip, engage the locking cap with the driveshaft nut so that one of its cut-outs is aligned with the driveshaft hole. Secure the cap in position with the R-clip.
26 Refit the roadwheel, then lower the vehicle to the ground and tighten the roadwheel bolts to the specified torque.

3 Front hub bearings – renewal

Note: *The bearing is a sealed, pre-adjusted and pre-lubricated, double-row roller type, and is intended to last the car's entire service life without maintenance or attention. Never overtighten the driveshaft nut beyond the specified torque wrench setting in an attempt to 'adjust' the bearing.*
Note: *A press will be required to dismantle and rebuild the assembly; if such a tool is not available, a large bench vice and spacers (such as large sockets) will serve as an adequate substitute. The bearing's inner races are an interference fit on the hub; if the inner race remains on the hub when it is pressed out of the hub carrier, a knife-edged bearing puller will be required to remove it. A new bearing retaining circlip must be used on refitting.*
1 Remove the swivel hub assembly as described in Section 2.
2 Support the swivel hub securely on blocks or in a vice. Using a tubular spacer which bears only on the inner end of the hub flange, press the hub flange out of the bearing. If the bearing's outboard inner race remains on the hub, remove it using a bearing puller (see note above).
3 Extract the bearing retaining circlip from the inner end of the swivel hub assembly **(see illustration)**.
4 Where necessary, refit the inner race back in position over the ball cage, and securely support the inner face of the swivel hub. Using a tubular spacer which bears only on the inner race, press the complete bearing assembly out of the swivel hub.
5 Thoroughly clean the hub and swivel hub, removing all traces of dirt and grease, and polish away any burrs or raised edges which might hinder reassembly. Check both for cracks or any other signs of wear or damage, and renew them if necessary. Renew the circlip, regardless of its apparent condition.
6 On reassembly, apply a light film of oil to the bearing outer race and hub flange shaft, to aid installation of the bearing.
7 Securely support the swivel hub, and locate the bearing in the hub. Press the bearing fully

2.24 Where the driveshaft nut needs to be staked, stake it firmly into the driveshaft with a hammer and punch

3.3 Front hub bearing retaining circlip (arrowed)

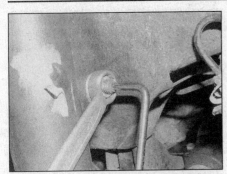

4.3 Retain the balljoint shank and unscrew the nut securing the anti-roll bar connecting link to the strut

4.5 Unscrew the nut and withdraw the lower arm balljoint clamp bolt

4.6 Unscrew the nut and withdraw the strut clamp bolt from the swivel hub

into position, ensuring that it enters the hub squarely, using a tubular spacer which bears only on the bearing outer race.

8 Once the bearing is correctly seated, secure the bearing in position with the new circlip, ensuring that it is correctly located in the groove in the swivel hub.

9 Securely support the outer face of the hub flange, and locate the swivel hub bearing inner race over the end of the hub flange. Press the bearing onto the hub, using a tubular spacer which bears only on the inner race of the hub bearing, until it seats against the hub shoulder. Check that the hub flange rotates freely, and wipe off any excess oil or grease.

10 Refit the swivel hub assembly as described in Section 2.

4.7 Pull down on the lower arm and peg it in position by inserting a socket (arrowed) between the top of the arm and subframe

| 4 | **Front suspension strut –** removal and refitting |

Removal

Note: *All self-locking nuts disturbed on removal must be renewed as a matter of course. These include the track rod balljoint nut, lower suspension arm balljoint clamp bolt nut, anti-roll bar connecting link nut and the swivel hub clamp bolt nut.*

1 Chock the rear wheels of the car and firmly apply the handbrake. Jack up the front of the car and support it on axle stands (see *Jacking and vehicle support*). Remove the appropriate front roadwheel.

2 Slacken and remove the bolt securing the support bracket (where fitted) to the top of the swivel hub.

3 Unscrew the nut and free the anti-roll bar connecting link (where fitted) from the strut **(see illustration)**. Discard the nut – a new one must be used on refitting.

4 Slacken and remove the nut securing the steering gear track rod balljoint to the swivel hub, and release the balljoint tapered shank using a balljoint separator.

5 Slacken and remove the suspension lower arm balljoint clamp bolt and nut **(see illustration)**. Discard the nut – a new one must be used on refitting.

6 Undo the nut and withdraw the swivel hub-to-suspension strut clamp bolt **(see**

illustration). Discard the nut – a new one must be used on refitting.

7 Pull down on the lower arm to free its balljoint from the swivel hub **(see Tool Tip in Section 2)**. Once the balljoint is freed from the swivel hub, peg the lower arm in position by inserting a suitable socket in between the top of the arm inner end and the subframe **(see illustration)**.

8 Recover the protector plate from lower arm balljoint.

9 Free the swivel hub assembly from the end of the strut. If the swivel hub is a tight fit on the strut, use a large flat-bladed screwdriver to carefully open up the clamp a little. Position the swivel hub assembly clear of the strut and seat it on the lower arm balljoint **(see illustration)**. Tie the upper end of the hub assembly securely to the body to ensure no excess strain is placed on the brake hose or driveshaft joints.

10 Unscrew the strut upper mounting bolts then manoeuvre the strut out from underneath the wheelarch and remove it from the vehicle **(see illustrations)**.

Refitting

11 Manoeuvre the strut assembly into position. Locate its upper mounting plate correctly on the body and refit the upper mounting bolts.

12 Slide the hub assembly fully onto the suspension strut, aligning the split in the hub clamp with the lug on the base of the strut.

4.9 Free the swivel hub assembly from the base of the strut and locate it back on the lower arm balljoint

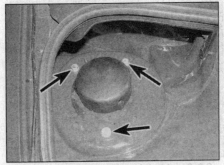

4.10a Unscrew the upper mounting bolts (arrowed) . . .

4.10b . . . then manoeuvre the strut out from underneath the wheelarch

10

4.12 Ensure the strut is correctly located in the swivel hub then tighten its clamp bolt nut to the specified torque

Also ensure that the stop bosses on the strut are in contact with the top surface of the swivel hub. Insert the swivel hub-to-suspension strut clamp bolt then fit a new nut and tighten it to the specified torque **(see illustration)**.

13 Fit the protector plate to the lower arm balljoint **(see illustration)**.

14 Align the lower arm balljoint with the swivel hub. Remove the socket (used to peg the arm in position) and seat the balljoint shank correctly in the swivel hub, aligning the protector plate tang with the hub slot. Insert the clamp bolt then fit the new nut and tighten to the specified torque.

15 Engage the track rod balljoint in the swivel hub, then fit a new retaining nut and tighten it to the specified torque.

16 Locate the anti-roll bar connecting link (where fitted) in the strut bracket. Fit the new

4.13 Refit the protector plate to the lower arm balljoint

nut to the link and tighten it to the specified torque.

17 Refit the bracket (where fitted) to the top of the swivel hub, and tighten its retaining bolt securely.

18 Refit the roadwheel, then lower the vehicle to the ground and tighten the road-wheel bolts to the specified torque.

5 Front suspension strut – overhaul

⚠️ **Warning: Before attempting to dismantle the front suspension strut, a suitable tool to hold the coil spring in compression must be obtained. Adjustable coil spring compressors are readily-available, and are**

recommended for this operation. Any attempt to dismantle the strut without such a tool is likely to result in damage or personal injury.

Note: *A new mounting plate nut must be used on reassembly.*

1 Remove the strut as described in Section 4.

2 Clean away all external dirt, then mount the strut upright in a vice.

3 Fit the spring compressors, and compress the coil spring until all tension is relieved from the upper spring seat **(see illustration)**.

4 Remove the cap then slacken the upper mounting plate nut whilst retaining the shock absorber piston with an Allen key **(see illustrations)**. Remove the mounting plate nut and washer. Discard the nut – a new one must be fitted on reassembly.

5 Lift off the mounting plate, bearing, upper spring seat and flat washer **(see illustrations)**.

6 Remove the coil spring then slide off the piston dust cover and rubber damper stop **(see illustration)**.

7 With the strut now dismantled, examine all the components for wear, damage or deformation, and check the upper bearing for smoothness of operation. Renew any of the components as necessary.

8 Examine the strut for signs of fluid leakage. Check the strut piston for signs of pitting along its entire length, and check the strut body for signs of damage. While holding it in an upright position, test the operation of the strut by moving the piston through a full stroke, and then through short

5.3 Compress the coil spring using spring compressors until all spring pressure is relieved from the seats

5.4a Remove the cap . . .

5.4b . . . then slacken the upper mounting plate nut whilst retaining the strut piston

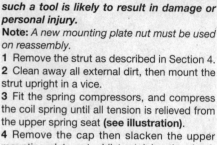

5.5a Lift off the upper mounting plate . . .

5.5b . . . followed by the bearing (1), upper spring seat (2) and flat washer (3)

5.6 Slide the dust cover and rubber bump stop off the piston

5.12 Fit the coil spring, ensuring its end is correctly located against the stop (arrowed) on the lower seat

5.13a Fit the flat washer . . .

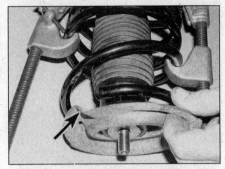

5.13b . . . then fit the upper spring seat, positioning its stop (arrowed) against the spring end

strokes of 50 to 100 mm. In both cases, the resistance felt should be smooth and continuous. If the resistance is jerky, or uneven, or if there is any visible sign of wear or damage to the strut, renewal is necessary.

9 If any doubt exists about the condition of the coil spring, carefully remove the spring compressors, and check the spring for distortion and signs of cracking. Renew the spring if it is damaged or distorted, or if there is any doubt as to its condition.

10 Inspect all other components for signs of damage or deterioration, and renew any that are suspect.

11 Ensure all components are clean and dry then slide the rubber damper stop and dust cover onto the strut.

12 Fit the coil spring ensuring its end is correctly located against the stop on the lower seat (see illustration).

13 Fit the flat washer to the piston then install the upper spring seat. Position the upper spring seat stop against the spring end (see illustrations).

14 Fit the bearing to the upper seat then fit the upper mounting plate. Fit the washer and new nut and tighten it to the specified torque (see illustrations).

15 Ensure the spring ends are still correctly positioned against their stops then carefully release the spring compressor and remove it from the strut.

16 Seat the damper stop and dust cover correctly in the upper spring seat.

17 Refit the strut as described in Section 4.

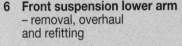

6 Front suspension lower arm
– removal, overhaul and refitting

Removal

Note: *A new lower arm balljoint clamp bolt nut and lower arm mounting bolt nuts will be required on refitting.*

1 Chock the rear wheels of the car and firmly apply the handbrake. Jack up the front of the car and support it on axle stands (see *Jacking and vehicle support*). Remove the appropriate front roadwheel.

5.14a Fit the washer . . .

2 Slacken and remove the suspension lower arm balljoint clamp bolt and nut (see illustration). Discard the nut – a new one must be used on refitting.

3 Slacken and remove the front and rear mounting nuts and bolts securing the lower arm to the subframe (see illustration). Discard the nuts – new ones must be used on refitting.

4 Free the lower arm balljoint from the swivel hub and remove the arm from the vehicle, taking care not to lose the protector plate from balljoint (see **Tool Tip in Section 2**).

Overhaul

5 Thoroughly clean the lower arm and the area around the arm mountings, removing all traces of dirt and underseal if necessary, then check carefully for cracks, distortion or any other signs of wear or damage, paying particular attention to the pivot bushes. The pivot bushes are a press-fit in the arm and can

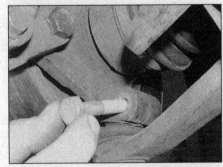

6.2 Unscrew the nut and withdraw the balljoint clamp bolt from the swivel hub

5.14b . . . and the new upper mounting plate nut, tightening it to the specified torque

be renewed separately. However, bush renewal requires the use of a hydraulic press and suitable mandrels and should therefore be entrusted to a Peugeot dealer.

6 Check that the lower arm balljoint moves freely, without any sign of roughness; check also that the balljoint gaiter shows no sign of deterioration, and is free from cracks and splits. The gaiter is available separately but if the balljoint is damaged, the lower arm will have to be renewed.

Refitting

7 Refit the protector plate to the balljoint then manoeuvre the lower arm assembly into position. Engage the balljoint shank with the swivel hub, aligning the protector plate tang with the hub slot, then insert the front and rear mounting bolts from above.

8 Fit the new nuts to the lower arm mounting bolts and tighten them to the specified torque.

6.3 Unscrew the nuts and remove the lower arm mounting bolts (rear bolt shown) from the top of the subframe

10

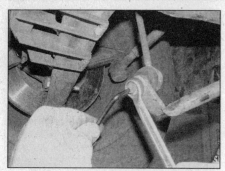

8.3 Unscrew the nuts and free the connecting link from each end of the anti-roll bar

8.4 Unscrew the nuts and bolts securing the anti-roll bar mounting clamps to the subframe

9.2 Retain the balljoint shanks with a Torx wrench whilst slackening the connecting link nuts

9 Ensure the balljoint is correctly seated in the swivel hub then insert the clamp bolt. Fit a new nut to the clamp bolt and tighten it to the specified torque.

10 Refit the roadwheel, then lower the vehicle to the ground and tighten the roadwheel bolts to the specified torque.

7 Front suspension lower arm balljoint – removal and refitting

1 The balljoint is integral with the lower arm. The gaiter is available separately but if the balljoint is worn or damaged the lower arm will have to be renewed (see Section 6).

8 Front suspension anti-roll bar – removal and refitting

Removal

Note: *New anti-roll bar mounting bolt and connecting link nuts will be needed on refitting.*

1 Chock the rear wheels, firmly apply the handbrake, then jack up the front of the vehicle and support it on axle stands (see *Jacking and vehicle support*).

2 On petrol engine models, remove the exhaust system intermediate pipe (see Chapter 4A).

3 On all models, undo the nuts securing the left- and right-hand connecting links to the anti-roll bar **(see illustration)**. Retain the connecting link balljoint with a Torx key to prevent rotation as the nut is slackened. Discard the nuts, new ones should be used on refitting, and position both connecting links clear of the anti-roll bar.

4 Slacken and remove the two anti-roll bar mounting clamp retaining bolts and nuts **(see illustration)**. Discard the nuts – new ones must be used on refitting.

5 Free both mounting both clamps from the subframe then manoeuvre the anti-roll bar out from underneath the vehicle. Remove the mounting bushes from the bar.

6 Carefully examine the anti-roll bar components for signs of wear, damage or

deterioration, paying particular attention to the mounting bushes. Renew worn components as necessary.

Refitting

7 Fit the rubber mounting bushes to the anti-roll bar, ensuring that the flats on the inside of each bush engage with the corresponding flats on the anti-roll bar and the bush split is facing towards the rear.

8 Offer up the anti-roll bar, and manoeuvre it into position on the subframe.

9 Ensure the mounting bushes are still correctly engaged with the bar flats then refit the mounting clamps. Hook the end of each clamp into on the subframe and engage the clamps with the bushes. Install the mounting clamp bolts and fit the new nuts, tightening them lightly only.

10 Refit the connecting links to the anti-roll bar ends and fit the new nuts, tightening them to the specified torque.

11 Tighten the anti-roll bar mounting clamp bolts to the specified torque.

12 On petrol engine models refit the exhaust system intermediate pipe (see Chapter 4A).

13 On completion, lower the vehicle to the ground.

9 Front suspension anti-roll bar connecting link – removal and refitting

Removal

Note: *New connecting link securing nuts must be used on refitting.*

1 Firmly apply the handbrake, then jack up the front of the car and support it on axle stands (see *Jacking and vehicle support*). Remove the roadwheel to improve access to the link.

2 Slacken and remove the nuts securing the connecting link to the strut and anti-roll bar, and remove the link from the vehicle **(see illustration)**. Retain the link balljoint shank with a Torx key to prevent rotation as the nut is slackened.

3 Examine the connecting link for signs of damage, paying particular attention to the mounting bushes or balljoints (as applicable). If any sign of damage is found, renew if

necessary. It is not possible to renew the bushes or balljoints separately. Note that the connecting link retaining nuts must be renewed as a matter of course.

Refitting

4 Manoeuvre the connecting link into position and engage it with the anti-roll bar and strut. Fit the new nuts to the connecting link and tighten to the specified torque.

5 Refit the roadwheel then lower the vehicle to the ground and tighten the wheel bolts to the specified torque.

10 Rear hub assembly – removal and refitting

1 The rear hub is an integral part of the brake drum. Refer to Chapter 9 for details on brake drum removal and refitting.

11 Rear hub bearings – renewal

Note: *The bearing is intended to last the car's entire service life without maintenance or attention. Never overtighten the hub nut beyond the specified torque wrench setting, in an attempt to 'adjust' the bearings.*

1 Remove the rear brake drum (Chapter 9).

2 Extract the bearing retaining circlip from the centre of the brake drum **(see illustration)**.

11.2 Extract the rear hub bearing circlip

11.3 Prise out the hub seal seating ring from the rear of the drum

11.4 Using a socket and drawbolt arrangement to draw the bearing out from the drum

11.8a Locate the new bearing in the drum . . .

11.8b . . . and draw it squarely into position

11.10a Fit the new hub seal seating ring to the rear of the drum . . .

11.10b . . . and tap it squarely into position

3 Prise out the hub seal seating ring from the rear of the drum **(see illustration)**.

4 Securely support the outer face of the drum hub, then press or drive the bearing out of position, using a tubular drift which bears on the bearing inner race. Alternatively, the bearing can be removed using an improvised tool made up from a suitable socket or tube, washers, nut and a suitable long bolt or threaded rod **(see illustration)**.

5 Thoroughly clean the hub, removing all traces of dirt and grease, and polish away any burrs or raised edges which might hinder reassembly. Check the hub for cracks or any other signs of wear or damage, and renew them if necessary. The bearing, circlip and seal seating ring must be renewed whenever they are disturbed. Note that a replacement bearing kit is available from Peugeot dealers.

6 Examine the stub axle shaft for signs of wear or damage, and if necessary renew it. The stub axle is an interference fit in the trailing arm, and can either be tapped out of position, using a hammer and a soft-metal drift, or pushed out using a heavy-duty bearing puller. When installing the new stub axle, align its splines with those of the trailing arm, and drive or press it fully into position in the arm.

7 On reassembly, apply a light film of clean engine oil to the bearing outer race, to aid installation of the bearing.

8 Securely support the inner face of the drum hub, and locate the bearing in the hub bore. Press the bearing fully into position, ensuring it enters the hub squarely, using a tubular spacer which bears only on the bearing outer

race. Alternatively, the bearing can be drawn into position with the improvised tool used previously, but note that a different socket or tube will be required, to bear on the bearing outer race **(see illustrations)**.

9 Ensure that the bearing is correctly seated against the hub shoulder, and secure it in position with the new circlip. Ensure that the circlip is correctly seated in its hub groove.

10 Tap the new hub seal seating ring into position in the rear of the hub, taking care not to damage the seal seating surface **(see illustrations)**.

11 Refit the brake drum (see Chapter 9) using the new seal.

12 Rear suspension components – general

1 Although it is possible to remove the rear suspension torsion bars, trailing arms and anti-roll bar independently of the complete rear axle assembly, it is essential to have certain special tools available to complete the work successfully.

2 Due to the complexity of the tasks, and the requirement for special tools to accurately set the suspension geometry on refitting, the removal and refitting of individual rear suspension components is considered to be beyond the scope of DIY work, and should be entrusted to a Peugeot dealer.

3 Procedures for removal and refitting of the rear shock absorbers, and the complete rear

axle assembly are given in Sections 13 and 14 respectively.

13 Rear shock absorber – removal, testing and refitting

Removal

Note: *New shock absorber mounting nuts must be used on refitting.*

1 Chock the front wheels, then jack up the rear of the vehicle and support it on axle stands (see *Jacking and vehicle support*). Remove the relevant rear roadwheel.

2 Using a trolley jack, raise the trailing arm until the shock absorber is slightly compressed.

3 Slacken and remove the nuts and washers from both the upper and lower shock absorber mounting bolts **(see illustrations)**.

13.3a Slacken and remove the upper . . .

10

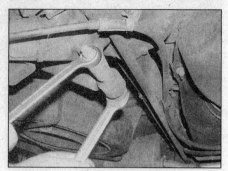

13.3b . . . and lower mounting nuts and bolts and remove the rear shock absorber

4 Withdraw the mounting bolts, noting which way round they are fitted, and manoeuvre the shock absorber out from underneath the vehicle.

Testing

5 Examine the shock absorber for signs of fluid leakage or damage. Test the operation of the shock absorber, while holding it in an upright position, by moving the piston through a full stroke and then through short strokes of 50 to 100 mm. In both cases, the resistance felt should be smooth and continuous. If the resistance is jerky, or uneven, or if there is any visible sign of wear or damage, renewal is necessary. Also check the rubber mounting bushes for damage and deterioration. Renew the complete unit if any damage or excessive wear is evident; the mounting bushes are not available separately. Inspect the shanks of the mounting bolts for signs of wear or damage, and renew as necessary.

Refitting

6 Prior to refitting the shock absorber, mount it upright in the vice, and operate it fully through several strokes in order to prime it. Apply a smear of multi-purpose grease to both the shock absorber mounting bolts.
7 Manoeuvre the shock absorber into position, and insert its mounting bolts. Fit the new nuts to the mounting bolts, but do not tighten them yet.
8 Measure the distance between the shock absorber bolt head centres, and adjust the position of the jack under the trailing arm until

a distance of 317.5 mm is obtained between the bolt centres. Once the trailing arm is correctly positioned, tighten the upper and lower mounting bolt nuts to the specified torque.
9 Refit the roadwheel, then lower the car to ground and tighten the roadwheel bolts to the specified torque.

14 Rear axle assembly – removal, overhaul and refitting

Removal

1 Firmly chock the front wheels, then jack up the rear of the vehicle and support it on axle stands (see *Jacking and vehicle support*). Remove both rear roadwheels, then lower the spare wheel out from underneath the rear of the vehicle, and unhook the wheel carrier.
2 Remove the relevant exhaust system components and heat shield(s) (see the relevant part of Chapter 4).
3 Referring to Chapter 9, fully slacken the handbrake cable adjuster nut and detach both handbrake cables from the lever plate. From underneath the vehicle, work along the length of each cable, and free them from any retaining clips which secure them to the vehicle underbody. Note the routing of the cables to ensure correct refitting.
4 Where necessary, disconnect the ABS wheel sensors at the wiring connectors, and free the sensor wiring from any retaining clips securing them to the vehicle underbody.
5 Trace the brake pipes back from the backplates to their unions on/in front of the axle **(see illustration)**. Wipe clean the area around the unions then slacken the union nuts and disconnect the pipes. Plug the hose/pipe ends and valve unions (as applicable), to minimise fluid loss and prevent the entry of dirt into the hydraulic system.
6 Make a final check that all necessary components have been disconnected and positioned so that they will not hinder the removal procedure, then position a trolley jack beneath the centre of the rear axle assembly. Raise the jack until it is supporting the weight of the axle.

7 Slacken and remove the four bolts and washers securing the axle mounting bushes to the vehicle underbody **(see illustrations)**.
8 Lower the jack and axle assembly out of position, and remove it from underneath the car.

Overhaul

9 Examine the rear axle mountings for signs of damage or deterioration of the mounting rubber. If any mounting shows signs of damage or deterioration, all four mountings should be renewed as a set; do not renew the mountings individually. The mountings are a press-fit in the crossmember; renewal requires the use of a hydraulic press and suitable mandrels and should therefore be entrusted to a Peugeot dealer.

Refitting

10 Position the rear axle assembly onto the jack and carefully raise it up into position, taking care not to crush the brake pipes or trap the cables/wiring.
11 Align the axle mountings with the vehicle underbody and refit the mounting bolts, tightening them to the specified torque.
12 Referring to Chapter 9, carry out the following.
a) Reconnect the brake pipes, tightening the union nuts to the specified torque. Ensure the pipes/hoses are correctly routed and retained by all the relevant clips
b) Reconnect the handbrake cables to the lever, ensuring they are correctly routed and retained by all the relevant clips.
c) On models with ABS, reconnect the rear wheel sensor wiring connectors, ensuring the wiring is correctly routed and retained by all the relevant clips.
13 Refit the rear section of the exhaust system (see the relevant part of Chapter 4).
14 Refit the spare wheel and carrier.
15 Refit the roadwheels then lower the vehicle to the ground and tighten the wheel bolts to the specified torque.
16 Bleed the complete braking system hydraulic circuit as described in Chapter 9 then adjust the handbrake cable.
17 If the axle assembly has been overhauled/renewed, have the vehicle ride height checked at the earliest opportunity.

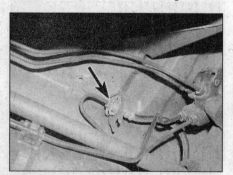

14.5 Rear brake pipe union (arrowed) on the right-hand side of the axle

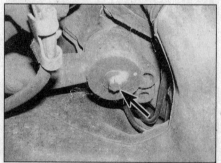

14.7a Rear axle front mounting bolt (arrowed)

14.7b Rear axle rear mounting bolt (arrowed)

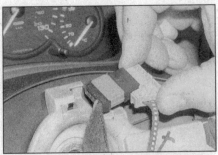

16.9a On models with a driver's airbag, unclip the horn wiring connector from the wheel . . .

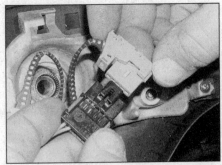

16.9b . . . then disconnect the connector and remove the wiring

16.10 Slacken and remove the steering wheel retaining bolt

15 Vehicle ride height – checking

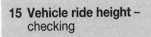

1 Checking of the vehicle ride height requires the use of Peugeot special tools to accurately compress the suspension in a suspension checking bay.
2 The operation should be entrusted to a Peugeot dealer, as it not possible to carry out checking accurately without the use of the appropriate tools.

16 Steering wheel – removal and refitting

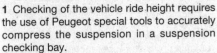

Note: *Models equipped with an airbag have the word AIRBAG stamped on the steering wheel pad.*

Models without an airbag

Removal

1 Set the front wheels in the straight-ahead position, and release the steering lock by inserting the ignition key.
2 Carefully ease off the steering wheel centre pad, then slacken and remove the steering wheel retaining bolt.
3 Mark the steering wheel and steering column shaft in relation to each other, then lift the steering wheel off the column splines.

 HAYNES HINT *If the wheel is tight, tap it up near the centre, using the palm of your hand, or twist it from side-to-side, whilst pulling to release it from the shaft splines.*

Refitting

4 Ensure that the indicator switch stem is in its central position (failure to do this could lead to the steering wheel lug breaking the switch tab) then engage the wheel with the column splines, aligning the mark made on removal.
5 Clean the threads of the steering wheel bolt

then apply a drop of locking compound (Peugeot recommend Loctite Frenetanch) to its threads. Fit the retaining bolt and tighten it to the specified torque.
6 Refit the centre pad to the wheel.

Models with an airbag

 Warning: Refer to the precautions given in Chapter 12 about the airbag system before proceeding.

Removal

7 Remove the airbag unit from the steering wheel (see Chapter 12).
8 Set the front wheels in the straight-ahead position, and release the steering lock by inserting the ignition key.
9 Unclip the horn wiring connector from the wheel then disconnect the connector and remove the horn wiring **(see illustrations)**.
10 Slacken and remove the steering wheel retaining bolt **(see illustration)**.
11 Mark the steering wheel and steering column shaft in relation to each other then carefully lift wheel off the column splines. As the wheel is removed, pass the horn and airbag wiring connectors down through the wheel, taking care not to strain the wiring **(see illustration)**.

 HAYNES HINT *If the wheel is tight, tap it up near the centre, using the palm of your hand, or twist it from side-to-side, whilst pulling to release it from the shaft splines.*

16.11 Free the steering wheel from the column and remove it, taking care not to strain the horn/airbag wiring

Refitting

12 Prior to refitting, ensure the airbag contact unit is correctly centralised (see Chapter 12, Section 23).
13 Ensure that the indicator switch stem is in its central position (failure to do this could lead to the steering wheel lug breaking the switch tab) then pass the airbag unit and horn wiring up through the wheel. Engage the wheel the column splines, aligning the mark made on removal.
14 Clean the threads of the steering wheel retaining bolt and apply a drop of locking compound (Peugeot recommend Loctite Frenetanch) to its threads. Fit the bolt and tighten it to the specified torque **(see illustration)**.
15 Reconnect the horn wiring then clip the connector back onto the steering wheel.
16 Refit the airbag unit as described in Chapter 12.

17 Steering column – removal, inspection and refitting

Removal

1 Disconnect the battery negative terminal.
2 Remove the steering wheel (see Section 16).
3 Rotate the fastener a quarter-of-a-turn (90°) and remove the lower cover from the driver's side of the facia.
4 Undo the retaining screws and free the

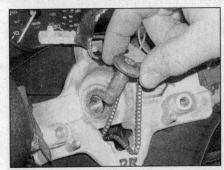

16.14 Treat the threads of the steering wheel bolt with locking compound prior to refitting

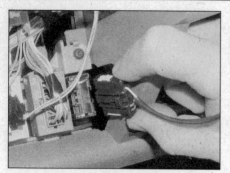

17.4 Disconnect the audio unit control stalk wiring connector and remove the lower shroud

17.7 Unclip the immobiliser ring from the ignition switch/steering lock

17.8a Undo the retaining screws (arrowed) . . .

lower shroud from the column. Trace the audio unit control stalk back to its wiring connector then disconnect the connector and remove the shroud and switch as an assembly **(see illustration)**.

5 Unclip and remove the upper shroud from the steering column.

6 On models equipped with an airbag, remove the contact unit from the column as described in Chapter 12.

7 On all models, carefully unclip the immobiliser ring and free it from the ignition switch/steering column lock **(see illustration)**.

8 Slacken and remove the three screws securing the combination switch bracket to the top of the column. Disconnect the wiring connectors from the base of the switches and remove the bracket assembly **(see illustrations)**.

9 Release the retaining clips and disconnect the ignition switch wiring connectors from the fusebox and wiring harness **(see illustration)**.

10 Free the wiring harness from the steering column cover then unclip the cover and remove it from the steering column **(see illustration)**.

11 Expand the ends of the safety clip and

remove it from the base of the steering column **(see illustrations)**. Using paint or a suitable marker pen, make alignment marks between the column and steering gear pinion. Slacken and remove the nut and clamp bolt and detach the column from the steering gear pinion.

12 Slacken and remove the column upper mounting nuts and lower mounting bolts then manoeuvre the column out of position **(see illustrations)**.

Inspection

Note: *New steering columns are supplied with*

17.8b . . . and remove the combination switch bracket assembly, disconnecting the switch wiring connectors

17.9 Trace the ignition switch back to its wiring connectors (lift the retaining clip to disconnect the connector – arrowed)

17.10 Unclip and remove the cover from the steering column

17.11a Unclip the ends (arrowed) of the safety clip . . .

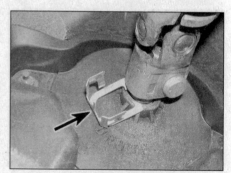

17.11b . . . then slide the clip (arrowed) off the base of the steering column

17.12a Slacken and remove the upper mounting nuts . . .

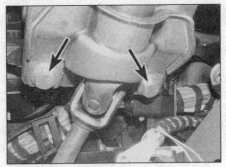

17.12b . . . and lower mounting bolts . . .

17.12c . . . and remove the steering column from the vehicle

a safety clip fitted to the upper universal joint to protect the joint during handling. Remove this clip once the column is correctly installed.

13 The steering column incorporates a telescopic safety feature. In the event of a front-end crash, the shaft collapses and prevents the steering wheel injuring the driver. Before refitting the steering column, examine the column and mountings for signs of damage and deformation, and renew as necessary.

14 Check the steering shaft for signs of free play in the column bushes, and check the universal joints for signs of damage or roughness in the joint bearings. If any damage or wear is found on the steering column universal joints or shaft bushes, the column must be renewed as an assembly.

Refitting

15 Manoeuvre the column into position and engage it with its upper mounting studs. Fit

the upper mounting nuts and lower bolts tighten them lightly only.

16 Release the column height adjustment lever then tighten the column upper mounting nuts to the specified torque. Lock the height adjustment mechanism again then tighten the lower mounting bolts to the specified torque.

17 Engage the column universal joint with the steering gear pinion, aligning the marks made on removal, and secure it in position with the safety clip. Refit the clamp bolt and nut and tighten it to the specified torque.

18 Securely reconnect the ignition switch wiring connectors then clip the cover back onto the column. Ensure the cover is correctly fitted and clip the wiring harness back into position.

19 Reconnect the wiring to the combination switches then seat the bracket assembly back on the column. Securely tighten the bracket screws.

20 Clip the immobiliser sensor ring back onto the ignition switch/steering lock.

21 On models with an airbag, refit the contact unit as described in Chapter 12.

22 On all models, reconnect the audio unit control switch wiring connector then refit the upper and lower shrouds to the column and securely tighten the retaining screws.

23 Refit the steering wheel (Section 16) then reconnect the battery.

18 Ignition switch/ steering column lock – removal and refitting

Removal

1 Disconnect the battery negative terminal.

2 Rotate the fastener a quarter-of-a-turn (90°) and remove the lower cover from the driver's side of the facia **(see illustration)**.

3 Undo the retaining screws and free the lower shroud from the column. Trace the audio unit control stalk back to its wiring connector then disconnect the connector and remove the shroud and switch as an assembly.

4 Unclip and remove the upper shroud from the steering column **(see illustration)**.

5 Carefully unclip the immobiliser ring and free it from the ignition switch/steering column lock **(see illustration)**.

6 Release the retaining clips and disconnect the ignition switch wiring connectors from the fusebox and wiring harness **(see illustrations)**.

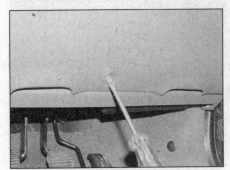

18.2 Rotate then fastener 90° and remove the lower cover from the facia

18.4 Unclip and remove the upper shroud from the steering column

18.5 Free the immobiliser ring from the lock

18.6a Disconnect the ignition switch wiring connectors from the fusebox (arrowed) . . .

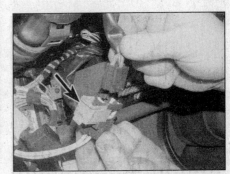

18.6b . . . and wiring harness (arrowed)

10

18.7 Slacken and remove the retaining screw from the front of the lock housing

18.9 With the key correctly positioned, depress the detent clip (arrowed) and withdraw the lock from the steering column

7 Slacken and remove the retaining screw from the front of the ignition switch/steering column lock housing **(see illustration)**.

8 Insert the ignition key and rotate it so that it is aligned with the mark positioned halfway between the A and M marks on the barrel.

9 With the key correctly positioned, depress the lock detent clip then withdraw the lock from the steering column **(see illustration)**.

Refitting

10 Align the key with the mark positioned halfway between the A and M marks then feed the wiring through the steering column lock housing and seat the lock barrel in position. Refit the retaining screw and tighten it securely.

11 Securely reconnect the ignition switch wiring connectors then check the operation of the switch and steering lock.

12 Clip the immobiliser sensor ring back onto the ignition switch/steering lock.

13 Reconnect the audio unit control switch wiring connector then refit the upper and lower shrouds to the column and securely tighten the retaining screws.

14 Refit the lower cover to the facia then reconnect the battery.

19 Steering gear assembly – removal, overhaul and refitting

Removal

Note: *New steering gear mounting studs and nuts and track rod balljoint nuts will be required on refitting. A balljoint separator tool will be required for this operation. On models*

19.5 Feed and return pipe clamp bolt (arrowed) – models with power steering

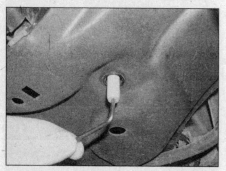

19.7b ... then unscrew the mounting studs ...

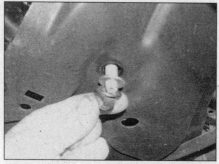

19.7a Unscrew the steering gear nuts and washers from the base of the subframe ...

19.7c ... and recover the washers fitted between the steering gear and top of the subframe

with power steering, new O-rings will also be required for the pipe-to-steering gear unions.

1 Working inside the vehicle, expand the ends of the safety clip and remove it from the base of the steering column **(see illustrations 17.11a and 17.11b)**. Using paint or a suitable marker pen, make alignment marks between the column and steering gear pinion. Slacken and remove the nut and clamp bolt and detach the column from the steering gear pinion. Free the inner rubber seal from the bulkhead and remove it from the steering gear.

2 Chock the rear wheels, firmly apply the handbrake, then jack up the front of the vehicle and support on axle stands (see *Jacking and vehicle support*). Remove both front roadwheels. Where necessary, remove the retaining bolts, screws and clips and remove the undercover (where fitted) from beneath the engine/transmission unit.

3 Slacken and remove the nuts securing the steering gear track rod balljoints to the swivel hubs, and release the balljoint tapered shanks using a universal balljoint separator. Discard the nuts; new ones must be used on refitting.

4 On petrol engine models, remove the exhaust system intermediate pipe as described in Chapter 4A. On 2.0 litre diesel engine models unscrew the nuts securing the exhaust mounting bracket to the rear of the subframe.

5 On models equipped with power steering, using brake hose clamps, clamp both the supply and return flexible hoses to minimise fluid loss. Slacken and remove the bolt securing the fluid feed and return pipe clamp to the steering gear **(see illustration)**. Free the pipes from the steering gear assembly; be prepared for fluid spillage, and position a suitable container beneath the pipes whilst unscrewing the union nuts. Plug the pipe ends and steering gear orifices, to prevent fluid leakage and to keep dirt out of the hydraulic system. Note that new sealing rings for the pipes must be used on refitting.

6 On all models, slacken and remove the nut and bolt securing the engine/transmission unit rear mounting link to the mounting.

7 Slacken and remove the nuts and washers securing the steering gear to the subframe. Once the nuts are removed, unscrew the mounting studs from the underside of the steering gear and recover the washers fitted between the steering gear and subframe **(see illustrations)**. Discard the studs and nuts; new ones should be used on refitting.

8 Support the subframe assembly with a jack then slacken and remove the four bolts securing the subframe to the vehicle body **(see illustrations)**. Lower the subframe slightly to enable access to be gained to the steering gear.

9 Free the steering gear outer rubber seal from the bulkhead then manoeuvre the steering gear from underneath the driver's side wheelarch, positioning the subframe clear as necessary.

19.8a Front subframe front mounting bolt (arrowed)

19.8b Front subframe rear mounting bolt (arrowed)

Overhaul

10 Examine the steering gear assembly for signs of wear or damage, and check that the rack moves freely throughout the full length of its travel, with no signs of roughness or excessive free play between the steering gear pinion and rack. It is possible to overhaul the steering gear assembly housing components, but this task should be entrusted to a Peugeot dealer. The only components which can be renewed easily by the home mechanic are the steering gear gaiters, the track rod balljoints and the track rods. Track rod, track rod balljoint and steering gear gaiter renewal procedures are covered in Sections 24, 23 and 20 respectively.

11 On models with power steering, inspect all the steering gear fluid unions for signs of leakage, and check that all union nuts are securely tightened. Also examine the steering gear hydraulic ram for signs of fluid leakage or damage, and if necessary renew it.

12 Inspect the inner and outer rubber seals for signs of damage or deterioration and renew as necessary.

Refitting

13 Engage the outer rubber seal with the steering gear. On right-hand drive models fit the seal so the DD slot in the seal is engaged with the tab on the steering gear; on left-hand drive models fit the seal so the DG slot is engaged with the steering gear tab **(see illustration)**.

14 Ensure the outer rubber seal is correctly installed then manoeuvre the steering gear into position. Position the washers in between the steering gear and subframe then align the steering gear with the subframe. Fit the new mounting studs, ensuring they pass through the washers, and tighten them to the specified torque **(see illustration)**.

15 Seat the outer seal correctly on the bulkhead then align the subframe with its mountings. Refit the subframe mounting bolts and tighten them to the specified torque.

16 Fit the washers and new mounting nuts to the steering gear studs and tighten to the specified torque.

17 Refit the engine/transmission rear mounting link bolt and nut and tighten to the specified torque (see the relevant part of Chapter 2).

18 On models with power steering, remove the O-rings from the ends of the feed and return pipe unions. Fit the new O-rings, lubricating them with a smear of power

steering fluid, then ease them back into position in the steering gear. Ensure both pipes are correctly located then refit the clamp bolt and tighten to the specified torque.

19 On petrol engine models, refit the exhaust intermediate pipe (see Chapter 4A). On 2.0 litre diesel engine models, locate the exhaust mounting bracket in the subframe and securely tighten its retaining nuts.

20 On all models, locate the track rod balljoints back in the swivel hubs. Fit the new nuts to the balljoints and tighten them to the specified torque.

21 Refit the roadwheels then lower the vehicle to the ground and tighten the wheel bolts to the specified torque.

22 Refit the inner rubber seal ensuring it is correctly engaged with the bulkhead and steering gear pinion. Engage the column universal joint with the steering gear pinion, aligning the marks made on removal, and secure it in position with the safety clip. Refit the clamp bolt and nut, tightening it to the specified torque.

23 On models with power steering, remove the hose clamps (where fitted) from the power steering hoses, then top-up the fluid reservoir and bleed the hydraulic system as described in Section 21.

24 On all models, on completion check and, if necessary, adjust the front wheel alignment as described in Section 25.

20 Steering gear rubber gaiters – renewal

1 Remove the track rod balljoint as described in Section 23.

2 To improve access to the left-hand gaiter, remove the battery and battery tray (see Chapter 5A).

3 Mark the correct fitted position of the gaiter on the track rod. Free the breather pipe from the inner edge of the gaiter, then release the retaining clips and slide the gaiter off the steering gear housing and track rod end.

4 Thoroughly clean the track rod and the steering gear housing, using fine abrasive paper to polish off any corrosion, burrs or

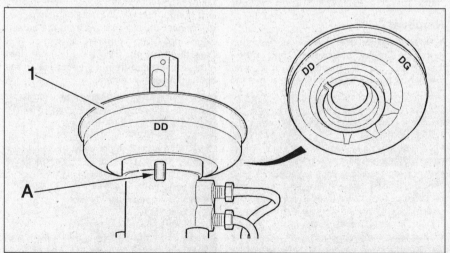

19.13 On right-hand drive models fit the outer seal (1) so that its DD slot is engaged with the tab (A) on the steering gear housing (on left-hand drive models align the DG slot with the tab)

19.14 Fit the new studs to the steering gear, ensuring they pass through the washers

10

22.2a On 1.9 litre diesel engines remove the fasteners from the right-hand side . . .

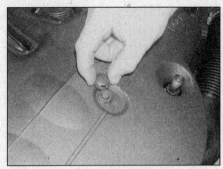

22.2b . . . and top of the engine cover . . .

22.2c . . . then lift the cover off from the engine

sharp edges, which might damage the new gaiter's sealing lips on installation. Scrape off all the grease from the old gaiter, and apply it to the track rod inner balljoint. (This assumes that grease has not been lost or contaminated as a result of damage to the old gaiter. Use fresh grease if in doubt – Peugeot recommend Total N3924 or N3945.)

5 Carefully slide the new gaiter onto the track rod end, and locate it on the steering gear housing, ensuring the breather pipe union is uppermost. Align the outer edge of the gaiter with the mark made on the track rod prior to removal, then secure it the gaiter in position with new retaining clips. Ensure the gaiter is securely fitted then reconnect the breather pipe.

6 Refit the track rod balljoint as described in Section 23. Where necessary, install the battery (see Chapter 5A).

21 Power steering system – bleeding

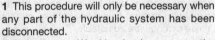

1 This procedure will only be necessary when any part of the hydraulic system has been disconnected.

2 Referring to Weekly checks, remove the fluid reservoir filler cap, and top-up with the specified fluid to the C level mark.

3 With the engine stopped, slowly move the steering from lock-to-lock several times to purge out the trapped air, then top-up the level in the fluid reservoir. Repeat this

procedure until the fluid level in the reservoir does not drop any further.

4 Start the engine and allow it to idle for a few minutes without turning the steering wheel. Keep fluid level topped up whilst the engine idles. Once the fluid level stabilises, slowly move the steering from lock-to-lock several times to purge out any remaining air in the system. Repeat this procedure until bubbles cease to appear in the fluid reservoir.

5 If, when turning the steering, an abnormal noise is heard from the fluid lines, it indicates that there is still air in the system. Check this by turning the wheels to the straight-ahead position and switching off the engine. If the fluid level in the reservoir rises, then air is present in the system, and further bleeding is necessary.

6 Once all traces of air have been removed from the power steering hydraulic system, turn the engine off and allow the system to cool. Once cool, check that the fluid level is correct (see Weekly checks), topping-up if necessary.

22 Power steering pump – removal and refitting

Removal

1 Release the drivebelt tension as described in the relevant part of Chapter 1, and unhook the drivebelt from the pump pulley. The power steering pump is mounted directly above the

alternator, on the front of the engine. Unclip and remove the screenwash reservoir neck to improve access to the pump.

2 On diesel engine models, remove the engine cover. On 1.9 litre engines, remove the fasteners from the right-hand side and top of the engine cover then lift off the cover, taking care not to lose its mounting rubbers (see illustrations); on 2.0 litre engines remove the fasteners (rotate them 90° to release them) and lift off the engine cover.

3 Slacken and remove the bolt securing the feed pipe clip to the side of the pump.

4 Wipe clean the area around the feed pipe union on the top of the pump. Unscrew the union nut and detach the pipe from the pump; be prepared for some fluid spillage as the pipe is disconnected, and plug the pipe end and pump unions, to minimise fluid loss and prevent the entry of dirt into the system (see illustration). Note: Access to the union nut is awkward; Peugeot produce a special socket (0720E) to enable the nut to the slackened/tightened.

5 Slacken and remove the front and rear bolts securing the pump to its mounting bracket (see illustration).

6 Free the pump from the bracket and (where necessary) recover the spacer from the rear mounting. Release the retaining clip, and disconnect the return hose from the base of the pump, being prepared for fluid spillage (see illustration). Plug the hose end then remove the pump from the vehicle and drain the fluid reservoir contents.

22.4 Unscrew the nut and disconnect the feed pipe from the power steering pump

22.5 The pump front mounting bolts are accessed through the holes in the drivebelt pulley

22.6 Lift the pump away from its mounting bracket and disconnect the fluid return hose (arrowed) from the base of the pump

Refitting

7 Manoeuvre the pump into position and securely reconnect the return hose.

8 Ensure the spacer (where fitted) is correctly fitted to the rear mounting then seat the pump on its bracket.

9 Apply a drop of locking compound (Peugeot recommend the use of Loctite Frenetanch) to the threads of the pump lower front mounting bolt then refit all the bolts. Tighten the front (drivebelt pulley end) mounting bolts to the specified torque first, then tighten the rear mounting bolts to the specified torque.

10 Reconnect the feed pipe to the pump and screw the union nut in a few turns. Refit the bolt securing the pipe clip to the pump then tighten the union nut to the specified torque followed by the clip bolt.

11 Refit the drivebelt to the pump pulley as described in the relevant part of Chapter 1.

12 Refill the fluid reservoir with fresh fluid then bleed the hydraulic system as described in Section 21.

23 Track rod balljoint – removal and refitting

Removal

Note: *A new track rod balljoint nut must be used on refitting.*

1 Apply the handbrake, then jack up the front of the vehicle and support it on axle stands (see *Jacking and vehicle support*). Remove the appropriate front roadwheel.

2 If the balljoint is to be re-used, use a straight-edge and a scriber, or similar, to mark its relationship to the track rod.

3 Hold the track rod, and unscrew the balljoint locknut by a quarter of a turn. Do not move the locknut from this position, as it will serve as a handy reference mark on refitting.

4 Slacken and remove the nut securing the track rod balljoint to the swivel hub, and release the balljoint tapered shank using a universal balljoint separator **(see illustration)**. Discard the nut – a new one must be used when refitting.

5 Counting the **exact** number of turns necessary to do so, unscrew the balljoint from the track rod end.

6 Count the number of exposed threads between the end of the balljoint and the locknut, and record this figure. If a new balljoint is to be fitted, unscrew the locknut from the old balljoint.

7 Carefully clean the balljoint and the threads. Renew the balljoint if its movement is sloppy or too stiff, if excessively worn, or if damaged in any way; carefully check the stud taper and threads. If the balljoint gaiter is damaged, the complete balljoint assembly must be renewed; it is not possible to obtain the gaiter separately.

Refitting

8 If a new balljoint is to be fitted, screw the locknut onto its threads, and position it so that the same number of exposed threads are visible, as was noted prior to removal **(see illustration)**. **Note:** *Peugeot give an initial setting for the locknut if both balljoints are to be renewed; the locknut should be positioned so the specified length of thread is visible between the balljoint and locknut.*

9 Screw the balljoint into the track rod by the number of turns noted on removal. This should bring the balljoint locknut to within a quarter of a turn from the locknut, with the alignment marks that were made on removal (if applicable) lined up.

10 Refit the balljoint shank to the swivel hub, then fit a new retaining nut and tighten it to the specified torque.

11 Refit the roadwheel, then lower the vehicle to the ground and tighten the roadwheel bolts to the specified torque.

12 Check and, if necessary, adjust the front wheel toe setting as described in Section 25, then tighten the balljoint locknut to the specified torque.

24 Track rod – removal and refitting

Removal

Note: *Access to the track rod inner balljoints is poor with the steering gear installed. To improve access remove the steering gear as described in Section 19.*

Note: *Peugeot manufacture a special wrench (0707) which fits the track rod balljoint enabling it to be easily unscrewed from the steering rack.*

1 Remove the track rod balljoints as described in Section 23.

2 Disconnect the breather pipe then release the retaining clips and slide the steering gear gaiter off the end of the track rod – refer to Section 20 for further information. It is recommended that the gaiter is renewed, regardless of its apparent condition.

3 Unscrew the track rod inner balljoint from the steering rack end, preventing the steering rack from turning by holding the steering rack with a pair of grips using a stout cloth to protect the rack surface. Take great care not to mark the surfaces of the rack and balljoint.

4 Remove the track rod assembly and examine its inner balljoint for signs of slackness or tight spots, and check that the track rod itself is straight and free from damage. If necessary, renew the track rod.

Refitting

5 Screw the track rod inner balljoint into the steering rack, and tighten it to the specified torque whilst retaining the steering rack with a pair of grips, using a stout cloth to protect against damage. Again, take great care not to

23.4 Releasing a track rod balljoint using a balljoint separator

damage or mark the track rod balljoint or steering rack.

6 Carefully slide the new gaiter onto the track rod end, and locate it on the steering gear housing, ensuring the breather pipe union is uppermost. Align the outer edge of the gaiter with the mark made on the track rod prior to removal, then secure it the gaiter in position with new retaining clips. Ensure the gaiter is securely fitted then reconnect the breather pipe.

7 Refit the track rod balljoint as described in Section 23.

25 Wheel alignment and steering angles – general information

General

1 A car's steering and suspension geometry is defined in four basic settings – all angles are expressed in degrees (toe settings are also expressed as a measurement); the relevant settings are camber, castor, steering axis inclination, and toe-setting. With the exception of front wheel toe-setting, none of these settings are adjustable.

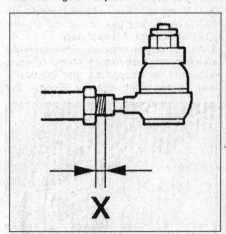

23.8 The initial setting for a track rod balljoint is made by measuring the amount of exposed thread (X) visible

Models with manual steering – X = 18 mm
Models with power steering – X = 13 mm

25.10 Adjusting the front wheel toe setting

Front wheel toe setting – checking and adjustment

2 Due to the special measuring equipment necessary to accurately check the wheel alignment, and the skill required to use it properly, checking and adjustment is best left to a Peugeot dealer or similar expert. Note that most tyre-fitting shops now possess sophisticated checking equipment. The following is provided as a guide, should the owner decide to carry out a DIY check.

3 The front wheel toe setting is checked by measuring the distance between the front and rear inside edges of the roadwheel rims. Proprietary toe measurement gauges are available from motor accessory shops. Adjustment is made by screwing the balljoints in or out of their track rods, to alter the effective length of the track rod assemblies.

4 For **accurate** checking, the vehicle **must** be at the kerb weight, ie, unladen and with a full tank of fuel, and the ride height must be correct (see Section 15).

5 Before starting work, check first that the tyre sizes and types are as specified, then check the tyre pressures and tread wear, the roadwheel run-out, the condition of the hub bearings, the steering wheel free play, and the condition of the front suspension components (see the relevant part of Chapter 1). Correct any faults found.

6 Park the vehicle on level ground, check that the front roadwheels are in the straight-ahead position, then rock the rear and front ends to settle the suspension. Release the handbrake, and roll the vehicle backwards 1 metre, then forwards again, to relieve any stresses in the steering and suspension components.

7 Measure the distance between the front edges of the wheel rims and the rear edges of the rims. Subtract the front measurement from the rear measurement, and check that the result is within the specified range.

8 If adjustment is necessary, apply the handbrake, then jack up the front of the vehicle and support it securely on axle stands (see *Jacking and vehicle support*). Turn the steering wheel onto full-left lock, and record the amount of exposed thread on the right-hand track rod balljoint. Now turn the steering onto full-right lock, and record the number of threads on the left-hand balljoint. If there is the same amount of thread visible on both sides, then subsequent adjustment should be made equally on both sides. If there are more thread is visible on one side than the other, it will be necessary to compensate for this during adjustment. **Note:** *Peugeot give an initial setting for the length of visible thread on each balljoint* **(see illustration 23.8)**. *It is most important that after adjustment, the same amount of thread is visible on each track rod end.*

9 First clean the track rod balljoint threads; if they are corroded, apply penetrating fluid before starting adjustment. Release the rubber gaiter outer clips (where necessary), and peel back the gaiters; apply a smear of grease to the inside of the gaiters, so that both are free, and will not be twisted or strained as their respective track rods are rotated.

10 Use a straight-edge and a scriber or similar to mark the relationship of each track rod to its balljoint then, holding each track rod in turn, unscrew its locknut fully **(see illustration)**.

11 Alter the length of the track rods, bearing in mind the note made in paragraph 8. Screw them onto or off of the balljoints, rotating the track rod using an open-ended spanner fitted to the flats provided on the track rod. Shortening the track rods (screwing them onto their balljoints) will reduce toe-in/increase toe-out.

12 When the setting is correct, hold the track rods and tighten the balljoint locknuts to the specified torque. Check the length of each track rod is equal by measuring the amount of exposed thread is equal on both balljoints. If they are not the same, then the adjustment has not been made equally, and problems will be encountered with tyre scrubbing in turns; also, the steering wheel spokes will no longer be horizontal when the wheels are in the straight-ahead position.

13 If the track rod lengths are the same, lower the vehicle to the ground and recheck the toe setting; re-adjust if necessary. When the setting is correct, tighten the track rod balljoint locknuts to the specified torque. Ensure that the rubber gaiters are seated correctly, and are not twisted or strained, and secure them in position with new retaining clips (where necessary).

Chapter 11
Bodywork and fittings

Contents

Degrees of difficulty

Easy, suitable for novice with little experience	Fairly easy, suitable for beginner with some experience	Fairly difficult, suitable for competent DIY mechanic	Difficult, suitable for experienced DIY mechanic	Very difficult, suitable for expert DIY or professional

Specifications

Torque wrench settings	Nm	lbf ft
Bonnet release lever bolt	6	4
Facia mounting bolts	19	14
Front seat mounting bolts	25	18
Rear seat back mounting bolts	23	17
Seat belt/inertia reel mounting bolts	30	22

1 General information

1 The bodyshell is made of pressed steel sections, and is available in both three- and five-door Hatchback versions. Most components are welded together, but some use is made of structural adhesives. The front wings are bolted on.

2 The bonnet, doors and some other vulnerable panels are made of zinc-coated metal, and are further protected by being coated with an anti-chip primer prior to being sprayed.

3 Extensive use is made of plastic materials, mainly in the interior, but also in exterior components. The front and rear bumpers and the front grille are injection-moulded from a synthetic material which is very strong, and yet light. Plastic components such as wheelarch liners are fitted to the underside of the vehicle, to improve the body's resistance to corrosion.

2 Maintenance – bodywork and underframe

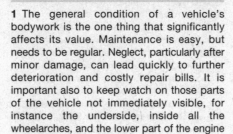

1 The general condition of a vehicle's bodywork is the one thing that significantly affects its value. Maintenance is easy, but needs to be regular. Neglect, particularly after minor damage, can lead quickly to further deterioration and costly repair bills. It is important also to keep watch on those parts of the vehicle not immediately visible, for instance the underside, inside all the wheelarches, and the lower part of the engine compartment.

2 The basic maintenance routine for the bodywork is washing – preferably with a lot of water, from a hose. This will remove all the loose solids which may have stuck to the vehicle. It is important to flush these off in such a way as to prevent grit from scratching the finish. The wheelarches and underframe need washing in the same way, to remove any accumulated mud which will retain moisture and tend to encourage rust. Paradoxically enough, the best time to clean the underframe and wheelarches is in wet weather, when the mud is thoroughly wet and soft. In very wet weather, the underframe is usually cleaned of large accumulations automatically, and this is a good time for inspection.

3 Annually, preferably just prior to winter, the underbody should be washed down and any damage to the wax coating repaired using underseal.

4 After washing paintwork, wipe off with a chamois leather to give an unspotted clear finish. A coat of clear protective wax polish will give added protection against chemical pollutants in the air. If the paintwork sheen has dulled or oxidised, use a cleaner/polisher combination to restore the brilliance of the shine. This requires a little effort, but such dulling is usually caused because regular washing has been neglected. Care needs to be taken with metallic paintwork, as a special non-abrasive cleaner/polisher is required to avoid damage to the finish. Always check that the door and ventilator opening drain holes

11

and pipes are completely clear, so that water can be drained out. Brightwork should be treated in the same way as paintwork. Windscreens and windows can be kept clear of the smeary film which often appears, by the use of proprietary glass cleaner. Never use any form of wax or other body or chromium polish on glass.

3 Maintenance – upholstery and carpets

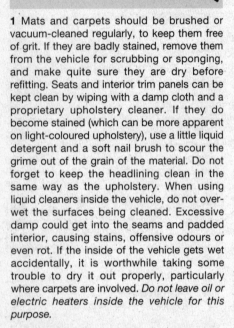

1 Mats and carpets should be brushed or vacuum-cleaned regularly, to keep them free of grit. If they are badly stained, remove them from the vehicle for scrubbing or sponging, and make quite sure they are dry before refitting. Seats and interior trim panels can be kept clean by wiping with a damp cloth and a proprietary upholstery cleaner. If they do become stained (which can be more apparent on light-coloured upholstery), use a little liquid detergent and a soft nail brush to scour the grime out of the grain of the material. Do not forget to keep the headlining clean in the same way as the upholstery. When using liquid cleaners inside the vehicle, do not over-wet the surfaces being cleaned. Excessive damp could get into the seams and padded interior, causing stains, offensive odours or even rot. If the inside of the vehicle gets wet accidentally, it is worthwhile taking some trouble to dry it out properly, particularly where carpets are involved. *Do not leave oil or electric heaters inside the vehicle for this purpose.*

4 Minor body damage – repair

Repairs of minor scratches in bodywork

1 If the scratch is very superficial, and does not penetrate to the metal of the bodywork, repair is very simple. Lightly rub the area of the scratch with a paintwork renovator, or a very fine cutting paste, to remove loose paint from the scratch, and to clear the surrounding bodywork of wax polish. Rinse the area with clean water.

2 Apply touch-up paint to the scratch using a fine paint brush; continue to apply fine layers of paint until the surface of the paint in the scratch is level with the surrounding paintwork. Allow the new paint at least two weeks to harden, then blend it into the surrounding paintwork by rubbing the scratch area with a paintwork renovator or a very fine cutting paste. Finally apply wax polish.

3 Where the scratch has penetrated right through to the metal of the bodywork, causing the metal to rust, a different repair technique is required. Remove any loose rust from the

bottom of the scratch with a penknife, then apply rust-inhibiting paint, to prevent the formation of rust in the future. Using a rubber or nylon applicator, fill the scratch with bodystopper paste. If required, this paste can be mixed with cellulose thinners, to provide a very thin paste which is ideal for filling narrow scratches. Before the stopper-paste in the scratch hardens, wrap a piece of smooth cotton rag around the top of a finger. Dip the finger in cellulose thinners, and quickly sweep it across the surface of the stopper-paste in the scratch; this will ensure that the surface of the stopper-paste is slightly hollowed. The scratch can now be painted over as described earlier in this Section.

Repairs of dents in bodywork

4 When deep denting of the vehicle's bodywork has taken place, the first task is to pull the dent out, until the affected bodywork almost attains its original shape. There is little point in trying to restore the original shape completely, as the metal in the damaged area will have stretched on impact, and cannot be reshaped fully to its original contour. It is better to bring the level of the dent up to a point which is about 3 mm below the level of the surrounding bodywork. In cases where the dent is very shallow anyway, it is not worth trying to pull it out at all. If the underside of the dent is accessible, it can be hammered out gently from behind, using a mallet with a wooden or plastic head. Whilst doing this, hold a suitable block of wood firmly against the outside of the panel, to absorb the impact from the hammer blows and thus prevent a large area of the bodywork from being 'belled-out'.

5 Should the dent be in a section of bodywork which has a double skin, or some other factor making it inaccessible from behind, a different technique is called for. Drill several small holes through the metal inside the area – particularly in the deeper section. Then screw long self-tapping screws into the holes, just sufficiently for them to gain a good purchase in the metal. Now the dent can be pulled out by pulling on the protruding heads of the screws with a pair of pliers.

6 The next stage of the repair is the removal of the paint from the damaged area, and from an inch or so of the surrounding 'sound' bodywork. This is accomplished most easily by using a wire brush or abrasive pad on a power drill, although it can be done just as effectively by hand, using sheets of abrasive paper. To complete the preparation for filling, score the surface of the bare metal with a screwdriver or the tang of a file, or alternatively, drill small holes in the affected area. This will provide a really good 'key' for the filler paste.

7 To complete the repair, see the Section on filling and respraying.

Repairs of rust holes or gashes in bodywork

8 Remove all paint from the affected area, and from an inch or so of the surrounding

'sound' bodywork, using an abrasive pad or a wire brush on a power drill. If these are not available, a few sheets of abrasive paper will do the job most effectively. With the paint removed, you will be able to judge the severity of the corrosion, and therefore decide whether to renew the whole panel (if this is possible) or to repair the affected area. New body panels are not as expensive as most people think, and it is often quicker and more satisfactory to fit a new panel than to attempt to repair large areas of corrosion.

9 Remove all fittings from the affected area, except those which will act as a guide to the original shape of the damaged bodywork (eg headlight shells etc). Then, using tin snips or a hacksaw blade, remove all loose metal and any other metal badly affected by corrosion. Hammer the edges of the hole inwards, in order to create a slight depression for the filler paste.

10 Wire-brush the affected area to remove the powdery rust from the surface of the remaining metal. Paint the affected area with rust-inhibiting paint; if the back of the rusted area is accessible, treat this also.

11 Before filling can take place, it will be necessary to block the hole in some way. This can be achieved by the use of aluminium or plastic mesh, or aluminium tape.

12 Aluminium or plastic mesh, or glass-fibre matting, is probably the best material to use for a large hole. Cut a piece to the approximate size and shape of the hole to be filled, then position it in the hole so that its edges are below the level of the surrounding bodywork. It can be retained in position by several blobs of filler paste around its periphery.

13 Aluminium tape should be used for small or very narrow holes. Pull a piece off the roll, trim it to the approximate size and shape required, then pull off the backing paper (if used) and stick the tape over the hole; it can be overlapped if the thickness of one piece is insufficient. Burnish down the edges of the tape with the handle of a screwdriver or similar, to ensure that the tape is securely attached to the metal underneath.

Bodywork repairs – filling and respraying

14 Before using this Section, see the Sections on dent, minor scratch, rust holes and gash repairs.

15 Many types of bodyfiller are available, but generally speaking, those proprietary kits which contain a tin of filler paste and a tube of resin hardener are best for this type of repair; some can be used directly from the tube. A wide, flexible plastic or nylon applicator will be found invaluable for imparting a smooth and well-contoured finish to the surface of the filler.

16 Mix up a little filler on a clean piece of card or board – measure the hardener carefully (follow the maker's instructions on the pack), otherwise the filler will set too

rapidly or too slowly. Using the applicator, apply the filler paste to the prepared area; draw the applicator across the surface of the filler to achieve the correct contour and to level the surface. As soon as a contour that approximates to the correct one is achieved, stop working the paste – if you carry on too long, the paste will become sticky and begin to 'pick-up' on the applicator. Continue to add thin layers of filler paste at 20-minute intervals, until the level of the filler is just proud of the surrounding bodywork.

17 Once the filler has hardened, the excess can be removed using a metal plane or file. From then on, progressively-finer grades of abrasive paper should be used, starting with a 40-grade production paper, and finishing with a 400-grade wet-and-dry paper. Always wrap the abrasive paper around a flat rubber, cork, or wooden block – otherwise the surface of the filler will not be completely flat. During the smoothing of the filler surface, the wet-and-dry paper should be periodically rinsed in water. This will ensure that a very smooth finish is imparted to the filler at the final stage.

18 At this stage, the 'dent' should be surrounded by a ring of bare metal, which in turn should be encircled by the finely 'feathered' edge of the good paintwork. Rinse the repair area with clean water, until all of the dust produced by the rubbing-down operation has gone.

19 Spray the whole area with a light coat of primer – this will show up any imperfections in the surface of the filler. Repair these imperfections with fresh filler paste or bodystopper, and once more smooth the surface with abrasive paper. If bodystopper is used, it can be mixed with cellulose thinners, to form a really thin paste which is ideal for filling small holes. Repeat this spray-and-repair procedure until you are satisfied that the surface of the filler, and the feathered edge of the paintwork, are perfect. Clean the repair area with clean water, and allow to dry fully.

20 The repair area is now ready for final spraying. Paint spraying must be carried out in a warm, dry, windless and dust-free atmosphere. This condition can be created artificially if you have access to a large indoor working area, but if you are forced to work in the open, you will have to pick your day very carefully. If you are working indoors, dousing the floor in the work area with water will help to settle the dust which would otherwise be in the atmosphere. If the repair area is confined to one body panel, mask off the surrounding panels; this will help to minimise the effects of a slight mismatch in paint colours. Bodywork fittings (eg chrome strips, door handles etc) will also need to be masked off. Use genuine masking tape, and several thicknesses of newspaper, for the masking operations.

21 Before commencing to spray, agitate the aerosol can thoroughly, then spray a test area (an old tin, or similar) until the technique is mastered. Cover the repair area with a thick coat of primer; the thickness should be built up using several thin layers of paint, rather than one thick one. Using 400 grade wet-and-dry paper, rub down the surface of the primer until it is really smooth. While doing this, the work area should be thoroughly doused with water, and the wet-and-dry paper periodically rinsed in water. Allow to dry before spraying on more paint.

22 Spray on the top coat, again building up the thickness by using several thin layers of paint. Start spraying at the top of the repair area, and then, using a side-to-side motion, work downwards until the whole repair area and about 2 inches of the surrounding original paintwork is covered. Remove all masking material 10 to 15 minutes after spraying on the final coat of paint.

23 Allow the new paint at least two weeks to harden, then, using a paintwork renovator or a very fine cutting paste, blend the edges of the paint into the existing paintwork. Finally, apply wax polish.

Plastic components

24 With the use of more and more plastic body components by the vehicle manufacturers (eg bumpers. spoilers, and in some cases major body panels), rectification of more serious damage to such items has become a matter of either entrusting repair work to a specialist in this field, or renewing complete components. Repair of such damage by the DIY owner is not really feasible, owing to the cost of the equipment and materials required for effecting such repairs. The basic technique involves making a groove along the line of the crack in the plastic, using a rotary burr in a power drill. The damaged part is then welded back together, using a hot air gun to heat up and fuse a plastic filler rod into the groove. Any excess plastic is then removed, and the area rubbed down to a smooth finish. It is important that a filler rod of the correct plastic is used, as body components can be made of a variety of different types (eg polycarbonate, ABS, polypropylene).

25 Damage of a less serious nature (abrasions, minor cracks etc) can be repaired by the DIY owner using a two-part epoxy filler repair material. Once mixed in equal proportions, this is used in similar fashion to the bodywork filler used on metal panels. The filler is usually cured in twenty to thirty minutes, ready for sanding and painting.

26 If the owner is renewing a complete component himself, or if he has repaired it with epoxy filler, he will be left with the problem of finding a suitable paint for finishing which is compatible with the type of plastic used. At one time, the use of a universal paint was not possible, owing to the complex range of plastics encountered in body component applications. Standard paints, generally speaking, will not bond to plastic or rubber satisfactorily. However, it is now possible to obtain a plastic body parts finishing kit which consists of a pre-primer treatment, a primer and coloured top coat. Full instructions are normally supplied with a kit, but basically, the method of use is to first apply the pre-primer to the component concerned, and allow it to dry for up to 30 minutes. Then the primer is applied, and left to dry for about an hour before finally applying the special-coloured top coat. The result is a correctly-coloured component, where the paint will flex with the plastic or rubber, a property that standard paint does not normally posses.

5 Major body damage – repair

1 Where serious damage has occurred, or large areas need renewal due to neglect, it means that complete new panels will need welding-in, and this is best left to professionals. If the damage is due to impact, it will also be necessary to check completely the alignment of the bodyshell, and this can only be carried out accurately by a Peugeot dealer using special jigs. If the body is left misaligned, it is primarily dangerous, as the car will not handle properly, and secondly, uneven stresses will be imposed on the steering, suspension and possibly transmission, causing abnormal wear, or complete failure, particularly to such items as the tyres.

6 Front bumper – removal and refitting

Removal

1 Open the bonnet. For improved access, apply the handbrake, then jack up the front of the vehicle and support securely on axle stands (see *Jacking and vehicle support*).

2 Remove the four fasteners (pull out the centre pin then remove the complete fastener) securing the grille panel to the top of the front panel. Release the lower retaining clips and unclip the grille panel from the front trim panel in an upwards direction **(see illustrations)**.

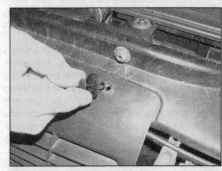

6.2a Pull out the centre pins and remove the fasteners securing the grille panel in position . . .

11

6.2b . . . then release the lower retaining clips (arrowed) and unclip the grille panel from the bumper in an upwards direction

6.3a Undo the retaining screws (arrowed) . . .

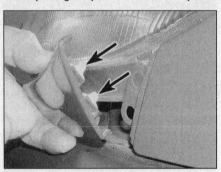

6.3b . . . then unclip each end of the panel from the wing . . .

3 Slacken and remove the retaining screws securing the front trim panel in position. Carefully unclip the trim panel from the inner edge of each headlight then unclip the ends of the panel from each wing and remove the panel from the vehicle (see illustrations).

4 Slacken and remove the three bumper upper retaining bolts (see illustration).

5 Undo the screws securing the front section of the left-hand wheelarch liner to the base of the bumper. Remove the fasteners securing the liner section to the body then manoeuvre the front section of the liner out from underneath the wing (see illustrations).

6 Remove the front section of the right-hand wheelarch liner in the same way.

7 Unscrew the nut securing each end of the bumper to the wings, and the two bolts securing the base of the bumper to the body (see illustrations).

8 On models with foglights, disconnect the battery negative lead, then disconnect the foglight wiring connectors (see illustration).

9 Carefully free the bumper ends from the wings and withdraw the bumper from the front of the vehicle (see illustration). On models equipped with headlight washers, disconnect the washer hose as the bumper is removed.

6.3c . . . and remove the front trim panel from the vehicle

6.4 Slacken and remove the three bumper retaining bolts

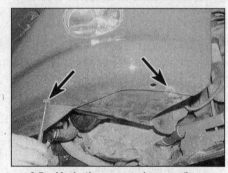

6.5a Undo the screws (arrowed) . . .

6.5b . . . then pull out the centre pins and remove the retaining fasteners . . .

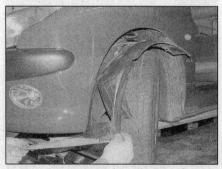

6.5c . . . and remove the front section of each wheelarch liner

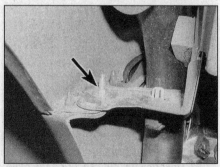

6.7a Unscrew the nut (arrowed) securing the bumper ends to each wing . . .

6.7b . . . and the bolts securing the base of the bumper to the body

6.8 On models with front foglights, disconnect the wiring connector from each foglight

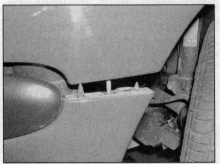

6.9 Free each end of the bumper from the wings and remove the bumper from the vehicle

Refitting

10 Refitting is a reversal of removal, ensuring the bumper is correctly engaged with the wings.

7 Rear bumper – removal and refitting

Removal

1 For improved access, chock the front wheels, then jack up the rear of the vehicle and support securely on axle stands (see *Jacking and vehicle support*).
2 Open the tailgate, and remove the three bumper upper retaining screws.
3 Undo the screw securing the right-hand wheelarch inner shield to the base of the bumper then remove the retaining fastener fasteners (pull out the centre pin then remove the complete fastener) and manoeuvre the shield out of position **(see illustrations)**. Remove the left-hand shield in the same way.
4 Working under the bumper, unscrew the two nuts securing the base of the bumper to the body and the nut securing each end of the bumper in position **(see illustrations)**.
5 Free the ends of the bumper and remove the bumper from the vehicle, disconnecting the wiring connector from the rear foglight **(see illustration)**.

Refitting

6 Refitting is a reversal of removal.

8 Bonnet – removal, refitting and adjustment

Removal

1 Open the bonnet and have an assistant support it, then, using a pencil or felt tip pen, mark the outline of each bonnet hinge relative to the bonnet, to use as a guide on refitting.
2 Disconnect the windscreen washer fluid hose from its connector then unclip the hose from the bonnet **(see illustrations)**.

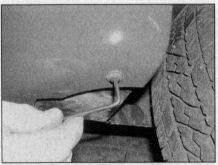

7.3a Undo the retaining screw . . .

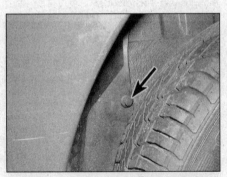

7.3b . . . then remove the fastener (arrowed) . . .

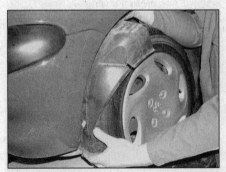

7.3c . . . and remove the wheelarch inner shield from the rear bumper

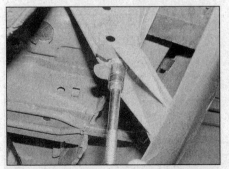

7.4a Unscrew the nuts securing the base of the bumper to the vehicle . . .

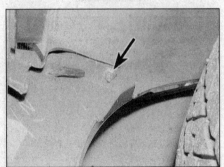

7.4b . . . and the nut securing each end of the bumper to the body

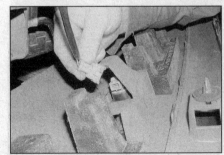

7.5 Remove the rear bumper from the vehicle, disconnecting the wiring connector from the foglight

11

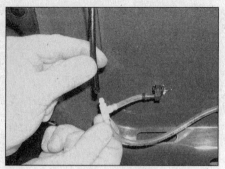

8.2a Disconnect the washer fluid hose from its connector . . .

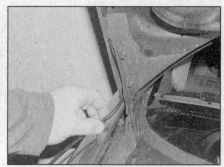

8.2b . . . and unclip the hose from the bonnet

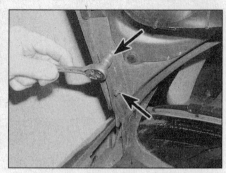

8.3 Unscrew the nuts (arrowed) securing the bonnet to the hinges and remove the bonnet from the vehicle

3 Unscrew the bonnet retaining nuts and, with the help of the assistant, carefully lift the bonnet from the vehicle **(see illustration)**. Store the bonnet out of the way in a safe place.
4 Inspect the bonnet hinges for signs of wear and free play at the pivots, and if necessary renew. Each hinge is secured to the body by two bolts. On refitting, apply a smear of multi-purpose grease to the hinges.

Refitting and adjustment

5 With the aid of an assistant, offer up the bonnet and loosely fit the retaining bolts. Align the hinges with the marks made on removal, then tighten the retaining nuts securely. Reconnect the windscreen washer hose and clip it securely to the bonnet.
6 Close the bonnet, and check for alignment with the adjacent panels. If necessary, slacken the hinge bolts and re-align the bonnet to suit. Once the bonnet is correctly aligned, tighten the hinge bolts securely.
7 Once the bonnet is correctly aligned, check that the bonnet fastens and releases in a satisfactory manner.

9 Bonnet release cable – removal and refitting

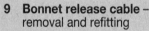

Removal

1 Remove the bonnet lock as described in Section 10.

2 Remove the retaining clips and free the outer cable from the front panel **(see illustration)**. Tie a length of string to the end of the cable then work back along the cable, freeing it from any retaining clips whilst noting its correct routing. Free the cable grommet from the bulkhead.
3 On left-hand drive models, to improve access to the release lever, remove the built-in systems interface (BSI) unit from the base of the fusebox (see Chapter 12).
4 On all models, reach up under the facia and unscrew the bolt securing the bonnet release lever to the body **(see illustration)**.
5 Withdraw the release lever and cable assembly from the vehicle. When the end of the cable appears, untie the string and leave it in position; it can then be used to draw the cable back into position on refitting.

Refitting

6 Prior to refitting, lubricate the cable grommet with a silicone-based spray lubricant.
7 Tie the string to the end of the cable then use the string to draw the cable through the bulkhead and into the engine compartment.
8 Ensure the cable is correctly routed and retained by all the necessary clips then untie the string. Pull the cable grommet through and seat it correctly in the bulkhead.
9 Ensure the grommet is correctly located then seat the release cable lever correctly on the body, tightening its retaining bolt to the specified torque. On left-hand drive models,

refit the built-in system interface (BSI) unit (see Chapter 12).
10 Seat the outer cable correctly in the front panel. Ensure the cable is correctly routed then secure it in position with all the retaining clips.
11 Refit the bonnet lock as described in Section 10.

10 Bonnet lock – removal and refitting

Removal

1 Open the bonnet.
2 Remove the four fasteners (pull out the centre pin then remove the complete fastener) securing the grille panel to the top of the front panel. Release the lower retaining clips and unclip the grille panel from the front trim panel in an upwards direction **(see illustrations 6.2a and 6.2b)**.
3 Trace the wiring back from the lock switch (where fitted) to its wiring connector. Free the connector from its retaining clip and separate the two halves of the connector **(see illustration)**.
4 Unscrew the retaining bolts and free the lock from the front panel then unclip the release cable and remove the lock from the vehicle **(see illustrations)**.

Refitting

5 Attach the lock to the release cable then

9.2 Release the retaining clips (arrowed) and free the bonnet release cable from the front panel

9.4 Bonnet release lever bolt (arrowed)

10.3 Disconnecting the bonnet lock switch wiring connector

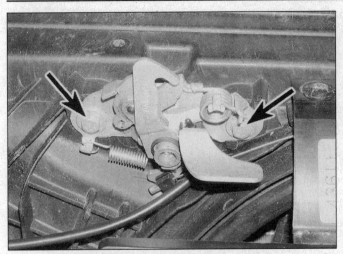

10.4a Unscrew the bolts (arrowed) . . .

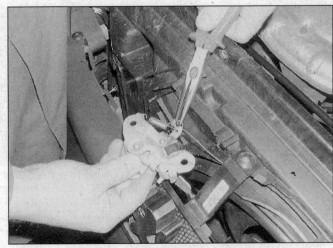

10.4b . . . then free the bonnet lock from the front panel and disconnect the release cable

seat the lock on the front panel and securely tighten its retaining bolts.

6 Reconnect the lock switch wiring connector and clip the connector onto the front panel.

7 Check the operation of the bonnet lock then refit the grille panel and secure it in position with the fasteners.

11 Door –
removal, refitting and adjustment

Front door

Removal

1 Disconnect the battery negative lead.

2 Open the door then unscrew the bolt securing the door check strap to the pillar **(see illustration)**.

3 Rotate the door wiring harness connector locking ring anti-clockwise and disconnect the connector from the socket in the door pillar **(see illustration)**.

4 Have an assistant support the door, then unscrew the pivot pins from the upper and lower hinges **(see illustration)**. The door can then be removed from the vehicle.
Caution: The door is heavy.

5 If necessary, with the door removed, undo

the retaining bolts and remove the hinges from the body and door **(see illustrations)**. Take care not to lose the hinge locating dowels.

Refitting

6 If the hinges were removed, ensure the locating dowels are in position, then refit the hinges to the body and door. Tighten the hinge retaining bolts securely. If the paintwork around the hinges has been damaged, paint the affected area with a suitable touch-up brush to prevent corrosion.

7 Lubricate the hinge pivot pins with multi-purpose grease. With the aid of an assistant,

offer up the door to the vehicle taking care not to damage the paintwork. Refit the pivot pins to the upper and lower hinges and tighten them securely.

8 Reconnect the door wiring connector and secure it in position by rotating the locking ring until the index marks align.

9 Seat the check link on the pillar and securely tighten its retaining bolt.

10 Reconnect the battery then close the door and check the door alignment.

Adjustment

11 Close the door and check its alignment with the surrounding panels. The hinges are

11.2 Unscrew the bolt securing the check strap to the door pillar

11.3 Rotate the locking ring anti-clockwise and disconnect the door connector from the pillar

11.4 Unscrew the hinge pins and remove the door from the vehicle

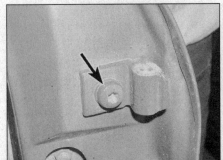

11.5a The hinges are secured to the door by a single bolt . . .

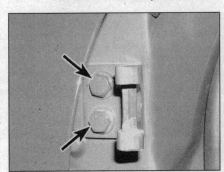

11.5b . . . and to the pillar by two bolts (arrowed)

11.14 Rotate the locking ring anti-clockwise and disconnect the door wiring connector

11.16 Unscrew the hinge pins and remove the rear door

located on dowels (unless they have been removed) so it is not possible to slacken the hinge bolts and reposition the hinges on the door/body. If the door is not correctly aligned, check the hinges are not worn or damaged. If necessary, remove the door and renew the hinges.

12 If adjustment is necessary, remove the door and unbolt the hinge from the body. Refit the hinge to the body without the locating dowels, tightening the hinge bolts lightly, and install the door. Align the door correctly with its surrounding panels then tighten the hinge bolts securely; the bolts can be accessed from behind the wheelarch once the liner has been freed.

Rear door

Removal

13 Disconnect the battery negative lead.
14 Open the front door to gain access to the rear door wiring harness connector. Rotate the connector locking ring anti-clockwise and disconnect the connector from the socket in the door pillar **(see illustration)**.
15 Unscrew the bolt securing the door check strap to the pillar.
16 Have an assistant support the door, then unscrew the pivot pins from the upper and lower hinges **(see illustration)**. The door can then be removed from the vehicle.
Caution: The door is heavy.
17 If necessary, with the door removed, undo the retaining bolts and remove the hinges from the body and door. Take care not to lose

the locating dowel fitted to the door side of the hinge.

Refitting

18 If the hinges were removed, ensure the locating dowel is in position, then refit the hinges to the body and door. Ensure the hinges are correctly located then tighten their retaining bolts securely. If the paintwork around the hinges has been damaged, paint the affected area with a suitable touch-up brush to prevent corrosion.
19 Lubricate the hinge pivot pins with multi-purpose grease. With the aid of an assistant, offer up the door to the vehicle taking care not to damage the paintwork. Refit the pivot pins to the upper and lower hinges and tighten them securely.
20 Reconnect the door wiring connector and secure it in position by rotating the locking ring until the index marks align.
21 Seat the check link on the pillar and securely tighten its retaining bolt.
22 Reconnect the battery then close the door and check the door alignment.

Adjustment

23 Close the door and check its alignment with the surrounding panels. The door side of the hinge is located on a dowel (unless it has been removed) and the body side of the hinges has built-in locating pin, so it is not possible to slacken the hinge bolts and reposition the hinges on the door/body. If the door is not correctly aligned, check the hinges are not worn or damaged. If necessary, remove the door and renew the hinges.

24 If adjustment is necessary, remove the door and door hinges. Enlarge the hinge locating pin holes in the pillar slightly using a drill. Refit the hinges to the door without the locating dowels and refit the hinges to the pillar. Lightly tighten the hinge bolts and install the door. Align the door correctly with its surrounding panels then tighten the hinge bolts securely.

---

12 Door inner trim panel –
removal and refitting

Removal

Note: *Door trim panel design varies according to the specification level of the vehicle and therefore some of the trim panel fasteners locations on your vehicle may be different to those shown in the accompanying illustrations.*

1 Fully lower the window glass then disconnect the battery negative terminal. Proceed as described under the relevant sub-heading.

Front door

2 Carefully unclip the exterior mirror inner trim panel from the front of the door. On models with manually-adjusted mirrors, remove the rubber gaiter from the adjustment handle prior to unclipping the trim panel. Rotate the tweeter speaker (where fitted) to free it from the panel then remove the panel from the vehicle **(see illustrations)**.
3 On models with manually-operated windows, pull the window winder regulator handle off its spindle and remove it, along with the spacer.
4 Carefully prise out the door lock inner handle surround from the panel **(see illustration)**.
5 Slacken and remove the retaining screws from the front edge of the trim panel.
6 Slacken and remove the screw securing the trim panel pocket to the door **(see illustration)**.
7 Make a final check that all the retaining screws have been removed then carefully unclip the base of the trim panel from the door

12.2a Unclip the exterior mirror inner trim panel from the door

12.2b Rotate the tweeter speaker (where fitted) to free it from the mirror panel

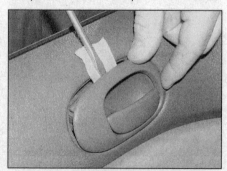

12.4 Carefully prise out the handle surround from the trim panel

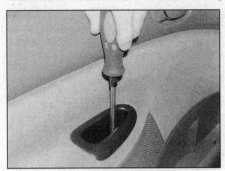

12.6 Undo the screw securing the trim panel pocket in position

12.7 Unclip the base of the trim panel from the door then remove the panel in an upwards direction

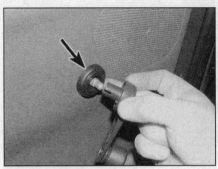

12.8 On models with manual windows, pull off the regulator handle and remove the spacer (arrowed)

and manoeuvre it upwards and away from the door **(see illustration).**

Rear door

8 On models with manually-operated windows, pull the window winder regulator handle off its spindle **(see illustration).**
9 Carefully prise out the door lock inner handle surround from the panel **(see illustration).**
10 Slacken and remove the retaining screw securing the trim panel pocket to the door.
11 Carefully unclip the base of the trim panel from the door and manoeuvre it upwards and away from the door **(see illustration).**

Refitting

12 Refitting is a reversal of removal. Prior to refitting, check the trim panel retaining studs for signs of damage and renew any which were broken on removal.

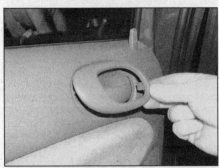

12.9 Unclip the inner handle surround from the trim panel

12.11 Unclip the base of the trim panel from the door then remove the panel in an upwards direction

loudspeaker and housing will need to be removed from the door (see Chapter 12) before the insulation panel can be removed.
3 Slide the handle forwards, to unclip it from the door, then detach it from the end of the link rod **(see illustration).**

Refitting

4 Engage the handle with the link rod then clip the handle securely into the door.
5 Check the operation of the handle and lock assembly then securely stick the insulation panel back to the door **(see illustrations).**
Note: *If a new insulation panel is being fitted, remove all traces of the original adhesive from the door with a suitable solvent. Align the new panel with the door then install the alignment peg(s) before carefully sticking the panel to the door, ensuring its is not creased or torn. On the rear door, refit he loudspeaker (see Chapter 12).*

---

13 Door handle and lock components – removal and refitting

Door lock inner handle

Removal

1 Remove the inner trim panel as described in Section 12.
2 Remove the alignment peg(s) from the top of the foam insulation panel then carefully peel/cut the panel away from the door sufficiently to gain access to the handle and lock **(see illustrations). Note:** *This is likely to result in the insulation panel being torn or damaged. If this is the case, remove the panel completely and discard it and obtain a new panel for use on refitting. On the rear door the*

13.2a Remove the alignment peg(s) . . .

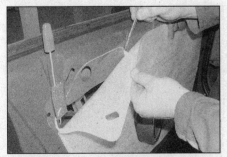

13.2b . . . then carefully cut the insulation panel away from the door to gain access to the handle/lock (front door shown)

13.3 Free the inner handle from the door and unhook it from the end of the link rod

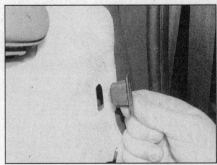

13.5a Install the alignment peg(s) . . .

13.5b ... then stick the insulation panel securely to the door, taking care not to crease or tear it (rear door shown)

6 Refit the inner trim panel as described in Section 12.

Front door lock

Removal

7 Remove the inner handle and lock cylinder from the door as described elsewhere in this section.
8 Fully raise the window glass.
9 Free the inner handle link rod from its guide **(see illustration)**.
10 Unclip and detach the exterior handle link rod from the lock.
11 Peel the lock button foam guide away from the door so it is free to be removed with the lock assembly **(see illustration)**.
12 Slacken and remove the three screws securing the lock to the door **(see illustration)**.
13 Manoeuvre the lock out of position then

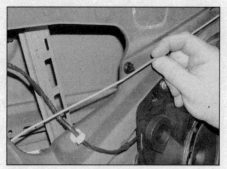

13.9 Unclip the handle link rod from its guide

release the retaining clip and disconnect the wiring connector **(see illustration)**.

Refitting

14 Refitting is the reverse of removal. Prior to sticking the insulation panel to the door, reconnect the battery and check the operation of the lock and handles. If all is well stick the panel securely in position (see paragraph 5) then refit the trim panel (Section 12).

Front door exterior handle

Removal

Note: *A pop rivet gun and suitable rivets will be required on refitting.*

15 Remove the inner trim panel as described in Section 12.
16 Remove the alignment peg(s) from the top of the foam insulation panel then carefully peel/cut the panel away from the door sufficiently to gain access to the handle and

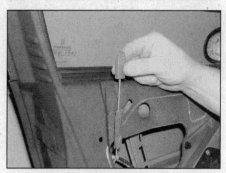

13.11 Free the lock button foam guide from the door

lock. **Note:** *This is likely to result in the insulation panel being torn or damaged. If this is the case, remove the panel completely, discard it and obtain a new panel for use on refitting.*
17 Fully raise the window glass.
18 Unclip and detach the exterior handle link rod from the lock.
19 Lift the handle then carefully drill the heads off the pop rivets securing the handle to the door **(see illustration)**.
Caution: Take care not to damage the handle/door when drilling out the rivets.

Refitting

20 Refitting is the reverse of removal, securing the handle in position with new pop rivets. Prior to sticking the insulation panel to the door, reconnect the battery and check the operation of the lock and handles. If all is well stick the panel securely in position (see paragraph 5) then refit the trim panel (Section 12).

Front door lock cylinder

Removal/refitting using the special tool

Note: *This procedure requires the use of Peugeot special lock removal tool. A suitable alternative can be made by brazing a medium-size self-tapping screw to the end of a piece of rod.*

21 Open the door. Prise out the plug from the rear of the door to gain access to the lock cylinder retaining clip **(see illustration)**.
22 Carefully insert the removal tool in through the door aperture and screw it securely into the retaining clip **(see illustration)**.

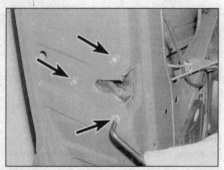

13.12 Undo the screws (arrowed) securing the lock to the door

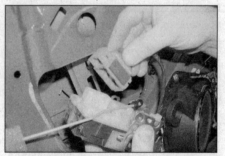

13.13 Manoeuvre the lock assembly out of position then lift the retaining clip and disconnect its wiring connector

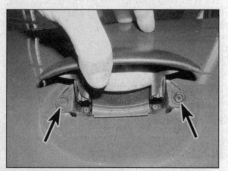

13.19 Door handle is secured in position with pop rivets (arrowed)

13.21 Remove the plug from the rear of the front door ...

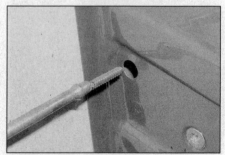

13.22 ... then insert the removal tool in through the hole and screw it into the lock cylinder retaining clip

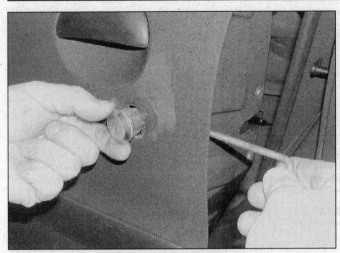

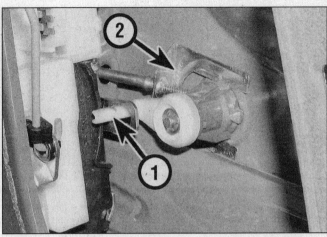

13.23 Pull the tool to the rear to release the retaining clip then manoeuvre the lock cylinder out of position

13.24 Ensure the lock cylinder pin (1) engages correctly with the lock then secure the lock cylinder in position by sliding the retaining clip (2) back into position (shown with panel removed)

23 Pull on the tool to release the retaining clip from the lock cylinder then manoeuvre the lock cylinder out of position (see illustration). Whilst the lock cylinder is removed, leave the removal tool in position.

24 Ensure the lock cylinder seal is in good condition then manoeuvre the cylinder into position. Engage the lock cylinder pin with the lock then seat the cylinder in the door. Hold the lock cylinder firmly against the door then secure it in position by sliding the retaining clip onto the lock. Ensure the lock cylinder is securely retained by the clip then check the operation of the lock assembly (see illustration). Unscrew the removal tool from the retaining clip then refit the access plug to the door. Note: *Do not remove the tool from the retaining clip until you are certain the lock cylinder and retaining clip are correctly fitted.*

Removal/refitting without the special tool

25 Remove the inner trim panel as described in Section 12.

26 Remove the alignment peg(s) from the top of the foam insulation panel then carefully peel/cut the panel away from the door sufficiently to gain access to the handle and lock. Note: *This is likely to result in the insulation panel being torn or damaged. If this*

is the case, remove the panel completely, discard it and obtain a new panel for use on refitting.

27 Fully raise the window glass.

28 Slide the retaining clip off the lock cylinder then manoeuvre the cylinder out from the door.

29 Refitting is the reverse of removal. Prior to sticking the insulation panel to the door, reconnect the battery and check the operation of the lock and handles. If all is well stick the panel securely in position (see paragraph 5) then refit the trim panel (Section 12).

Rear door lock

Removal

30 Remove the inner handle as described in paragraphs 1 to 3.

31 Fully raise the window glass.

32 Free the inner handle link rod from its guide.

33 Unclip the inner locking button pivot from the door (see illustration). Free the button link rod from its guide and ease the button out of its foam guide so it is free to be removed with the lock.

34 Slacken and remove the three screws securing the lock to the door (see illustration).

35 Release the retaining clip and disconnect the wiring connector from the lock then manoeuvre the lock assembly out of position (see illustration).

Refitting

36 Refitting is the reverse of removal. Prior to sticking the insulation panel to the door, reconnect the battery and check the operation of the lock and handles. If all is well stick the panel securely in position (see paragraph 5) then refit the trim panel (Section 12).

Rear door exterior handle

Removal

Note: *A pop rivet gun and suitable rivets will be required on refitting.*

37 Lift the handle then carefully drill the heads off the pop rivets securing the handle to the door. The handle can then be removed from the door.

Caution: *Take care not to damage the handle/door when drilling out the rivets.*

Refitting

38 Refitting is the reverse of removal, securing the handle in position with new pop rivets.

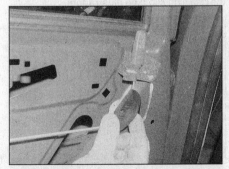

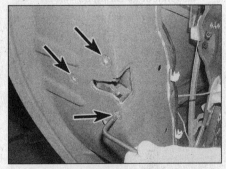

13.33 Unclip the inner locking button pivot from the door and free the button from its foam guide

13.34 Remove the retaining screws (arrowed) . . .

13.35 . . . then disconnect the wiring connector and manoeuvre the lock out from the rear door

11

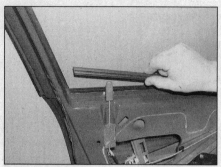

14.3 Remove the inner sealing strip from the top of the door

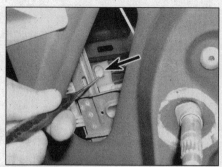

14.5a Depress the retaining clip (arrowed) and slide the window glass out from the regulator guide . . .

14.5b . . . then lift it out from the door

14 Door window glass and regulator – removal and refitting

Removal

1 Remove the inner trim panel as described in Section 12.

2 Remove the alignment peg(s) from the top of the foam insulation panel then carefully peel/cut the panel away from the door sufficiently to gain access to the regulator and window glass **(see illustrations 13.2a and 13.2b)**. **Note:** *This is likely to result in the insulation panel being torn or damaged. If this is the case, remove the panel completely and discard it and obtain a new panel for use on refitting. On the rear door the loudspeaker and housing will need to be removed from the door (see Chapter 12) before*

the insulation panel can be removed.

Window glass

3 Remove the inner sealing strip from the top of the door, noting which way around it is fitted **(see illustration)**.

4 Position the window approximately two-thirds of the way down so access can be gained to the glass retaining clip(s) on the regulator guide(s) (the front window has two clips and guides, the rear window one).

5 Depress the retaining clip(s) with a screwdriver then release the window glass from the regulator guide(s) and carefully manoeuvre it upwards and out from the top of the door **(see illustrations)**.

Window regulator

Note: *A pop rivet gun and suitable rivets will be required on refitting.*

6 Position the window approximately two-thirds of the way down so access can be gained to the glass retaining clip(s) on the regulator guide(s) (the front window has two clips and guides, the rear window one).

7 Depress the retaining clip(s) with a screwdriver then release the window glass from the regulator guide(s). Slide the window glass fully up and hold it in position by taping it to the door frame **(see illustration)**.

8 On models with electric windows, release the retaining clip and disconnect the wiring connector from the regulator motor **(see illustration)**.

9 On all models, carefully drill the heads off the pop rivets securing the regulator mechanism to the door. If the front door regulator is being removed, it will also be necessary to unclip the regulator cable clip from the door **(see illustrations)**.

Caution: Take care not to damage the regulator/door when drilling out the rivets.

10 Free the regulator mechanism from the door and manoeuvre it out of position **(see illustration)**.

Refitting

Window glass

11 Manoeuvre the glass back into position in the door and engage it with the regulator guide(s). Ensure the glass is securely retained by the guide clip(s) (as applicable).

12 Refit the inner sealing strip to the top of the door, ensuring it is the correct way around.

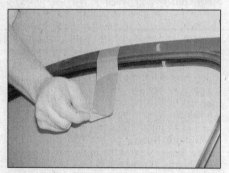

14.7 Release the window glass from the regulator and tape it to the top of the door frame

14.8 On models with electric windows disconnect the wiring connector from the regulator motor

14.9a Carefully drill the heads off all the pop rivets securing the regulator to the door

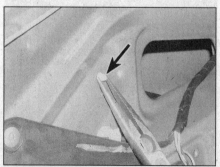

14.9b If the front door regulator is being removed free the cable clip from the door

14.10 Manoeuvre the regulator out through the door aperture

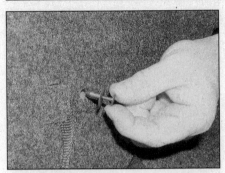

15.3 Pull out the centre pin and remove the fastener securing the luggage compartment side trim panel to the body

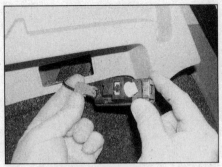

15.4 Remove the courtesy light from the left-hand upper trim panel and disconnect it from the wiring connector

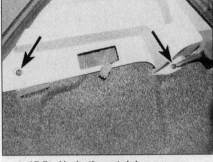

15.5a Undo the retaining screws (arrowed) . . .

13 Check the operation of the window then securely stick the insulation panel back to the door. **Note:** *If a new insulation panel is being fitted, remove all traces of the original adhesive from the door with a suitable solvent. Align the new panel with the door then install the alignment pegs before carefully sticking the panel to the door, ensuring its is not creased or torn* **(see illustrations 13.5a and 13.5b).** *On the rear door, refit he loudspeaker (see Chapter 12).*
14 Refit the inner trim panel as described in Section 12.

Window regulator

15 Remove the remnants of the original rivets from the regulator/door.
16 Manoeuvre the regulator into position in the door and align it with its mountings. **Note:** *If the front door mechanism is being installed, take great care not to twist the regulator cables on installation.*
17 Ensure the regulator is correctly positioned then secure it in position with new pop rivets.
18 Remove the tape then slide the window glass down and engage it with the regulator guide(s). Ensure the glass is securely retained by the guide clip(s) (as applicable).
19 Reconnect the wiring connector (where necessary) then check the operation of the window before securely sticking the insulation panel back to the door. **Note:** *If a new insulation panel is being fitted, remove all traces of the original adhesive from the door*

with a suitable solvent. Align the new panel with the door then install the alignment peg(s) before carefully sticking the panel to the door, ensuring its is not creased or torn* **(see illustrations 13.5a and 13.5b).** *On the rear door, refit he loudspeaker (see Chapter 12).*
20 Refit the inner trim panel as described in Section 12.

15 Tailgate and support struts – removal and refitting

Tailgate

Removal

Note: *Obtain a connector to enable the tailgate washer hose to be joined on refitting.*
1 Open the tailgate then disconnect the battery negative lead.
2 Fold down the rear seats then remove the parcel shelf.
3 Remove the fastener(s) (pull out the centre pin then remove the complete fastener) and free the luggage compartment left-hand side trim panel from the body to gain access to the tailgate wiring connector **(see illustration).**
4 Remove the luggage compartment courtesy light from the upper trim panel and disconnect it from the wiring connector **(see illustration).**
5 Slacken and remove the retaining screws

15.5b . . . then unclip the left-hand upper trim panel from the body

securing the left-hand upper trim panel to the rear pillar then unclip the panel and free it from the body **(see illustrations).**
6 Unscrew the bolt securing the tailgate earth lead to the rear pillar then lift the retaining clip and disconnect the tailgate wiring harness connector. Release the wiring from its retaining clips then free the wiring harness grommet from the body and withdraw the wiring **(see illustrations).**
7 Free the tailgate washer hose grommet from the right-hand side of the body and cut the tailgate washer hose; a connector will be required to rejoin the hose on refitting **(see illustration). Note:** *If it is not wished to cut the washer hose, remove the high-level stoplight (see Chapter 12, Section 7) then withdraw the hose from the tailgate.*

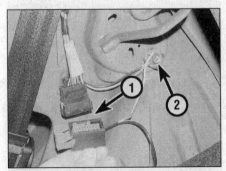

15.6a Disconnect the tailgate wiring harness connector (1) and unbolt the earth lead (2) . . .

15.6b . . . then free the wiring harness grommet from the body and withdraw the wiring

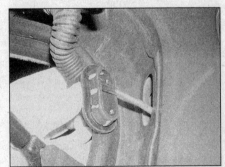

15.7 Free the washer hose grommet from the right-hand side of the body and cut the tailgate washer hose

11

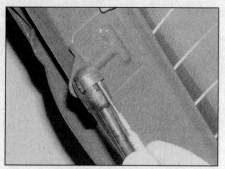

15.8 Lift the retaining clip and detach each support strut from the tailgate

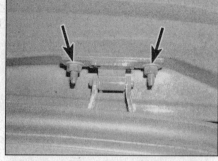

15.9 Unscrew the nuts securing the tailgate to the hinges and remove the tailgate

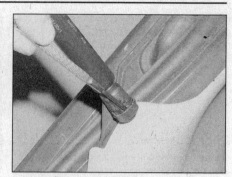

15.13 Lift the retaining clips and free the support strut from its balljoints

8 Have an assistant support the tailgate then carefully lift the retaining clips and detach both support struts from the tailgate (**see illustration**).

9 Unscrew the nuts securing the hinges to the tailgate, then carefully remove the tailgate from the vehicle (**see illustration**).

10 Inspect the hinges for signs of wear or damage. If renewal is necessary, free the tailgate sealing strip from the top of its aperture then carefully unclip the upper trim panel from the rear of the roof. Carefully peel back the headlining to gain access to the hinge nuts. Draw around the outline of each hinge then undo the retaining nuts and remove the hinges from the vehicle. Fit the new hinges, aligning them with the marks made prior to removal, and securely tighten the hinge retaining nuts. Clip the headlining back into position and refit the upper trim panel. Ensure the panel is correctly refitted

then seat the sealing strip back on the body.

Refitting
11 Refitting is a reversal of removal. Prior to refitting the trim panels, reconnect the battery and check the operation of all the tailgate electrical components. On completion, ensure the tailgate is correctly aligned with its surrounding panels; adjustments can be made by slackening the hinge bolts and reposition the tailgate and by adjusting the tailgate rubber buffers.

Support struts

Removal
12 Support the tailgate in the open position, with the help of an assistant, or using a stout piece of wood.
13 Using a small flat-bladed screwdriver, carefully lift the retaining clips and unhook the support strut from its balljoints (**see illustration**).

Refitting
14 Refitting is a reversal of removal ensuring the strut is fitted the correct way around and is securely held by its retaining clips.

16 Tailgate lock components – removal and refitting

Removal
1 Open the tailgate then disconnect the battery negative terminal.
2 Carefully unclip the inner trim panel from the tailgate. Proceed as described under the relevant sub-heading.

Lock assembly
3 Unclip the lock link rod from the handle assembly (**see illustration**).
4 Unscrew the two retaining screws and remove the lock from the tailgate (**see illustrations**).

Lock handle
5 Unclip the lock link rod from the handle assembly.
6 Disconnect the wiring connector from the central locking motor.
7 Unscrew the two retaining nuts then manoeuvre the handle assembly out of position. If necessary the outer trim strip can then be unclipped and removed from the tailgate (**see illustrations**).

Refitting
8 Refitting is the reverse of removal ensuring

16.3 Unclip the link rod from the handle . . .

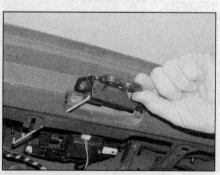

16.4b . . . and remove the lock assembly from the tailgate

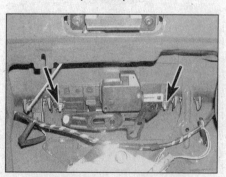

16.4a . . . then undo the retaining screws (arrowed) . . .

16.7a Undo the retaining nuts (arrowed) . . .

16.7b . . . and remove the lock handle from the tailgate

the link rod is securely reconnected. Check the operation of the lock and handle before refitting the trim panel.

17 Central locking components – removal and refitting

Door lock motor

1 Each door lock motor is integral with the lock assembly and cannot be renewed separately. If the motor is faulty, the complete lock assembly must be renewed (see Section 13).

Tailgate lock motor

2 Carefully unclip the inner trim panel from the tailgate.
3 Disconnect the wiring connector then undo the retaining screw and remove the motor from the tailgate lock handle (**see illustration**).
4 Refitting is the reverse of removal. Check the operation of the motor before refitting the trim panel.

Electronic control unit (ECU)

5 The central locking system control unit (ECU) and the remote signal receiver are an integral part of the built-in systems interface (BSI) unit. Refer to Chapter 12 for removal and refitting details.

Remote control transmitter batteries

6 Using a small screwdriver, carefully prise the two halves of the transmitter apart, and remove the battery, noting which way round it is fitted.
7 Fit the new battery, ensuring that it is fitted the correct way round; the battery and transmitter terminals are marked + and – to avoid confusion. Clip the transmitter back together and check the operation of the transmitter. If the transmitter does not function correctly, reprogram the unit as follows.
a) Press and hold the transmitter locking button until the indicator light on the transmitter stops flashing then release the button. The indicator light should remain on.
b) With the indicator light lit, press the locking button twice then insert the key and turn on the ignition. Wait at least three seconds then switch the ignition off. The transmitter should now be reprogrammed and function as normal.

18 Electric window components renewal – general information

Window switches

1 Refer to Chapter 12.

Window winder motors

2 At the time of writing is was unclear

16.7c With the lock handle removed, the outer trim strip can be unclipped

whether the window winder motors were available separately or whether the complete regulator assembly would have to be renewed. Refer to your Peugeot dealer for the latest information. Regulator removal and refitting is described in Section 14.

19 Exterior mirrors and associated components – removal and refitting

Manually-adjusted mirror

1 Remove the rubber gaiter from the mirror adjustment handle, then carefully unclip the mirror inner trim panel from the door. Where necessary, rotate the tweeter speaker (where fitted) to free it from the panel then remove the panel from the vehicle.
2 Slacken and remove the three retaining screws and remove the mirror from the door.

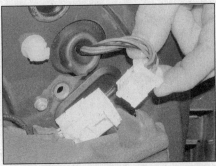

19.5 Disconnect the mirror wiring connector . . .

19.6b . . . and remove the mirror assembly from the door

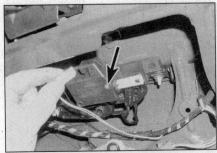

17.3 Disconnect the wiring connector then undo the retaining screw (arrowed) and remove the tailgate lock motor

Recover the rubber seal which is fitted between the door and mirror; if the seal is damaged, it must be renewed.
3 Refitting is the reverse of removal, ensuring the seal is correctly positioned.

Electrically-operated mirror

4 Carefully unclip the mirror inner trim panel from the door. Where necessary, rotate the tweeter speaker to free it from the panel then remove the panel from the vehicle (**see illustrations 12.2a and 12.2b**).
5 Disconnect the mirror wiring connector (**see illustration**).
6 Slacken and remove the three retaining screws and remove the mirror from the door. Recover the rubber seal which is fitted between the door and mirror; if the seal is damaged, it must be renewed (**see illustrations**).
7 Refitting is the reverse of removal, ensuring the seal is correctly positioned (**see illustration**).

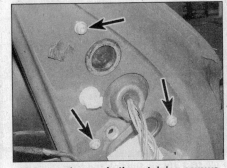

19.6a . . . then undo the retaining screws (arrowed) . . .

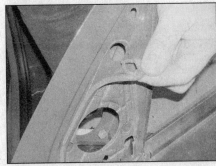

19.7 On refitting, ensure the mirror seal is correctly fitted

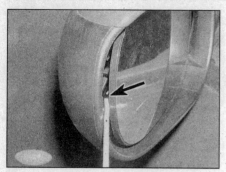

19.8 Unhook the mirror glass retaining clip (arrowed) . . .

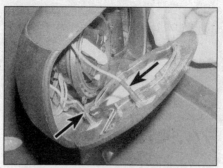

19.9 . . . then unclip the glass and disconnect the wiring connectors (arrowed) from the heating element

19.10 Ensure the retaining clip is correctly fitted before refitting the glass to the housing

Mirror glass

Note: *The mirror glass is clipped in position. Removal of the glass is likely to result in breakage if carried out carelessly. It is advisable to wear gloves when carrying out this procedure.*

8 Tilt the mirror glass fully inwards. Insert a small flat-bladed screwdriver inbetween the outer edge of the mirror glass and housing, and unhook the retaining clip from the rear of the mirror **(see illustration)**.

9 Once the clip has been released, carefully unclip the glass from the motor/adjuster. Take great care when removing the glass; do not use excessive force as the glass is easily broken. Remove the glass from the mirror, where necessary, disconnecting the wiring connectors from the mirror heating element **(see illustration)**.

10 On refitting, ensure the retaining clips is correctly fitted to the rear of the glass then reconnect the wiring (where necessary) and clip the glass onto the mirror/adjuster, taking care not to break it **(see illustration)**. Ensure the glass is clipped securely into position and adjust as necessary.

Mirror switch

11 Refer to Chapter 12.

Mirror motor

12 Remove the mirror glass as described above.

13 Undo the retaining screws and free the motor from the housing. Disconnect the wiring and remove the motor.

14 Refitting is the reverse of removal.

Outside temperature sensor

Note: *This is fitted to the passenger side mirror.*

15 Remove the mirror glass as described above.

16 Undo the retaining screws and free the motor from the mirror housing.

17 Slacken and remove the two screws from the base of the mirror housing **(see illustration)**.

18 Carefully, taking great care not to damage the plastic, ease the temperature sensor out from the base of the mirror housing.

19 Mark the sensor wires for identification then cut the wires and remove the sensor.

20 Refitting is the reverse of removal, ensuring the sensor wires are correctly reconnected (Peugeot recommend that the wires are soldered) and insulated.

20 Rear quarter window (three-door models) – removal and refitting

Window glass

Removal

1 From inside the vehicle, slacken and remove the screw securing the window to the opening catch and recover the nut and rubber washer from the outside of the window **(see illustrations)**.

2 Support the glass, then remove the screws, nuts and rubber washers securing the glass panel to the hinges. Remove the window from the vehicle.

Refitting

3 Refitting is the reverse of removal, ensuring the rubber washers are correctly positioned between the window and nuts.

Window hinges

Removal

4 Remove the button from the seat belt upper mounting height adjuster then undo the retaining screw and remove the trim cover from the mounting.

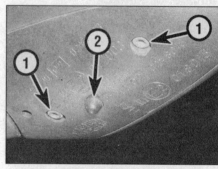

19.17 Mirror housing screws (1) and temperature sensor (2)

5 Unscrew the mounting bolt and free the belt from the height adjuster.

6 Unclip the top of the pillar upper trim panel and free it from the pillar.

7 Undo the screw securing the window to the hinge and recover the nut and rubber washer from the outside of the window. Slacken and remove the screw securing the hinge to the body and remove the hinge.

Refitting

8 Refitting is the reverse of removal, ensuring the rubber washers are correctly positioned between the window and nuts. Prior to refitting the trim panel, ensure the window is correctly aligned with its surrounding panels.

Window opening catch

Note: *A pop rivet gun and suitable rivets will be required on refitting.*

20.1a On three-door models, undo the screw securing the rear quarter window to the catch . . .

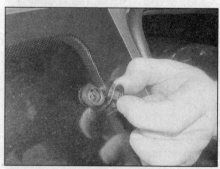

20.1b . . . and recover the nut and rubber washer from the outside of the glass

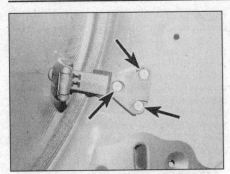

20.11 Rear quarter window catch is secured to the body by three pop rivets (arrowed)

Removal

9 Peel back the luggage compartment side trim panel then slacken and remove the rear pillar upper trim panel retaining screws. Unclip the panel and free it from the body to gain access to the catch.

10 Slacken and remove the screw securing the catch to the window and recover the nut and rubber washer from the outside of the window **(see illustrations 20.1a and 20.1b)**.

11 Carefully drill the heads off the pop rivets securing the catch to the body and remove the catch from the vehicle **(see illustration)**.

Caution: Take care not to damage the catch/body when drilling out the rivets.

Refitting

12 Refitting is the reverse of removal, securing the catch to the body with new pop rivets. Ensure the rubber washer is correctly positioned between the nut and window.

21 Windscreen and tailgate glass – general information

1 These areas of glass are secured by the tight fit of the weatherstrip in the body aperture, and are bonded in position with a special adhesive. Renewal of such fixed glass is a difficult, messy and time-consuming task, which is considered beyond the scope of the home mechanic. It is difficult, unless one has plenty of practice, to obtain a secure, waterproof fit. Furthermore, the task carries a high risk of breakage; this applies especially to the laminated glass windscreen. In view of this, owners are strongly advised to have this sort of work carried out by one of the many specialist windscreen fitters.

22 Sunroof – general information

1 Due to the complexity of the sunroof mechanism, considerable expertise is needed to repair, replace or adjust the sunroof components successfully. Removal of the roof first requires the headlining to be removed

which is a complex and tedious operation in itself. Therefore, any problems with the sunroof should be referred to a Peugeot dealer.

23 Body exterior fittings – removal and refitting

Wheelarch liners and body under-panels

1 The various plastic covers fitted to the underside of the vehicle are secured in position by a mixture of screws, nuts and retaining clips, and removal will be fairly obvious on inspection. Work methodically around the panel, removing its retaining screws and clips until the panel is free and can be removed from the underside of the vehicle. Most clips used on the vehicle are simply prised out of position. Other clips can be released by unscrewing/prising out the centre pins then removing the clip **(see illustration)**.

2 On refitting, renew any retaining clips that may have been broken on removal and ensure the panel is securely retained by all the necessary fasteners.

Body trim strips and badges

3 The various body trim strips and badges are held in position with a special adhesive tape. Removal requires the trim/badge to be heated, to soften the adhesive, and then cut away from the surface. Due to the high risk of damage to the vehicle paintwork during this operation, it is recommended that this task should be entrusted to a Peugeot dealer.

24 Seats – removal and refitting

 Warning: On models with side airbags (a side airbag label will be attached to the trim on the side of the seat base if side airbags are fitted), refer to the precautions given in Chapter 12 before proceeding.

24.2 Slide the front seat fully forwards and unscrew the rear mounting bolts . . .

23.1 The most commonly used fastener is removed by pulling out its centre pin then removing the complete fastener

Front seat

Removal

1 On models with side airbags, disconnect the battery negative terminal and wait at least two minutes before proceeding. Reach in under the seat and disconnect the wiring connector from the side airbag unit.

2 Slide the seat fully forwards then slacken and remove the bolts securing the rear of the seat rails in position **(see illustration)**.

3 Slide the seat fully backwards then slacken and remove the seat rail front mounting bolts **(see illustration)**.

4 Carefully manoeuvre the seat out of position.

Refitting

5 Manoeuvre the seat into position and securely reconnect its wiring connector(s) (where necessary).

6 Fit the seat rail front mounting bolts, tightening them lightly only, then slide the seat forwards and install the rear mounting bolts. Tighten the rear mounting bolts to the specified torque then slide the seat backwards again and tighten the front mounting bolts to the specified torque.

7 On models with side airbags, on completion, reconnect the battery. With the driver's door open, switch on the ignition from outside the vehicle whilst standing clear of the airbag/seat belt. Check the operation of the airbag warning light.

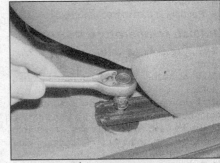

24.3 . . . then slide the seat fully backwards and remove its front mounting bolts

11

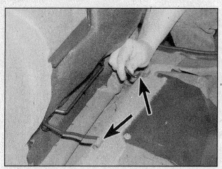

24.8 Fold the rear seat cushion forwards and unhook its pivot clip ends (arrowed) from the floor

Rear seat cushions

Removal

8 Tilt the rear seat cushion forwards. Unhook the pivot clip ends from the body and remove the seat cushion from the vehicle **(see illustration)**.

Refitting

9 Refitting is the reverse of removal.

Rear seat back

Removal

10 Tilt the rear seat cushions forwards.
11 Unscrew the bolts securing the seat back centre mounting brackets to the floor **(see illustration)**.
12 Working in the luggage compartment, unscrew the bolt securing the smaller section seat back outer mounting bracket to the floor then release the seat catch and remove the seat back from the vehicle **(see illustration)**.
13 If the rear seat centre belt is fitted to the seat and the larger seat back is being removed, unbolt the belt lower mounting from the floor.
14 Unscrew the bolt securing the larger section seat back outer mounting bracket to the floor then release the seat catch and remove the larger seat back from the vehicle.

Refitting

15 Refit the larger seat back and lightly tighten its outer mounting bracket bolt.
16 Install the smaller seat back and fit its outer bracket bolt. Clip both seat backs in

24.12 . . . and the outer bracket to the floor

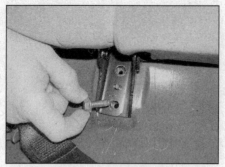

24.11 Unscrew the bolts securing the rear seat back centre brackets . . .

position then refit the centre mounting bracket bolts. With all bolts correctly fitted, go around and tighten them to the specified torque.
17 Where necessary, refit the centre belt lower mounting bolt and tighten to the specified torque.
18 Lower the seat cushions into position.

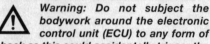

25 Front seat belt tensioning mechanism – general information and precautions

1 Most models covered in this manual are fitted with a front seat belt tensioner system. The system is designed to instantaneously take up any slack in the seat belt in the case of a sudden frontal impact, therefore reducing the possibility of injury to the front seat occupants. Each front seat belt is fitted with the system, the tensioner being an integral part of the seat belt inertia reel.
2 The seat belt tensioners are operated by a an electronic control unit (ECU) which is located behind the centre console. On models with a driver/passenger airbag, the ECU also operates the driver/passenger airbag (as applicable – see Chapter 12 for information on the airbag systems). The ECU contains a sensor which is triggered by a frontal impact above a pre-determined force. Lesser impacts, including impacts from behind, will not trigger the system.
3 When the mechanism is triggered, the fuel inside the tensioner cylinder ignites. This force retracts the inertia reel mechanism slightly, removing all slack from the seat belt, before locking it in position. The strength of the explosion is calibrated to retract the seat belt sufficiently to securely retain the occupant of the seat without forcing them into the seat. Once the tensioner has been triggered, the seat belt will be permanently locked and the assembly will have to be renewed.
4 Note the following warnings before contemplating any work on the front seat belts.

⚠ **Warning: Before carrying out any operations on the front seat belt tensioning mechanism, disconnect the battery negative terminal and wait at least two minutes. Remove the centre console (see Section 28) then release the**

retaining clip and disconnect the wiring connector(s) from the seat belt tensioning/airbag system electronic control unit (ECU) (see Chapter 12). On completion of work, securely reconnect the ECU wiring connector(s) then refit the centre console. Ensure no one is inside the vehicle when the battery is reconnected then, with the driver's door open, switch on the ignition from outside the vehicle whilst standing clear of the airbag/seat belt. Check the operation of the airbag warning light.

⚠ **Warning: If the seat belt inertia reel is dropped, it must be renewed, even if it has suffered no apparent damage.**

⚠ **Warning: Do not allow any solvents to come into contact with the tensioner mechanism.**

⚠ **Warning: Do not subject the bodywork around the electronic control unit (ECU) to any form of shock as this could accidentally trigger the seat belt tensioner/airbag system.**

⚠ **Warning: Do not subject the inertia reel assembly to temperatures in excess of 100ºC.**

⚠ **Warning: Peugeot recommend that the front seat belts must be renewed every ten years.**

26 Seat belt components – removal and refitting

⚠ **Warning: Refer to the precautions given in Section 25 before proceeding.**

Front – three-door models

Removal

1 Disconnect the battery negative terminal and wait at least two minutes. Remove the centre console (see Section 28) then release the retaining clip and disconnect the wiring connector from the seat belt tensioning/airbag system electronic control unit (ECU) (see Chapter 12).
2 Prise off the trim cap from the lower belt anchorage bolt then slacken and remove the bolt and washer. Free the anchorage bar from the body then slide off the washer and free the bar from the seat belt. Recover the spacer and trim cap fitted between the anchorage bar mounting and body **(see illustrations)**.
3 Remove the button from the seat belt upper mounting height adjuster then undo the retaining screw and remove the trim cover from the mounting. Unscrew the mounting bolt and free the belt from the height adjuster **(see illustrations)**.
4 Unclip the top of the pillar upper trim panel then free the panel from the seat belt and remove it from the vehicle **(see illustration)**. If necessary, the height adjuster mechanism can then be unbolted from the pillar.
5 Lift out the parcel shelf then remove the seat

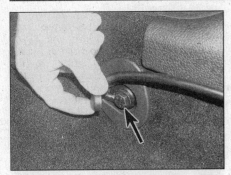

26.2a On three-door models, remove the trim cap and unscrew the mounting bolt (arrowed) . . .

26.2b . . . then free the anchorage bar from the body and recover the washer (arrowed)

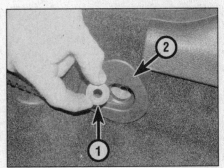

26.2c Recover the spacer (1) and trim cap (2) fitted between the anchorage bar and body

26.3a Remove the height adjuster button then undo the retaining screw (arrowed) and remove the trim cover from the seat belt upper mounting

26.3b Unscrew the mounting bolt and free the seat belt from the height adjuster

26.4 Unclip the upper trim panel from the pillar and free it from the seat belt

cushion and back as described in Section 24.

6 Prise off the trim cap from the rear seat belt lower mounting bolt then slacken and remove the bolt and washer. Free the belt and recover the spacer fitted between the belt and body **(see illustrations)**.

7 Peel back the luggage compartment side trim panel then slacken and remove the upper trim panel retaining screws. Unclip the panel and free it from the rear seat belt **(see illustrations)**. If the left-hand panel is being removed, it will also be necessary to remove the courtesy light from the panel.

8 Open the rear quarter window and free the window sealing strip from the top of the rear seat side trim panel. Unclip the side trim panel from the body then free the seat belt guide and seat belt from the panel and remove the panel from the vehicle **(see illustrations)**.

9 Disconnect the wiring connector from the seat belt tensioner mechanism **(see illustration)**.

10 Slacken and remove the inertia reel mounting bolt and remove the seat belt assembly from the vehicle.

26.6a Remove the trim cap then unscrew the rear seat belt lower mounting bolt . . .

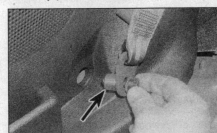

26.6b . . . and recover the spacer (arrowed) fitted between the belt and body

26.7a Undo the retaining screws (arrowed) . . .

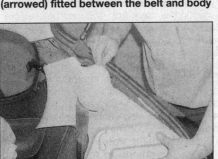

26.7b . . . then unclip the upper trim panel from the rear pillar

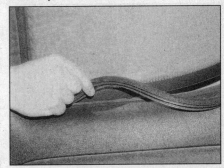

26.8a Free the window sealing strip from the top of the panel . . .

11

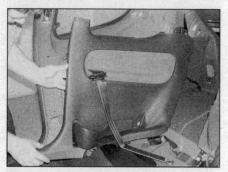

26.8b ... and unclip the rear seat side trim panel from the body

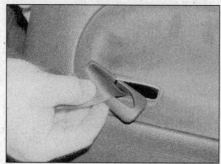

26.8c Unclip the seat belt guide then free the trim panel from the seat belt

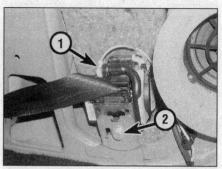

26.9 Front seat belt inertia reel tensioner wiring connector (1) and mounting bolt (2)

Refitting

11 Refitting is a reversal of removal, ensuring the mounting bolts are tightened to the specified torque and the tensioner wiring

connector is securely reconnected. Ensure the trim panels are clipped securely in position and are correctly located behind the edges of the sealing strips

Front – five-door models

Removal

12 To improve access, remove the relevant front seat as described in Section 24.
13 Remove the trim cap from the seat belt lower mounting bolt then slacken and remove the mounting bolt and washer **(see illustration)**.
14 Remove the button from the seat belt upper mounting height adjuster then undo the retaining screw and remove the trim cover from the mounting. Unscrew the mounting bolt and free the belt from the height adjuster **(see illustrations)**.
15 Unclip the upper trim panel from the pillar

and free it from the seat belt then unclip the lower trim panel from the pillar **(see illustrations)**. If necessary, the height adjuster mechanism can also be unbolted from the pillar.
16 Disconnect the wiring connector from the seat belt tensioner mechanism **(see illustration)**.
17 Slacken and remove the inertia reel mounting bolt and remove the seat belt assembly from the vehicle **(see illustration)**.

Refitting

18 Refitting is a reversal of removal, ensuring the mounting bolts are tightened to the specified torque and the tensioner wiring connector is securely reconnected. Ensure the trim panels are clipped securely in position and are correctly located behind the edges of the sealing strips.

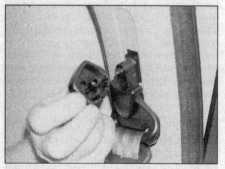

26.13 On five-door models, prise off the trim cap then slacken and remove the seat belt lower mounting bolt

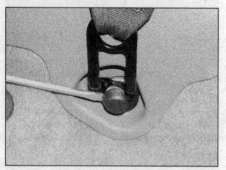

26.14a Unclip the button from the height adjuster lever ...

26.14b ... then undo the retaining screw and remove the trim cover (arrowed)

26.14c Unscrew the upper mounting bolt and free the seat belt from the height adjuster

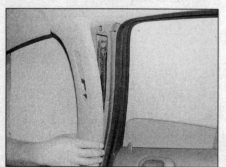

26.15a Unclip the upper trim panel from the pillar ...

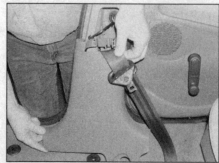

26.15b ... then free the lower trim panel from the pillar and belt

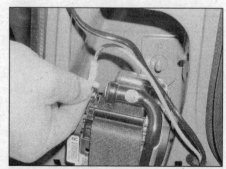

26.16 Disconnect the wiring connector from the seat belt tensioner mechanism ...

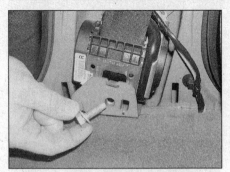

26.17 . . . then unscrew the inertia reel mounting bolt and remove the seat belt

Rear side belt – three-door models

Removal

19 Remove the parcel shelf.

20 Remove the rear seat back as described in Section 24.

21 Prise off the trim cap from the rear seat belt lower mounting bolt then slacken and remove the bolt and washer. Free the belt and recover the spacer fitted between the belt and body **(see illustrations 26.6a and 26.6b)**.

22 Remove the fastener (pull out the centre pin then remove the complete fastener) and free the luggage compartment side trim panel from the body to gain access to the inertia reel.

23 Slacken and remove the retaining screws securing the rear pillar upper trim panel in position. Unclip the panel from the body and free it from the seat belt; if the left-hand panel is being removed, it will also be necessary to remove the courtesy light from the panel **(see illustrations 26.7a and 26.7b)**.

24 Unscrew the seat belt upper mounting bolt and recover the spacer fitted between the belt and body **(see illustration)**.

25 Slacken and remove the inertia reel mounting bolt and remove the seat belt assembly from the vehicle **(see illustration)**.

Refitting

26 Refitting is a reversal of removal. Ensure that all washers and/or spacers are positioned as noted before removal, and tighten all mounting bolts to the specified torque. Ensure

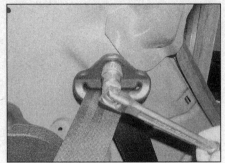

26.24 Unscrew the bolt and free the rear seat belt upper mounting from the body

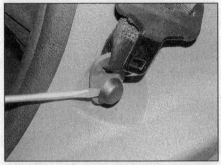

26.29a On five-door models, prise off the trim cap . . .

the trim panels are clipped securely in position and are correctly located behind the edges of the sealing strips.

Rear side belt – five-door models

Removal

27 Remove the parcel shelf.

28 Remove the rear seat back as described in Section 24.

29 Remove the trim cap then unscrew the seat belt lower mounting bolt and washer. Recover the spacer fitted between the belt and body **(see illustrations)**.

30 Remove the fastener(s) (pull out the centre pin then remove the complete fastener) and free the luggage compartment side trim panel from the body to gain access to the inertia reel.

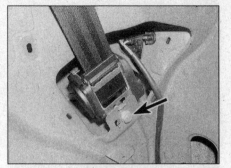

26.25 Rear seat belt inertia reel mounting bolt (arrowed)

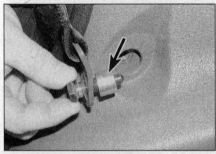

26.29b . . . then unscrew the lower mounting bolt and recover the spacer (arrowed) fitted between the belt and body

31 Slacken and remove the retaining screws securing the rear pillar upper trim panel in position **(see illustrations)**. Unclip the panel from the body and free it from the seat belt; if the left-hand panel is being removed, it will also be necessary to remove the courtesy light from the panel.

32 Unscrew the seat belt upper mounting bolt and recover the spacer fitted between the belt and body **(see illustration)**.

33 Slacken and remove the inertia reel mounting bolt and remove the seat belt assembly from the vehicle.

Refitting

34 Refitting is a reversal of removal, ensuring the mounting bolts are tightened to the specified torque. Ensure the trim panels are clipped securely in position and are correctly located behind the edges of the sealing strips.

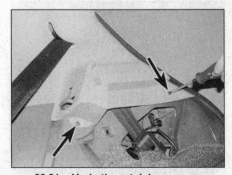

26.31a Undo the retaining screws (arrowed) . . .

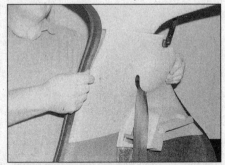

26.31b . . . then unclip the upper trim panel from the rear pillar

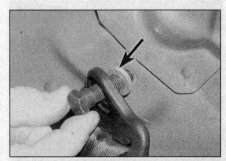

26.32 Unscrew the upper mounting bolt and recover the spacer (arrowed) fitted between the belt and body

11

Rear belt buckles and lap belt

Removal

35 The assemblies can simply be unbolted from the floor panel, after folding the rear seat cushion forwards **(see illustration)**. Note the locations of any washers and spacers, to ensure correct refitting.

Refitting

36 Refitting is a reversal of removal. Ensure that all washers and/or spacers are positioned as noted before removal, and tighten all mounting bolts to the specified torque.

Rear centre belt – later models with inertia reel

Note: *New headrest guides will be required on refitting.*

Removal

37 Remove the seat back as described in Section 24.
38 Depress the locking buttons and slide out the rear headrests from the seat back.
39 Remove the headrest guides from the seat. To do this, grab each guide firmly and rotate it to break its retaining tabs then pull it out of the seat assembly. If this fails to remove the guides, saw off the guide head whilst taking great care not to damage the seat upholstery (as a precaution, make up a protective template out of cardboard and fit this between the saw and upholstery).
40 Undo the retaining screws and remove the seat belt trim cover from the top of the seat.

27.6 Unclip the glovebox lid from its retaining clips and remove it from the facia

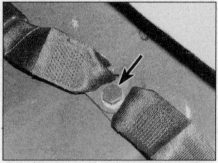

26.35 The rear seat belt buckles and lap belt are bolted to the floor

41 Unclip the upholstery from the sides and top of the seat back and peel back the foam to gain access to the inertia reel. Unbolt the inertia reel and remove the belt from the seat.

Refitting

42 Refitting is the reverse of removal, ensuring the upholstery and headrest guides are securely clipped in position. Refit the seat back as described in Section 24.

27 Interior trim – removal and refitting

Interior trim panels

1 The interior trim panels are retained using either or various types of trim fastener, usually studs or clips.
2 Check that there are no other panels overlapping the one to be removed; usually there is a sequence that has to be followed that will become obvious on close inspection. Where the panel is next to a door/window sealing strip, if necessary, free the sealing strip from the body to ensure it does not hinder panel removal.
3 Remove all obvious fasteners, such as screws. If the panel will not come free, it is held by hidden clips or fasteners. These are usually situated around the edge of the panel and are released by prising the panel away from the body. The best way of releasing such clips without the correct tool, is to use a large flat-bladed screwdriver to carefully release the panel, taking care not to damage the panel or paintwork.
4 When removing a panel **never** use excessive force or the panel may be damaged; always check carefully that all fasteners have been removed or release before attempting to remove the panel.
5 Refitting is the reverse of removal. Prior to refitting check the condition of all retaining clips and renew any which show signs of damage or deterioration. Ensure the panel is securely clipped in position and retained by all the necessary fasteners and screws to prevent annoying rattles and squeaks. Where the panel is next to a door/window sealing strip, ensure the it is correctly located behind the edge of the strip.

Glovebox

6 Open up the glovebox lid then carefully unclip the base of the lid from its retaining clips. Free the lid stays from the glovebox compartment and remove the lid from the facia **(see illustration)**.
7 Slacken and remove the glovebox compartment retaining screws, noting the correct fitted locations of the lid retaining clips **(see illustrations)**.
8 Free the glovebox compartment from the facia then manoeuvre it downwards and out from under the facia **(see illustration)**. Where necessary, disconnect the wiring connectors from the glovebox light and switch as the compartment is removed.
9 Refitting is the reverse of removal.

Carpets

10 The passenger compartment floor carpet is in one piece, and is secured at its edges by screws or various types of clips.
11 Carpet removal and refitting is reasonably straightforward, but time-consuming, due to the fact that all adjoining trim panels must be removed first, as must components such as the seats and centre console.

Headlining

12 The headlining is bonded to the roof, and can be withdrawn only once all fittings such as the grab handles, sun visors, overhead console, windscreen, centre and rear pillar trim panels, and associated panels have been removed. The

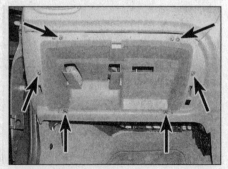

27.7a Slacken and remove the retaining screws (arrowed) . . .

27.7b . . . noting the correct fitted direction of the retaining clips fitted to the lower screws . . .

27.8 . . . then manoeuvre the glovebox compartment out of position

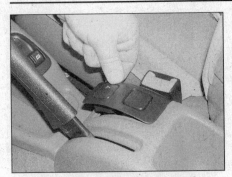

28.1a Unclip the switches from the console rear section . . .

28.1b . . . and disconnect the wiring

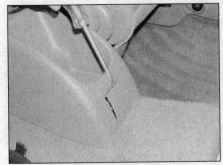

28.2a Unclip the access cover . . .

28.2b . . . then slacken and remove the retaining screw . . .

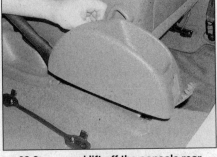

28.2c . . . and lift off the console rear section

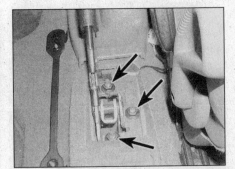

28.3 Unscrew the nuts (arrowed) and free the handbrake lever from the floor

door, tailgate and sunroof aperture weatherstrips will also have to be prised clear.

13 Note that headlining removal requires considerable skill and experience if it is to be carried out without damage, and is therefore best entrusted to an expert (the headlining must also be heated with a hot air gun to soften the adhesive and carefully prised away from the roof).

28 Centre console – removal and refitting

Removal

1 Carefully, taking care not to mark the switch or console, prise the switch(es) out from the rear section of the centre console. Disconnect the wiring connector(s) and remove the switch(es) **(see illustrations)**.

2 Unclip the access cover from the rear of the centre console rear section to gain access to the retaining screw. Undo the retaining screw and remove the console rear section from the vehicle **(see illustrations)**.

3 Unscrew the handbrake lever mounting nuts and free the handbrake lever from the floor, taking care not to strain the cables **(see illustration)**. If necessary, referring to Chapter 9, slacken the cable adjuster nut to obtain maximum freeplay in the cables to enable the lever to be moved.

4 On manual transmission models, unclip the gearchange lever gaiter from the console **(see illustration)**.

5 On automatic transmission models, carefully unclip the selector lever surround from the console **(see illustration)**.

6 On models with electric front windows/ electrically-operated exterior mirrors, carefully

28.4 On manual transmission models unclip the gearchange lever gaiter from the console

28.6a Carefully prise out the window/mirror switch assembly . . .

prise out the window/mirror switch out from the centre console front section. Disconnect the wiring connector and remove the switch **(see illustrations)**.

7 On models without electric front windows/

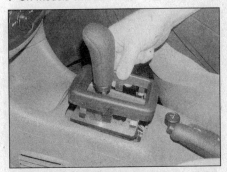

28.5 On automatic transmission models unclip the selector lever surround from the console

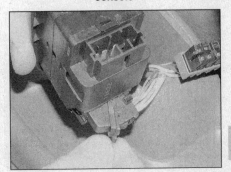

28.6b . . . and disconnect its wiring connectors

11

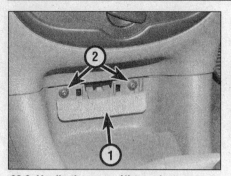

28.8 Unclip the cover (1) to gain access to the console front retaining screws (2)

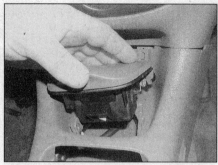

28.9a Remove the ashtray assembly . . .

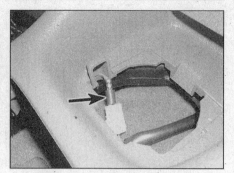

28.9b . . . and free the illumination bulbholder from the console

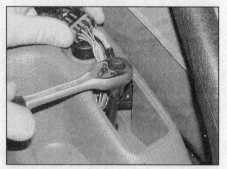

28.10a Unscrew the front screws and rear nut . . .

28.10b . . . then manoeuvre the console front section out of position

retaining nut. Lift the rear of the console front section and disconnect the wiring connectors from the cigarette lighter. Free the front of the console from the facia and manoeuvre it out of position (see illustrations).

Refitting

11 Refitting is the reverse of removal, noting the following.
  a) Ensure the wiring is correctly routed and securely reconnected.
  b) Tighten the handbrake lever mounting nuts to the specified torque (see Chapter 9). Check and, if necessary, adjust the handbrake adjustment before refitting the console rear section.
  c) On completion check the operation of all the switches.

mirrors, unclip and remove the storage compartment from the console.
8 On all models, unclip the trim cover from the front of the console to gain access to the front retaining screws (see illustration).

9 Remove the ashtray and unclip the ashtray illumination bulbholder from the console (see illustrations).
10 Slacken and remove the console front section front retaining screws and the rear

29 Facia panel assembly – removal and refitting

Removal

HAYNES HiNT *Attach an identification label to each wiring connector as it is disconnected. The labels can then be used on refitting to ensure that all wiring is correctly routed through the relevant facia apertures.*

1 Disconnect the battery negative terminal.
2 Remove the centre console (see Section 28).
3 Remove the steering column as described in Chapter 10.
4 Remove the following components as described in Chapter 12.
  a) Instrument panel.
  b) Clock/multi-function unit.
  c) Facia switch panel.
  d) Audio unit.
5 Slacken and remove the retaining screws securing the top of the centre vent panel to the facia. Carefully unclip the panel and remove it from the facia (see illustrations).
6 Slacken and remove the four screws then release the upper retaining clip(s) and free the heating/ventilation control unit from the facia (see illustrations).

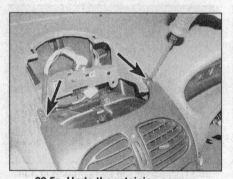

29.5a Undo the retaining screws (arrowed) . . .

29.5b . . . then unclip the centre vent panel from the facia

29.6a Undo the retaining screws (arrowed) . . .

29.6b . . . then unclip the heating/ventilation control unit from the facia

29.7a Unscrew the two bolts (arrowed) securing the facia to the heating/ventilation housing . . .

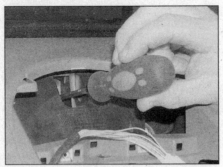

29.7b . . . and the single bolt securing it to the body

29.9 Unscrew the bolt (arrowed) and detach the facia earth lead from the floor

7 Unscrew the two bolts securing the centre of the facia to the heating/ventilation housing and upper bolt securing the facia to the body (see illustrations).

8 Unscrew the bolt securing the facia centre mounting bracket to the floor and the two bolts securing the bracket to the facia frame.

9 Unscrew the bolt and detach the facia panel earth lead from the floor (see illustration).

10 Release the retaining clips and disconnect the facia harness wiring connectors located next to the fusebox. Unclip the brown-coloured connector and the black-coloured connector from the bracket (see illustrations).

11 Unscrew the facia mounting bolt located in the instrument panel aperture (see illustration).

12 Carefully prise out the end covers from the left- and right-hand end of the facia. Disconnect the aerial lead from its connector located behind the passenger side cover (see illustrations).

13 Unscrew the bolts securing the left- and right-hand ends of the facia to the bulkhead.

14 With the aid of an assistant, lift the facia up slightly then manoeuvre it away from the bulkhead, freeing it from the heating/ventilation housing and control panel (see illustration).

Refitting

15 Manoeuvre the facia into position, ensuring the wiring connectors are correctly routed through the necessary facia apertures. Locate the facia correctly on the bulkhead, ensuring that the facia vents engage correctly with the heating/ventilation housing. Also ensure the control panel is correctly engaged with the facia.

16 Refit the bolts securing the facia ends to the bulkhead, the facia bolt located in the instrument panel aperture and the bolt securing the centre mounting bracket to the floor. Tighten all bolts by hand then tighten them to the specified torque in the following order.

a) Centre mounting bracket bolt-to-body bolt.
b) Left-and right-hand end bolts.
c) Instrument panel aperture bolt.

29.10a Disconnect the facia harness wiring connectors located next to the fusebox . . .

29.10b . . . then unclip the brown and black wiring connectors (arrowed) and from the facia bracket

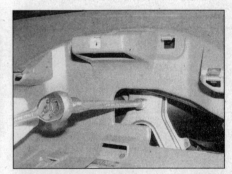

29.11 Unscrew the facia mounting bolt located in the instrument panel aperture

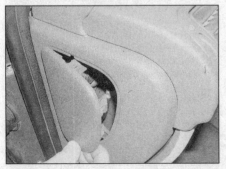

29.12a Unclip the left- and right-hand end covers from the facia

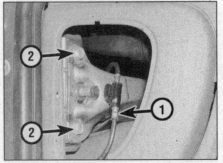

29.12b Aerial lead connector (1) and facia left-hand end mounting bolts (2)

29.14 Removing the facia assembly

11

d) Centre mounting bracket-to-facia bracket bolts

17 Reconnect the aerial lead to the connector located at the passenger end of the facia then refit the end covers to the facia.

18 Clip the brown and black connectors back onto the facia bracket then securely reconnect all the facia wiring connectors.

19 Reconnect the facia and wiring harness earth leads to the floor, tightening the retaining bolt securely.

20 Refit the bolts and screws securing the facia to the heating/ventilation housing and control panel, tightening them securely.

21 Clip the centre vent panel into position and secure it in position with the retaining screws.

22 Refit the audio unit, facia switch panel, clock/multi-function unit and instrument panel, as described in Chapter 12.

23 Refit the steering column as described in Chapter 10.

24 Refit the centre console as described in Section 28.

25 Reconnect the battery. With the driver's door open, switch on the ignition from outside the vehicle whilst standing clear of the airbag/seat belt. Check the operation of the airbag warning light then check that all electrical components and switches function correctly.

Chapter 12
Body electrical systems

Contents

Degrees of difficulty

Easy, suitable for novice with little experience	**Fairly easy,** suitable for beginner with some experience	**Fairly difficult,** suitable for competent DIY mechanic 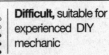	**Difficult,** suitable for experienced DIY mechanic	**Very difficult,** suitable for expert DIY or professional

Specifications

General

System type . . . . 12-volt negative earth

Bulbs

	Type	Wattage
Headlights:		
Models with combined dip/main beam bulb	H4	60/55
Models with separate main and dipped beam bulbs	H7	55
Front foglight	H1	55
Front sidelights	Push-fit	5
Direction indicator light	Bayonet	21
Direction indicator side repeater	Push-fit	5
Stop/tail light	Bayonet	21/5
Rear foglight	Bayonet	21
Reversing light	Bayonet	21
Number plate light	Push-fit	5

Torque wrench settings

	Nm	lbf ft
Airbag system:		
Control unit retaining nuts	8	6
Driver's airbag retaining screws	10	7
Passenger airbag retaining nuts	4	3
Tailgate wiper motor:		
Spindle nut	25	18
Wiper arm nut	20	15
Windscreen wiper arm nut	25	18

12

1 General information

⚠️ **Warning: Before carrying out any work on the electrical system, read through the precautions given in 'Safety first!' at the beginning of this manual, and in Chapter 5A.**

1 The electrical system is of 12-volt negative earth type. Power for the lights and all electrical accessories is supplied by a lead-acid type battery, which is charged by the alternator.

2 This Chapter covers repair and service procedures for the various electrical components not associated with the engine. Information on the battery, alternator and starter motor can be found in Chapter 5A.

3 It should be noted that, prior to working on any component in the electrical system, the battery negative terminal should first be disconnected, to prevent the possibility of electrical short-circuits and/or fires.

2 Electrical fault finding – general information

Note: *Refer to the precautions given in 'Safety first!' and in Section 1 of this Chapter before starting work. The following tests relate to testing of the main electrical circuits, and should not be used to test delicate electronic circuits (such as anti-lock braking systems), particularly where an electronic control unit (ECU) is used.*

General

1 A typical electrical circuit consists of an electrical component, any switches, relays, motors, fuses, fusible links or circuit breakers related to that component, and the wiring and connectors which link the component to both the battery and the chassis. To help to pinpoint a problem in an electrical circuit, wiring diagrams are included at the end of this Chapter.

2 Before attempting to diagnose an electrical fault, first study the appropriate wiring diagram, to obtain a more complete understanding of the components included in the particular circuit concerned. The possible sources of a fault can be narrowed down by noting whether other components related to the circuit are operating properly. If several components or circuits fail at one time, the problem is likely to be related to a shared fuse or earth connection.

3 Electrical problems usually stem from simple causes, such as loose or corroded connections, a faulty earth connection, a blown fuse, a melted fusible link, or a faulty relay (refer to Section 3 for details of testing relays). Visually inspect the condition of all fuses, wires and connections in a problem circuit before testing the components. Use the wiring diagrams to determine which terminal connections will need to be checked, in order to pinpoint the trouble-spot.

4 The basic tools required for electrical fault finding include a circuit tester or voltmeter (a 12-volt bulb with a set of test leads can also be used for certain tests); a self-powered test light (sometimes known as a continuity tester); an ohmmeter (to measure resistance); a battery and set of test leads; and a jumper wire, preferably with a circuit breaker or fuse incorporated, which can be used to bypass suspect wires or electrical components. Before attempting to locate a problem with test instruments, use the wiring diagram to determine where to make the connections.

5 To find the source of an intermittent wiring fault (usually due to a poor or dirty connection, or damaged wiring insulation), a 'wiggle' test can be performed on the wiring. This involves wiggling the wiring by hand, to see if the fault occurs as the wiring is moved. It should be possible to narrow down the source of the fault to a particular section of wiring. This method of testing can be used in conjunction with any of the tests described in the following sub-Sections.

6 Apart from problems due to poor connections, two basic types of fault can occur in an electrical circuit – open-circuit, or short-circuit.

7 Open-circuit faults are caused by a break somewhere in the circuit, which prevents current from flowing. An open-circuit fault will prevent a component from working, but will not cause the relevant circuit fuse to blow.

8 Short-circuit faults are caused by a 'short' somewhere in the circuit, which allows the current flowing in the circuit to 'escape' along an alternative route, usually to earth. Short-circuit faults are normally caused by a breakdown in wiring insulation, which allows a feed wire to touch either another wire, or an earthed component such as the bodyshell. A short-circuit fault will normally cause the relevant circuit fuse to blow.

Finding an open-circuit

9 To check for an open-circuit, connect one lead of a circuit tester or voltmeter to either the negative battery terminal or a known good earth.

10 Connect the other lead to a connector in the circuit being tested, preferably nearest to the battery or fuse.

11 Switch on the circuit, bearing in mind that some circuits are live only when the ignition switch is moved to a particular position.

12 If voltage is present (indicated either by the tester bulb lighting or a voltmeter reading, as applicable), this means that the section of the circuit between the relevant connector and the battery is problem-free.

13 Continue to check the remainder of the circuit in the same fashion.

14 When a point is reached at which no voltage is present, the problem must lie between that point and the previous test point with voltage. Most problems can be traced to a broken, corroded or loose connection.

Finding a short-circuit

15 To check for a short-circuit, first disconnect the load(s) from the circuit (loads are the components which draw current from a circuit, such as bulbs, motors, heating elements, etc).

16 Remove the relevant fuse from the circuit, and connect a circuit tester or voltmeter to the fuse connections.

17 Switch on the circuit, bearing in mind that some circuits are live only when the ignition switch is moved to a particular position.

18 If voltage is present (indicated either by the tester bulb lighting or a voltmeter reading, as applicable), this means that there is a short-circuit.

19 If no voltage is present, but the fuse still blows with the load(s) connected, this indicates an internal fault in the load(s).

Finding an earth fault

20 The battery negative terminal is connected to 'earth' – the metal of the engine/transmission and the car body – and most systems are wired so that they only receive a positive feed, the current returning via the metal of the car body. This means that the component mounting and the body form part of that circuit. Loose or corroded mountings can therefore cause a range of electrical faults, ranging from total failure of a circuit, to a puzzling partial fault. In particular, lights may shine dimly (especially when another circuit sharing the same earth point is in operation), motors (eg, wiper motors or the radiator cooling fan motor) may run slowly, and the operation of one circuit may have an apparently-unrelated effect on another. Note that on many vehicles, earth straps are used between certain components, such as the engine/transmission and the body, usually where there is no metal-to-metal contact between components, due to flexible rubber mountings, etc.

21 To check whether a component is properly earthed, disconnect the battery, and connect one lead of an ohmmeter to a known good earth point. Connect the other lead to the wire or earth connection being tested. The resistance reading should be zero; if not, check the connection as follows.

22 If an earth connection is thought to be faulty, dismantle the connection, and clean back to bare metal both the bodyshell and the wire terminal or the component earth connection mating surface. Be careful to remove all traces of dirt and corrosion, then use a knife to trim away any paint, so that a clean metal-to-metal joint is made. On reassembly, tighten the joint fasteners securely; if a wire terminal is being refitted, use serrated washers between the terminal and the bodyshell, to ensure a clean and secure connection. When the connection is

remade, prevent the onset of corrosion in the future by applying a coat of petroleum jelly or silicone-based grease, or by spraying on (at regular intervals) a proprietary ignition sealer or water-dispersant lubricant.

3 Fuses and relays – general information

Fuses

1 Fuses are designed to break a circuit when a predetermined current is reached, in order to protect the components and wiring which could be damaged by excessive current flow. Any excessive current flow will be due to a fault in the circuit, usually a short-circuit (see Section 2).

2 The majority of fuses are located behind the lower cover on the driver's side of the facia. Additional fuses (including the larger, higher-rated fuses) are located in the fuse/relay box on the left-hand side of the engine compartment.

3 To gain access to the facia fuses, rotate the cover fastener through 90º then remove the cover from the facia **(see illustrations)**. To gain access to the fuses in the engine compartment, simply unclip the cover from the fuse/relay box.

4 A list of circuits each fuse protects is given on the fusebox cover.

5 To remove a fuse, first switch off the circuit concerned (or the ignition), then pull the fuse out of its terminals **(see illustrations)**. The wire within the fuse should be visible; if the fuse has blown it will be broken or melted.

6 Always renew a fuse with one of the correct rating, never use a fuse with a different rating from that specified. The fuse rating is stamped on the top of the fuse, the fuses are also colour-coded as follows. Refer to the wiring diagrams for details of the fuse ratings and the circuits protected.

Colour	Rating
Orange	5A
Red	10A
Blue	15A
Yellow	20A
Clear or white	25A
Green	30A

7 Never renew a fuse more than once without tracing the source of the trouble. If the new fuse blows immediately, find the cause before renewing it again; a short to earth as a result of faulty insulation is most likely. Where a fuse protects more than one circuit, try to isolate the fault by switching on each circuit in turn (where possible) until the fuse blows again. Always carry a supply of spare fuses of each relevant rating on the vehicle; a spare of each rating should be clipped into the fusebox.

Relays

8 The majority of relay functions are incorporated into the built-in system interface

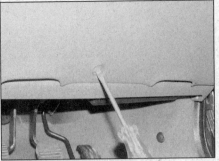

3.3a Rotate the fastener 90º . . .

(BSI) unit (see Section 24). Other relays are located in the fuse/relay box in the engine compartment and the cooling fan relay(s) is/are located in front panel **(see illustrations)**.

9 If a circuit or system controlled by a relay develops a fault and the relay is suspect, operate the system. If the relay is functioning, it should be possible to hear it 'click' as it is energised. If this is the case, the fault lies with the components or wiring of the system. If the relay is not being energised, then either the relay is not receiving a main supply or a switching voltage, or the relay itself is faulty. Testing is by the substitution of a known good unit, but be careful – while some relays are identical in appearance and in operation, others look similar but perform different functions.

10 To remove a relay, first ensure that the relevant circuit is switched off. The relay can

3.5a Using the removal tool supplied to remove a fuse

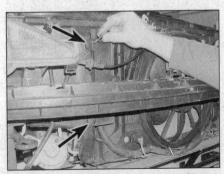

3.8a Remove the fasteners (arrowed) and remove the relay plate . . .

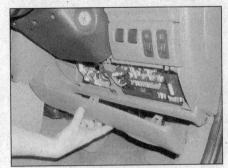

3.3b . . . then remove the lower cover to gain access to the fusebox

then simply be pulled out from the socket, and pushed back into position.

4 Switches – removal and refitting

Note: *Disconnect the battery negative lead before removing any switch, and reconnect the lead after refitting the switch.*

Ignition switch/ steering column lock

1 Refer to Chapter 10.

Steering column combination switches

2 Rotate the fastener a quarter-of-a-turn (90º) and remove the lower cover from the driver's side of the facia.

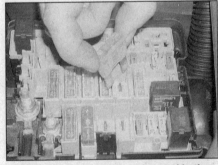

3.5b Additional fuses are located in the fuse/relay box in the engine compartment

3.8b . . . from the front panel to gain access to the cooling fan relays (arrowed)

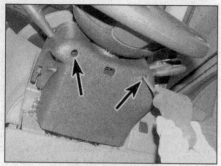

4.3a Undo the retaining screws (arrowed) then free the lower shroud from the steering column . . .

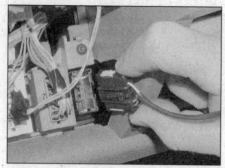

4.3b . . . disconnect the audio unit control stalk wiring connector and remove the shroud

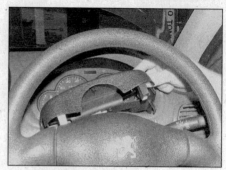

4.3c Unclip the upper shroud and remove it from the column

3 Undo the retaining screws and free the lower shroud from the column. Trace the audio unit control stalk wiring back to its connector then disconnect the connector and remove the shroud and switch as an assembly. Unclip and remove the upper shroud from the steering column **(see illustrations)**.

4 To remove an individual switch assembly, remove the retaining screws then slide the switch out of its holder, disconnecting the wiring connector as it becomes accessible **(see illustrations)**.

5 To remove the complete switch and mounting bracket assembly it will first be necessary to remove the steering wheel (see Chapter 10). On models with a driver's airbag also remove the contact unit as described in Section 23. On all models, undo the retaining screws then remove the assembly from the top of the steering column, disconnecting the wiring connectors from the switches **(see illustrations)**.

6 Refitting is the reverse of removal, ensuring the wiring connectors are securely reconnected.

Audio unit control stalk switch

7 Rotate the fastener a quarter-of-a-turn (90°) and remove the lower cover from the driver's side of the facia.

8 Undo the retaining screws and free the lower shroud from the column. Trace the audio unit control stalk wiring back to its connector then disconnect the connector and remove the shroud and switch as an assembly **(see illustrations 4.3a and 4.3b)**.

9 Undo the retaining screws and separate the audio control switch and lower shroud **(see illustration)**.

10 Refitting is a reversal of removal, ensuring that the switch wiring is routed as noted before removal.

Facia-mounted switches

11 Rotate the fastener a quarter-of-a-turn (90°) and remove the lower cover from the driver's side of the facia.

12 Unclip the switch panel from the facia and disconnect the wiring connectors from the switches. Each individual switch can then be unclipped and remove from the panel **(see illustrations)**.

13 Refitting is the reverse of removal.

Hazard warning light switch

14 Carefully unclip the clock/multi-function unit surround from the top of the facia and remove it, disconnecting the wiring connector from the hazard warning light switch **(see illustration)**.

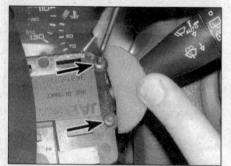

4.4a To remove an individual switch, undo the screws (arrowed) . . .

4.4b . . . then slide the switch out of the holder and disconnect its wiring connector

4.5a To remove the complete assembly, undo the retaining screws (arrowed) . . .

4.5b . . . then lift off the switch and bracket assembly, disconnecting its wiring connectors

4.9 Undo the screws (arrowed) and remove the audio unit switch from the lower shroud

4.12a Unclip the switch panel from the facia . . .

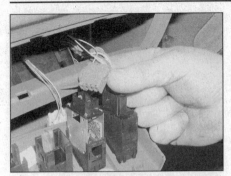

4.12b . . . and disconnect the switch wiring connectors

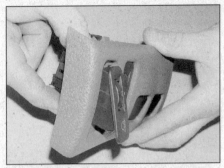

4.12c Each individual switch can then be pushed out of the panel

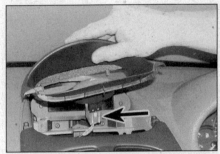

4.14 Unclip clock/multi-function unit surround from the facia and disconnect the hazard warning light switch wiring connector (arrowed) . . .

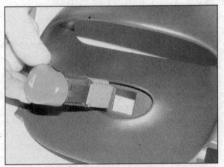

4.15 . . . the switch can then be unclipped from the surround

4.17 Carefully prise the switch out from the console . . .

4.18 . . . and disconnect its wiring connectors

15 Unclip the switch and remove it from the surround (see illustration).
16 Refitting is the reverse of removal.

Centre console-mounted switches

17 Carefully, taking care not to mark the switch or console, prise the relevant switch assembly out from the centre console (see illustration).
18 Disconnect the switch from the wiring connector(s) and remove it from the vehicle (see illustration).
19 Refitting is the reverse of removal.

Heating/ventilation control panel switches

20 The switches are an integral part of the heater/ventilation control panel, and cannot be renewed separately. If any switch is faulty,

the complete control panel must be renewed – refer to Chapter 3 for details.

Overhead console switches

21 The overhead console switches are an integral part of the courtesy light unit(s). If a switch is faulty the light unit will have to be renewed (see Section 6).

Stop-light switch

22 Refer to Chapter 9.

Handbrake warning light switch

23 Remove the rear section of the centre console as described in Chapter 11.
24 Carefully unclip the warning light switch from the floor and disconnect it from the wiring connector (see illustrations). Note: If there is insufficient slack in the wiring to enable this to be done, it will be necessary to

free the handbrake lever from the floor (see Chapter 9). Access to the wiring connector can then be gained reaching in through the lever aperture.
25 Refitting is the reverse of removal.

Courtesy light switch

26 The courtesy light switches are an integral part of the door lock assemblies. Refer to Chapter 11 for door lock removal and refitting details.

Luggage compartment light switch

27 Open the tailgate then carefully unclip the tailgate inner trim panel.
28 Disconnect the wiring connector from the switch then undo the retaining bolt and remove the switch from the tailgate (see illustration).

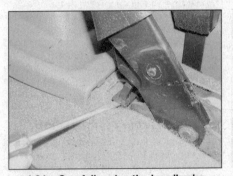

4.24a Carefully prise the handbrake warning light switch out from the floor . . .

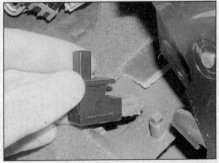

4.24b . . . and disconnect it from the wiring connector

4.28 Disconnect the wiring connector then undo the bolt (arrowed) and remove the switch from the tailgate

12

5.2 Unclip the washer reservoir filler neck to improve access to the right-hand headlight unit

29 Refitting is the reverse of removal, ensuring the trim panel is correctly fitted to the tailgate.

Windscreen wiper rain sensor switch

30 Carefully unclip the rear view mirror housing from its mounting on the inside of the windscreen by pushing it gently upwards.
31 Disconnect the wiring connector then carefully release the side retaining clips and remove the rain sensor from the windscreen.
Caution: Do not touch the rain sensor lens or the windscreen glass in the area of the sensor. These areas must be kept spotlessly clean if the sensor is to function correctly.
32 Refitting is the reverse of removal, ensuring the sensor is securely retained by its clips. If a new sensor is being fitted, it will be necessary to remove the protective film from the sensor prior to installation. On completion, check the

sensor operation by spraying the screen with water (wiper stalk in the auto position).

Glovebox illumination light switch

33 Open the glovebox lid.
34 Carefully prise the switch out of position then disconnect it from the wiring connector.
35 Refitting is the reverse of removal.

5 Bulbs (exterior lights) – renewal

General

1 Whenever a bulb is renewed, note the following points:
a) *Disconnect the battery negative lead before starting work.*
b) *Remember that, if the light has just been in use, the bulb may be extremely hot.*
c) *Always check the bulb contacts and holder, ensuring that there is clean metal-to-metal contact between the bulb and its live(s) and earth. Clean off any corrosion or dirt before fitting a new bulb.*
d) *Wherever bayonet-type bulbs are fitted (see Specifications), ensure that the live contact(s) bear firmly against the bulb contact.*
e) *Always ensure that the new bulb is of the correct rating, and that it is completely clean before fitting it; this applies particularly to headlight/foglight bulbs (see below).*

Headlight

Note: On models with ABS, it may be necessary to remove the LH headlamp completely (as described is Section 7) to gain access to the bulb.

2 To improve access to the right-hand headlight, unclip the filler neck from the washer reservoir **(see illustration)**.
3 On models with a combined dipped/main beam bulb, disconnect the wiring connector from the rear of the headlight bulb then remove the rubber dust cover from the headlight unit, noting its correct fitted location **(see illustrations)**.
4 On models with separate dipped and main beam bulbs, release the retaining clip then remove the access cover from the rear of the headlight unit. Disconnect the wiring connector from the relevant bulb.
5 On all models, unhook the ends of the bulb retaining clip and release it from the rear of the headlight unit. Withdraw the bulb **(see illustrations)**.
6 When handling the new bulb, use a tissue or clean cloth to avoid touching the glass with the fingers; moisture and grease from the skin can cause blackening and rapid failure of this type of bulb. If the glass is accidentally touched, wipe it clean using methylated spirit.
7 Install the new bulb, ensuring that its locating tabs are correctly seated in the light cut-outs, and secure it in position with the retaining clip.
8 On models with a combined dipped/main beam bulb, refit the rubber dust cover, ensuring it is correctly seated on the headlight unit and bulb, then reconnect the bulb wiring connector.
9 On models with separate dipped and main beam bulbs, reconnect the wiring connector. Ensure the seal is in good condition then securely refit the access cover to the headlight unit.
10 Where necessary, clip the filler neck securely back onto the washer reservoir.

Front sidelight

11 Rotate the bulbholder and free it from the rear of the headlight unit. The bulb is of the capless (push-fit) type, and can be removed by simply pulling it out of the holder **(see illustrations)**.

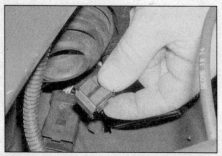

5.3a On models with a combined dip/main beam bulb, disconnect the wiring connector . . .

5.3b . . . then remove the rubber dust cover from the headlight

5.5a Unhook the retaining clip (arrowed) . . .

5.5b . . . then remove the bulb

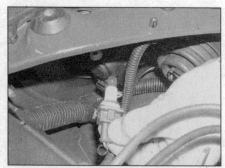

5.11a Free the sidelight bulbholder from the rear of the headlight . . .

5.11b . . . then pull the bulb out from the holder

5.14 Rotate the cover anti-clockwise and remove it from the foglight (shown with bumper removed for clarity)

5.15 Disconnect the wiring connector from the bulb . . .

12 Refitting is the reverse of the removal procedure, ensuring that the bulbholder seal is in good condition.

Front foglight

13 Rotate the wheel onto full lock then open the flap in the wheelarch liner to gain access to the rear of the foglight unit.
14 Rotate the cover anti-clockwise and remove it from the foglight **(see illustration)**.
15 Disconnect the wiring connector from the foglight bulb **(see illustration)**.
16 Unhook the end of the bulb retaining clip and release it from the rear of the foglight unit **(see illustration)**. Withdraw the bulb.
17 When handling the new bulb, use a tissue or clean cloth to avoid touching the glass with the fingers; moisture and grease from the skin can cause blackening and rapid failure of this type of bulb. If the glass is accidentally

touched, wipe it clean using methylated spirit.
18 Install the new bulb, ensuring that its locating tabs are correctly seated in the light cut-outs. Secure the bulb in position with the retaining clip then reconnect the wiring connector.
19 Ensure the seal is in good condition then securely refit the cover to the rear of the foglight unit. Securely close the wheelarch liner flap.

Front direction indicator

20 Rotate the bulbholder and free it from the top of the headlight unit **(see illustration)**. The bulb is a bayonet-fit in the holder, and can be removed by pressing it in and rotating it anti-clockwise.
21 Refitting is the reverse of the removal procedure, ensuring that the bulbholder seal is in good condition.

Front direction indicator side repeater

22 Push the light unit to one side, to free its retaining clips, then ease it out from the front wing **(see illustration)**.
23 Rotate the bulbholder anti-clockwise and free it from the rear of the light. The bulb is of the capless (push-fit) type, and can be removed by simply pulling it out of the holder **(see illustrations)**.
24 Refitting is a reversal of the removal procedure.

Rear light

25 Remove the fastener(s) (pull out the centre pin then remove the complete fastener) and free the luggage compartment side trim panel from the body to gain access to the rear of the light unit **(see illustration)**.

5.16 . . . then unhook the retaining clip and withdraw the foglight bulb

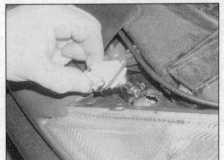

5.20 Rotate the direction indicator bulbholder to free it from the headlight

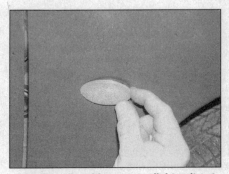

5.22 Ease the side repeater light unit out from the wing . . .

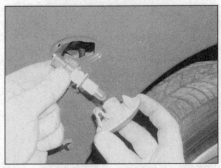

5.23a . . . then free the bulbholder from the light . . .

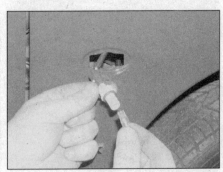

5.23b . . . and pull out the bulb

5.25 Pull out the centre pin then remove the fastener securing the luggage compartment side trim panel in position

12

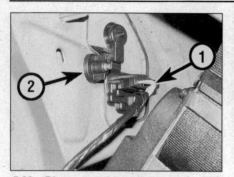

5.26a Disconnect the wiring connector (1) then unscrew the wing nut (2) . . .

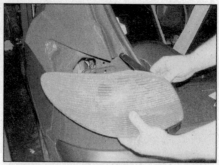

5.26b . . . and remove the rear light unit

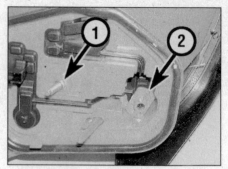

5.27a Unscrew the bulbholder nut (1) using the tool (2) supplied . . .

5.27b . . . if the tool has not been used before it will still be moulded onto the light unit

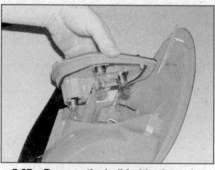

5.27c Remove the bulbholder from the light unit . . .

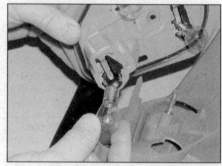

5.28 . . . and remove the relevant bulb by pressing it in and rotating it anti-clockwise

26 Disconnect the wiring connector from the light unit then unscrew the wing nut and remove the light unit from the vehicle (see illustrations).
27 Unscrew the bulbholder retaining nut and

5.31a Rotate the bulbholder anti-clockwise to free it from the light unit . . .

remove the bulbholder from the light unit. The nut can be unscrewed using the tool supplied which is clipped to the rear of the light unit; if the tool has never been used it will still be moulded to the rear light shell; break the tab to release it (see illustrations).
28 All the bulbs have bayonet fittings. The relevant bulb can be removed by pressing it in and rotating it anti-clockwise (see illustration). Note that the stop/taillight bulb has offset pins to ensure it is fitted the correct way around.
29 Refitting is the reverse of removal, ensuring the light unit and bulbholder seals are in good condition.

Rear foglight

30 Reach up behind the bumper then release the retaining clip and push the light unit out from the rear bumper.

31 Rotate the bulbholder anti-clockwise and free it from the rear of the light unit. The bulb is a bayonet-fit in the holder, and can be removed by pressing it in and rotating it anti-clockwise (see illustrations).
32 Refitting is the reverse of the removal procedure, ensuring the bulbholder seal is in good condition.

High-level stop light

33 Remove the light unit as described in Section 7.
34 Release the retaining clips and detach the light unit from the bulbholder. Each bulb (there are five in total) is of the capless (push-fit) type, and can be removed by simply pulling it out of the bulbholder (see illustrations).
35 Refitting is the reverse of removal. Do not overtighten the light unit retaining nuts as the plastic is easily broken.

5.31b . . . then remove the bulb by pressing it in and rotating it anti-clockwise

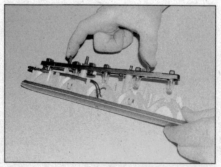

5.34a Unclip the bulbholder from the rear of the high-level stop light . . .

5.34b . . . and pull out the relevant bulb

5.36a Carefully unclip the lens from the number plate light . . .

5.36b . . . and pull out the bulb

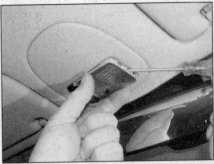
6.2 Carefully prise the courtesy light unit out of position

Number plate light

36 Carefully unclip and remove the lens from the number plate light unit. The bulb is of the capless (push-fit) type, and can be removed by simply pulling it out of the light unit (see illustrations).
37 Refitting is the reverse of the removal procedure, ensuring that the lens is securely clipped in position.

6 Bulbs (interior lights) – renewal

General

1 Refer to Section 5, paragraph 1.

Courtesy light and map reading light

2 Using a flat bladed-screwdriver, carefully ease the light unit out of position and disconnect it from the wiring connector (see illustration).
3 Release the bulbholder from the light unit. The bulb is of the capless (push-fit) type, and can be removed by simply pulling it out of the bulbholder (see illustrations).
4 Refitting is the reverse of the removal procedure

Instrument panel illumination/warning lights

5 Remove the instrument panel as described in Section 9.
6 Twist the relevant bulbholder anti-clockwise and remove it from the rear of the instrument panel (see illustration). All bulbs are integral with their holders.
7 Ensure the new bulb is off the correct rating then securely fit the holder to the rear of the instrument panel.
8 Refit the instrument panel as described in Section 9.

Heating/ventilation control panel illumination bulb

Manual heater control panel

9 Remove the control panel as described in Chapter 3.
10 Pull off the knob from the air recirculation flap lever (see illustration).

6.3a Free the bulbholder from the rear of the light . . .

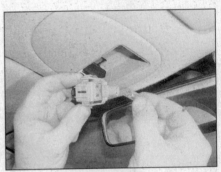
6.3b . . . then pull the bulb out from its holder

11 Carefully release the retaining clips and separate the two halves of the control panel. The illumination bulbs can then be pulled out of position (see illustrations).
Caution: Do not use excessive force when separating the control panel as the panel is easily broken. Do not attempt to remove the LEDs from the control panel these are an integral part of the panel and cannot be renewed separately.

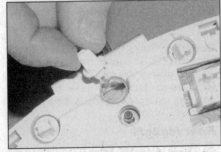
6.6 Rotate the bulbholder anti-clockwise and remove it from the rear of the instrument panel

6.10 Pull off the knob from the air recirculation lever . . .

6.11a . . . then carefully release the retaining clips (arrowed) . . .

6.11b . . . and separate the two halves of the heating/ventilation manual control panel

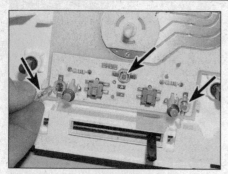

6.11c The illumination bulbs (arrowed) can then be pulled out

6.15 Unclip the clock/multi-function unit surround from the facia and disconnect the switch wiring connector (arrowed)

6.16 Rotate the relevant bulbholder anti-clockwise and remove it from the unit

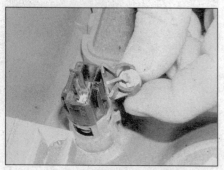

6.22 Unclip the illumination light assembly from the cigarette lighter . . .

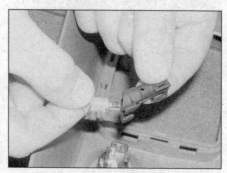

6.23 . . . and free the bulbholder

12 Fit the new bulb(s) then reassemble the control panel, engaging the control knobs with their shafts. Check the operation of the panel controls and switches then refit the knob to the recirculation lever.

13 Refit the control panel as described in Chapter 3.

Automatic climate control system control panel

14 At the time of writing no information it was unclear whether the illumination bulbs were an integral part of the control panel or whether they could be renewed separately. Refer to your Peugeot dealer for the latest available information. Control panel removal and refitting is described in Chapter 3.

Clock/multi-function unit illumination bulb

15 Carefully unclip the clock/multi-function

unit surround from the top of the facia and remove it, disconnecting the wiring connector from the hazard warning light switch **(see illustration)**.

16 Rotate the relevant bulbholder anti-clock-wise and remove it from the top of the clock/multi-function unit **(see illustration)**. The bulb is integral with the holder.

17 Securely fit the new bulbholder then reconnect the switch wiring connector and clip the surround back into position.

Centre console ashtray illumination bulb

18 Unclip the ashtray and remove it from the centre console.

19 Free the bulbholder from the console and pull the bulb out from its holder.

20 Securely fit the new bulb to its holder then clip the holder back into position on the console. Refit the ashtray.

Cigarette lighter illumination bulb

21 Remove the centre console as described in Chapter 11.

22 Carefully release retaining clips and slide the illumination light assembly off the base of the lighter, taking care not to break its electrical contacts **(see illustration)**.

23 Unclip the bulbholder from the base of the assembly then pull the bulb out from the holder **(see illustration)**.

24 Fit the new bulb then clip the bulbholder back into the assembly.

25 Slide the light assembly onto the metal insert and clip it securely onto the plastic outer.

26 Ensure the cigarette lighter is correctly assembled then refit the centre console

Switch illumination bulbs

27 All of the switches are fitted with illumination bulbs. On most switches, these bulbs are an integral part of the switch and cannot be renewed separately. Bulb renewal will therefore require renewal of the complete switch assembly (see Section 4).

7 Exterior light units – removal and refitting

Note: *Disconnect the battery negative lead before removing any light unit, and reconnect the battery after refitting light unit.*

Headlight

1 Open the bonnet. If the left-hand headlight is being removed, pull out the retaining clip pin and remove the air intake water deflector from the top of the headlight unit **(see illustration)**.

2 Remove the four fasteners (pull out the centre pin then remove the complete fastener) securing the grille panel to the top of the front panel. Release the lower retaining clips and unclip the grille panel from the front trim panel in an upwards direction **(see illustrations)**.

3 Slacken and remove the retaining screws securing the front trim panel in position. Carefully unclip the trim panel from the inner edge of each headlight then unclip the ends of

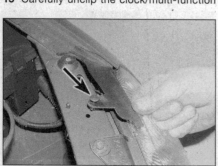

7.1 If the left-hand headlight is being removed, pull up the retaining clip pin and remove the air intake deflector

7.2a Pull out the centre pin and remove each fastener securing the grille panel in position . . .

7.2b . . . then release the retaining clips (arrowed) and remove the panel in an upwards direction

7.3a Undo the retaining screws (arrowed) . . .

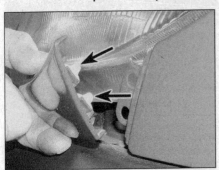

7.3b . . . then unclip the panel ends from the wings . . .

7.3c . . . and remove the front trim panel from the vehicle

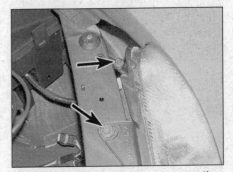

7.4a Slacken and remove upper mounting bolts (arrowed) . . .

7.4b . . . and lower mounting bolt (arrowed) . . .

the panel from each wing and remove the panel from the vehicle (see illustrations).
4 Slacken and remove the three mounting bolts and free the headlight unit from its mounting pin. Disconnect the wiring connectors from the headlight unit then manoeuvre the unit out of position (see illustrations).
5 On models equipped with a headlight levelling system, if necessary, remove the motor from the rear of the light unit by rotating it anti-clockwise and carefully unclipping its balljoint from the rear of the reflector unit (see illustration).
6 Prior to refitting, ensure the levelling system motor (where fitted) is correctly installed.

7 Offer up the headlight unit and securely reconnect its wiring connectors.
8 Align the headlight bracket with the mounting pin on the outer edge of the body then seat the headlight in position, ensuring its locating tab is correctly located in the cut-out in the wing (see illustration).
9 Refit the headlight mounting bolts. Tighten all the bolts lightly then securely tighten the bolts in the following order.
a) Upper, outermost bolt.
b) Lower bolt.
c) Upper, innermost bolt
10 Check the operation of the headlight then clip the front trim panel into position and

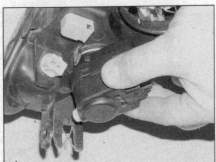

7.4c . . . then disconnect the wiring connectors and remove the headlight unit

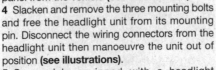

7.5 Rotate the levelling motor and unclip it from the rear of the unit

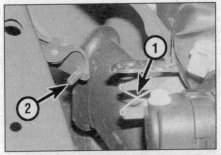

7.8 Ensure the headlight bracket (1) engages correctly with the pin (2) when refitting the headlight unit

12

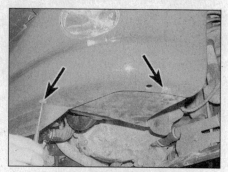

7.12a Remove the retaining screws (arrowed) . . .

7.12b . . . and fasteners . . .

7.12c . . . and manoeuvre the front section of the wheelarch liner out from under the wing

7.13 Disconnect the wiring connector from the foglight . . .

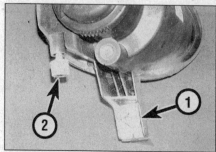

7.14 . . . then undo the retaining screw (1) and remove the foglight from the front bumper (note the adjuster – 2)

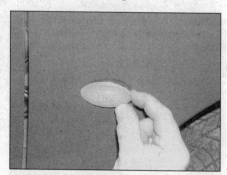

7.16 Ease the side repeater light out from the wing . . .

securely tighten its retaining screws. Clip the grille panel onto the trim panel and secure it in position with the fasteners.

11 Check the headlight beam alignment using the information given in Section 8.

Front foglight

12 Undo the screws securing the front section of the relevant wheelarch liner to the base of the bumper. Remove the fasteners securing the liner section to the body then manoeuvre the front section of the liner out from underneath the wing **(see illustrations)**.
13 Disconnect the wiring connector from the foglight **(see illustration)**.
14 Undo the lower retaining screw then free the foglight unit and remove it from the bumper **(see illustration). Note:** *If the left-hand foglight is being removed, remove the air cleaner housing intake duct to improve access to the light unit (see Chapter 4A or 4B).*
15 Refitting is the reverse of removal. If necessary adjust the foglight aim using the adjuster on the rear of the light unit.

Front direction indicator side repeater light

16 Push the light unit to one side, to free its retaining clips, then ease it out from the wing panel **(see illustration)**.
17 Disconnect the wiring connector and remove the light unit from the vehicle **(see illustration)**.
18 Refitting is a reversal of the removal procedure.

Rear light unit

19 Remove the fastener(s) (pull out the centre pin then remove the complete fastener) and free the luggage compartment side trim panel from the body to gain access to the rear of the light unit **(see illustration)**.
20 Disconnect the wiring connector from the light unit then unscrew the wing nut and remove the light unit from the vehicle **(see illustrations)**.
21 Refitting is the reverse of removal, ensuring the light unit seal is in good condition.

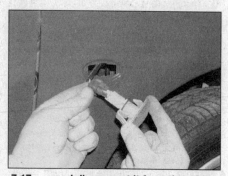

7.17 . . . and disconnect it from the wiring connector

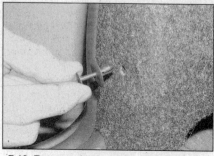

7.19 Remove the fastener and peel back the luggage compartment side trim panel to gain access to the rear light

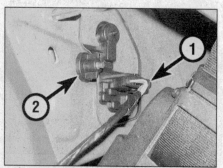

7.20a Disconnect the wiring connector (1) then unscrew the wing nut (2) . . .

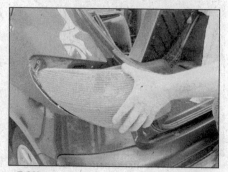

7.20b . . . and remove the rear light unit

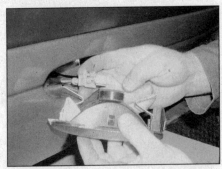

7.23 Push the rear foglight unit out from the bumper and disconnect its wiring connector

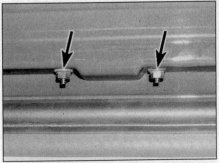

7.25 Unscrew the retaining nuts (arrowed) then push the high-level stop light out of position

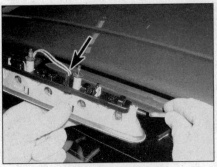

7.26 Disconnect the washer hose and wiring connector (arrowed) then remove the light unit from the tailgate

7.29a Release the retaining clips and push the number plate light unit out of the tailgate . . .

7.29b . . . then disconnect its wiring connector

Rear foglight

22 Reach up behind the bumper then release the retaining clip and push the light unit out from the rear bumper.
23 Disconnect the wiring connector and remove the light unit from the vehicle (see illustration).
24 Refitting is the reverse of the removal procedure.

High-level stop light

25 Open the tailgate the unscrew the nuts securing the light unit to the tailgate (see illustration). Carefully push on the light unit studs to ease the unit out from the tailgate spoiler.
26 Disconnect the washer hose and wiring connector and remove the light unit from the tailgate (see illustration).

27 Refitting is the reverse of removal. Do not overtighten the light unit retaining nuts as the plastic is easily broken.

Number plate light

28 Open the tailgate then carefully unclip the inner trim panel from the tailgate.
29 Release the retaining clips then push the relevant light unit out from the tailgate. Disconnect the wiring connector and remove the light unit (see illustrations).
30 Refitting is the reverse of removal.

<table>
<tr><td>8</td><td>Headlight beam alignment – general information</td></tr>
</table>

1 Accurate adjustment of the headlight beam is only possible using optical beam-setting equipment, and this work should therefore be carried out by a Peugeot dealer or suitably-equipped workshop.
2 For reference, the headlights can be adjusted using a suitable-sized Allen key to rotate the adjuster assemblies fitted to the rear of each light unit. The outer adjuster alters the vertical height of the beam, whilst the inner adjuster alters the horizontal position of the beam (see illustration).
3 On models equipped with headlight levelling, ensure the adjuster switch is set to position 0 before the headlights are adjusted. On models not equipped with headlight levelling, ensure the manual adjuster on the rear of each headlight unit is set to position 0 before adjustment (where fitted).

<table>
<tr><td>9</td><td>Instrument panel – removal and refitting</td><td></td></tr>
</table>

Removal

1 Disconnect the battery negative terminal.
2 To improve access, release the height adjuster lever and fully lower the steering column.
3 Starting at the bottom of the shroud, carefully unclip the shroud and remove it from the facia (see illustration).
4 Slacken and remove the instrument panel retaining screw (see illustration).

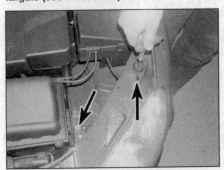

8.2 Headlight beam adjustment screw locations (arrowed). The outer screw is accessed through the hole in the panel

9.3 Unclip the instrument panel shroud from the facia (shown with steering wheel removed for clarity)

9.4 Undo the retaining screw . . .

9.5 . . . then unclip and remove the instrument panel, disconnecting its wiring connectors (arrowed)

5 Remove the instrument panel assembly from the facia, disconnecting the wiring connectors as they become accessible **(see illustration)**.

Refitting

6 Securely reconnect the wiring connectors to the instrument panel and clip the panel back into position in the facia. Refit the panel retaining screw, tightening it securely.
7 Clip the instrument panel shroud back onto the facia.
8 Reconnect the battery and check the operation of the panel warning lights to ensure they are functioning correctly.

10 Instrument panel components – removal and refitting

At the time of writing, it was unclear if any of the instrument panel components were available separately. Refer to your Peugeot dealer for the latest parts information; they will advise you on the best course of action should the instrument(s) develop a fault.

11 Clock/multi-function unit – removal and refitting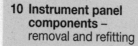

Removal

1 Disconnect the battery negative terminal.
2 Carefully unclip the clock/multi-function unit surround from the top of the facia and remove it, disconnecting the wiring connector from the hazard warning light switch **(see illustration)**.
3 Undo the retaining screws then remove the clock/multi-function unit, disconnecting its wiring connector as it becomes accessible **(see illustrations)**.

Refitting

4 Reconnect the wiring connector then seat the clock/multi-function unit back in position. Refit the unit retaining screws, tightening them securely.

5 Reconnect the wiring connector to the hazard warning light switch then clip the surround back onto the facia.

12 Cigarette lighter – removal and refitting

Removal

1 Remove the centre console as described in Chapter 11.
2 Carefully release retaining clips and slide the illumination light assembly off the base of the lighter, taking great care not to break its electrical contacts **(see illustration)**.
3 Pull out the lighter element then release the tangs and push out the metal insert. The plastic outer section can then be removed from the console **(see illustrations)**.

Refitting

4 Align the plastic outer section tab with the cut-out then insert it into the console.
5 Align the bulbholder contact on the metal insert with the holder tangs on the plastic outer then clip the insert into position.
6 Slide the illumination light assembly onto the metal insert and clip it securely onto the plastic outer.
7 Ensure the cigarette lighter is correctly assembled then refit the centre console as described in Chapter 11.

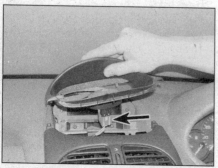

11.2 Unclip the clock/multi-function unit surround from the facia and disconnect the wiring connector (arrowed)

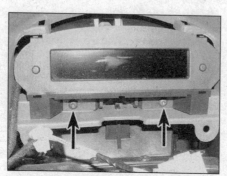

11.3a Undo the retaining screws (arrowed) . . .

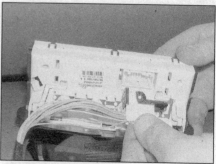

11.3b . . . and remove the clock/multi-function unit, disconnecting its wiring connectors

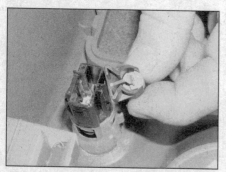

12.2 Unclip the illumination light assembly from the cigarette lighter

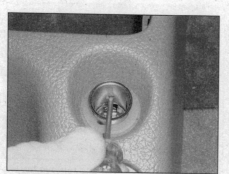

12.3a Unclip and remove the metal insert . . .

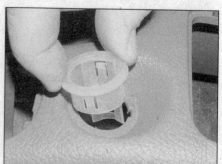

12.3b . . . then slide out the plastic outer section

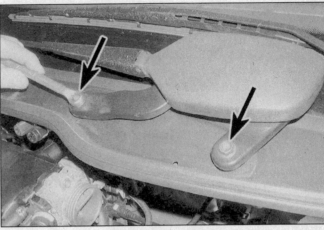

13.2 Horn mounting nut (1) and wiring connector (2) (viewed from front with bumper removed)

14.2 On right-hand drive models the driver's side wiper arm has a dual pivot arrangement (arrowed)

13 Horn –
removal and refitting

Removal

1 The horn is located behind the front bumper, on the right-hand side. To gain access, firmly apply the handbrake then jack up the front of the vehicle, and support it securely on axle stands (see *Jacking and vehicle support*).

2 Disconnect the wiring connector(s) then slacken the mounting nut and remove the horn from the vehicle **(see illustration)**.

14.3 Using a puller to free a wiper arm from its spindle

Refitting

3 Refitting is a reversal of removal.

14 Wiper arm –
removal and refitting

Note: *The wiper arms are a very tight fit on their spindles and it is likely that a puller will be needed to remove them safely, without damage.*

Removal

1 Operate the wiper motor, then switch it off so that the wiper arm returns to the at-rest position. Stick tape to the screen alongside the wiper blade to ensure correct refitment.

2 Lift up the wiper arm spindle nut cover (where fitted) then slacken and remove the spindle nut. On right-hand drive models the driver's side wiper arm incorporates a linkage at its lower end and is also fixed to a pivot by a second nut; remove this nut as well **(see illustration)**.

3 Lift the blade off the glass, and pull the wiper arm off its spindle. If the arm is very tight, free it from the spindle using a suitable puller **(see illustration)**.

Refitting

4 Ensure that the wiper arm and spindle splines are clean and dry, then refit the arm to the spindle, aligning the wiper blade with the tape fitted on removal.

5 Refit the spindle nut, tightening it securely, and clip the nut cover (where fitted) back into position.

15 Windscreen wiper motor and linkage –
removal and refitting

Removal

1 Disconnect the battery negative lead.

2 Remove the wiper arms (see Section 14).

3 On petrol engine models, remove the air cleaner housing to inlet manifold intake duct to improve access (see Chapter 4A).

4 Free the sealing strip from the top of the bulkhead then, starting at the inner end and working outwards, carefully unclip the left-hand section of the water deflector panel. Free the panel from the right-hand section and remove it from base of the windscreen **(see illustrations)**.

5 Unscrew the mounting bolt, located directly beneath the wiper motor **(see illustration)**.

15.4a Free the sealing strip from the top of the bulkhead . . .

15.4b . . . then unclip and remove the left-hand section of the water deflector panel (retaining clips arrowed)

15.5 Slacken and remove the mounting bolt from beneath the wiper motor

15.6a Unscrew the nut and remove the washer from each wiper spindle

15.6b Disconnect the wiring connector ...

15.6c ... then manoeuvre the wiper motor assembly out of position

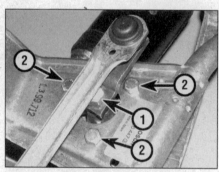

15.7 Wiper motor shaft nut (1) and retaining bolts (2)

6 Unscrew the retaining nut and washer from each wiper arm spindle then free the wiper motor assembly from the body. Disconnect the wiring connector then manoeuvre the assembly out of position **(see illustrations)**.

7 If necessary, mark the relative positions of the motor shaft and crank, then unscrew the retaining nut and washer and free the wiper linkage from the motor spindle **(see illustration)**. Unscrew the motor retaining bolts and separate the motor and linkage.

Refitting

8 Refitting is a reversal of removal, ensuring all fasteners are securely tightened. Ensure the water deflector panel is securely clipped in position prior to refitting the wiper arms.

16 Tailgate window wiper motor – removal and refitting

Removal

Note: *A pop rivet gun and suitable rivets will be required on refitting.*

1 Disconnect the battery negative lead.

2 Remove the wiper arm (see Section 14), then unscrew the wiper motor spindle nut.

3 Open the tailgate then unclip the inner trim panel from the tailgate.

4 Using a 7.5 mm drill, carefully drill the heads off the pop rivets securing the wiper motor bracket to the tailgate **(see illustration)**. To prevent the rivets falling into the tailgate, position a cloth on either side of the motor.

Caution: Take care not to damage the motor and tailgate when drilling out the rivets.

5 With the three rivets removed, disconnect the wiring connector and remove the wiper motor from the tailgate **(see illustration)**. Take care not to lose the collars from the motor mounting rubbers.

6 Remove the wiper motor sealing grommet from the tailgate glass.

7 Remove the cloths and recover the remnants of each rivet from the motor bracket/tailgate. Ensure all traces of rivet are removed.

8 If necessary, undo the three bolts and separate the wiper motor and bracket **(see illustration)**.

Refitting

9 Prior to refitting check the sealing grommet and rubber mountings for signs of damage or deterioration and renew as necessary.

10 Ensure the rubber grommet is correctly fitted to the tailgate glass, and the rubber mountings and collars are correctly fitted to the motor mounting bracket **(see illustrations)**.

11 Manoeuvre the wiper motor into position and secure it in position with new pop rivets.

16.4 Carefully drill the heads of the rivets (arrowed) securing the wiper motor bracket to the tailgate

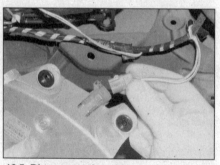

16.5 Disconnect the wiring connector and remove the wiper motor assembly from the tailgate

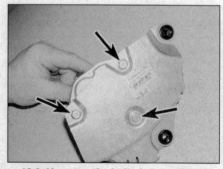

16.8 Unscrew the bolts (arrowed) and separate the wiper motor and bracket

16.10a Ensure the rubber grommet is correctly fitted to the tailgate glass ...

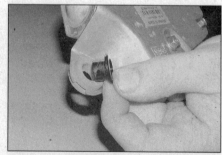

16.10b ... and the mounting rubbers and collars are correctly fitted to the motor mounting bracket

Tighten the wiper motor spindle nut to the specified torque wrench setting.

12 Reconnect the wiring connector to the motor then refit the trim panel to the tailgate.

13 Refit the wiper arm as described in Section 14 then reconnect the battery.

17 Washer system components – removal and refitting

1 The washer reservoir is located behind the right-hand front wing and supplies both the windscreen and tailgate washers via the same pump. On models equipped with headlight washers, the reservoir also supplies the headlight washer jets via an additional pump.

Washer fluid reservoir

2 Working in the engine compartment, unclip the filler neck from the reservoir **(see illustration)**.

3 Jack up the front of the vehicle, and support it securely on axle stands (see *Jacking and vehicle support*). To improve access, remove the right-hand roadwheel.

4 Undo the screws securing the front section of the right-hand wheelarch liner to the base of the bumper. Remove the fasteners securing the liner section to the body then manoeuvre the front section of the liner out from underneath the wing.

5 On models with front foglights, remove the right-hand foglight unit (see Section 7).

6 Note the correct fitted location of the washer hoses (if necessary, mark them for identification purposes) then disconnect the hoses from the washer pump(s) **(see illustration)**.

7 Disconnect the wiring connector(s) from the washer pump(s) **(see illustration)**.

8 Slacken and remove the retaining bolt then free the reservoir from the body and manoeuvre it out from underneath the wing **(see illustration)**.

9 Refitting is the reverse of removal, ensuring that the hoses are securely reconnected. Refill the reservoir and check for leaks.

Washer pump

10 Proceed as described in paragraphs 3 to 7

17.2 Unclip the filler neck and remove it from the washer fluid reservoir

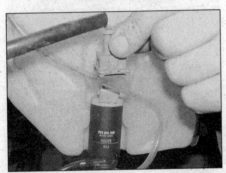

17.7 . . . and wiring connector from the washer pump

and disconnect the hose(s) and wiring connector from the pump (there is no need to remove the foglight).

11 Position a container beneath the reservoir to catch the washer fluid as the pump is removed.

12 Carefully ease the pump out from the reservoir, and recover its sealing grommet **(see illustrations)**. Wash off any spilt fluid with cold water.

13 Refitting is the reverse of removal, using a new sealing grommet if the original shows signs of damage or deterioration. Refill the reservoir and check the pump grommet for leaks on completion.

Windscreen washer jet

14 Open the bonnet to gain access to the base of the windscreen washer jets.

17.6 Disconnect the washer hoses . . .

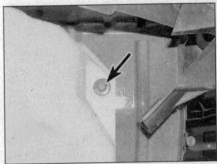

17.8 Unscrew the mounting bolt (arrowed – shown with bumper removed) and remove the washer fluid reservoir

Disconnect the washer hose(s) from the relevant jet, then depress the retaining clips and ease the jet out of position.

15 On refitting, securely connect the jet to the hose then clip it into the bonnet. Check the operation of the jet. If necessary, adjust the nozzles using a pin aiming one nozzle to a point slightly above the centre of the swept area of the screen and the other to a point slightly below the centre point to ensure complete coverage.

Tailgate washer jet

16 Remove the high-level stoplight unit as described in Section 7.

17 Release the retaining clips and detach the light unit from the bulbholder **(see illustration)**.

17.12a Ease the washer pump out of position . . .

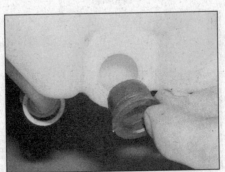

17.12b . . . and remove the sealing grommet from the reservoir

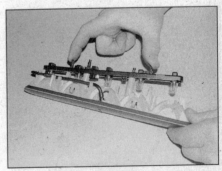

17.17 Unclip the bulbholder from the rear of the high-level stop light

12

18 Disconnect the washer hose from the jet then free the jet from the light unit, by rotating it a quarter-of-a-turn **(see illustrations)**.

19 Refitting is the reverse of removal. Do not overtighten the light unit retaining nuts as the plastic is easily broken. The washer jet is not adjustable.

Headlight washer jet

20 Remove the bumper as described in Chapter 11.

21 Disconnect the washer hose from the washer jet then unscrew the retaining nuts and remove the jet from the bumper.

22 Refitting is the reverse of removal.

18 Audio unit/CD autochanger – removal and refitting

Note: *The following procedure is for the range of equipment fitted by Peugeot.*

Audio unit

Removal

1 Ensure the audio unit is switched off.

2 Insert a small screwdriver/punch into the hole on each side of the unit and pushing it in until the clip releases **(see illustration)**.

3 Once both retaining clips have been released, slide the audio unit out of position. Disconnect the wiring connections and aerial lead and remove the unit from the vehicle **(see illustration)**.

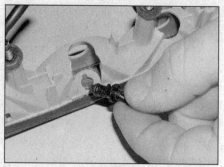

17.18a Disconnect the washer hose . . .

17.18b . . . then rotate the washer jet 90° and remove it from the light

Refitting

4 Prior to refitting, reset the audio unit retaining clips.

5 Securely reconnect the aerial lead and wiring connectors then slide the unit back into position, taking care not to trap the wiring.

6 Switch on the unit and enter the security code (see *Audio unit anti-theft system* section in the Reference section at the end of this manual).

CD autochanger

Removal

7 Remove the screws and/or fastener(s) (pull out the centre pin then remove the complete fastener) and free the luggage compartment side trim panel from the body to gain access to the CD autochanger **(see illustrations)**.

8 Slide the CD autochanger unit out of its

mounting bracket then release the retaining clip and disconnect its wiring connector **(see illustrations)**.

9 If necessary, the mounting bracket can then be unbolted from the body.

Refitting

10 Refitting is the reverse of removal.

19 Loudspeakers – removal and refitting

Removal

Front door speaker

1 Remove the door inner trim panel as described in Chapter 11.

18.2 Release the retaining clips by inserting a screwdriver/punch into each of the holes . . .

18.3 . . . then withdraw the audio unit from facia and disconnect its wiring connectors and aerial lead (arrowed)

18.7a Remove the screw and hook . . .

18.7b . . . and the fasteners and peel back the luggage compartment side trim panel to gain access to the CD autochanger

18.8a Slide the CD autochanger out of its bracket . . .

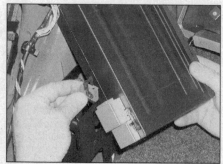

18.8b . . . then disconnect its wiring connector

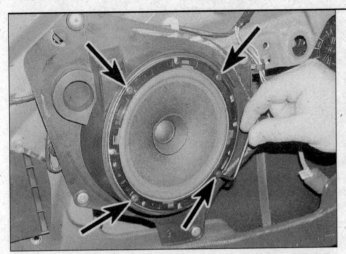

19.2a Undo the retaining screws (arrowed) . . .

19.2b . . . then remove the front door speaker from its housing, disconnecting its wiring connector

2 Slacken and remove the retaining screws then remove the speaker from the door, disconnecting the wiring connector as it becomes accessible (see illustrations).

3 If necessary, carefully drill the heads off the pop rivets securing the speaker housing to the door then remove the housing.

Caution: Take care not to damage the housing and door when drilling out the rivets.

Front door tweeter

4 Carefully unclip the exterior mirror inner trim panel from the front of the door (see illustration). On models with manually-adjusted mirrors, remove the rubber gaiter from the adjustment handle prior to unclipping the trim panel.

5 Rotate the tweeter speaker to free it from the trim panel and disconnect it from the wiring connector (see illustration).

Rear speaker – five-door models

Note: *A pop rivet gun and suitable rivets will be required on refitting.*

6 Remove the door inner trim panel as described in Chapter 11.

7 Carefully drill the heads off the pop rivets securing the speaker assembly to the door.

8 Release the retaining clips then free the speaker from its housing, disconnecting the wiring connector as it becomes accessible (see illustration).

9 If necessary, the speaker housing can then be unclipped and removed from the door (see illustration).

Rear speaker – three-door models

10 Lift out the parcel shelf then remove the seat cushion and back as described in Chapter 11.

11 Peel back the luggage compartment side trim panel then slacken and remove the upper trim panel retaining screws. Unclip the panel and free it from the rear seat belt. If the left-hand panel is being removed, it will also be necessary to remove the courtesy light from the panel (see illustrations).

19.4 Unclip the mirror inner trim panel from the door . . .

19.5 . . . and rotate the tweeter speaker to free it from the panel

19.8 Drill out the pop rivets then unclip the speaker from the rear door and disconnect its wiring connector

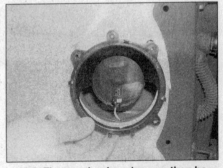

19.9 The speaker housing can then be unclipped and removed from the door

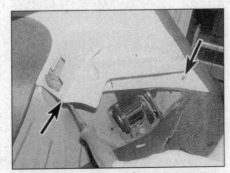

19.11a On three-door models, undo the retaining screws (arrowed) . . .

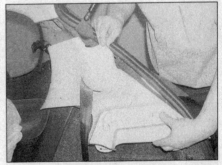

19.11b . . . then unclip the upper trim panel from the rear pillar

12

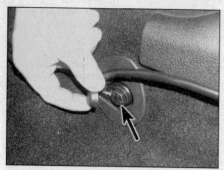

19.12a Remove the trim cap and unscrew the mounting bolt (arrowed) . . .

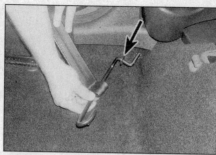

19.12b . . . then free the anchorage bar from the body and recover the washer (arrowed)

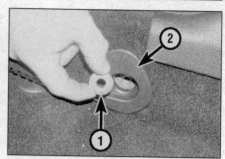

19.12c Recover the spacer (1) and trim cap (2) fitted between the anchorage bar and body

19.13a Remove the height adjuster button then undo the retaining screw (arrowed) and remove the trim cover from the seat belt upper mounting

19.13b Unscrew the mounting bolt and free the seat belt from the height adjuster

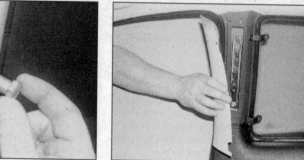

19.14 Unclip the upper trim panel from the pillar and free it from the seat belt

12 Prise off the trim cap from the front seat belt lower anchorage bolt then slacken and remove the bolt and washer. Free the anchorage bar from the body then slide off the washer and free the bar from the seat belt. Recover the spacer and trim cap fitted between the anchorage bar mounting and body **(see illustrations)**.

13 Remove the button from the seat belt upper mounting height adjuster then undo the retaining screw and remove the trim cover from the mounting. Unscrew the mounting bolt and free the belt from the height adjuster **(see illustrations)**.

14 Unclip the top of the pillar upper trim panel then free the panel from the seat belt and remove it from the vehicle **(see illustration)**.

15 Prise off the trim cap from the rear seat belt lower mounting bolt then slacken and remove the bolt and washer. Free the belt and recover the spacer fitted between the belt and body **(see illustrations)**.

16 Open the rear quarter window and free the window sealing strip from the top of the rear seat side trim panel. Unclip the side trim panel from the body then free the seat belt guide and seat belt from the panel and remove the panel from the vehicle **(see illustrations)**.

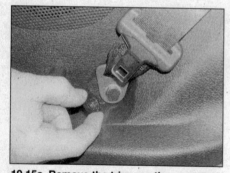

19.15a Remove the trim cap then unscrew the rear seat belt lower mounting bolt . . .

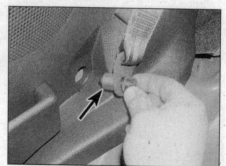

19.15b . . . and recover the spacer (arrowed) fitted between the belt and body

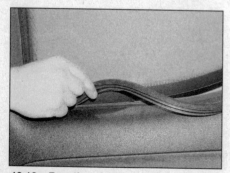

19.16a Free the window sealing strip from the top of the panel . . .

19.16b . . . and unclip the rear seat side trim panel from the body

19.16c Unclip the seat belt guide then free the trim panel from the seat belt

17 If necessary, remove the foam insulation ring from around the speaker to gain access to the speaker screws **(see illustration)**.
18 Slacken and remove the retaining screws then remove the speaker from the body, disconnecting the wiring connector as it becomes accessible.

Refitting

19 Refitting is a reversal of removal, ensuring the seat belt mounting bolts are tightened to the specified torque (see Chapter 11). Ensure the trim panels are clipped securely in position and are correctly located behind the edges of the sealing strips.

20 Radio aerial –
removal and refitting

Removal

1 The aerial is a screw-fit in its base and is easily removed.
2 To remove the complete aerial on models where the aerial is mounted on the rear of the roof, open the tailgate then free the tailgate sealing strip from the top of its aperture. Carefully unclip the upper trim panel from the rear of the roof and peel back the headlining to gain access to the aerial nut.
3 To remove the complete aerial on models where the aerial is at the front of the roof, carefully prise the courtesy light out of position, disconnecting it from the wiring

19.17 Peel back the foam insulation ring to gain access to the speaker screws

connector, then unclip the light surround from the headlining **(see illustrations)**.
4 Remove the insulating cap then slacken and remove the nut **(see illustrations)**. Detach the aerial lead and lift the aerial off from the roof, complete with its rubber seal.

Refitting

5 Refitting is the reverse of removal.

21 Engine immobiliser and anti-theft alarm system – general information

Note: *This information is applicable only to the systems fitted by Peugeot as standard equipment.*

Engine immobiliser

1 An engine immobiliser system is fitted as

standard to all models and the system is operated automatically every time the ignition key is inserted/removed.
2 The immobiliser system ensures the vehicle can only be started using the original Peugeot ignition key. The key contains an electronic chip (transponder) which is programmed with a code. When the key is inserted into the ignition switch it uses the current present in the sensor ring (which is fitted to the ignition switch housing) to send a signal to the immobiliser electronic control unit (ECU). The ECU is incorporated into the built-in systems interface (BSI) unit (see Section 24). The ECU checks this code every time the ignition is switched on. If the key code does not match the ECU code, the ECU will disable the starter, fuel and ignition (as applicable) to prevent the engine being started.
3 When the vehicle is new, a confidential security card is supplied along with the other vehicle documentation. This card contains the security code which your Peugeot dealer requires when carrying out any work on the immobiliser system. Keep this card in a safe place at home; never store it in the vehicle. If the ignition key is lost, a new one can be obtained from a Peugeot dealer. Take the confidential security card and all the existing keys along to your Peugeot dealer who will supply a new key and reprogram all the keys with a new security code; this will render the lost key useless.
Caution: Without the confidential security card, it will not be possible to have the keys and immobiliser system reprogrammed.

HAYNES HINT *If you have purchased the vehicle second-hand, as a precaution have all the keys and the immobiliser system reprogrammed with a new security code. This will ensure the keys in your possession are the only ones able to start the vehicle and render all other keys useless.*

4 Any problems with the engine immobiliser system should be referred to a Peugeot dealer.

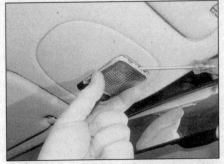

20.3a Where the aerial is mounted at the front of the roof, prise out the courtesy light . . .

20.3b . . . and disconnect it from the wiring connector . . .

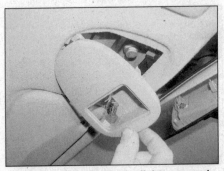

20.3c . . . then unclip the light surround

20.4a Remove the insulating cap . . .

20.4b . . . then unscrew the aerial retaining nut (arrowed)

Anti-theft alarm system

5 Most models covered in this were also equipped with an anti-theft alarm system as standard equipment. The system was available as a option on all other models. The alarm is automatically armed when the deadlocking is set using the remote central locking transmitter and is disarmed when the doors are unlocked using the remote transmitter. The alarm system has switches on the bonnet, tailgate and each of the doors and also has ultrasonic sensing, which detects movement inside the vehicle, via sensors mounted on either side of the vehicle interior.

6 When the system is activated, the direction indicators will flash continuously for two seconds and the indicator light on the alarm switch, fitted to the rear section of the centre console, will flash continuously. **Note:** *If the bonnet, tailgate or one of the doors are not properly closed when the alarm is set, the siren will sound briefly. If the bonnet/ tailgate/door (as applicable) is properly closed within 45 seconds the alarm will activate. If not the alarm will remain disarmed.*

7 If for some reason the remote central locking transmitter fails whilst the alarm is armed, the alarm can be disarmed using the key. To do this, open the door with the key, then enter the vehicle, noting that the alarm will sound as the door is opened. Insert the key and switch on the ignition, the immobiliser will recognise the key and will switch off the alarm.

8 If required, the ultrasonic sensing facility of the alarm can be switched off, whilst retaining the switched side of the system. To switch off the ultrasonic sensing, with the ignition switched off, depress the alarm switch (mounted on the rear section of the centre console) until the alarm indicator light on the switch is continuously lit. Get out of the vehicle and operate the deadlocking function using the remote transmitter to arm the alarm. The direction indicators will flash as normal but only the switched (door, tailgate and bonnet) side of the alarm system will be operational. This facility is useful, as it allows you to leave the windows/sunroof open, and still arm the alarm. If the windows/sunroof are left open with the ultra-sonic sensing not switched off, the alarm may be falsely triggered by a gust of wind.

9 Prior to disconnecting the battery, the alarm system should be disabled; this will prevent the alarm sounding when the battery is disconnected/reconnected. To do this, switch on the ignition then immediately depress and hold the alarm switch for two seconds; the indicator light on the switch should then flash rapidly for approximately three seconds indicating the alarm has been disabled. Switch off the ignition and disconnect the battery negative terminal. Once the battery has been reconnected, operate the deadlocking with the remote transmitter then

unlock the vehicle. The alarm will be set as normal, the next time the deadlocking is set.

10 Should the alarm system become faulty, the vehicle should be taken to a Peugeot dealer for examination.

22 Airbag system – general information and precautions

Driver and passenger airbags

1 Both a driver's and passenger airbag are fitted as standard to some models in the range, on other models they were available as an optional extra. Models fitted with a driver's airbag have the word AIRBAG stamped on the airbag unit (fitted to the centre of the steering wheel). Models also equipped with a passenger airbag also have the word airbag stamped on the passenger airbag unit (fitted to the facia unit). The airbag system comprises of the airbag unit(s) (complete with gas generators), the control unit (with an integral impact sensor) and a warning light in the instrument panel.

2 The airbag system is triggered in the event of a heavy frontal impact above a predetermined force, depending on the point of impact. The airbag is then inflated within milliseconds, and forms a safety cushion between the driver and steering wheel and (where fitted) the passenger and facia. This prevents contact between the upper body and wheel/facia, and therefore greatly reduces the risk of injury. The airbag then deflates almost immediately. The control unit also operates the front seat belt tensioner mechanisms at the same time (see Chapter 11).

3 Every time the ignition is switched on, the airbag control unit performs a self-test. The self-test takes approximately six seconds and during this time the warning light in the instrument panel will be illuminated. After the self-test is complete, the warning light will go out (unless the passenger airbag unit has been deactivated – see paragraph 4). If the warning light fails to come on, remains illuminated after the self-test period, or comes on at any time when the vehicle is being driven, there is a fault in the airbag system. The vehicle should be taken to a Peugeot dealer for examination at the earliest possible opportunity.

4 Most vehicles with a passenger airbag are equipped with a disabling switch on the facia. The switch is operated using the ignition key and switches off the passenger airbag (it is not possible to disable the driver's airbag) to enable a rear-facing child seat to be installed in the passenger seat. Whilst the passenger airbag is disabled, the airbag warning light on the instrument panel will remain illuminated all the time.

⚠ **Warning:** *Before carrying out any operations on the airbag system, disconnect the battery negative*

terminal and wait at least two minutes. Remove the centre console (see Chapter 11) then release the retaining clip and disconnect the wiring connector(s) from the airbag control unit; if necessary remove the facia panel bracket mounting bolt to gain the clearance necessary to disconnect the connector. When the operations are complete, securely reconnect the control unit and tighten the facia bracket bolt to the specified torque (where removed) then refit the centre console (see Chapter 11). Make sure no one is inside the vehicle when the battery is reconnected then, with the driver's door open, switch the ignition on from outside vehicle and check the operation of the airbag warning light.

⚠ *Warning: Do not subject the area of the body around the control unit to any form of shock which could trigger the system.*

⚠ *Warning: Note that the airbags must not be subjected to temperatures in excess of 100ºC. When the airbag is removed, ensure that it is stored the correct way up to prevent possible inflation.*

⚠ *Warning: Do not allow any solvents or cleaning agents to contact the airbag assemblies. They must be cleaned using only a damp cloth.*

⚠ *Warning: The airbags and control unit are both sensitive to impact. If either is dropped or damaged they should be renewed.*

⚠ *Warning: Disconnect the airbag control unit wiring connector prior to using arc welding equipment on the vehicle.*

⚠ *Warning: On models with a passenger airbag, never fit a rear-facing child seat to the front passenger seat unless the passenger airbag has been disabled (see paragraph 4).*

⚠ *Warning: Peugeot recommend that the airbag units be renewed every ten years.*

Side airbags

5 On some models, in addition to the driver and passenger airbag units, side airbags are also fitted to the seat back of each front seat (a side airbag label will be attached to the trim on the side of the seat base if side airbags are fitted). Each airbag unit has its own control unit which is mounted onto the vehicle body on the outside of each front seat. The side airbags are not linked in anyway and operate individually.

6 The relevant side airbag is triggered in the event of a heavy side impact above a predetermined force. The airbag is then inflated within milliseconds, and forms a safety cushion between the driver/passenger (as applicable) and the door. This prevents contact between the upper body and door, and therefore greatly reduces the risk of

23.3a Undo the retaining screws then lift the airbag unit away from the steering wheel . . .

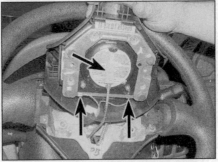

23.3b . . . and disconnect its wiring connectors (arrowed)

23.9 Unclip the glovebox lid from its retaining clips and remove it from the facia

injury. The airbag then deflates almost immediately.

7 Every time the ignition is switched on, the control units performs a self-test. The self-test takes approximately six seconds and during this time the side airbag warning light in the instrument panel will be illuminated. After the self-test is complete, the warning light will go out. If the warning light fails to come on, remains illuminated after the self-test period, or comes on at any time when the vehicle is being driven, there is a fault in the airbag system. The vehicle should be taken to a Peugeot dealer for examination at the earliest possible opportunity.

⚠️ *Warning: Before carrying out any operations on the front seats, disconnect the battery negative terminal and wait at least two minutes. Reach in under the seats and disconnect the wiring connector from the side airbag unit of each seat. When the operations are complete, reconnect the wiring connectors to the airbags. Make sure no one is inside the vehicle when the battery is reconnected then, with the driver's door open, switch the ignition on from outside vehicle and check the operation of the airbag warning light.*

⚠️ *Warning: Do not subject the area of the body around the control units to any form of shock which could trigger the system.*

⚠️ *Warning: Note that the airbags must not be subjected to temperatures in excess of 100ºC.*

⚠️ *Warning: The side airbags and control units are sensitive to impact. If either is dropped or damaged they should be renewed.*

⚠️ *Warning: Disconnect the side airbag control unit wiring connectors prior to using arc welding equipment on the vehicle.*

⚠️ *Warning: Peugeot recommend that the airbag units be renewed every ten years.*

23 Airbag system components – removal and refitting

⚠️ *Warning: Refer to the precautions given in Section 23 before carrying out the following operations.*

Driver's airbag

Removal

1 Disconnect the battery negative terminal and wait at least two minutes. Remove the centre console (see Chapter 11) then release the retaining clip and disconnect the wiring connector(s) from the airbag control unit **(see illustration 23.22)**. If necessary, remove the facia bracket lower mounting bolt to gain the clearance necessary to disconnect the connector.

2 Slacken and remove the two airbag unit retaining screws from the rear of the steering

wheel, rotating the wheel as necessary to gain access to the screws.

3 Return the steering wheel to the straight-ahead position, then carefully lift the airbag unit away from the wheel, disconnecting the wiring connectors as they become accessible **(see illustrations)**.

⚠️ *Warning: Do not knock or drop the airbag unit and store it the correct way up with its padded surface uppermost.*

Refitting

4 Securely reconnect the wiring connectors then seat the airbag unit in the steering wheel, ensuring the wiring does not become trapped.

5 Fit the airbag unit retaining screws and tighten them evenly and progressively to the specified torque.

6 Securely reconnect the airbag control unit wiring connector(s). Refit the facia mounting bracket bolt (where removed), tightening it to the specified torque, then refit the centre console (see Chapter 11). Make sure no one is inside the vehicle then reconnect the battery. With the driver's door open, switch the ignition on from outside vehicle and check the operation of the warning light.

Passenger airbag

Removal

7 Disconnect the battery negative terminal and wait at least two minutes. Remove the centre console (see Chapter 11) then release the retaining clip and disconnect the wiring connector(s) from the airbag control unit **(see illustration 23.22)**. If necessary, remove the facia bracket lower mounting bolt to gain the clearance necessary to disconnect the connector.

8 Remove the audio unit as described in Section 18.

9 Open up the glovebox lid then carefully unclip the base of the lid from its retaining clips. Free the lid stays from the glovebox compartment and remove the lid from the facia **(see illustration)**.

10 Slacken and remove the glovebox compartment retaining screws, noting the correct fitted locations of the lid retaining clips **(see illustrations)**.

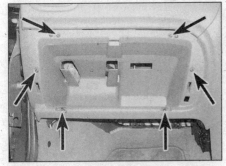

23.10a Slacken and remove the retaining screws (arrowed) . . .

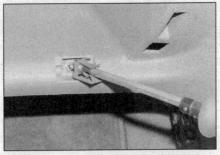

23.10b . . . noting the correct fitted direction of the retaining clips fitted to the lower screws . . .

12

23.11 . . . then manoeuvre the glovebox compartment out of position

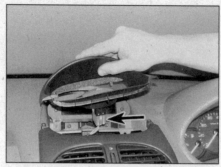

23.12 Unclip the clock/multi-function unit surround from the facia and disconnect the switch wiring connector (arrowed)

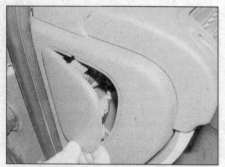

23.14 Unclip the end cover from the passenger end of the facia . . .

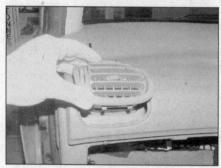

23.15 . . . then prise out the passenger end vent

11 Free the glovebox compartment from the facia then manoeuvre it downwards and out from under the facia **(see illustration)**. Where necessary, disconnect the wiring connectors from the glovebox light and switch as the compartment is removed.
12 Carefully unclip the clock/multi-function unit surround from the top of the facia and remove it, disconnecting the wiring connector from the hazard warning light switch **(see illustration)**.
13 Slacken and remove the retaining screws securing the top of the centre vent panel to the facia. Carefully unclip the panel and

remove it from the facia.
14 Prise out the end cover from the passenger end of the facia **(see illustration)**.
15 Carefully prise the vent out from the passenger end of the facia, taking great care not to mark the vent or facia **(see illustration)**.
16 Rotate the fastener through 90° and remove the lower cover from the driver's side of the facia.
17 Trace the passenger airbag unit wiring back across the facia, freeing it from the retaining clips, and disconnect it from the wiring connector located next to the fusebox.
18 Working through the glovebox aperture,

slacken and remove the seven retaining screws securing the airbag panel to the rear of the facia and the four nuts securing the passenger airbag in position **(see illustration)**. The airbag panel and unit can then be removed from the facia, taking care not to strain the airbag wiring.

Refitting

19 Fit the airbag unit and panel to the facia, ensuring the wiring is correctly routed. Fit all the retaining screws and tighten the airbag unit nuts to the specified torque.
20 Secure the airbag wiring in position with the retaining clips and securely reconnect its wiring connector.
21 The remainder of refitting is the reverse of removal. On completion, securely reconnect the airbag control unit wiring connector(s). Refit the facia mounting bracket bolt (where removed), tightening it to the specified torque, then refit the centre console (see Chapter 11). Make sure no one is inside the vehicle then reconnect the battery. With the driver's door open, switch the ignition on from outside vehicle and check the operation of the warning light.

Airbag control unit

Removal

22 Disconnect the battery negative terminal and wait at least two minutes. Remove the centre console (see Chapter 11) then release the retaining clip and disconnect the wiring connector(s) from the airbag control unit **(see illustration)**. If necessary, remove the facia bracket lower mounting bolt to gain the clearance necessary to disconnect the connector.
23 Unscrew the retaining nuts then remove the control unit from the vehicle.

Refitting

24 Refit the control unit, making sure the arrow on the top of the unit is pointing towards the front of the vehicle. Refit the

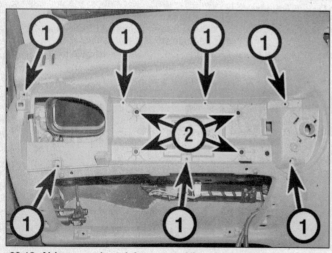

23.18 Airbag panel retaining screw (1) and passenger airbag unit nut (2) locations

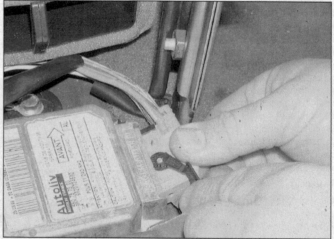

23.22 Release the retaining clip and disconnect the wiring connector from the airbag control unit

23.30a Undo the retaining screws securing the lower shroud to the steering column . . .

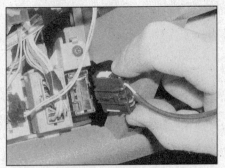

23.30b . . . then disconnect the audio unit control stalk wiring connector and remove the shroud

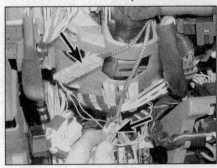

23.32 Free the contact unit wiring connectors (arrowed) from the steering column and disconnect them

control unit retaining nuts and tighten them to the specified torque.

25 Securely reconnect the airbag control unit wiring connector(s).

26 Refit the facia mounting bracket bolt (where removed), tightening it to the specified torque, then refit the centre console (see Chapter 11). Make sure no one is inside the vehicle then reconnect the battery. With the driver's door open, switch the ignition on from outside vehicle and check the operation of the warning light.

Driver's airbag unit wiring contact unit

Removal

27 Remove the driver's airbag as described in paragraphs 1 to 3.

28 Remove the steering wheel as described in Chapter 10. Ensure the front wheels are pointing in the straight-ahead position.

29 Rotate the fastener a quarter-of-a-turn (90°) and remove the lower cover from the driver's side of the facia.

30 Undo the retaining screws and free the lower shroud from the column. Trace the audio unit control stalk back to its wiring connector then disconnect the connector and remove the shroud and switch as an assembly **(see illustrations)**.

31 Unclip and remove the upper shroud from the steering column.

32 Unclip the contact unit wiring connectors from the column then release the retaining clips and separate the two halves of each connector **(see illustration)**.

33 Release the retaining clip and carefully free the immobiliser ring from the ignition switch/steering column lock.

34 Slacken and remove the retaining screws and remove the contact unit from the top of the steering column taking care not to strain the wiring **(see illustrations)**.

Refitting

35 Prior to refitting it is necessary to ensure the contact unit is correctly centralised, with the arrow markings on the top of the unit correctly aligned, and that the front wheels are pointing in the straight-ahead position. If there is any doubt about the unit position, rotate the contact insert

in a clockwise direction until resistance is felt. From this point, rotate the insert back through two to two and a half rotations until the arrow markings on the top surface of the unit are correctly aligned; the wiring harness will now be at the bottom. Do not rotate the unit from now onwards.

36 Slide the contact unit into position, making sure its wiring is correctly routed, and engage it with the switch housing on the column. Ensure that the contact ring is correctly seated then refit its retaining screws, tightening them securely.

37 Reconnect the contact unit wiring connectors then clip the connectors back onto the bracket.

38 Reconnect the audio unit control stalk wiring connector then refit the shrouds to the steering column. Ensure the wiring is not trapped by the shrouds then refit and securely tighten the lower shroud screws.

39 Refit the steering wheel as described in Chapter 10, then refit the airbag unit as described in paragraphs 4 to 6.

Side airbag unit

40 Removal and refitting of the side airbag units should be entrusted to a Peugeot dealer. The seat must be dismantled to enable the airbag unit to removed/refitted.

Side airbag control unit

Removal

41 Remove the relevant front seat as described in Chapter 11.

23.34a Undo the retaining screws (arrowed) . . .

42 Referring to Section 26 of Chapter 11, on three-door models remove the rear seat side trim panel as described in paragraphs 2 to 8, and on five-door models remove the pillar upper and lower trim panels as described in paragraphs 12 to 15.

43 On all models, peel back the carpet to gain access to the side airbag control unit.

44 Disconnect the wiring connector then undo the retaining nuts and remove the control unit from the vehicle.

Refitting

45 Refitting is the reverse of removal, tightening the control unit retaining nuts to the specified torque.

24 Built-in systems interface (BSI) unit – general information, removal and refitting

General information

1 The built-in systems interface (BSI) unit is an electronic control unit which controls a variety of functions, normal controlled by individual control units and relays. The BSI unit is located behind the lower cover on the driver's side of facia where it is situated directly beneath the fusebox; the unit has six fuses plugged into it. The BSI unit controls the following functions (not all functions are fitted to all models).

   a) *Direction indicator/hazard warning lights.*
   b) *Windscreen/tailgate wiper motors.*

23.34b . . . then remove the contact unit, taking care not to strain the wiring

12

24.5 Unclip the cover from the base of the fusebox to gain access to the BSI unit (shown with facia removed for clarity)

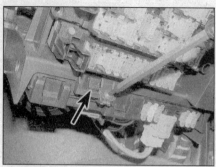

24.6a Undo the retaining screw then release the retaining clip (arrowed) . . .

24.6b . . . and free the BSI unit from the base of the fusebox

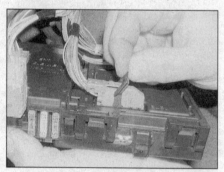

24.7 Release the retaining clips then disconnect the wiring connectors and remove the BSI unit

c) Rear screen heating element.
d) Immobiliser system.
e) Anti-theft alarm system.
f) Lights-on/ignition key warning buzzer.
g) Central locking/deadlocking, including the remote central locking receiver.

h) Door open indicator.
i) Courtesy light delay timer.
j) Automatic transmission audible warning system.

2 Should any of the above functions become faulty, first check the condition of the fuses. If this fails to locate the problem, take the vehicle to a Peugeot dealer for testing. The only satisfactory way to test the BSI unit is by substitution with another unit which is know to be functioning correctly.

Removal

3 Disconnect the battery negative terminal.
4 Rotate the fastener a quarter-of-a-turn (90º) and remove the lower cover from the driver's side of the facia.
5 Carefully unclip the protective cover from the underside of the fusebox to gain access to the BSI unit **(see illustration)**.
6 Undo the retaining screw then release the retaining clip and pivot the BSI unit downwards to free it from the base of the fusebox **(see illustrations)**.
7 Release the retaining clips then disconnect all the wiring connectors and remove the BSI unit from the vehicle **(see illustration)**.

Refitting

8 Refitting is the reverse of removal, ensuring the wiring connectors are all securely reconnected.

25 Satellite navigation system – general information

1 A satellite navigation system was offered as an optional extra on some models. The navigation unit and remote control are located in the glovebox. Refer to the manufacturer's handbook supplied with the vehicle for operating instructions. Any problems with the system must be referred to a Peugeot dealer.

Peugeot 206 wiring diagrams

Diagram 1

Key to symbols

Bulb		Item no.	**2**
Switch		Pump/motor	
Multiple contact switch (ganged)		Earth and location	
Fuse/ fusible link	F5	Gauge/meter	
Resistor		Diode	
Variable resistor		Wire splice or soldered joint	
Connecting wires		Solenoid actuator	
Light emitting diode (LED)			

Wire identifier and colour (Orange). Note: colours may not resemble actual vehicle due to variations in production!

— CC05 (OR) —

Connections to other circuits. Direction of arrow denotes current flow.

▶ A

Diagram 3, Arrow A
High beam warning light

Screened cable

Dashed outline denotes part of a larger item, containing in this case an electronic or solid state device.
C2 - connector pin identification.
2VE - 2 pin green connector.

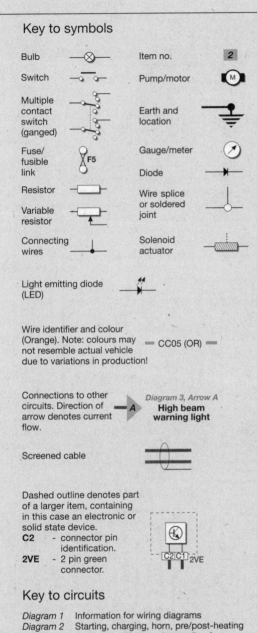

C2 C1 2VE

Key to circuits

Diagram 1	Information for wiring diagrams
Diagram 2	Starting, charging, horn, pre/post-heating
Diagram 3	Pre/post heating, engine cooling fan
Diagram 4	Engine cooling fan, temp. gauge, seat belt warning light
Diagram 5	Warning lights and gauges
Diagram 6	Exterior lighting
Diagram 7	Exterior lighting continued, buzzer, interior lighting
Diagram 8	Interior lighting continued, headlight levelling
Diagram 9	Clock, cigar lighter, sunroof, audio system
Diagram 10	Audio system, electric windows
Diagram 11	Rear windows, heated rear window and mirrors
Diagram 12	Wash/wipe system, ABS
Diagram 13	Central locking
Diagram 14	Airbags, heater blower, air conditioning
Diagram 15	HDi Diesel engine management (part 1 of 2)
Diagram 16	HDi Diesel engine management (part 2 of 2)
Diagram 17	Magneti Marelli MM1AP fuel injection
Diagram 18	Bosch MP7.2 fuel injection

4 Engine fuse box

Fuse	Rating	Circuit protected
MF1	70A	Built in systems interface supply
MF2	40A	Fan
MF3	-	Additional heating
MF4	-	Spare
MF8	70A	Supply passenger comp. fuse box
MF9	50A	Built in systems interface supply
MF10	40A	Main and dipped beam
MF11	60A	Supply passenger comp. fuse box (models with rear power windows)
MF12	50A	Ignition switch power supply
MF13	40A	Ignition switch power supply
MF16	30A	ABS
MF17	30A	ABS
F5	20/30A	Horn, sidelights, front foglight
F6	10/20A	Heated seats, heating, ventilation, running lights
F7	5/20A	Fan
F14	5/30A	Running lights, headlight wash, diagnostic socket
F18	-	Spare
F19	-	Spare
F20	-	Spare
F21	5A	Coolant thermostat, heating, ventilation
F22	-	Spare
F23	5A	ABS
F24	5A	Engine management, pre-heat unit, air flow sensor
F25	10A	Fuel pump
F26	10/30A	Engine man. fuel pump, oxygen sensor, EGR
F27	-	Engine man.
F28	5A	Throttle housing heater
F29	30A	Air pump
F30	10A	RH foglight, foglight warning light
F31	10A	LH foglight
F32	10A	Reversing lights, vehicle speed sensor, diesel pump, auto. gearbox electrohydraulic block, additional heating
F33	10A	Automatic gearbox
F34	5/15A	Oxygen sensor

5 Passenger fuse box (28 fuse)

Fuse	Rating	Circuit protected
F1	SH	Pretensioner unit, front and side airbags, BSI supply
F2	5A	Instrument cluster
F3	-	Spare
F4	5A	Built in systems interface (BSI)
F5	-	Spare
F6	5A	Engine management control unit, immobiliser
F7	15A	Spare
F8	10A	Coolant temp. unit, instrument panel, hazard warning, clock, multi/func. display, courtesy light
F9	5A	Built in systems interface (BSI)
F10	-	Spare
F11	10A	LH stop light, high level stop light
F12	10A	RH stop light
F13	-	Spare
F14	30A	Rear electric windows
F15	20A	Luggage compartment illumination, tow-bar supply
F16	-	Spare
F17	-	Spare
F18	10A	Number plate light, lighter illumination, clock, multifunction display, interior illum.
F19	5A	Rear foglights
F20	-	Spare
F21	-	Spare
F22	10A	Glove box light, map reading light, courtesy light, clock or multi/func. display, instrument panel, on-board navigation system, rear electric windows, rain sensor
F23	20A	Cigar lighter
F24	15A	Radio
F25	20A	Windscreen wiper and rear wiper
F26	-	Spare
F27	5A	Built in systems interface (BSI)
F28	-	Spare

25 Passenger fuse box (12 fuse)

Fuse	Rating	Circuit protected
F29	10A	LH main beam
F30	10A	RH main beam, main beam warning light
F31	10A	LH dipped beam
F32	10A	RH dipped beam, dipped beam warning light
F33	5A	Headlight wash
F34	10A	LH side/tail light
F35	10A	RH side/tail light
F36	-	Spare
F37	5A	Coolant temperature unit
F38	5A	Fan, pressostat
F39	-	Spare
F40	20/40A	Heating, ventilation

H32036

12

Wire colours

BA	White	**OR**	Orange
BE	Blue	**RG**	Red
BG	Beige	**RS**	Pink
GR	Grey	**VE**	Green
JN	Yellow	**VI**	Mauve
MR	Brown	**VJ**	Green/
NR	Black		Yellow

★ Alternative wiring

Key to items

1 Battery
2 Ignition switch
3 Instrument cluster
  a = alternator warning light
  b = speedometer
  c = tachometer
  d = glow plug warning light
  e = control unit
4 Engine fusebox
  a = horn relay (if fitted)
5 Passenger fusebox (28 fuse)
6 Starter motor
7 Alternator
8 Diagnostic connector
9 Built in systems interface (BSI)
10 Multifunction switch
  a = horn switch
11 Horn switch
12 Horn
13 Steering wheel rotary connector
14 TDC sensor
15 Vehicle speed sensor
16 Injection supply relay
17 Pre-heat control unit
18 Glow plugs
19 Diesel injection pump
  a = control unit
  b = EGR load lever switch
  c = advance correction solenoid
20 Oil pressure switch
21 Post heat relay
22 EGR function supply relay
23 Post heat thermal switch
24 EGR valve

Diagram 2

H32037

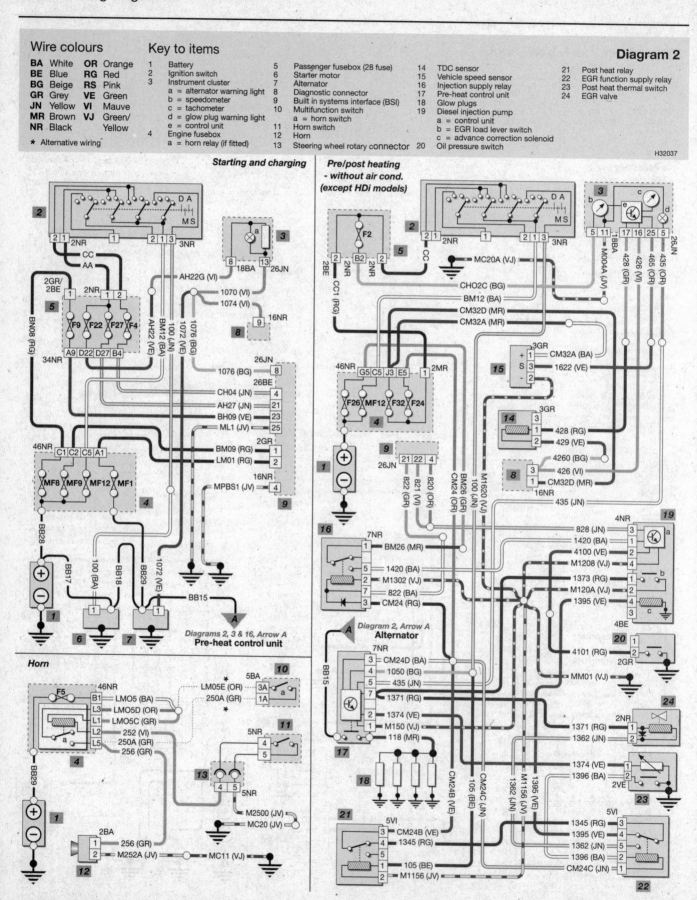

Starting and charging

Pre/post heating
- without air cond.
(except HDi models)

Diagrams 2, 3 & 16, Arrow A
Pre-heat control unit

Diagram 2, Arrow A
Alternator

Horn

Wire colours

BA	White	**OR**	Orange
BE	Blue	**RG**	Red
BG	Beige	**RS**	Pink
GR	Grey	**VE**	Green
JN	Yellow	**VI**	Mauve
MR	Brown	**VJ**	Green/
NR	Black		Yellow

Key to items

1	Battery	5	Passenger fusebox (28 fuse)	18	Glow plugs	24	EGR valve
2	Ignition switch	6	Starter motor	19	Diesel injection pump	30	Air cond. cut-off control unit
3	Instrument cluster	7	Alternator		a = control unit	31	Cooling fan motor

1 Battery
2 Ignition switch
3 Instrument cluster
  b = speedometer
  c = tachometer
  d = glow plug warning light
  e = control unit
4 Engine fusebox
  b = low speed fan supply relay

5 Passenger fusebox (28 fuse)
6 Starter motor
7 Alternator
8 Diagnostic connector
9 Built in systems interface (BSI)
14 TDC sensor
15 Vehicle speed sensor
16 Injection supply relay
17 Pre-heat control unit

18 Glow plugs
19 Diesel injection pump
  a = control unit
  b = EGR load lever switch
  c = advance correction solenoid
20 Oil pressure switch
21 Post heat relay
22 EGR function supply relay
23 Post heat thermal switch

24 EGR valve
30 Air cond. cut-off control unit
31 Cooling fan motor
32 Cooling fan thermal switch
33 Diesel engine management ECU
34 Engine management double
  function relay

Diagram 3

H32038

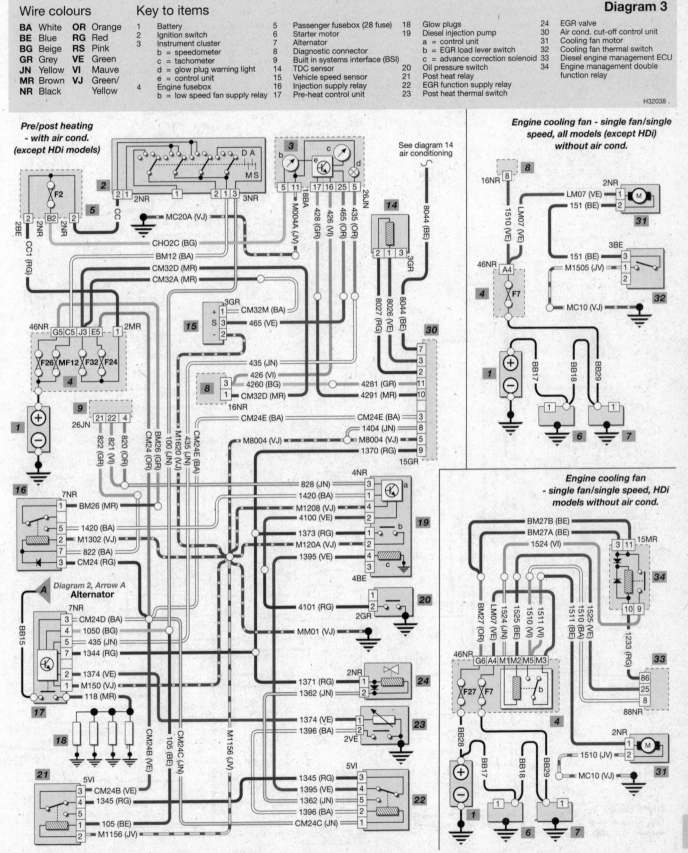

Pre/post heating - with air cond. (except HDi models)

Engine cooling fan - single fan/single speed, all models (except HDi) without air cond.

Engine cooling fan - single fan/single speed, HDi models without air cond.

Diagram 2, Arrow A Alternator

See diagram 14 air conditioning

12

Wire colours

BA	White	**OR**	Orange
BE	Blue	**RG**	Red
BG	Beige	**RS**	Pink
GR	Grey	**VE**	Green
JN	Yellow	**VI**	Mauve
MR	Brown	**VJ**	Green/
NR	Black		Yellow

Key to items

1 Battery
2 Ignition switch
3 Instrument cluster
  e = control module
  f = coolant temp. gauge
  g = stop warning light
  h = seat belt warning light
4 Engine fusebox

5 Passenger fusebox (28 fuse)
8 Diagnostic connector
25 Passenger fusebox (12 fuse)
31 Cooling fan motor
33 Engine management control unit
34 Engine management double function relay
38 Air cond. coolant temp. unit
39 Low speed fan supply relay

40 High speed fan supply relay
41 Twin speed fan resistor
42 Air cond. coolant temp. thermistor
43 Pressostat
44 Air cond. compressor
45 Coolant temp. sensor/switch
46 Seat belt switch

Diagram 4

H32039

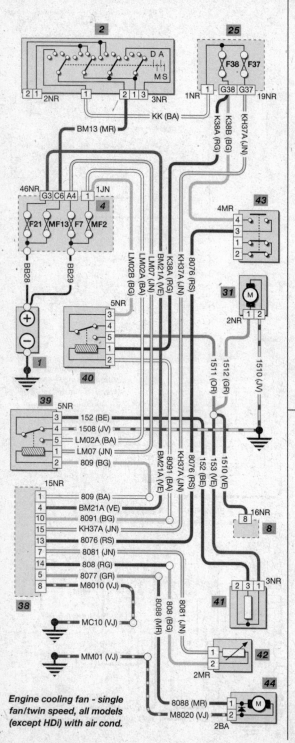

Engine cooling fan - single fan/twin speed, all models (except HDi) with air cond.

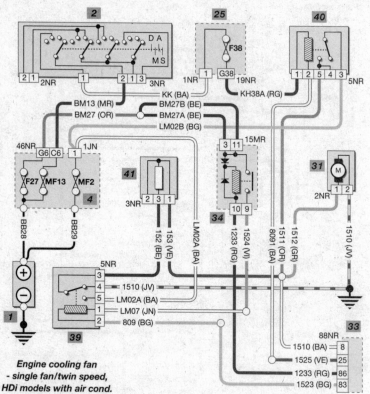

Engine cooling fan - single fan/twin speed, HDi models with air cond.

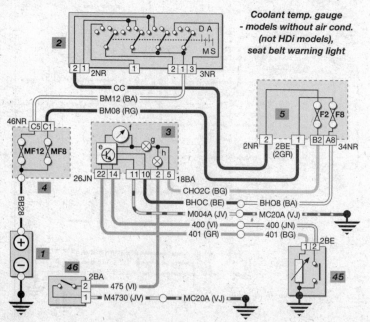

Coolant temp. gauge - models without air cond. (not HDi models), seat belt warning light

Wire colours

BA	White	OR	Orange
BE	Blue	RG	Red
BG	Beige	RS	Pink
GR	Grey	VE	Green
JN	Yellow	VI	Mauve
MR	Brown	VJ	Green/
NR	Black		Yellow

* Alternative wiring

Key to items

1 Battery
2 Ignition switch
3 Instrument cluster
  e = control module
  f = coolant temp. gauge
  g = stop warning light
  h = low coolant level warning light
  j = oil level gauge
  k = oil temp. gauge
  l = fuel gauge

3 Instrument cluster (continued)
  m = low oil pressure warning light
  n = handbrake/low brake fluid warning light
  o = low fuel warning light
4 Engine fusebox
5 Passenger fusebox (28 fuse)
33 Engine management control unit
38 Air cond. coolant temp. unit
42 Air cond. coolant temp. thermistor
45 Coolant temp. sensor/switch (alternative)

46 Engine coolant temp. sensor
47 Engine coolant level unit
48 Oil pressure switch
49 Engine oil temp./level sensor (alternative)
50 Oil level sensor
51 Oil temp. sensor/thermal switch
52 Fuel gauge sender unit/fuel pump
53 Handbrake switch
54 Brake fluid level switch

Diagram 5

H32040

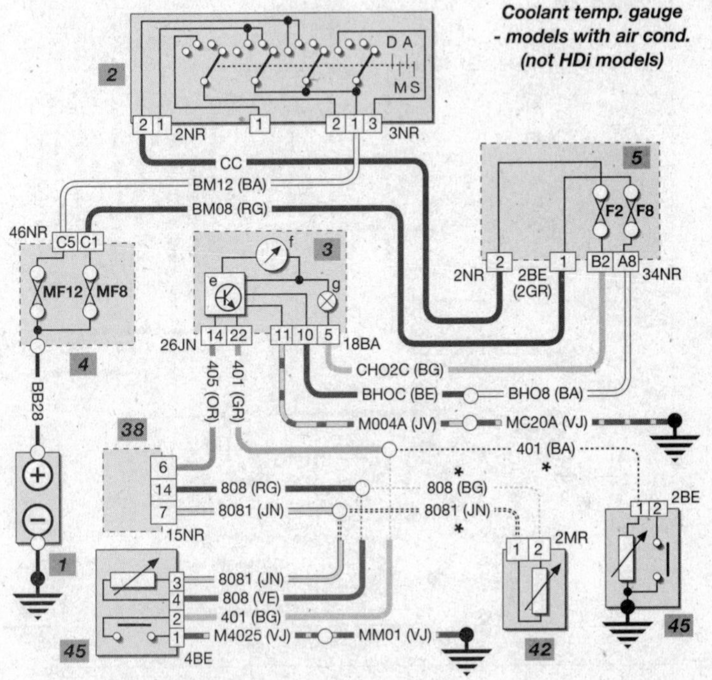

Coolant temp. gauge - models with air cond. (not HDi models)

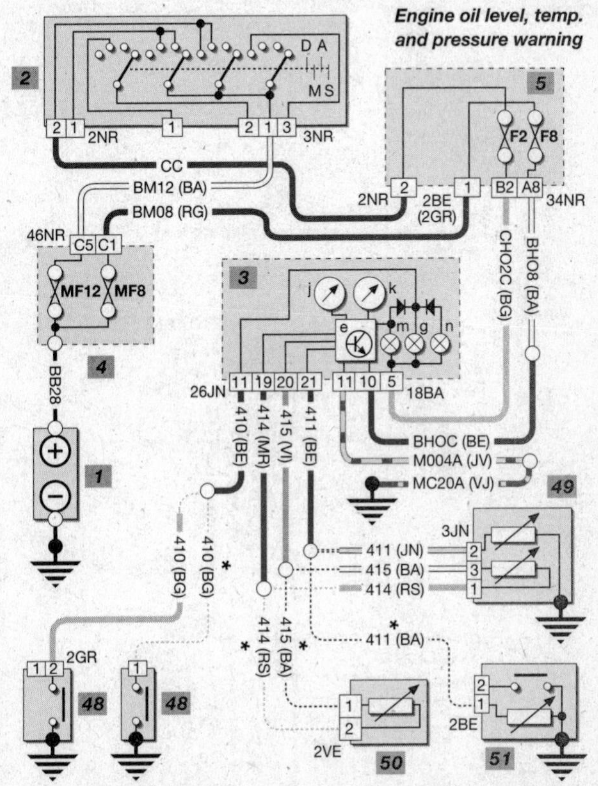

Engine oil level, temp. and pressure warning

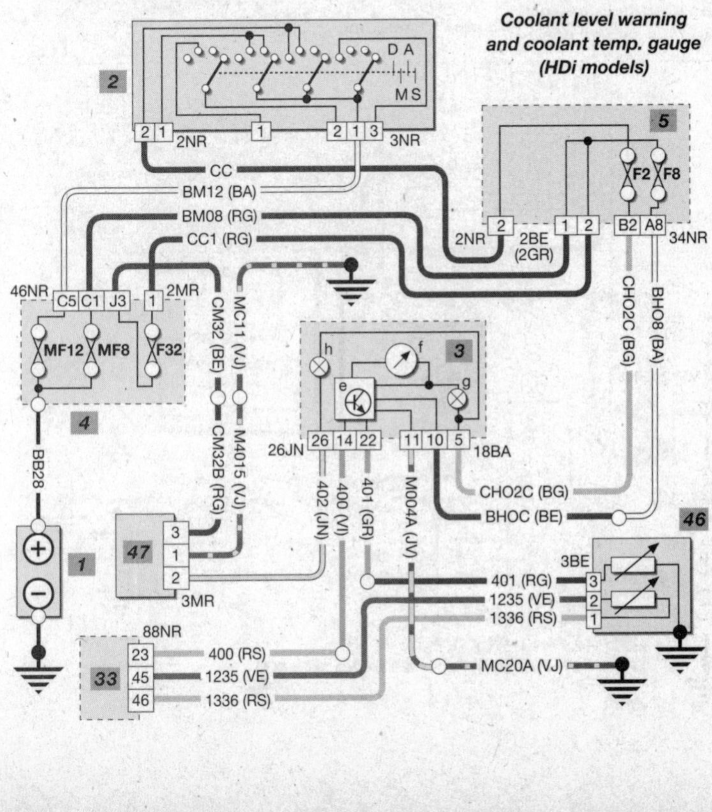

Coolant level warning and coolant temp. gauge (HDi models)

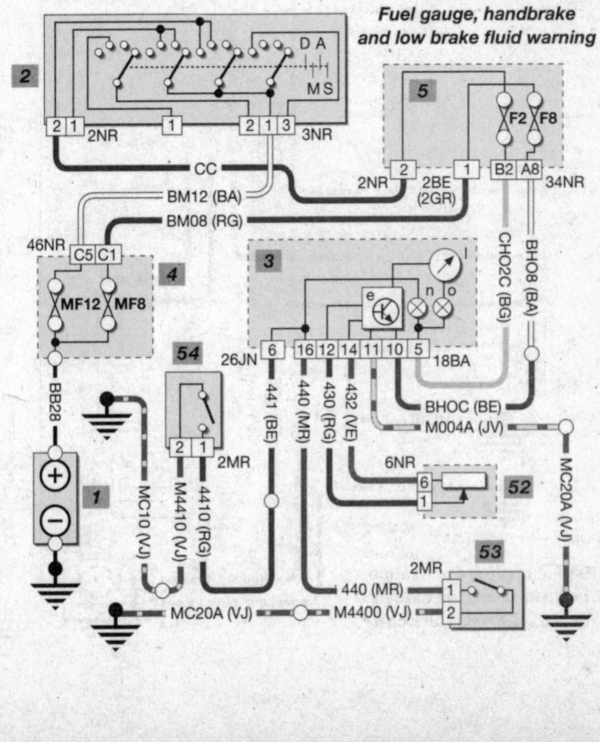

Fuel gauge, handbrake and low brake fluid warning

12

Wire colours

BA	White	OR	Orange
BE	Blue	RG	Red
BG	Beige	RS	Pink
GR	Grey	VE	Green
JN	Yellow	VI	Mauve
MR	Brown	VJ	Green/
NR	Black		Yellow

* Alternative wiring

Key to items

1 Battery
2 Ignition switch
3 Instrument cluster
   p = dipped beam warning light
   q = main beam warning light
   r = front foglight warning light
   s = rear foglight warning light
4 Engine fusebox
   c = front foglight relay
5 Passenger fusebox (28 fuse)

25 Passenger fusebox (12 fuse)
60 Reversing light switch (manual)
61 Stop light switch
62 High level brake light
63 LH rear light cluster
   a = reversing light
   b = stop light
   c = tail light
64 RH rear light cluster
   (items a to c as above)

65 Number plate light
66 LH front side light
67 RH front side light
68 Multifunction switch
   a = side/headlight switch
   b = dipped/main beam switch
   c = headlight flasher
   e = rear foglight switch
   f = front foglight switch
69 LH headlight

70 RH headlight
71 Rear foglight
72 LH front foglight
73 RH front foglight
74 Reversing light switch (auto.)

Diagram 6

H32041

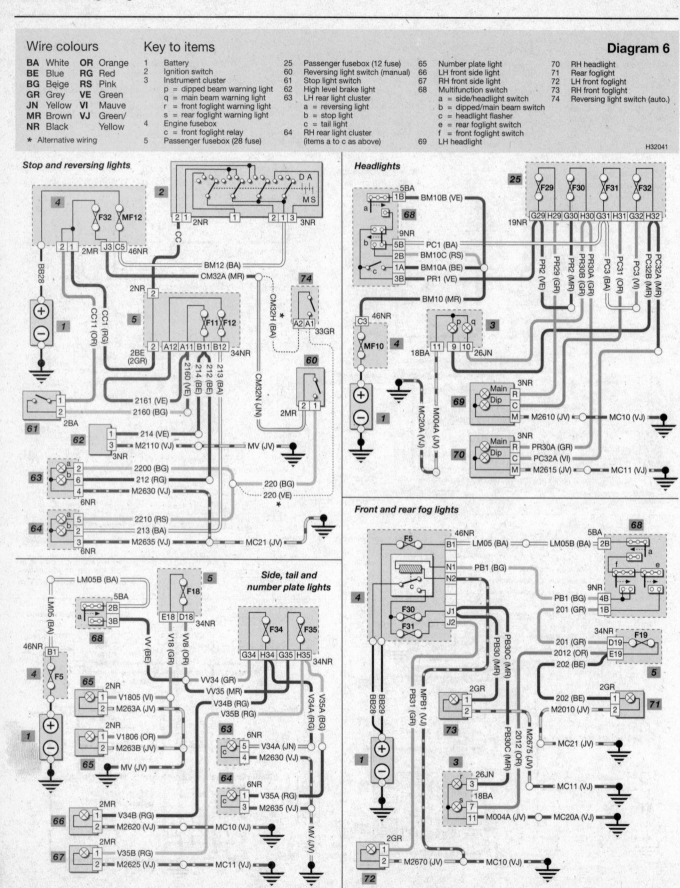

Stop and reversing lights

Headlights

Front and rear fog lights

Side, tail and number plate lights

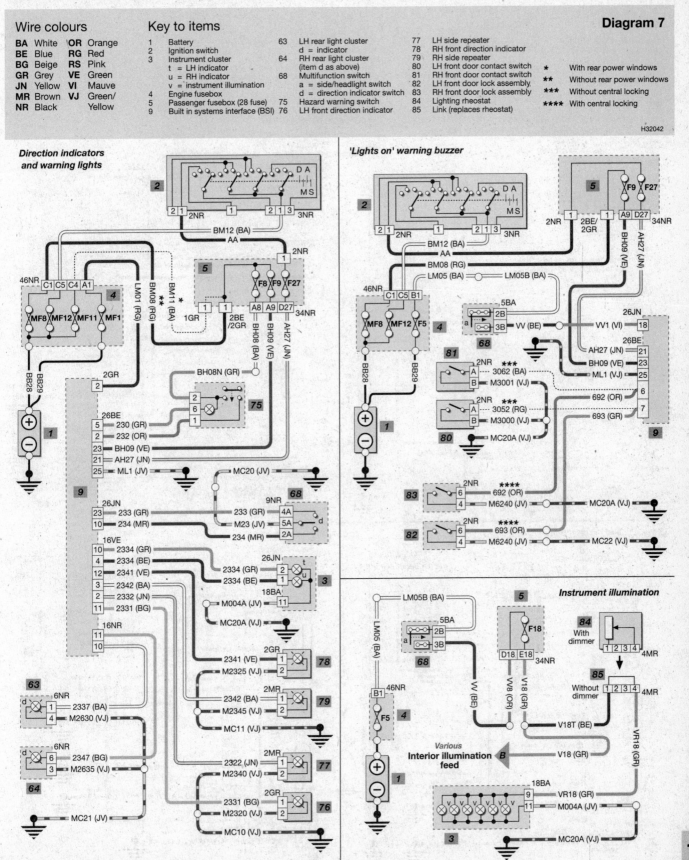

Diagram 7

Wire colours

BA	White	OR	Orange
BE	Blue	RG	Red
BG	Beige	RS	Pink
GR	Grey	VE	Green
JN	Yellow	VI	Mauve
MR	Brown	VJ	Green/
NR	Black		Yellow

Key to items

1 Battery
2 Ignition switch
3 Instrument cluster
 t = LH indicator
 u = RH indicator
 v = instrument illumination
4 Engine fusebox
5 Passenger fusebox (28 fuse)
9 Built in systems interface (BSI)

63 LH rear light cluster
 d = indicator
64 RH rear light cluster
 (item d as above)
68 Multifunction switch
 a = side/headlight switch
 d = direction indicator switch
75 Hazard warning switch
76 LH front direction indicator

77 LH side repeater
78 RH front direction indicator
79 RH side repeater
80 LH front door contact switch
81 RH front door contact switch
82 LH front door lock assembly
83 RH front door lock assembly
84 Lighting rheostat
85 Link (replaces rheostat)

* With rear power windows
** Without rear power windows
*** Without central locking
**** With central locking

H32042

Direction indicators and warning lights

'Lights on' warning buzzer

Instrument illumination

12

Wire colours

BA	White	OR	Orange
BE	Blue	RG	Red
BG	Beige	RS	Pink
GR	Grey	VE	Green
JN	Yellow	VI	Mauve
MR	Brown	VJ	Green/
NR	Black		Yellow

Key to items

1. Battery
2. Ignition switch
4. Engine fusebox
5. Passenger fusebox (28 fuse)
9. Built in systems interface (BSI)
68. Multifunction switch
   a = side/headlight switch
80. LH front door contact switch
81. RH front door contact switch
82. LH front door lock assembly

83. RH front door lock assembly
87. Interior light
88. Map reading light
89. Luggage compartment light
90. Luggage compartment light switch
91. Glove box light
92. Glove box light switch
93. Headlight levelling control switch
94. LH headlight levelling motor
95. RH headlight levelling motor

Diagram 8

H32043

Map reading light and interior light (models without central locking)

Map reading light and delayed interior light (models with central locking)

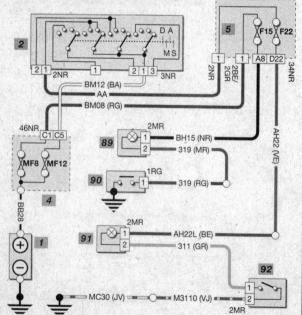

Glove box and luggage compartment light

Headlight levelling

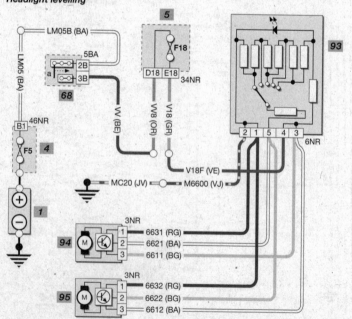

Wire colours

BA	White	**OR**	Orange
BE	Blue	**RG**	Red
BG	Beige	**RS**	Pink
GR	Grey	**VE**	Green
JN	Yellow	**VI**	Mauve
MR	Brown	**VJ**	Green/
NR	Black		Yellow

Key to items

1   Battery
2   Ignition switch
4   Engine fusebox
5   Passenger fusebox (28 fuse)
9   Built in systems interface (BSI)
98   Cigar lighter
99   Clock
100   Audio unit (2030 model)
101   Satellite controls
102   Electric aerial module
103   LH rear speaker
104   LH tweeter
105   Passenger's front door speaker
106   RH rear speaker
107   RH tweeter
108   Driver's front door speaker
109   Sunroof assembly

* With rear power windows
** Without rear power windows
*** Alternative wiring

Diagram 9

H32044

Clock and cigar lighter

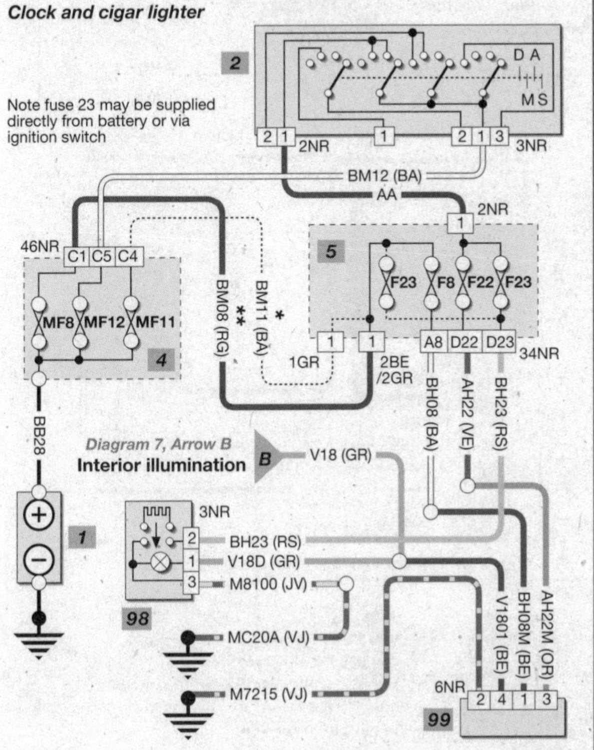

Note fuse 23 may be supplied directly from battery or via ignition switch

Diagram 7, Arrow B
Interior illumination

Power sunroof

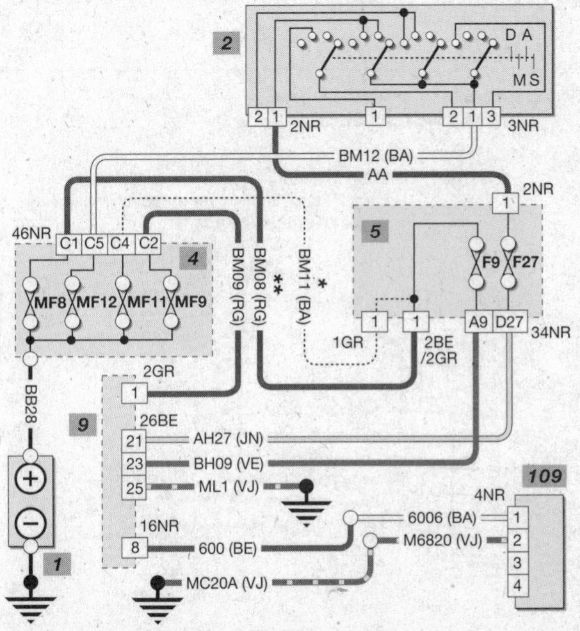

Audio unit - 2030 model

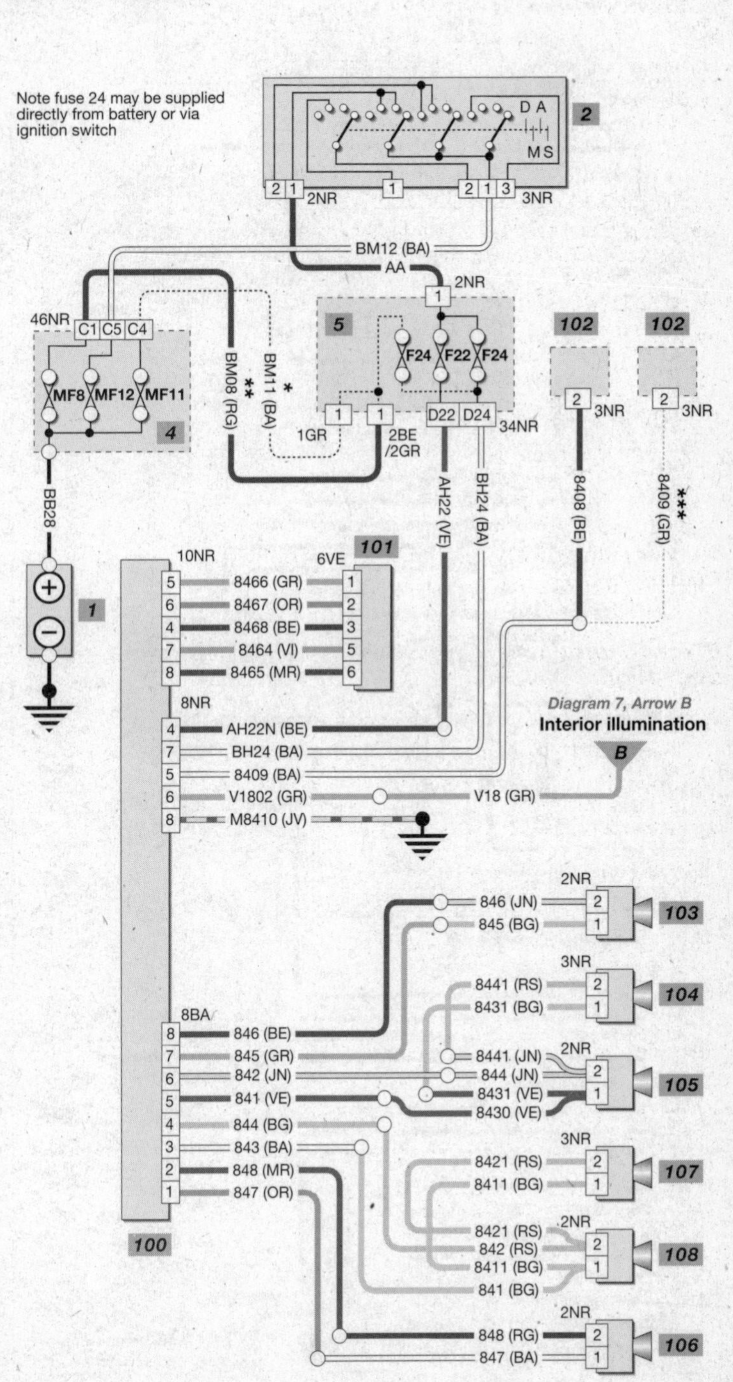

Note fuse 24 may be supplied directly from battery or via ignition switch

Diagram 7, Arrow B
Interior illumination

12

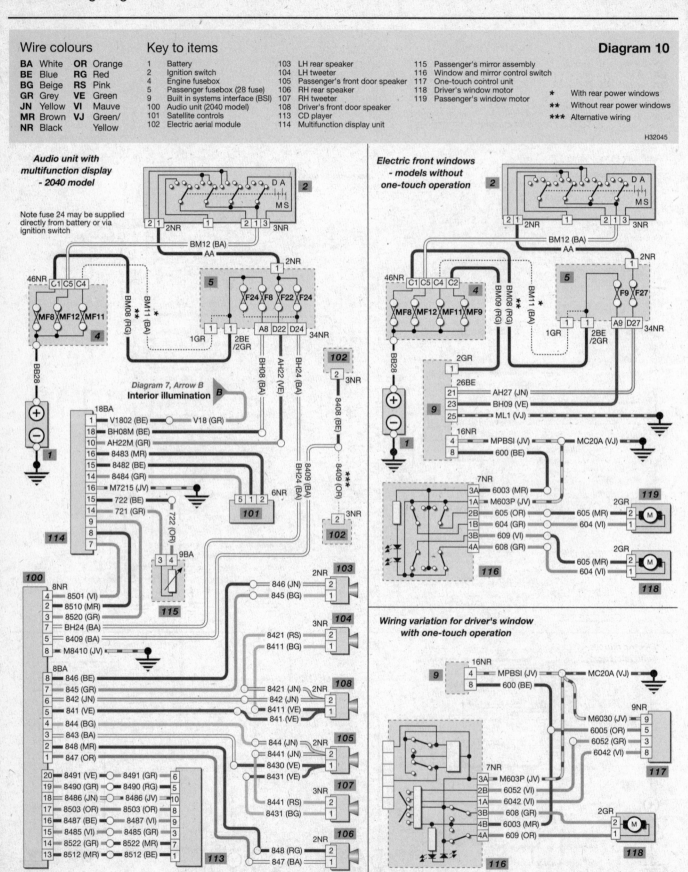

Wire colours

BA	White	OR	Orange
BE	Blue	RG	Red
BG	Beige	RS	Pink
GR	Grey	VE	Green
JN	Yellow	VI	Mauve
MR	Brown	VJ	Green/
NR	Black		Yellow

Key to items

1   Battery
2   Ignition switch
4   Engine fusebox
5   Passenger fusebox (28 fuse)
9   Built in systems interface (BSI)
100 Audio unit (2040 model)
101 Satellite controls
102 Electric aerial module
103 LH rear speaker
104 LH tweeter
105 Passenger's front door speaker
106 RH rear speaker
107 RH tweeter
108 Driver's front door speaker
113 CD player
114 Multifunction display unit
115 Passenger's mirror assembly
116 Window and mirror control switch
117 One-touch control unit
118 Driver's window motor
119 Passenger's window motor

*   With rear power windows
**   Without rear power windows
***   Alternative wiring

Diagram 10

H32045

Audio unit with
multifunction display
- 2040 model

Note fuse 24 may be supplied
directly from battery or via
ignition switch

Diagram 7, Arrow B
Interior illumination

Electric front windows
- models without
one-touch operation

Wiring variation for driver's window
with one-touch operation

Wire colours

BA	White	**OR**	Orange
BE	Blue	**RG**	Red
BG	Beige	**RS**	Pink
GR	Grey	**VE**	Green
JN	Yellow	**VI**	Mauve
MR	Brown	**VJ**	Green/
NR	Black		Yellow

Key to items

1	Battery
2	Ignition switch
4	Engine fusebox
5	Passenger fusebox (28 fuse)
6	Starter motor
7	Alternator
9	Built in systems interface (BSI)
115	Passenger's mirror assembly
116	Mirror and window control switch
125	Driver's mirror assembly
126	Rear function locking relay
127	Rear window isolator switch
128	LH rear window switch
129	LH rear window motor
130	RH rear window switch
131	RH rear window motor
132	Heated rear window
133	Heater panel

Diagram 11

H32046

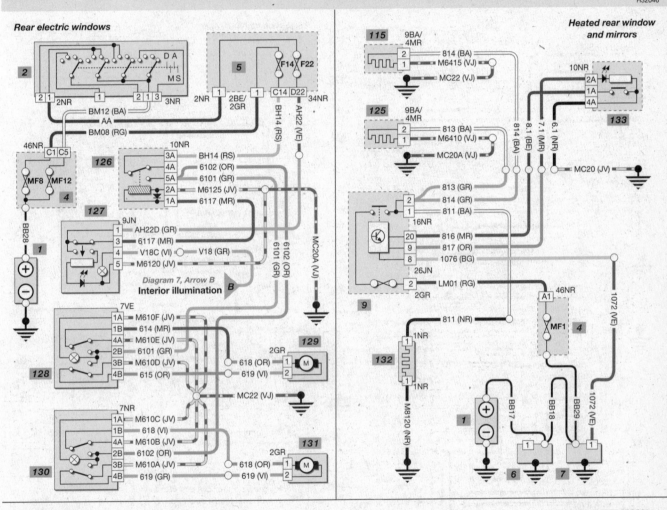

Rear electric windows

Heated rear window and mirrors

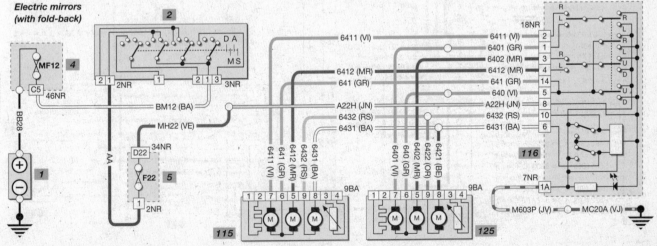

Electric mirrors (with fold-back)

12

Wire colours

BA	White	OR	Orange
BE	Blue	RG	Red
BG	Beige	RS	Pink
GR	Grey	VE	Green
JN	Yellow	VI	Mauve
MR	Brown	VJ	Green/
NR	Black		Yellow

Key to items

1 Battery
2 Ignition switch
3 Instrument cluster
  e = control unit
  w = ABS warning light
4 Engine fusebox
5 Passenger fusebox (28 fuse)
8 Diagnostic connector
9 Built in systems interface (BSI)

61 Stop light switch
135 Rain sensor (if fitted)
136 Front wiper motor
137 Rear wiper motor
138 washer pump
139 Wash/wipe switch
  a = horn switch (not used)
  b = rear wiper switch
  c = washer switch

139 Wash/wipe switch (continued)
  d = front wiper switch
140 ABS control unit
141 LH rear wheel sensor
142 RH rear wheel sensor
143 LH front wheel sensor
144 RH front wheel sensor

*   With rear power windows
** Without rear power windows

Diagram 12

H32047

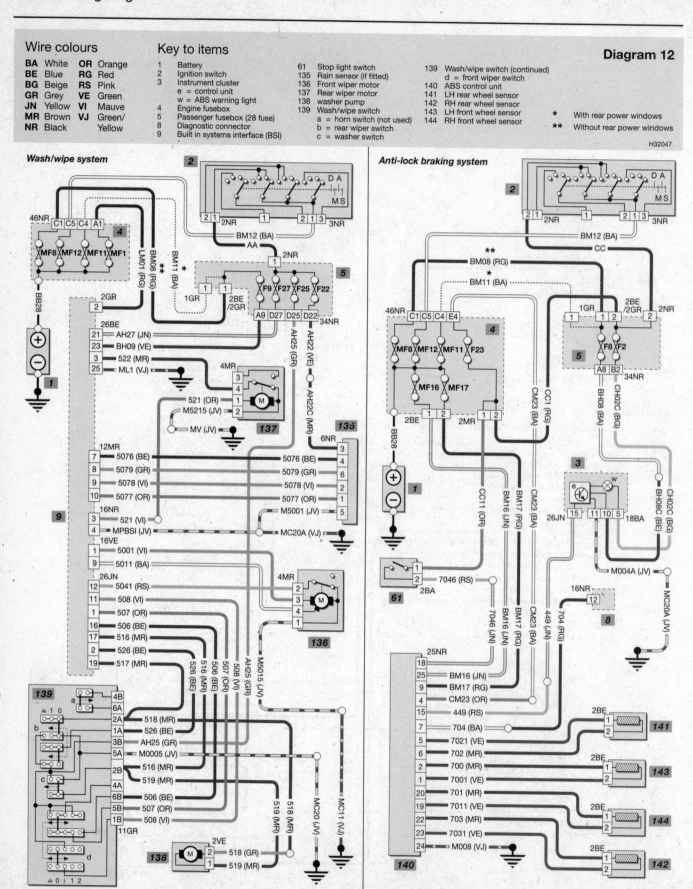

Wash/wipe system

Anti-lock braking system

Wire colours

BA	White	**OR**	Orange
BE	Blue	**RG**	Red
BG	Beige	**RS**	Pink
GR	Grey	**VE**	Green
JN	Yellow	**VI**	Mauve
MR	Brown	**VJ**	Green/
NR	Black		Yellow

Key to items

1   Battery
2   Ignition switch
4   Engine fusebox
5   Passenger fusebox (28 fuse)
9   Built in systems interface (BSI)
147 LH front door lock motor assembly
148 RH front door lock motor assembly
149 LH rear door lock assembly
150 RH rear door lock assembly
151 Boot/tailgate lock

Diagram 13

*   With rear power windows
**   Without rear power windows
***   With deadlocking
****   Without deadlocking

H32048

Central locking

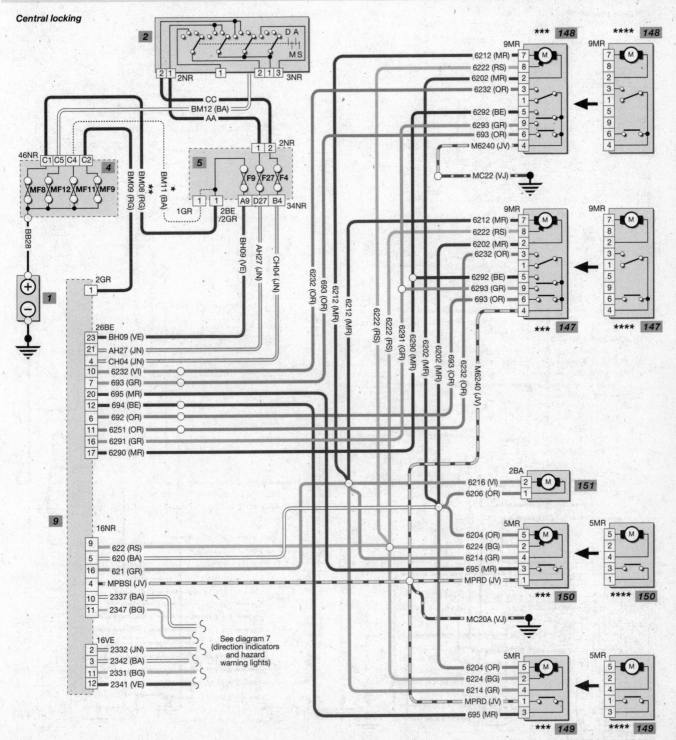

12

Wire colours

BA	White	**OR**	Orange
BE	Blue	**RG**	Red
BG	Beige	**RS**	Pink
GR	Grey	**VE**	Green
JN	Yellow	**VI**	Mauve
MR	Brown	**VJ**	Green/
NR	Black		Yellow

Key to items

1	Battery
2	Ignition switch
3	Instrument cluster
	x = airbag warning light
	y = side airbag warning light
4	Engine fusebox
	d = engine running relay
5	Passenger fusebox (28 fuse)
6	Starter motor
7	Alternator
8	Diagnostic connector
13	Steering wheel rotary connector
25	Passenger fusebox (12 fuse)
38	A/C coolant temp. unit
42	A/C coolant temp. thermistor
43	Pressostat
44	A/C compressor
133	Heater panel
155	Airbag control unit
156	Driver's airbag
157	Passenger's airbag
158	Driver's seatbelt pretensioner
159	Passenger's seatbelt pretensioner
160	LH side airbag
161	RH side airbag
162	LH side airbag control unit
163	RH side airbag control unit
164	Heater blower resistor
165	Heater blower motor
166	Passenger's airbag disable switch
167	Passenger compartment electronic thermostat
168	Evaporator thermistor

Diagram 14

H32049

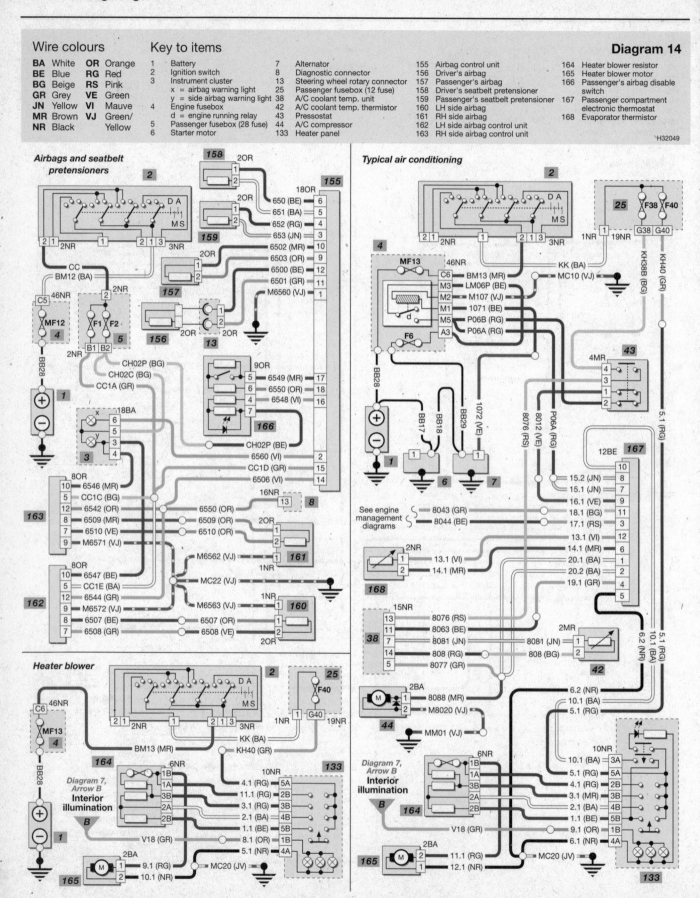

Airbags and seatbelt pretensioners

Typical air conditioning

Heater blower

Diagram 7, Arrow B
Interior illumination

Wire colours

BA	White	**OR**	Orange
BE	Blue	**RG**	Red
BG	Beige	**RS**	Pink
GR	Grey	**VE**	Green
JN	Yellow	**VI**	Mauve
MR	Brown	**VJ**	Green/
NR	Black		Yellow

Key to items

1 Battery
2 Ignition switch
3 Instrument cluster
  d = glow plug warning light
  e = control unit
  z = engine management warning light
4 Engine fusebox
  d = engine running relay
5 Passenger fusebox (28 fuse)
8 Diagnostic connector
33 Engine management contol unit
34 Double function relay
172 Pressure regulator (high pressure)
173 3rd piston cut-out solenoid
174 EGR butterfly solenoid
175 EGR solenoid
176 Engine coolant temperature sensor
177 Cruise control clutch switch

Diagram 15

H32050

HDi Diesel engine management system (part 1 of 2)

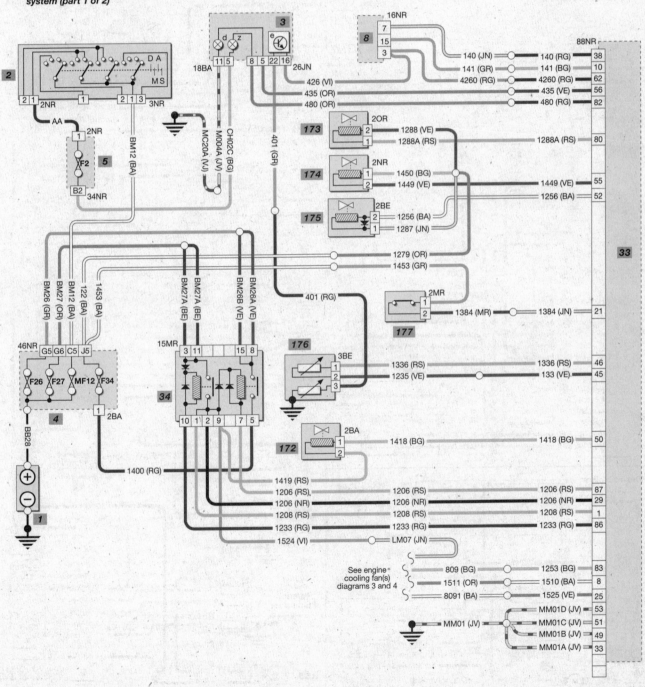

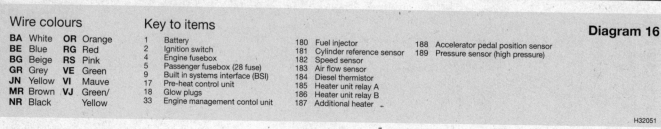

Wire colours

BA	White	**OR**	Orange
BE	Blue	**RG**	Red
BG	Beige	**RS**	Pink
GR	Grey	**VE**	Green
JN	Yellow	**VI**	Mauve
MR	Brown	**VJ**	Green/
NR	Black		Yellow

Key to items

1   Battery
2   Ignition switch
4   Engine fusebox
5   Passenger fusebox (28 fuse)
9   Built in systems interface (BSI)
17 Pre-heat control unit
18 Glow plugs
33 Engine management contol unit

180 Fuel injector
181 Cylinder reference sensor
182 Speed sensor
183 Air flow sensor
184 Diesel thermistor
185 Heater unit relay A
186 Heater unit relay B
187 Additional heater

188 Accelerator pedal position sensor
189 Pressure sensor (high pressure)

Diagram 16

H32051

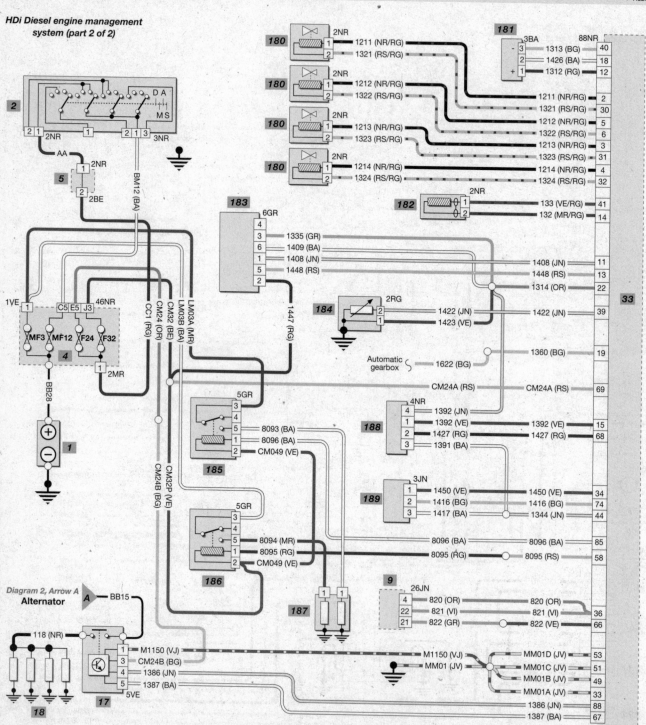

HDi Diesel engine management system (part 2 of 2)

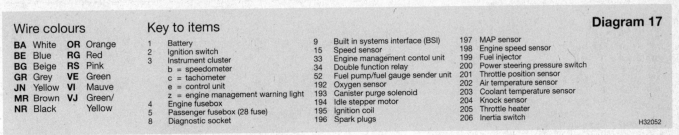

Wire colours

BA	White	**OR**	Orange
BE	Blue	**RG**	Red
BG	Beige	**RS**	Pink
GR	Grey	**VE**	Green
JN	Yellow	**VI**	Mauve
MR	Brown	**VJ**	Green/
NR	Black		Yellow

Key to items

1 Battery
2 Ignition switch
3 Instrument cluster
  b = speedometer
  c = tachometer
  e = control unit
  z = engine management warning light
4 Engine fusebox
5 Passenger fusebox (28 fuse)
8 Diagnostic socket

9 Built in systems interface (BSI)
15 Speed sensor
33 Engine management contol unit
34 Double function relay
52 Fuel pump/fuel gauge sender unit
192 Oxygen sensor
193 Canister purge solenoid
194 Idle stepper motor
195 Ignition coil
196 Spark plugs

197 MAP sensor
198 Engine speed sensor
199 Fuel injector
200 Power steering pressure switch
201 Throttle position sensor
202 Air temperature sensor
203 Coolant temperature sensor
204 Knock sensor
205 Throttle heater
206 Inertia switch

Diagram 17

H32052

MM1AP fuel injection system

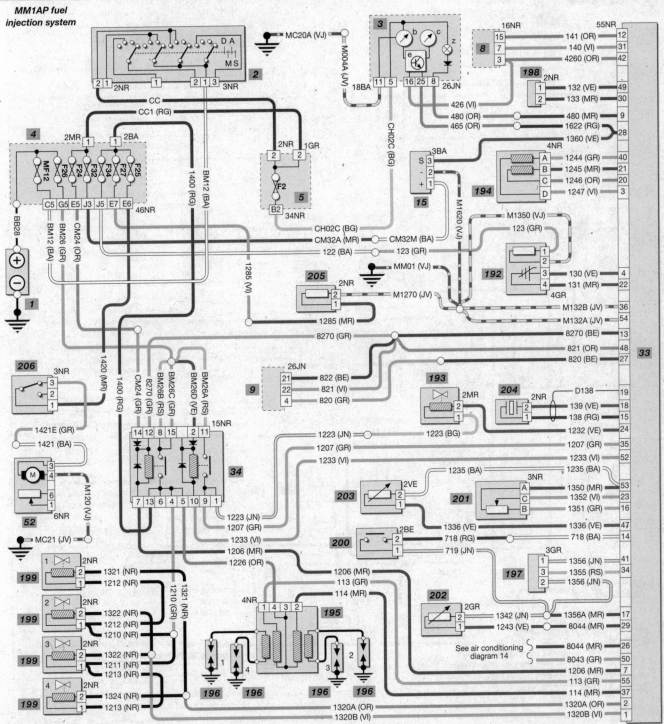

12

Wire colours

BA	White	OR	Orange
BE	Blue	RG	Red
BG	Beige	RS	Pink
GR	Grey	VE	Green
JN	Yellow	VI	Mauve
MR	Brown	VJ	Green/
NR	Black		Yellow

Key to items

1	Battery
2	Ignition switch
3	Instrument cluster
b	= speedometer
c	= tachometer
e	= control unit
z	= engine man. warning light
4	Engine fusebox
5	Passenger fusebox (28 fuse)
8	Diagnostic socket
9	Built in systems interface (BSI)
15	Speed sensor
33	Engine management control unit
34	Double function relay
52	Fuel pump/fuel gauge sender unit
192	Oxygen sensor
193	Canister purge solenoid
194	Idle stepper motor
195	Ignition coil
196	Spark plugs
197	MAP sensor
198	Engine speed sensor
199	Fuel injector
200	Power steering pressure switch
201	Throttle position sensor
202	Air temperature sensor
203	Coolant temperature sensor
204	Knock sensor
205	Throttle heater
206	Inertia switch

Diagram 18

H32053

Bosch MP7.2 Motronic fuel injection system

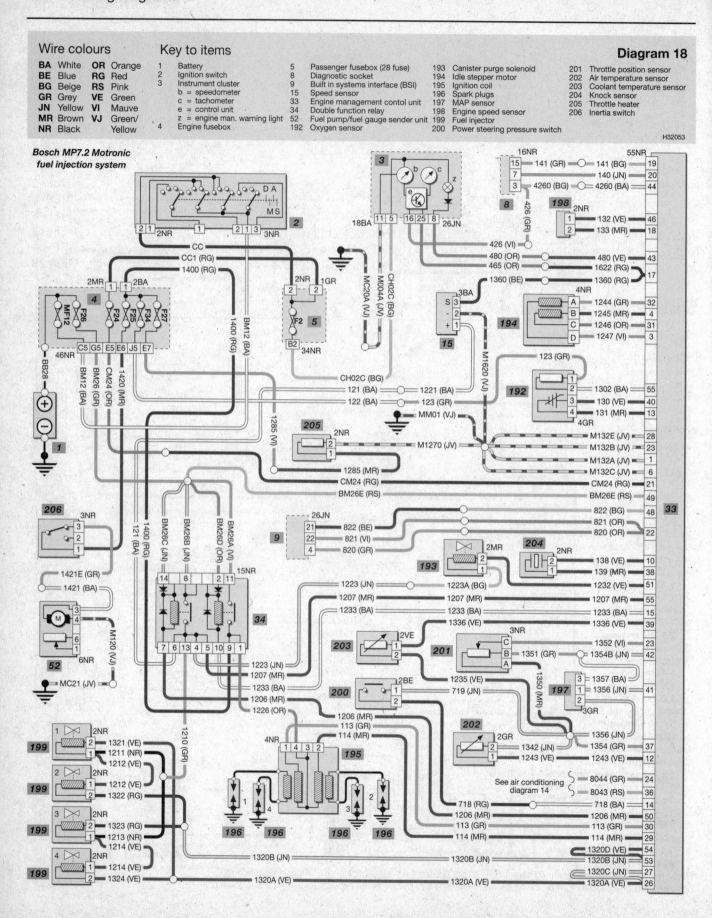

Dimensions and weights

Note: *All figures are approximate, and may vary according to model. Refer to manufacturer's data for exact figures.*

Dimensions
Overall length	3822 mm
Overall width (excluding mirrors)	1673 mm
Overall height (unladen)	1435 mm
Wheelbase	2445 mm

Weights
Kerb weight:
Petrol engine models:
- 1.1 litre engine — 985 kg
- 1.4 litre engine — 1055 kg
- 1.6 litre engine — 1100 kg

Diesel engine models:
- 1.9 litre engine — 1084 kg
- 2.0 litre engine — 1145 kg

Maximum gross vehicle weight*:
Petrol engine models:
- 1.1 litre engine — 1405 kg
- 1.4 litre engine — 1480 kg
- 1.6 litre engine — 1525 kg

Diesel engine models:
- 1.9 litre engine — 1525 kg
- 2.0 litre engine — 1585 kg

Maximum gross train (vehicle and trailer) weight*:
Petrol engine models:
- 1.1 litre engine — 1920 kg
- 1.4 litre engine — 2395 kg
- 1.6 litre engine — 2440 kg

Diesel engine models:
- 1.9 litre engine — 2440 kg
- 2.0 litre engine — 2500 kg

Maximum towing weight**:
Unbraked trailer:
- 1.1 litre petrol engine model — 485 kg
- 1.4 litre petrol engine model — 525 kg
- 1.6 litre petrol engine model — 550 kg
- 1.9 litre diesel engine model — 540 kg
- 2.0 litre diesel engine model — 570 kg

Braked trailer:
- 1.1 litre petrol engine model — 700 kg
- All other models — 1100 kg

*Refer to the Vehicle Identification Plate for the exact figures for your vehicle – see 'Vehicle identification'
**Ensure the combined weight of the trailer and vehicle never exceeds the gross train weight when towing.

Conversion factors

Length (distance)

Inches (in)	x 25.4	=	Millimetres (mm)	x 0.0394 =	Inches (in)
Feet (ft)	x 0.305	=	Metres (m)	x 3.281 =	Feet (ft)
Miles	x 1.609	=	Kilometres (km)	x 0.621 =	Miles

Volume (capacity)

Cubic inches (cu in; in³)	x 16.387	=	Cubic centimetres (cc; cm³)	x 0.061	Cubic inches (cu in; in³)
Imperial pints (Imp pt)	x 0.568	=	Litres (l)	x 1.76	Imperial pints (Imp pt)
Imperial quarts (Imp qt)	x 1.137	=	Litres (l)	x 0.88	Imperial quarts (Imp qt)
Imperial quarts (Imp qt)	x 1.201	=	US quarts (US qt)	x 0.833	Imperial quarts (Imp qt)
US quarts (US qt)	x 0.946	=	Litres (l)	x 1.057	US quarts (US qt)
Imperial gallons (Imp gal)	x 4.546	=	Litres (l)	x 0.22	Imperial gallons (Imp gal)
Imperial gallons (Imp gal)	x 1.201	=	US gallons (US gal)	x 0.833	Imperial gallons (Imp gal)
US gallons (US gal)	x 3.785	=	Litres (l)	x 0.264	US gallons (US gal)

Mass (weight)

Ounces (oz)	x 28.35	=	Grams (g)	x 0.035 =	Ounces (oz)
Pounds (lb)	x 0.454	=	Kilograms (kg)	x 2.205 =	Pounds (lb)

Force

Ounces-force (ozf; oz)	x 0.278	=	Newtons (N)	x 3.6 =	Ounces-force (ozf; oz)
Pounds-force (lbf; lb)	x 4.448	=	Newtons (N)	x 0.225 =	Pounds-force (lbf; lb)
Newtons (N)	x 0.1	=	Kilograms-force (kgf; kg)	x 9.81 =	Newtons (N)

Pressure

Pounds-force per square inch (psi; lbf/in²; lb/in²)	x 0.070	=	Kilograms-force per square centimetre (kgf/cm²; kg/cm²)	x 14.223 =	Pounds-force per square inch (psi; lbf/in²; lb/in²)
Pounds-force per square inch (psi; lbf/in²; lb/in²)	x 0.068	=	Atmospheres (atm)	x 14.696 =	Pounds-force per square inch (psi; lbf/in²; lb/in²)
Pounds-force per square inch (psi; lbf/in²; lb/in²)	x 0.069	=	Bars	x 14.5 =	Pounds-force per square inch (psi; lbf/in²; lb/in²)
Pounds-force per square inch (psi; lbf/in²; lb/in²)	x 6.895	=	Kilopascals (kPa)	x 0.145 =	Pounds-force per square inch (psi; lbf/in²; lb/in²)
Kilopascals (kPa)	x 0.01	=	Kilograms-force per square centimetre (kgf/cm²; kg/cm²)	x 98.1 =	Kilopascals (kPa)
Millibar (mbar)	x 100	=	Pascals (Pa)	x 0.01 =	Millibar (mbar)
Millibar (mbar)	x 0.0145	=	Pounds-force per square inch (psi; lbf/in²; lb/in²)	x 68.947 =	Millibar (mbar)
Millibar (mbar)	x 0.75	=	Millimetres of mercury (mmHg)	x 1.333 =	Millibar (mbar)
Millibar (mbar)	x 0.401	=	Inches of water (inH₂O)	x 2.491 =	Millibar (mbar)
Millimetres of mercury (mmHg)	x 0.535	=	Inches of water (inH₂O)	x 1.868 =	Millimetres of mercury (mmHg)
Inches of water (inH₂O)	x 0.036	=	Pounds-force per square inch (psi; lbf/in²; lb/in²)	x 27.68 =	Inches of water (inH₂O)

Torque (moment of force)

Pounds-force inches (lbf in; lb in)	x 1.152	=	Kilograms-force centimetre (kgf cm; kg cm)	x 0.868 =	Pounds-force inches (lbf in; lb in)
Pounds-force inches (lbf in; lb in)	x 0.113	=	Newton metres (Nm)	x 8.85 =	Pounds-force inches (lbf in; lb in)
Pounds-force inches (lbf in; lb in)	x 0.083	=	Pounds-force feet (lbf ft; lb ft)	x 12 =	Pounds-force inches (lbf in; lb in)
Pounds-force feet (lbf ft; lb ft)	x 0.138	=	Kilograms-force metres (kgf m; kg m)	x 7.233 =	Pounds-force feet (lbf ft; lb ft)
Pounds-force feet (lbf ft; lb ft)	x 1.356	=	Newton metres (Nm)	x 0.738 =	Pounds-force feet (lbf ft; lb ft)
Newton metres (Nm)	x 0.102	=	Kilograms-force metres (kgf m; kg m)	x 9.804 =	Newton metres (Nm)

Power

Horsepower (hp)	x 745.7	=	Watts (W)	x 0.0013 =	Horsepower (hp)

Velocity (speed)

Miles per hour (miles/hr; mph)	x 1.609	=	Kilometres per hour (km/hr; kph)	x 0.621 =	Miles per hour (miles/hr; mph)

Fuel consumption*

Miles per gallon, Imperial (mpg)	x 0.354	=	Kilometres per litre (km/l)	x 2.825 =	Miles per gallon, Imperial (mpg)
Miles per gallon, US (mpg)	x 0.425	=	Kilometres per litre (km/l)	x 2.352 =	Miles per gallon, US (mpg)

Temperature

Degrees Fahrenheit = (°C x 1.8) + 32

Degrees Celsius (Degrees Centigrade; °C) = (°F - 32) x 0.56

* It is common practice to convert from miles per gallon (mpg) to litres/100 kilometres (l/100km), where mpg x l/100 km = 282

Spare parts are available from many sources, including maker's appointed garages, accessory shops, and motor factors. To be sure of obtaining the correct parts, it may sometimes be necessary to quote the vehicle identification number. If possible, it can also be useful to take the old parts along for positive identification. Items such as starter motors and alternators maybe available under a service exchange scheme – any parts returned should be clean.

Our advice regarding spare part sources is:

Officially-appointed garages

This is the best source of parts which are peculiar to your car, and are not otherwise generally available (eg, badges, interior trim, certain body panels, etc). It is also the only place at which you should buy parts if the vehicle is still under warranty.

Accessory shops

These are very good places to buy materials and components needed for the maintenance of your car (oil, air and fuel filters, spark plugs, light bulbs, drivebelts, oils and greases, brake pads, touch-up paint, etc). Components of this nature sold by a reputable shop are of the same standard as those used by the car manufacturer.

Besides components, these shops will also sell tools and general accessories, usually have convenient opening hours, charge lower prices, and can often be found close to home. Some accessory shops also have parts counters where components needed for almost any repair job can be purchased or ordered.

Motor factors

Good factors will stock all the more important components which wear out comparatively quickly and can sometimes supply individual components needed for the overhaul of a larger assembly. They may also handle work such as cylinder block reboring, crankshaft regrinding and balancing, etc.

Tyre and exhaust specialists

These outlets may be independent or members of a local or national chain. They frequently offer competitive prices when compared with a main dealer or local garage, but it will pay to obtain several quotes before making a decision. Also ask what 'extras' may be added to the quote – for instance, fitting a new valve and balancing the wheel are both often charged on top of the price of a new tyre.

Other sources

Beware of parts or materials obtained from market stalls, car boot sales or similar outlets. Such items are not invariably sub-standard, but there is little chance of compensation if they do prove unsatisfactory. In the case of safety-critical components such as brake pads there is the risk not only of financial loss but also of an accident causing injury or death.

Vehicle identification

Modifications are a continuing and unpublicised process in vehicle manufacture, quite apart from major model changes. Spare parts manuals and lists are compiled upon a numerical basis, the individual vehicle identification numbers being essential for correct identification of the part concerned.

When ordering spare parts, always give as much information as possible. Quote the car model, year of manufacture, body and engine numbers as appropriate.

The *vehicle identification number (VIN) plate* is inside the luggage compartment, riveted onto the rear of the body (just beneath the tailgate lock). The plate carries the vehicle identification number (VIN) and vehicle weight information **(see illustration)**.

The *vehicle identification number (VIN)* is also stamped onto the rear of the body, on the right-hand side of the VIN plate and onto the left-hand side of the engine compartment bulkhead where it is visible through the base of the windscreen **(see illustrations)**.

The engine number is situated on the front face of the cylinder block, and can be found in the following locations:

a) *On petrol engines the engine number is located on the left-hand side of the*

cylinder block. The number is either stamped directly onto the block or is stamped onto a plate which is riveted to the block.

b) *On diesel engines the engine number is stamped on the base of the cylinder block on the flat surface located on the left-hand side of the oil filter/cooler.*

Note: *The first part of the engine number gives the engine code – eg KFX.*

The paint code is on the label stuck to the top of the left-hand suspension turret.

Vehicle identification number (VIN) plate is fixed to the rear of the luggage compartment

The vehicle identification number is also stamped onto the rear of the body, on the right-hand side of the VIN plate . . .

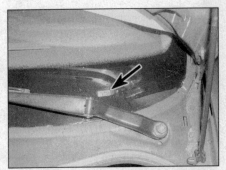

. . . and on the left-hand side of the bulkhead where it is visible through the windscreen

Whenever servicing, repair or overhaul work is carried out on the car or its components, observe the following procedures and instructions. This will assist in carrying out the operation efficiently and to a professional standard of workmanship.

Joint mating faces and gaskets

When separating components at their mating faces, never insert screwdrivers or similar implements into the joint between the faces in order to prise them apart. This can cause severe damage which results in oil leaks, coolant leaks, etc upon reassembly. Separation is usually achieved by tapping along the joint with a soft-faced hammer in order to break the seal. However, note that this method may not be suitable where dowels are used for component location.

Where a gasket is used between the mating faces of two components, a new one must be fitted on reassembly; fit it dry unless otherwise stated in the repair procedure. Make sure that the mating faces are clean and dry, with all traces of old gasket removed. When cleaning a joint face, use a tool which is unlikely to score or damage the face, and remove any burrs or nicks with an oilstone or fine file.

Make sure that tapped holes are cleaned with a pipe cleaner, and keep them free of jointing compound, if this is being used, unless specifically instructed otherwise.

Ensure that all orifices, channels or pipes are clear, and blow through them, preferably using compressed air.

Oil seals

Oil seals can be removed by levering them out with a wide flat-bladed screwdriver or similar implement. Alternatively, a number of self-tapping screws may be screwed into the seal, and these used as a purchase for pliers or some similar device in order to pull the seal free.

Whenever an oil seal is removed from its working location, either individually or as part of an assembly, it should be renewed.

The very fine sealing lip of the seal is easily damaged, and will not seal if the surface it contacts is not completely clean and free from scratches, nicks or grooves. If the original sealing surface of the component cannot be restored, and the manufacturer has not made provision for slight relocation of the seal relative to the sealing surface, the component should be renewed.

Protect the lips of the seal from any surface which may damage them in the course of fitting. Use tape or a conical sleeve where possible. Lubricate the seal lips with oil before fitting and, on dual-lipped seals, fill the space between the lips with grease.

Unless otherwise stated, oil seals must be fitted with their sealing lips toward the lubricant to be sealed.

Use a tubular drift or block of wood of the appropriate size to install the seal and, if the seal housing is shouldered, drive the seal down to the shoulder. If the seal housing is unshouldered, the seal should be fitted with its face flush with the housing top face (unless otherwise instructed).

Screw threads and fastenings

Seized nuts, bolts and screws are quite a common occurrence where corrosion has set in, and the use of penetrating oil or releasing fluid will often overcome this problem if the offending item is soaked for a while before attempting to release it. The use of an impact driver may also provide a means of releasing such stubborn fastening devices, when used in conjunction with the appropriate screwdriver bit or socket. If none of these methods works, it may be necessary to resort to the careful application of heat, or the use of a hacksaw or nut splitter device.

Studs are usually removed by locking two nuts together on the threaded part, and then using a spanner on the lower nut to unscrew the stud. Studs or bolts which have broken off below the surface of the component in which they are mounted can sometimes be removed using a stud extractor. Always ensure that a blind tapped hole is completely free from oil, grease, water or other fluid before installing the bolt or stud. Failure to do this could cause the housing to crack due to the hydraulic action of the bolt or stud as it is screwed in.

When tightening a castellated nut to accept a split pin, tighten the nut to the specified torque, where applicable, and then tighten further to the next split pin hole. Never slacken the nut to align the split pin hole, unless stated in the repair procedure.

When checking or retightening a nut or bolt to a specified torque setting, slacken the nut or bolt by a quarter of a turn, and then retighten to the specified setting. However, this should not be attempted where angular tightening has been used.

For some screw fastenings, notably cylinder head bolts or nuts, torque wrench settings are no longer specified for the latter stages of tightening, "angle-tightening" being called up instead. Typically, a fairly low torque wrench setting will be applied to the bolts/nuts in the correct sequence, followed by one or more stages of tightening through specified angles.

Locknuts, locktabs and washers

Any fastening which will rotate against a component or housing during tightening should always have a washer between it and the relevant component or housing.

Spring or split washers should always be renewed when they are used to lock a critical component such as a big-end bearing retaining bolt or nut. Locktabs which are folded over to retain a nut or bolt should always be renewed.

Self-locking nuts can be re-used in non-critical areas, providing resistance can be felt when the locking portion passes over the bolt or stud thread. However, it should be noted that self-locking stiffnuts tend to lose their effectiveness after long periods of use, and should then be renewed as a matter of course.

Split pins must always be replaced with new ones of the correct size for the hole.

When thread-locking compound is found on the threads of a fastener which is to be re-used, it should be cleaned off with a wire brush and solvent, and fresh compound applied on reassembly.

Special tools

Some repair procedures in this manual entail the use of special tools such as a press, two or three-legged pullers, spring compressors, etc. Wherever possible, suitable readily-available alternatives to the manufacturer's special tools are described, and are shown in use. In some instances, where no alternative is possible, it has been necessary to resort to the use of a manufacturer's tool, and this has been done for reasons of safety as well as the efficient completion of the repair operation. Unless you are highly-skilled and have a thorough understanding of the procedures described, never attempt to bypass the use of any special tool when the procedure described specifies its use. Not only is there a very great risk of personal injury, but expensive damage could be caused to the components involved.

Environmental considerations

When disposing of used engine oil, brake fluid, antifreeze, etc, give due consideration to any detrimental environmental effects. Do not, for instance, pour any of the above liquids down drains into the general sewage system, or onto the ground to soak away. Many local council refuse tips provide a facility for waste oil disposal, as do some garages. If none of these facilities are available, consult your local Environmental Health Department, or the National Rivers Authority, for further advice.

With the universal tightening-up of legislation regarding the emission of environmentally-harmful substances from motor vehicles, most vehicles have tamperproof devices fitted to the main adjustment points of the fuel system. These devices are primarily designed to prevent unqualified persons from adjusting the fuel/air mixture, with the chance of a consequent increase in toxic emissions. If such devices are found during servicing or overhaul, they should, wherever possible, be renewed or refitted in accordance with the manufacturer's requirements or current legislation.

OIL CARE
FOLLOW THE CODE

OIL BANK LINE
0800 66 33 66
www.oilbankline.org.uk

Note: It is antisocial and illegal to dump oil down the drain. To find the location of your local oil recycling bank, call this number free.

The jack supplied with the vehicle should only be used for changing the roadwheels – see *Wheel changing* at the front of this manual. When carrying out any other kind of work, raise the vehicle using a hydraulic (or 'trolley') jack, and always supplement the jack with axle stands at the vehicle jacking points.

When using a hydraulic jack or axle stands, always position the jack head or axle stand head under one of the relevant jacking points; the jacking point is the area in between the cut-outs on the sill **(see illustration)**. Use a block of wood between the jack or axle stand and the sill – the block of wood should have a groove cut into it, into which the welded flange of the sill will locate.

Do not attempt to jack the vehicle under the front crossmember, the sump, or any of the suspension components.

The jack supplied with the vehicle locates in the jacking points on the underside of the sills – see *Wheel changing*. Ensure that the jack head is correctly engaged before attempting to raise the vehicle.

Never work under, around, or near a raised vehicle, unless it is adequately supported in at least two places.

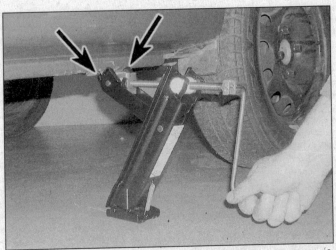

Jacking points are between the cut-outs (arrowed) on the base of the sill (shown with the vehicle jack in position)

Audio unit anti-theft system

The audio unit fitted as standard equipment by Peugeot is equipped with a built-in security code, to deter thieves. If the power source to the unit is cut, the anti-theft system will activate. Even if the power source is reconnected, the audio unit will not function until the correct security code has been entered. Therefore, if you do not know the correct security code for the audio unit, **do not** disconnect the battery negative terminal, or remove the audio unit from the vehicle.

To enter the security code first switch the unit on; the display will show 'Code'. The security code can then be entered using the station buttons 1 to 6 on the unit. For example if the code is 5345; press button 5, followed by button 3, button 4 and finally button 5. Once the correct code is displayed, the audio unit will automatically come on. If you make a mistake when entering one of the first three digits of the security code; switch the audio unit off and start again.

If an incorrect code is entered, the display will show four dashes, after which the radio will be locked for between 5 minutes and an hour, depending on how many attempts have been made. If an incorrect code is entered, the audio unit must be switched on and left untouched until the display shows the 'Code' prompt again, and allows you to re-enter the security code

If the security code is lost or forgotten, seek the advice of your Peugeot dealer. On presentation of proof of ownership, a Peugeot dealer will be able to provide you with a new code.

Introduction

A selection of good tools is a fundamental requirement for anyone contemplating the maintenance and repair of a motor vehicle. For the owner who does not possess any, their purchase will prove a considerable expense, offsetting some of the savings made by doing-it-yourself. However, provided that the tools purchased meet the relevant national safety standards and are of good quality, they will last for many years and prove an extremely worthwhile investment.

To help the average owner to decide which tools are needed to carry out the various tasks detailed in this manual, we have compiled three lists of tools under the following headings: *Maintenance and minor repair*, *Repair and overhaul*, and *Special*. Newcomers to practical mechanics should start off with the *Maintenance and minor repair* tool kit, and confine themselves to the simpler jobs around the vehicle. Then, as confidence and experience grow, more difficult tasks can be undertaken, with extra tools being purchased as, and when, they are needed. In this way, a *Maintenance and minor repair* tool kit can be built up into a *Repair and overhaul* tool kit over a considerable period of time, without any major cash outlays. The experienced do-it-yourselfer will have a tool kit good enough for most repair and overhaul procedures, and will add tools from the *Special* category when it is felt that the expense is justified by the amount of use to which these tools will be put.

Maintenance and minor repair tool kit

The tools given in this list should be considered as a minimum requirement if routine maintenance, servicing and minor repair operations are to be undertaken. We recommend the purchase of combination spanners (ring one end, open-ended the other); although more expensive than open-ended ones, they do give the advantages of both types of spanner.

☐ *Combination spanners:*
Metric - 8 to 19 mm inclusive
☐ *Adjustable spanner - 35 mm jaw (approx.)*
☐ *Spark plug spanner (with rubber insert) - petrol models*
☐ *Spark plug gap adjustment tool - petrol models*
☐ *Set of feeler gauges*
☐ *Brake bleed nipple spanner*
☐ *Screwdrivers:*
Flat blade - 100 mm long x 6 mm dia
Cross blade - 100 mm long x 6 mm dia
Torx - various sizes (not all vehicles)
☐ *Combination pliers*
☐ *Hacksaw (junior)*
☐ *Tyre pump*
☐ *Tyre pressure gauge*
☐ *Oil can*
☐ *Oil filter removal tool*
☐ *Fine emery cloth*
☐ *Wire brush (small)*
☐ *Funnel (medium size)*
☐ *Sump drain plug key (not all vehicles)*

Repair and overhaul tool kit

These tools are virtually essential for anyone undertaking any major repairs to a motor vehicle, and are additional to those given in the *Maintenance and minor repair* list. Included in this list is a comprehensive set of sockets. Although these are expensive, they will be found invaluable as they are so versatile - particularly if various drives are included in the set. We recommend the half-inch square-drive type, as this can be used with most proprietary torque wrenches.

The tools in this list will sometimes need to be supplemented by tools from the *Special* list:

☐ *Sockets (or box spanners) to cover range in previous list (including Torx sockets)*
☐ *Reversible ratchet drive (for use with sockets)*
☐ *Extension piece, 250 mm (for use with sockets)*
☐ *Universal joint (for use with sockets)*
☐ *Flexible handle or sliding T "breaker bar" (for use with sockets)*
☐ *Torque wrench (for use with sockets)*
☐ *Self-locking grips*
☐ *Ball pein hammer*
☐ *Soft-faced mallet (plastic or rubber)*
☐ *Screwdrivers:*
Flat blade - long & sturdy, short (chubby), and narrow (electrician's) types
Cross blade – long & sturdy, and short (chubby) types
☐ *Pliers:*
Long-nosed
Side cutters (electrician's)
Circlip (internal and external)
☐ *Cold chisel - 25 mm*
☐ *Scriber*
☐ *Scraper*
☐ *Centre-punch*
☐ *Pin punch*
☐ *Hacksaw*
☐ *Brake hose clamp*
☐ *Brake/clutch bleeding kit*
☐ *Selection of twist drills*
☐ *Steel rule/straight-edge*
☐ *Allen keys (inc. splined/Torx type)*
☐ *Selection of files*
☐ *Wire brush*
☐ *Axle stands*
☐ *Jack (strong trolley or hydraulic type)*
☐ *Light with extension lead*
☐ *Universal electrical multi-meter*

Sockets and reversible ratchet drive

Brake bleeding kit

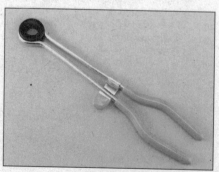

Torx key, socket and bit

Hose clamp

Angular-tightening gauge

Special tools

The tools in this list are those which are not used regularly, are expensive to buy, or which need to be used in accordance with their manufacturers' instructions. Unless relatively difficult mechanical jobs are undertaken frequently, it will not be economic to buy many of these tools. Where this is the case, you could consider clubbing together with friends (or joining a motorists' club) to make a joint purchase, or borrowing the tools against a deposit from a local garage or tool hire specialist. It is worth noting that many of the larger DIY superstores now carry a large range of special tools for hire at modest rates.

The following list contains only those tools and instruments freely available to the public, and not those special tools produced by the vehicle manufacturer specifically for its dealer network. You will find occasional references to these manufacturers' special tools in the text of this manual. Generally, an alternative method of doing the job without the vehicle manufacturers' special tool is given. However, sometimes there is no alternative to using them. Where this is the case and the relevant tool cannot be bought or borrowed, you will have to entrust the work to a dealer.

- [ ] *Angular-tightening gauge*
- [ ] *Valve spring compressor*
- [ ] *Valve grinding tool*
- [ ] *Piston ring compressor*
- [ ] *Piston ring removal/installation tool*
- [ ] *Cylinder bore hone*
- [ ] *Balljoint separator*
- [ ] *Coil spring compressors (where applicable)*
- [ ] *Two/three-legged hub and bearing puller*
- [ ] *Impact screwdriver*
- [ ] *Micrometer and/or vernier calipers*
- [ ] *Dial gauge*
- [ ] *Stroboscopic timing light*
- [ ] *Dwell angle meter/tachometer*
- [ ] *Fault code reader*
- [ ] *Cylinder compression gauge*
- [ ] *Hand-operated vacuum pump and gauge*
- [ ] *Clutch plate alignment set*
- [ ] *Brake shoe steady spring cup removal tool*
- [ ] *Bush and bearing removal/installation set*
- [ ] *Stud extractors*
- [ ] *Tap and die set*
- [ ] *Lifting tackle*
- [ ] *Trolley jack*

Buying tools

Reputable motor accessory shops and superstores often offer excellent quality tools at discount prices, so it pays to shop around.

Remember, you don't have to buy the most expensive items on the shelf, but it is always advisable to steer clear of the very cheap tools. Beware of 'bargains' offered on market stalls or at car boot sales. There are plenty of good tools around at reasonable prices, but always aim to purchase items which meet the relevant national safety standards. If in doubt, ask the proprietor or manager of the shop for advice before making a purchase.

Care and maintenance of tools

Having purchased a reasonable tool kit, it is necessary to keep the tools in a clean and serviceable condition. After use, always wipe off any dirt, grease and metal particles using a clean, dry cloth, before putting the tools away. Never leave them lying around after they have been used. A simple tool rack on the garage or workshop wall for items such as screwdrivers and pliers is a good idea. Store all normal spanners and sockets in a metal box. Any measuring instruments, gauges, meters, etc, must be carefully stored where they cannot be damaged or become rusty.

Take a little care when tools are used. Hammer heads inevitably become marked, and screwdrivers lose the keen edge on their blades from time to time. A little timely attention with emery cloth or a file will soon restore items like this to a good finish.

Working facilities

Not to be forgotten when discussing tools is the workshop itself. If anything more than routine maintenance is to be carried out, a suitable working area becomes essential.

It is appreciated that many an owner-mechanic is forced by circumstances to remove an engine or similar item without the benefit of a garage or workshop. Having done this, any repairs should always be done under the cover of a roof.

Wherever possible, any dismantling should be done on a clean, flat workbench or table at a suitable working height.

Any workbench needs a vice; one with a jaw opening of 100 mm is suitable for most jobs. As mentioned previously, some clean dry storage space is also required for tools, as well as for any lubricants, cleaning fluids, touch-up paints etc, which become necessary.

Another item which may be required, and which has a much more general usage, is an electric drill with a chuck capacity of at least 8 mm. This, together with a good range of twist drills, is virtually essential for fitting accessories.

Last, but not least, always keep a supply of old newspapers and clean, lint-free rags available, and try to keep any working area as clean as possible.

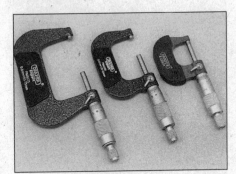
Micrometers

Dial test indicator ("dial gauge")

Strap wrench

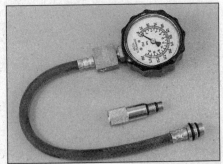
Compression tester

Fault code reader

This is a guide to getting your vehicle through the MOT test. Obviously it will not be possible to examine the vehicle to the same standard as the professional MOT tester. However, working through the following checks will enable you to identify any problem areas before submitting the vehicle for the test.

Where a testable component is in borderline condition, the tester has discretion in deciding whether to pass or fail it. The basis of such discretion is whether the tester would be happy for a close relative or friend to use the vehicle with the component in that condition. If the vehicle presented is clean and evidently well cared for, the tester may be more inclined to pass a borderline component than if the vehicle is scruffy and apparently neglected.

It has only been possible to summarise the test requirements here, based on the regulations in force at the time of printing. Test standards are becoming increasingly stringent, although there are some exemptions for older vehicles.

An assistant will be needed to help carry out some of these checks.

The checks have been sub-divided into four categories, as follows:

1 Checks carried out **FROM THE DRIVER'S SEAT**

2 Checks carried out **WITH THE VEHICLE ON THE GROUND**

3 Checks carried out **WITH THE VEHICLE RAISED AND THE WHEELS FREE TO TURN**

4 Checks carried out on **YOUR VEHICLE'S EXHAUST EMISSION SYSTEM**

1 Checks carried out **FROM THE DRIVER'S SEAT**

Handbrake

☐ Test the operation of the handbrake. Excessive travel (too many clicks) indicates incorrect brake or cable adjustment.

☐ Check that the handbrake cannot be released by tapping the lever sideways. Check the security of the lever mountings.

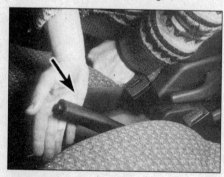

Footbrake

☐ Depress the brake pedal and check that it does not creep down to the floor, indicating a master cylinder fault. Release the pedal, wait a few seconds, then depress it again. If the pedal travels nearly to the floor before firm resistance is felt, brake adjustment or repair is necessary. If the pedal feels spongy, there is air in the hydraulic system which must be removed by bleeding.

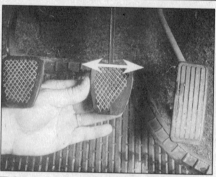

☐ Check that the brake pedal is secure and in good condition. Check also for signs of fluid leaks on the pedal, floor or carpets, which would indicate failed seals in the brake master cylinder.

☐ Check the servo unit (when applicable) by operating the brake pedal several times, then keeping the pedal depressed and starting the engine. As the engine starts, the pedal will move down slightly. If not, the vacuum hose or the servo itself may be faulty.

Steering wheel and column

☐ Examine the steering wheel for fractures or looseness of the hub, spokes or rim.

☐ Move the steering wheel from side to side and then up and down. Check that the steering wheel is not loose on the column, indicating wear or a loose retaining nut. Continue moving the steering wheel as before, but also turn it slightly from left to right.

☐ Check that the steering wheel is not loose on the column, and that there is no abnormal

movement of the steering wheel, indicating wear in the column support bearings or couplings.

Windscreen, mirrors and sunvisor

☐ The windscreen must be free of cracks or other significant damage within the driver's field of view. (Small stone chips are acceptable.) Rear view mirrors must be secure, intact, and capable of being adjusted.

☐ The driver's sunvisor must be capable of being stored in the "up" position.

MOT test checks REF•9

Seat belts and seats

Note: *The following checks are applicable to all seat belts, front and rear.*

☐ Examine the webbing of all the belts (including rear belts if fitted) for cuts, serious fraying or deterioration. Fasten and unfasten each belt to check the buckles. If applicable, check the retracting mechanism. Check the security of all seat belt mountings accessible from inside the vehicle.

☐ Seat belts with pre-tensioners, once activated, have a "flag" or similar showing on the seat belt stalk. This, in itself, is not a reason for test failure.

☐ The front seats themselves must be securely attached and the backrests must lock in the upright position.

Doors

☐ Both front doors must be able to be opened and closed from outside and inside, and must latch securely when closed.

2 Checks carried out WITH THE VEHICLE ON THE GROUND

Vehicle identification

☐ Number plates must be in good condition, secure and legible, with letters and numbers correctly spaced – spacing at (A) should be at least twice that at (B).

☐ The VIN plate and/or homologation plate must be legible.

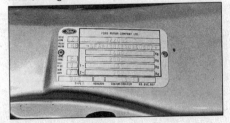

Electrical equipment

☐ Switch on the ignition and check the operation of the horn.

☐ Check the windscreen washers and wipers, examining the wiper blades; renew damaged or perished blades. Also check the operation of the stop-lights.

☐ Check the operation of the sidelights and number plate lights. The lenses and reflectors must be secure, clean and undamaged.

☐ Check the operation and alignment of the headlights. The headlight reflectors must not be tarnished and the lenses must be undamaged.

☐ Switch on the ignition and check the operation of the direction indicators (including the instrument panel tell-tale) and the hazard warning lights. Operation of the sidelights and stop-lights must not affect the indicators - if it does, the cause is usually a bad earth at the rear light cluster.

☐ Check the operation of the rear foglight(s), including the warning light on the instrument panel or in the switch.

☐ The ABS warning light must illuminate in accordance with the manufacturers' design. For most vehicles, the ABS warning light should illuminate when the ignition is switched on, and (if the system is operating properly) extinguish after a few seconds. Refer to the owner's handbook.

Footbrake

☐ Examine the master cylinder, brake pipes and servo unit for leaks, loose mountings, corrosion or other damage.

☐ The fluid reservoir must be secure and the fluid level must be between the upper (**A**) and lower (**B**) markings.

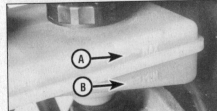

☐ Inspect both front brake flexible hoses for cracks or deterioration of the rubber. Turn the steering from lock to lock, and ensure that the hoses do not contact the wheel, tyre, or any part of the steering or suspension mechanism. With the brake pedal firmly depressed, check the hoses for bulges or leaks under pressure.

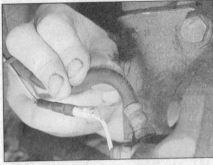

Steering and suspension

☐ Have your assistant turn the steering wheel from side to side slightly, up to the point where the steering gear just begins to transmit this movement to the roadwheels. Check for excessive free play between the steering wheel and the steering gear, indicating wear or insecurity of the steering column joints, the column-to-steering gear coupling, or the steering gear itself.

☐ Have your assistant turn the steering wheel more vigorously in each direction, so that the roadwheels just begin to turn. As this is done, examine all the steering joints, linkages, fittings and attachments. Renew any component that shows signs of wear or damage. On vehicles with power steering, check the security and condition of the steering pump, drivebelt and hoses.

☐ Check that the vehicle is standing level, and at approximately the correct ride height.

Shock absorbers

☐ Depress each corner of the vehicle in turn, then release it. The vehicle should rise and then settle in its normal position. If the vehicle continues to rise and fall, the shock absorber is defective. A shock absorber which has seized will also cause the vehicle to fail.

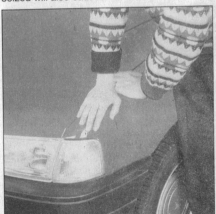

Exhaust system

☐ Start the engine. With your assistant holding a rag over the tailpipe, check the entire system for leaks. Repair or renew leaking sections.

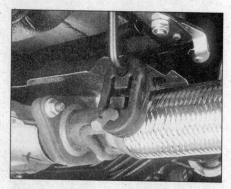

3 Checks carried out
WITH THE VEHICLE RAISED AND THE WHEELS FREE TO TURN

Jack up the front and rear of the vehicle, and securely support it on axle stands. Position the stands clear of the suspension assemblies. Ensure that the wheels are clear of the ground and that the steering can be turned from lock to lock.

Steering mechanism

☐ Have your assistant turn the steering from lock to lock. Check that the steering turns smoothly, and that no part of the steering mechanism, including a wheel or tyre, fouls any brake hose or pipe or any part of the body structure.

☐ Examine the steering rack rubber gaiters for damage or insecurity of the retaining clips. If power steering is fitted, check for signs of damage or leakage of the fluid hoses, pipes or connections. Also check for excessive stiffness or binding of the steering, a missing split pin or locking device, or severe corrosion of the body structure within 30 cm of any steering component attachment point.

Front and rear suspension and wheel bearings

☐ Starting at the front right-hand side, grasp the roadwheel at the 3 o'clock and 9 o'clock positions and rock gently but firmly. Check for free play or insecurity at the wheel bearings, suspension balljoints, or suspension mountings, pivots and attachments.

☐ Now grasp the wheel at the 12 o'clock and 6 o'clock positions and repeat the previous inspection. Spin the wheel, and check for roughness or tightness of the front wheel bearing.

☐ If excess free play is suspected at a component pivot point, this can be confirmed by using a large screwdriver or similar tool and levering between the mounting and the component attachment. This will confirm whether the wear is in the pivot bush, its retaining bolt, or in the mounting itself (the bolt holes can often become elongated).

☐ Carry out all the above checks at the other front wheel, and then at both rear wheels.

Springs and shock absorbers

☐ Examine the suspension struts (when applicable) for serious fluid leakage, corrosion, or damage to the casing. Also check the security of the mounting points.

☐ If coil springs are fitted, check that the spring ends locate in their seats, and that the spring is not corroded, cracked or broken.

☐ If leaf springs are fitted, check that all leaves are intact, that the axle is securely attached to each spring, and that there is no deterioration of the spring eye mountings, bushes, and shackles.

☐ The same general checks apply to vehicles fitted with other suspension types, such as torsion bars, hydraulic displacer units, etc. Ensure that all mountings and attachments are secure, that there are no signs of excessive wear, corrosion or damage, and (on hydraulic types) that there are no fluid leaks or damaged pipes.

☐ Inspect the shock absorbers for signs of serious fluid leakage. Check for wear of the mounting bushes or attachments, or damage to the body of the unit.

Driveshafts (fwd vehicles only)

☐ Rotate each front wheel in turn and inspect the constant velocity joint gaiters for splits or damage. Also check that each driveshaft is straight and undamaged.

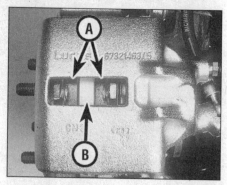

Braking system

☐ If possible without dismantling, check brake pad wear and disc condition. Ensure that the friction lining material has not worn excessively, (A) and that the discs are not fractured, pitted, scored or badly worn (B).

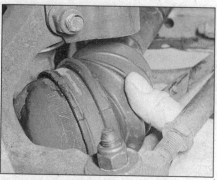

☐ Examine all the rigid brake pipes underneath the vehicle, and the flexible hose(s) at the rear. Look for corrosion, chafing or insecurity of the pipes, and for signs of bulging under pressure, chafing, splits or deterioration of the flexible hoses.

☐ Look for signs of fluid leaks at the brake calipers or on the brake backplates. Repair or renew leaking components.

☐ Slowly spin each wheel, while your assistant depresses and releases the footbrake. Ensure that each brake is operating and does not bind when the pedal is released.

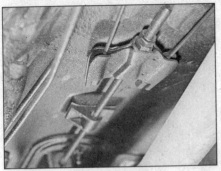

☐ Examine the handbrake mechanism, checking for frayed or broken cables, excessive corrosion, or wear or insecurity of the linkage. Check that the mechanism works on each relevant wheel, and releases fully, without binding.

☐ It is not possible to test brake efficiency without special equipment, but a road test can be carried out later to check that the vehicle pulls up in a straight line.

Fuel and exhaust systems

☐ Inspect the fuel tank (including the filler cap), fuel pipes, hoses and unions. All components must be secure and free from leaks.

☐ Examine the exhaust system over its entire length, checking for any damaged, broken or missing mountings, security of the retaining clamps and rust or corrosion.

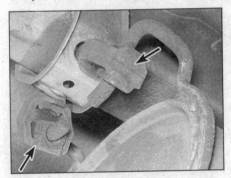

Wheels and tyres

☐ Examine the sidewalls and tread area of each tyre in turn. Check for cuts, tears, lumps, bulges, separation of the tread, and exposure of the ply or cord due to wear or damage. Check that the tyre bead is correctly seated on the wheel rim, that the valve is sound and properly seated, and that the wheel is not distorted or damaged.

☐ Check that the tyres are of the correct size for the vehicle, that they are of the same size and type on each axle, and that the pressures are correct.

☐ Check the tyre tread depth. The legal minimum at the time of writing is 1.6 mm over at least three-quarters of the tread width. Abnormal tread wear may indicate incorrect front wheel alignment.

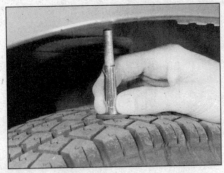

Body corrosion

☐ Check the condition of the entire vehicle structure for signs of corrosion in load-bearing areas. (These include chassis box sections, side sills, cross-members, pillars, and all suspension, steering, braking system and seat belt mountings and anchorages.) Any corrosion which has seriously reduced the thickness of a load-bearing area is likely to cause the vehicle to fail. In this case professional repairs are likely to be needed.

☐ Damage or corrosion which causes sharp or otherwise dangerous edges to be exposed will also cause the vehicle to fail.

4 Checks carried out on YOUR VEHICLE'S EXHAUST EMISSION SYSTEM

Petrol models

☐ Have the engine at normal operating temperature, and make sure that it is in good tune (ignition system in good order, air filter element clean, etc).

☐ Before any measurements are carried out, raise the engine speed to around 2500 rpm, and hold it at this speed for 20 seconds. Allow the engine speed to return to idle, and watch for smoke emissions from the exhaust tailpipe. If the idle speed is obviously much too high, or if dense blue or clearly-visible black smoke comes from the tailpipe for more than 5 seconds, the vehicle will fail. As a rule of thumb, blue smoke signifies oil being burnt (engine wear) while black smoke signifies unburnt fuel (dirty air cleaner element, or other carburettor or fuel system fault).

☐ An exhaust gas analyser capable of measuring carbon monoxide (CO) and hydrocarbons (HC) is now needed. If such an instrument cannot be hired or borrowed, a local garage may agree to perform the check for a small fee.

CO emissions (mixture)

☐ At the time of writing, for vehicles first used between 1st August 1975 and 31st July 1986 (P to C registration), the CO level must not exceed 4.5% by volume. For vehicles first used between 1st August 1986 and 31st July 1992 (D to J registration), the CO level must not exceed 3.5% by volume. Vehicles first

used after 1st August 1992 (K registration) must conform to the manufacturer's specification. The MOT tester has access to a DOT database or emissions handbook, which lists the CO and HC limits for each make and model of vehicle. The CO level is measured with the engine at idle speed, and at "fast idle". The following limits are given as a general guide:

At idle speed -
CO level no more than 0.5%
At "fast idle" (2500 to 3000 rpm) -
CO level no more than 0.3%
(Minimum oil temperature 60ºC)

☐ If the CO level cannot be reduced far enough to pass the test (and the fuel and ignition systems are otherwise in good condition) then the carburettor is badly worn, or there is some problem in the fuel injection system or catalytic converter (as applicable).

HC emissions

☐ With the CO within limits, HC emissions for vehicles first used between 1st August 1975 and 31st July 1992 (P to J registration) must not exceed 1200 ppm. Vehicles first used after 1st August 1992 (K registration) must conform to the manufacturer's specification. The MOT tester has access to a DOT database or emissions handbook, which lists the CO and HC limits for each make and model of vehicle. The HC level is measured with the engine at "fast idle". The following is given as a general guide:

At "fast idle" (2500 to 3000 rpm) -
HC level no more than 200 ppm
(Minimum oil temperature 60ºC)

☐ Excessive HC emissions are caused by incomplete combustion, the causes of which can include oil being burnt, mechanical wear and ignition/fuel system malfunction.

Diesel models

☐ The only emission test applicable to Diesel engines is the measuring of exhaust smoke density. The test involves accelerating the engine several times to its maximum unloaded speed.

Note: It is of the utmost importance that the engine timing belt is in good condition before the test is carried out.

☐ The limits for Diesel engine exhaust smoke, introduced in September 1995 are:
Vehicles first used before 1st August 1979:
Exempt from metered smoke testing, but must not emit "dense blue or clearly visible black smoke for a period of more than 5 seconds at idle" or "dense blue or clearly visible black smoke during acceleration which would obscure the view of other road users".
Non-turbocharged vehicles first used after 1st August 1979: 2.5m⁻¹
Turbocharged vehicles first used after 1st August 1979: 3.0m⁻¹

☐ Excessive smoke can be caused by a dirty air cleaner element. Otherwise, professional advice may be needed to find the cause.

Engine

- ☐ Engine fails to rotate when attempting to start
- ☐ Engine rotates, but will not start
- ☐ Engine difficult to start when cold
- ☐ Engine difficult to start when hot
- ☐ Starter motor noisy or excessively-rough in engagement
- ☐ Engine starts, but stops immediately
- ☐ Engine idles erratically
- ☐ Engine misfires at idle speed
- ☐ Engine misfires throughout the driving speed range
- ☐ Engine hesitates on acceleration
- ☐ Engine stalls
- ☐ Engine lacks power
- ☐ Engine backfires
- ☐ Oil pressure warning light on with engine running
- ☐ Engine runs-on after switching off
- ☐ Engine noises

Cooling system

- ☐ Overheating
- ☐ Overcooling
- ☐ External coolant leakage
- ☐ Internal coolant leakage
- ☐ Corrosion

Fuel and exhaust systems

- ☐ Excessive fuel consumption
- ☐ Fuel leakage and/or fuel odour
- ☐ Excessive noise or fumes from exhaust system

Clutch

- ☐ Pedal travels to floor – no pressure or very little resistance
- ☐ Clutch fails to disengage (unable to select gears)
- ☐ Clutch slips (engine speed rises, with no increase in vehicle speed)
- ☐ Judder as clutch is engaged
- ☐ Noise when depressing or releasing clutch pedal

Manual transmission

- ☐ Noisy in neutral with engine running
- ☐ Noisy in one particular gear
- ☐ Difficulty engaging gears
- ☐ Jumps out of gear
- ☐ Vibration
- ☐ Lubricant leaks

Automatic transmission

- ☐ Fluid leakage
- ☐ Transmission fluid brown, or has burned smell
- ☐ General gear selection problems
- ☐ Transmission will not downshift (kickdown) on full throttle
- ☐ Engine won't start in any gear, or starts in gears other than P or N
- ☐ Transmission slips, shifts roughly, is noisy, or has no drive in forward or reverse gears

Driveshafts

- ☐ Clicking or knocking noise on turns (at slow speed on full-lock)
- ☐ Vibration when accelerating or decelerating

Braking system

- ☐ Vehicle pulls to one side under braking
- ☐ Noise (grinding or high-pitched squeal) when brakes applied
- ☐ Excessive brake pedal travel
- ☐ Brake pedal feels spongy when depressed
- ☐ Excessive brake pedal effort required to stop vehicle
- ☐ Judder felt through brake pedal or steering wheel when braking
- ☐ Brakes binding
- ☐ Rear wheels locking under normal braking

Suspension and steering systems

- ☐ Vehicle pulls to one side
- ☐ Wheel wobble and vibration
- ☐ Excessive pitching and/or rolling around corners, or during braking
- ☐ Wandering or general instability
- ☐ Excessively-stiff steering
- ☐ Excessive play in steering
- ☐ Lack of power assistance
- ☐ Tyre wear excessive

Electrical system

- ☐ Battery will not hold a charge for more than a few days
- ☐ Ignition/no-charge warning light stays on with engine running
- ☐ Ignition/no-charge warning light fails to come on
- ☐ Lights inoperative
- ☐ Instrument readings inaccurate or erratic
- ☐ Horn inoperative, or unsatisfactory in operation
- ☐ Windscreen/tailgate wipers failed, or unsatisfactory in operation
- ☐ Windscreen/tailgate washers failed, or unsatisfactory in operation
- ☐ Electric windows inoperative, or unsatisfactory in operation
- ☐ Central locking system inoperative, or unsatisfactory in operation

Introduction

The vehicle owner who does his or her own maintenance according to the recommended service schedules should not have to use this section of the manual very often. Modern component reliability is such that, provided those items subject to wear or deterioration are inspected or renewed at the specified intervals, sudden failure is comparatively rare. Faults do not usually just happen as a result of sudden failure, but develop over a period of time. Major mechanical failures in particular are usually preceded by characteristic symptoms over hundreds or even thousands of miles. Those components which do occasionally fail without warning are often small and easily carried in the vehicle.

With any fault-finding, the first step is to decide where to begin investigations. Sometimes this is obvious, but on other occasions, a little detective work will be necessary. The owner who makes half a dozen haphazard adjustments or replacements may be successful in curing a fault (or its symptoms), but will be none the wiser if the fault recurs, and ultimately may have spent more time and money than was necessary. A calm and logical approach will

be found to be more satisfactory in the long run. Always take into account any warning signs or abnormalities that may have been noticed in the period preceding the fault – power loss, high or low gauge readings, unusual smells, etc – and remember that failure of components such as fuses or spark plugs may only be pointers to some underlying fault.

The pages which follow provide an easy-reference guide to the more common problems which may occur during the operation of the vehicle. These problems and their possible causes are grouped under headings denoting various components or systems, such as Engine, Cooling system, etc. The Chapter and/or Section which deals with the problem is also shown in brackets. Whatever the fault, certain basic principles apply. These are as follows:

Verify the fault. This is simply a matter of being sure that you know what the symptoms are before starting work. This is particularly important if you are investigating a fault for someone else, who may not have described it very accurately.

Don't overlook the obvious. For example, if

the vehicle won't start, is there fuel in the tank? (Don't take anyone else's word on this particular point, and don't trust the fuel gauge either!) If an electrical fault is indicated, look for loose or broken wires before digging out the test gear.

Cure the disease, not the symptom. Substituting a flat battery with a fully-charged one will get you off the hard shoulder, but if the underlying cause is not attended to, the new battery will go the same way. Similarly, changing oil-fouled spark plugs (petrol models) for a new set will get you moving again, but remember that the reason for the fouling (if it wasn't simply an incorrect grade of plug) will have to be found and corrected.

Don't take anything for granted. Particularly, don't forget that a 'new' component may itself be defective (especially if it's been rattling around in the boot for months), and don't leave components out of a fault diagnosis sequence just because they are new or recently-fitted. When you do finally diagnose a difficult fault, you'll probably realise that all the evidence was there from the start.

Engine

Engine fails to rotate when attempting to start

☐ Battery terminal connections loose or corroded (*Weekly checks*).
☐ Battery discharged or faulty (Chapter 5A).
☐ Broken, loose or disconnected wiring in the starting circuit (Chapter 5A).
☐ Defective starter motor (Chapter 5A).
☐ Starter pinion or flywheel/driveplate ring gear teeth loose or broken (Chapter 2A or 2B and 5A).
☐ Engine earth strap broken or disconnected (Chapter 5A).

Engine rotates, but will not start

☐ Fuel tank empty.
☐ Battery discharged (engine rotates slowly) (Chapter 5A).
☐ Battery terminal connections loose or corroded (*Weekly checks*).
☐ Worn, faulty or incorrectly-gapped spark plugs – petrol models (Chapter 1A).
☐ Preheating system faulty – diesel models (Chapter 5C).
☐ Engine management system fault – petrol models (Chapter 4A).
☐ Air in fuel system – diesel models (Chapter 4B).
☐ Fuel injector/injection pump fault – diesel models (Chapter 4B).
☐ Low cylinder compressions (Chapter 2A or 2B).
☐ Major mechanical failure (eg camshaft drive) (Chapter 2A or 2B).

Engine difficult to start when cold

☐ Battery discharged (Chapter 5A).
☐ Battery terminal connections loose or corroded (*Weekly checks*).
☐ Worn, faulty or incorrectly-gapped spark plugs – petrol models (Chapter 1A).
☐ Preheating system faulty – diesel models (Chapter 5C).
☐ Engine management system fault – petrol models (Chapter 4A).
☐ Fast idle valve incorrectly adjusted – 1.9 litre diesel model (Chapter 4B).
☐ Fuel injector/injection pump fault – diesel models (Chapter 4B).

Engine difficult to start when hot

☐ Engine management system fault – petrol models (Chapter 4A).
☐ Fuel injector/injection pump fault – diesel models (Chapter 4B).
☐ Low cylinder compressions (Chapter 2A or 2B).

Starter motor noisy or excessively-rough in engagement

☐ Starter pinion or flywheel/driveplate ring gear teeth loose or broken (Chapters 2A or 2B and 5A).
☐ Starter motor mounting bolts loose or missing (Chapter 5A).
☐ Defective starter motor (Chapter 5A).

Engine starts, but stops immediately

☐ Vacuum leak at the throttle housing/inlet manifold – petrol models (Chapter 4A).
☐ Engine management system fault – petrol models (Chapter 4A).
☐ Air in fuel system – diesel models (Chapter 4B).
☐ Fuel injector/injection pump fault – diesel models (Chapter 4B).

Engine idles erratically

☐ Vacuum leak at the throttle housing/inlet manifold – petrol models (Chapter 4A).
☐ Worn, faulty or incorrectly-gapped spark plugs – petrol models (Chapter 1A).
☐ Engine management system fault – petrol models (Chapter 4A).
☐ Air in fuel system – diesel models (Chapter 4B).
☐ Fuel injector/injection pump fault – diesel models (Chapter 4B).
☐ Uneven or low cylinder compressions (Chapter 2A or 2B).
☐ Camshaft lobes worn (Chapter 2A or 2B).
☐ Timing belt incorrectly fitted (Chapter 2A or 2B).

Engine misfires at idle speed

☐ Worn, faulty or incorrectly-gapped spark plugs – petrol models (Chapter 1A).
☐ Vacuum leak at the throttle housing/inlet manifold – petrol models (Chapter 4A).
☐ Engine management system fault – petrol models (Chapter 4A).
☐ Faulty injector(s) – diesel models (Chapter 4B).
☐ Uneven or low cylinder compressions (Chapter 2A or 2B).
☐ Disconnected, leaking, or perished crankcase ventilation hoses (Chapter 4C).

Engine misfires throughout the driving speed range

☐ Fuel filter blocked (Chapter 1A or 1B).
☐ Fuel pump faulty (Chapter 4A or 4B).
☐ Fuel tank vent blocked, or fuel pipes restricted (Chapter 4A or 4B).
☐ Worn, faulty or incorrectly-gapped spark plugs – petrol models (Chapter 1A).
☐ Vacuum leak at the throttle housing/inlet manifold – petrol models (Chapter 4A).
☐ Engine management system fault – petrol models (Chapter 4A).
☐ Fuel injector/injection pump fault – diesel models (Chapter 4B).
☐ Faulty ignition HT coil – petrol models (Chapter 5B).
☐ Uneven or low cylinder compressions (Chapter 2A or 2B).

Engine hesitates on acceleration

☐ Worn, faulty or incorrectly-gapped spark plugs – petrol models (Chapter 1A).
☐ Vacuum leak at the throttle housing/inlet manifold – petrol models (Chapter 4A).
☐ Engine management system fault – petrol models (Chapter 4A).
☐ Fuel injector/injection pump fault – diesel models (Chapter 4B).

Engine (continued)

Engine stalls

- ☐ Fuel filter blocked (Chapter 1A or 1B).
- ☐ Fuel pump faulty (Chapter 4A or 4B).
- ☐ Fuel tank vent blocked, or fuel pipes restricted (Chapter 4A or 4B).
- ☐ Worn, faulty or incorrectly-gapped spark plugs – petrol models (Chapter 1A).
- ☐ Vacuum leak at the throttle housing/inlet manifold – petrol models (Chapter 4A).
- ☐ Engine management system fault – petrol models (Chapter 4A).
- ☐ Fuel injector/injection pump fault – diesel models (Chapter 4B).

Engine lacks power

- ☐ Timing belt incorrectly fitted (Chapter 2A or 2B).
- ☐ Fuel filter blocked (Chapter 1A or 1B).
- ☐ Fuel pump faulty (Chapter 4A or 4B).
- ☐ Uneven or low cylinder compressions (Chapter 2A or 2B).
- ☐ Worn, faulty or incorrectly-gapped spark plugs – petrol models (Chapter 1A).
- ☐ Vacuum leak at the throttle housing/inlet manifold – petrol models (Chapter 4A).
- ☐ Engine management system fault – petrol models (Chapter 4A).
- ☐ Fuel injector/injection pump fault – diesel models (Chapter 4B).
- ☐ Brakes binding (Chapters 1A or 1B and 9).
- ☐ Clutch slipping (Chapter 6).

Engine backfires

- ☐ Timing belt incorrectly fitted (Chapter 2A or 2B).
- ☐ Vacuum leak at the throttle housing/inlet manifold – petrol models (Chapter 4A).
- ☐ Engine management system fault – petrol models (Chapter 4A).

Oil pressure warning light on with engine running

- ☐ Low oil level, or incorrect oil grade (*Weekly checks*).
- ☐ Faulty oil pressure warning light switch (Chapter 5A).
- ☐ Worn engine bearings and/or oil pump (Chapter 2C).
- ☐ High engine operating temperature (Chapter 3).
- ☐ Oil pressure relief valve defective (Chapter 2A or 2B).
- ☐ Oil pick-up strainer clogged (Chapter 2A or 2B).

Engine runs-on after switching off

- ☐ Excessive carbon build-up in engine (Chapter 2C).
- ☐ High engine operating temperature (Chapter 3).
- ☐ Engine management system fault – petrol models (Chapter 4A).
- ☐ Fuel injection pump fault – diesel models (Chapter 4B).

Engine noises

Pre-ignition (pinking) or knocking during acceleration or under load

- ☐ Engine management system fault – petrol models (Chapter 4A).
- ☐ Incorrect grade of spark plug – petrol models (Chapter 1A).
- ☐ Incorrect grade of fuel – petrol models (Chapter 4A).
- ☐ Vacuum leak at the throttle housing/inlet manifold – petrol models (Chapter 4A).
- ☐ Excessive carbon build-up in engine (Chapter 2C).

Whistling or wheezing noises

- ☐ Leaking inlet manifold or throttle housing gasket – petrol models (Chapter 4A).
- ☐ Leaking vacuum hose (Chapters 4A or 4B and 9).
- ☐ Blowing cylinder head gasket (Chapter 2A or 2B).

Tapping or rattling noises

- ☐ Worn valve gear or camshaft (Chapter 2A or 2B).
- ☐ Ancillary component fault (coolant pump, alternator, etc) (Chapters 3, 5A, etc).

Knocking or thumping noises

- ☐ Worn big-end bearings (regular heavy knocking, perhaps less under load) (Chapter 2C).
- ☐ Worn main bearings (rumbling and knocking, perhaps worsening under load) (Chapter 2C).
- ☐ Piston slap (most noticeable when cold) (Chapter 2C).
- ☐ Ancillary component fault (coolant pump, alternator, etc) (Chapters 3, 5A, etc).

Cooling system

Overheating

- ☐ Insufficient coolant in system (*Weekly checks*).
- ☐ Thermostat faulty (stuck closed) (Chapter 3).
- ☐ Radiator core blocked, or grille restricted (Chapter 3).
- ☐ Electric cooling fan or sensor faulty (Chapter 3).
- ☐ Pressure cap faulty (Chapter 3).
- ☐ Inaccurate temperature gauge/sensor (Chapter 3).
- ☐ Airlock in cooling system (Chapter 1A or 1B).
- ☐ Engine management system fault – petrol models (Chapter 4A).

Overcooling

- ☐ Thermostat faulty (stuck open) (Chapter 3).
- ☐ Inaccurate temperature gauge/sensor (Chapter 3).

External coolant leakage

- ☐ Deteriorated or damaged hoses or hose clips (Chapter 1A or 1B).
- ☐ Radiator core or heater matrix leaking (Chapter 3).
- ☐ Pressure cap faulty (Chapter 3).
- ☐ Coolant pump leaking (Chapter 3).
- ☐ Boiling due to overheating (Chapter 3).
- ☐ Core plug leaking (Chapter 2C).

Internal coolant leakage

- ☐ Leaking cylinder head gasket (Chapter 2A or 2B).
- ☐ Cracked cylinder head or cylinder bore (Chapter 2A, 2B or 2C).

Corrosion

- ☐ Infrequent draining and flushing (Chapter 1A or 1B).
- ☐ Incorrect coolant mixture or inappropriate coolant type (Chapter 1A or 1B).

Fuel and exhaust systems

Excessive fuel consumption

- ☐ Air filter element dirty or clogged (Chapter 1A or 1B).
- ☐ Engine management system fault – petrol models (Chapter 4A).
- ☐ Faulty injector(s) – diesel models (Chapter 4B).
- ☐ Tyres under-inflated (*Weekly checks*).
- ☐ Brakes binding (Chapters 1A or 1B and 9).

Fuel leakage and/or fuel odour

- ☐ Damaged or corroded fuel tank, pipes or connections (Chapter 4A or 4B).

Excessive noise or fumes from exhaust system

- ☐ Leaking exhaust system or manifold joints (Chapters 1A or 1B and 4A or 4B).
- ☐ Leaking, corroded or damaged silencers or pipe (Chapters 1A or 1B and 4A or 4B).
- ☐ Broken mountings causing body or suspension contact (Chapters 1A or 1B and 4A or 4B).

Clutch

Pedal travels to floor – no pressure or very little resistance

☐ Broken clutch cable/faulty self-adjusting mechanism – cable-operated clutch (Chapter 6).
☐ Air in hydraulic system/faulty master or slave cylinder – hydraulically operated clutch (Chapter 6).
☐ Broken clutch release bearing or fork (Chapter 6).
☐ Broken diaphragm spring in clutch pressure plate (Chapter 6).

Clutch fails to disengage (unable to select gears)

☐ Faulty self-adjusting mechanism – cable-operated clutch (Chapter 6).
☐ Air in hydraulic system/faulty master or slave cylinder – hydraulically operated clutch (Chapter 6).
☐ Clutch disc sticking on gearbox input shaft splines (Chapter 6).
☐ Clutch disc sticking to flywheel or pressure plate (Chapter 6).
☐ Faulty pressure plate assembly (Chapter 6).
☐ Clutch release mechanism worn or incorrectly assembled (Chapter 6).

Clutch slips (engine speed rises, with no increase in vehicle speed)

☐ Faulty self-adjusting mechanism – cable-operated clutch (Chapter 6).
☐ Faulty hydraulic release system – hydraulically operated clutch (Chapter 6).
☐ Clutch disc linings excessively worn (Chapter 6).
☐ Clutch disc linings contaminated with oil or grease (Chapter 6).
☐ Faulty pressure plate or weak diaphragm spring (Chapter 6).

Judder as clutch is engaged

☐ Clutch disc linings contaminated with oil or grease (Chapter 6).
☐ Clutch disc linings excessively worn (Chapter 6).
☐ Clutch cable sticking or frayed – cable-operated clutch (Chapter 6).
☐ Faulty or distorted pressure plate or diaphragm spring (Chapter 6).
☐ Worn or loose engine or gearbox mountings (Chapter 2A or 2B).
☐ Clutch disc hub or gearbox input shaft splines worn (Chapter 6).

Noise when depressing or releasing clutch pedal

☐ Worn clutch release bearing (Chapter 6).
☐ Worn or dry clutch pedal bushes (Chapter 6).
☐ Faulty pressure plate assembly (Chapter 6).
☐ Pressure plate diaphragm spring broken (Chapter 6).
☐ Broken clutch disc cushioning springs (Chapter 6).

Manual transmission

Noisy in neutral with engine running

☐ Input shaft bearings worn (noise apparent with clutch pedal released, but not when depressed) (Chapter 7A).*
☐ Clutch release bearing worn (noise apparent with clutch pedal depressed, possibly less when released) (Chapter 6).

Noisy in one particular gear

☐ Worn, damaged or chipped gear teeth (Chapter 7A).*

Difficulty engaging gears

☐ Clutch fault (Chapter 6).
☐ Worn or damaged gear linkage (Chapter 7A).
☐ Worn synchroniser units (Chapter 7A).*

Jumps out of gear

☐ Worn or damaged gear linkage (Chapter 7A).
☐ Worn synchroniser units (Chapter 7A).*
☐ Worn selector forks (Chapter 7A).*

Vibration

☐ Lack of oil (Chapters 1 and 7A).
☐ Worn bearings (Chapter 7A).*

Lubricant leaks

☐ Leaking differential output oil seal (Chapter 7A).
☐ Leaking housing joint (Chapter 7A).*
☐ Leaking input shaft oil seal (Chapter 7A).
*Although the corrective action necessary to remedy the symptoms described is beyond the scope of the home mechanic, the above information should be helpful in isolating the cause of the condition, so that the owner can communicate clearly with a professional mechanic.

Automatic transmission

Note: *Due to the complexity of the automatic transmission, it is difficult for the home mechanic to properly diagnose and service this unit. For problems other than the following, the vehicle should be taken to a Peugeot dealer service department.*

Fluid leakage

☐ Automatic transmission fluid is usually dark in colour. Fluid leaks should not be confused with engine oil, which can easily be blown onto the transmission by airflow.
☐ To determine the source of a leak, first remove all built-up dirt and grime from the transmission housing and surrounding areas using a degreasing agent, or by steam-cleaning. Drive the vehicle at low speed, so airflow will not blow the leak far from its source. Raise and support the vehicle, and determine where the leak is coming from.

Transmission fluid brown, or has burned smell

☐ Transmission fluid level low, or fluid in need of renewal (Chapter 1A and 7B).

General gear selection problems

☐ Chapter 7B deals with checking and adjusting the selector cable on automatic transmissions. The following are common problems which may be caused by a poorly-adjusted cable:

a) Engine starting in gears other than Park or Neutral.
b) Indicator panel showing a gear other than that being used.
c) Vehicle moves when in Park or Neutral.
d) Poor gear shift quality or erratic gear changes.
☐ Refer to Chapter 7B for the selector cable adjustment procedure.

Transmission will not downshift (kickdown) at full throttle

☐ Low transmission fluid level (Chapter 1A).
☐ Incorrect selector cable adjustment (Chapter 7B).

Engine won't start in any gear, or starts in gears other than Park or Neutral

☐ Incorrect multi-function switch adjustment (Chapter 7B).
☐ Incorrect selector cable adjustment (Chapter 7B).

Transmission slips, shifts roughly, is noisy, or has no drive in forward or reverse gears

☐ There are many probable causes for the above problems, but the home mechanic should be concerned with only one possibility – fluid level. Before taking the vehicle to a dealer or transmission specialist, check the fluid level as described in Chapter 1A. Correct the fluid level as necessary, or change the fluid. If the problem persists, professional help will be necessary.

Driveshafts

Clicking or knocking noise on turns (at slow speed on full-lock)

☐ Lack of constant velocity joint lubricant, possibly due to damaged gaiter (Chapter 8).
☐ Worn outer constant velocity joint (Chapter 8).

Vibration when accelerating or decelerating

☐ Worn inner constant velocity joint (Chapter 8).
☐ Bent or distorted driveshaft (Chapter 8).
☐ Worn intermediate bearing (Chapter 8).

Braking system

Note: *Before assuming that a brake problem exists, make sure that the tyres are in good condition and correctly inflated, that the front wheel alignment is correct, and that the vehicle is not loaded with weight in an unequal manner. Apart from checking the condition of all pipe and hose connections, any faults occurring on the anti-lock braking system should be referred to a Peugeot dealer for diagnosis.*

Vehicle pulls to one side under braking

☐ Worn, defective, damaged or contaminated brake pads/shoes on one side (Chapter 9).
☐ Seized or partially-seized front brake caliper/wheel cylinder piston (Chapter 9).
☐ A mixture of brake pad/shoe lining materials fitted between sides (Chapter 9).
☐ Brake caliper or backplate mounting bolts loose (Chapter 9).
☐ Worn or damaged steering or suspension components (Chapters 1A or 1B and 10).

Noise (grinding or high-pitched squeal) when brakes applied

☐ Brake pad or shoe friction lining material worn down to metal backing (Chapters 1A or 1B and 9).
☐ Excessive corrosion of brake disc or drum. May be apparent after the vehicle has been standing for some time (Chapter 9).
☐ Foreign object (stone chipping, etc) trapped between brake disc and shield (Chapter 9).

Excessive brake pedal travel

☐ Inoperative rear brake self-adjust mechanism (Chapter 9).
☐ Faulty master cylinder (Chapter 9).
☐ Air in hydraulic system (Chapter 9).
☐ Faulty vacuum servo unit (Chapter 9).

Brake pedal feels spongy when depressed

☐ Air in hydraulic system (Chapter 9).
☐ Deteriorated flexible rubber brake hoses (Chapters 1A or 1B and 9).
☐ Master cylinder mounting nuts loose (Chapter 9).
☐ Faulty master cylinder (Chapter 9).

Excessive brake pedal effort required to stop vehicle

☐ Faulty vacuum servo unit (Chapter 9).
☐ Disconnected, damaged or insecure brake servo vacuum hose (Chapter 9).
☐ Primary or secondary hydraulic circuit failure (Chapter 9).
☐ Seized brake caliper or wheel cylinder piston(s) (Chapter 9).
☐ Brake pads or brake shoes incorrectly fitted (Chapter 9).
☐ Incorrect grade of brake pads or brake shoes fitted (Chapter 9).
☐ Brake pads or brake shoe linings contaminated (Chapter 9).

Judder felt through brake pedal or steering wheel when braking

☐ Excessive run-out or distortion of discs/drums (Chapters 9).
☐ Brake pad or brake shoe linings worn (Chapters 1A or 1B and 9).
☐ Brake caliper or brake backplate mounting bolts loose (Chapter 9).
☐ Wear in suspension or steering components or mountings (Chapters 1A or 1B and 10).

Brakes binding

☐ Seized brake caliper or wheel cylinder piston(s) (Chapter 9).
☐ Incorrectly-adjusted handbrake mechanism (Chapter 9).
☐ Faulty master cylinder (Chapter 9).

Rear wheels locking under normal braking

☐ Rear brake shoe linings contaminated (Chapters 1A or 1B and 9).
☐ Faulty brake pressure regulator (Chapter 9).

Suspension and steering

Note: *Before diagnosing suspension or steering faults, be sure that the trouble is not due to incorrect tyre pressures, mixtures of tyre types, or binding brakes.*

Vehicle pulls to one side

- ☐ Defective tyre (*Weekly checks*).
- ☐ Excessive wear in suspension or steering components (Chapters 1A or 1B and 10).
- ☐ Incorrect front wheel alignment (Chapter 10).
- ☐ Damage to steering or suspension components (Chapter 1A or 1B).

Wheel wobble and vibration

- ☐ Front roadwheels out of balance (vibration felt mainly through the steering wheel) (Chapters 1A or 1B and 10).
- ☐ Rear roadwheels out of balance (vibration felt throughout the vehicle) (Chapters 1A or 1B and 10).
- ☐ Roadwheels damaged or distorted (Chapters 1A or 1B and 10).
- ☐ Faulty or damaged tyre (*Weekly checks*).
- ☐ Worn steering or suspension joints, bushes or components (Chapters 11A or 1B and 10).
- ☐ Wheel bolts loose (Chapters 1A or 1B and 10).

Excessive pitching and/or rolling around corners, or during braking

- ☐ Defective shock absorbers (Chapters 1A or 1B and 10).
- ☐ Broken or weak spring and/or suspension part (Chapters 1A or 1B and 10).
- ☐ Worn or damaged anti-roll bar or mountings (Chapter 10).

Wandering or general instability

- ☐ Incorrect front wheel alignment (Chapter 10).
- ☐ Worn steering or suspension joints, bushes or components (Chapters 1A or 1B and 10).
- ☐ Roadwheels out of balance (Chapters 1A or 1B and 10).
- ☐ Faulty or damaged tyre (*Weekly checks*).
- ☐ Wheel bolts loose (Chapters 1A or 1B and 10).
- ☐ Defective shock absorbers (Chapters 1A or 1B and 10).

Excessively-stiff steering

- ☐ Lack of steering gear lubricant (Chapter 10).
- ☐ Seized track rod end balljoint or suspension balljoint (Chapters 1A or 1B and 10).
- ☐ Broken or incorrectly-adjusted auxiliary drivebelt – power steering (Chapter 1A or 1B).
- ☐ Incorrect front wheel alignment (Chapter 10).
- ☐ Steering gear or column bent or damaged (Chapter 10).

Excessive play in steering

- ☐ Worn steering column intermediate shaft universal joint (Chapter 10).
- ☐ Worn steering track rod end balljoints (Chapters 1A or 1B and 10).
- ☐ Worn steering gear (Chapter 10).
- ☐ Worn steering or suspension joints, bushes or components (Chapters 1A or 1B and 10).

Lack of power assistance

- ☐ Broken or incorrectly-adjusted auxiliary drivebelt (Chapter 1A or 1B).
- ☐ Incorrect power steering fluid level (*Weekly checks*).
- ☐ Restriction in power steering fluid hoses (Chapter 1A or 1B).
- ☐ Faulty power steering pump (Chapter 10).
- ☐ Faulty steering gear (Chapter 10).

Tyre wear excessive

Tyre treads exhibit feathered edges

- ☐ Incorrect toe setting (Chapter 10).

Tyres worn in centre of tread

- ☐ Tyres over-inflated (*Weekly checks*).

Tyres worn on inside and outside edges

- ☐ Tyres under-inflated (*Weekly checks*).

Tyres worn on inside or outside edges

- ☐ Incorrect camber/castor angles (wear on one edge only) (Chapter 10).
- ☐ Worn steering or suspension joints, bushes or components (Chapters 1A or 1B and 10).
- ☐ Excessively-hard cornering.
- ☐ Accident damage.

Tyres worn unevenly

- ☐ Tyres/wheels out of balance (*Weekly checks*).
- ☐ Excessive wheel or tyre run-out (Chapter 1A or 1B).
- ☐ Worn shock absorbers (Chapters 1A or 1B and 10).
- ☐ Faulty tyre (*Weekly checks*).

Electrical system

Note: For problems associated with the starting system, refer to the faults listed under 'Engine' earlier in this Section.

Battery won't hold a charge for more than a few days

☐ Battery defective internally (Chapter 5A).
☐ Battery terminal connections loose or corroded (*Weekly checks*).
☐ Auxiliary drivebelt broken, worn or incorrectly adjusted (Chapter 1A or 1B).
☐ Alternator not charging at correct output (Chapter 5A).
☐ Alternator or voltage regulator faulty (Chapter 5A).
☐ Short-circuit causing continual battery drain (Chapters 5A and 12).

Ignition/no-charge warning light stays on with engine running

☐ Auxiliary drivebelt broken, worn, or incorrectly adjusted (Chapter 1A or 1B).
☐ Internal fault in alternator or voltage regulator (Chapter 5A).
☐ Broken, disconnected, or loose wiring in charging circuit (Chapter 5A).

Ignition/no-charge warning light fails to come on

☐ Warning light bulb blown (Chapter 12).
☐ Broken, disconnected, or loose wiring in warning light circuit (Chapter 12).
☐ Alternator faulty (Chapter 5A).

Lights inoperative

☐ Bulb blown (Chapter 12).
☐ Corrosion of bulb or bulbholder contacts (Chapter 12).
☐ Blown fuse (Chapter 12).
☐ Faulty relay (Chapter 12).
☐ Broken, loose, or disconnected wiring (Chapter 12).
☐ Faulty switch (Chapter 12).

Instrument readings inaccurate or erratic

Instrument readings increase with engine speed

☐ Faulty voltage regulator (Chapter 12).

Fuel or temperature gauges give no reading

☐ Faulty gauge sensor unit (Chapter 3).
☐ Wiring open-circuit (Chapter 12).
☐ Faulty gauge (Chapter 12).

Fuel or temperature gauges give continuous maximum reading

☐ Faulty gauge sensor unit (Chapter 3).
☐ Wiring short-circuit (Chapter 12).
☐ Faulty gauge (Chapter 12).

Horn inoperative, or unsatisfactory in operation

Horn operates all the time

☐ Horn push either earthed or stuck down (Chapter 12).
☐ Horn cable-to-horn push earthed (Chapter 12).

Horn fails to operate

☐ Blown fuse (Chapter 12).
☐ Cable or cable connections loose, broken or disconnected (Chapter 12).
☐ Faulty horn (Chapter 12).

Horn emits intermittent or unsatisfactory sound

☐ Cable connections loose (Chapter 12).
☐ Horn mountings loose (Chapter 12).
☐ Faulty horn (Chapter 12).

Windscreen/tailgate wipers failed, or unsatisfactory in operation

Wipers fail to operate, or operate very slowly

☐ Wiper blades stuck to screen, or linkage seized or binding (Chapters 1A or 1B and 12).
☐ Blown fuse (Chapter 12).
☐ Cable or cable connections loose, broken or disconnected (Chapter 12).
☐ Faulty built-in system interface (BSI) unit (Chapter 12).
☐ Faulty wiper motor (Chapter 12).

Wiper blades sweep over too large or too small an area of the glass

☐ Wiper arms incorrectly positioned on spindles (Chapter 12).
☐ Excessive wear of wiper linkage (Chapter 12).
☐ Wiper motor or linkage mountings loose or insecure (Chapter 12).

Wiper blades fail to clean the glass effectively

☐ Wiper blade rubbers worn or perished (*Weekly checks*).
☐ Wiper arm tension springs broken, or arm pivots seized (Chapter 12).
☐ Insufficient windscreen washer additive to adequately remove road film (Weekly checks).

Electrical system (continued)

Windscreen/tailgate washers failed, or unsatisfactory in operation

One or more washer jets inoperative

- [ ] Blocked washer jet (*Weekly checks*).
- [ ] Disconnected, kinked or restricted fluid hose (Chapter 12).
- [ ] Insufficient fluid in washer reservoir (*Weekly checks*).

Washer pump fails to operate

- [ ] Broken or disconnected wiring or connections (Chapter 12).
- [ ] Blown fuse (Chapter 12).
- [ ] Faulty washer switch (Chapter 12).
- [ ] Faulty washer pump (Chapter 12).

Washer pump runs for some time before fluid is emitted from jets

- [ ] Faulty one-way valve in fluid supply hose (Chapter 12).

Electric windows inoperative, or unsatisfactory in operation

Window glass will only move in one direction

- [ ] Faulty switch (Chapter 12).

Window glass slow to move

- [ ] Regulator seized or damaged, or in need of lubricant (Chapter 11).
- [ ] Door internal components or trim fouling regulator (Chapter 11).
- [ ] Faulty motor (Chapter 11).

Window glass fails to move

- [ ] Blown fuse (Chapter 12).
- [ ] Broken or disconnected wiring or connections (Chapter 12).
- [ ] Faulty motor (Chapter 11).

Central locking system inoperative, or unsatisfactory in operation

Complete system failure

- [ ] Blown fuse (Chapter 12).
- [ ] Broken or disconnected wiring or connections (Chapter 12).
- [ ] Faulty built-in system interface (BSI) unit (Chapter 12).

Door/tailgate locks but will not unlock, or unlocks but will not lock

- [ ] Broken or disconnected link rod(s) (Chapter 11).
- [ ] Faulty lock motor (Chapter 11).

One lock fails to operate

- [ ] Broken or disconnected wiring or connections (Chapter 12).
- [ ] Faulty lock motor (Chapter 11).
- [ ] Broken, binding or disconnected link rod(s) (Chapter 11).

A

ABS (Anti-lock brake system) A system, usually electronically controlled, that senses incipient wheel lockup during braking and relieves hydraulic pressure at wheels that are about to skid.

Air bag An inflatable bag hidden in the steering wheel (driver's side) or the dash or glovebox (passenger side). In a head-on collision, the bags inflate, preventing the driver and front passenger from being thrown forward into the steering wheel or windscreen.

Air cleaner A metal or plastic housing, containing a filter element, which removes dust and dirt from the air being drawn into the engine.

Air filter element The actual filter in an air cleaner system, usually manufactured from pleated paper and requiring renewal at regular intervals.

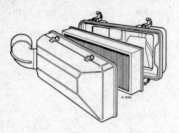

Air filter

Allen key A hexagonal wrench which fits into a recessed hexagonal hole.

Alligator clip A long-nosed spring-loaded metal clip with meshing teeth. Used to make temporary electrical connections.

Alternator A component in the electrical system which converts mechanical energy from a drivebelt into electrical energy to charge the battery and to operate the starting system, ignition system and electrical accessories.

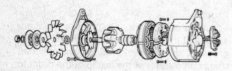

Alternator (exploded view)

Ampere (amp) A unit of measurement for the flow of electric current. One amp is the amount of current produced by one volt acting through a resistance of one ohm.

Anaerobic sealer A substance used to prevent bolts and screws from loosening. Anaerobic means that it does not require oxygen for activation. The Loctite brand is widely used.

Antifreeze A substance (usually ethylene glycol) mixed with water, and added to a vehicle's cooling system, to prevent freezing of the coolant in winter. Antifreeze also contains chemicals to inhibit corrosion and the formation of rust and other deposits that

would tend to clog the radiator and coolant passages and reduce cooling efficiency.

Anti-seize compound A coating that reduces the risk of seizing on fasteners that are subjected to high temperatures, such as exhaust manifold bolts and nuts.

Anti-seize compound

Asbestos A natural fibrous mineral with great heat resistance, commonly used in the composition of brake friction materials. Asbestos is a health hazard and the dust created by brake systems should never be inhaled or ingested.

Axle A shaft on which a wheel revolves, or which revolves with a wheel. Also, a solid beam that connects the two wheels at one end of the vehicle. An axle which also transmits power to the wheels is known as a live axle.

Axle assembly

Axleshaft A single rotating shaft, on either side of the differential, which delivers power from the final drive assembly to the drive wheels. Also called a driveshaft or a halfshaft.

B

Ball bearing An anti-friction bearing consisting of a hardened inner and outer race with hardened steel balls between two races.

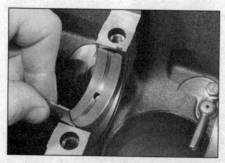

Bearing

Bearing The curved surface on a shaft or in a bore, or the part assembled into either, that permits relative motion between them with minimum wear and friction.

Big-end bearing The bearing in the end of the connecting rod that's attached to the crankshaft.

Bleed nipple A valve on a brake wheel cylinder, caliper or other hydraulic component that is opened to purge the hydraulic system of air. Also called a bleed screw.

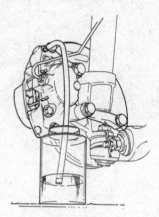

Brake bleeding

Brake bleeding Procedure for removing air from lines of a hydraulic brake system.

Brake disc The component of a disc brake that rotates with the wheels.

Brake drum The component of a drum brake that rotates with the wheels.

Brake linings The friction material which contacts the brake disc or drum to retard the vehicle's speed. The linings are bonded or riveted to the brake pads or shoes.

Brake pads The replaceable friction pads that pinch the brake disc when the brakes are applied. Brake pads consist of a friction material bonded or riveted to a rigid backing plate.

Brake shoe The crescent-shaped carrier to which the brake linings are mounted and which forces the lining against the rotating drum during braking.

Braking systems For more information on braking systems, consult the *Haynes Automotive Brake Manual*.

Breaker bar A long socket wrench handle providing greater leverage.

Bulkhead The insulated partition between the engine and the passenger compartment.

C

Caliper The non-rotating part of a disc-brake assembly that straddles the disc and carries the brake pads. The caliper also contains the hydraulic components that cause the pads to pinch the disc when the brakes are applied. A caliper is also a measuring tool that can be set to measure inside or outside dimensions of an object.

Camshaft A rotating shaft on which a series of cam lobes operate the valve mechanisms. The camshaft may be driven by gears, by sprockets and chain or by sprockets and a belt.

Canister A container in an evaporative emission control system; contains activated charcoal granules to trap vapours from the fuel system.

Canister

Carburettor A device which mixes fuel with air in the proper proportions to provide a desired power output from a spark ignition internal combustion engine.

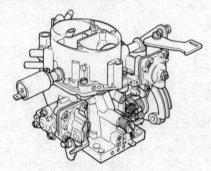

Carburettor

Castellated Resembling the parapets along the top of a castle wall. For example, a castellated balljoint stud nut.

Castellated nut

Castor In wheel alignment, the backward or forward tilt of the steering axis. Castor is positive when the steering axis is inclined rearward at the top.

Catalytic converter A silencer-like device in the exhaust system which converts certain pollutants in the exhaust gases into less harmful substances.

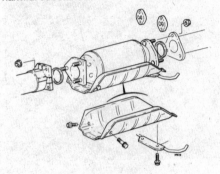

Catalytic converter

Circlip A ring-shaped clip used to prevent endwise movement of cylindrical parts and shafts. An internal circlip is installed in a groove in a housing; an external circlip fits into a groove on the outside of a cylindrical piece such as a shaft.

Clearance The amount of space between two parts. For example, between a piston and a cylinder, between a bearing and a journal, etc.

Coil spring A spiral of elastic steel found in various sizes throughout a vehicle, for example as a springing medium in the suspension and in the valve train.

Compression Reduction in volume, and increase in pressure and temperature, of a gas, caused by squeezing it into a smaller space.

Compression ratio The relationship between cylinder volume when the piston is at top dead centre and cylinder volume when the piston is at bottom dead centre.

Constant velocity (CV) joint A type of universal joint that cancels out vibrations caused by driving power being transmitted through an angle.

Core plug A disc or cup-shaped metal device inserted in a hole in a casting through which core was removed when the casting was formed. Also known as a freeze plug or expansion plug.

Crankcase The lower part of the engine block in which the crankshaft rotates.

Crankshaft The main rotating member, or shaft, running the length of the crankcase, with offset "throws" to which the connecting rods are attached.

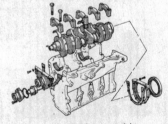

Crankshaft assembly

Crocodile clip See Alligator clip

D

Diagnostic code Code numbers obtained by accessing the diagnostic mode of an engine management computer. This code can be used to determine the area in the system where a malfunction may be located.

Disc brake A brake design incorporating a rotating disc onto which brake pads are squeezed. The resulting friction converts the energy of a moving vehicle into heat.

Double-overhead cam (DOHC) An engine that uses two overhead camshafts, usually one for the intake valves and one for the exhaust valves.

Drivebelt(s) The belt(s) used to drive accessories such as the alternator, water pump, power steering pump, air conditioning compressor, etc. off the crankshaft pulley.

Accessory drivebelts

Driveshaft Any shaft used to transmit motion. Commonly used when referring to the axleshafts on a front wheel drive vehicle.

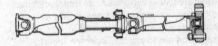

Driveshaft

Drum brake A type of brake using a drum-shaped metal cylinder attached to the inner surface of the wheel. When the brake pedal is pressed, curved brake shoes with friction linings press against the inside of the drum to slow or stop the vehicle.

Drum brake assembly

E

EGR valve A valve used to introduce exhaust gases into the intake air stream.

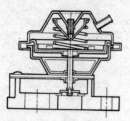

EGR valve

Electronic control unit (ECU) A computer which controls (for instance) ignition and fuel injection systems, or an anti-lock braking system. For more information refer to the *Haynes Automotive Electrical and Electronic Systems Manual*.

Electronic Fuel Injection (EFI) A computer controlled fuel system that distributes fuel through an injector located in each intake port of the engine.

Emergency brake A braking system, independent of the main hydraulic system, that can be used to slow or stop the vehicle if the primary brakes fail, or to hold the vehicle stationary even though the brake pedal isn't depressed. It usually consists of a hand lever that actuates either front or rear brakes mechanically through a series of cables and linkages. Also known as a handbrake or parking brake.

Endfloat The amount of lengthwise movement between two parts. As applied to a crankshaft, the distance that the crankshaft can move forward and back in the cylinder block.

Engine management system (EMS) A computer controlled system which manages the fuel injection and the ignition systems in an integrated fashion.

Exhaust manifold A part with several passages through which exhaust gases leave the engine combustion chambers and enter the exhaust pipe.

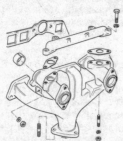

Exhaust manifold

F

Fan clutch A viscous (fluid) drive coupling device which permits variable engine fan speeds in relation to engine speeds.

Feeler blade A thin strip or blade of hardened steel, ground to an exact thickness, used to check or measure clearances between parts.

Feeler blade

Firing order The order in which the engine cylinders fire, or deliver their power strokes, beginning with the number one cylinder.

Flywheel A heavy spinning wheel in which energy is absorbed and stored by means of momentum. On cars, the flywheel is attached to the crankshaft to smooth out firing impulses.

Free play The amount of travel before any action takes place. The "looseness" in a linkage, or an assembly of parts, between the initial application of force and actual movement. For example, the distance the brake pedal moves before the pistons in the master cylinder are actuated.

Fuse An electrical device which protects a circuit against accidental overload. The typical fuse contains a soft piece of metal which is calibrated to melt at a predetermined current flow (expressed as amps) and break the circuit.

Fusible link A circuit protection device consisting of a conductor surrounded by heat-resistant insulation. The conductor is smaller than the wire it protects, so it acts as the weakest link in the circuit. Unlike a blown fuse, a failed fusible link must frequently be cut from the wire for replacement.

G

Gap The distance the spark must travel in jumping from the centre electrode to the side

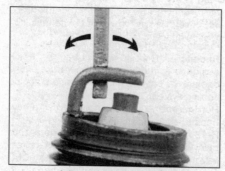

Adjusting spark plug gap

electrode in a spark plug. Also refers to the spacing between the points in a contact breaker assembly in a conventional points-type ignition, or to the distance between the reluctor or rotor and the pickup coil in an electronic ignition.

Gasket Any thin, soft material - usually cork, cardboard, asbestos or soft metal - installed between two metal surfaces to ensure a good seal. For instance, the cylinder head gasket seals the joint between the block and the cylinder head.

Gasket

Gauge An instrument panel display used to monitor engine conditions. A gauge with a movable pointer on a dial or a fixed scale is an analogue gauge. A gauge with a numerical readout is called a digital gauge.

H

Halfshaft A rotating shaft that transmits power from the final drive unit to a drive wheel, usually when referring to a live rear axle.

Harmonic balancer A device designed to reduce torsion or twisting vibration in the crankshaft. May be incorporated in the crankshaft pulley. Also known as a vibration damper.

Hone An abrasive tool for correcting small irregularities or differences in diameter in an engine cylinder, brake cylinder, etc.

Hydraulic tappet A tappet that utilises hydraulic pressure from the engine's lubrication system to maintain zero clearance (constant contact with both camshaft and valve stem). Automatically adjusts to variation in valve stem length. Hydraulic tappets also reduce valve noise.

I

Ignition timing The moment at which the spark plug fires, usually expressed in the number of crankshaft degrees before the piston reaches the top of its stroke.

Inlet manifold A tube or housing with passages through which flows the air-fuel mixture (carburettor vehicles and vehicles with throttle body injection) or air only (port fuel-injected vehicles) to the port openings in the cylinder head.

J

Jump start Starting the engine of a vehicle with a discharged or weak battery by attaching jump leads from the weak battery to a charged or helper battery.

L

Load Sensing Proportioning Valve (LSPV) A brake hydraulic system control valve that works like a proportioning valve, but also takes into consideration the amount of weight carried by the rear axle.
Locknut A nut used to lock an adjustment nut, or other threaded component, in place. For example, a locknut is employed to keep the adjusting nut on the rocker arm in position.
Lockwasher A form of washer designed to prevent an attaching nut from working loose.

M

MacPherson strut A type of front suspension system devised by Earle MacPherson at Ford of England. In its original form, a simple lateral link with the anti-roll bar creates the lower control arm. A long strut - an integral coil spring and shock absorber - is mounted between the body and the steering knuckle. Many modern so-called MacPherson strut systems use a conventional lower A-arm and don't rely on the anti-roll bar for location.
Multimeter An electrical test instrument with the capability to measure voltage, current and resistance.

N

NOx Oxides of Nitrogen. A common toxic pollutant emitted by petrol and diesel engines at higher temperatures.

O

Ohm The unit of electrical resistance. One volt applied to a resistance of one ohm will produce a current of one amp.
Ohmmeter An instrument for measuring electrical resistance.
O-ring A type of sealing ring made of a special rubber-like material; in use, the O-ring is compressed into a groove to provide the sealing action.

O-ring

Overhead cam (ohc) engine An engine with the camshaft(s) located on top of the cylinder head(s).
Overhead valve (ohv) engine An engine with the valves located in the cylinder head, but with the camshaft located in the engine block.
Oxygen sensor A device installed in the engine exhaust manifold, which senses the oxygen content in the exhaust and converts this information into an electric current. Also called a Lambda sensor.

P

Phillips screw A type of screw head having a cross instead of a slot for a corresponding type of screwdriver.
Plastigage A thin strip of plastic thread, available in different sizes, used for measuring clearances. For example, a strip of Plastigage is laid across a bearing journal. The parts are assembled and dismantled; the width of the crushed strip indicates the clearance between journal and bearing.

Plastigage

Propeller shaft The long hollow tube with universal joints at both ends that carries power from the transmission to the differential on front-engined rear wheel drive vehicles.
Proportioning valve A hydraulic control valve which limits the amount of pressure to the rear brakes during panic stops to prevent wheel lock-up.

R

Rack-and-pinion steering A steering system with a pinion gear on the end of the steering shaft that mates with a rack (think of a geared wheel opened up and laid flat). When the steering wheel is turned, the pinion turns, moving the rack to the left or right. This movement is transmitted through the track rods to the steering arms at the wheels.
Radiator A liquid-to-air heat transfer device designed to reduce the temperature of the coolant in an internal combustion engine cooling system.
Refrigerant Any substance used as a heat transfer agent in an air-conditioning system. R-12 has been the principle refrigerant for many years; recently, however, manufacturers have begun using R-134a, a non-CFC substance that is considered less harmful to the ozone in the upper atmosphere.

Rocker arm A lever arm that rocks on a shaft or pivots on a stud. In an overhead valve engine, the rocker arm converts the upward movement of the pushrod into a downward movement to open a valve.
Rotor In a distributor, the rotating device inside the cap that connects the centre electrode and the outer terminals as it turns, distributing the high voltage from the coil secondary winding to the proper spark plug. Also, that part of an alternator which rotates inside the stator. Also, the rotating assembly of a turbocharger, including the compressor wheel, shaft and turbine wheel.
Runout The amount of wobble (in-and-out movement) of a gear or wheel as it's rotated. The amount a shaft rotates "out-of-true." The out-of-round condition of a rotating part.

S

Sealant A liquid or paste used to prevent leakage at a joint. Sometimes used in conjunction with a gasket.
Sealed beam lamp An older headlight design which integrates the reflector, lens and filaments into a hermetically-sealed one-piece unit. When a filament burns out or the lens cracks, the entire unit is simply replaced.
Serpentine drivebelt A single, long, wide accessory drivebelt that's used on some newer vehicles to drive all the accessories, instead of a series of smaller, shorter belts. Serpentine drivebelts are usually tensioned by an automatic tensioner.

Serpentine drivebelt

Shim Thin spacer, commonly used to adjust the clearance or relative positions between two parts. For example, shims inserted into or under bucket tappets control valve clearances. Clearance is adjusted by changing the thickness of the shim.
Slide hammer A special puller that screws into or hooks onto a component such as a shaft or bearing; a heavy sliding handle on the shaft bottoms against the end of the shaft to knock the component free.
Sprocket A tooth or projection on the periphery of a wheel, shaped to engage with a chain or drivebelt. Commonly used to refer to the sprocket wheel itself.

Starter inhibitor switch On vehicles with an automatic transmission, a switch that prevents starting if the vehicle is not in Neutral or Park.

Strut See MacPherson strut.

T

Tappet A cylindrical component which transmits motion from the cam to the valve stem, either directly or via a pushrod and rocker arm. Also called a cam follower.

Thermostat A heat-controlled valve that regulates the flow of coolant between the cylinder block and the radiator, so maintaining optimum engine operating temperature. A thermostat is also used in some air cleaners in which the temperature is regulated.

Thrust bearing The bearing in the clutch assembly that is moved in to the release levers by clutch pedal action to disengage the clutch. Also referred to as a release bearing.

Timing belt A toothed belt which drives the camshaft. Serious engine damage may result if it breaks in service.

Timing chain A chain which drives the camshaft.

Toe-in The amount the front wheels are closer together at the front than at the rear. On rear wheel drive vehicles, a slight amount of toe-in is usually specified to keep the front wheels running parallel on the road by offsetting other forces that tend to spread the wheels apart.

Toe-out The amount the front wheels are closer together at the rear than at the front. On front wheel drive vehicles, a slight amount of toe-out is usually specified.

Tools For full information on choosing and using tools, refer to the *Haynes Automotive Tools Manual*.

Tracer A stripe of a second colour applied to a wire insulator to distinguish that wire from another one with the same colour insulator.

Tune-up A process of accurate and careful adjustments and parts replacement to obtain the best possible engine performance.

Turbocharger A centrifugal device, driven by exhaust gases, that pressurises the intake air. Normally used to increase the power output from a given engine displacement, but can also be used primarily to reduce exhaust emissions (as on VW's "Umwelt" Diesel engine).

U

Universal joint or U-joint A double-pivoted connection for transmitting power from a driving to a driven shaft through an angle. A U-joint consists of two Y-shaped yokes and a cross-shaped member called the spider.

V

Valve A device through which the flow of liquid, gas, vacuum, or loose material in bulk may be started, stopped, or regulated by a movable part that opens, shuts, or partially obstructs one or more ports or passageways. A valve is also the movable part of such a device.

Valve clearance The clearance between the valve tip (the end of the valve stem) and the rocker arm or tappet. The valve clearance is measured when the valve is closed.

Vernier caliper A precision measuring instrument that measures inside and outside dimensions. Not quite as accurate as a micrometer, but more convenient.

Viscosity The thickness of a liquid or its resistance to flow.

Volt A unit for expressing electrical "pressure" in a circuit. One volt that will produce a current of one ampere through a resistance of one ohm.

W

Welding Various processes used to join metal items by heating the areas to be joined to a molten state and fusing them together. For more information refer to the *Haynes Automotive Welding Manual*.

Wiring diagram A drawing portraying the components and wires in a vehicle's electrical system, using standardised symbols. For more information refer to the *Haynes Automotive Electrical and Electronic Systems Manual*.

Note: *References throughout this index are in the form 'Chapter number' • 'Page number'*

Haynes Manuals – The Complete List

Title	Book No.
ALFA ROMEO	
Alfa Romeo Alfasud/Sprint (74 - 88) up to F	0292
Alfa Romeo Alfetta (73 - 87) up to E	0531
AUDI	
Audi 80 (72 - Feb 79) up to T	0207
Audi 80, 90 (79 - Oct 86) up to D & Coupe (81 - Nov 88) up to F	0605
Audi 80, 90 (Oct 86 - 90) D to H & Coupe (Nov 88 - 90) F to H	1491
Audi 100 (Oct 82 - 90) up to H & 200 (Feb 84 - Oct 89) A to G	0907
Audi 100 & A6 Petrol & Diesel (May 91 - May 97) H to P	3504
Audi A4 (95 - Feb 00) M to V	3575
AUSTIN	
Austin A35 & A40 (56 - 67) *	0118
Austin Allegro 1100, 1300, 1.0, 1.1 & 1.3 (73 - 82)*	0164
Austin Healey 100/6 & 3000 (56 - 68) *	0049
Austin/MG/Rover Maestro 1.3 & 1.6 (83 - May 95) up to M	0922
Austin/MG Metro (80 - May 90) up to G	0718
Austin/Rover Montego 1.3 & 1.6 (84 - 94) A to L	1066
Austin/MG/Rover Montego 2.0 (84 - 95) A to M	1067
Mini (59 - 69) up to H	0527
Mini (69 - Oct 96) up to P	0646
Austin/Rover 2.0 litre Diesel Engine (86 - 93) C to L	1857
BEDFORD	
Bedford CF (69 - 87) up to E	0163
Bedford/Vauxhall Rascal & Suzuki Supercarry (86 - Oct 94) C to M	3015
BMW	
BMW 1500, 1502, 1600, 1602, 2000 & 2002 (59 - 77)*	0240
BMW 316, 320 & 320i (4-cyl) (75 - Feb 83) up to Y	0276
BMW 320, 320i, 323i & 325i (6-cyl) (Oct 77 - Sept 87) up to E	0815
BMW 3-Series (Apr 91 - 96) H to N	3210
BMW 3- & 5-Series (sohc) (81 - 91) up to J	1948
BMW 520i & 525e (Oct 81 - June 88) up to E	1560
BMW 525, 528 & 528i (73 - Sept 81) up to X	0632
CITROËN	
Citroën 2CV, Ami & Dyane (67 - 90) up to H	0196
Citroën AX Petrol & Diesel (87 - 97) D to P	3014
Citroën BX (83 - 94) A to L	0908
Citroën C15 Van Petrol & Diesel (89 - Oct 98) F to S	3509
Citroën CX (75 - 88) up to F	0528
Citroën Saxo Petrol & Diesel (96 - 01) N to X	3506
Citroën Visa (79 - 88) up to F	0620
Citroën Xantia Petrol & Diesel (93 - 98) K to S	3082
Citroën XM Petrol & Diesel (89 - 00) G to X	3451
Citroën Xsara Petrol & Diesel (97 - Sept 00) R to W	3751
Citroën ZX Diesel (91 - 98) J to S	1922
Citroën ZX Petrol (91 - 98) H to S	1881
Citroën 1.7 & 1.9 litre Diesel Engine (84 - 96) A to N	1379
FIAT	
Fiat 126 (73 - 87) *	0305
Fiat 500 (57 - 73) up to M	0090
Fiat Bravo & Brava (95 - 00) N to W	3572
Fiat Cinquecento (93 - 98) K to R	3501
Fiat Panda (81 - 95) up to M	0793
Fiat Punto Petrol & Diesel (94 - Oct 99) L to V	3251
Fiat Regata (84 - 88) A to F	1167
Fiat Tipo (88 - 91) E to J	1625
Fiat Uno (83 - 95) up to M	0923
Fiat X1/9 (74 - 89) up to G	0273
FORD	
Ford Anglia (59 - 68) *	0001
Ford Capri II (& III) 1.6 & 2.0 (74 - 87) up to E	0283

Title	Book No.
Ford Capri II (& III) 2.8 & 3.0 (74 - 87) up to E	1309
Ford Cortina Mk III 1300 & 1600 (70 - 76) *	0070
Ford Cortina Mk IV (& V) 1.6 & 2.0 (76 - 83) *	0343
Ford Cortina Mk IV (& V) 2.3 V6 (77 - 83) *	0426
Ford Escort Mk I 1100 & 1300 (68 - 74) *	0171
Ford Escort Mk I Mexico, RS 1600 & RS 2000 (70 - 74)*	0139
Ford Escort Mk II Mexico, RS 1800 & RS 2000 (75 - 80)*	0735
Ford Escort (75 - Aug 80) *	0280
Ford Escort (Sept 80 - Sept 90) up to H	0686
Ford Escort & Orion (Sept 90 - 00) H to X	1737
Ford Fiesta (76 - Aug 83) up to Y	0334
Ford Fiesta (Aug 83 - Feb 89) A to F	1030
Ford Fiesta (Feb 89 - Oct 95) F to N	1595
Ford Fiesta (Oct 95 - 01) N-reg. onwards	3397
Ford Focus (98 - 01) S to Y	3759
Ford Granada (Sept 77 - Feb 85) up to B	0481
Ford Granada & Scorpio (Mar 85 - 94) B to M	1245
Ford Ka (96 - 02) P-reg. onwards	3570
Ford Mondeo Petrol (93 - 99) K to T	1923
Ford Mondeo Diesel (93 - 96) L to N	3465
Ford Orion (83 - Sept 90) up to H	1009
Ford Sierra 4 cyl. (82 - 93) up to K	0903
Ford Sierra V6 (82 - 91) up to J	0904
Ford Transit Petrol (Mk 2) (78 - Jan 86) up to C	0719
Ford Transit Petrol (Mk 3) (Feb 86 - 89) C to G	1468
Ford Transit Diesel (Feb 86 - 99) C to T	3019
Ford 1.6 & 1.8 litre Diesel Engine (84 - 96) A to N	1172
Ford 2.1, 2.3 & 2.5 litre Diesel Engine (77 - 90) up to H	1606
FREIGHT ROVER	
Freight Rover Sherpa (74 - 87) up to E	0463
HILLMAN	
Hillman Avenger (70 - 82) up to Y	0037
Hillman Imp (63 - 76) *	0022
HONDA	
Honda Accord (76 - Feb 84) up to A	0351
Honda Civic (Feb 84 - Oct 87) A to E	1226
Honda Civic (Nov 91 - 96) J to N	3199
HYUNDAI	
Hyundai Pony (85 - 94) C to M	3398
JAGUAR	
Jaguar E Type (61 - 72) up to L	0140
Jaguar MkI & II, 240 & 340 (55 - 69) *	0098
Jaguar XJ6, XJ & Sovereign; Daimler Sovereign (68 - Oct 86) up to D	0242
Jaguar XJ6 & Sovereign (Oct 86 - Sept 94) D to M	3261
Jaguar XJ12, XJS & Sovereign; Daimler Double Six (72 - 88) up to F	0478
JEEP	
Jeep Cherokee Petrol (93 - 96) K to N	1943
LADA	
Lada 1200, 1300, 1500 & 1600 (74 - 91) up to J	0413
Lada Samara (87 - 91) D to J	1610
LAND ROVER	
Land Rover 90, 110 & Defender Diesel (83 - 95) up to N	3017
Land Rover Discovery Petrol & Diesel (89 - 98) G to S	3016
Land Rover Series IIA & III Diesel (58 - 85) up to C	0529
Land Rover Series II, IIA & III Petrol (58 - 85) up to C	0314
MAZDA	
Mazda 323 (Mar 81 - Oct 89) up to G	1608
Mazda 323 (Oct 89 - 98) G to R	3455
Mazda 626 (May 83 - Sept 87) up to E	0929
Mazda B-1600, B-1800 & B-2000 Pick-up (72 - 88) up to F	0267
Mazda RX-7 (79 - 85) *	0460

Title	Book No.
MERCEDES-BENZ	
Mercedes-Benz 190, 190E & 190D Petrol & Diesel (83 - 93) A to L	3450
Mercedes-Benz 200, 240, 300 Diesel (Oct 76 - 85) up to C	1114
Mercedes-Benz 250 & 280 (68 - 72) up to L	0346
Mercedes-Benz 250 & 280 (123 Series) (Oct 76 - 84) up to B	0677
Mercedes-Benz 124 Series (85 - Aug 93) C to K	3253
Mercedes-Benz C-Class Petrol & Diesel (93 - Aug 00) L to W	3511
MG	
MGA (55 - 62) *	0475
MGB (62 - 80) up to W	0111
MG Midget & AH Sprite (58 - 80) up to W	0265
MITSUBISHI	
Mitsubishi Shogun & L200 Pick-Ups (83 - 94) up to M	1944
MORRIS	
Morris Ital 1.3 (80 - 84) up to B	0705
Morris Minor 1000 (56 - 71) up to K	0024
NISSAN	
Nissan Bluebird (May 84 - Mar 86) A to C	1223
Nissan Bluebird (Mar 86 - 90) C to H	1473
Nissan Cherry (Sept 82 - 86) up to D	1031
Nissan Micra (83 - Jan 93) up to K	0931
Nissan Micra (93 - 99) K to T	3254
Nissan Primera (90 - Aug 99) H to T	1851
Nissan Stanza (82 - 86) up to D	0824
Nissan Sunny (May 82 - Oct 86) up to D	0895
Nissan Sunny (Oct 86 - Mar 91) D to H	1378
Nissan Sunny (Apr 91 - 95) H to N	3219
OPEL	
Opel Ascona & Manta (B Series) (Sept 75 - 88) up to F	0316
Opel Ascona (81 - 88) (Not available in UK see Vauxhall Cavalier 0812)	3215
Opel Astra (Oct 91 - Feb 98) (Not available in UK see Vauxhall Astra 1832)	3156
Opel Astra & Zafira Diesel (Feb 98 - Sept 00) (See Astra & Zafira Diesel Book No. 3797)	
Opel Astra & Zafira Petrol (Feb 98 - Sept 00) (See Vauxhall/Opel Astra & Zafira Petrol Book No. 3758)	
Opel Calibra (90 - 98) (See Vauxhall/Opel Calibra Book No. 3502)	
Opel Corsa (83 - Mar 93) (Not available in UK see Vauxhall Nova 0909)	3160
Opel Corsa (Mar 93 - 97) (Not available in UK see Vauxhall Corsa 1985)	3159
Opel Frontera Petrol & Diesel (91 - 98) (See Vauxhall/Opel Frontera Book No. 3454)	
Opel Kadett (Nov 79 - Oct 84) up to B	0634
Opel Kadett (Oct 84 - Oct 91) (Not available in UK see Vauxhall Astra & Belmont 1136)	3196
Opel Omega & Senator (86 - 94) (Not available in UK see Vauxhall Carlton & Senator 1469)	3157
Opel Omega (94 - 99) (See Vauxhall/Opel Omega Book No. 3510)	
Opel Rekord (Feb 78 - Oct 86) up to D	0543
Opel Vectra (Oct 88 - Oct 95) (Not available in UK see Vauxhall Cavalier 1570)	3158
Opel Vectra Petrol & Diesel (95 - 98) (Not available in UK see Vauxhall Vectra 3396)	3523
PEUGEOT	
Peugeot 106 Petrol & Diesel (91 - 01) J to X	1882
Peugeot 205 Petrol (83 - 97) A to P	0932
Peugeot 206 Petrol and Diesel (98 - 01) S to X	3757
Peugeot 305 (78 - 89) up to G	0538

* Classic reprint

Title	Book No.
Peugeot 306 Petrol & Diesel (93 - 99) K to T	3073
Peugeot 309 (86 - 93) C to K	1266
Peugeot 405 Petrol (88 - 97) E to P	1559
Peugeot 405 Diesel (88 - 97) E to P	3198
Peugeot 406 Petrol & Diesel (96 - 97) N to R	3394
Peugeot 505 (79 - 89) up to G	0762
Peugeot 1.7/1.8 & 1.9 litre Diesel Engine (82 - 96) up to N	0950
Peugeot 2.0, 2.1, 2.3 & 2.5 litre Diesel Engines (74 - 90) up to H	1607

PORSCHE
Title	Book No.
Porsche 911 (65 - 85) up to C	0264
Porsche 924 & 924 Turbo (76 - 85) up to C	0397

PROTON
Title	Book No.
Proton (89 - 97) F to P	3255

RANGE ROVER
Title	Book No.
Range Rover V8 (70 - Oct 92) up to K	0606

RELIANT
Title	Book No.
Reliant Robin & Kitten (73 - 83) up to A	0436

RENAULT
Title	Book No.
Renault 4 (61 - 86) *	0072
Renault 5 (Feb 85 - 96) B to N	1219
Renault 9 & 11 (82 - 89) up to F	0822
Renault 18 (79 - 86) up to D	0598
Renault 19 Petrol (89 - 94) F to M	1646
Renault 19 Diesel (89 - 96) F to N	1946
Renault 21 (86 - 94) C to M	1397
Renault 25 (84 - 92) B to K	1228
Renault Clio Petrol (91 - May 98) H to R	1853
Renault Clio Diesel (91 - June 96) H to N	3031
Renault Clio Petrol & Diesel (May 98 - May 01) R to Y	3906
Renault Espace Petrol & Diesel (85 - 96) C to N	3197
Renault Fuego (80 - 86) *	0764
Renault Laguna Petrol & Diesel (94 - 00) L to W	3252
Renault Mégane & Scénic Petrol & Diesel (96 - 98) N to R	3395
Renault Mégane & Scénic (Apr 99 - 02) T-reg onwards	3916

ROVER
Title	Book No.
Rover 213 & 216 (84 - 89) A to G	1116
Rover 214 & 414 (89 - 96) G to N	1689
Rover 216 & 416 (89 - 96) G to N	1830
Rover 211, 214, 216, 218 & 220 Petrol & Diesel (Dec 95 - 98) N to R	3399
Rover 414, 416 & 420 Petrol & Diesel (May 95 - 98) M to R	3453
Rover 618, 620 & 623 (93 - 97) K to P	3257
Rover 820, 825 & 827 (86 - 95) D to N	1380
Rover 3500 (76 - 87) up to E	0365
Rover Metro, 111 & 114 (May 90 - 98) G to S	1711

SAAB
Title	Book No.
Saab 90, 99 & 900 (79 - Oct 93) up to L	0765
Saab 95 & 96 (66 - 76) *	0198
Saab 99 (69 - 79) *	0247
Saab 900 (Oct 93 - 98) L to R	3512
Saab 9000 (4-cyl) (85 - 98) C to S	1686

SEAT
Title	Book No.
Seat Ibiza & Cordoba Petrol & Diesel (Oct 93 - Oct 99) L to V	3571
Seat Ibiza & Malaga (85 - 92) B to K	1609

SKODA
Title	Book No.
Skoda Estelle (77 - 89) up to G	0604
Skoda Favorit (89 - 96) F to N	1801
Skoda Felicia Petrol & Diesel (95 - 01) M to X	3505

SUBARU
Title	Book No.
Subaru 1600 & 1800 (Nov 79 - 90) up to H	0995

SUNBEAM
Title	Book No.
Sunbeam Alpine, Rapier & H120 (67 - 76) *	0051

SUZUKI
Title	Book No.
Suzuki SJ Series, Samurai & Vitara (4-cyl) (82 - 97) up to P	1942
Suzuki Supercarry & Bedford/Vauxhall Rascal (86 - Oct 94) C to M	3015

TALBOT
Title	Book No.
Talbot Alpine, Solara, Minx & Rapier (75 - 86) up to D	0337
Talbot Horizon (78 - 86) up to D	0473
Talbot Samba (82 - 86) up to D	0823

TOYOTA
Title	Book No.
Toyota Carina E (May 92 - 97) J to P	3256
Toyota Corolla (Sept 83 - Sept 87) A to E	1024
Toyota Corolla (80 - 85) up to C	0683
Toyota Corolla (Sept 87 - Aug 92) E to K	1683
Toyota Corolla (Aug 92 - 97) K to P	3259
Toyota Hi-Ace & Hi-Lux (69 - Oct 83) up to A	0304

TRIUMPH
Title	Book No.
Triumph Acclaim (81 - 84) *	0792
Triumph GT6 & Vitesse (62 - 74) *	0112
Triumph Herald (59 - 71) *	0010
Triumph Spitfire (62 - 81) up to X	0113
Triumph Stag (70 - 78) up to T	0441
Triumph TR2, TR3, TR3A, TR4 & TR4A (52 - 67)*	0028
Triumph TR5 & 6 (67 - 75) *	0031
Triumph TR7 (75 - 82) *	0322

VAUXHALL
Title	Book No.
Vauxhall Astra (80 - Oct 84) up to B	0635
Vauxhall Astra & Belmont (Oct 84 - Oct 91) B to J	1136
Vauxhall Astra (Oct 91 - Feb 98) J to R	1832
Vauxhall/Opel Astra & Zafira Diesel (Feb 98 - Sept 00) R to W	3797
Vauxhall/Opel Astra & Zafira Petrol (Feb 98 - Sept 00) R to W	3758
Vauxhall/Opel Calibra (90 - 98) G to S	3502
Vauxhall Carlton (Oct 78 - Oct 86) up to D	0480
Vauxhall Carlton & Senator (Nov 86 - 94) D to L	1469
Vauxhall Cavalier 1300 (77 - July 81) *	0461
Vauxhall Cavalier 1600, 1900 & 2000 (75 - July 81) up to W	0315
Vauxhall Cavalier (81 - Oct 88) up to F	0812
Vauxhall Cavalier (Oct 88 - 95) F to N	1570
Vauxhall Chevette (75 - 84) up to B	0285
Vauxhall Corsa (Mar 93 - 97) K to R	1985
Vauxhall/Opel Corsa (Apr 97 - Oct 00) P to X	3921
Vauxhall/Opel Frontera Petrol & Diesel (91 - Sept 98) J to S	3454
Vauxhall Nova (83 - 93) up to K	0909
Vauxhall/Opel Omega (94 - 99) L to T	3510
Vauxhall Vectra Petrol & Diesel (95 - 98) N to R	3396
Vauxhall/Opel 1.5, 1.6 & 1.7 litre Diesel Engine (82 - 96) up to N	1222

VOLKSWAGEN
Title	Book No.
Volkswagen 411 & 412 (68 - 75) *	0091
Volkswagen Beetle 1200 (54 - 77) up to S	0036
Volkswagen Beetle 1300 & 1500 (65 - 75) up to P	0039
Volkswagen Beetle 1302 & 1302S (70 - 72) up to L	0110
Volkswagen Beetle 1303, 1303S & GT (72 - 75) up to P	0159
Volkswagen Beetle Petrol & Diesel (Apr 99 - 01) T reg onwards	3798
Volkswagen Golf & Bora Petrol & Diesel (April 98 - 00) R to X	3727
Volkswagen Golf & Jetta Mk 1 1.1 & 1.3 (74 - 84) up to A	0716
Volkswagen Golf, Jetta & Scirocco Mk 1 1.5, 1.6 & 1.8 (74 - 84) up to A	0726
Volkswagen Golf & Jetta Mk 1 Diesel (78 - 84) up to A	0451
Volkswagen Golf & Jetta Mk 2 (Mar 84 - Feb 92) A to J	1081
Volkswagen Golf & Vento Petrol & Diesel (Feb 92 - 96) J to N	3097
Volkswagen LT vans & light trucks (76 - 87) up to E	0637
Volkswagen Passat & Santana (Sept 81 - May 88) up to E	0814
Volkswagen Passat Petrol & Diesel (May 88 - 96) E to P	3498
Volkswagen Passat 4-cyl Petrol & Diesel (Dec 96 - Nov 00) P to X	3917
Volkswagen Polo & Derby (76 - Jan 82) up to X	0335
Volkswagen Polo (82 - Oct 90) up to H	0813
Volkswagen Polo (Nov 90 - Aug 94) H to L	3245
Volkswagen Polo Hatchback Petrol & Diesel (94 - 99) M to S	3500
Volkswagen Scirocco (82 - 90) up to H	1224
Volkswagen Transporter 1600 (68 - 79) up to V	0082
Volkswagen Transporter 1700, 1800 & 2000 (72 - 79) up to V	0226
Volkswagen Transporter (air-cooled) (79 - 82) up to Y	0638
Volkswagen Transporter (water-cooled) (82 - 90) up to H	3452
Volkswagen Type 3 (63 - 73) *	0084

VOLVO
Title	Book No.
Volvo 120 & 130 Series (& P1800) (61 - 73) *	0203
Volvo 142, 144 & 145 (66 - 74) up to N	0129
Volvo 240 Series (74 - 93) up to K	0270
Volvo 262, 264 & 260/265 (75 - 85) *	0400
Volvo 340, 343, 345 & 360 (76 - 91) up to J	0715
Volvo 440, 460 & 480 (87 - 97) D to P	1691
Volvo 740 & 760 (82 - 91) up to J	1258
Volvo 850 (92 - 96) J to P	3260
Volvo 940 (90 - 96) H to N	3249
Volvo S40 & V40 (96 - 99) N to V	3569
Volvo S70, V70 & C70 (96 - 99) P to V	3573

AUTOMOTIVE TECHBOOKS
Title	Book No.
Automotive Air Conditioning Systems	3740
Automotive Brake Manual	3050
Automotive Carburettor Manual	3288
Automotive Diagnostic Fault Codes Manual	3472
Automotive Diesel Engine Service Guide	3286
Automotive Electrical and Electronic Systems Manual	3049
Automotive Engine Management and Fuel Injection Systems Manual	3344
Automotive Gearbox Overhaul Manual	3473
Automotive Service Summaries Manual	3475
Automotive Timing Belts Manual – Austin/Rover	3549
Automotive Timing Belts Manual – Ford	3474
Automotive Timing Belts Manual – Peugeot/Citroën	3568
Automotive Timing Belts Manual – Vauxhall/Opel	3577
Automotive Welding Manual	3053
In-Car Entertainment Manual (3rd Edition)	3363

* Classic reprint

CL13.4/02

Preserving Our Motoring Heritage

<
The Model J Duesenberg Derham Tourster. Only eight of these magnificent cars were ever built – this is the only example to be found outside the United States of America

Almost every car you've ever loved, loathed or desired is gathered under one roof at the Haynes Motor Museum. Over 300 immaculately presented cars and motorbikes represent every aspect of our motoring heritage, from elegant reminders of bygone days, such as the superb Model J Duesenberg to curiosities like the bug-eyed BMW Isetta. There are also many old friends and flames. Perhaps you remember the 1959 Ford Popular that you did your courting in? The magnificent 'Red Collection' is a spectacle of classic sports cars including AC, Alfa Romeo, Austin Healey, Ferrari, Lamborghini, Maserati, MG, Riley, Porsche and Triumph.

A Perfect Day Out

Each and every vehicle at the Haynes Motor Museum has played its part in the history and culture of Motoring. Today, they make a wonderful spectacle and a great day out for all the family. Bring the kids, bring Mum and Dad, but above all bring your camera to capture those golden memories for ever. You will also find an impressive array of motoring memorabilia, a comfortable 70 seat video cinema and one of the most extensive transport book shops in Britain. The Pit Stop Cafe serves everything from a cup of tea to wholesome, home-made meals or, if you prefer, you can enjoy the large picnic area nestled in the beautiful rural surroundings of Somerset.

> John Haynes O.B.E., Founder and Chairman of the museum at the wheel of a Haynes Light 12.

<
Graham Hill's Lola Cosworth Formula 1 car next to a 1934 Riley Sports.

The Museum is situated on the A359 Yeovil to Frome road at Sparkford, just off the A303 in Somerset. It is about 40 miles south of Bristol, and 25 minutes drive from the M5 intersection at Taunton.
Open 9.30am - 5.30pm (10.00am - 4.00pm Winter) 7 days a week, *except Christmas Day, Boxing Day and New Years Day*
Special rates available for schools, coach parties and outings Charitable Trust No. 292048